Charles L. Hinkle
University of Colorado

Esther F. Stineman
Yale University

CASES
IN
MARKETING
MANAGEMENT
Issues for the 1980s

Prentice-Hall, Inc., Englewood Cliffs, New Jersey 07632

Library of Congress Cataloging in Publication Data

HINKLE, CHARLES L.
 Cases in marketing management.

 Includes bibliographical references.
 1. Marketing—Management—Case studies. I. Stineman,
Esther (date). II. Title.
HF5415.13.H57 1984   658.8   83-19109
ISBN 0-13-115600-4

Editorial/production supervision and
  interior design: **Joan Foley**
Cover design: **Ben Santora**
Manufacturing buyer: **Ed O'Dougherty**

© 1984 by Prentice-Hall, Inc., Englewood Cliffs, New Jersey 07632

Printed in the United States of America

10 9 8 7 6 5 4 3 2 1

ISBN 0-13-115600-4

PRENTICE-HALL INTERNATIONAL, INC., *London*
PRENTICE-HALL OF AUSTRALIA PTY. LIMITED, *Sydney*
EDITORA PRENTICE-HALL DO BRASIL, LTDA., *Rio de Janeiro*
PRENTICE-HALL CANADA INC., *Toronto*
PRENTICE-HALL OF INDIA PRIVATE LIMITED, *New Delhi*
PRENTICE-HALL OF JAPAN, INC., *Tokyo*
PRENTICE-HALL OF SOUTHEAST ASIA PTE. LTD., *Singapore*
WHITEHALL BOOKS LIMITED, *Wellington, New Zealand*

CONTENTS

PART II   STRATEGIES AND TACTICS: DESIGNING, ASSEMBLING, AND IMPLEMENTING THE MARKETING MIX

Product

Price

Place

Promotion

PART III   INTEGRATING AND ADMINISTERING MARKETING AND CORPORATE STRATEGIES

PREFACE

THE PURPOSES
AND PROCESSES
OF CASE ANALYSIS

The authors hope that using this volume will help you to enrich your perspective on the so-called "real world" of business, one in which perhaps you and many of your group are already experienced. As you examine, study, and discuss these cases, developed in organizations being tested daily in the crucible of the marketplace, these four learning objectives, at least, seem reasonable:

1. To understand how managers' backgrounds and values affect their contributions to and views of policies and procedures
2. To understand the impact of different management policies and practices upon various types of organizations and to distinguish between effective and ineffective policies under differing circumstances
3. To grasp how marketing and the different functional areas of business (e.g., finance and production) are interrelated
4. To understand both the theoretical and applied aspects of information decision systems for marketing management and to use various standard and special sources of data for analyses

A principal goal of using case studies in management education is to stimulate direct involvement in the process of finding, defining, and analyzing issues and problems, which may be stated directly or merely implied in the case narrative, and developing recommendations and programs for the organization. Tackling real business problems is viewed as an excellent means of developing practitioners in the art of management. The approach has several implications for your preparation and participation, among them the following:

1. You increase your learning benefits with thorough preparation efforts before class and through participation in class discussion.
2. You develop problem-finding and analytic skills in a critical, although usually not hostile, atmosphere. The process helps to build both a willingness to risk stating conclusions and an ability to overcome fears of making and admitting mistakes.
3. You sharpen the capacity to recognize management's assumptions and to develop your own, in real situations presented in case formats.
4. You learn and teach along with the instructor whose central mission is to orchestrate the group's interaction, to stimulate ideas, and to guide discussion—in other words, to help you develop your ideas.

THE MARKETING AUDIT

As you examine the case—skimming first for highlights and then reading it thoroughly, preferably twice, for understanding—and list the principal features relating to what you see as the central issues, several tentative solutions may evolve.

The following suggestions are intended to help you examine the case, to pinpoint problem areas, and to devise solutions and recommendations:

1. Examine the firm's management, services, financial structure, and general and specific goals. Remember that companies do not do things; people do. Consider the managers' value systems, and estimate their impact upon objectives, policies, and strategies.
2. Take the customers' viewpoints and try to understand such factors as the following:
   a. **Who** are the customers? Classify them according to pertinent socioeconomic, demographic, and marketing characteristics.
   b. **What** products and services do they use?
   c. **Where** do they buy these products and services? Consider market geography, regional differences, and types of companies patronized.
   d. **When** do they buy? What is the frequency of use? Time of the day and week? Are there seasonal (cyclical) influences?
   e. **How** do they buy? Is help required to make the purchase? Do customers seek advice because of their lack of experience? Does personal selling play an important role?

    f. **Why** do they buy? You may not be able to infer motivations, but you can consider related literature, findings of the behavioral sciences, and your experiences that pertain to the product and/or service and to the circumstances in the case.

3. Define the nature of the product-service.
   a. What are its similarities to, and differences from, competitive offerings?
   b. After carefully evaluating how people choose and use the products and services, ask the question, "How can the firm's marketing system adapt its product-service capabilities to the requirements of the buying/using system?"
4. Given the composition of markets and the company's product-service capabilities, what seem to be the most desirable ways to close the gap between company and customers?
   a. What marketing elements—services, research, advertising, personal selling, publicity—are available?
   b. Will marketing operations provide adequately for the flow of the product-service, the return money flow, and an information flow?
5. By now you should be able to define, and rank order by urgency, the problems facing the firm. List all those issues that are important; pay particular attention to those that are critical.
6. Lay out a proposed program, maintaining an acceptable cost-price-profit relationship. Justify your preferred solution. Balance the risks and potential returns in keeping with corporate policies and available resources.

This section suggests but one way of approaching the tasks of case analysis; it is not intended as a formula to be followed by rote. You will wish to alter techniques for different situations. In developing analyses and solutions, make assumptions that you consider to be necessary and that are reasonable.

Since perfect information is never available, you might wish to seek case-related information, but *it is preferable to deal with the study as it is presented rather than acquire postcase data on the company.* Perfect answers are hard to come by, and since there may be two or more acceptable solutions to a case problem, not only the solution itself but also the manner in which it is derived is important.

By objective, systematic, and thorough diagnosis, analysis, and preparation, you will be able to defend your ideas and enhance your skills and will contribute to the learning of others in the class as well.

A SIMPLIFIED PLANNING MODEL

Exhibit 1 portrays conceptually the phases of planning, which can be used for a one-year budgeting cycle or expanded to embrace a long-term perspective, beginning with articulating (or examining it if there already is one) the organization's statement of purpose, its mission. The situation, or strengths-weak-

Exhibit 1
Phases of Planning

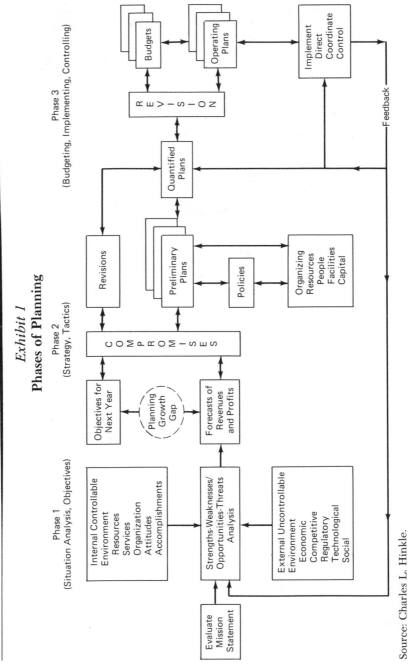

Source: Charles L. Hinkle.

nesses/opportunities-threats (SWOT), analysis should be considered for almost every case in this book.

Leaping to judgments before examining the fundamentals of a situation often leads to unwarranted conclusions, and the recommendations based on such a superficial examination can instigate egregious circumstances. Before jumping into a business strategy for a going concern, develop an idea of what the current strategy is and how well, overall, the organization is doing. If possible, infer from the case information a mission statement; in short, try to answer the question, "What business are they in?" Expressing an answer to this query is an excellent starting point from which to go about the tasks of evaluating the firm's past, present, and future. However, if it is a fledgling enterprise, such as A. Poe Designs, or just a concept, such as High Flight Resort, and no history exists, a suitable starting task would be to draft your version of a mission-and-role statement for the entrepreneur. Following that, it may be worthwhile to consider a basic set of policies to guide management.

The goals and objectives of a business ideally are governed by its policies and implemented through planned practices. Policies and courses of corporate action might include a code of ethics, a plan for expanding into new territories, an approach to advertising and publicity, attitudes toward employees, viewpoints on promotion, and many other variables. Policies are ideas, attitudes, and philosophies, as distinguished from procedures or methods.

Management policies are the responsibility of the owner or board of directors, and in many organizations these policies are developed and approved by an executive committee of the board and put into effect and interpreted by the chief executive officer. In some organizations, the CEO develops the policies as a means of communicating intent and fundamental directions.

For an example of how one large and very successful company views this matter of philosophy, policies, and objectives, you might wish to review the Hewlett-Packard case, which indicates how one firm has approached developing general objectives.

DATA ANALYSIS

When analyzing the quantitative data in a case, remember that the words "figure" and "fictitious" both derive from the same Latin infinitive, *fingere*. Temper conclusions drawn from the superficial appearance of data with good judgment, being aware that even more important than the actual numbers is what management will believe or distrust about them. Some of the case studies you will analyze in this text provide large amounts of information, qualitative and quantitative, but do not require its use. That choice is up to you. A combination of analytical tools and personal judgments is often necessary.

PRECLASS CASE PREPARATION SESSIONS

Unless you spend the time and effort necessary to study a case before the class session, the classroom experience will not provide maximum returns for you, and others will not receive the benefit of your ideas. Small-group preparation periods allow time for "teams" to go over the case in a preliminary fashion before the whole class convenes. Everyone should read the case before a prep session. In these "warm-up" get-togethers, a number of erroneous ideas and solutions can be filtered out, bringing each person to a greater level of understanding before the entire class gets into the act, thus accelerating the learning process. Rather than arriving at a consensus, it is expected that members of prep groups will interact constructively with each other and come out with conclusions that, while based principally on independent thinking, will have the benefit of others' thoughts.

Intellectual income for you will be directly related to the thoroughness of your individual study and the intensity of your involvement in preliminary sessions and classroom discussions.

RESPONSIBILITIES OF PRECLASS PREPARATION LEADERS

In getting ready for the case prep session, the discussion leader

1. Thoroughly reads and analyzes the case
2. Develops thought-provoking questions to focus group attention upon important pros and cons in the case situation

During the discussion, the leader

1. Helps group members to get organized for the work session
2. States the basics of the problem
3. Encourages reticent members to participate
4. Discourages private conversations
5. Focuses and guides discussion
   a. Maintains logical progression, pushing toward solutions
   b. Summarizes key points

In directing and coordinating case preparation activity, the attitude that you display will significantly influence results. So employ your helpful traits—be dynamic, genial, interested, and responsible.

PREPARING WRITTEN ANALYSES

Your instructor will have his or her own special evaluation procedure for critiquing your written anlyses, so these criteria are offered as preliminary guidelines only. We would suggest, however, that you check your analysis of each case for the following:

1. Coverage of key institutional strategic issues
2. Coverage of key marketing management strategic issues
3. Use of facts in the case, plus your own assumptions
4. Coverage of other functional areas (finance, production, etc.) when appropriate to the situation
5. Clear priorities for action
6. A clear and feasible plan for implementing recommendations
7. Adequate consideration of alternatives and recognition of shortcomings of recommendations
8. Application of concepts presented by authors in course textbook, if any, and of ideas and frameworks developed in class discussion
9. Use of exhibits and appendixes to aid the reader
10. Attention to writing: grammar, spelling, mechanics, and flow of ideas

And, finally, we wish you the best of luck in deconstructing these cases designed to challenge your skills in articulating significant strategies to be applied to marketing decisions in the 1980s.

Charles Hinkle
Colorado Springs

ACKNOWLEDGMENTS

Some cases in this volume were drafted by contributing writers who are acknowledged here under "primary authorship," indicating that the person being recognized was responsible in a substantial way for that particular writeup. Following that, recognition is given to individuals in various organizations who collaborated with the authors by orchestrating visits, arranging interviews with key persons, and providing resource materials. It will become clear to the reader, by quotations and references in the studies, that substantial credit is owed to many individuals who made this collection possible.

PRIMARY AUTHORSHIP

A. Poe Designs, Inc. Susan Maples is president, Maples Enterprises, a management consulting organization, and instructor in marketing at Metropolitan State College, Denver.

The Chinook Bookshop Marshall Sprague, author-historian, is a well-known chronicler of the West.

Compassion International Stephen Sorenson is an author and editor and public relations manager of the subject organization.

Julie Research Laboratories   Artist Dick Hafer is the cartoonist who helped to develop the booklets used as centerpieces of this study.

Omega Medical Products   Dr. Neil M. Ford is a member of the graduate business school faculty, University of Wisconsin, and Bonnie J. Queram is an M.B.A. graduate of that institution. Permission was granted by Richard D. Irwin, publisher of *Sales Force Management,* 1981, in which the previous version of this study appeared.

Penrose Hospitals   Michael B. Guthrie, M.D., is director of medical affairs for Penrose Hospitals.

Semester at Sea   Dr. Lloyd Lewan is director of academic affairs, Institute for Shipboard Education, University of Pittsburgh.

Springville Y/USO   Dr. Robert Knapp is a member of the business school faculty, University of Colorado, Colorado Springs.

U.S. Government and the Auto Industry   Dr. Jerry M. Calton, a member of the business school faculty, University of Colorado, Colorado Springs, developed this study as part of a research effort directed by Charles Summer, faculty member of the University of Washington business schoool.

COLLABORATIVE SUPPORT

DeLorean Motor Company   Mike Knepper, director of public relations, and Carol Winkler, administrative assistant to John Z. DeLorean.

Democratic Socialist Republic of Sri Lanka   Inspiration provided by Sam Wijesinha, secretary of the Parliament, Sri Lanka.

Hewlett-Packard Company   John Riggen, general manager of the Colorado Springs Division of Hewlett-Packard.

Kentucky Fried Chicken   Gregg M. Reynolds, vice president of public affairs.

Julie Research Laboratories   Pamela Spencer, administrative assistant to Loebe Julie.

L. L. Bean, Inc.   D. Kilton Andrew, Jr., public affairs spokesperson for the firm.

Mary Kay Cosmetics, Inc.   Dick Bartlett, vice president of marketing; Dean Meadors, director of public relations; and J. Eugene Stubbs, chief financial officer.

National Sporting Goods Association   Thomas B. Doyle, director of information and research.

Robinson Associates, Inc.   The firm's president, Patrick J. Robinson.

Time Inc./Seagram   Dr. Robert Schreiber, director of research, Magazine Group, Time Inc.

Walt Disney World EPCOT Center   Erwin D. Okun, vice president of public relations, Walt Disney Productions.

DISCLAIMER

All case studies are intended to provide a basis for classroom discussion; none purports to illustrate correct or incorrect, appropriate or inappropriate, management policies and practices.

CASE TOPICS, TEXT REFERENCES, AND SEQUENCE OF CONTENTS

TWO REFERENCE TABLES

The first of the two tables in this introductory material outlines the marketing subject matter contained in the cases and provides other taxonomic descriptors. The second table presents references to related chapters in six marketing management textbooks frequently adopted for upper-division college courses in marketing strategy and for M.B.A. marketing management courses. If you wish to investigate chapters in textbooks other than those listed, the headings of Table 1 provide useful leads.

SEQUENCE OF CASES

Since the majority of these case studies spans more than one of the listed core topics of marketing management, labeling them uniquely was, in some instances, necessarily arbitrary. Several cases could fit under one rubric as easily as under another.

The first major division of the book embraces the role of marketing, strategic planning and marketing management, and evaluation of market opportunities. Unavoidably overlapping this portion is the next major division

Table 1

CASE CATEGORIES AND MARKETING TOPICS

	CONSUMER	INDUSTRIAL	TANGIBLE (PRODUCT)	INTANGIBLE (SERVICE)	PRODUCT/SERVICE DECISIONS	PRICING	ADVERTISING/PUBLIC RELATIONS	PERSONAL SELLING	SALES MANAGEMENT	LEGAL, SOCIAL ISSUES	MARKETING RESEARCH	PLACEMENT RESEARCH	RETAILING (CHANNELS)	CORPORATE STRATEGY	MANAGEMENT VALUES	NOT FOR PROFIT
Adolph Coors Company	x		x		x	x	x		x	x	x			x	x	
A. Poe Designs, Inc.	x		x		x	x		x			x	x				
Apple Computer, Inc.	x	x	x		x	x	x		x		x			x	x	
Bell Labs/The Writer's Workbench		x		x	x	x			x		x			x	x	
Celestial Seasonings, Inc.	x		x		x		x	x	x	x	x			x		
The Chinook Bookshop	x		x		x		x	x	x			x		x		
Citizens Bank & Trust		x		x	x	x	x	x	x		x			x		
The Colorado Daily, Inc.	x		x		x				x	x				x	x	x
Compassion International	x			x			x			x					x	x
DeLorean Motor Company	x		x		x	x	x				x			x	x	
Delta Air Lines	x	x		x	x	x	x	x	x		x			x	x	
Democratic Socialist Republic of Sri Lanka		x		x	x	x	x							x	x	x
Digital Products Corporation		x	x		x	x	x				x			x		
Early Winters Ltd.	x		x		x	x	x				x		x	x	x	
Hewlett-Packard Company		x	x		x		x	x						x	x	
High Flight Resort	x			x	x	x	x	x	x	x				x	x	
Julie Research Laboratories		x	x		x	x	x							x	x	
Kentucky Fried Chicken	x		x		x	x	x						x	x		
L. L. Bean, Inc.	x		x		x	x	x	x					x	x	x	
Mary Kay Cosmetics, Inc.	x		x					x	x	x					x	
Measurement Research and Development, Inc.		x	x					x	x		x			x		
Mighty Dog	x		x			x	x									
National Revenue Corporation		x		x	x	x	x									
National Sporting Goods Association		x		x	x					x				x		
Omega Medical Products		x	x					x	x							
Penrose Hospitals		x		x			x			x	x		x	x	x	x
Pipes and Tobaccos Unlimited		x		x	x	x	x	x					x	x	x	
Powell/Kleinschmidt		x		x			x	x						x	x	
Robinson Associates, Inc.		x		x				x			x			x	x	
Round The Corner Restaurants, Inc.	x		x		x	x	x			x			x	x		
Semester at Sea	x			x		x	x	x						x		x
Springville Y/USO	x			x	x	x					x		x	x	x	x
Time, Inc./Seagram		x		x			x				x					
U.S. Government and the Auto Industry	x	x	x							x				x	x	
Walt Disney World—EPCOT Center	x			x		x	x							x		

2

Table 2
REFERENCES TO MARKETING TEXTBOOKS

	DOUGLAS J. DALRYMPLE AND LEONARD J. PARSONS, MARKETING MANAGEMENT: TEXT AND CASES, 2ND ED. (NEW YORK: JOHN WILEY, 1980).	KENNETH R. DAVIS, MARKETING MANAGEMENT, 4th ED. (NEW YORK: JOHN WILEY, 1981).	JOSEPH P. GUILTINAN AND GORDON W. PAUL, MARKETING MANAGEMENT: STRATEGIES AND PROGRAMS (NEW YORK: McGRAW-HILL, 1982).
Adolph Coors Company	Chs. 4, 6, 7, 8, 10, 12, 13	Chs. 1, 2, 3, 4, 5, 7, 8, 12, 13, 14	Chs. 2, 4, 6, 7, 8, 9, 13, 15
A. Poe Designs, Inc.	Chs. 2, 3, 6, 9, 11	Chs. 7, 8, 9, 13	Chs. 3, 6, 7, 11, 13
Apple Computer, Inc.	Chs. 3, 4, 5, 7, 8, 9, 13	Cas. 2, 3, 5, 6, 8, 9, 12, 13	Chs. 3, 4, 6, 7, 8, 9, 11, 13, 15
Bell Labs/The Writer's Workbench	Chs. 1, 5, 6, 7, 8, 9	Chs. 2, 3, 7, 8, 9, 10, 13, 14	Chs. 2, 3, 6, 7, 8, 9, 11, 13
Celestial Seasonings, Inc.	Chs. 4, 5, 6, 7, 8	Chs. 2, 4, 6, 7, 8, 11, 12, 14	Chs. 2, 3, 6, 7, 9, 10, 11, 13, 15
The Chinook Bookshop	Chs. 4, 7, 10, 11	Chs. 8, 9, 11, 12	Chs. 2, 3, 6, 10, 11, 14
Citizens Bank & Trust	Chs. 1, 3, 5, 6, 8, 11	Chs. 2, 3, 7, 8, 11, 12, 13	Chs. 2, 3, 6, 7, 8, 9, 10, 12, 13, 14, 15
The Colorado Daily, Inc.	Chs. 1, 4, 5, 8, 9, 13	Chs. 2, 4, 7, 8, 13	Chs. 2, 3, 6, 7, 8, 10
Compassion International	Chs. 4, 5, 10	Chs. 4, 7, 12, 14	Chs. 2, 3, 5, 9, 10, 11, 15
DeLorean Motor Company	Chs. 4, 5, 6, 7, 8, 9, 10, 13	Chs. 4, 5, 8, 9, 12, 13, 14	Chs. 2, 3, 6, 7, 8, 9, 11
Delta Airlines	Chs. 3, 4, 5, 8, 9, 10, 13	Chs. 2, 4, 5, 8, 9, 11, 12, 13	Chs. 2, 3, 4, 5, 6, 7, 8, 9, 10, 15
Democratic Socialist Republic of Sri Lanka	Chs. 5, 8, 10, 11	Chs. 8, 11, 12, 13, 14	Chs. 2, 6, 7, 8, 9, 12, 15
Digital Products Corporation	Chs. 6, 9, 10, 11	Chs. 8, 9, 11, 12	Chs. 2, 6, 7, 8, 9, 12
Early Winters Ltd.	Chs. 2, 4, 5, 7, 8, 10	Chs. 2, 7, 8, 9, 12, 13	Chs. 2, 3, 6, 7, 8, 9, 10, 15
Hewlett-Packard Company	Chs. 1, 6, 11, 13	Chs. 1, 2, 14, 15	Chs. 1, 2, 7, 13, 14
High Flight Resort	Chs. 2, 3, 4, 5, 6, 10, 11, 13	Chs. 3, 5, 7, 8, 11, 12, 13, 14	Chs. 2, 3, 6, 7, 8, 9, 10, 12, 13, 15
Julie Research Laboratories	Chs. 4, 8, 10, 11, 13	Chs. 1, 11, 12, 13	Chs. 8, 9, 12, 15
Kentucky Fried Chicken	Chs. 4, 6, 8, 10	Chs. 6, 7, 8, 12, 13, 14	Chs. 2, 3, 6, 7, 8, 9, 13
L. L. Bean, Inc.	Chs. 3, 6, 7, 8, 9, 10	Chs. 2, 3, 4, 8, 12, 13	Chs. 2, 3, 4, 6, 7, 8, 9, 10, 13, 15
Mary Kay Cosmetics, Inc.	Chs. 4, 11, 13	Chs. 1, 4, 8, 11	Chs. 2, 3, 6, 7, 12, 15
Measurement Research and Development, Inc.	Chs. 4, 5, 6, 8, 9, 11, 12	Chs. 2, 3, 7, 8, 9, 11, 14	Chs. 2, 3, 4, 6, 8, 12, 13, 15
Mighty Dog	Chs. 3, 4, 5, 8, 10	Chs. 2, 3, 4, 8, 12, 13	Chs. 3, 6, 8, 9, 10, 15
National Revenue Corporation	Chs. 4, 8, 10, 11	Chs. 8, 11, 12, 13	Chs. 8, 9, 12, 15
National Sporting Goods Association	Chs. 4, 6, 7, 11, 12	Chs. 3, 4, 5, 11	Chs. 2, 3, 12, 13, 15
Omega Medical Products	Chs. 2, 4, 9, 11	Chs. 1, 2, 4, 7, 8, 10, 12	Chs. 2, 3, 6, 7, 8, 9, 13, 15
Penrose Hospitals	Chs. 1, 2, 4, 6, 7, 10, 13	Chs. 2, 8, 9, 11, 13	Chs. 3, 6, 7, 8, 9, 10, 12, 13, 14
Pipes and Tobaccos Unlimited	Chs. 4, 5, 7, 8, 10, 11	Chs. 2, 6, 11, 12, 14	Chs. 2, 3, 6, 9, 10, 12, 13, 14, 15
Powell/Kleinschmidt	Chs. 1, 5, 10, 11, 12	Chs. 2, 3, 7, 8	Chs. 2, 3, 6, 7, 10, 13, 15
Robinson Associates, Inc.	Chs. 2, 4, 6, 7, 11	Chs. 2, 3, 7, 8	Chs. 2, 3, 5, 6, 9, 10, 13, 14, 15
Round The Corner Restaurants, Inc.	Chs. 1, 2, 3, 4, 5, 6, 8, 10	Chs. 2, 4, 7, 8, 12, 13	Chs. 2, 3, 5, 6, 9, 10, 13, 14, 15
Semester at Sea	Chs. 4, 5, 8, 10, 11	Chs. 4, 5, 8, 10, 11, 12, 13	Chs. 2, 3, 6, 7, 8, 9, 10, 13, 15
Springville Y/USO	Chs. 2, 4, 8, 9, 12	Chs. 2, 3, 7, 8, 13	Chs. 2, 3, 6, 7, 8, 13, 14, 15
Time, Inc./Seagram	Chs. 2, 3, 4	Chs. 7, 12	Chs. 4, 9, 10, 13
U.S. Government and the Auto Industry	Chs. 4, 13	Ch. 1	Ch. 15
Walt Disney World—EPCOT Center	Chs. 3, 4, 5, 6, 7, 8, 12	Chs. 2, 5, 8, 13	Chs. 2, 4, 6, 7, 8, 10, 13

Table 2 (Cont.)

REFERENCES TO MARKETING TEXTBOOKS

	G. DAVID HUGHES, MARKETING MANAGEMENT: A PLANNING APPROACH (READING, MASS.: ADDISON-WESLEY, 1978).	PHILIP KOTLER, MARKETING MANAGEMENT: ANALYSIS, PLANNING, AND CONTROL, 5TH ED. (ENGLEWOOD CLIFFS, N.J.: PRENTICE-HALL, 1984).	MAURICE I. MANDELL AND LARRY J. ROSENBERG, MARKETING (ENGLEWOOD CLIFFS, N.J.: PRENTICE-HALL, 1981).
Adolph Coors Company	Chs. 3, 4, 7, 10, 11, 12, 13, 15, 19	Chs. 2, 4, 7, 8, 10, 12, 15, 16, 19, 24	Chs. 5, 7, 8, 11, 12, 14, 19, 21
A. Poe Designs, Inc.	Chs. 2, 3, 11, 12, 14, 16, 17	Chs. 4, 8, 9, 10, 15, 16, 18, 21	Chs. 5, 11, 14, 16, 20, 21
Apple Computer, Inc.	Chs. 3, 5, 6, 8, 10, 11, 12, 13, 14, 15, 17, 18	Chs. 4, 5, 8, 11, 14, 15, 16, 17, 20, 24	Chs. 3, 5, 7, 9, 10, 11, 14, 16, 19, 21
Bell Labs/The Writer's Workbench	Chs. 2, 3, 4, 5, 8, 9, 11, 12, 13, 14	Chs. 1, 5, 6, 8, 9, 12, 15, 16, 17, 19, 22	Chs. 2, 5, 7, 10, 11, 13, 15, 18, 20, 21
Celestial Seasonings, Inc.	Chs. 2, 3, 4, 5, 6, 11, 12, 14, 15, 17	Chs. 2, 4, 8, 9, 10, 12, 14, 15, 18, 20, 24	Chs. 4, 5, 7, 8, 11, 16, 19, 21
The Chinook Bookshop	Chs. 2, 3, 6, 9, 11, 12, 17, 19	Chs. 2, 4, 8, 15, 18, 19, 20, 21, 24	Chs. 5, 7, 8, 11, 16, 19, 20
Citizens Bank & Trust	Chs. 2, 3, 4, 5, 6, 8, 12, 13, 15, 16, 19	Chs. 5, 6, 8, 9, 10, 15, 16, 20, 21, 22, 24	Chs. 2, 3, 5, 7, 10, 11, 14, 19, 20, 21
The Colorado Daily, Inc.	Chs. 2, 3, 4, 7, 9, 12, 13	Chs. 4, 5, 6, 8, 10, 12, 15, 16, 24	Chs. 4, 5, 7, 8, 10, 11, 14, 21
Compassion International	Chs. 2, 3, 15	Chs. 4, 6, 8, 9, 19, 20, 24	Chs. 2, 4, 5, 8, 11, 19, 20, 21, 22
DeLorean Motor Company	Chs. 4, 5, 10, 11, 12, 13, 14, 15, 18	Chs. 4, 6, 8, 9, 10, 12, 15, 16, 17, 20	Chs. 4, 5, 6, 7, 9, 11, 14, 19, 21
Delta Airlines	Chs. 2, 3, 5, 6, 8, 10, 11, 12, 13, 14, 15	Chs. 2, 3, 4, 5, 6, 8, 12, 14, 15, 16, 17, 20, 21, 22, 24	Chs. 3, 4, 6, 7, 9, 10, 11, 14, 15, 19, 20, 21
Democratic Socialist Republic of Sri Lanka	Chs. 2, 7, 9, 10, 11, 12, 13, 15, 18	Chs. 2, 3, 5, 8, 9, 10, 14, 15, 16, 20, 21	Chs. 3, 4, 5, 7, 10, 11, 13, 19, 20, 21
Digital Products Corporation	Chs. 2, 3, 4, 8, 11, 14, 16, 19	Chs. 5, 8, 10, 11, 12, 15, 18, 21, 23, 24	Chs. 5, 7, 10, 11, 14, 17, 20, 21, 22

Early Winters Ltd.	Chs. 2, 3, 11, 12, 13, 15, 17	Chs. 4, 6, 8, 9, 10, 14, 15, 18, 20, 24	Chs. 5, 7, 12, 14, 19, 21
Hewlett-Packard Company	Chs. 2, 4, 5, 12, 16, 18	Chs. 1, 2, 5, 9, 10, 12, 14, 21, 24	Chs. 2, 5, 10, 11, 20, 23
High Flight Resort	Chs. 2, 3, 6, 9, 10, 12, 13, 15, 16	Chs. 2, 3, 4, 6, 8, 9, 10, 12, 15, 16, 20, 21, 22	Chs. 2, 3, 5, 7, 9, 11, 13, 18, 21
Julie Research Laboratories	Chs. 10, 13, 15, 16	Chs. 2, 3, 5, 16, 21	Chs. 3, 5, 7, 13, 19, 20
Kentucky Fried Chicken	Chs. 4, 12, 13, 15	Chs. 2, 4, 9, 10, 16, 20, 24	Chs. 2, 8, 11, 13, 19, 21
L. L. Bean, Inc.	Chs. 2, 3, 5, 6, 12, 13, 15, 19	Chs. 4, 6, 8, 9, 10, 12, 14, 15, 16, 18, 20, 24	Chs. 5, 12, 14, 17, 19, 20, 21
Mary Kay Cosmetics, Inc.	Chs. 10, 12, 16	Chs. 3, 4, 8, 9, 21, 24	Chs. 3, 5, 6, 7, 9, 20
Measurement Research and Development, Inc.	Chs. 2, 3, 8, 9, 10, 11	Chs. 1, 5, 9, 12, 14, 14, 15, 17, 21, 22, 24	Chs. 2, 5, 6, 7, 10, 12, 13, 19, 20, 21, 22
Mighty Dog	Chs. 3, 6, 12, 13, 14, 15, 17	Chs. 4, 8, 9, 12, 15, 16, 20, 23	Chs. 5, 6, 7, 9, 11, 14, 19, 21
National Revenue Corporation	Chs. 13, 15, 16	Chs. 3, 5, 8, 13, 16, 20, 21, 22, 24	Chs. 5, 7, 10, 13, 19, 20
National Sporting Goods Association	Chs. 2, 3, 12, 13, 16	Chs. 1, 2, 5, 6, 8, 9, 10, 13, 16, 21, 24	Chs. 2, 7, 10, 11, 13, 20, 21
Omega Medical Products	Chs. 3, 8, 11, 16	Chs. 2, 5, 6, 9, 20, 21, 23	Chs. 2, 5, 10, 20, 21, 22
Penrose Hospitals	Chs. 2, 3, 4, 6, 9, 12, 15	Chs. 3, 4, 6, 8, 9, 10, 12, 24	Chs. 2, 3, 4, 6, 7, 9, 10, 11, 13, 19, 20, 21
Pipes and Tobaccos Unlimited	Chs. 3, 5, 9, 11, 16	Chs. 4, 6, 8, 9, 12, 19, 21	Chs. 5, 7, 9, 11, 14, 16, 20, 21
Powell/Kleinschmidt	Chs. 2, 3, 4, 5, 8, 15, 16	Chs. 1, 5, 6, 8, 9, 12, 19, 20, 21, 22	Chs. 2, 4, 5, 7, 10, 11, 19, 20, 21
Robinson Associates, Inc.	Chs. 2, 3, 8, 11, 12, 16	Chs. 2, 5, 6, 7, 8, 9, 12, 19, 21, 24	Chs. 2, 5, 7, 10, 11, 19, 20, 21
Round The Corner Restaurants, Inc.	Chs. 2, 3, 4, 5, 6, 12, 13, 15, 19	Chs. 4, 6, 8, 9, 10, 12, 15, 16, 20, 24	Chs. 2, 5, 6, 7, 9, 11, 14, 16, 19, 21
Semester at Sea	Chs. 2, 3, 10, 11, 12, 13, 15, 16	Chs. 4, 8, 9, 13, 14, 15, 16, 20, 21, 24	Chs. 3, 4, 5, 6, 7, 9, 11, 13, 19, 20, 21
Springville Y/USO	Chs. 2, 3, 6, 12, 13	Chs. 2, 4, 5, 6, 7, 9, 10	Chs. 3, 4, 5, 6, 7, 9, 10, 11, 14, 18, 20, 21
Time, Inc./Seagram	Chs. 3, 11, 15	Chs. 6, 7, 8, 20	Chs. 5, 7, 9, 19, 21
U.S. Government and the Auto Industry	Ch. 10	Ch. 3	Ch. 3
Walt Disney World—EPCOT Center	Chs. 3, 4, 5, 10, 11, 12, 13, 15, 18	Chs. 4, 8, 9, 10, 13, 16, 20, 24	Chs. 5, 6, 7, 9, 11, 14, 19

related to strategies and tactics—designing, assembling, and implementing the mix: product, price, distribution, and promotion (including advertising, personal selling, and sales management decisions and programs). In the final group of cases, we are back full circle to developing and integrating marketing and corporate strategies and tactics, with emphasis on evaluating internal strengths and weaknesses of the organization and assessing opportunities and threats—forces largely beyond management's control—in the external environment.

case

1

HEWLETT-PACKARD COMPANY

In 1939 Hewlett-Packard (HP) had one invention, an audio oscillator designed by Bill Hewlett, that was sold by engineers to other engineers to solve practical electronic measurement problems. The direct descendant of that original company business became an instrument line comprising over 3,000 products, still sold in the same manner—head-to-head discussions and problem-solving sessions with customers. There was a noticeable difference, however: for many years, formal marketing functions were not explicit parts of the organizational structure. In contrast, for fiscal year 1981, the company spent 15 cents of every sales dollar on marketing functions related to selling business and scientific computers, analytical and measuring instruments, electronic medical equipment, components, and hand-held calculators. The company began advertising on prime-time television, and its advertising placements in popular business periodicals steadily increased as corporate technological advancements expanded dramatically and planners began examining a wider array of potential markets.

In 1981, HP had more than 200 sales and service offices in over 80 cities throughout the United States and in 30 foreign countries. It sold through a network of 80 distributorships in certain countries where there were no company sales or service offices. There were 50,000 industrial and commercial customers, numerous educational and scientific institutions, and a variety of medical organizations doing business with the company. Virtually all products were

sold directly through HP's own sales force, with marketing operations supported by approximately 3,300 field sales engineers as well as 14,000 individuals
providing field service and administrative support. Orders originating outside
of the United States accounted for 48 percent of total company orders in fiscal
1981.[1]

New products were seen to be the keys to growth. In them, HP invested
more than 9 cents of every sales dollar in 1981. This funding level was traditional at the company, placing it among the top U.S. industrial organizations
ranked by proportion of sales invested in product development. It may not
seem surprising, then, that about 70 percent of total 1981 orders were for
products developed after 1977.[2]

Noted for its ability to innovate by nurturing small entrepreneurial
units—an apt term might be "corporateurs"—while undergoing extraordinary
growth, the company achieved total sales of $4.25 billion in the year ended
October 31, 1982.[3] Although the firm's rapid growth might occasionally col-
lide with its entrepreneurial spirit,[4] basic policies and objectives continually
evolved at HP to guide the corporation's directions and behavior. A summary
of these principles is presented in this case study to afford a framework for examining the implications of corporate philosophy and operating objectives for
designing marketing policies and strategies.

HEWLETT-PACKARD: STATEMENT OF CORPORATE OBJECTIVES[5]

Distributed to many requesters annually, both inside HP and to outsiders, and
considered by many observers to be an excellent model for formulating principles and general objectives, the pamphlet on which this section is based was
endorsed in January 1982, by David Packard, chairman of the board, William
R. Hewlett, chairman of the executive committee, and John Young, president
and chief executive officer.

> *The achievements of an organization are the result of the combined ef-
> forts of each individual in the organization working toward common ob-
> jectives. These objectives should be realistic, should be clearly understood
> by everyone in the organization, and should reflect the organization's
> basic character and personality.*

[1]Hewlett-Packard Company Form 10-K, fiscal year ended October 31, 1981.
[2]1981 Annual Report.
[3]1982 Annual Report.
[4]"Can John Young Redesign Hewlett-Packard?" *Business Week*, December 6, 1982, pp. 72–
78.
[5]HP publication, distributed both inside and outside the company, upon which this entire
section is based, Palo Alto, California, 1982.

If the organization is to fulfill its objectives, it should strive to meet certain other fundamental requirements:

First, there should be highly capable, innovative people throughout the organization. Moreover, these people should have the opportunity— through continuing programs of training and education—to upgrade their skills and capabilities. This is especially important in a technical business where the rate of progress is rapid. Techniques that are good today will be outdated in the future, and people should always be looking for new and better ways to do their work.

Second, the organization should have objectives and leadership which generate enthusiasm at all levels. People in important management positions should not only be enthusiastic themselves, they should be selected for their ability to engender enthusiasm among their associates. There can be no place, especially among the people charged with management responsibility, for half-hearted interest or half-hearted effort.

Third, the organization should conduct its affairs with uncompromising honesty and integrity. People at every level should be expected to adhere to the highest standards of business ethics, and to understand that anything less is totally unacceptable. As a practical matter, ethical conduct cannot be assured by written policies or codes; it must be an integral part of the organization, a deeply ingrained tradition that is passed from one generation of employees to another.

Fourth, even though an organization is made up of people fully meeting the first three requirements, all levels should work in unison toward common objectives, recognizing that it is only through effective, cooperative effort that the ultimate in efficiency and achievement can be obtained.

It has been our policy at Hewlett-Packard not to have a tight military-type organization, but rather, to have overall objectives which are clearly stated and agreed upon, and to give people the freedom to work toward those goals in ways they determine best for their own areas of responsibility.

Our Hewlett-Packard objectives were initially published in 1957. Since then they have been modified from time to time, reflecting the changing nature of our business and social environment. This booklet represents the latest updating of our objectives. We hope you find them informative and useful.

1. Profit

Objective To achieve sufficient profit to finance our company growth and to provide the resources we need to achieve our other corporate objectives.

Commentary   In our economic system, the profit we generate from our operations is the ultimate source of the funds we need to prosper and grow. It is the one absolutely essential measure of our corporate performance over the long term. Only if we continue to meet our profit objective can we achieve our other corporate objectives.

Our long-standing policy has been to reinvest most of our profits and to depend on this reinvestment, plus funds from employee stock purchases and other cash flow items, to finance our growth.

Profits vary from year to year, of course, reflecting changing economic conditions and varying demands for our products. Our needs for capital also vary, and we depend on short-term loans to meet those needs when profits or other cash sources are inadequate. However, loans are costly and must be repaid; thus, our objective is to rely on reinvested profits as our main source of capital.

Meeting our profit objective requires that we design and develop each and every product so that it is considered a good value by our customers, yet is priced to include an adequate profit. Maintaining this competitiveness in the marketplace also requires that we perform our manufacturing, marketing and administrative functions as economically as possible.

Profit is not something that can be put off until tomorrow; it must be achieved today. It means that myriad jobs be done correctly and efficiently. The day-to-day performance of each individual adds to—or subtracts from—our profit. Profit is the responsibility of all.

2. Customers

Objective   To provide products and services of the highest quality and the greatest possible value to our customers, thereby gaining and holding their respect and loyalty.

Commentary   The continued growth and success of our company will be assured only if we offer our customers innovative products that fill real needs and provide lasting value, and that are supported by a wide variety of useful services, both before and after sale.

Satisfying customer needs requires the active participation of everyone in the company. It demands a total commitment to *quality*, a commitment that begins in the laboratory and extends into every phase of our operations. Products must be designed to provide superior performance and long, trouble-free service. Once in production, these products must be manufactured at a reasonable cost and with superior workmanship.

Careful attention to quality not only enables us to meet or exceed customer expectations, but it also has a direct and substantial effect on our operating costs and profitability. Doing a job right the first time, and doing it consistently, sharply reduces costs and contributes significantly to higher productivity and profits.

Once a quality product is delivered to the customer, it must be supported with prompt, efficient services of the same high quality.

Good communications are essential to an effective field sales effort. Because of our broad and growing line of products, very often several sales teams will be working with a single customer. These teams must work closely to assure that the products recommended best fulfill the customer's overall, long-term needs. Moreover, HP customers must feel that they are dealing with one company, a company with common policies and services, and one that has a clear understanding of their needs and a genuine interest in providing proper, effective solutions to their problems.

3. Fields of Interest

Objective   To build on our strengths in the company's traditional fields of interest and to enter new fields only when it is consistent with the basic purpose of our business and when we can assure ourselves of making a needed and profitable contribution to the field.

Commentary   Our company's growth has been generated by a strong commitment to research and development, and has been accomplished in two ways—first, by providing a steady flow of new products to markets in which we are already well established and, second, by expanding our technology into fields that are new but related to our traditional ones. The evolution of the HP product line is a reflection of this two-dimensional growth.

Our first products were electronic measuring instruments used primarily by engineers and scientists. In time we extended our range of products to include solid-state components and instrumentation for the fields of medicine and chemical analysis. Recognizing our customers' needs to gather and assimilate large quantities of measurement data, we developed a family of computers to complement HP measuring devices. By linking measurement and computational technologies, we gained added strength in our traditional, technically-oriented markets and began to serve the broader needs of business and industry.

Today, the interactive capabilities of Hewlett-Packard instruments and systems enable our customers—decision makers in business as well as in technical fields—to gain ready access to essential information, to put it into meaningful form, and to use it effectively in improving the productivity of themselves and their organizations. Helping these customers achieve better results is the unifying purpose of our business. The areas we serve build on each other to add strength to our company and provide additional values to our customers. This guides our interests, our organization and our marketing philosophy.

The broad scope of HP technology often provides opportunities for our company to expand into new fields. Before entering a new field, however, we must satisfy ourselves that it is consistent with our business purpose and that it affords us the opportunity to make a significant *contribution.* This requires that we have not only the technology to create truly innovative and needed products, but that we also have the capability to manufacture and market them effectively and at a reasonable profit.

4. Growth

Objective   To let our growth be limited only by our profits and our ability to develop and produce innovative products that satisfy real customer needs.

Commentary   How large should a company become? Some people feel that when it has reached a certain size there is no point in letting it grow further. Others feel that bigness is an objective in itself. We do not believe that large size is important for its own sake; however, for at least two basic reasons, continuous growth in sales *and* profits is essential for us to achieve our other objectives.

In the first place, we serve a dynamic and rapidly growing segment of our technological society. To remain static would be to lose ground. We cannot maintain a position of strength and leadership in our fields without sustained and profitable growth.

In the second place, growth is important in order to attract and hold high caliber people. These individuals will align their future only with a company that offers them considerable opportunity for personal progress. Opportunities are greater and more challenging in a growing company.

5. Our People

Objective   To help HP people share in the company's success which they make possible; to provide job security based on their performance; to insure them a safe and pleasant work environment; to recognize their individual achievements; and to help them gain a sense of satisfaction and accomplishment from their work.

Commentary   We are proud of the people we have in our organization, their performance, and their attitude toward their jobs and toward the company. The company has been built around the individual, the personal dignity of each, and the recognition of personal achievements.

Relationships within the company depend upon a spirit of cooperation among individuals and groups, and an attitude of trust and understanding on the part of managers toward their people. These relationships will be good only if employees have faith in the motives and integrity of their peers, supervisors and the company itself.

On occasion, situations will arise where people have personal problems which temporarily affect their performance or attitude, and it is important that people in such circumstances be treated with sympathy and understanding while the problems are being resolved.

Job security is an important HP objective. Over the years, the company has achieved a steady growth in employment by consistently developing good new products, and by avoiding the type of contract business that requires hiring many people, then terminating them when the contract expires. The company wants HP people to have stable, long-term careers—dependent, of course upon satisfactory job performance.

Another objective of HP's personnel policies is to enable people to share in the company's success. This is reflected in a pay policy and in employee benefit programs that place us among the leaders in our industry.

There is also a strong commitment at HP to the concept of equal opportunity and affirmative action, not only in hiring but also in providing opportunities for advancement. Advancement is based solely upon individual initiative, ability and demonstrated accomplishment. Since we promote from within whenever possible, managers at all levels must concern themselves with the proper development of their people, and should give them ample opportunity—through continuing programs of training and education—to broaden their capabilities and prepare themselves for more responsible jobs.

The physical well-being of our people has been another important concern of HP's since the company's founding. With the growing complexity and diversity of our research and manufacturing processes, we must be especially vigilant in maintaining a safe and healthful work environment.

We want people to enjoy their work at HP and to be proud of their accomplishments. This means we must make sure that each person receives the recognition he or she needs and deserves. In the final analysis, people at all levels determine the character and strength of our company.

6. Management

Objective   To foster initiative and creativity by allowing the individual great freedom of action in attaining well-defined objectives.

Commentary   In discussing HP operating policies, we often refer to the concept of "management by objective." By this we mean that, insofar as possible, each individual at each level in the organization should make his or her own plans to achieve company objectives and goals. After receiving supervisory approval, each individual should be given a wide degree of freedom to work within the limitations imposed by these plans, and by our general corporate policies. Finally, each person's performance should be judged on the basis of how well these individually established goals have been achieved.

The successful practice of "management by objective" is a two-way street. Management must be sure that each individual understands the immediate objectives, as well as corporate goals and policies. Thus a primary HP management responsibility is communication and mutual understanding. Conversely, employees must take sufficient interest in their work to want to plan it, to propose new solutions to old problems, to stick their necks out when they have something to contribute. "Management by objective," as opposed to management by directive, offers opportunity for individual freedom and contribution; it also imposes an obligation for everyone to exercise initiative and enthusiasm.

In this atmosphere it is important to recognize that cooperation between individuals and between operating units is essential to our growth and success. Although our operations are decentralized, we are a *single* company whose overall strength is derived from mutually helpful relationships and frequent interaction among our dispersed but interdependent units.

It is important, as well, for everyone to recognize there are some policies which must be established and maintained on a company-wide basis. We welcome recommendations on these company-wide policies from all levels, but we expect adherence to them at all times.

7. Citizenship

Objective   To honor our obligations to society by being an economic, intellectual and social asset to each nation and each community in which we operate.

Commentary   All of us should strive to improve the environment in which we live. As a corporation operating in many different communities throughout the world, we must make sure that each of these communities is better for our presence. This means identifying our interests with those of the community; it means applying the highest standards of honesty and integrity to all our relationships with individuals and groups; it means enhancing and protecting the physical environment, building attractive plants and offices of which the community can be proud; it means contributing talent, time and financial support to worthwhile community projects.

Each community has its particular set of social problems. Our company must help to solve these problems. As a major step in this direction, we must strive to provide worthwhile employment opportunities for people of widely different backgrounds. Among other things, this requires positive action to seek out and employ members of disadvantaged groups, and to encourage and guide their progress toward full participation at all position levels.

As citizens of their community, there is much that HP people can and should do to improve it—either working as individuals or through such groups as churches, schools, civic or charitable organizations. In a broader sense, HP's "community" also includes a number of business and professional organizations, whose interests are closely identified with those of the company and its individual employees. These, too, are deserving of our support and participation. In all cases, supervisors should encourage HP people to fulfill their personal goals and aspirations in the community as well as attain their individual objectives within HP.

At a national level, it is essential that the company be a good corporate citizen of each country in which it operates. Moreover, our employees, as individuals, should be encouraged to help in finding solutions to national problems by contributing their knowledge and talents.

The betterment of our society is not a job to be left to a few; it is a responsibility to be shared by all.

Your Task:

Evaluate the usefulness of these objectives as a foundation for marketing planning.

KENTUCKY FRIED CHICKEN

The ubiquitous visage of Colonel Sanders conjures up taste-tantalizing images of a product that helped to launch the fast-food industry that has spread internationally from its U.S. roots. While many quick-service restaurant organizations were in the doldrums in 1982, Kentucky Fried Chicken (KFC) was enjoying a real growth of 2 percent, its fourth consecutive year of real growth, and store remodeling and new store development programs were underway throughout the system. Having recovered from a serious downward slide, KFC was transformed into a bright star in parent Heublein's portfolio of businesses.

REVERSING A DOWNWARD SPIRAL

The turnaround and revival of an upward trend was credited to the application of strategic planning concepts. Richard P. Mayer, KFC-USA's chairman and chief executive officer, waxed enthusiastic when asked to comment upon the way change was implemented. "That change has been fundamental and far reaching, encompassing even our overseas operations. Let me give you a brief perspective: first, KFC's vital statistics—worldwide sales for fiscal year 1981 exceeded $2 billion from the more than 6,000 Kentucky Fried Chicken stores in some 51 nations. In the United States alone, we operate more than 800 company-owned units, and we franchise another 3,600, a total of 4,400 domestic stores employing 67,000 people.

"Today, KFC is healthy, strong, and outperforming the industry, but it wasn't always so. A few years ago, KFC was dying. Wall Street had written us off. Competition was not taking us seriously. During those dark days, 1976 through 1978, our key business indicators were going down fast! Per store average sales were declining at an annual rate of 3 percent. Store-level pretax profits dropped at a 26 percent annual rate."

Exhibit 1 depicts graphically the factors described by Mr. Mayer: sales volume, store profit, and total earnings, for fiscal years 1976 through 1981. The chairman commented that in 1976 franchisees were outperforming the company-owned operations and were openly dissatisfied, even hostile. Customers were shifting to competitors in droves. Then came the restoration. "I am pleased to say that instead of dying, KFC has become one of the healthiest chains in the industry. From fiscal year 1979 (pointing to the chart in Exhibit 1), our per store average sales have shot upward at an annual rate of 14.5 percent with no end in sight. Store-level pretax profits increased 24 percent each year. Overall earnings from KFC have more than tripled."

KFC's real sales growth, adjusted for inflation and pricing, was up an average of 6 percent annually from 1979 onward, compared with 1.5 percent for

Exhibit 1

KFC AVERAGE STORE SALES

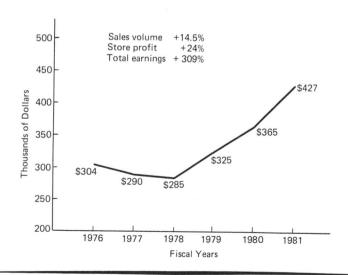

the industry, all accompanied by improved share of market. Mayer was visibly pleased: "We are increasing our market share, thanks to KFC's superior quality, service, cleanliness, and value. Many industry analysts view the change as the biggest turnaround in the fast-food industry."

VALUE OF THE PROCESS

Mayer warmed easily to the subject of how these events were brought about by the process of planning. "Strategic planning in and of itself did not turn the business around, but people working on actions derived from the plan did. The key words, I think, are 'planning' and 'process.' By moving through the strategic planning process, with exhaustive analyses, we realistically redefined our mission and objectives and developed high-leverage strategies and action plans to change our future.

"In executing the system overhaul at KFC, planners—staff and line management—conducted an intensive examination of the environment, competition and resources, both competitors' and KFC's.

"Fortunately, the overall environmental outlook was favorable, particularly for chicken-based products; still, the examination revealed intensifying competition in the quick-service restaurant [QSR] industry. While industry growth in the late 1960s and early seventies was fueled mainly by market expansion through new store development, we saw a mature industry focusing more and more on market share growth. In retrospect, we saw clearly that in 1977 KFC was not positioned or managed to exploit the chicken segment. This incongruity grew from management's view of the company as a food service conglomerate, which had diversified into a number of businesses, such as a seafood chain, a Mexican food chain, and related equipment and supply businesses. At that time we were also one of the world's largest producers of fresh broilers.

"With all these businesses to be looked after, one outcome was that KFC had received a disproportionately low share of attention. Also, there was very little 'hard information' available on KFC.

"As our analysis progressed from the environment and competition to the opportunities and threats, and strengths and limitations of our businesses, a number of conclusions emerged," Mayer recounted. "Marketing management had totally underestimated the degree of difficulty in building new business in segments where prospering giants existed. Our relative share in nonchicken businesses was nonexistent, and we faced well-entrenched competitors with favorable economics and insulation. KFC was, however, the leader in its segment with a share advantage about 5 times that of our leading competitor. Nevertheless, competition was rapidly eroding that advantage. We simply had not exploited the advantages of our leadership role."

REDEFINING THE CORPORATE MISSION

Based on these conclusions and other data from the environment, KFC's mission was redefined to capitalize on the company's strengths. The new mission was "to become the strongest, most profitable, and fastest-growing chain in the chicken segment of the QSR industry." The president collaborated with others in drafting this changed definition of what KFC was about. "The impact of this seemingly simplistic redefinition cannot be overstated. It set the tone and direction for the entire organization and required all efforts to focus on strategies required to fulfill this mission. Subsequently, the portfolio of businesses we had been pursuing was ruthlessly pared so we could concentrate on the one with strategic opportunity and strength—KFC."

RESEARCHING KFC'S PRESENT AND FUTURE

To provide the detail needed upon which to base analyses and programs, the company undertook massive proprietary research ranging from national attitude and usage studies to product testing of KFC's and competitive products. The task teams also examined competitors' annual reports, Form 10-Ks, and other secondary data to develop a picture of KFC's juxtaposition to success models. Several findings resulted from this effort: "Our chicken was not consistent, sometimes old and dry, sometimes over- or undercooked, and only occasionally 'finger-lickin' good.' Our cole slaw, mashed potatoes, and dinner roll all got poor marks, and frequently our hot foods weren't hot and the cold foods weren't very cold. Our prices were too high, our service was not fast and at times was absolutely surly. On price, nobody could remember what our advertising theme was but they usually recalled that we offered frequent discounts. But that's not all of the worst: our stores were perceived as being out of date—ugly and not clean. Our competitors outscored us by a wide margin in most respects. And, as you might expect with all these negatives, earnings, even in our best stores, were below our competitions'. Our pretax was falling. Other than that, things were pretty good.

"Obviously, past marketing management had led KFC to the brink of disaster. We had ignored the fundamentals of success in the food and restaurant industry. Quality. Service. Cleanliness. Value on the absolute basis and relative to competition. All these were absent in the equation of success."

Mayer concluded that the organization had lost touch with consumers and had lost sight of the threats in KFC's environment. Competitors were outflanking them. Examining why this was permitted to happen, Mr. Mayer continued his comments on ignoring the basics of good business. "Instead of learning why the core chicken business was weak, marketing had attempted to offset declining sales by introducing new products and discounting prices and raising prices from time to time to meet short-term sales and profit goals. This was a scenario for disaster. New products further weakened store operations by loading them with more products to project, cook, and hold. It was a vicious circle. Our efficiency base disintegrated. All these largely unplanned and irrelevant actions violated many principles of strategic planning.

"Had strategic planning processes been applied, with the proper commitment and discipline by management, these outcomes would have been predicted and could have been avoided. Yet, despite what might seem like overwhelming difficulties, Kentucky Fried Chicken had opportunities, principally the attractiveness of the chicken segment of the QSR market and our distribution and share advantage versus all chicken competitors. Further, research showed clearly that we were differentiated in the mind of the marketplace because of our proprietary product, the Colonel's Original Recipe chicken. When it is prepared correctly, our fried chicken evokes awesome consumer loyalty. Further, we knew that inefficiency and profit problems could be fixed, as demonstrated by our analysis-of-success models."

KFC's intensive review of its strengths and weaknesses confirmed to management that the new mission was achievable; the environmental review identified the critical issues that needed to be resolved to reach management's objectives, especially the principal marketing objective: to satisfy the fried chicken customer better than KFC's competitors could. The focus was changed to excelling in comparison with those stores that served primarily chicken. "However," Mayer affirmed, "we did not ignore indirect competitors like hamburger chains that dabbled in chicken as a sideline."

IMPLEMENTING CHANGE

Altering its programming to overcome lost ground in the area of consumer satisfaction meant that KFC management had to concentrate on fixing what had gone wrong over the period of decline. The chairman continued: "For example, we had to improve the quality of our products starting with chicken and extending through all side items. It was essential to adopt a strict policy of service and cleanliness in our stores. The value of the product offering had to be upped. And we faced the herculean tasks of improving the appearance of our 4,400 badly outdated stores. It was clear to all of us, upon reflection, that every one of these activities involved marketing."

Although it was apparent that Dick Mayer's enthusiasm was equal to the leadership role he must play to conduct such a wide-ranging and expensive program, the road would be tortuous. But the payoff potential was significant; perhaps the very survival of the company was at stake. Just improving the chicken would be far from simple.

He was pleased with the process: "I'll give you a sense of how we tracked through one area, improving our chicken. We were very specific when moving from strategies to plans, continually asking and answering questions until there weren't any questions left ... only answers. For instance, *How* are we going to offer the best possible chicken? The answer? We are going to standardize and cook it the Colonel's way. Another question: How are we going to get our employees to do that? Answer: We are going to train them better. Question: How are we going to do that? We will develop a systemwide training program, so that everyone will be taught exactly the right procedures. And who, then, is going to develop this tool? That was not easy to answer, but we decided that our Research and Development, Operations Engineering, and Training departments would collaborate on that one. When will it be done? Within six months, clearly an impossible schedule, but one that was met brilliantly with a state-of-the-art system. Finally, how will we know—objectively—when we've succeeded? Again, not an easy answer, but we knew that sales would be an uncertain indicator, so we decided to institute a program of inspections by mystery shoppers, who would visit stores and anonymously rate product quality."

Achieving a consensus on all these issues and on how to attack the problems proved difficult, and several doubters had to be won over as the ideas were implemented in the field. And this dimension was but one of the many that emerged.

To provide a sense of the breadth of activities in which the various task groups and management teams became involved, Mayer pointed out other areas that required intensive analysis, decisions, and planning. "We needed to increase store efficiency and profitability to a level that would place us in the top 10 percent of the industry. We had to translate all improvement programs to our franchisees, who are a large and diverse group—we have more franchisees than any other concept.

"If I have made the strategic planning process sound like unromantic hard work, with almost infinite attention to detail, then I have described it properly as I see it. This process carefully identifies the business leverage points, what must be done, who is going to do it, when they are going to do it, and last but not least, appropriate goals and means of measuring outcomes. That we did this well separates our action plan from the ordinary sort of wish book."

KFC's chief executive made it clear that providing for continuing review is an integral part of successful planning, lest many jobs go undone. He related how the KFC management committee met monthly to go through all elements in the action plans to identify programs that were not on schedule. "The managers responsible for each element did not have a very receptive audience for complaints, but they got a very attentive audience for actions that were being taken to get projects back on track. Monthly reviews of plans, which numbered in the hundreds, often took three days. Six- and seven-day weeks at KFC were the rule. Turning around a 6,000-store, worldwide system was a mammoth job. But, as you know, the KFC story had a happy ending or, perhaps I should call it, a new beginning."

CHANGING THE ROLE OF MARKETING

As he explained how strategic planning placed new demands on every department in the KFC organization, Mayer elaborated on its impact on the marketing function. "For marketing, a number of things changed. Data and definitions needed by strategic planning created a work load burden and posed a threat as traditional marketing turf was encroached upon. For example, strategic planning required marketing to define realistically the served market for KFC, to define how competition should be classified, to assess accurately the strengths and weaknesses of both KFC and its key competitors, and, where data voids existed, to structure research for enlightening the organization. The strategic planning process clearly reduced marketing's ability to 'do your own thing.' As more people knew precisely what was going on, there was less tap dancing and more accountability in the marketing function. Short-term profit tactics that would weaken the business were rejected. All menu and pricing proposals required exhaustive marketing analysis before they were submitted.

"These proposals were reviewed by top management in the light of *long-term* strategic goals, not quarter-to-quarter earnings spikes. Unbelievable as it may seem during the period of our greatest sales and earnings decline, we cut our prices to reestablish our price-value relationship, which consumer research showed was poor. Marketing management at KFC has been charged with the goal of marketing only the highest-quality products, at a good value, and with an excellent financial return. In short, marketing has been required to become more well-rounded team players working toward a common and clearly defined business goal. These new demands on marketing's skills neither stifled creativity nor resulted in mediocre marketing programs. Instead they became productive catalysts for change. As you can see, the results have been impressive."

The chairman explained how the chain's new advertising campaign was an outcome of enhanced creativity, because the advertising accurately reflected how KFC repositioned itself in a highly competitive market in moves that reflected the strategic mission of the company. One such television commercial, for example, showed a successful NFL place kicker repeatedly practicing his specialty. After a long boot between the goal posts, he exclaims enthusiastically, "I do kickin' right . . . they do chicken right!" The commercial draws a parallel between the place kicker's and Kentucky Fried Chicken's concentration on their respective specialties and implies that concentration leads to success.

Dick Mayer explained that the introduction of the strategic planning process broadened and increased marketing's role: "Today, we view our marketing people as 'strategic marketers,' because they fully embrace and use strategic planning as a very solid foundation for their work. Our best marketing people have become even better after involvement in the planning process. In fact, they quickly saw the logic and applied this tool to improve the business and, not so incidentally, their careers. On the other hand, the weaker performers who never saw the light are now tap dancing on someone else's stage, not ours.

"Our Marketing Department has never been stronger, more effective, and more motivated than it is today. And, although we are concentrating on the impact of planning on marketing, all others were similarly impacted because strategic planning clarified not only the direction and goals of the company but also facilitated the allocation of resources and helped balance demands across *all* functions. The result? KFC is not a dead bird, but is soaring like an eagle!"

EPILOGUE

KFC's atmosphere in 1982 was optimistic as the aura of success extended to franchisees, which voted to increase their contribution to network TV advertising from 1.5 percent of sales to 2.0 percent, and to parent Heublein, which happily announced that real growth for KFC in 1982 was running at a rate of 2 percent while performance for much of the industry was either flat or declining. In the fall of 1982, plans were announced for the chain to launch U.S.-style drive-in restaurants in the United Kingdom, commencing with new sites at the edge of town, rather than competing head on with other fast-food restaurants found mainly in business district locations. KFC was also planning to expand its stores in Japan—350 already in operation—and in Australia, where there were 200 stores.

Your Task:

Based on Mr. Mayer's comments and your research into the QSR industry, advise KFC's management on marketing issues they presently face.

case

3

A. POE DESIGNS, INC.

My involvement with A. Poe Designs began at a cocktail party for past and present members of the governor's staff. I was a past staff member who had left public service to return to the business arena. While listening to a number of "political" conversations, I heard someone talking about profits, margins, and a new business venture, and I gravitated to that side of the room to find the source of this interesting conversation. I was surprised to find a past working associate, Ann Poe, who had left political life a few years before I had, was married, had a child, and was trying to begin a business in her home, combining career and family responsibilities. An artist and fine seamstress, Ann was designing and manufacturing women's fabric purses and fabric-lined picnic baskets, with accessories. As she put it, "I've been working on this project, off and on, for about two years now, and I still don't have a clear idea of how to get these items on the market. I don't have any business background and am not the selling type, so I'm really at a standstill."

The project sounded interesting, so after more discussion I volunteered my assistance. I was teaching at a local college and thought I could spare some time to lend a hand. Little did I realize what lay ahead of us. Our experience together might be best termed a "quest for focus."

BACKGROUND OF THE PRODUCT

The line of A. Poe Designs included three sizes of women's handbags, a brief-case for women, and accessories in the three purse colors of blue, salmon, and green. The accessories were seen primarily as loss leaders used to stimulate the purchase of the handbags, not necessarily to generate profit. These accessories, made in the same fabric as the purse to match the item chosen, included a matching glasses case and a zippered makeup case. The purse sizes combined functionality with fashion to create a purse size for virtually any use. The smaller purse might be used for day or evening, while the medium-sized purse would be perfect for "the woman who has everything" and carries it with her. The larger tote was an ideal bag for an exercise/aerobics class or as a diaper bag. All items were machine washable ensuring ease of care and unlimited use in or out of doors. With the accessories designed to complement the item selected and purchased, each creation offered an additional incentive for purchase.

I had asked Ann about the care of the fabric since shrinkage or fading could ruin the product's reputation and her business as well. "Oh, I get the fabric from a domestic manufacturer," she continued. "He seems reliable but won't quilt the fabric; so I use a local quilter to do each ream for me. The small floral prints are basically a French pattern and are very similar to the Pierre Dioux designs; however, my fabric is at least half the price of theirs. I've washed all the purses that I've made so far and they come out just fine, no shrinkage or bleeding; but as for fading, I'm not sure what they'll do. I did make one for my mother-in-law a few years ago and she uses it all the time. She's never said anything about fading, so I assume fading isn't a problem—this is really fine fabric."

I was also curious about her picnic baskets and how she saw those items fitting into the purse line; one normally doesn't see purses and picnic baskets in the same line. "Well, I had a lot of excess fabric that didn't have the contrasting trim, so I used it to line some picnic baskets and make table cloths with matching napkins," she continued. "It used up most of my excess fabric and people were selling them on consignment; so I decided to keep making them until I found some other use for my excess fabric that didn't have the contrasting design." She explained further: "You see, the body of the purse is made with the floral fabric. When I purchase the floral fabric, it has a contrasting design along two borders. Of course, I have more floral fabric than contrast, so I use the excess floral fabric for the accessories and the picnic baskets."

MARKET EVALUATION

I proposed that Ann do some market testing to determine what items and colors in the line appealed to potential customers. We tested a group of 200 women on the campus where I taught. Since research funds were limited, we segmented our market group to younger women. We felt that this group would give us a reliable measure of the product's acceptance. The results demonstrated that blue was the favored color with salmon coming in as a very close second. The most popular size was more difficult to determine since the smaller and medium-sizes were almost equal in demand preference. The larger tote was well received but not as a purse. The picnic baskets were well liked but not at our suggested price levels. The following data summarize results of the research:

Question 1: If purchasing this product, which size would you choose?

SIZE PREFERENCE		
	Number	Percentage
Small purse	85	43.5%
Medium purse	83	42.5
Large tote	32	16.0

Question 2: If purchasing this product, which color would you choose?

COLOR PREFERENCE		
	Number	Percentage
Azure blue	81	40.5%
Salmon red	77	38.5
Medium green	42	21.0

Question 3: What price range do you apply to each size/item?

PRICE PREFERENCE		
	Range	Percentage
Small purse	$20–$35	80%
Medium purse	30– 40	75
Large tote	40– 50	65
Briefcase	40– 50	40

Although the purses were favorably received, only 80 percent of those tested would purchase at the suggested prices. The briefcase suffered the most with only 40 percent of those tested willing to spend that much for a fabric briefcase.

Question 4: Of what is your current purse made?

CURRENT PURSE MATERIAL		
	Number	Percentage
Leather	70	35%
Fabric	80	40
Other	50	25

This test was completed during the spring and summer, which can explain the high number of fabric purses recorded.

Question 5: Where do you purchase your purses, totes, or related items?

PURCHASE POINT		
	Number	Percentage
Department store	107	53.5%
Women's store/boutique	62	31.0
Specialty store	23	11.5
Mail order/catalog	8	4.0

This group showed a high percentage of purchases in department stores over specialty stores. It should be noted as well that many specialty stores are in the area of this college campus.

Question 6: What is the average price of your purses?

AVERAGE PRICE OF PURCHASE		
	Number	Percentage
Between $15 and $18	7	3.5%
Between $19 and $22	20	10.0
Between $23 and $26	23	11.5
Between $26 and $29	53	26.5
Over $30	97	48.5

Question 7: Would you purchase this purse/briefcase?

PURCHASE RATE		
	Number	Percentage
Yes	184	92%
No	16	8

The overwhelming majority of persons tested would purchase the product; and they normally spent over $30 for their purse purchases.

Question 8: Would you purchase this purse/briefcase for these prices?

PRICE/PURCHASE RATE			
	Yes	No	Yes Percentage
Small purse	$25	196	4	98.0%
Medium purse	35	156	44	78.0
Large tote	40	102	98	51.0
Briefcase	40	80	120	40.0

The demand for each product dropped off drastically when high price levels were reached. Value added was not perceived sufficient to justify the higher prices.

Question 9: What do you see as the quality measure of these products?

QUALITY RATING		
	Number	Percentage
Excellent	172	86%
Good/Fair	26	13
Poor	2	1

Question 10: What would cause you *not* to purchase these products?

PRODUCT LIMITATIONS	
	Percentage
Fabric does not last	62%
Fabric could fade or shrink	45
Needs care instructions	47
Questioned guarantee if any	53

The area of most concern was that of the construction and its ability to withstand use and proper routine care.

Question 11: What is your opinion of the picnic basket?

PICNIC BASKET PERCEPTIONS		
	Number	Percentage
More than favorable	185	92.5%
Favorable	15	7.5
Unfavorable	0	—

All those tested liked the picnic basket both in terms of overall construction and contents.

Question 12: Would you purchase these baskets if you felt the price correct?

PURCHASE RATE		
	Number	Percentage
Yes	195	97.5%
No	5	2.5

The vast majority saw a personal use for the picnic baskets and would use them as well as purchase them if they found the price acceptable.

Question 13: Would you purchase the picnic basket for these prices?

PRICE/PURCHASE RATE				Yes
		Yes	No	Percentage
Small	$100	55	145	27.5%
Large	150	20	180	10.0

Clearly, the price was too high.

DISTRIBUTION

We discussed several methods of distribution, ranging from mail order to consignment distribution and even personal selling, which Ann had basically used for the past year. I asked her who was currently buying her purses and how purchasers found out about them. "Most of the orders come from my mother-in-law's friends. She travels a great deal. People see her tote and ask her where she got it, and that leads to my getting a few orders. Normally, people will ask for a tote with the matching little purse. There's a lot of demand for that among the cruise ship set."

We decided to try the women's boutiques to see how they might feel about distributing our handbags. The area we chose was characterized by households with incomes ranging between $70,000 and $100,000. We started by personally contacting each boutique. After 10 contacts and 2 sales, we decided that this technique was far too expensive.

I asked Ann, "Do you know of anyone who could put together a photo layout/mailer for us? How about your friend who works as a printer downtown?" That weekend we took several photos of the line in use and in traditional display pose, and Ann's printer friend mounted the shots that we selected and printed selling copy.

Armed with 10 sets of the photo layout, we compiled a list of the most likely and largest customers of women's clothing and accessories. The next step was to compose a sales letter and enclose the layouts to send to prospects. Each "packet" also contained a "fact sheet" to explain the product, its prices and options, in the case of the picnic basket, and an order sheet. We had reduced our costs from $27.00 for a personal call to $7.00 for the direct-mail technique.

The choice of selective distribution rather than intensive or exclusive was based upon the assumption that our demographic segment was not quite priced at the exclusive end of the market, which would require more value added on the part of the product and increased promotional coverage to communicate this exclusivity of ownership, therefore increasing our costs. Our costs prevented pricing at a level low enough to merit distribution through larger department stores, which would require us to sell to them for less and would create demand that we could not meet at the current level of production. Until production increased considerably, selective distribution seemed well-fitted to our capabilities and suited the image of the product.

Choosing the selective mode of distribution was also based on our need for relative control of the line and its development as well as the need for increased compatibility within the line. By distributing in only fine women's shops, the perceived quality of the product benefited as did the reputation of the store in distributing only selective items. The knowledge that only other fine women's shops would be carrying this line increased the owner's desire to carry the line as well. This then ensured compatibility among the distributors and harmony within the channel.

COSTS AND PRICING

After approaching several potential distributors, we found a major problem—keystoning. A typical dialogue between Ann and a store owner will illustrate:

Ann: *We're asking $20 for the small purse, $25 for the medium, and $30 for the ladies' tote. (Ann had arrived at these prices by keystoning her price relative to her cost, i.e., if it cost her $8 to make the small purse, she sold it for $16.)*

Owner: *Oh. That's a bit high for me. You see I keystone my prices. If you sell the small to me for $20, I sell it for $40. So the tote would run $60; and I don't think I can get that for the tote, not even if I threw in the matching makeup case for free!*

Ann: *Well, what do you think might be a reasonable price that would give you an equitable margin?*

Owner: *I'd say about $12 for the small, $14 for the medium, and $19 for the large tote.*

Ann: *I couldn't sell them that cheap, I'd only make about $4 per purse.*

Owner: *Well, what are you selling the picnic baskets for?*

Ann: *$100 for the picnic basket for two and $150 for the basket for four.*

Owner: *You're way out of my range there. I'm afraid I can't take any of the line.*

It was plain to see that the prices must be adjusted and the line expanded to include another "enticer." Since many people who purchased the tote got the small purse to match, we decided to make a briefcase to stimulate demand for the smaller purse as well. We then analyzed our costs (itemized in Exhibit 1) and reduced them to lower our price. The new prices ranged from $16 for the small purse, $20 for the medium, $30 for the tote, and $30 for the brief-

Exhibit 1

PRODUCTION COSTS AND WHOLESALE PRICES

ITEM	LABOR*	MATERIALS	TOTAL	WHOLESALE PRICE
Small purse	$ 3.00	$ 5.00	$ 8.00	$ 16.00
Medium purse	3.00	7.00	10.00	20.00
Large tote	5.00	10.00	15.00	30.00
Ladies' briefcase	5.00	10.00	15.00	30.00
Glasses case	.50	1.00	1.50	3.00
Makeup case	.75	1.25	2.00	4.00
Picnic basket for 2	10.00	30.00	40.00	80.00
Picnic basket for 4	10.00	40.00	50.00	100.00

*Computed at $3.50 per hour.

Exhibit 2

THE COLLECTION

Bags of uncommon quality. Made of the finest domestic cotton, treated with Dupont Teflon. Machine washable in cold water. Line dry. A variety of sizes to meet your every need. Available in three delightful colors: salmon red, loden green, and azure blue. Bags are fully lined, with a zipper closure and reinforced bottom. Accessories are also available.

The briefcase is fully lined with a large inside pouch and a zipper pocket.

Price List		Accessories	
Ladies' briefcase	$30.00	Glasses case	$3.00
10" x 16"		Fully lined with a	
Ladies' tote	$30.00	velcro closure	
Size: Approx. 9" high x		Makeup bag	$4.00
18" long		6" x 9", fully lined	
Ladies' medium bag	$20.00	with a zipper closure	
Size: Approx. 7" high x			
14" long			
Ladies' small bag	$16.00		
Size: Approx. 5" high x			
10" long			

Exhibit 3

PICNIC BASKET DESCRIPTION

Baskets are made of Hong Kong rattancore and peel. They are fully lined with quilted, reinforced weaver's cloth (50 percent cotton, 50 percent polyester). The lining can be easily removed for washing. Napkins and tablecloth are made of cotton and are also machine washable. Plates, mugs, and storage containers are made of durable plastic and are dishwasher safe on the top rack. Also included is a waiter's corkscrew, cheese knife/spreader, and chopsticks. Matching flatware and handmade cutting board are available at additional cost.

Prices	Options
Picnic basket for four, $100 each	Cutting board, $5
Basket size: 20" x 14" x $8^{1}/_{2}$"	Flatware, $3 per place setting
Picnic basket for two, $80 each	
Basket size: 18" x $12^{1}/_{2}$" x 7"	

case. We priced the glasses case at $3 and the makeup bag at $4. We marked the large picnic basket down to $100 and the picnic basket for two to $80. Since we felt that the $16 matching purse would stimulate their sale, we priced the tote and briefcase around $30 (see Exhibits 2 and 3).

PROMOTION

The next pressing issue was promotion. Because of limited funding, promotion was restricted to personal calling and mailing. (The purse is a small purchase, relative to other wardrobe expenses, and advertising seemed an unaffordable luxury.) As I told Ann, "This market segment is relatively homogeneous in terms of needs and demography. The only purpose for advertising, therefore, would be to differentiate this purse among other handbags or to cultivate a 'fad' of some sort. Since the achievement of either of these objectives might push demand beyond what we can supply, I'd suggest that we test the market first to see if there is a need for advertising and what type would be the most effective."

Our promotion strategy, then, relied heavily on direct mail to generate demand from store owners. Direct mail was chosen based upon some secondary research by my students. Their research uncovered some interesting facts concerning direct mail:

1. Seventy-five percent of the people who receive direct mail feel favorable about it.
2. Eighty times more leads result from direct mail than from ads placed in newspapers or magazines.
3. Mail's total share of all advertising budgets has increased 46 percent in the past five years.
4. The cost of direct-mail advertising is .0073 times the total cost of a personal call, on the average.
5. The Direct Mail Marketing Association (DMMA) ran ads for nine years to offer a mailing list Name Removal Service. Some 163,000 people accepted the offer to have their names removed from mailing lists for a $5 fee. Yet 200,000 people responded by asking to be put on **more** lists.

It appeared that mail marketing promised great growth in the future both as a channel of advertising for A. Poe Designs and as a sales medium to potential ultimate purchasers. We considered also exploring this avenue to determine if mail-order houses such as Lands' End or L. L. Bean might be interested in distributing the A. Poe Design Line.

CONCLUSION

My job was done—providing focus and direction to help Ann make a go of her idea. We had tested the market, adjusted costs and prices, developed the product fact sheets and order forms, and created direct-mail selling packets. My final recommendation was that she lower her prices even further to ensure greater success. Basically, I wanted to see the wholesale prices come down about 30 percent, but Ann was reluctant. So the prices remained as shown in Exhibits 2 and 3.

Ann's final comment: "I never knew there was so much to do to begin a simple, small business. It's amazing how much preparation time you spend before you even begin to make a sale. If most people knew how much time and money it takes, I doubt they would begin their own businesses. But at least the hard part is over; now all I have to do is sell."

Your Task:

Analyze the consultant's role for Ann Poe Designs. Where does Ann Poe go from here?

POWELL/KLEINSCHMIDT

Donald D. Powell expressed the belief that architectural firms can improve their practice of management. "Being a competent architect does not mean that one is capable of managing a firm. Many architects, scrambling for business against hundreds of others seeking the same jobs, are often eager to cut fees to get contracts, frequently hovering near the break-even point for months at a time, gradually laying off staff, and ultimately closing their doors. The supposed rule-of-thumb fee of 10 percent of a structure's value no longer holds, and often the higher the cost of the structure, the lower the percentage charged, as competition for projects intensifies. Few firms have well-structured sales plans, waiting instead for business to walk in the door. When the outlook is bleak, the staff is underpaid and there is turnover with too few people to handle projects. Also, uncontrollable costs are rising rapidly, such as insurance for errors and omissions, with annual premiums often costing 8 to 10 percent of the coverage.

"Talent is the main requirement for entering this business. Our focus as interior designers is on how to use the building as contrasted to the building architect's emphasis on getting it constructed. But it takes money, of course, and most beginning architectural firms are undercapitalized." Powell was explaining how, in 1976, he and Robert D. Kleinschmidt made the transition from working all their professional lives at the nationally known firm of Skidmore, Owings & Merrill (SOM), to organizing Powell/Kleinschmidt (P/K) in the crowded design marketplace. Starting with 2 individuals, then growing to 12 in 1982, the partners intended to limit the size of their organization because, in Powell's words, "We are a small group of architecturally trained specialists, and I don't expect we'll alter the management structure much beyond appointing Gregory Patterson, who was made a principal last year. However, we look forward to electing a designer as principal."

All the P/K design/production staff in 1982 were architects, and most were SOM alumni as well. Victoria Behm, who came aboard in 1981 to help develop the marketing function, also had the credentials and experience that added to her credibility with the firm's professionals.

Donald Powell graduated in architecture from the University of Minnesota, spent 2 years in the Air Force, worked 6 months in Minneapolis, and served on the team that designed the United States Air Force Academy. He exercised his talents for 15 years at SOM, having started there as an associate designer.

Robert Kleinschmidt did his undergraduate work in architecture at the University of Illinois, Urbana, followed by an M.A. in design at Columbia University after which he spent 6 months in Europe, studying design and evaluating products that would later become a part of his detail work and colorist orientation in Chicago. "Don's role is more managerial," Kleinschmidt remarked, "so he is happiest during the conceptual stages of a project, work that I *can* do but Don does better. This provides a good balance: when Don's interest wanes, after the planning is completed, I'm excited to begin with design development and the implementation details, and thus see the total project take shape. And I also enjoy the marketing aspects."

A brief visit at Powell/Kleinschmidt is enough to convince anyone that Chicago is clearly this firm's kind of town, with its legendary dynamism, its North Michigan Avenue known to shoppers and others as the "magnificent mile," top-notch restaurants, the Cubs, Bears, and Black Hawks, the world's tallest building, great newspapers, renowned institutions of higher learning, one of the world's busiest airports, remarkable museums—a city with a fascinating history and a powerful future.

A look at the new skyscrapers appearing on Chicago's horizon reminds one that highrise configurations are changing and that Chicago is a leader in that shift. Geometry has begun to reform, from the boxes that Wright scorned, to curves and nontraditional approaches, including recognition of the worth of older structures. "Snakeskin" skyscrapers offer alternatives not available in predecessor structures that once dominated the scene, and interior spaces pose dramatic challenges for designers who are confronted with a variety of arrangement possibilities beyond the classic box.

ROLE OF THE INTERIOR DESIGNER

Despite his reputation for establishing trends in buildings, Frank Lloyd Wright objected to being called the "father of modern architecture" and often inveighed against the "sterility," as he called it, of some of the boxlike houses and stark steel skyscrapers that began dotting cityscapes in the post–World War II era. He professed disliking cities, so it was not accidental that most of his effort was spent on designing homes, churches, museums, hotels—buildings that do not dominate skylines. P/K thrives not on designing massive buildings but, rather, on developing people spaces inside them.

"In the early 1940s, architecture became a major tool in developing cities, but it took a while for space planning the interior layouts and finishes to be considered in any terms other than square footage," observed Powell. "As interior designers, we are concerned with a building module, the environmental factors that affect the human condition—air conditioning, lighting, sound, floors and floor coverings, electrical and telephone outlet placement, and window treatments. In other words, we are responsible for everything inside the front door. Skidmore has been a leader in this movement of developing people spaces. This is important to all employees, even, by way of example, for data processing managers and programmers who are really assistants to their machines; the workspace they occupy reflects status, or lack of it, in the organization."

P/K seemed to be the beneficiary of a minor miracle when, at slightly more than one year of age and with seven on the staff, the firm was commissioned by Prudential Insurance Company of America to design, first, a 260,000-square-foot operations facility in Merrillville, Indiana, and soon thereafter one even larger in scope—Prudential's North Central Operations Center in Plymouth, Minnesota, a 385,000-square-foot interior project in a new building. The latter required three years to complete, from the planning/design stage through installation of all the furnishings and equipment. P/K was hired to work in concert with the building architects as a total building team from the outset of the project, to do the space planning and interior design, select base building materials, organize a graphics and signage program, and develop a sizable art collection, plus compile a 10-volume maintenance manual dealing with the entire design process for in-house use.

As Kleinschmidt put it, "We are collaborators not competitors with the architect, and we avoid intruding into the relationship between the primary architect and the building's owner. Their efforts and ours are complementary. Specializing in what we've chosen to do has given us a niche in the market that few seemed to be interested in, but it's what we are best qualified to do."

"I cannot say we are unique," said Powell, responding to laudatory comments about the company's ability to get large commissions even before proving its credibility, "because the design process at P/K differs scarcely at all from other architectural/design firm approaches. For example, we first set goals and try to identify potential problems of the project, and then we estimate budgets and time horizons for various stages of the proposed project. Budgets and time always produce conflict; they're the most unpleasant dimensions in the earlier phases. Following that, we undertake comprehensive programming interviews with executives and others to get inputs for putting together the space calculations and the needs of various departments, including interactions among people who will use the space we design. We diagram these interactions to help everyone visualize the flows. Once client approval is given in this, the conceptual phase, we get into the particulars of systems furniture, other furnishings, colors, and materials—all the elements that will be most visible to those in the finished space.

"After all these tasks are completed, a formal presentation, complete with budgets and time schedules, is assembled and a presentation is made to the client. We typically show three conceptual design schemes: our preferred solution, a variation on that theme that is close but not exactly the same concept, and a radical departure from our recommended approach. After client acceptance, we make a final design, with details; then we develop the architectural drawing phase with the required specifications and send it out for bid to the various contractors to complete the project."

Exhibits 1, 2, 3, and 4 are descriptions of interiors designed by Powell/ Kleinschmidt.

GETTING STARTED

Powell explained P/K's modest beginnings: "We each invested $5,000 cash and $25,000 in securities as initial capital. Harris Bank let us lease space while finishing off the space with very little money up front for construction. In searching for space, we looked at lofts, hoping to share with others in the overhead burden; we considered older buildings, lower in rent than newer space, but we could not find the kind of space we needed; we finally settled on this prime, central location in Chicago's central business district. It has a clean openness, north light, and other amenities. The design features in our office demonstrate what we can do and that we will have the same concern for clients' needs. In other words, we need a working area that makes a statement. Most architects get along with low-quality surroundings. I just never wanted to have to say to a client, 'Forgive us for living in this slum, but don't worry, we'll do great things for you.'

"However, we worked in a friend's architect office the first six months and handled office matters in my apartment, with a former co-worker typing for us after her regular office hours. This was minimally satisfactory until we moved into our present offices in April and May of 1977."

During the first six months the partnership billed between $4,500 and $6,000 a month. Accounting was simple and the firm was not complex.

Bob Kleinschmidt remembered early struggles just to get the word out: "A lot of effort that first six months was spent letting the world know we had left SOM, that we were on our own and ready to do business. Then a friend of Don's, while at work on a Prudential project, mentioned our names. We prepared a brochure and forwarded it to the director of interior design. Prudential wanted evidence we could serve their needs. We couldn't meet in Don's apartment or at our friend's office, so our banker friends at Harris Bank loaned us a conference room, a table, and some chairs."

"We took a lighthearted approach," interjected Don Powell, "and humorously presented our case that P/K could come through for Prudential. Fortunately, they had a sense of humor, thought we were gutsy, and asked us to visit Minneapolis to see their executives. Quickly, we called people who had

---

Exhibit 1

DESCRIPTION OF P/K OFFICES IN DOWNTOWN CHICAGO

These offices for interior architecture practice are the embodiment of orderliness and openness; they combine a utilitarianism of purpose with a gracefulness of plan and design. The glass light at the front door, flanked by seasonal flowering plants, invites the visitor and client to enter.

Materials and fabrics were chosen to provide a neutral background so that color may come from the architects' work projects. Walls, upholstered in limousine cloth (a wool flannel), are "tackable," to facilitate study and display of current work in progress.

A 6 foot high English brown oak storage unit 25 feet in length divides the office's executive-administrative space from the drafting room. The reception area functions as a holding space for clients and manufacturers' representatives, office manager space, and coat storage. With tackable walls for drawings and presentations, the conference area may also be used for slide programs, while the partners' area, with a contemporary version of a traditional partner's desk, affords private space for confidential exchange and private space.

A color and materials laboratory is equipped with storage space and a variety of lighting types for evaluating fabrics and materials samples.

The drafting room, a model of functional design, has 12 custom-built work stations. Leather-tufted cushions on the window seats provide for rest space, catalog viewing, or informal conference with a colleague. Files and library material are built into the work stations. The drafting table surfaces are plastic laminated for ease of maintenance. All components combine to make for efficiency and professionalism of the highest order.

Exhibit 2

DESCRIPTION OF ILLINOIS HOUSING DEVELOPMENT AUTHORITY PROJECT*

Among Powell/Kleinschmidt projects, the Illinois Housing Development Authority is unique. The degree of involvement was complete, from the initial request to help the Authority find suitable space to assisting in negotiating the terms of the lease, planning and designing the space, obtaining bids, and coordinating and supervising the entire move.

To identify office space that would be efficient and functional, attractive but not ostentatious, and at the same time cost effective, Powell/Kleinschmidt compiled a list of 30 sites and inspected approximately half the suggested locations. The space chosen is linear in proportion and provides excellent adaptability to all the requirements of the Illinois Housing Development Authority.

In establishing the design philosophy, notice was taken of the corporate structure, which consists of a high proportion of managerial positions to clerical workers. The client was also concerned that the design provide for acoustical privacy and be reflective of the Authority's role as a public body.

In addition to providing work areas for approximately 90 employees, including offices for the director, deputy director, legal counsel, and other executives, space is allotted to a reception area, a multipurpose conference area, a computer room, and storage.

Acoustic movable partitions were specified in three heights that tier downward to conform to the window sill height along the exterior wall, thereby affording more light and view into interior spaces.

The work stations consist of plastic laminated panels, metal desks and files, and various models of the Krueger vertebrae chair, which, at the time, was its largest installation. The beige color palette deepens and intensifies as one moves closer to the exterior windows and walls. A plant program enhances the environment, as does the art program that includes the use of project renderings as art. The interiors are further enlivened by an ever-changing group of works of art on loan from the School of the Art Institute of Chicago.

*Area of 22,500 square feet, completed April 1979.

Exhibit 3

DESCRIPTION OF AMERICAN STEEL FOUNDRIES PROJECT*

When the 25-year-old offices of American Steel Foundries, a division of Amsted Industries, were found to be inadequate, the company decided to relocate all of its five departments. With the aid of Powell/Kleinschmidt, American Steel reassessed future space requirements for its 150 employees.

Each of the five divisions—product engineering, finance, marketing, manufacturing, and industrial relations—had distinctive requirements. They shared general common goals, however, in wishing to provide a fresh environment that would engender a sense of uplift, brightness, and cheerfulness. The project included a reception area, executive offices, two conference rooms, a full-service computer room on a raised floor system, and an extensive file section.

The client decided to adopt the open office concept throughout, permitting a visitor to grasp the entire plan at a glance. The color and materials scheme of neutral gray carpet, walls painted in shades of gray, and white work stations is enlivened with bright accent colors of red, yellow, blue, green, orange, and purple for fabrics on the work station panel enclosures and furniture.

The reception room repeats the use of bold vivid colors with red wool fabric, custom designed by Powell/Kleinschmidt, on walls flowing to the built-in sofa and black chairs for sharp contrast.

In a few instances, the client resolved to use existing specialized furniture and other equipment, freshened by electrostatically applied paint to ensure that it would be compatible with the new. The choice of materials was also dictated by the necessity for ease of maintenance. In high-traffic areas, vinyl wall covering, Antron nylon carpet, and heavy-duty upholstery were specified. In spite of a rather high worker density, the acoustical effect is one of quiet.

To give a sense of completeness and a look of quality to the entire project, extensive use is made of live plants and trees. An art program, contemporary in character to reflect the fresh surroundings, has also been installed. Original works of art are placed in the offices of the president and upper-level management; elsewhere, framed posters of high quality are hung, including two groups of Vasarely prints that effectively modulate and brighten corridor walls.

The response to the newly designed spaces has been enthusiastic and has resulted in a high level of performance.

*Area of 32,000 square feet, completed July 1980.

Exhibit 4

DESCRIPTION OF THE
PRUDENTIAL INSURANCE COMPANY OF AMERICA
PROJECT AT MERRILLVILLE, INDIANA*

Wanting to be assured of a reliable quality work force, the Prudential Insurance Company of America decided to build one of its key satellite facilities in Merrillville, Indiana. A company-ordered survey had confirmed this sought-for benefit.

The structure, designed for 1,150 employees, is built on the open office concept. The building materials consist of precast concrete in tones of beige, black slate flooring, white plaster walls and ceilings, and metal surfaces of stainless steel, complemented by intense shades of red, yellow, blue, and green, all set against a background of flannel-gray carpet and lighter-toned work stations.

Entrance to the Prudential Merrillville offices is gained via a bridge through a three-story greenhouse, after which the visitor comes to the main reception area. Here the focal point is a specially commissioned black and white painting by the artist Al Held; the intersecting and overlapping geometric forms suggest depth and space.

For a maximum of flexibility the concept of open office planning was adopted, while offices and conference rooms were clustered around service cores, relating to function of operation in a three-part hierarchy of circulation area, clerical staff, and managerial staff. To keep vistas free, no offices were built along the exterior; rather, all are interior.

On the first floor, work stations for four staff members form an H-cluster; 42-inch high panels assure that vision is unimpaired and at the same time provide tack surface plus screening for paperwork organizers. Floors are covered with carpet tiles. Large masses of green plants help to break the rigidity of the work station pattern.

A free-standing wall of frameless glass, darkly tinted, separates the reception area from the third floor executive area. Ultramarine blue wool Jacquard, woven with the company's Rock of Gibraltar logo, was designed for the reception wall panels. This same fabric is repeated in the bright thematic colors in the interior offices and conference room.

A regional art program was employed for the principal offices and conference rooms, with each occupant and department selecting its own artwork. For the public spaces several large paintings, tapestries, and sculptures were commissioned by artists of established reputation. To reduce the length of corridors, a consequence of the arrangement of offices, and to interrupt the monotony of line, neon light sculptures by the artist Chryssa were mounted in tinted Plexiglas boxes, allowing the shapes to be reflected in double and multiple images.

Exhibit 4 (Cont.)

Located above the lobby entrance, the main seminar room is equipped with projection facilities and can be subdivided by means of retractable white oak panel walls into three smaller rooms.

In summary, the overriding concern and challenge of the architectural design was to create an environment for the entire company staff that would be pleasing and workable, one in which each employee would feel a productive and significant member of the Prudential organization.

*Area of 260,000 square feet, completed September 1978.

---

previously expressed interest in joining our firm, we put together a slide show and went on the offensive. Next, the Prudential executives visited Chicago, where Harris Bank let us show what we had done for them, including the west tower, that took some five years to finish.

"Mr. Harris invited us in, walked around his desk, sat on the edge of it, and turned to the visiting Prudential team: 'Gentlemen,' he stated, 'you have the opportunity to hire Powell and Kleinschmidt, an option few people have. I assure you that Harris Bank is backing them completely.' The Prudential people were practically bowled over, and I must admit Bob and I were surprised, too. But that did it! Mr. Harris immediately established our credibility, in a way we never could have, with this large, conservative company. It was just a stroke of luck that he was in and was willing to go out on a limb for us."

P/K was awarded the Prudential contract, winning in competition with three other aspirants. As Powell put it, "Before we got settled into the office, we began full-blast. There was no time to get organized; it was all we could do to keep up with the job. Then, three months into that activity, Prudential hired us for yet another major project—they recognized our uniqueness. The North Central Plymouth Operations [NCPO] was the largest project either of us had ever worked on. It was exciting, and it gave us needed credibility. We became known as a firm that does a thorough, complete job with unique but conservative solutions, all the while working closely with decision makers.

"Sometimes we are criticized for our projects looking similar to each other," Powell continued; "this is surprising since we do take into account clients' quirks and idiosyncrasies, and we do attempt to express the regionalism of each project we undertake. The criticism is sometimes that we produce starkness when some prefer frills. But we are not into antiquities or into style for style's sake. With all our clients, money *is* an object. We always sell our reasons for selecting certain features—we don't sell 'better designs' but concentrate on the merits that have long-lasting implications for the owner.

"Prudential imposed no stipulations from an aesthetic viewpoint but did participate every step of the way in budgeting and space planning on all of our

Prudential projects. P/K was given a specific dollar amount that could be spent for each work station and an overall budget figure that was not to be exceeded," according to the project manager, Greg Patterson. The company presented the architects with strict guidelines delineating the square footage per work station at various hierarchical levels. For example, on NCPO the average open offices were to have about 135 square feet each and private offices 210 square feet. Nearby conference rooms were identically sized and could be converted into offices if needed. In pleasant contrast to the linear grid of work stations, closed spaces in the facility were trapezoidally shaped.

Bob Kleinschmidt orchestrated the art program. "This was the second time the client entrusted an art program's development to an outside concern; previously all were assembled in house. The first was Prudential in Merrillville, Indiana, also awarded to Powell/Kleinschmidt." Credit was given to a Prudential vice president, Oren McDonald, for being the crucial factor in the program's success and seeing to it that sufficient funds were allocated to art. "We bought about 300 works, including approximately 50 on special commission for specific spaces. We came in under budget. Our payment was flat fee for this service. No percentages were involved. Prudential even did the paperwork and accounting on that part of the project."

He continued, "I focus on establishing and maintaining working relationships with furniture manufacturers, product designers, textile and fiber specialists, graphic designers, horticulturists, and artists, but I consider it everyone's responsibility at P/K. These interactions enable P/K to obtain higher-quality products at budget-conscious figures, whether it's something as elementary as floor coverings and work stations or as critical as accessories and art objects."

The partners cited 1980 billings of $600,000 and expected to reach $750,000 in 1982, a far cry from earlier days when they felt the queasiness that most experience when forsaking the tidiness, security, and steady paychecks of a large, established firm for the uncertain world of the entrepreneur who must sink or swim in a fiercely competitive environment. The economy could well temper these financial goals.

APPOINTING A MARKETING CONSULTANT

"When Bob Kleinschmidt visited the offices of Chicago's AIA [American Institute of Architects] chapter, to seek our help in finding someone to assist P/K's marketing efforts, he explained the firm's needs and I asked if he would take a look at my résumé [see Appendix A]. After receiving Bob's letter outlining what my responsibilities would be [Appendix B], I accepted and resigned my post as office manager at the Institute." Victoria Behm began her new duties shortly thereafter, working at P/K three days weekly.

Warm and outgoing, the marketing director introduced herself as

"Vicki" to clients and prospects, displaying an informal demeanor well suited to the P/K environment. "I read all the magazines that come in here—about 15 every month—on art, interior work, architecture, and others, some foreign. When I started here I did not know who in Chicago was doing which projects. I had to become literate by researching these and other publications and calling a lot of people directly to get prospectuses on their projects so I could prepare before calling on them.

"I read *The Wall Street Journal, The New York Times,* the *Chicago Tribune, Crane's Business World,* "Chicago Real Estate Advisor," and others. After I go through them, they are circulated to others. Of course, if any jobs we would have been interested in are in the news, it is already too late. But we use it as information to contact developers and let them know we are interested in future work."

(At that point in the meeting, Don Powell interrupted to ask that Ms. Behm and the casewriter shift to another area, to make way for a client who was coming in for an update report on a project. The office hummed with conversation almost constantly as people conferred with each other.)

"One unique thing about P/K," Vicki commented, "is that Don and Bob are involved in every facet of all projects. For example, when Greg, Bob, and I go to a meeting, the client sometimes fears that he won't see *us* again and that a novice draftsman will take over from that point. Not so at P/K. We are well aware that clients like to work with the top partner, so that's why the two principals here are involved in every important meeting with all our clients."

The marketing director removed a folder from the desk and pulled out a page headed "marketing phrases" (Exhibit 5). "I wrote down these statements for the staff to use in talking to prospects. This is just so everyone will be constantly alert to leads and opportunities and will be able to interact in a positive way with the people they're talking to. Then, here's a presentation checklist [Exhibit 6] that helps us make sure to cover everything in a marketing presentation to clients and prospects. It helps presenters from P/K to stay on track, to be thorough, and to be brief."

Vicki enjoyed contacting potential customers. "I called one developer—a tough gentleman who lives in both London and Chicago. It took me six weeks of research to prepare to call him, and he was on one of those horrible speakerphones that broadcast all over the place. I told him, 'we are very interested in your plans and would like to show you our work.' He yelled back, 'We have a firm and are not interested!' Then I said, 'But we feel that executives like you see the importance of offices and have a feeling that you must make important decisions and need several options to look at.' I had come back with a compliment to overcome his objection. He mellowed and we had a pleasant conversation.

"I get the AIA newsletters and participate in AIA functions. Last summer, for example, we had an AIA marketing seminar—that's while I was director of AIA—strictly focusing on interior design. I try to attend as many seminars as I can, but when they cost above $400, that's the cutoff point—we can't afford it."

While P/K, unlike Mr. Wright, shies away from small-scale residential kinds of assignments, they do share his negativism toward the amount of help provided architects by the American Institute of Architects. Although AIA paid him homage when he died ("He has been a teacher to us all"), he thought less kindly of what he called the establishment as embodied in the Institute, once characterizing some if its members as lethargic and "afraid to go out without their rubbers." P/K does see the Institute as providing a "sense of affiliation," but neither partner was active in the Chicago chapter, viewing its purpose at one point in the recent past as getting mutual consent among members not to cut fees, according to Behm.

"I keep detailed records of who at P/K made presentations and where and who talks to which clients and prospects. Nothing like this was being done before I came. All this sort of thing is preliminary intelligence, necessary before making other contacts. And it impresses prospects when we have gone to a lot of effort to do all this and can talk intelligently about their businesses and projects. Sometimes we send small gifts to those who have done us favors; for example, I sent some perfume to a real estate saleswoman who did us some favors with a developer we've been courting," recounted Ms. Behm.

Exhibit 5

MARKETING "PHRASES"

1. "We are unique in that a design partner is involved in every project from the initial stages to final installation."
   "We have minimal turnover of staff."
2. "We have a staff of 10 architects who work easily and effectively with the architect of the building."
3. "I realize that you are extremely busy and I appreciate your returning my call."
4. "We feel that executives, like you, see the importance of options."
5. "We have experience in
   Office interiors
   Bank interiors
   Residential interiors
   Restaurant design
   Computer facility planning
   Locating specific tenant space for clients
   etc."

Note: Tailor phrases to needs of prospect.

Exhibit 6

MARKETING PRESENTATION CHECKLIST

1. **Small firm** (10 full-time, 1 part-time) consisting of all staff members trained as architects. Very minimal **turnover.**
2. **Partner involvement** on every project in every stage.
3. Can work efficiently within various **budget** amounts.
4. **Wide spectrum** of project experience (small to large).
5. **Full scope** of services depending on needs. There are 15 stages:

- *Establishment of program
- Allocation of space
- Schematic design
- *Space planning
- Development of colors and materials
- Design development
- *Budget allocation
- Working drawings
- Specifications
- *Bidding
- Bid evaluation
- Monitoring of manufacturing
- *Supervision of installation
- Assistance with move in
- *Final tune-up

Note: *May wish to emphasize these (or others). Relax, listen, avoid details; limit remarks to less than 30 minutes.

The director of marketing maintained a file of 3" × 5" cards listing details on contacts and a file folder with articles and the like pertaining to the client. "We've talked of getting a computerized system for all this information, but I don't think we are quite ready for that. We are, after all, only 12 people right now. Some larger firms have gone on the computer for storing marketing information. But with my manual file, I have instant retrieval and can carry it with me."

The cheeriness of P/K's environment was reflected in Ms. Behm's infectious laughter and pervasive enthusiasm in discussing the merits of the firm and her efforts to promote its services. "If anything happened to this file," she concluded, "we would all be up a creek!"

The firm had just begun organized, occasional mailings to a selected list of names. "A very important part of marketing," Vicki introduced the subject

Exhibit 7

PROMOTIONAL LETTERS TO CLIENTS, PROSPECTS, AND FRIENDS

LETTER TO CLIENTS

It is with pleasure that we are sending you reprints of two articles from the October 1981 issue of **Interior Design.** We are elated at this favorable mention, but of equal importance, we are grateful to have been associated with clients and projects that have been challenging, stimulating, and fulfilling. And because the strongest endorsements come from a satisfied clientele, we would welcome your recommendation in informing prospective clients about our firm.

Season's Greetings and best wishes for a prosperous new year from all of us at Powell/Kleinschmidt.

LETTER TO PROSPECTS

We are pleased to send you reprints of two articles from the October 1981 issue of **Interior Design.** By publishing these accounts side by side, our small staff's capability of designing projects of all sizes is effectively demonstrated.

Powell/Kleinschmidt's role is helping clients identify their needs and wishes, and our commitment is to designs that embody these requirements through function, comfort, durability, and timelessness. If you are planning either new construction or a program of refurbishment, we would be delighted to assist you.

Season's Greetings and best wishes for a prosperous new year from all of us at Powell/Kleinschmidt.

LETTER TO FRIENDS

To paraphrase Robert Burns, the two enclosed reprints from the October 1981 issue of **Interior Design** offer us a "chance to see ourselves as ID sees us." Some of the editorial observations represent minor flights of fancy, but on the whole we are truly elated at the favorable coverage.

Exhibit 7 (Cont.)

The fact that our small staff is capable of designing a project of the scope of Prudential Plymouth and do it with style, holding to budget, and completing it on schedule is gratifying. We want to share the articles with you, our special friends, and hope you enjoy reading them.

In retrospect, we are profoundly pleased for a year of opportunity and fulfillment and now, at year's end, may this season of beauty be a season of happiness.

Best wishes from all of us at Powell/Kleinschmidt.

---

of promotional efforts, "is to reach a client or prospect as many times as possible. But you don't want to blow everything on one huge bulk mailing, to just anyone; it has to be targeted. For example, we bought a thousand overrun copies of the *ID*[1] feature article at a cost to us of $500 and we mail them to clients and some prospects. This is very good ammunition, because there's a little different psychology when a third party says how great you are and when you say it yourself. For this mailing I did different kinds of letters, and Dorothy [Dorothy Ver Steeg, special projects director, whose background in literature was being put to good use at P/K] composed them [Exhibit 7].

"Bob and Don were reluctant to come right out and ask our clients to recommend, but Dorothy and I feel that the satisfied customers are the best referrals we can get."

Pointing to an 8½" square envelope containing photo brochures of projects by Powell/Kleinschmidt, "Those cost about $22.50 each, so we mail few of them. We do, however, present them personally when the occasion warrants.

"Some architects feel that it is undignified to advertise and worry that their images will suffer. Actually, the AIA has no policies in the code against advertising—I'm talking about using the mass media, primarily, because most firms do the special kinds of things we've been talking about—but nobody in Chicago is doing it. Also, I think that a lot of the advertising that has been done has not been done well, so maybe that's why architects would rather not attempt it.

"Who could compete with a full-page, four-color advertisement that a large firm might be able to place in *Fortune?* But we should not forget that architects consider themselves to be artists, and artists don't want to denigrate their work by common forms of hard sell. It makes them very uncomfortable.

[1]"Prudential Insurance Offices," *Interior Design,* October 1981, pp. 258–275.

"But that isn't all. Publicity like the *Interior Design* piece is seen mostly by other architects, not by clients and prospects, unless we close the gap. So that's why we go for overruns and reprints and use our mailing lists as well as we can.

"In the brief time I've been here, I can't trace any business directly to the contacts I've made. But I make as many calls as I can to contact everyone from developer owners, brokers, secretaries . . . sometimes just to ask how business is. And I have to develop good judgment as to who is susceptible to what kinds of contact. I don't want them to see me as a pest. For example, almost all brokers get into their offices by 8:30, so I start my calls just before their regular business day begins."

Just before rushing away to an appointment, Vicki mentioned awards: "Another aspect of our whole marketing effort is our awards program. I take care of entering projects in awards competitions. This hasn't been a major thrust until now, but I'm here and have the materials, and we all agree it's one way of getting recognition. Very inexpensive, too. Only costs about $30 to $50 for submitting an application, and a win means we can send out another promotion. Even the AIA competitions get a lot of recognition here in Chicago, and it's very important we get that kind of local exposure."

EPILOGUE

In January 1982, Ms. Behm notified the casewriter that "I will be gradually phasing out my contract with Powell/Kleinschmidt. No hard feelings, I assure you. One of my other clients, Fujikawa, Conterato, and Lohan [FCL] has made me a tremendous offer to do marketing and supervise the graphics for them. They are Mies van der Rohe's successor firm and number about 100 employees in Dallas and Chicago. . . . I am sorry to leave the wonderful environment of P/K, but I feel this new opportunity will be challenging and fulfilling." The people-oriented principals of P/K were pleased at Vicki's good fortune, because they strongly believed in supporting the personal goals of staff members, even if it meant losing a valuable person, but they were disappointed to lose her effectiveness. Both Don Powell and Bob Kleinschmidt pondered the situation and wondered what steps they should take next.

Your Task:

Advise P/K about how to approach the future, from a marketing point of view, after first presenting them with a review of the strengths and weaknesses of their recent efforts to organize and implement a marketing function in the firm. Be prepared to discuss with Messrs. Powell and Kleinschmidt the threats and opportunities, as you see them, of proceeding with and without a "formal" marketing function in the company.

Appendix A

RÉSUMÉ: VICTORIA BEHM

Education

1967–1971, B.A., University of Missouri-Columbia, Design
1971–1973, M.A., UMC, Journalism and Design
1972, Independent Study in Design, Northern Europe, UMC
1974, Rensselaer Polytechnic Institute, Troy, N.Y., Writing
1973–1977, Graduate courses in Journalism, UMC

Professional

1981 to present, Victoria Behm Design, Chicago, Illinois
1980, American Institute of Architects, Chicago, Illinois
1977, National Trust for Historic Preservation, Chicago; Frank Lloyd
  Wright Home and Studio Foundation, Oak Park
1971, University of Missouri-Columbia

Teaching

1972–1974, University of Missouri-Columbia, Columbia College

Honors/Awards

Curator's Award, Dean's List, Falsetti-Hoffman Scholarship, Gamma Delta
  Phi, Upsilon Omicron

Memberships

American Institute of Architects, Washington, D.C.
Society of Typographic Arts, Chicago, Illinois
Women in Design, Chicago, Illinois

Accounts Served

National Trust for Historic Preservation, Chicago, Illinois
AIA Journal, Washington, D.C.
Frank Lloyd Wright Home and Studio Foundation, Oak Park, Illinois
Aubrey Greenburg & Associates, Chicago, Illinois
University of Missouri-Columbia, Missouri
Stephens College, Columbia, Missouri
Kenneth Schroeder & Associates, Chicago, Illinois
Lee Strickland & Associates, Chicago, Illinois
Chicago Architectural Foundation, Chicago, Illinois
Ginkgo Tree Bookshop, Oak Park, Illinois
Lee's Carpet, Detroit, Michigan

Appendix A (Cont.)

Marsh, Jefferson City, Missouri
Energy Research and Development Administration, Argonne, Illinois
Logan Square Economic Development Corporation, Chicago, Illinois
Powell/Kleinschmidt, Inc., Chicago, Illinois
Smith Laboratories, Inc., Rosemont, Illinois
Brownstein Associates, St. Louis, Missouri
FCL, Architects, Inc., Chicago, Illinois
Darrell Rist-Yates, Chicago, Illinois

Appendix B

LETTER OF RESPONSIBILITIES
TO VICTORIA BEHM

July 16, 1981

Miss Victoria Behm
1514 N. Wieland
Chicago, Illinois 60610

Dear Vicki:

This letter will constitute an agreement between you as an independent contractor and Powell/Kleinschmidt, Inc., which is engaging you as a consultant in the area of marketing the services and programs of P/K as interior architects (interior design and furnishing of buildings).

1. The objectives of the services to be provided by the director of marketing (future defined DM) are to accomplish the following:
   a. To implement and develop affirmative marketing programs for the services of P/K, both direct and indirect.
   b. To obtain immediate short-term projects and jobs for P/K.
   c. To develop future projects and jobs or the potential for such jobs for P/K that are both medium-range and long-range in nature.
   d. To relieve the principal shareholders and officers of P/K from the present demand placed on their time and energy to marketing efforts for and on behalf of P/K, so that their time may be put to different use.

2. The services to be rendered by DM to P/K are as follows:
   a. Define the potential markets for the services of P/K, including, but not limited to, real estate developers, the owners and/or tenants of professional and institutional office buildings or offices,

Appendix B (Cont.)

limited residential work, and restoration and refurbishment of buildings.

b. Seek out and make initial contacts with potential clients within the defined markets and conduct preliminary interviews with the prospective clients for P/K's service; make report and recommendations in connection therewith to P/K.

c. Follow through on leads, client recommendations and other contacts with the objective of developing jobs and new clients for P/K as a result thereof.

d. Develop and implement a program for increasing awareness of P/K's services within the desired market area, including direct mailings, promotional letters, and direct telephone calls to prospective clients.

e. Prepare and distribute advantageous articles on P/K in newspapers and general circulation, business and professional periodicals, and other publications.

f. Preparation and coordination of presentations, slide shows, and maintenance of the slide library all come under jurisdiction of the DM. The entry to competitions and the furthering of visibility of the firm are additional areas of responsibility.

g. In addition, DM will prepare and make weekly reports to Robert D. Kleinschmidt, vice president of P/K, or such other officer as P/K may appoint for purposes of keeping P/K fully advised on the achievement of the objectives described in this Agreement and the specific steps taken by DM or to be taken by DM in connection therewith.

The DM has no authority and is not entitled to enter into any contracts or agreements by or on behalf of P/K or which may have the effect of binding P/K or its assets and that the sole authority to enter into such contracts or agreements is lodged in the officers of P/K.

HIGH FLIGHT RESORT

As the Delta flight approached Atlanta, Karen and Bernard Lee, although decidedly weary after a week's skiing at one of the more prestigious resorts in the western United States, talked animatedly of their newly hatched plans to become limited partners in developing a new and different skiing haven. It all started when Karen's former law school classmate and other friends of long standing who shared a 16-person condominium during the week became disgusted with standing in lift lines, paying $22 daily for tickets, gulping down tasteless food in a crowded subterranean ptomaine tavern, and picking their way precariously across poorly maintained, and alternately icy and muddy, walkways. Also, their favorite chairlift had broken down twice during the week, forcing them to take to the intermediate slopes for most of each day.

Among the group that had skied together annually for more than a decade were two attorneys, an electronics firm's owner, a stockbroker, two doctors, and three high-level executives, all of whom felt sanguine about the prospects of banding together, investing perhaps $50,000 to $100,000 of seed money each, and financing the remainder through loans and venture capital to launch their dream. The clincher of the deal was immediate availability of a friend and fellow skier's nonworking ranch, covering 3,840 acres, and contiguous on one side to abandoned timberland and on the other to a U.S. Forest Service area that happened to be marked, along with a dozen or more other sites in the state, as a potential ski area. Mining operations on the ranch in the late

1970s and early 1980s were shut down as markets changed to reflect what many supposed to be long-term stability of petroleum prices. There are numerous creeks on the property, a trout stream, and a sizable river that is part of the ranch's boundary line.

Nature has endowed the region with magnificent mountain ranges offering unparalleled winter recreational potential. There are over 50 ski areas in the state, counting all the private, civic organization, and city-sponsored areas, some with little more than a hill and a poma lift and rope tow. Of the 32 areas classified as "major," most operate daily and a few only on weekends. Major vacation areas include such destination resorts as Aspen, Vail, Breckenridge, Steamboat, Keystone, Copper Mountain, Winter Park, Crested Butte, Purgatory, and Telluride. Acreage for the proposed resort is relatively isolated in the southwestern part of the state, over an hour's drive from Telluride and Purgatory. An airport about 125 miles distant, served by one major and two trunk airlines, is linked to the potential resort by a four-lane U.S. highway and a two-lane paved state road that is maintained in good condition. Bus transportation is available daily.

Conversation in the group had been stimulated by the glow from a crackling fire and ample mulled wine—it was easy to dismiss such comments as "snow tractors cost $130,000," "snowmaking systems would cost millions," "chairlifts are over $500,000," and "we'll have to contract for an environmental impact study—I hear they cost $50,000." When the subject of staffing arose, one of the corporate executives, a Bostonian, remarked, "I was told that Killington—a top-notch organization—employs a traveling sales force of over 20 people and a marketing director. We've got to have the organizational structure and good people to make it go!" Next day, the lung-searing frosty air and hot coffee helped clear morning-after fuzziness, but enthusiasm was undiminished. Their audacious idea spurred further deliberations.

Regarding the environmental impact statement, there was concern about the changing regulatory mood in Washington and how their hopes of quick approval might be affected. Interior Department ideologue, Secretary James Watt, appeared to be making headway diluting the environmental strictness of the former Carter administration, easing regulations and making decisions that favored development. However, his tactics were increasingly assailed by the so-called "green lobby," made up of such organizations as the National Wildlife Federation, the Wilderness Society, and the Sierra Club. The Sierra Club became sufficiently distressed in 1981 to organize a document, signed by over 1 million people, petitioning for removal of Watt from office. Many citizens alleged that Secretary Watt was oblivious to the destruction of America's parks and, at various public gatherings where the secretary appeared, brandished such printed slogans as "Save a tree, ax Watt." Nevertheless, the eager entrepreneurs believed that they could make an excellent case for their project and that little direct grass-roots opposition would materialize.

Thinking of a suitable model after which to pattern their "dream," they considered Vail. Celebrating its twentieth birthday in 1982, Vail, 100 miles west of Denver, was the epitome of popular ski areas, with its 27-foot annual snowfall and 10 square miles of skiing terrain. They knew starting "even" with Vail would be impossible, with its gondola, surface lift, 3 triple and 13 double chairlifts, 89 runs, 65 lodging facilities with 15,000 beds, 74 restaurants and bars, 5 indoor tennis courts, 30 swimming pools, and 4 child care centers. Also, Vail's ski school was renowned, and its ski touring trails abundant. "Perhaps," one of the physicians offered, "we should consider another model, say, Telluride?" And so the brainstorming went.

The Chicago lawyer added a note of caution: "In 1972 my husband and I and our two children could visit Vail for a week's ski vacation and spend $1,500, air fare and all; next trip we'll spend about $3,800 for the same package. Air fare, lodging, and lift tickets have gone up faster than the Consumer Price Index. I think we should exercise prudence and realize that only those with plenty of discretionary income will be able to afford it. Leisure time alone won't create the demand; money is the fundamental and key ingredient."

What they would settle for provoked spirited disagreement: slopes offering world-class skiing on terrain varying from broad, gentle grades to steep mogul chutes, perhaps 25 trails on about 500 acres, to start with. Some thought a gondola and 4 or 5 double chairlifts would be a good beginning. Soon they concluded that a lot more information was needed about break-even volume and about all the services required to form a well-rounded and attractive resort. Also, in their enthusiasm, they must not overlook the need to serve all skill levels—beginner, intermediate, and expert. And what facilities, they pondered, would be required to attract summer tourists to help cover overhead costs? This was a separate question.

The would-be partners believed that in addition to traditional ski-area services, it could be desirable and profitable to include helicopter skiing as well. This would be for the few who possess both technique and endurance—strong skiers who want that "something extra" that only untouched deep powder can offer, something that cannot be found at traditional resorts even when snowfall is steady and substantial, the slopes perfectly groomed, and the skiers few in number. For the past three years, four of the group had spent one of their two or three annual skiing vacations carving serpentine tracks on mountainsides in the Canadian Rockies. Based on their experiences of having paid $2,000 each for a six-day package, they concluded, however, that only the upscale aficionados would be prospects for heli-skiing.

"One thing you can take my word for," the ranch owner said, "daytime temperatures are usually comfortable, the snow falls light and dry at that 9,000-foot elevation, and we can expect an average of 350 inches of powder throughout the season. And we are close enough for Telluride and Purgatory customers to patronize us. Also, I estimate there are 300 to 400 rooms available at nearby motels and lodges within 25 miles, to help take care of the traffic until development begins at High Flight." "High Flight" was the tentative name submitted by one of the discussants, and quickly seconded by another because the owner had been a jet fighter pilot. There was common consent.

"It sounds romantic," said a third, "and signifies what we plan to offer: a Rocky Mountain high."

Your Task:

The enthusiastic skiers cum entrepreneurs have asked you for advice. They want your insights about what strategic issues they ought to consider before proceeding further with the idea. Propose a framework for a strengths-weaknesses, opportunities-threats analysis. The U.S. Forest Service and Colorado Ski Country USA have provided you with the following figures (Exhibit 1):

Exhibit 1

SKIER VISITS FOR THE STATE OF COLORADO

SEASON	VISITS	% CHANGE
1953–54	192,500	—
1954–55	204,640	6.3%
1955–56	264,051	29.0
1956–57	274,225	3.9
1957–58	338,499	23.4
1958–59	386,298	14.1
1959–60	458,549	18.7
1960–61	451,223	−1.6
1961–62	571,125	26.6
1962–63	562,235	−1.6
1963–64	817,518	45.4
1964–65	1,102,690	34.9
1965–66	1,168,159	5.9
1966–67	1,410,641	20.8
1967–68	1,813,210	28.5
1968–69	2,329,546	28.5
1969–70	2,741,101	17.7
1970–71	2,997,953	9.4
1971–72	3,260,155	8.7
1972–73	3,974,250	21.9
1973–74	4,304,787	8.3
1974–75	5,194,720	20.7
1975–76	5,965,172	14.8
1976–77	3,653,409	−38.8
1977–78	6,648,866	82.0
1978–79	7,215,316	8.5
1979–80	7,887,181	9.3
1980–81	5,498,962	−30.3
1981–82	7,622,182	38.6

Be prepared to discuss with your clients alternative design concepts for their "product." Should they go "utilitarian" or "luxurious"? What target markets should they consider? How can they analyze potential in those segments? What marketing mix would you suggest for each? Assume that it will be a destination resort, not close enough to population centers for one-day roundtrips.

As you contemplate a meeting with several of the intended principals, it is December 30, 1982 and "CBS Morning News" has just reported that ski operators in the Northeast, plagued by unseasonably warm weather, have lost $16 million in the past week, while ski resort managers in the Rocky Mountains are complaining because holiday skiers have been unable to reach them, following the Christmas blizzard.

case

6

CELESTIAL SEASONINGS, INC.

STATEMENT OF PHILOSOPHY

Celestial Seasonings is a consumer packaged goods company committed to marketing internally manufactured, health-oriented, high-quality products to the consumer and sold via health food and mass market outlets. Our job is to serve consumers by filling voids in the marketplace with quality products that consumers want. Our mission is to solve major health problems according to our corporate definition. Our objective: a healthy, nourished, disease-free, exercised public.

Under the name Celestial Seasonings, the product line and style of magic is set for the future. We sell high-quality products with the most beautiful packaging possible. Each package is sprinkled with bits of wisdom and is designed to give consumers an added bonus ... Lighthearted Philosophy.

For stockholders our objective is a minimum sales growth of 27 percent compounded annually with a minimum of 27 percent growth in earnings. Celestial offers shareholders the opportunity to reap financial reward while getting people healthy.

For our employees, our objective is to build a strong and stable company with dynamic opportunity for upward mobility through loyalty, pursuit of excellence, hard work, and quality. This company is dedicated to mutual reward systems based on the achievement of worthwhile and aggressive goals. We remain loyal to the continual search and practice of advanced management systems that build working bridges between exempt and nonexempt employees, believing that a united, fully utilized work force can accomplish far-reaching objectives with work satisfaction and mutual reward for all. Our philosophy encourages creative, productive, possibility thinking throughout the organization.

In summary, the foundation of Celestial Seasonings is based on serving health needs through good products and expressed in a beautiful form. Our profit will increase 100-fold by dedicating our total efforts to these ends, which in turn will make this world a better place for our children and our children's children.[1]

BOULDER, COLORADO, 1982

Boulder, Colorado, is a sleepy but fashionable town located north of Denver on the Front Range of the Rocky Mountains. During the early 1970s, hippies trudged through its streets lugging worn backpacks and sleeping bags, many of them living from hand to mouth supporting themselves by panhandling or selling "dope" to university students around The Hill area of town. Today, Boulder presents a more affluent face to visitors. The hippies have either left town or have cashed in their patched jeans for snappier, more socially acceptable though casual attire—Chemise La Coste shirts and L. L. Bean chinos, for example. Many have joined the ranks of the young professionals and zip around the town in foreign-made cars, said to be better than domestic models for mountain driving.

Jogging and bicycling are popular Boulder pastimes. Former marathon Olympic star Frank Shorter is now a local businessman selling chic running shorts and shoes in his own shop on the Mall, which marks the center of town. Most of the youthful, health-conscious people in town are glad not to have a ragtag population marring their peaceful local scenes of outdoor cafés and trendy businesses done up in natural cedar or red brick façades. Casualness seems to be a fetish.

CELESTIAL SEASONINGS BACKGROUND

In this idyllic setting Mr. Mo Siegel, president and co-founder of Celestial Seasonings, Inc., reigns over his herb tea kingdom, an empire that includes among its all-natural products such innovative no-caffeine offerings as Red Zinger,

[1]Source: Corporate files.

Mandarin Orange Spice, and Cinnamon Rose herb teas, graphically tricked out in flamboyant fantasy packaging (see Appendix A). Celestial competes in its own small market, the $75-million-a-year herb tea share of all tea sales, with other counterculturally costumed competitors—Select, San Francisco Herbs, Lipton, and the rest. The purchaser of Siegel's tantalizingly titled teas buys not only a beverage to sustain body but messages from such unlikely and diverse sources as Abraham Lincoln and Sophia Loren to sustain the soul. "Please write, we like to respond. We are interested in your suggestions, ideas, queries, quotations, and short essays for use on the packages," invites a box-top bit of prose. Mo Siegel, himself an inveterate collector of quotations, includes pithy morsels of wit and wisdom in business correspondence. Under the cable and Telex information on a recent Siegel letter, the reader is treated to some Goethe: "Whatever liberates our spirit without giving us self-control is disastrous."

Mr. Siegel sits at mission control site between a portrait of Lincoln on one wall and the Iced Delight bear on the other. He has little reason to meditate on disasters these days with his closely held Celestial Seasonings now dominating the domestic herbal tea market with annual earnings of more than $1 million. Sales to foreign markets have leapt to 6 percent of Celestial's total current annual sales. Still a dwarf in the overall $825 million black tea market, Celestial at $23 million a year in sales has stunned the big tea marketers by making steady inroads into major supermarket chains, gourmet, and health stores, and into foreign markets during the late 1970s and early 1980s.

Tea giants such as Thomas J. Lipton, until as recently as 1980, tended to discount Celestial's entrepreneurs as amateurs playing flower-child games in a tough marketplace. Now Lipton and others look at Celestial, a company that has experienced a high growth rate, as a feisty wunderkind to emulate and contend with. Lipton in 1982 began marketing herb teas packaged in rainbow colors at prices close to Celestial's—about 5½ cents a bag, although Lipton packaged its herbals in packs of 16, while Celestial preferred the 24-teabag format.

The compelling Mr. Siegel was the subject of wide-ranging publicity.[2] He popped up regularly on television programs such as "Merv Griffin" and "Donahue," and business magazines took turns publishing a colorful sketch of the president who was given to quotable remarks as he ruminated aloud. "We have an obligation to make the shelves astonishing! to keep magic alive," he said when asked about Celestial Seasonings' devotion to creative packaging. "We must continue to create beautiful, outstanding-quality packaging with truthful writings." Later he told the casewriters upon entering the elegant Celestial board room, "We want Louvre quality in our artwork," and "If Walt Disney could do it better, we aren't interested" (Exhibit 1).

[2]See Eric Morgenthaler, "From Hippies to $16 Million a Year, *The Wall Street Journal*, May 6, 1981; "What's Brewing at Celestial," *Money*, January 1981; Margaret Thoren, "It Wasn't the Bankers' Cup of Tea...," *The Christian Science Monitor*, April 21, 1981; and Barth David Schwartz, "How to Make a Million Doing Your Own Thing," *Fortune*, June 4, 1979, among others.

Exhibit 1

CELESTIAL SEASONINGS GRAPHICS

An ancient tea for the tensions of a modern world.

"For 2,000 years my ancestors have sipped ginseng tea when they wanted to relax.

"So I have followed carefully their wise advice, combing the steppes of Siberia and the vast reaches of China to find the rarest and best ginseng. And from it, I've made one of the most relaxing herb teas in the world: Emperor's Choice.

"Of course, an emperor's taste requires a delicious tea, too.

"So I combined the best cinnamon, licorice root, rosehips and other herbs and spices. And created a flavor to please the most discerning royal palate.

"And I made my tea without caffeine. Or anything artificial.

"Try Emperor's Choice. You'll see why my ancestors said: 'A few sips of this delicious tea everyday can help chase the woes of the world away.'"

—The Emperor

Available in your favorite health or natural food store.

CELESTIAL SEASONINGS HERB TEAS

NO CAFFEINE
WITH GINSENG

24 TEA BAGS

EMPEROR'S CHOICE™

Naturally caffeine free.
For your good health.

Some of the press that Siegel received suggested that the success realized for Celestial "just sort of happened." In fact, Mo Siegel is a very ambitious person, addicted to reading management books, Drucker one of his favorites. "I like big rather than small," he admitted to us with a gleam in his eye. Then he explained how he recruited outside of Celestial to professionalize management, hiring a regional manager from Lipton and a plant manager from General Mills. Along the way he recruited a vice president of PepsiCo for his marketing team and brought in a chief engineer from Pepperidge Farm. Celestial's head tea brand manager was recruited from Quaker Oats, another from Vaseline Intensive Care, and still another from Samsonite. Clearly, Siegel sought marketing expertise for the company from proven training camps. He followed marketing stories of large companies as if they were detective novels: "Tylenol is bright," and "Johnson & Johnson is as good as P and G." And his strategy was pragmatic: "We don't have the time or the money to test in the same way as Quaker."

His objectives for the company were specific and hardhitting. In 1981, which was "the first year for our real-live-moving-growing marketing department," Siegel decided that any product line not reaching $10 million in sales in five years should be discontinued. Other objectives included the achievement of a 30 percent increase of tea sales in standard units; a broadening of grocery volume from 35 percent to 55 percent on at least four items; and the expansion of tea section placements from 15 percent to 30 percent on Sleepytime, Mandarin Orange Spice, Cinnamon Rose, Country Apple, Iced Delight, Red Zinger, Almond Sunset, Emperor's Choice, Peppermint, and the variety-pack four flavors.

Siegel believed that Celestial should continue expanding trial tastings among nonusers and increase the frequency of consumption among users from 1 to 2 cups each day. Since Colorado was Celestial's most active market area, Siegel's 1981 goals stated that the company needed "to determine upside volume potential outside of Colorado." Finally, and perhaps most important since Siegel claimed he was not interested in being a "food company" but was interested in preventive health care, Celestial targeted an improvement in its position in health food stores through a carefully orchestrated shelf management program in 1981 and 1982.

Siegel is not particularly modest about what he thinks are Celestial's most successful characteristics. At the top of the list he counts the distinctive and unique aspects of Celestial, including quality, packaging, products, names, and writings. In the "tricky herb industry" because of the adverse publicity about herbs and regulatory difficulties, he believes that he has accomplished no small feat in achieving the "highest quality standards in the herb industry." Because health products, not food, is the area in which he is interested, Siegel believes Celestial's success to be inextricably tied to its provision of a "real alternative to other caffeinated hot beverages." That the company has embraced a "wide variety of flavors and product concepts" he believes is all to the good. The lead products in Celestial have a strong consumer positioning and best of all—from Mo Siegel's perspective of the health-focused "corporateur" as he terms himself—Celestial's products remain all natural and health oriented. Exhibit 2 summarizes Celestial's strengths, weaknesses, and strategies for the 1980s as seen by top management.

Not that everything is coming up rosehips, however. Celestial has experienced its share of problems. A brief and abortive romance with a product called Salad Snacks failed to meet quality control standards. Juice products, despite great corporate hopes, could not make a go of it.

Exhibit 2

STRENGTHS, WEAKNESSES, AND STRATEGIES OF CELESTIAL SEASONINGS

Strengths

Growth via health consciousness
Strong consumer loyalty
Financial stability and excellent gross margins
Distinctive packaging
Readily acceptable flavor varieties
Significantly higher brand awareness than the competition
Professional management
Vertical integration: from raw product to finished teabag

Weaknesses

Extensive product line
Premium product line
No line pricing
24-teabag count
Compressed timetables

Strategies for the 1980s. Continue to take the leadership position in

Unique packaging
Inventing blended herb teas
Offering the largest selection of blended teas
Offering special packs
Ability to sample
Offering the best quality herb teas
Marketing solution teas, for example, Sleepytime

Observed Siegel, "The caution is that we deal with limited resources, both people and finances, and we cannot effectively execute against multiple priorities especially when the objectives are not compatible with our central corporate mission. The key is maximum sales effectiveness. An example of the dilution of resources was the introduction of BreakAway during the major drive for Iced Delight—no one's fault—and penetrating a new channel of distribution—placing Salad Snacks in produce departments—without adequate development of our basic business. Launching VITA during the key prewinter sales drive on Herb Tea would have been a similar mistake."

Mo Siegel hardly underestimates the importance of marketing. One of his trump suits has been a strategy of strong and consistent marketing to the health foods market segment. As markets drift away from hot caffeinated products, there Celestial will be. The sweet dream of high coffee prices has always kept spirits high at the tea factory, and the strong growth of health food stores has been a trend that fueled the Celestial team's marketing enthusiasm. With increasing professionalization of the team, however, no one is naïve enough to think that people can rest on their tea leaves and achieve continuing growth. Rather, the annual building of new distribution channels is seen as a perennial strategic topic as are plans to develop a wider product mix (Exhibit 3). Always Celestial is striving to improve its professional approach to sales and marketing.

MARKETERS AND MARKETING AT CELESTIAL

Keith Brenner, a pleasant, self-assured Canadian—some might say slightly arrogant—became vice president of marketing at Celestial in 1980. Before that, marketing at Celestial had been strictly an in-house, family affair. Brenner, who owned his own beverage manufacturing company in Canada, met Mo Siegel at a food show. He worked with Celestial first as a consultant, assisting the company in its attempt to enter the natural beverage market, an effort that flopped. Although Brenner hoped to work in general management, he was asked by Siegel to head the marketing function of the organization. He has not put aside his preference to get into general management where he could be involved in finance and production as well as marketing.

Besides his stint as a beverage manufacturer Brenner acquired an impressive set of credentials from his work with Pepsi Cola in Canada and with General Foods. Like Siegel, he attained success early. At 32 he was a vice president and general manager for Pepsi Cola, globetrotting for a three-year period to Pepsi operations in South Africa and the Philippines as well as serving in Canada. He cited as his major reason for joining Siegel and Celestial "the opportunity to impact a healthy growing concern instead of attempting to climb the ladder in a vast corporation."

Exhibit 3

ADVERTISING FOR A NEW (1982) PRODUCT

Delicious to the core.

Before you decide on your favorite Celestial Seasonings Herb Tea, try this one.

Country Apple Herb Tea is a delicious blend of apples, rosehips and cinnamon enhanced by hibiscus flowers and chamomile, with absolutely no caffeine.

The flavor of Country Apple unfolds with each sip, as the aroma of orchards takes you back to breezy afternoons in the country and all your fondest memories.

Try our new Country Apple Herb Tea. Then pick your Celestial favorite.

Both Brenner and Siegel believe in the Celestial mystique: "Our goal is to manufacture only healthful, nutritional products—nothing artificial." At Brenner's urging, Celestial planned to abandon its sole caffeine product, Morning Thunder: "Since Celestial Seasonings' customers are a segment based upon their penchant for natural food products, a clean bill of health with customers will be strengthened by severing ties with caffeine."

As for his marketing efforts, Brenner terms Celestial "an alternative kind of company which has achieved success without hammering people with incessant advertising. We tell a simple story in a colorful way, only the truth, not embellished with a lot of hoopla."

Brenner professes a belief that "Celestial's success was a major reason why Lipton decided to enter the herb tea market. Instead of thinking that such competition works to Celestial's detriment, we credit the Lipton move to raising overall public awareness of products such as ours. In fact, the Lipton competition creates a bigger market for everyone." Brenner is sanguine about growth possibilities for Celestial even though teas was a low-growth category, according to the marketing vice president, 1 percent annual growth, the same as the population growth rate. "Any extra we get has to come out of somebody else's business, but there is a trend by large stores to stock more nutritional foods . . . health foods and the like . . . which is good for us. This will help us reach our target of 25 percent annual growth, compounded, but only through 1985, I believe, with our present product line. This means that to continue meeting our objective we must develop new ideas—beyond herbal teas." Brenner's overall strategy for growth in 1982 was succinct: "First, we widen our grocery distribution base with tea section placement. This has been difficult, but it gets easier as we get stronger. Second, we go after consumer awareness and trial through the use of Sunday supplement coupons, trial packages, and displays. Last, we move more strongly into the iced tea market, which is three times larger than that for hot tea."

Regarding trips into the marketplace, Brenner has confessed, "I do get into the field occasionally, but not enough." Like Siegel, he is emphatic that one distribution channel cannot be sacrificed to another. "We had 100 percent distribution in the health food outlets, so we moved into the supermarkets. But we are not neglecting our health food outlets."

LIFE AT THE TEA FACTORY

The music of James Taylor wafted through the tea factory on a typical day in 1982 as Italian-made machinery moved the teas 24 hours a day on a computerized schedule. This new equipment made it possible to pack the major Celestial blends into horizontal boxes, found by market testing to lure the purchaser more effectively than vertical packages. Employees in production appeared to be blissfully engaged in their tasks. The cafeteria awaited them at some point in their shift, with a meal of natural foods—soup, salad, granola cookies, and a selection from the company's herb tea line. Mo Siegel, who frequently dresses in shorts and a sports shirt for the office, and rides his bicycle to work, stresses quality of the workplace.

If it is possible to tell something about a person or an organization by surveying the reading material that is strewn about, perhaps the following survey of books and magazines in the Celestial Seasonings' employee waiting room offers some insights: Pierre Teilhard de Chardin's *Man's Place in Nature;* M. Scott Myer's *Every Employee a Manager: More Meaningful Work Through Job Enrichment;* works by Drucker and Toffler; and copies of the periodicals *New Health, New Age, Prevention, Runner, New West, Runner's World,* and *Processed Prepared Foods.*

In one section of the main plant, Marelynn W. Zipser, Ph.D., a food technologist and the mother of Mandarin Orange Spice, Cinnamon Rose, Iced Delight, and BreakAway, presides over herbs and test tubes in a pristine but cheery testing laboratory. As manager of new product development, Zipser reports directly to Brenner. "I take the concept and turn it into reality," she explained. Among her research and development tasks, Dr. Zipser conducts taste panels—mainly among women's groups and employees—to test the latest reactions to Celestial's expanding product lines. Quality and taste of the tea are as important to Celestial as other major points of difference with their competition: packaging style and graphics, the number of teabags per box, premium pricing, and channels of distribution. Thus, Celestial taste tests against Select, Alvita, Golden Harvest, Health Valley, Traditionals, San Francisco Herbs, Worthington, Horizon, and other regional and local brands in the health food market as well as Bigelow, Lipton, and Magic Mountain in the grocery market.

Systematic product development grew out of Mo Siegel's demands for specific types of products that he and Brenner instructed Zipser and her group to conjure up in the laboratory. "Conservative planning plus optimistic action plus intelligent work equals success" is a favorite Siegel maxim, which seems eminently practicable in the laboratory part of the tea factory.

HISTORY OF CELESTIAL

In the beginning were the herbs. Siegel, his wife Peggy, and sidekick Wyck Hay pioneered the operation by gathering Colorado mountain herbs with other friends "for fun" and selling them to local health food stores. These were the early days of health food awareness of the late 1960s and early 1970s, and Siegel and Hay's philosophy then was to provide a pleasant living for themselves and a congenial group of Boulder comrades by selling a product that was good for people. "One of the things we found in Europe is that people who live to 100 drink a lot of herb tea and eat herbs continually," Siegel states.

The company's appellation, derived from the fanciful nickname of a female friend who participated in the early days of Celestial's movement into what some have termed "cosmic capitalism," suggests the tone and tempo of those early times. Celestial began as a relatively tranquil cottage business in which Siegel, Peggy, and friends patiently stuffed the heady concoctions of orange peel, wild cherry bark, rosehips, hibiscus flowers, lemon grass, and peppermint into hand-sewn, hand-stamped muslin bags with solicitous instructions to buyers as to the particulars of brewing and steeping, along with a reminder to them that a bit of honey would enhance flavor. This early, successful blend, entitled Red Zinger, propelled Celestial out of the cottage and into a corporate setting. In 1982 Celestial required six buildings to house its manufacturing, warehousing of herbs and spices from 35 countries, and other functions.

From the outset, Celestial espoused causes and amplified these from its boxes—reminding customers about a foundation needing support to protect vanishing species of flowers, sometimes warning about world hunger, and promoting save the whales or other conservational causes. Celestial saw itself as having an instructive, positivistic mission, perhaps as important as its more pedestrian, grocery-focused one. "Happiness is the only thing we can give without having" and other messages of its kind became inherent aspects of Celestial's packaging concepts. But such aphorisms were more to Celestial than a way of selling tea. Siegel's enterprise was a mission (see Appendix B, a brief biography).

With lots of help from his friends, Siegel organized a corporate structure based on communitarian concerns and centered on quality-of-life issues: concern with providing employees enough time for family and leisure, flexitime, pleasant working conditions, and many more. As the alternative to business that they were, the merry band was not quite able to do away with a hierarchical structure, and they developed a seven-person board of directors, most of them major stockholders, to hold down the fort. Living was easy then with only a few blends in their tea portfolio, and only 50 or so stockholders in the entire corporation.

MOVING INTO THE 1980S

Red Zinger was ultimately joined by some 40 other herbals, including a new tea in 1982, Almond Sunset: "a wonderfully romantic blend of herbs with the soothing natural flavor of almonds. A delicate blend of lovely things like rich roasted carob, barley and chickory root; spiced with cinnamon, sunny orange peel and a hint of anise seed. . . . Almond Sunset will remind you of holiday cookies baking in the oven of a farmhouse kitchen." Introduction of new products was carefully considered; Celestial's marketing and advertising budget was expected to be $5 million in 1982.

Seeking to market Celestial more aggressively, Siegel recognized the "be big or bust" paradigm that has ruled decision making at the larger beverage companies and the expansion imperative that was its corollary. New products, including body care preparations and vitamins, loom large in Siegel's mind as he looks toward product expansion and toward a goal of 27 percent compounded annual growth (Exhibit 4) with anticipated sales of $50 million by the mid-1980s.

As time went on Celestial people gave less attention to the fun-and-games enterprises of more carefree years, for instance, the world-famous Red Zinger bicycle races, a promotional activity the company sponsored from 1975 to 1980 because "Mo Siegel is into bikes." The races underscored a long-time Siegel belief that if more people rode bikes as their only transportation, the world would be a better place. "Celestial Seasonings is dedicated to improving the quality of life on this planet, having a major concern in environmental life," he wrote in literature promoting the Red Zinger Bicycle Classic. In 1980, however, it became an issue of bicycle races or teas for Celestial, just as it became an issue of hiring executives with sophisticated managerial expertise versus possible corporate extinction. Case in point: in the summer of 1980 the company came close to being swallowed by General Mills due to one disgruntled, major stockholder's wish to rid himself of $1 million worth of Celestial's stock. Siegel saved the day by borrowing money to purchase the stock himself.

Exhibit 4

ANNUAL CHANGES IN DOLLAR SALES, FISCAL 1973–1982
(net sales in thousands of dollars)

FISCAL YEAR	DOLLAR SALES	
	Amount	Increase
1973	$ 70	—
1974	293	+320%
1975	1,316	+350
1976	2,930	+125
1977	5,636	+ 92
1978	8,887	+ 58
1979	10,524	+ 18
1980	11,557	+ 10
1981	16,662	+ 44
1982	23,327	+ 40

Source: Celestial Seasonings records.

Exhibit 5

MARKET SHARE (in $)
ESTIMATED U.S. HERBAL TEA MARKET,
1978–1980

	1978	1979	1980
Celestial Seasonings	38%	33%	30%
Magic Mountain	5	12	11
Lipton	—	—	8
Bigelow	—	4	8
G.N.C.	4	4	4
Other	53	47	39

Source: Company records.

In hiring heavyweight marketing types like Keith Brenner to draft a new marketing strategy, the main component being to move the herbal teas out of the less trafficked, speciality sections of grocery stores into the mainline beverage sections, Mo Siegel underscored his ambition to be big rather than small. Siegel and Brenner shared a perception that "the 35- to 50-year-old market remains to be captured if Celestial is to be truly successful." See Exhibit 5 for estimated herbal tea market shares from 1978 to 1980.

There were significant changes in Celestial's corporate culture once new management began to join the firm. Several members of the original cadre left the company presumably because of the new style of life at the tea factory. Although Siegel continued promoting quality of work life, his corporateurial mind was on priority markets for Celestial and criteria for selecting such markets. He reread his Drucker and listened to his cassette tape course on strategic planning. And he repeated to himself a six-word formula: "Concentrate on preventive health care foods." If such foods were curative in nature, so much the better.

A LOOK TO THE FUTURE

To keep the team spirit alive, Mo Siegel retreats frequently with his top staff members to discuss possible new directions for Celestial Seasonings. "We must operate in a basically unfriendly environment as retailers become more self-assured as to their position in relation to manufacturers." In the periodic strategic planning sessions in scenic and secluded Colorado resort areas, top managers at Celestial concentrate in 2½-hour segments on such tough-to-ana-

Exhibit 6

ORGANIZATIONAL STRUCTURE

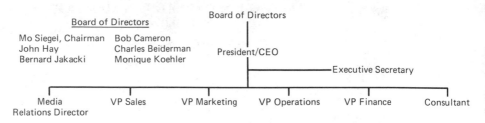

Board of Directors

Board of Directors	
Mo Siegel, Chairman	Bob Cameron
John Hay	Charles Beiderman
Bernard Jakacki	Monique Koehler

President/CEO

Executive Secretary

Media Relations Director — VP Sales — VP Marketing — VP Operations — VP Finance — Consultant

Exhibit 7

1982 PHOTOGRAPH OF MO SIEGEL, PRESIDENT/CEO

"I want to help change the course of American business, I want to help make all forms of Art more available to the American people, and I want to get the word out on health and fitness."

Mo Siegel, President
CELESTIAL SEASONINGS, INC.

Exhibit 8

DISTILLATION OF MO'S IDEAS FOR SUCCESSFUL LIVING

MO SIEGEL
THE HERB TEA MAN

ON SUCCESSFUL LIVING:

IDEAS: The best ideas are the ones that fill a need. If people want to make money, start with an idea that fills a need for someone else. Do something useful!

GOALS: I'm a believer in goal-setting. If you know what you want, it's pretty hard to lose.

FAILURES: I've had plenty. You've got to learn to accept them. You're going to fail sometimes. Don't be afraid of it.

HARD WORK: Be persistent. Work hard, but use your intelligence.

HIRING: Never hire anyone else unless they're smarter than you are in the area in which they're going to be working for you.

MARKETING: What does the public think of it? Is it good for other people?

BELIEVING: You could do something you don't believe in, but it really takes the fun out of it. I've had some hard times along the way, and if I didn't believe in the product, I would have sold the company a long time ago.

HEALTH: People are tired of paying doctors, and they want to stay healthy. I see people around the country getting more interested in prevention.

INCENTIVES: If we want the labor force to work well, why not let them own part of it?

LABOR: Create a condition in which the work force feels better about their lives. What is good for labor should be good for management and vice versa.

FAITH: There is only one place to have faith and that is in God. The disapointments that are hardest to bear are those that never come. Faith in an active life is a positive attitude.

Source: Company's 1982 press kit.

MO SIEGEL
THE HERB TEA MAN

MO'S STEPS TO SUCCESSFUL LIVING

1. Do something worthwhile for someone else.

2. Have faith, maintain a positive attitude.

3. Learn the art of setting goals, what you want.

4. It isn't enough to work hard, you must work SMART!

5. Do not be afraid to fail.

6. Don't take yourself too seriously.

7. Stay healthy.

8. Believe in and be dedicated to quality.

9. Do not be afraid to take a risk.

10. Family love and support maintain stability and help you keep priorities in perspective.

lyze questions as, What business are we in? What business should we be in? What is our company philosophy? Is our philosophy changing and if so in what ways? Who are our customers and how are segments changing? What are Celestial's strengths and weaknesses? What threats and opportunities face us over the next several years? Is caffeine compatible with Celestial? What are our criteria for business development?

Underlying the retreats' agendas was Siegel's own ambition for the company: "To be a billion dollars in sales at the turn of the century."

Exhibit 6 depicts Celestial Seasonings' organizational structure; Exhibit 7 is a photograph of the founder; and Exhibit 8, from Celestial's press kit, summarizes some of Mo's reflections for successful living.

Your Task:

Assume that Messrs. Siegel and Brenner and others have invited you to join them at a year-end 1982 planning retreat so you can provide an outsider's perspectives regarding the issues facing Celestial. As you approach the assignment, you are looking at one of their recent apple-green packages of Sleepytime Herb Tea, which features a lovable bear dozing by the fire, a pot of tea by its side. Only slightly to the left of its machine-readable bar coding on the back of the packet appears a saying, perhaps prophetic, by Schumacher: "Every increase of needs tends to increase dependence on outside forces over which one cannot have control, and therefore increases existential fear . . .".

Appendix A

DESCRIPTION OF SELECTED PRODUCTS

CELESTIAL SEASONINGS

AMERICA'S #1 SELLING HERB TEA

SLEEPYTIME®: Our No. 1 Selling Herb Tea — The perfect before bedtime drink. A great non-caffeinated tea with chamomile, spearmint leaves and lemon grass with seven other herbs. Helps you relax and wind down from a hectic day. Designed to round off the day's rough edges. Its sweet flowered flavor can be enjoyed by young and old.

MANDARIN ORANGE SPICE: One of our most popular teas. The delicious flavor of imported natural mandarin oranges makes this tea drinkable any time of day. We captured a tangy citrus flavor with just the right spice bouquet by combining orange peels, hibiscus flowers, rosehips, blackberry leaves and a touch of sweet cloves, a flavor you will also enjoy iced.

CINNAMON ROSE™: A bright, refreshing tea that combines the sweet explosion of imported cinnamon with the naturally round flavors of rosehips, orange peels, blackberry leaves and sweet cloves. A uniquely flavored herbal blend that is excellent both hot or cold.

COUNTRY APPLE™: The luscious apple flavor unfolds with every sip. The aroma of Country Apple Herb Tea will take you back to breezy afternoons in a country orchard. Truly an apple adventure, combining rosehips and hibiscus flowers for a bit of tartness, chamomile and chicory for smoothness and body, plus cinnamon and nutmeg for just the right touch of spice.

ALMOND SUNSET™: Our newest tea, a romantic blend of herbs with the soothing natural flavor of almonds. A delicate blend of rich roasted carob, barley and chicory root; spiced with cinnamon, sunny orange peel and a hint of anise seed. A taste for almond lovers of all ages.

RED ZINGER®: A Celestial tradition, imitated often but never equalled. The deep ruby red color, the tangy citrus flavor, the powerful bolt of flavor. All these combine to make Red Zinger a unique herbal soft drink enjoyed by young and old alike. Red Zinger is an indescribale brew that can only be appreciated by tasting it.

Soothing teas for a nervous world.®

Appendix B

MR. SIEGEL'S RÉSUMÉ AND MISSION

1780 55th Street
Boulder, Colorado 80301 U.S.A.
(303) 449-3779

Cable: CELESEAS BLDR
TWX: 910-940-3448

MO SIEGEL
630 Spruce Street
Boulder, Colorado 80302
(303) 447-9599

Business Address: 1780 - 55th Street
          Boulder, Colorado 80301
            (303) 449-3779

EDUCATIONAL HISTORY

1967
and on-going

Attended parochial schools; attended numerous college courses; completed numerous professional CEO and executive seminars and courses.

On-going

Independent Study - I am a devoted and perpetual student of the health sciences, business management, religion, philosophy, and government. I am currently engaged in authoring a series of programs for political reform in the United States which began with the publication of the essay "Fire in the American People".

1979

Travel Study - I sponsored a three-week, 5,000 mile study-tour of health and nutrition through the Soviet Union with special focus on "The Garden of the Centenarians" in the Trans-Caucasian Republic of Azerbaijan and Georgia, home of the "long dwellers."

1980

Travel Study - I completed a three week interior study tour of China, involving the study of food production and Chinese herbal science.

Other travels include North America, Central America, South America, Europe, Middle East, and Asia.

EMPLOYMENT HISTORY

1968 to
1970

Owner, health food store; first mate, commercial fishing vessel, Key West, Fla.; harmonica playing sandwich board advertiser; carrot juicer salesman.

Appendix B (Cont.)

- 2 -

1970 to
present

Founder, President and Chairman of the Board,
Celestial Seasonings Herb Tea Company, Boulder
Colorado.

My responsibilities at Celestial Seasonings
include planning, organizing and directing the
over-all growth and development of the company;
providing executive management to the divisions
of Operations, Marketing, Sales, Human Resources,
and Finance.

My principal goals have been to ensure the
achievement of all corporate objectives and
the fulfillment of all responsibilities to
employees, shareholders, and customers by
directing all executive decisions affecting
the current and long-range operations of the
company.

PERSPECTIVE ON CELESTIAL SEASONINGS

In 1971 Celestial Seasonings sold a grand
total of 10,000 hand-sewn tea bags, containing
hand-picked Rocky Mountain herbs, to a small
group of health food stores.

Celestial now imports herbs from 35 countries
for use in blends which are milled at the
Boulder plant at a rate of over 4 million
pounds per year . . .

In 1982 Celestial will manufacture and serve
700 million tea bags and the fiscal year sales
will exceed twenty-five million dollars . . .

Celestial Seasonings Herb Teas are available
in more than 35,000 retail outlets throughout
the world including 60% of all U.S. supermarkets
and foreign distribution in Canada, Australia,
New Zealand, and Great Britain.

PROFESSIONAL ACCOMPLISHMENTS

Founder of America's finest International Class
stage bicycle race; formerly the Red Zinger Bicycle
Classic, now the Coors Classic.

Podium Speaker at the Democratic National Convention
1980; served on the Rules Committee of the Democratic
National Party, 1980.

Keynote Speaker for numerous professional, religious,
and civic organizational activities.

Appendix B (Cont.)

- 3 -

Guest appearances on <u>ABC-TV's "Success, It Can Be Yours,</u>
<u>PM Magazine, Donahue, Donahue on Today,</u> HBO's <u>"Money Matters"</u>,
<u>Merv Griffin, Mike Douglas, Dinah Shore, Sandy Freeman, USam,</u>
<u>700 Club, Cable Health Network.</u>

Featured in <u>People Magazine, Sports Illustrated, Wall Street</u>
<u>Journal, Fortune Magazine, Money Magazine, BusinessWeek</u>
<u>Magazine, New York Times, Los Angeles Times, San Francisco</u>
<u>Chronicle, Boston Globe, Chicago Sun-Times, Christian</u>
<u>Science Monitor, Washington Post, Denver Post, Rocky Mountain</u>
<u>News, Seattle Times, Minneapolis Tribune, In-Flight Magazines,</u>
<u>US Magazine, San Jose Mercury News, Seattle Post Intelligencer.</u>

CHARACTER SKETCHES

Abiding concern...The health and fitness of the American
people. Political reform.

Personal Heroes...Jesus, Abraham Lincoln, Walt Disney, Thomas J.
Watson (founder of IBM), Dr. Kenneth Cooper (founder of the
Aerobics Institute), Eddie Merckx (six-time Tour de France
champion).

Quote..."I want Celestial Seasonings to enter the 21st
century as one of America's leading corporations."

Favorite tea bag homily..."Angels can fly because they
take themselves lightly."

Quote..."Where we go in the hereafter, depends on what
we go after here."

Dream...of the day when the typical American employee
enjoys the dignity and the equity he has earned and
deserves.

Hoped for epitaph..."Mo Siegel was a good father."

Explanation of insatiable appetite for social and
business advance...Because I don't believe that when
St. Peter asks me, "Mo, what have you done with your
life?", that it will be sufficient to reply, "Well,
I cornered the herb tea market."

Quote..."I want to help change the course of American
business, I want to help make all forms of Art more
available to the American People, and I want to get
the word out on health and fitness."

case

7

MEASUREMENT RESEARCH AND DEVELOPMENT, INC.

"The question is, Should we develop, manufacture, and sell this transducer to industry?" David Jennison was conducting a meeting of his engineering staff. Jennison was vice president and general manager of the Product Development and Manufacturing Department of Measurement Research and Development, Inc. (MRD), a company formed in the mid-1960s by a group of research scientists who had left their posts at various scientific laboratories in the United States and Europe to become entrepreneurs.

The transducer under consideration could measure the proximity of a metallic plate relative to the face of the device. This feat was accomplished by driving the sensor with a 1 megaHertz (MHz) signal that induced eddy currents in the metallic plate. The resulting electrical signal was inversely proportional to the distance between the sensor face and the metallic plate. Movements of 1 micro inch—about 0.01 the amount a copper penny expands when held in one's hand—could be measured accurately and with highly reliable repeatability.

Some measurement applications that MRD engineers thought would be useful to industry were vibrating motion of structures at frequencies up to 40 KHz (kiloHertz); eccentricity of rotating shafts; shake table motion; thickness, buckle, and flatness of metal; oil film thickness; and other precision deflection, motion, and position applications. A tested quality control application was that of measuring the thickness of Teflon coatings on parts of telephone assemblies. Measurement accuracy was not lessened by water or oil media between the sensor and the metallic object being sensed, and there was negligible effect from temperature, humidity, moisture, and pressure.

Field tests, in experimental settings, demonstrated the instrument's and associated electronics' reliability as key components in computer-controlled process applications; with robot systems; and as stand-alone sensors, with digital readouts, in automated quality-assurance procedures. Engineers in the test companies' production and laboratory facilities were favorably impressed, most reporting performance superior to that achieved with existing equipment.

COMPANY BACKGROUND

MRD, based upon its founders' analytic talents in nucleonics and related scientific fields, quickly developed a reputation for competency and earned a spot as one of the top 100 defense contractors. The organizers wished to provide facilities and a favorable environment for conducting research and development studies, believing that they could eventually design and manufacture measurement and test equipment, initially to fulfill their DOD contracts and later to sell to industry as spinoff products. By the mid-1970s, MRD's product capabilities included research, design, testing, production, and on-site evaluation of measurement instrumentation.

Product development comprised activities in electromechanical devices, such as the system that MRD was considering making and selling, nuclear test and neutron instrumentation, and ceramic materials. Diversification was a goal of the manufacturing group.

Corporate officers, both at MRD and at the company that acquired them soon after they started, were proud of the organization's ability to integrate scientific disciplines with applied engineering and of their reputation for providing highly competent, responsive, and uniquely integrated project teams to solve complex problems.

MRD competence included weapons systems analysis (vulnerability, reliability, effectiveness, countermeasures, materials); phenomenology (nuclear radiation effects, meteorology, hydrodynamics, thermodynamics, electromagnetic fields and waves, and high-voltage discharges); and data processing (software and consulting services).

Along with other electronics companies' representatives, MRD's scientists met regularly in 1982 with top electronic warfare (EW) personnel and Defense Department staff to help decide upon U.S. responses to anticipated increased sophistication of U.S.S.R. target-tracking radar systems in surface-to-air missiles and interceptor aircraft. American outlays for EW research and development were predicted to increase by 15 to 20 percent annually over the ensuing 10 years, most of this, according to several experts, slated for equipment purchases. MRD was a high-tech defense analysis contractor but did not manufacture EW hardware.

PRODUCT PLANNING MEETING

Besides David Jennison, also present at the meeting were George Benson, electrical engineer, in charge of designing and developing the instrument and its related electronics; Julie Pendegrast, a recent electrical engineering graduate of Rensselaer Polytechnic Institute, hired by Benson a few months earlier; John Hooper, a Ph.D. physicist and one of the company's organizers, previously headed a government research facility in New Mexico; Helen Brezneski, formerly a technician at the company, promoted in 1980 to assistant production manager in the manufacturing group; and Henry Gallagher, primarily experienced in aircraft and radar-site management while a colonel in the Air Force, employed in 1980 as sales manager for MRD's product development and manufacturing group.

Jennison continued: "We must decide whether to go ahead with this effort and, if we proceed, what are the next steps? What uncertainties must be resolved? So, let's share ideas."

"Well," George Benson spoke with conviction and enthusiasm, "we know that our studies in nuclear effects and other hostile environments give us an obvious edge. No competitor is state of the art like us, a point we've proved with the high-temperature pressure gauges. I bet I'm speaking for all of us in saying we ought to go full steam ahead."

"I agree with you, George, up to a point," Julie said, "but most of the company's experience has been with DOD and in other applications for the government. What we're talking about now is a departure. Industrial applications for the sensor are different from what we've dealt with in the past, and MRD isn't as well known as others who are already in the markets we want to sell to."

"True," added Hooper, "we may not be able to go at this the same way we have with DOD customers because what has been successful with our friends in the nuclear testing business probably won't work for industrial buyers—I'm talking primarily about marketing approaches. Speaking for the operating committee, I'm also concerned about other risks that can't be ignored."

"What risks, John?" asked Benson.

"Financial risks," Hooper responded. "We have some development money, but not much to spare unless the payoff potential is fairly high and reasonably certain. Then, too, I'm referring to the risk of damaging MRD's national reputation if the new instrumentation doesn't perform in the industrial setting according to our high standards. We became one of the top 100 prime contractors by delivering top-quality work, on time, to DOD."

Brezneski, who had been listening intently, interjected, "I was afraid you were doubtful of our ability to produce and deliver the system on time. Is that the main point, or is it more a matter of instrument performance?"

"A little of both, Helen," replied Hooper. "We have had some problems recently turning out components that function within specifications. And the EW group has received a few complaints about slipped deadlines on their reports; they blame this on delays in manufacturing delivery of test units to support the study contracts. However, David tells me those problems were mainly in getting units out of the calibration lab and all of that is running smoothly now."

"I can tell you, when it comes to performance," Benson stated, "there is no problem, John. This sensor has absolutely superior specs and will easily get the low-level measurements required for industry's mechanical engineering types. And you know the old saying about pioneers—they're the ones with arrows in their backs. But competitors won't be close behind us on this one because we have the superior technology and a good lead time. Our lab results and reports from government users make me totally optimistic. Further. . ."

Jennison interrupted: "Nevertheless, George, there is a difference between lab testing and field use, which is what Julie was referring to. And the market study last month tells us that the kinds of users we'll have to contact have different needs from present customers. We're still having difficulty getting our MRD pressure systems accepted for field tests by industry, so why should it be any different with this one? Hank tells me that forecasting sales will be a guessing game the first couple of years."

Henry Gallagher expressed a quandary: "I wonder if sales reps will be able to shift gears to call on different kinds of prospects for the new system. The market research study shows we aren't well known to the markets we are interested in; that means a lot of missionary effort. As it is, I'm having trouble motivating the reps to cover R&D labs that send inquiry cards for our proven products. Market coverage is spotty, any way you look at it. And with the company's stated intent to distribute in Japan and Europe, a lot of gearing up will have to be done in advertising and for other kinds of selling. It'll be a new ball game."

Benson's enthusiasm was unchecked: "I was wondering, Hank, if we shouldn't make this a separate effort, maybe even hire a sales manager to run the show, hire new reps, get someone to do the advertising for us, and do sophisticated sales planning."

On this note, the two-hour discussions began to wind down, with a consensus that several tasks remained: additional market analysis, evaluation of alternative strategies for domestic and foreign sales of all products, and consideration of changes in the rep organization and in the advertising program.

"There's one other concept we might reserve for a future agenda," Jennison concluded, "and that's the notion of this department becoming a separate division, or a full-fledged subsidiary, because we actually have a separate business from the other businesses in the company. John and I have discussed it, and if it's reasonably . . ."

He was stopped by Hooper: "I meant to bring those statements with me tonight, Dave, but I forgot to pick them up from accounting. We're not sure how fairly they represent your group's status, but they ought to be close enough for planning. By the way, I told them to add in that work you just finished for us on the Navy contract; I think it was around $100,000. Tell you what, I'll send those financial statements to you Monday." The summary Hooper referred to is presented in Appendix A.

"Thanks, John," said Jennison, and turning to his staff, "Have a nice weekend, gang. See you Monday." As the others filed out, animatedly discussing how close they were to having the new product perfected, Jennison ruminated over MRD's lack of marketing experience, the multitude of tasks that lay ahead, and the limited time in which to get them all done. At 9:30 P.M., after analyzing inventory data, sorting out his calendar for the coming week, and making a note to himself to review the consultant's report before the staff's next meeting on the new product effort, he locked the office and bade goodnight to the security guard.

Appendix B presents a condensed version of the consultant's executive summary, along with two diagrams—one a conceptual view of future income sources and the other a model for responding to inquiries, said to be a problem urgently in need of attention—which were to serve as items for discussion at a forthcoming meeting between MRD management and the consulting group.

OTHER PROBLEMS FACED BY JENNISON

While attending various group meetings at MRD, it became apparent to the casewriter that several issues should be addressed along with the ones posed in the product planning session. Some of these were

1. Space available for assembly was crowded.
2. There was lack of standardization on sensors; with the exception of displacement transducers most systems were custom-built.
3. With no stock items, delivery dates were gradually lengthening, and, as assemblers worked longer hours to meet schedules, defects and rejections from the calibration laboratory increased.
4. Parts outages were gradually increasing.
5. Time lags in responding to requests for quotations (RFQs) were increasing, although negative effects, based on customer feedback, seemed negligible.
6. Requests were increasing for calibration lab technicians to shorten time spent on their function; attempts to shortcut calibration procedures were leading to organizational conflicts, defective shipments, increased service costs, and dissatisfied customers.
7. A current large job shop assembly contract, which was producing immediate cash flow, was being given more attention by quality control personnel than the somewhat longer-term transducer operation.

Your Task:

1. As you interpret the situation, in what business is MRD operating? Jennison's unit?
2. Based on information given in the case study, including appendices, evaluate the product development and manufacturing group's planning to introduce their product to industrial markets.
3. Given the financial information, what are the risks involved and what potential gains might be realized in forming a separate organization?
4. What information would help Jennison, Hooper, and the others to conceptualize more clearly their strengths and weaknesses and the external threats and opportunities facing their company? What information do they need and how should they use it?
5. How could they construct a business plan that would enable them to make the transition from an engineering to a marketing orientation? What major obstacles face them in attempts to make necessary changes?

In your analysis and recommendations, consider the interaction of organizational (engineering, departmental, corporate, parent), financial, and external market variables.

Appendix A

TO: John Hooper

FROM: Accounting/Finance Department

The accompanying exhibits represent the accounting department's best current estimates of what the balance sheet and operating statement figures would be if the product manufacturing group had been separate from the rest of MRD for the year just ended and for the two previous fiscal years.

Please note that we've added the subcontract orders done mainly in the machine shop and temporary production area. That amount brings the revenue estimate to approximately $800,000. The percentages for the last year are comparable to those reported by such companies as Dun & Bradstreet and Robert Morris Associates for electronics companies in the same size range as MRD.

Finally, we have attached ratio calculations, and because we thought you and Mr. Jennison might be interested in some return-on-net-worth calculations, we put together the RONW chart.

BALANCE SHEET

	FY JUST ENDED		TWO YEARS AGO		THREE YEARS AGO	
	Amount	% of Total	Amount	% of Total	Amount	% of Total
ASSETS						
Cash	$ 40,000	8%	$ 50,000	10%	$ 15,000	6.5%
Marketable securities	5,000	1	20,000	4	2,500	1.1
Receivables, net	150,000	30	175,000	35	50,000	21.7
Inventory, net	155,000	31	140,000	28	50,000	21.7
Total current assets	$350,000	70%	$385,000	77%	$117,500	51.0%
Plant and equipment, net	$150,000	30%	$115,000	23%	$112,500	49.0%
Total assets	$500,000	100%	$500,000	100%	$230,000	100.0%
CLAIMS ON ASSETS						
Bank loans (short-term notes)	$ 25,000	5%	$ 50,000	10%	$ 5,000	2.2%
Accounts payable (suppliers)	75,000	15	80,000	16	15,000	6.5
Income taxes (provision for)	10,000	2	10,000	2	2,500	1.1
Current maturities (long-term debt)	25,000	5	25,000	5	25,000	10.9
Total current debt	$135,000	27%	$165,000	33%	$ 47,500	20.7%
Long-term debt	115,000	23	140,000	28	165,000	71.7
Total net worth	250,000	50	195,000	39	17,500	7.6
Total claims	$500,000	100%	$500,000	100%	$230,000	100.0%

OPERATING STATEMENT

	FY JUST ENDED		TWO YEARS AGO		THREE YEARS AGO	
Net sales	$800,000	100%	$950,000	100%	$255,000	100%
Cost of sales	520,000	65	665,000	70	179,000	70
Gross profit	280,000	35%	285,000	30%	76,000	30%
Selling, delivery expense	96,000	12	114,000	12	30,600	12
Officers' salaries	72,000	9	66,500	7	64,000	25
Other general administrative expenses	64,000	8	76,000	8	20,400	8
Profit (loss) before taxes	$ 48,000	6%	$ 28,500	3%	($ 39,000)	(15%)

Note: The Product Development and Manufacturing Department's sales have been running at about 3 percent of total MRD revenues, increasing from 1 percent 5 years ago. Corporate revenues have risen at a compounded rate of 12 percent annually for the past 10 years.

RATIOS CALCULATED FROM FINANCIAL STATEMENTS

FACTORS AND RATIOS	CURRENT YEAR	LAST YEAR	TWO YEARS AGO
Profit margin	.06	.03	−.153
Capital turnover	1.6	1.9	1.1
Return on assets	.096	.057	−.168
Leverage	2.00	2.564	13.143
Return on equity	.192	.146	−2.21
Net profit to net worth	.192	.146	−2.23
Net profit to net sales	.06	.03	−.153
Net sales to fixed assets	5.33	8.26	2.27
Net sales to net worth	3.2	4.87	14.57
Current ratio	2.59	2.33	2.47
Acid test	1.44	1.48	1.42
Receivables to working capital	.697	.795	.714
Inventory to working capital	.721	.636	.714
Collection period	68.44 days	67.24 days	71.57 days
Net sales to inventory	5.16	6.79	5.1
Net sales to working capital	3.72	4.32	3.64
Long-term liability to working capital	.535	.636	2.357
Debt to net worth	1.00	1.56	12.14
Current liabilities to net worth	.540	.846	2.71
Fixed assets to net worth	.600	.590	6.43

Figure 1

FLOW DIAGRAM OF RETURN-ON-NET-WORTH CALCULATIONS (DATA FOR LAST FISCAL YEAR)

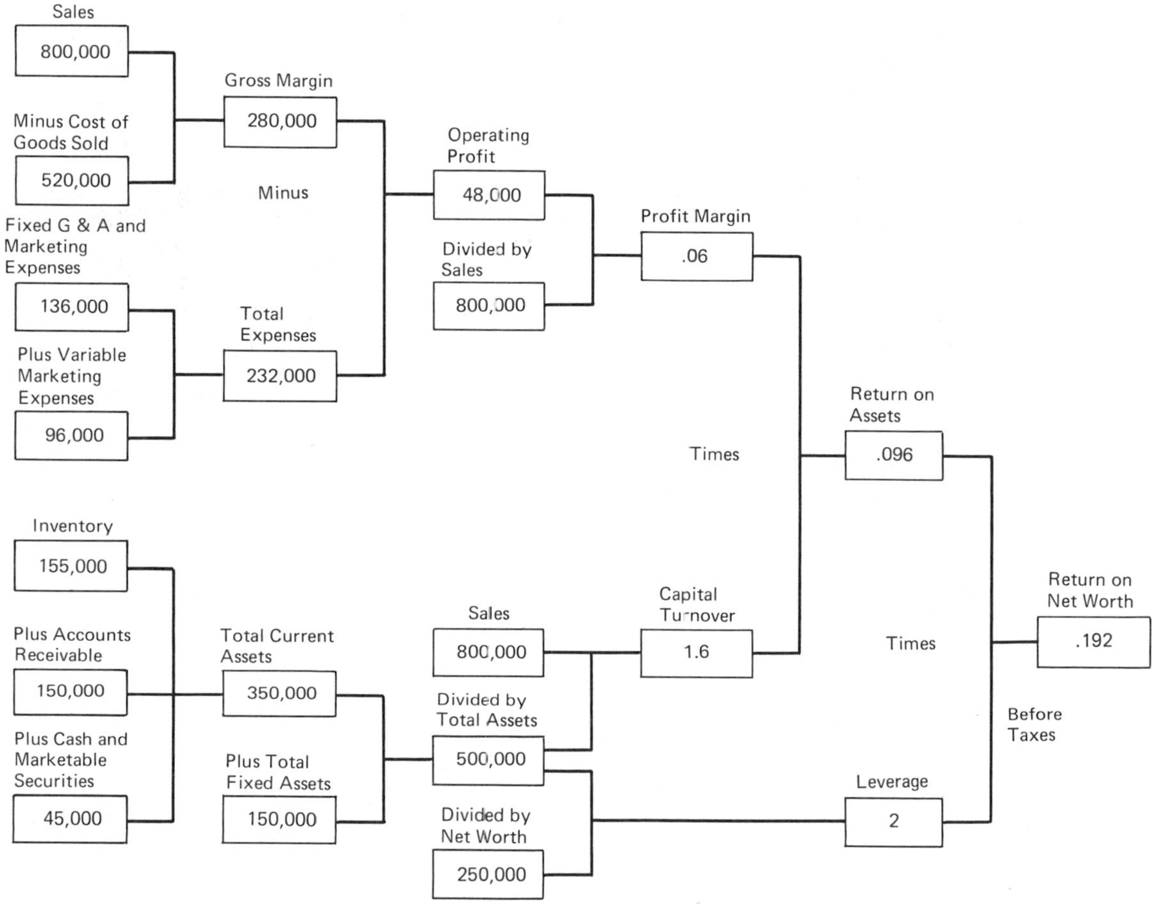

Appendix B

CONSULTANT'S REPORT TO MRD: EXECUTIVE SUMMARY

OBJECTIVES OF THE MARKET SURVEY

1. To help evaluate general potential in the industrial (commercial as opposed to government) sector for MRD's displacement transducers.
2. To find out from those respondents who classed themselves as prospective purchasers of transducers which product characteristics they considered to be most important.
3. To discover respondents' opinions of the displacement measuring systems produced by various companies. A related objective here was to find out the extent of awareness of MRD.

CONCLUSIONS

Potential exists in most standard industrial classifications (SICs) surveyed, with major potential in the following:

SIC 3511	Steam engines; steam, gas, and hydraulic turbines; and steam, gas, and hydraulic turbine generator set units
SIC 3522	Farm machinery and equipment
SIC 3531	Construction machinery and equipment
SIC 3611	Electric measuring instruments and test equipment
SIC 3621	Motors and generators
SIC 3622	Industrial controls
SIC 3711	Motor vehicles
SIC 3712	Passenger car bodies
SIC 3721	Aircraft
SIC 3722	Aircraft engines and engine parts
SIC 3811	Engineering, laboratory, and scientific and research instruments and associated equipment
SIC 3821	Mechanical measuring and controlling instruments, except automatic temperature controls.

RANKING OF IMPORTANCE OF PRODUCT FEATURES

In descending order, output linearity, temperature stability, price of complete system, noncontacting feature, and frequency response (the last

Appendix B (Cont.)

two were rated equally). Obviously, their needs differ greatly from current buyers of MRD systems.

RESPONDENTS' PERCEPTIONS OF COMPANIES AND PRODUCTS

Two major producers were very well known, and their systems were rated as excellent; four others were known to many, but their measuring systems were considered to be inferior to the top two; MRD was next to last in the group of five least known companies; respondents "guessed" the company's transducers to be high in both quality and price.

SURVEY RESPONSE RATE AND USER CATEGORY

A total of 614 responses were received from a sample of 1,629 (about 38 percent), of whom 320 (about 52 percent) classed themselves as potential buyers of MRD systems. This figure is weighted neither by the number of systems each lab and plant might use nor by the urgency of need.

RESPONSE BY STATES

MRD's coverage appears to be adequate in a few higher-potential states, but inadequate in most. The territory already assigned to one nuclear instrumentation representative accounts for 29 percent of total potential respondents, and that covered by another nuclear rep group equals 16 percent of potential measured by the survey. However, it is unlikely, because they primarily sell nuclear products, that these reps cover more than 20 percent of MRD transducer prospects. We recommend that literature packets be sent immediately to all those indicating any interest at all and that telephone calls be made to the group expressing a high level of interest.

Please note Figure 1, which, although arguable, portrays our schematic of potential revenue sources and their relationships to a yet-to-be-defined revenue target. When we meet to discuss this report, setting sales targets should be on the agenda. Figure 2 gets at what we talked about on the phone—an urgent need to streamline the process of responding to inquiries. This file, currently manual, should be on magnetic tape, purged regularly, and used as a control and planning tool.

Figure 1

A CONCEPTUAL VIEW OF FUTURE INCOME SOURCES

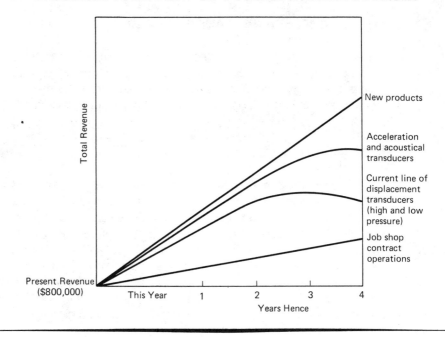

Figure 2

THE MRD INQUIRY CARD KIT

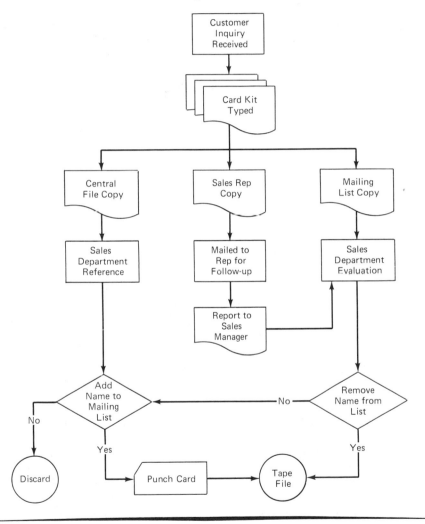

case

8

THE COLORADO DAILY, INC.

The Colorado Daily, Inc., with offices on the University of Colorado campus and in downtown Boulder, styles itself "a Boulder alternative since 1892." An independent morning newspaper with a target audience of both the University of Colorado and the Boulder communities, the *Daily* had a 1982 circulation of about 20,000, with 12,000 copies distributed at locations on campus and 8,000 copies at off-campus points. The *Daily* is a free paper, although a small subscription list has been maintained, accounting for $2,000 in revenues annually.

The Colorado Daily, Inc., which includes New Morning Composition (NMC),[1] a production subsidiary, and *Audience,* a free weekly publication containing entertainment listings, is a not-for-profit corporation. Expenses are met through advertising revenues, which came to almost $700,000 in 1981. Because the paper is tied closely to its University of Colorado student readers (although it receives no money or official support from the university), its production is somewhat seasonal. During the 1981–1982 school year the *Daily* produced a newspaper averaging 20 to 24 pages (during the summer, there was a reduction to about 12 pages) and employed a staff of 60 in its total opera-

[1]New Morning Composition was phased out in 1982.

tion, including 20 at New Morning. *Audience* publishes throughout the summer months at its normal size, retaining its full staff.

Various stages of production of the *Daily* and *Audience* take place throughout the year at several locations. Editorial offices for the newspaper are at the University Memorial Center on campus; business and advertising offices are located off campus in the NMC location; printing, at still another location, is done by Intermountain Color, a Boulder business firm. *Audience*, located in downtown Boulder, uses video display terminals (VDTs) in the *Daily* offices on campus for setting its listings and articles.

Managing editor Tim Lange, in his early thirties, has been with the *Daily* sporadically from the early 1970s. He left the *Daily* in 1976 and returned to assume his present assignment in 1980. He sees himself as left of liberal, although his world view has changed considerably from the early 1970s radicalism for which he evinces nostalgia: "We were involved in city politics from a radical student perspective in the early 1970s. We supported bikeways; we wanted the city council to take a stand on the impeachment of Richard Nixon; we wanted people on the city council who would push issues. In my opinion, students are a lot less aware now about politics and life in general than we were then. For us who were involved in the antiwar movement, the period was a crucible for testing our ideas of political organization, and for the men, maybe the women, too, it was a test of courage and personhood. It was dangerous. There are a lot of older people here now (in their thirties) who find it hard to identify with these students.

"In the early 1970s, you could go to jail. There were some real dangers involved. Students don't have that today. Students come here very ignorant of life. They are interested in grades; from what I have seen they are not interested in academics and learning. It is the rare student who asks a question. They are interested in getting a job. Now students don't want to engage in dialogue. They just write down what the professor says."

Lange's office decor testifies to the left-liberal politics that have characterized the journalism practiced at the *Daily* since the early 1970s. Bumper stickers and posters ornament the crumbling plaster proclaiming "Reagan for Shah," "Robin Hood Was Right," and "Pogo for President."[2] The managing editor has no secretary. On his door is tacked the statement, "If you have an appointment, welcome (if not, please make an appointment)."

When questioned why he was editing a paper on a university campus, which in the 1980s had little of the radicalism that excited him and his co-workers in the Vietnam war years of the 1970s, Tim Lange spoke of the environment: "My philosophy about the *Daily* has changed over the years. This is my last chance to be in a news organization where I have a lot of say. People here are really concerned about being both good writers and good reporters—

[2]In mid-1982, repainting was underway in the *Daily*'s offices.

are concerned about journalism—and want to work in an atmosphere that allows them creativity and does not just dispatch them to one boring assignment after another, which is what happens in other places. In the next two years if the *Daily* can become a community newspaper in the large sense—the university and the Boulder community—then I may stick around for a few more years."

Lange and his staff in the editorial department, now in their late twenties and early thirties, recognized the problems they would face if they decided to turn the paper into a publication reflecting their own image and likeness. The *Daily* is neither written nor managed by students; yet, many in Boulder see it strictly as a student newspaper, a perception that is a source of irritation for writers and editors. Says one editor, "A lot of people say—Oh, you're from the CU paper—you're from the campus paper." They don't take you seriously; they think you are 18 years old, and they treat you as if you don't know what you're talking about. I'd like to move off campus and change the name of the paper."

For Lange, confusion over the mission and organization of the paper is something he lives with: "When students come to campus they may think that the *Daily* is a student newspaper, but they find out that it is not if they read it regularly. Most people do not understand the history, the workings, or how the organization is set up. We are open to students working for us. Years ago we set up a screening program. We would let people write, and if they worked out, then they had the opportunity to come on permanently, and some students do end up on the paid staff after they graduate. If they can write a sentence, we can probably teach them the rest. If they can't, we can't."

HISTORY AND ORGANIZATION
OF THE COLORADO DAILY

After publishing for 69 years, the *Daily* was established as a nonprofit corporation in 1972 (under the Colorado Nonprofit Corporation Act of 1967) mainly because the university's Board of Regents decided that the publication was "too liberal." Lange recalls that people in the state perceived the staff as "a bunch of commies." In those days, according to Lange, at the *Daily* "all politicians were thought to be jerks." Rightwingers at the *Daily* in the early 1970s were McGovernites. The Board of Regents reportedly feared that libel suits might arise from articles published in the newspaper and saw the change as a way out of a potentially risky situation. This move pleased the *Daily* writers and editors who were annoyed by interference from such conservative powers in the state as Joseph Coors, the brewing scion.

It was in the mid-1970s that the business and editorial departments of the newspaper began their rivalry. Editorial staff perceived business personnel as interested only in making money. Business perceived editorial people as financial incompetents. Exhibit 1 depicts the *Daily's* organization in 1982. (The board of directors was reduced to six after NMC was disbanded, and there is no requirement that only employees serve on the board.)

Exhibit 1

COLORADO *DAILY* ORGANIZATION CHART

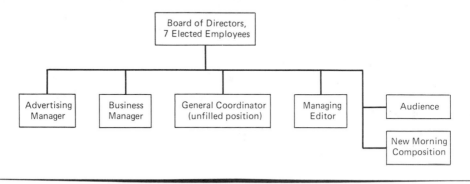

In 1973, the board established New Morning Composition as a wholly owned subsidiary of the Colorado Daily, Inc., primarily for the purpose of doing the composition for the Colorado *Daily* newspaper, to reduce costs of printing. New Morning also did some "outside" commercial work—about 20 percent of sales—with the *Daily* and *Audience* accounting for 80 percent of revenues.

After *Preview,* an entertainment weekly in Boulder, folded in 1978 the Colorado Daily, Inc., saw an informational gap in the community and created the new entertainment magazine, *Audience,* in 1979. It, too, is a wholly owned subsidiary of The Colorado Daily, Inc., one that the corporation expects will yield "large returns on our investment in the very near future."[3]

FINANCE AND ACCOUNTING

Exhibit 2 includes summary financial statistics for 1971 through 1981. Although in the fiscal year ending May 31, 1980, a loss was reported, Business Manager Cindy Dziekan chalked this up to a failure to raise advertising rates for the university and the community to compensate for inflation. About 95 percent of income was derived from local and university advertising. In April 1980 advertising rates were increased substantially, and the paper began to

[3]*Audience* earned net income of $11,000 in 1982, its first profitable year.

Exhibit 2

SELECTED INCOME AND EXPENSE SUMMARY FIGURES, 1971–1981

(fiscal year ending May 31)

	1971	1972	1973	1974	1975	1976	1977	1978	1979	1980	1981
Income											
Local advertising	$ 74,757	$119,286	$153,441	$170,148	$256,275	$307,985	$334,675	$389,418	$475,937	$345,650	$386,023
National advertising	13,116	11,634	12,403	10,421	9,672	22,036	23,473	35,848	42,025	41,096	43,971
University	28,997	30,624	29,814	44,092	70,782	76,425	81,831	96,465	109,167	99,003	107,585
Classified	23,124	30,024	39,662	46,414	52,383	52,220	53,516	52,773	57,912	63,576	68,514
Special sections	3,834	895	529	919	8,110	6,198	5,441	7,968	7,238	58,374*	74,405
Subscriptions	1,371	1,272	216	945	1,607	1,402	2,009	2,162	2,061	2,343	1,785
Other	—	—	1,526	370	738	2,596	2,123	2,991	26,976	16,200	23,670
Total income	$145,199	$193,735	$237,591	$273,309	$399,566	$468,862	$503,068	$587,625	$721,316	$626,242	$705,953
Expenses											
Salaries, wages, and commisions	$ 42,532	$ 61,007	$ 68,914	$ 89,017	$130,919	$136,052	$147,167	$171,589	$184,793	$190,231	$201,712
Printing and composing	84,771	98,377	127,352	135,678	194,120	214,502	224,578	248,875	272,591	281,142	291,964
Bad debts	4,703	2,261	2,428	4,649	9,132	14,009	17,904	15,781	18,754†	16,024	16,631
Other	—	20,456	30,140	33,051	68,789§	67,210	68,871	93,316	161,082‡	187,017	189,275
Total expenses	$147,537	$182,101	$228,834	$262,395	$402,960	$431,773	$458,520	$532,561	$637,220	$674,414	$699,582
Profit (loss)	($2,338)	$ 11,634	$ 8,757	$ 10,914	($3,394)	$ 37,089	$ 44,547	$ 55,015	$ 84,096	($48,172)	$ 6,371

*Advertising sales for special editions, including the *Audience* entertainment guide, are distributed (separately from Colorado *Daily*) throughout Boulder County.
†Estimated.
‡Increased expenses reflect start-up of *Audience*, depreciation increases for new composition equipment, and launching the short-lived University of Colorado at Denver edition of the *Daily*.
§Reflects acquisition of New Morning Composition.

see profits again. In Dziekan's words, "We are at about $4.65-per-column-inch break-even. The reason it's so high is that the university is charged so little, so we have to make it up with local advertisers. There are a lot of university people who run their ads at substantially less than it costs us to publish the ads. About 10 percent of our ads are from the university. They are charged $3.75 a column inch."

Ms. Dziekan, who came to the Colorado Daily, Inc., in 1978, after five years with a CPA firm, is chiefly responsible for diagnosing and healing financial ailments in the corporation. Under her tutelage budgets are prepared for the spring, summer, and fall, and finances are closely watched. "For the fiscal year beginning June 1, 1980," she commented, "we are doing better than budgeted and significantly better than in the prior fiscal year. We budget for modest profits and channel the rest back into the betterment of the *Daily* and its employees by way of wages, benefits, and general overall improvements to the newspaper. The Colorado Daily, Inc., has also ventured out in other areas such as *Audience* and, at one time, a Denver campus edition of the Colorado *Daily*. The Denver edition ceased publication in 1979 as the demand for a student newspaper on that campus was not great enough to support its publication.

"Although cash flow problems were occasionally troublesome," Dziekan said, "the *Daily* has always paid its bills on time. Printing invoices, for example, are paid within 21 days of receipt. All other invoices are paid within 30 days of receipt. At this point, we have no bills due in excess of 30 days. We have a ready reserve account with the bank, but we have been able to meet all our cash requirements through collection of accounts receivable."

Previous to Dziekan's joining the staff, there was a succession of business managers, and students who had some business background were recruited to handle the books. "It was chaos. When I came in March 1979, they had not done a financial statement since November 1978. They had not done a bank reconciliation. There was no continuity since the previous business people, which wasn't really a problem because I wouldn't have continued doing it the way it had been done. It took me about a year to tie things up and get it going. I know how financial statements should be prepared—what records need to be kept and what things need to be done. Some of the student help did not even know what a set of books looked like."

Still, Dziekan was not sanguine about the overall understanding of the financial situation at the *Daily*. "Most people here probably have problems reconciling their own personal bank statement at the end of the month," she says, "let alone reading a financial statement."

THE COLORADO DAILY'S ENVIRONMENT

People who have stayed with the *Daily* over the years like living near the mountains and enjoy working in a creative environment where the rule of thumb is that you can write what you like if you write it well and truthfully.

The average age on the editorial staff is 28. Fifteen of the editorial people are paid, and of those the highest-paid person receives just under $7.00 per hour. Most are in the range from $4.90 to $5.18 hourly. Although everyone who writes has a gasoline allowance, only people who work at least 20 hours have a health plan. The editorial department sees itself as having the greatest stake in the organization, according to Lange: "We are in the process of making big changes and the editorial department is the catalyst, partly because it is the people on the editorial staff who have been here the longest, and we're the ones most interested in making this a newspaper where we can work for a long time. For some of the business and ad staff people, this is more or less a stepping stone, a learning situation for them. Their rationale is different from ours." Another editorial staffer put it this way, "If advertising were in control, we would be turning out shoppers, and that's it."

Kathy Kaiser, an editor who has been with the *Daily* intermittently since 1973, feels that she has grown up with the paper. (See Exhibit 3 for a condensed experience summary.) She and Lange work together closely; both believe that the paper needs to "grow up." As she summed it up, "The *Daily* has led in the issues: it was against the war in Vietnam; we were one of two papers in 1980 who endorsed Barry Commoner for president. Now we are changing our focus from environment and politics to business, even thinking of doing a column on businesses around Boulder, which we would not have done 10 years ago. Environment is a regular beat rather than a special column. We need to do more on housing as well as stories that interest us, even if they do sound idealistic. I don't operate on the premise that we want to get more readers—we do plan to get more comics—but I want to do things that interest *me*."

Kaiser philosophically accepts the altered ambience around the *Daily* offices: "Things have changed around the *Daily*. It used to be that after work we all used to party together and do a lot of things together. Now people go back to their wives and families and husbands and kids—it's not the same group. We have gotten 10 years older; the median age is 28 now. We are still able to get really good reporters. I started to work for the *Daily* for pay following graduation after working as a student since 1971. Though I don't know what the students think of us, I have some ideas. Sometimes students will come up and say 'We had this great fraternity party last week—will you write about it?' And I say, 'No, we won't write about it unless something newsworthy happened.' They think of us as a campus paper. At moments I feel badly that they don't have their little campus paper. We're professionals. Maybe students deserve a paper that tells them 'there's going to be a big bash here.' I don't want to be the one to do it," said Kaiser emphatically.

Kaiser and Lange have seen a gradual metamorphosis of the paper into a community newspaper since the mid-1970s. Because students won the right to vote in 1971, the paper began to cover city issues aligned to liberal political factions in Boulder. The liberal group eventually became a winning faction in Boulder, so the separation that the *Daily* used to editorialize about in its pages

Exhibit 3

RÉSUMÉ: KATHY KAISER
(selected points)

Experience

— Newsletter editor, Larimer-Weld Regional Council of Governments
— Proofreader, University of Colorado Publication Services
— Proofreader, copy editor (freelance) for **Boulder Monthly**
— Copy editor, managing editor, **Colorado Daily**
— Assistant editor, **Rocky Mountain Magazine**
— Member, Board of Directors, **Frontiers: A Journal of Women Studies**
— Associate editor, **Mountain Gazette**
— Typesetter, proofreader, and paste-up person at New Morning Composition
— Freelance writer, numerous published articles

Awards

— Colorado Press Women and National Federation of Press Women

---

became irrelevant. Lange sees the separation of the 1970s as "a false dichotomy" in the 1980s: "The university is the backbone of the city, because 20,000 students and 5,000 faculty and staff represent a sizable chunk of the 80,000 total population."

What Kaiser and Lange would like to do is to move off campus completely and to continue the *Daily,* targeting both to an audience of students and to the community-at-large. Kaiser sees the participatory management aspect of the *Daily* as vital to a strategy of moving off campus: "No one owns the *Daily.* We have a group of people who are unified and interested in the same things. To go off campus we would like to have a cohesive group of people who think alike and who have the same goals. We seem to have a business manager who tacitly supports what we are doing, an advertising manager interested in the same thing, and an editorial staff that is together."

Kaiser and Lange both recognize that if the paper is to move off campus, on-campus circulation must be retained and an off-campus circulation of another 12,000 must be realized. This means that they would need an additional circulation of 4,000 since they are currently distributing 8,000 in Boulder. The idea would be to continue with a free distribution, a point underscored by Kaiser: "We are a free paper. We once tried to sell the paper for 10 or 15 cents some years ago, and our circulation dropped from 2,000 papers a day to 200.

But our production schedule is seasonal. In the fall at the beginning of the term, we often do a 24-page or a 28-page paper, but we go down to about 12 pages in the summer. You can't ask someone to pay for one page of ads, one page of classified, and very little editorial content. It's advantageous for us to publish a free paper because people will pick it up if only to read one article."

As Kaiser and Lange see it, the future for the *Daily* is in becoming an established alternative newspaper, perhaps a weekly. At present, there are only two alternative newspapers in Colorado—*The Rocky Mountain Journal*[2] and *Westword.* Lange sees the opportunities for a weekly alternative newspaper in Boulder this way: "Though a lot of newspapers have folded here, I believe Boulder is a place where an alternative weekly could succeed. Some people say that the reason they have folded is because the *Daily* is here. We siphon off a lot of advertising—$600,000 worth. The way to do that is to capitalize on that advertising; all you have to do is expand. One way may be to develop other products; we do have a typesetting facility that is underutilized right now and we have a lot of skill. There may be other things we could do that would subsidize the newspaper—other things like *Audience,* things around the communications industry, a weekly, or printing. I would like to see [the then] New Morning put in a small press—a job press."

Present competition comes from the *Boulder Daily Camera,*[4] a paper "read by most everyone in town," according to Lange and Kaiser, "because it is the only newspaper available." The managing editor continued the theme of circulation and advertising: "In some ways we see ourselves in competition with the *Camera* for the advertising dollar. What they are interested in at the *Camera* is sending 15 percent of the profits home to Miami each year. They are not really interested in coverage. Our interest is in coverage and in breaking even. There is no question that our local coverage is better than the *Camera*'s; our in-depth coverage is better. They develop a lethargy over there."

The median age of Boulder's population in 1982 was 26, and its median income was over $21,000. Lange believes there is an audience in the community waiting for his type of journalism and sees an ideal circulation for the *Daily* at 30,000 by 1987, with a predominantly off-campus readership: "We think that we can reach the audience in Boulder that comprises the scientific community, the hi-tech community—IBM, Storage Tech, and the "cocaine crowd"—people who come to Boulder for the quality of life. These are people in their late twenties and early thirties who did not go to the University of Colorado. Although we think we may be able to reach some blue-collar workers, as well, there are not very many of these in Boulder. Presently we probably have the liberal political community as our readers, the people who have been here for awhile—community leaders, people who are graduates, people who hate the *Camera*, the women's community, single parents. The divorce rate in Boulder is 50 percent; half the marriages here are dissolved.

[4]Owned by Knight-Ridder Newspapers, Inc., Miami.

"We did a short series on high technology in Boulder and received immediate response. We were just getting our feet wet on this type of story and received favorable comparison to the *Camera* on the series. We know this response reflects greater numbers than those from whom we heard—and bigger than the actual circulation that we have. I really don't know how you determine what your circulation is; that's going to be tough. We have one other disadvantage. The *Camera* has recently gone to morning circulation; before we had that morning slot to ourselves. Many people picked us up for that reason. To survive we have to know that there are at least 12,000 people out there who will pick us up."

Exhibit 4 shows the *Daily*'s front page, October 13, 1982, edition.

Although Lange is positive that an audience for a weekly alternative exists, he is uncertain about how to define and approach the audience, and he is less than confident about surveys. The last survey for the *Daily*—an insert—received only 63 replies. Kaiser and Lange count on content to generate the necessary readership. "Right now we are targeting beyond the campus group to the people we want to appeal to. That's why we are going to 8,000 off-campus circulation in the fall. We are going to have a person who spends full time on science and technical articles and reporting—businesses in the area and what's going on in the field. We will have four people covering city news in the fall." Circulation figures appear to be elusive, Lange finds: "When I use the term 'circulation,' that does not include the people who see a copy in someone's home or in a restaurant. We guess that our actual readership is closer to 25,000. There is no way you can audit free circulation very effectively."

There are people around the *Daily* who are committed to a certain type of alternative journalism, a view that they may find hard to revise even if a survey were to demonstrate that Boulder demands a different type of journalism from that they propose to deliver. Lange speaks for the editorial staff when he talks about fears of surveys: "Surveys may tell us to do what we will not. If we would have to make the paper a Chamber of Commerce house organ to get the advertising we need, then I would just as soon go and work for *The Rocky Mountain News*. There's no sense in staying here, or I could go on to one of those weeklies in other places, presumably, to get a job. In that case, I would rather do freelance work for natural-resources-specialized newspapers and journals."

Lange and Kaiser have watched the changing fortunes of alternative papers with interest in the last few years. Kaiser remembers a paper called *Borrowed Times* out of Missoula, Montana, that folded in 1980. "It used to cover antinuke stuff, health care and abortion, but nothing about local people—always diatribes against nuclear energy and things about natural childbirth." Although these are issues of concern to her, she is firm that papers have to publish what readers are concerned about—local news. "If people want to read environmental stuff they subscribe to *Audubon*; if they want political stuff they subscribe to *Nation*; but you pick up a local paper for local news be-

Exhibit 4

THE FRONT PAGE

County District 3 race — page 3

Colorado Daily

Vol. 30 No. 240   Wednesday, October 13, 1982   FREE

A "Hands Off Central America" mural has been set up in the University Memorial Center Fountain Area by the Boulder chapter of the Committee in Solidarity with the People of El Salvador to show worldwide solidarity with the People of El Salvador and to protest continued American military aid to the Salvadoran government.

Daily Photo by David Conserva

Flats relocation costs assessed
Nuclear weapons plant studied

By S.K. LEVIN
Colorado Daily Staff Writer

"The certainty that such a plant would not today be located at Rocky Flats, as well as our feelings that accidents will continue to occur even under the best of circumstances, dictates our belief that such a plant should not be located at Rocky Flats."

Following this 1975 conclusion by a government-appointed task force that looked into the health hazards of the Rocky Flats nuclear weapons plant south of Boulder, 2nd District Rep. Tim Wirth asked the U.S. Department of Energy to assess the impacts and costs of relocating the plutonium-manufacturing facility.

Four years later, the DOE, owner of the Rocky Flats plant, initiated such a study at a cost of $3.6 million.

Concern that the DOE would be assessing itself, however, led to Gov. Lamm's appointing in 1979 a watchdog committee — called the Blue Ribbon Citizen's Committee (BRCC) — to ensure that the DOE study was "thorough, complete and objective."

Tonight at 7 at the CU Fleming Law Building on campus, the BRCC, which has now evaluated several of the sub-studies in the DOE's overall study, will hold a public workshop for those who wish to review and comment upon the DOE and BRCC's evaluations prior to their being included in the final report.

The DOE study to be completed later this year, will include a determination of the risks associated with ongoing Rocky Flats operations as well as the costs and socioeconomic

continued on page 10

Economies on disaster track: Brown
U.S.-U.S.S.R. grain deal deterring nuke war

By JULITH JEDAMUS
Colorado Daily Staff Writer

A decade of managing a southern New Jersey tomato farm did just as much to train Lester Brown to see global environmental problems wholistically as his 10-year tenure at the U.S. Department of Agriculture and his academic studies, said the world-famous demographer during a meeting with CU faculty Monday.

Brown, president and senior researcher for the Worldwatch Institute, a Washington think-tank specializing in global environmental issues, spent two days on the CU campus this week discussing his research on U.S./Soviet grain trade interdependence and his latest book, *Building a Sustainable Society.*

The world's economies may be on a collision course with disaster unless policy-makers take stock of the deteriorating environmental resources that, combined with cheap oil, made many of the advances of the past few decades possible, Brown told a crowd of about 150 in the University Memorial Center Forum Room Monday night.

While the United States has "taken great pride," for example, in its doubling of agricultural production since the 1950s, Brown explained, "we are now paying the price for the methods of those gains" in the form of soil erosion, diminishing water resources and shrinking forests and grasslands. Up to one-third of U.S. cropland is losing topsoil at a rate that will undermine its long-term productivity.

"WE'VE PUT MORE pressure on world biological systems than they can stand," Brown said. Ultimately, this "biological deficit financing" will prove far more serious than

any fiscal crisis, he added, observing that many economists have "missed a major part of the analysis {of global problems} . . . if we can't protect environmental support systems, levels of unemployment will be meaningless."

Economic policies and social values that made good sense decades ago — such as having large families — will have to be abandoned by some countries in the future, Brown cautioned, citing China's drive toward one-child households. Resource "safety valves" such as petroleum-based fuels, fibers and packaging materials will soon become scarce, forcing a shift toward primary material conservation and recycling.

"We'll have to move beyond a throwaway society," Brown observed. "In a mature industrial society, recycled materials will become the primary resource supply," he said, pointing to Japan, where manufacturers convert U.S. scrap metal from "last year's Buick to this year's Toyota" and Norway, which has imposed a $100 deposit on cars that is refundable when the car is recycled.

THE POTENTIAL OF resource conservation and use of renewable energy supplies hasn't begun to be exploited, Brown said, and may have beneficial spinoff effects such as the gradual redistribution of populations to rural areas.

While oil is easily transportable, he explained, renewable energy resources (like oil's predecessor, coal), are not, requiring towns to cluster around areas where they are produced. In Brazil, for example, where one-fifth of the country's energy now comes from sugar cane, the ethanol industry is creating thousands of jobs in the countryside.

continued on page 8

Daily Photo by Emmett Jordan

Supply-side economics and a "blind faith in the free market" will lead to "destruction of world soils and deterioration of biological systems," demographer and Worldwatch President Lester Brown told a crowd of about 150 in the UMC Forum Room Monday night.

Chisholm to teach at CU
Visiting scholar in Women Studies Program

Shirley Chisholm, the first Black woman ever to be elected to Congress, has accepted an invitation to teach next summer at CU as a distinguished visiting scholar in the Women Studies Program.

Chisholm, who was first elected in 1968 to represent Brooklyn, N.Y.'s racially and ethnically diverse 12th Congressional District, is retiring from Congress this year. She is the senior Democratic woman in the U.S. House of Representatives and is the only woman and Black American to sit on the powerful House Rules Committee.

A spokeswoman for the CU Women Studies Program said Chisholm had formally accepted the CU offer as of Monday — out of a total of 29 requests for her services she received.

In 1972, Rep. Chisholm passed another "first" she was the first Black woman to run for President of the United States. She has been awarded 15 honorary degrees and is the author of many articles and two books, *Unbought and Unbossed* (1970) and *The Good Fight* (1973).

Chisholm will teach an upper-division Women's Studies course during the second session in 1983, from July 11 to Aug. 12 on women and public policy. She will likely also deliver a public lecture on the

topic.

Well known for her independent thinking and actions, Chisholm established herself as such from the beginning. When, as a freshman congresswoman in 1969, she was assigned to the House Agriculture Subcommittee on Forestry and Rural Villages, she placed an unprecedented amendment before the House removing her name from the assignment. She felt the committee had no relation to the needs and problems of her district. She succeeded, and was then assigned to the committee on Veterans Affairs.

A specialist in early childhood education and child welfare since her days as a schoolteacher and day care nursery director, Chisholm first entered public office in 1964, when she was elected to the New York State Assembly. She has a B.A. and an M.A. in education from Columbia University.

Chisholm will be one of five visiting scholars expected to teach at CU this summer; they will each be paid stipends of $5,000, plus $1,000 for living expenses.

—Karen Kos

SHIRLEY CHISHOLM

cause you want to find out why this restaurant closed, or what movie is playing, or what's going on in the city council." Kaiser believes that talking to people about the paper may be a viable survey technique. She would like to see the *Daily* talking to people at off-campus stands asking them, "Why are you picking this up? What do you like about the paper?"

She has definite ideas about the personality of the *Daily* as well as the ideal reader of the newspaper: "We could not change our basic personality at the *Daily* as liberals: support of women's rights, for example, and the environment. I couldn't write from a position in which I would support the growth of Boulder. People who apply for jobs here, however, know what the *Daily* is. However, if we found someone who was conservative, who wrote well, who was open-minded, and whom I liked, I wouldn't care. I would hire that person.

"Our ideal reader is someone between 18 and 35 who looks for an alternative from the straight *Boulder Daily Camera*. It's a group that's sensitive and intelligent, that has perhaps gone through the war in Vietnam. They are interested in the good life in Boulder, and they have changed like we all have, but they are still interested in issues. *They* are *us* because that is our age group. We would use ourselves as the norm. You have to."

Like Tim Lange, Kaiser finds the *Daily* a creative workplace, but at the same time she is frustrated by the present umbilical cord relationship to the University of Colorado campus. "In a sense I am trying to mold the paper into my own image. There are not a lot of places I could get away with that . . . what I am doing is saleable and viable. I like small towns; I like Boulder; I like the people at the *Daily;* I think that Boulder deserves a better paper."

Kathy Kaiser agrees with Tim Lange that the campuses of the 1980s lack the fiery forms of campus life a decade earlier. She admitted to mellowing over 10 years of working for the *Daily*, however, and was willing to make concessions: "Students now are more apolitical than they are left or right. I assume that female students are concerned about abortion and about birth control. It's a political issue. But my news focus is on softer news—cross-country skiing, things that are appealing to a younger audience who go to movies, who eat out, who do all the things we like to do. They're just like us."

Lange's content strategy for the *Daily* is to become a paper "with something for everyone." Since movement off campus and to a weekly format will not be possible unless the *Daily* attracts increased readership, the plan now is to deliver news about the university that will interest the general community, while presenting general interest and community news palatable to the university audience the *Daily* knows it already has.

In contrast to the editorial slant of the *Daily* 10 years ago, Editor Lange has moved away from the left in ways inconceivable for him or the paper in the days of radical campuses: "I am supportive of small corporations of $3 million or less. This community is supported by small corporations, and *this* corporation is supported by corporations that advertise. My old attitude used to be that people in corporations were creeps. No longer. I don't condone robber baronism in the 1980s, which I think we are seeing a lot of nationally, and it doesn't mean that I am super pro-capitalist now where I used not to be. I am realistic."

NEW MORNING COMPOSITION SHOP

New Morning Composition (NMC) was created by the *Daily* for the *Daily*. As a composition shop, the reputation of New Morning for doing commercial work hinged upon its prompt delivery of outside jobs, but because it had to be ready for the *Daily*'s work as well as for the *Audience*'s, it was difficult to sandwich in commercial jobs between jobs for the corporation. The *Daily* paid only break-even rates for composition. In September 1980, Colorado Daily, Inc., bought New Morning a new Mergenthaler linotype machine, a composition computer said to be the state of the art. Other equipment, however, was old and required updating—at costs of about $100,000 to bring everything up to a level that would ensure increased productivity. Facing these barriers, NMC was closed down.

Some people believe that if each reporter had a VDT on which to compose stories, much of the expensive composition work could be eliminated. Even though a VDT system costs more than $3,500 per terminal, it is not unusual for college newspapers to have several in their shops. Dziekan suggested that efficient VDT use was contingent upon the corporation's acquisition of a building. "The ideal situation would be to be located in one building. If we owned the building and had all the equipment we needed, we would be really going. We need a building in which all of the *Daily* and composition facilities could be in one physical location—we are lacking a computer capability because of our present situation. We are not using our visual display terminals efficiently because we are not in one location. *Audience* has come over here to put their copy on ours. We have two. We can't get a line between our office and their office, so that they could have their own VDT. If we were in one building we could just have separate lines between offices. As it is now, *Audience* has to come in at weird hours to meet their deadlines and to avoid conflict with our classifieds deadlines. Work has to be batched in such a way as to avoid problems with the *Daily*'s classifieds being put on the VDTs."

Although the business manager seemed certain that the editorial staff needed and wanted VDTs, one member of the editorial staff was negative about the terminals, worrying about the possible health hazards of using VDTs, but perhaps more practically, she did not like working with the machines: "I hate the VDTs and have a difficult time editing on them. You only have a portion of the story in front of you at one time. If you want to take a paragraph out and put it someplace else, it's complicated where if you have the story in your hand . . . it may just be a matter of getting adjusted to it. Also

I don't like the reports about the VDT being linked to glaucoma. We were going to buy more VDTs and all use them. Finances prevented this. As a member of the board, I would strongly oppose buying this equipment. I think most people on the board would probably look at the cost effectiveness of using them, even though they may not like them."

Certainly editorial staff would need training to use the VDTs. According to one company employee, "All our editorial people want to use VDTs. You are expected to know how to use this equipment when you go to a larger newspaper. But you need to use a VDT every day to know it backwards and forwards. Our classified people never lose anything on the VDT; our *Audience* people never lose anything. But the editorial people use it, say, one hour a week, and then it's 'How do I turn it on?' 'Which disk do I use?' 'How do I call this up?' It's more work than it's worth."

FILLING THE PAPER

The *Daily*, under its present editor, realizes that the only cost-efficient way of running a paper is to publish a "tight" paper, tightness being determined by the amount of advertising content. According to Lange, "A large paper running from 60 to 65 percent advertising is considered tight. The *Daily* management generally hopes to fill 55 percent of its paper with advertising, 45 percent with editorial content. The tighter the paper, the easier it is to fill. Editors at the *Daily* do not want to fill the paper with wire copy simply because they cannot write enough, although if a special editorial feature seems to merit heavy coverage, the *Daily* will run a looser paper."

It is important for advertising salespeople to gauge the percentage of advertising they must be prepared to sell well in advance, the trick being to avoid budgeting a paper that is either too small or too large. In the fall, the *Daily* usually plans for "fat" papers with a great deal of advertising when the students return to campus.

Because it cannot fill the paper simply with Boulder stories, the *Daily*, like other papers, relies on wire service material, favoring the Pacific News Service (PNS), which takes a liberal slant to many stories. Editor Lange believes that "PNS contains no rhetoric, however, and is careful with their sources." PNS packets of stories arrive in the *Daily* office twice each week. Lange observed, "We use a lot of it—for example, stuff on El Salvador. We don't want to run the same stuff that *The Wall Street Journal* or *The New York Times* is running." Reputed PNS links with the Institute for Policy Studies, a left-leaning thinktank, has never bothered the *Daily* people. In fact, half their wire service material is from PNS, which has had a reputation of covering topics and events that many services would not touch. They were the first with stories on My Lai, for example.

AUDIENCE MAGAZINE

Regarding *Audience* magazine, Business Manager Dziekan suggested it was naïve to expect a return on this investment so quickly. She believed that part of the discomfort some *Daily* people felt with *Audience* developed because they had never seen a business start from scratch the way that *Audience* did. (Exhibit 5 is a copy of the *Audience* contents page for July 10, 1981). "The problem, I think, is that the editorial staff is looking for dividends a little faster than is realistic. *Audience* replaces *Preview*, which folded. We are able to make *Audience* financially more successful than *Preview* ever was because of our low composition rate (at that time through New Morning) and a low printing rate because of the *Daily.* The business functions are all done over here for $200 per month—all business functions. Realistically, it costs us more to keep their books than that, but it is all merged with the *Daily.* Our person-hours have not increased to do this bookkeeping; so it has cost the *Daily* next to nothing to do the accounting for *Audience.* If it were an independent organization, it would be paying substantially more than it is now; so we were able to make *Audience* financially feasible where *Preview* had not been." The purpose of *Audience,* to reach a general public, was a way of expanding the *Daily* without expanding the newspaper portion of it. The editorial people at the *Daily* have felt that *Audience* and the *Daily* were completely separate entities in people's minds and doubt that many people in the Boulder community even understand the link between the two.

According to Lange, *Audience* never returned anything to the *Daily* while the *Daily* was subsidizing it. "They owe us about $30,000. Only five people work there. They were taking what we felt to be outrageous salaries (one person over $700 per week gross) at a time when the next highest person in the corporation made $320 gross. We felt that there was something wrong there. On the *Daily* we have five in our selling area; at *Audience* there are two." But Lange concedes, "The goals of *Audience* are different from ours. Its goals have never been laid out clearly to anyone. This needs to be done, and now it's hard to do because people are in place, and they say, 'Hey, we've been doing it this way; now what are you trying to do?' Yet the *Daily* editorial staff sees *Audience* as an investment, and the *Daily* goals come first. *Audience* has about 12,000 circulation."

There has been a question about *Audience*'s voice in the corporation. Should it be given a seat on the board? Some people in the editorial area of the *Daily* think not. The *Daily* should maintain control of its own editorial decisions, they say. Since *Audience* is a subsidiary, some feel that *Audience*'s active decision-making voice could ultimately weaken the *Daily.*

A board decision in 1981 resulted in the *Daily*'s paying the general manager of *Audience* a percentage of the profits as an incentive to productivity.

Exhibit 5

CONTENTS PAGE FROM *AUDIENCE*

CONTENTS

audience

JULY 10, 1981   VOL. 3 NO. 24

EDITOR	ART DIRECTOR	ADMINISTRATIVE ASSISTANT	SALES MANAGER	DISTRIBUTION	CONTRIBUTORS
Lois Canzonieri	Cathi Allen	Michelle Luzius	Stewart Ressler	V. E. Williams	R. Alan Rice, Jane C. Bryant,
			ACCOUNT REPRESENTATIVE		Jack Pommer, Marty Durlin
			Betsy Weber		

Meet John Reed, who will direct two Gilbert and Sullivan operettas on the CU-Boulder campus.

Leon Russell headlines John McEuen's First Annual Rocky Mountain Opry, July 18 at Red Rocks.

Audience, a complete guide of entertainment is published weekly by Audience, Inc. and distributed throughout Boulder County. Our offices are located at 2040 Broadway, Boulder, Colorado 80302. 444-4211.

We welcome information on your local events and will print on a space available basis. Reproduction without written permission is strictly prohibited. Editorial and advertising deadline: 5:00 p.m. Monday preceding Friday publication

Production by New Morning Composition. Printing by Intermountain Color.

Cover art: John McEuen's First Annual Rocky Mountain Opry is highlighted in this week's issue of **Audience.**

GREAT EXPECTATIONS

– Lois Canzonieri

I was listening to David Hartley on Boulder AM (KADE) this morning. This being Wednesday, he was heralding "hump day" in a seemingly endless week. After a three day holiday weekend everyone seems to move at half speed for the next ten days. Fortunately, the summer entertainment season is gearing up, designed to end my lethargy with a variety of offerings . . .

We learned this week that the Telluride Jazz Festival will be held this year, August 15-16. A number of top acts have been booked for the two-day festival: Freddie Hubbard, Richie Cole, Spyro Gyra, Kinesis, The Prosperity Jazz Band, and local favorites Rare Silk and New Moon. More details on the festival as they are released.

Closer to home, the theatre season is picking up.

I met John Reed this week at a brown bag lunch at the College of Music. Reed, a delightful character, is directing two Gilbert and Sullivan operettas on campus this summer. He's a veteran actor and director from the D'Oyly Carte Opera Company in London. He brings years of experience and a delightful collection of anecdotes to his summer troupe.

"Pirates of Penzance" and "Yeoman of the Guard" will be presented in repertory from Friday, July 10 through Saturday, July 25. Try to catch at least one of these shows, it is like stepping into another era — a welcome diversion.

While students were rehearsing Gilbert and Sullivan in the Music Hall, the Shakespeare troupe was putting finishing touches on their three productions: "Julius Caesar," "Taming of the Shrew," and "All's Well That Ends Well." We ran through one of the final rehearsals in the Mary Rippon Theatre on Tuesday evening. Unfortunately, rain and technical difficulties prevented a full dress rehearsal that evening, but the troupe was receiving final instructions on sets, props and costumes in preparation for their premiere July 14.

The twenty-four year old Colorado Shakespeare Festival attracts national attention and *Audience* will be reviewing each of the plays in upcoming weeks.

While planning activities to end (or alleviate) mid-summer doldrums, don't miss the two week humanities project "Between Two World Wars" offered by the Colorado Music Festival. Festival Director Giora Bernstein has chronicled the twenty year period at home and abroad in a series of lectures, films and concerts.

The last day of the series begins with a panel discussion entitled "The Cabaret as Artistic and Social Forum," with Kim Kowalke, Andrew Doe and Stephanie Cotsirilos in the Community House at Chautauqua at 4:30 p.m. Later in the day Stephanie Cotsirilos will be featured in a "Cabaret: Theatre Songs from Two Continents" at 8:30 p.m. in the Auditorium.

This is a unique opportunity to delve into the past through a variety of media. Call the Festival office for a complete schedule of films, lectures and performances, well worth your attendance.

INDEPENDENCE FOR THE DAILY

Although the *Daily* likes to think that the University of Colorado is nothing to them but a landlord, the fact is that their affiliation with the university gets them special favors in several quarters. For one, the owner of Intermountain Color as a staunch supporter of the university gives *Audience* and *Daily* a special printing rate. There is no way to predict how such preferential treatment might break down were the *Daily* to move from campus to become a community weekly rather than a university daily. (Exhibit 6 illustrates the *Daily*'s heavy orientation toward students.)

Speculation about such a move is a favorite topic at the *Daily* and even at the small potluck dinners that provide a forum for planning, where the members of business and editorial departments meet separately to plan the future of their organization. One issue that people frequently discuss is salaries. Editorial staff people consider their pay to be "ridiculously low." Since full staffing of the paper is dependent upon the calendar of the academic year, presently there is no way to guarantee year-round employment to most employees. Only the editor and the business manager and staff are full time. For editorial people, one of the major priorities is to upgrade salaries to keep first-rate reporters.

In 1981 the corporation purchased a new computer to handle business functions—accounts receivable, accounts payable, payroll—all accounting information. The old system was obsolete; no repair parts were available.

Lange, Kaiser, and other board members see no chance of moving into a new building for another three years, even if they could find one. But the more pressing problem has been determining for the future a clear-cut target audience and what the paper is to become. In the summer of 1981 the *Daily* board agreed to hire a "general coordinator." The Appendix contains the job description for this newly created position. At the time of the case research Dziekan had enough tasks to keep the new general coordinator busy for months: "I want to see historically our linage for the past 10 years. I want to set up several graphs on the size of the paper in relation to percentage to see whether it is make or break. We need a model so that the ad manager will know whether we should write a tight 20-page paper or a loose 24-page paper. We need to know whether we should jump four pages or hold at what we have." It remained to be seen whether a general coordinator would be able to infuse the *Daily* with the marketing savvy needed to draw a substantially larger audience with a new product, let alone to accomplish the many tasks that ranking staff members envisaged.

Because the *Daily* is a company in which employees play a direct role in shaping the future, it inspires a great deal of loyalty. Perhaps Cindy Dziekan hit upon the central issues when she summed up her relationship to the *Daily* and reviewed the paper's needs: "I don't think it's unusual for small newspapers to

Exhibit 6

TYPICAL CLASSIFIEDS APPEALING TO
STUDENT READERS OF THE *DAILY*

Classified

Soap

LET'S KEEP IT CLEAN - We reserve the right to edit or refuse any ads submitted to the Colorado Daily Classified Dept.

SLIDERS. What Soap is to love, SLIDERS are to softball. Every Monday in the Colorado Daily. Call 443-6272 for more Information.

AOPi's -THANKS for a fantastic year. It's been great. Get psyched for next year. I'll miss you all in September, but I'll see you in January. Love, Liz.

ANN BOX, Steve n Mike, Beer on Flagstaff. No BJ's Peanut Buster Parfait's - Glad we're on diet's. Bob Marley's Tribute to cookie breaks - were so fun. Man on a moped. Black... Bogus shoes - cool Neut's. Don't break the egg! Psychopatic laundry stealer don't mash - Marathon in October - not mashing toothpaste anyone. Num gumson 11th. Love, Twittete.

A HUMUNGOUS THANK-YOU to Tammy, Jim, Skip, Karen, Dean, Ben, Bine, Lori, Darin, Mary, Carla, Roxanne, Markus. Joe and everyone else who helped make my 20th FANTASTIC! Good luck on Finals! I love you all! Margaret.

AH HA: It's been great! Thanks for helping me to understand Willie, with whom I can't wait to spend the summer. Out there on the peanut farm, careful how you fall.

ANNIE, Happy B-day! Here's to your cute little buns, those Sunday dinner tours, and feeding the kittens. Get psyched for Sa. Love ya, Dave.

BOB, Best monk around, shame you can't keep the Robe this summer. Brother Chuck.

BRUCE - Throughout the year, many of flights on de plane we did seek; only to find ourselves up the old proverbial creek; I enjoyed the year except for "!!" Jimmy Buffet; But remember I'm a man, I learned how to rough it; from two free pizzas, we payed for with crime; to calling Fluff's bluff, practically all the time; not to much more I can afford to say; except have a good summer and Happy Birthday. Brad.

BARRY, HANK, & SAM: Have a good time at the BOULDER HIGH PROM, Boys. The Eskimo & The Kid.

BRENDA - Here's to a wonderful friend, I love ya, toots. Bobbin. p.s. Oreos and poolt-ables?!

BRIAN, BRUCE, Ed, Dan, Mark and even MEM, you guys are alright. Have a great summer. Ricardo.

Help Wanted

KATH,- BG and pizza, right or left? Laundry room door, 7-11, Journey (so to speak). Sightseeing after the wedding (so to speak). If someone knocks... Booboo and Pinky. Thanx for everything, roomie. I love ya. T.M.

KURT, Thank you for all. Remember the stars! We'll see ya, Julie.

KELLY H., Here's a Soap just for you. Good Luck on all of your finals, especially Paul P.'s class. Thanks for studying with me.

LARA, Soon I'll be a memory which you'll probably forget, but to me you're one which I'll never regret. If you need a job someday, call me - Love, Dan.

LINDA SELLERS - Best of luck in the future. You'll always be my number one roommate. I'll miss you. Love ya, Liz.

MAC - You made my day with the call and the roses... I only wish you were here to celebrate! Thanks for being such a good friend! Love, Marg.

MR. WONDERFUL - Though you've been here such a short time, you have left your imprint forever! No longer will your wisdom resound on the Editor's page, so here's to you: DAVID STEVENS, DAVID STEVENS, DAVID STEVENS. 2 out of 3 of us.

MARIANNE - Your very first Soap! Here's to Allenspark, Boulder Falls, Cabernet Sauvignon, Devo Daquiris, Easter Baskets, Friends & Lovers, The Gris, Herbie's, Insurance Money, John Adams, Kidnapping, Little Whorehouses, Midnight Swims, New York, Oktoberfest, Picnics, "You're so Queer!" Revealing Pictures, Scrapes II, 21, The Underworld, Vermont, The Walrus, XOXO, You & Me and Zinfandel! Write lots. I love you lots. Chris.

Colorado Daily
a boulder alternative since 1892

have a familial, almost emotional, attachment on the part of the staff. People who work for such independent newpapers have a very definite commitment to the paper; almost like it's theirs. I don't feel exactly that way because I am a business person, not an editorial person. I don't have the same emotional background that an editorial person has. I don't see any real direct relationship among editorial, business, and advertising. We are three different entities as far as what we look for.

"I look for financial success. Tim looks for editorial success. Advertising is the closest to business in that by looking for successful linage we in turn get financial success. We merge these aspects to make the paper go forward. If the paper is not financially successful, there will be no newspaper to publish. Realistically the others know that if we don't pay our bills and we don't make some money, the newspaper will fold."

Your Task:

Advise The Colorado Daily, Inc.'s board on these matters:

1. Have they been successful? Please comment.
2. How can the board develop strategic alternatives and reach agreement on the business's market posture? How can the key people gain commitment from editorial and business staff members on what directions they should take and how the objectives are to be achieved?
3. Formulate a tentative mission-and-role statement for the organization.
4. Explain your views of how the people in the **Daily** and the products themselves are interwoven. Or are they?
5. What are the implications for designing and implementing marketing strategies when the organization ostensibly practices democracy in decision making and planning? What impact does such an arrangement have on approaching strategy formulation and program development as an analytic and intellectual process?
6. In getting ready for your presentation to Lange, Kaiser, Dziekan, and the board of directors, prepare an evaluation of the Colorado **Daily's** strategy, local market, strengths and weaknesses, and opportunities and threats. Be prepared to comment on how well you think the staff has assessed its "industry" and other factors that affect the organization. Where are its flaws? What do you recommend?
7. Analyze the role of the incoming General Coordinator (GC).

Appendix

JOB DESCRIPTION, GENERAL COORDINATOR: COLORADO DAILY, INC.

GENERAL DESCRIPTION

The function of the general coordinator (GC) of the Colorado Daily, Inc., shall be to keep all phases of the operations of the corporation running smoothly and in complete coordination with each other. The coordinator should be, first and foremost, a communicator: transmitting, organizing, and storing the information generated by, and sought by, the different departments, including New Morning Composition and **Audience.**

The GC shall be a communicator, facilitator, historian, negotiator, financial analyst, diplomat, and spokesperson. The GC assumes a leadership role in the restricted sense that he or she carries out board policies and attempts to keep department managers focused on the board's priorities amid the daily operational struggle.

SPECIFIC DUTIES

The GC shall be a catalyst for positive change at the **Daily,** someone who focuses the energy of various departments into a coherent whole. The GC shall facilitate the group process to arrive at changes. The GC shall **not** serve as publisher, or as censor or superboss, but as a special manager with specific responsibilities. These shall include, but not be limited to

Promoting the Colorado **Daily** newspaper as an independent voice in the community.

Assessing the productivity of each department through consultation with managers and other personnel and proposing ways in which productivity can be increased.

Assessing capital needs.

Serving as property control manager and knowing the whereabouts and uses to which the corporation's real property is being put.

Serving as circulation manager. Day-to-day routine of distributing newspapers and **Audience** shall remain in the hands of the circulation staff. GC responsibility shall involve increasing off-campus circulation, monitoring appropriate drops, and doing readership surveys and demographic studies.

Advising on expansion.

Appendix (Cont.)

RELATIONSHIP WITH THE BOARD

The GC shall have a symbiotic relationship with the Board of Directors, feeding information, proposals, and ideas to the directors on the one hand and carrying out agreed-upon board policy on the other.

The GC's chief functions in relation to the board are to make board meetings productive and useful for directors and to be the board's chief agent. To this end, the coordinator should be involved with the flow of documents to and from the board, working with the secretary of the board to ensure that the directors and employees are well informed about the corporation.

The GC shall invest time and energy in a continuous statistical and business evaluation of the corporation, supplying the board with a constant stream of comprehensible information about the corporation's status, including analyses of performance as measured against similar institutions, corporate goals, and business forecasts.

The GC should research issues coming before the board, present information in writing before board meetings, and be ready and willing to carry out the board's collective will at the conclusion of deliberations. A typical presentation by the GC to the board should include an assessment of the problems and opportunities of the issue under discussion, what leaders and others in the corporation think about the issue, a list of alternatives, and usually, a recommendation. The GC shall attend all board meetings and should report on board meetings to staff managers, staff members, and other interested parties.

The GC shall assist the board in transforming policy decisions into concrete actions, acting with and through department managers. The coordinator shall represent the board in matters falling outside the direct jurisdictions of department managers, such as a printing contract.

THE GC AND DEPARTMENT MANAGERS

The GC shall work with department managers to carry out board policies and directives. The GC's primary responsibility will be to the Board of Directors. The GC shall serve as a communicator between and among managers and will help the communication process by organizing and chairing regular manager meetings. The coordinator shall work with managers to develop short- and mid-range strategies for the successful operation of the corporation.

The GC shall attempt to function as facilitator to resolve any dis-

Appendix (Cont.)

putes between departments or personnel. He or she shall have no hiring/
firing authority over managers. Although the GC shall try to resolve differences among managers consentually, he or she shall have final authority
(subject to board review) in all matters concerning the carrying out of
board policy. Managers shall remain responsible for the internal workings
of their departments.

POWERS

The GC shall have access to all the corporation's documents and
records. The GC shall have the cooperation of all employees; he or she
shall have the right to examine the activities of any department of employee of the corporation without prejudice.

The GC shall not be a voting member of the Board of Directors. He
or she shall not enter into any agreements or contracts binding on the
corporation without the knowledge or consent of the Board of Directors
but shall act as the board's agent once given consent.

case
9

DIGITAL PRODUCTS CORPORATION

ro•bot n. 1. a machine that resembles a man and does mechanical, routine tasks on command as though it were alive. 2. a person who
acts and responds in a mechanical, routine manner, usually subject to another's will; automation. 3. any machine or mechanical
device that operates automatically, with humanlike skill.[1]

The word "robotics" did not appear in the 1981 edition of *The American
Heritage Dictionary of the English Language.* The Robot Institute of America
had only a handful of members, including 10 manufacturers, as recently as
1978. When thinking of a robot, one's image may well be of the dictionary version—an R2D2, a machine that performs actions similar to those of a person—
and not a less spectacular electronic device that, in its own way, also emulates
human beings. Digital Products Corporation (DPC), far from a General Electric, Bendix, Unimation, or Hitachi—leaders in robot manufacturing and marketing—is not engaged in producing steel-collar workers or electronic movie
stars; rather, this Florida-based company has been responsible for helping a
major national retailer, the U.S. Army, morticians, and other institutions and
individuals use the telephone more efficiently.

---

[1]Jess Stein, ed., *The Random House Dictionary of the English Language, The Unabridged
Edition* (New York: Random House, 1967), p. 1239.

"We call it The TELSOL Electronic System.[2] It sells for $9,450," Marketing Vice President Burton J. Weiss said, "and can do the work of six full-time phone solicitors. We made it to be relatively maintenance free—the only moving parts are in the recording mechanism. All the rest is space-age technology." Exhibit 1 presents a list of features and specifications. A national network of distributors sells the automatic phone robot.

TELSOL is a telecomputer/automatic phone robot that can be programmed to call, talk to, and collect responses from people whose telephone numbers are selected by the owner. The manufacturer employs a team of pro-

[2]Also referred to as TELSOL Phone Robot in DPC's *1982 Annual Report.*

Exhibit 1

TELSOL FEATURES AND SPECIFICATIONS, 1982

FEATURES	SPECIFICATIONS	
Built-in monitor and lighted display; indicates number called while listening to response.	TELSOL	15½" wide × 23" deep × 6" high; 115/120 volts AC approximately 30 watts; 4-hour battery backup for number storage; phone line connector supplied. FCC Registration No.: AB3985-62472-P-C-E. Ringer Equivalence No.: 0.0A0.0B.
Enter up to 500 phone numbers at a time. It takes just 2 minutes to store them on standard cassette tapes for later use or reload them into the machine.		
Calls both local and long distance.		
Compatible with both touch-tone and dial phone systems.	Timer	Connects to TELSOL with cable supplied; battery powered.
Built-in FCC-registered coupler complies with telephone regulations.	Printer	12½" wide × 11" deep × 5" high. Connects to TELSOL with cable supplied; requires standard AC connection; requires approximately 40 watts.
Use your own announcements or our professionally prepared scripts.		
Patented voice activation waits for human response before beginning message.		
Voice activation provides efficient use of response tape.	SM-1	Single message unit used for notification message or a series of questions and recorded answers.
Stores unanswered calls for later use.		
Battery backup retains numbers in the event of power failure.	MM-1	Similar to SM-1 except may be used for up to seven different messages. While responses are played back, the display shows number contacted to allow correlation of answers to messages.
Easily attaches to direct phone lines.		
Timer permits unattended use during time periods when people are most available.		

Source: Corporate product brochure.

fessional scriptwriters and people who use their voices professionally to develop messages for use on the machine. It has found outlets for its electronic energies in notification, solicitation, collections, and marketing research/polling applications. Some example calling statements appear in Exhibit 2 for these various applications. The sales brochure claims:

> *Using the TELSOL personal communication system to tell your customers of sales, delivery schedules, and investment opportunities relieves your employees of making hundreds of routine calls and makes sure every customer receives the same cheerful message.*
>
> *It is an efficient means of notifying people and it has several advantages to you: it can improve your cash flow, increase traffic, reduce warehouse space requirements, and reduce dry service calls. These savings can be passed to your customers in the form of better service at lower costs, which, of course, leads to long-term price reductions.*

Exhibit 2

EXAMPLE STATEMENTS FOR VARIOUS TELSOL APPLICATIONS

Notification

Please pick up the merchandise you ordered from XYZ department store.
Our serviceperson will be at your home between 10 A.M. and noon on Monday.
Our special for this week is _____ .
There is a job available that requires your experience. Please call the XYZ employment office.
Mention this call when you visit our store, and you will receive a free _____ .

Solicitation

Would you be interested in a no obligation appraisal of your property?
Are you interested in the cost savings of having your carpet cleaned rather than replaced?
Did you know that 1 of 10 Americans will suffer a disabling accident on the job this year?
Would you like to receive a free discount coupon for _____?

Collections

Please call Mr. Jones at the XYZ Bank regarding an important matter.
We are certain you want to keep your credit record in good order.
We are certain that you would not want to lose your benefits after making so many payments.

Exhibit 2 (Cont.)

Market Research/Polling

What radio station do you listen to?
What's your favorite television program?
Are you registered to vote?

Weiss calls his Fort Lauderdale company "the undisputed champion of this market. It's the fifth medium—it goes beyond direct mail, newspapers, radio, and television. It's a moneysaver, but it isn't just efficient, it's also effective. TELSOL generates high response rates, and because it arouses people's curiosity, in many cases, it's better than its human counterparts." Weiss is proud of the company's reputation for customer backup, including a WATS line to Digital's Service Department. Documentation includes an illustrated step-by-step procedural manual, and the company provides what has been claimed to be "the strongest warranty in the industry."

TELSOL uses standard cassette tapes to record responses and holds numbers in memory, which are transferrable to standard cassettes for further use. Its memory stores up to 512 seven-digit numbers, has touch-tone and dial-pulse features, and provides for multiple question-and-answer sequences. Also, it will hold unanswered and busy numbers in abeyance, recalling them automatically. An electronic timer turns the unit on and off.

"That's important," observed Weiss, "and when owners have failed to turn it off, they've gotten some bad press because the system will keep on calling, regardless of the lateness of the hour, unless programmed to stop."

"Let's assume," Weiss expounds on the unit's versatility, "that you're a retailer who wants to promote a special sale to a few hundred customers. The 15-second tape could be used to make the basic announcement. Then, either from the credit files or some other source, consumers' phone numbers would be entered into the unit's memory—and the memory itself can also be used as a file for numbers from previous promotions. While all the clerks and department managers go about their business, TELSOL contacts the households and prints out the numbers that have been reached. We have found that where two-way dialogue is involved, people are intrigued enough to carry on a conversation with the machine. They don't resent it. Still, a bit of humor on the tape also helps to prevent people who might not like it from being upset."

If the person called is not cooperative, the system disconnects after non-responses to the first two questions and then proceeds to dial the next number.

TELSOL is lightweight and portable, making it easy to transport from place to place as needed. TELSOL is being used by a nationwide retailer, which by early 1982 had purchased over 1,000 units, making it the biggest customer to that point to install in its catalog departments to notify customers that their orders are ready to be picked up; a direct-sale home products firm, which prospects for new distributors and salespeople; and Army recruiters, who tell and sell via TELSOL in sparsely settled areas. All sorts of marketing research is conducted by the two-way feature in the device—asking and recording answers. It is also used for cold canvassing by some insurance firms; charity fundraisers find it helpful in boosting contributions; auto dealers call prospects to invite them in for a test drive; and a funeral home uses the device to advertise its preplanned burials.

"Our 1981 sales ran to about $4 million, and I believe we will exceed $6 million in fiscal 1982." Weiss has speculated that this number might double by 1985. "Once buyers find out the machine can be cost-justified in less than a year, we have their attention. I see TELSOL as a prime device to boost productivity, a goal that almost every business has today. We have competitors, but their equipment is not equal to ours."

DIGITAL PRODUCTS BACKGROUND

After sinking $40,000 into DPC stock, Marton Grossman, an ordained rabbi and owner of a housewares import business in New York City, was conversing with a friend and customer, Leopold Cohen, who owned a chain of women's dress shops and household goods stores in New Jersey. With its stock down to 12½ cents a share, DPC was staggering under $250,000 debt and was considering filing for bankruptcy under Chapter XI. Neither investor had an electronics background, but they decided then and there—it was June 1971—to buy the firm.

In 1980, after their company turned its first profit, there was discussion among analysts of its potential for profits of $20 million a year by 1990. The stock, if adjusted for a recent split, would have been selling at about $44 a share in early 1982.

TELSOL Phone Robot sales to distributors approximated $7 million in the year ended March 31, 1982, but certain distributors were depending upon reselling the units before paying DPC; so at year-end the company adopted a policy of recording sales to certain distributors on a cash basis. This change, plus the costs associated with rapid expansion of the TELSOL distribution network, resulted in a loss of $94,732 for the year. Exhibit 3 provides a review of selected financial data for the years 1977 to 1982.

Grossman and Cohen attribute the survival of their company to sales of TELSOL, but other products just beginning to earn their way have been added. One is Dial/Eze, a device that automatically dials and protects a user's satellite network telephone access and authorization code. Another is TW-3, a coin acceptor, promoted as jamproof, that "rejects 92 percent more slugs and foreign coins than other such devices" and that is adaptable for all types of U.S.

Exhibit 3

SUMMARY OF SELECTED FINANCIAL DATA FOR DPC, MARCH 31, 1977–1982

	1977	1978	1979	1980	1981	1982
Total assets	$384,213	$512,917	$427,048	$1,249,656	$2,432,449	$7,933,199
Long-term debt	761	165	—	—	—	645,000
Net sales	243,815	150,278	71,282	1,591,014	3,904,444	4,026,194
Income (loss) from continuing operations	(178,767)	(159,672)	(256,299)	321,871	833,814	(94,732)
Net income (loss)	(73,798)	(65,441)	(231,699)	479,106	813,670	(94,732)
*Per Share Data**						
Income (loss) from continuing operations	$(.05)	$(.05)	$(.08)	$.08	$.21	$(.02)
Net income	(.02)	(.02)	(.07)	.13	.21	(.02)
Cash dividends per common share	—	—	—	—	—	—

*Common shares and equivalents.

119

and foreign coins. In 1982, Bally became the coin device's exclusive distributor for Nevada, and the New Jersey Gaming Commission approved it for use and sale in that state.

Grossman, born in 1931 in Romania, was to survive World War II concentration camps, later arriving penniless in the United States. Cohen, born in 1916, learned business from running a production line in his parents' sewing factory before starting his own retail stores. Setting up two women's dress shops in Florida provided enough cash flow to help keep the electronics company afloat between 1974 and 1978. Then, in 1978, TELSOL was bought from a bankrupt company and refined by Digital's engineers before going on the market later that year. Its first application was a test use by the national retail chain for notifying customers that their catalog orders had arrived. Then, it would call later to tell them the purchase would be delivered, if the customer had chosen not to pick it up.

In June 1981, Digital Products moved to its new 17,500-square-foot facility designed to house administrative functions, manufacturing, engineering, and research and development. Assembly space in the new quarters would enable the company to increase production capacity for estimated needs covering the next five years. The organization was still lean in early 1982, with about 60 employees, including engineer David Bowers, one of the three founders who commented on the pre–Grossman/Cohen days, "Our engineering was fine; we just didn't have much business sense." Concluded Cohen, in remarking that their success stemmed from following business instincts and knowing whether or not an electronics product was worth selling, "Those judgments mattered a lot more than knowing how to build the products."

Believing, along with Cohen and Grossman, that "little guys can still do it," Burt Weiss reflected upon their success as he contemplated tentative marketing plans for 1983. "What," he wondered, "lies in store for TELSOL, specifically? Based on the current configuration of our distributor network, what can we do—what should we do—as a company to back them in their various marketplaces? What goals would be reasonable through 1985? And what of the five years after that—is it too early to think seriously about directions for TELSOL from 1986 to 1990? How can our marketing staff coordinate DPC's and distributors' efforts so we can achieve mutually acceptable targets in sales, profits, and growth? Finally, what kinds of competition should we be alert to, given that patent protection in this business is far from absolute?"

Your Task:

Advise Burt Weiss.

ROBINSON ASSOCIATES, INC.

Robinson Associates, Inc., is a full-service management consulting and marketing research firm and national clearinghouse for census data services. It has close ties to senior academic personnel at several leading universities. It brings together a professional interdisciplinary team ranging from social psychology to math and physics, from econometrics to engineering and business, from computer scientists to well-rounded generalists with experience in hands-on research in marketing, new product development, corporate strategy, and venture analysis.

This paragraph, from a 1982 Robinson Associates' (RAI) brochure conveys the firm's desired position in the field of management consulting and marketing research. It all began two decades earlier.

COMPANY BACKGROUND

In the early 1960s, the Marketing Science Institute (MSI) was founded in Philadelphia primarily through the energetic espousal of Thomas B. McCabe, Sr., chairman and chief executive officer of Scott Paper Company. MSI's mission was to advance the science of marketing. Numerous corporations added their names to the banner of sponsorship, and Patrick J. Robinson was appointed to be its director of management studies and, later, research director. Mr. McCabe's advocacy combined with support from Wroe Alderson, marketing theorist and Wharton professor, provided significant impetus for locating the Institute in Philadelphia and promoting an affiliation with the Wharton School and its faculty.

"Great care had been taken to avoid any domination of MSI by Wharton for fear of the Institute's becoming parochial in its interests, thus diluting its universal appeal as a center for advancing the development and applications of management science to supplement marketing art," Patrick Robinson recalled. "After Alderson's death, strong leadership was lacking to bring about a workable agreement, even though several of us thought affiliating with Wharton would be a suitable arrangement. Then an attractive suitor appeared in the person of Dean George Baker of the Harvard Graduate School of Business Administration [HBS] who proposed close ties with the proviso that MSI relocate to Boston. The offer from this respected institution was accepted by Mr. McCabe and MSI's trustees. Although I graduated from HBS, my family's preference was to remain in the Philadelphia area."

Several friends, Paul Green and Yoram (Jerry) Wind, professors at Wharton; Bent Stidsen, a Wharton Ph.D. candidate; and J. Minas, professor at University of Waterloo, who had been working with Robinson as Marketing Science Institute project consultants encouraged him to form a research consulting firm, a sort of "son of MSI," offering their participation as professional associates.

As Patrick Robinson remembered, "It didn't take much of a nudge to move me to make the commitment. Almost exactly 10 years earlier, Paul's and my mentor, Wroe Alderson, had persuaded me to leave my very satisfying position with Imperial Oil Limited [Esso/Exxon in Toronto, Canada] to join Alderson Associates as his successor. While that transition had not been achieved, I did join Mobil Oil in New York as head of integrated operations planning. Three years later, Wroe was instrumental in having me invited to Philadelphia as the newly formed MSI's research director. I made that transition in June 1963, although the actual title did not pass to me until about four and a half years later."

Asked about how the organization's role was developed, Robinson summed it up as follows: "RAI's mission statement was conceived over a series of discussions about alternative scenarios, but the primary thrust became that of concentrating on applying research and development momentum from work at MSI. It was exciting to contemplate being a catalyst for adopting and exploiting the commercial potential of applied mathematical psychology, experimental design, and systems simulation, based on behavioral measures and sensitivities."

The organizers assumed that several Institute sponsors and member companies would underwrite some pioneering applications of multidimensional scaling and related multivariate statistical analysis projects, which became the primary focus of RAI's interdisciplinary team efforts.

"Getting underway, however, proved to be a nontrivial challenge in 1969 at a time when money was tight and the timing seemed less than propitious," Robinson said.

Funds suppliers did not have the courtesy to array themselves in parade formation for Mr. Robinson's scrutiny and choice, but luck intervened. At a New Year's Eve dinner dance at his country club, Robinson chanced to be seated with a fellow member who was founder and head of a successful industrial engineering performance evaluation consulting organization. Sufficiently intrigued by the Robinson concept, the dinner companion offered to help secure a credit line from a local bank. Robinson continued: "Armed with this support, I went to a valued friend and leading corporation lawyer who set up the incorporation and arranged a lease so we could retain some of MSI's old office facilities at the University City Science Center. He also became corporate secretary. Then, with the help of a former MSI colleague, Professor Frank Carmone, I established computer operations and engaged a scientific programmer to maintain and operate our program library."

The practical expertise and high technology RAI brought to its prospects and clients consisted of many years experience in the conduct and teaching of management science and applied research in marketing and related corporate planning, venture analysis, physical distribution logistics, management information and control systems design, new product development, appraisal, and promotional positioning. Hard-cover books and monographs and other publications distilled findings resulting from expenditures of some half-million dollars annually at MSI. RAI's strategy was to run on the tracks laid down at MSI. The following goals, according to Robinson, continue to be paramount:

1. Offer an intimate knowledge of the consumer and industrial goods and services markets and channels of distribution.
2. Provide conceptual guidance for progressive business managers and researchers in considering the implications and demands of taking full account of the marketing management concept in product planning and market development.
3. Make available the sensitive new tools of perceptual and preference mapping, cluster analysis, and systems simulation for definitive measurement and analysis of people's choice behavior, "gap analysis," promotional positioning, and understanding of the competitive dynamics of market structure and semantics.
4. Provide creative and innovative consultation to brand and product managers and others concerned with performance improvements and the impact of change on company operations, organization, and information for decision support systems and adaptive experimentation in the marketplace.
5. Make available enhanced qualitative front-end-focused group interview (FGI) capabilities for understanding people's attitudes, motivations, semantics, occasions of use, and tentative hypotheses for further refinement and quantitative testing. (The modern framework of these FGIs included

two-way mirrors, plus video and audio taping of sessions for editing and content analysis. RAI psychologists focused on critical incidents, both favorable and adverse, plus convergence on possible causal relationships in the buying process, apparent barriers to entry, conventional wisdom concerning a given category, and its effective competition, plus any unfulfilled needs or expressed anxieties or frustrations.) Additionally, quantified choice and ranking tasks for subsequent perceptual and preference computer mapping of FGI respondents' mental models was offered as an augmentation to the basic qualitative service.

6. Stress implementation as the driving force of any assignment. RAI insisted, insofar as the bounds of good taste and business etiquette would permit, on asking so-what and what-if questions on the potential value of any anticipated end product of a research or counseling assignment.

Robinson reviewed the early phases of the firm's development: "Our first two years got off to a modest start. We were getting the word out on what could be done with our new technology and learning how we should present and price our differential advantage versus firms using more traditional methods. We traveled to client firms such as Lever Brothers, General Foods, British Petroleum, the American Bankers Association, Air Canada, RCA, Campbell Soup, Sears, Roebuck, Eastman Kodak, and others we were fortunate to attract. A project was often conceived, designed, priced, and sold in the course of a few hours' discussion and a handshake.

"In those early days, our in-house computer support came from Najma Khalid, a mathematically sophisticated professional who went on to advanced computer architecture consulting. She was followed by Mike DeVita, who came to us from a local computer science college. Senior project specialist was Stuart Jolly, whose background was math, physics, and Cornell's Ph.D. program in operations research. RAI's corporate treasurer, financial counselor, and investor was another HBS graduate and close friend, Bob Rogers, who devoted many evening and weekend hours to help our undercapitalized, fledgling business get started and stay on course while operations were grossing scarcely $200,000 annually."

After successfully negotiating a debenture refinancing through its bank, with the funding by an imaginative petroleum transportation company's president, Mr. Adrian S. Hooper, RAI was able to move from the University City Science Center, where it had been for a year, to offices in Bryn Mawr. "Engineering this move meant that none of our principal professionals would be more than 15 minutes from the office. We also wanted to have a more pleasant and congenial setting for client visits. This building is adjacent to the train station, less than 20 minutes from Philadelphia on the so-called 'Paoli Local,' which serves the Main Line. It's also within 10 minutes of the Pennsylvania Turnpike and just 35 minutes from the airport. First-class lodging and restaurants, as well as many historic sights such as Valley Forge, are within a 20-minute driving radius.

"RAI has always stressed the belief that there's nothing more practical than a good theory. For example, when a good mechanic or a physician examines symptoms, and decides what to do, theory is the framework for that judgment, and implementation is the means to obtaining results.

"During those early years, we hated to lose for the wrong reason; all right, if we were seen as too technical or even beyond a budgetary limit, but let us not lose because of our failure to communicate convincingly. Perhaps a prime example of falling on our collective faces occurred when we were invited to address Scott Paper's marketing research and brand management people. We pulled out all the stops.

"We had prepared elaborate slide materials and a presentation of market measurement and analysis tools and examples of end product visualizations of what we might do for Scott Paper. We even had custom built for us a cubic-foot lucite model of a three-dimensional perceptual-and-preference joint-space map of competing brand imagery and segmented ideal points to use in explaining how such a graphic picture could indeed be worth a thousand words. We also brought a 25-inch video monitor and video tape deck with excerpts from focused group interviews edited for the presentation, to be held in a conference room at Scott headquarters.

"There we were, six in number, including Paul Green and Jerry Wind. The meeting room was fully prepared at the appointed early starting time, with an anticipated half-day presentation ahead of us. It was all downhill from there. First, the audience was slow to assemble, apparently owing to unexpected demands on people's time. Then we got the word to proceed without waiting. We were also informed that certain key people present had to take part in a senior executive meeting and could only remain for 30 or 40 minutes. The rest of the morning we tried to cope with a shifting agenda for late arrivals and early departures—on top of the inherent challenge of being 'separated by our common language.' The best we ever got from this entire costly exercise was a report that an internal memorandum at Scott had sized RAI up as 'the best qualified marketing research firm in the country.' The memo went on to state that Scott would consider RAI favorably if its current suppliers didn't work out satisfactorily on some very large ongoing and pending assignments, including at least one reportedly in the six figures. What a disappointment!"

Researchers affiliated with MSI, and then with RAI, produced myriad articles and books stemming from their work. Publications were considered to be very important for a firm such as RAI, carrying much more influence, if published in appropriate journals, than advertisements and other promotion. This notoriety helped the firm to compete against large and aggressive competitors. Robinson mentioned a project conducted for International Air Transport Association (IATA):

"At the beginning of our second five-year period, RAI embarked on some particularly challenging major projects involving its full range of trademarked BEHAVIORMETRICS mathematical psychology tools. The most ambitious of these assignments was a six-country, cross-cultural, trade-off segmentation analysis of transatlantic air fares for IATA, headquartered in Geneva. The process of winning this contract involved our first major confrontation with a wide array of leading domestic and European research firms. We had to compete with many experienced firms nominated by IATA headquarters and by some 30 participating transatlantic air carriers. A few screening committee members favored dividing the project among several research firms. We argued strongly in favor of a single firm conducting all the research to have a common basis for cross-comparisons, market structure modeling, and forecasting the cross-elasticity of demand between scheduled carriers and charter flights—under a wide range of optional slates of competing air fare configurations. The final 40-page RAI proposal won the entire contract of approximately $300,000."

EXAMPLES OF PROJECTS

In discussing RAI's starting lineup of clients, Robinson described some early projects:

Lever Brothers

"Among our first clients was Lever Brothers in New York. We worked as a general sounding board consultant for some very receptive executives and researchers, including Alden Clayton, currently MSI's research director.

"One of the most fascinating Lever projects at that time involved a categorywide study of the use of fabric softeners in the wash. This ambitious challenge was commissioned directly by an imaginative senior vice president who felt that traditional research had not provided satisfactory insights into why roughly half the households in the United States used fabric softeners, while the other half did not.

"As often happens with our research, some of the results appear perfectly obvious *after* the fact, just like $E = mc^2$, not mb^2, I suppose. In this instance one 'obvious' finding was that fabric softeners soften clothes does indeed go without saying. Herein lies an example of its being sometimes just as important to know what *not* to do. On the other hand, we discovered that the key discriminating factors separating users from nonusers were task-related associations. We discovered the mental imagery of mainly female users associated with the activity 'using a fabric softener in your wash' as related to pleasurable or family-oriented activities such as airing out a room or bringing in fresh flowers or powdering a baby or wearing perfume. All these had a refreshing scent and rewarding or caring qualities. In contrast, the nonuser associated using a fabric softener with chorelike activities such as peeling potatoes or cleaning out a closet.

"The implications seemed clear: develop product features and position-ings, and supporting thematic and copy point appeals, designed to emphasize freshness and less chorelike effort in use, plus being a concerned parent giving pleasure to other family members. Passage of time has demonstrated a successful industrywide move in this direction."

DuPont/Canada

"The findings of the Lever project were somewhat reminiscent of an early MSI development project with DuPont of Canada in 1966 in connection with justification of a new plant for synthetic fibers for women's panties. Some members thought the way to achieve sufficient demand would be by dropping the price; others thought not. We were invited to try to help determine the relevant policy.

"In this prototype project, we used female respondents and a sample of various types, makes, and prices of panties as the stimulus set for gathering nonverbal similarities, judgments, and preference rankings. What emerged were six or seven distinctly different behavioral market segments, homogeneous within segment as revealed by the congruence of their perceptual and preference maps.

"In none of these segment maps was there any evidence of the classic economic unidimensional sensitivity to price. The simplest case partitioned all briefs into one cluster with another cluster of bikinis and a lone pettipant by itself. We called this simplistically oriented segment—rather uncharitably in retrospect—'Miss Plain Jane.' A much more challenging segment exhibited three clusters of panties—plus the outlying pettipant. Everyone from DuPont and MSI was completely baffled as to how to interpret this important segment's characteristic map. Only when I suggested that we let a typical respondent see the 'mirror of her mind' did the solution to the puzzle become 'obvious.' In fact, she instantly pointed out that one cluster contained 'dress-up panties,' one contained 'everyday panties,' and the remaining cluster, plus the lone pettipant, were 'unacceptable panties.'

"Aside from this categorical breakout, which accounted for one dimension in the two-dimensional map, the other dimension was immediately apparent to this respondent as quality. So each cluster had better and not-as-good panties. Furthermore, the highest-quality item in the entire stimulus set turned out to be the lone pettipant—over in the unacceptable category, yet highest in perceived quality of workmanship. We called this segment 'Miss Sophisticate.'

"The policy implications of this benchmark study seemed clear. Don't cut price to create new demand. Reinforce the tendency that many women are conditioned to accept of having a wardrobe for dress-up, from underwear to outerwear. Even if no one else sees you, you know yourself—besides you might faint and be taken to the hospital or who knows what! Furthermore, manufacturing matching panty and bra sets to resemble beachwear should have great appeal and might also influence the plainer dressers to be more so-cially aware and concerned about their total appearance, at least for dress-up occasions.

"We had also mapped words as a separate task to determine something of the imagery of the relevant semantics of fabric and style such as comfortable, sexy, durable, attractive, and the like. These maps were useful in providing timely input to the creative wordsmiths."

British Petroleum

One of RAI's initial clients was British Petroleum, when it came to the United States in search of a successful market entry to complement its antici-pated North Slope petroleum production bonanza in the Arctic. BP had pur-chased 10,000 Sinclair service stations and wanted the research consulting firm to help[1]

1. Identify the primary attitudes of representative groups of motorists toward service stations and their supplying petroleum companies.
2. Assess the perceived variability of service station purchasing environments, key buying influences, and dealer attitudes to identify significant marketing problems.
3. Suggest alternative advertising themes and related marketing policies and formulates to facilitate initial rebranding and future development of BP's retail sales in the United States.
4. Design potentially profitable supplemental analyses, fieldwork, and hypotheses for testing as inputs to the advertising creative process and to marketing planning.

Robinson related that, "In May of 1969, we conducted 21 focused group interviews throughout the eastern region from New England to Florida, among motorists and dealers. All interviews were both audio and videotaped and later content analyzed and indexed for critical incidents. These indexed incidents were then dubbed onto summary tapes of selected topics of concern to management. Specifically, the subject categories included multigrade gaso-line; product quality; self-service; TBA and other products; facilities; credit cards; promotions, games, and stamps; international/British; car care; price; trust; getting out of car; station personnel; and Sinclair's present image.

"Psychological and marketing policy interpretations of these highlights were then prepared topic by topic for strategic planning and policy interpre-tations in the context of the project objectives. A 20-minute final report pre-sentation was summarized on videotape to supplement overhead projector slides and discussion. Additionally, perceptual and preference maps were em-ployed to facilitate these interpretations and competitive and BP image-relat-ed questions.

[1]Adapted from corporate files.

"This intensive qualitative project was completed on schedule in only three months for a fee of approximately $50,000. It was instrumental in guiding management at a critical time while selecting an advertising agency, in deciding 'how British' to be, in burying Sinclair's dinosaur logo, and in introducing BP as a major retail gasoline brand. Only the prolonged delays in bringing the North Slope developments to fruition held up the orderly pursuit of market development goals that were carefully planned years earlier," Robinson concluded.

American Bankers Association

Another example of an early project, for the American Bankers Association, was a DELPHMAPP futures project focusing on the anticipated impact of computers and high-speed communications on the monetary and payment system—the so-called "checkless" or "less check" society. "At that time I was also serving as marketing and management science consultant to the ABA," Robinson recalled. Robinson and partner Paul Green met for a two-and-a-half-day executive retreat with senior bankers to consider the alternative future scenarios to the year 2000 for the commercial banking industry, combining traditional Rand Corporation Delphi procedures with RAI's multidimension scaling and related procedures.

The result of this project for Gerry Lowrey of the ABA executive staff and Gordon Jelliffe and his senior bank committee colleagues was a definitive action plan for research and development at ABA—including input to its decision to move its headquarters from New York to Washington, D.C. The likely impact of single-statement banking, preauthorized payments, overdraft banking, automated tellers, electronic funds transfer, and competitive demand deposit instruments were all foreseen and screened to reveal policy implications to suggest prudent allocation of Association resources and setting priorities to serve members.

Campbell Soup Company

One of RAI's first comprehensive perceptual and preference mapping projects was conducted for the former vice chairman of MSI, John McGlinn, executive vice president of Campbell Soup. "The resulting study proved to be a very stimulating challenge that brought high praise from the major advertising agency concerned—specifically from Larry Light, BBD&O's research vice president, and the Campbell Soup account group. The agency, and Campbell's 'red and white' label management, vigorously acted upon the findings, which had significant policy implications for product positioning, store promotions, thematic and copy point appeals, portion size packaging, and the complementary and substitutable roles of soup in the family menu," Robinson said.

"The completed report was first presented in 1971. Over the ensuing decade, this report has periodically provided sources of working hypotheses, innovations, and a benchmark for identifying significant trends and shifts in people's perceptions, preferences, and the mental associations of soup and serving occasions. Oddly enough, the study seemed to disappear in the mid-1970s and then to reemerge, quite by chance. In 1981, RAI was asked to present the findings once again and to provide fresh copies of the report.

"One of these presentation occasions involved an old friend, Horace Schwerin, who had achieved recognition for his syndicated commercial testing services. He had retired from his entrepreneurial career, becoming a stimulating maverick member of Campbell's management team. Among the ideas we surfaced together, in reviewing the 1971 'golden oldie,' were a number of surprisingly fresh insights with policy implications for the 1980s, respecting single-portion servings, the clustering of soup types in people's minds, the nourishing image of soup, and its suitability and role in various menu and serving occasions.

"While we conducted subsequent studies for Campbell," Robinson concluded, "none, it seems to me, came close to the scope and excitement of this early baseline investigation."

RCA

An example of a Robinson Associates' industrial marketing research project came when RCA was still committed to computers and to a new feature called "virtual memory." This ambitious crash project was commissioned by the Office of the President when considerable belt-tightening was under way throughout the RCA Computer Company.

Robinson reviewed a few particulars of the RCA effort: "For the client, a great deal was at stake, so we were given free rein to conduct the investigation in an effort to obtain strategic policy guidance at a most critical time. Consequently, Paul Green, Stu Jolly, and I spent considerable time trying to obtain every possible insight of potential value to management. One aspect that I was particularly keen on was an *objective* performance-space taxonomy, based on published engineering features, performance data, and costs for a wide array of competing hardware to contrast where different people 'were coming from' by using our *subjective* clustering routines. We had nine major customer categories, plus RCA sales representatives, some in-house product designers, market planners, and headquarter's respondents. This variety of respondents was designed to permit congruence analysis among the groups' perceptual clusters as well as against the objective clusters.

"Results were fascinating and revealing. We had understood that members of RCA management consciously planned their past strategy to go head on against IBM. However, to disguise the sponsorship of the project, we prepared our questionnaires so that IBM, RCA, and Univac were equally featured, and a number of other makes were also covered explicitly, but less prominently. In the final analysis, we concentrated on the RCA versus IBM perceptual and preference comparisons and statistically discriminating background characteristics as a basis for drawing our most important inferences. The policy implications seemed clear, and we hastened to put our presentation of findings before the chief executive officer and others.

"Trying to deliver our message to its intended audience at RCA's headquarters near Boston proved to be one of the most frustrating problems I've ever faced. The president's executive aide tried desperately to get the executive group together but was thwarted at the eleventh hour and fifty-ninth minute by news that RCA worldwide headquarters had just discharged the computer company president and planned to sell off the entire division. We were too late! We felt that we had thrown our best Sunday punch but had missed the target in a way that really hurt. When we work for a client, we think the results should be a win-win outcome. Here, we faced a lose-lose proposition if there ever was one.

"The loss for RAI almost became literally true when we sought our final payment for a completed assignment that no one knew anything about! It had indeed been a secret project—no recorded agreement, no purchase order, no verbal arrangements with accounts payable—nothing. I made several trips to RCA's Cherry Hill, New Jersey, procurement offices to plead our case. To make matters even worse, other suppliers with more conventional arrangements were apparently facing partial payments as settlements in full on the assumption of an insolvent situation. Eventually, we were paid, but only after other members of management read the hastily assembled final report, really just a hard copy of our overhead transparencies, because we hadn't planned on anything other than an oral report before a small, top-level audience.

"Two footnotes to this case came to light later: When Univac bought RCA's System 70 and other assets and its established customer base, Univac was able to utilize our findings to some extent—although the 'not-invented-here' resistance was noticeable among some of the entrenched sales management.

"Within the past several years, it was reported in the media that an internal 'bookkeeping error' of over $20 million came to light respecting how RCA's computer division had been doing prior to its dissolution. This discrepancy might have spelled the difference in top management's untimely decision to sell out; we can never know."

Ford Motor Company

"Another fascinating project was conducted for the Ford Motor Company, in collaboration with Rogers National Research, and involved gathering information to help design a new compact car, the Fairmont. This study slightly preceded the first major energy crisis in 1974 and focused on people who were already interested in a downsized or economy vehicle. This full-profile MULTIPLE TRADEOFF ANALYSIS research provided a significant lead in Ford's product planning once the energy crisis occurred and began to affect an even larger cross section of new car buyers. Subsequently, over 1 million Fairmonts were sold. A contributing factor to this success was the fact that, when the energy crisis struck, Ford was relatively well situated with its new car designed for compact car buyers." Robinson seemed pleased with these results.

SUMMARY OF RAI SERVICES

RAI's diversity was represented in its 1982 and 1983 brochures:

1982's Focus

Robinson ruminated, "In three decades computer technology has moved an incredible distance forward in helping to plot today's marketing decisions. Yet many companies use yesterday's methods. Yesterday's navigation method was to follow the compass, and yesterday's question was, 'Am I going in the right direction?' With today's sophisticated navigational systems the question could be, 'How do I steer through the rings of Saturn?' " In that year's brochure an impressive listing of computer software tools was begun with the assertion that "we created the word 'Behaviormetrics' for our own use . . .." Some of the methods and models listed are given in Exhibit 1.

1983's Focus

In addition to its customary emphasis on applied science in marketing, RAI turned the spotlight on other dimensions of its consulting expertise in the 1983 brochure: strategic planning, management consulting, business and opportunity audits, acquisitions and divestitures, trends assessment, expert testimony, and decision support systems design and software development. The apparent goal was to promote a broader array of services, responding, as Patrick Robinson put it, "to all of the important questions asked by management and to help make more manageable the complex environment of the 1980s, to sharpen skills, to enhance decisions, to make implementation more effective and efficient, and to improve performance in our client organizations." It was obvious in listening to Robinson describe his vision for RAI that the firm would continue to expand its presence as a consulting force in the fields of consumer durables and nondurables, industrial products, agricultural products, energy industries, information and electronics, finance and insurance, medical and pharmaceutical, communications, transportation, and other fields of endeavor.

Exhibit 1

METHODS AND MODELS USED BY ROBINSON ASSOCIATES, INC.*

DELPHMAPP. Quantitative extension of Delphi futures techniques for technological and social forecasting.

CONSCREEN. Perceptual and preference mapping, clustering and associated multivariate techniques.

SPEEDMARK. Nationally distributed test market simulation modeling for predicting brand switching and market shares.

MULTIPLE TRADEOFF ANALYSIS (MTA). RAI's unique version of conjoint measurement and related techniques for new product development and appraisal.

PRODUCT DEFICIENCY ANALYSIS (PDA). The definitive system for studying established products and their competitors in the search for relative weaknesses and potential improvements and repositionings.

MICROSTRUCTURED STUDY. Projectable qualitative/quantitative small-group research based on experimental design.

BENEMAX. A totally new set of five computer-based research procedures for aiding in the optimal design of advertising and promotional materials and the prediction of market impact.

POSSE. An integrated suite of 28 comprehensive programs with unmatched capabilities in quantitative policy optimization, potential market assessment, market segmentation, product positioning, and new product design or improvement.

*All methods and models are registered properties of RAI.

PEERING INTO THE FUTURE

Three quotations from RAI's 1983 datebook stood out as the casewriter browsed through this expensive promotional item distributed to the firm's numerous blue-chip clients:

> *It requires a very unusual mind to undertake the analysis of the obvious.*
> *—Alfred North Whitehead*

> *A distinction that does not further understanding is no distinction.*
> *—Goethe*

> *Analysis kills spontaneity. The grain once ground into flour springs and germinates no more.*
> *—Frederic Amiel*

To these pithy axioms, Patrick J. Robinson might respond that the obvious never is, that the distinction that furthers understanding is usually attainable by astute analysts working hand-in-glove with enlightened managers, and that analysis need not mean paralysis.

A visit with Patrick Robinson, whose unfailing enthusiasm often approaches an evangelical fervor, reveals the optimism of one who has observed marketing managers becoming increasingly involved in upper management and who has helped marketing research to grow as a strategic planning tool, particularly in larger corporations. Clearly, he views his craft as an integral part of "the art of the possible" in an intensifying search by many companies for new marketing opportunities and new product niches. More than ever before, upper-level managers concerned about improving performance are turning for surcease to investigative and analytic models with origins dating back to the advent of electronic computers. However, a credible claim to excellence in the consulting field is hard to come by; recognition such as that earned by RAI is exceptional, even though the firm, in terms of revenue, is far from ranking among the top 50 suppliers of research.

Robinson is tenacious: "Despite a few setbacks that have cropped up unexpectedly, we have adhered to the original set of precepts that guided our formation. That early philosophy remains unchanged as we continue diligently to improve service to RAI clients by enhancing research designs and demonstrating innovativeness in computer software. Our 25 full-time staff members are never satisfied with previous achievements—their attitude is 'onward and upward.' "

Your Task:

Share with Patrick J. Robinson and his staff your ideas on the following points:

1. What is the potential role of marketing research in developing and in executing corporate marketing plans? Please think about this in terms of profit and not-for-profit organizations.
2. RAI has worked primarily for large firms. Is there a profitable market for services like those offered by Robinson's firm in medium-sized and small-sized companies? How could you find out—what investigative approach would you recommend?
3. Is the expectation realistic that those who conduct the research, do the analysis, write the report, and prepare the clinical presentation deserve the undivided attention of managers who commission the project?
4. Pat Robinson appears to believe that decision makers need direction, specific guidance, and operational recommendations rather than just facts. Do you consider this to be presumptuous on his part? Why, or why not? Do you believe that facts, or what management is willing to believe about the so-called "facts," is more important? Please explain.
5. As you see it, why is research sometimes (perhaps often) misused by decision makers? If this happens, is it likely the researchers themselves are blameless?

6. Assuming that someone in a firm says, "Management's use of research around here is inversely related to the profitability of a brand," what is your speculation about possible reasons for that assertion?

7. In your opinion, what role could RAI play in designing an integrated marketing decision information system for a client? Are the talents of RAI best suited to the sorts of investigations described in the case study?

8. To what extent can marketing management and marketing research be categorized as scientific?

9. What are the strengths and weaknesses of RAI, Inc., as you see them?

10. If you were assigned to outline for Pat Robinson the major threats and most significant opportunities facing his firm for the remainder of the 1980s, what comments would you make?

case

11

WALT DISNEY WORLD EPCOT CENTER

An entire new era of Disney magic is about to dawn in every segment of our business—from films to outdoor recreation, from home entertainment to consumer products. . . . Fiscal 1981, with the second best results in the company's history, was a year of transition. . . . We experienced our 14th consecutive year of record revenues, a fact made all the more significant because those revenues passed the billion-dollar mark for the first time. . . . The decline in net income is attributable to two main factors: the disappointing domestic results of several live-action films and lower interest from investments resulting from planned Epcot Center expenditures.[1]

BACKGROUND

Revenue performance of the various corporate subsidiaries is presented in Exhibit 1.

Disneyland's attendance in 1981 was 11,343,000 off 2 percent from 1980, its twenty-fifth anniversary year. Walt Disney World was celebrating its tenth

[1]Adapted from *1981 Annual Report*, p. 1.

Exhibit 1

WALT DISNEY PRODUCTIONS AND SUBSIDIARIES: REVENUES EARNED BY VARIOUS DISNEY SUBSIDIARIES, 1977–1981
(in thousands)

	1977	1978	1979	1980	1981
Walt Disney World					
Admissions and rides	$100,792	$114,687	$121,276	$130,144	$139,326
Merchandise sales	72,906	86,860	101,856	116,187	121,465
Food sales	73,245	84,319	95,203	106,404	114,951
Lodging	39,902	44,972	54,043	61,731	70,110
Participant and other rentals	9,220	9,574	9,994	8,632	8,148
Other	4,453	5,226	7,251	10,279	11,436
Total revenues	$300,518	$345,638	$389,623	$433,377	$465,436
Theme park total attendance	13,057	14,071	13,792	13,783	13,221
Disneyland					
Admissions and rides	$ 65,913	$ 70,909	$ 75,758	$ 87,066	$ 92,065
Merchandise sales	39,485	49,312	60,235	72,140	79,146
Food sales	29,700	32,710	35,865	41,703	44,920
Participant and other rentals	4,784	4,676	5,266	5,432	5,603
Other	673	667	606	718	657
Total revenues	$140,555	$158,274	$177,730	$207,059	$222,391
Theme park total attendance	10,678	10,807	10,760	11,522	11,343
Walt Disney Travel Co.	$ 4,092*	$ 4,532*	$ 3,726*	$ 2,944	$ 3,984
Motion Pictures and Television					
Theatrical					
Domestic	$ 58,723	$ 69,010	$ 49,594	$ 63,350	$ 54,624
Foreign	36,585	57,912	57,288	78,314	76,279
Television					
Worldwide	22,750	25,213	27,903	19,736	43,672
Total revenues	$118,058	$152,135	$134,785	$161,400	$174,575
Consumer Products					
Telecommunications and nontheatrical	$20,714	$24,809	$29,240	$32,473	$ 43,379
Character merchandising	17,743	21,359	24,787	29,631	30,555
Publications	12,861	15,045	18,985	22,284	24,658
Records and music publishing	13,858	17,218	16,129	23,432	27,358
Other	1,426	2,133	1,768	1,905	12,704
Total revenues	$ 66,602	$ 80,564	$ 90,909	$109,725	$138,654

*Includes Celebrity Sports Center, which was sold in March 1979.

Source: 1981 Annual Report, p. 46.

Exhibit 2

SELECTED EVENTS IN THE HISTORY OF
WALT DISNEY PRODUCTIONS

1923	Walt Disney signs contract with M. J. Winkler in Los Angeles to produce series of "Alice Comedies."
1930	Mickey Mouse comic strip begins.
1937	*Snow White and the Seven Dwarfs,* first feature-length animated film, released. Received honorary Academy Award, 1939.
1940	*Fantasia* released.
1955	Disneyland opens in Anaheim, California (with Ronald Reagan performing as one of the official hosts).
1955	"Mickey Mouse Club" TV series begins.
1964	Walt Disney Productions begins acquisition of property near Orlando, Florida.
1966	Walt Disney outlines concept of EPCOT (Experimental Prototype Community of Tomorrow) in his final film appearance.
1966	Walt Disney dies.
1969	Walt Disney World construction begins with emphasis on the Magic Kingdom.
1971	Walt Disney World opens.
1971	Roy O. Disney dies.
1975	Walt Disney Productions announces Phase II of Walt Disney World with plans for EPCOT Center.
1979	EPCOT groundbreaking ceremonies held.
1980	Tokyo Disneyland construction begins.
1982	EPCOT Center opens.

Source: Adapted from corporate news release.

birthday, having amassed an attendance of 126 million. And the company was anticipating the spring 1983 debut of Tokyo Disneyland, being built on landfill in Tokyo harbor. Sixty years had witnessed a continuing growth of the Disney legend, some milestones of which are reflected in Exhibit 2.

EPCOT: "A PERMANENT WORLD'S FAIR"

EPCOT Center is described by its designers at WED Enterprises, the Disney engineering and design unit, as a "permanent World's Fair of imagination, discovery, education and exploration that will never be completed." Additional attractions being constructed will bring total costs of EPCOT Center to more than $1 billion by the end of the first year of operations, double the initial esti- mate of $500 million.

Eventually, additions to Future World and World Showcase are expected to encompass more than 500 acres at the site. EPCOT Center is located about three miles south of the world-famous Magic Kingdom, which has attracted nearly 140 million visitors from 100 countries during its first 11 years of opera- tions.

Walt Disney World officials estimate that EPCOT Center will attract some 8 million new admissions per year initially, bringing total annual atten- dance at the Central Florida resort and vacation property to around 20 million guests.

FUTURE WORLD

Future World, with six major pavilions and exhibit areas sponsored by leading U.S. companies, presents themes on communications, energy, transportation, agriculture, imagination, and technology. Participating companies include the Bell System, Exxon, General Motors, Kraft, Kodak, Sperry, and American Ex- press. In addition, American Express and Coca-Cola are sponsors of The Amer- ican Adventure, an imposing Georgian-style structure in the community of nine nations represented by World Showcase.

The pavilions of Future World, each uniquely designed to complement a theme subject, are dominated by Spaceship Earth, the symbol of EPCOT Cen- ter. Spaceship Earth is a shining geodesic sphere anchored on huge 15 foot high legs and towering a total of 180 feet. A ride-through attraction spiraling through the 17-story interior of the geosphere introduces visitors to the story of human progress through 40,000 years of communications advancements.

At the hub of Future World is CommuniCore, two crescent-shaped build- ings where guests can use a variety of advanced-design electronic devices for entertainment and information purposes, including a touch-sensitive video- disk system that provides instant audiovisual information on specific attrac- tions throughout EPCOT Center.

Surrounding CommuniCore are four separate theme-area pavilions, in- cluding World of Motion, shaped like a giant wheel six stories high; Universe of Energy, a pyramid-shaped building with rooftop solar cells that can generate up to 70,000 watts of direct-current power; The Land, with six acres under roof devoted to leading-edge agricultural methods and land use; and Journey into Imagination, with two truncated glass pyramids shaping the exterior and an interior where guests explore a fantasy world of creativity and participate in "creative" experiences using electronic devices.

All theme pavilions have ride-through attractions, some involving elabo- rately constructed scenes of historical events done with a whimsical touch and the use of lifelike "Audio-Animatronics" figures constructed by WED "imagineers." In World of Motion, for example, a used-chariot salesman in ancient Rome is busily slashing prices—in Roman numerals. Elsewhere, the first traffic jam involving the automobile is depicted.

In Universe of Energy, visitors ride in 97-passenger "theater cars" powered by solar energy through a prehistoric diorama illustrating the billion-year formation of fossil fuels. In The Land, a boat ride journeys through the different food-growing regions of the world and through greenhouses where lush crops are being grown in imaginative new ways.

Future World pavilions explore themes through demonstrations, participatory experiences, theatrical productions, unique motion pictures, and hundreds of elaborate special effects employing state-of-the-art technologies and projection techniques.

World Showcase

World Showcase, arranged around a 41-acre lagoon beyond Future World, presents the architectural, social, and cultural heritages of nine nations. In addition to The American Adventure, where a 29-minute theatrical production highlights American history, are "mininations" of Canada, the United Kingdom, France, Japan, Germany, Italy, China, and Mexico, each country represented by architectural landmarks and town scenes familiar to world travelers. Replicas range from an ornate Chinese temple and delicate Japanese pagoda to Italy's Doges' Palace and the steep-roofed Hotel du Canada. There's even a 100 foot high replica of the Eiffel Tower gracing scenes of Paris and the French provinces.

Commercial firms from participating countries have stocked a broad variety of merchandise from their native lands in their respective shopping areas. World Showcase countries also offer native cuisines and present artisans and performers dressed in traditional costumes. During a mile-long stroll of the World Showcase Promenade, visitors are entertained by a Mexican mariachi band, an Italian puppet show, or a German oompah band.

Each country's facilities are staffed with the aid of its own citizens, represented by a select group of international students participating in the World Showcase Fellowship Program, a unique work-study program directed by Walt Disney World.

Shows and Productions

Visual experiences at EPCOT Center include more than four hours of motion pictures in 31 shows, prepared at a cost in excess of $30 million. Disney film crews, shooting in 30 different countries, worked in 22 different formats, including 3-D, computer animation, laser graphics, and Circle-Vision 360. Presentation of the motion pictures requires 150 different projection systems.

Motion pictures have been enhanced by enveloping screens, digital sound, and, in some cases, projected odors of scenery. In a movie montage of basic energy sources in the Universe of Energy, even the 89 foot wide projection screen becomes animated with 100 programmable triangles, creating textures, patterns, and ripple effects of images.

Some 450 "Audio-Animatronics" characters range from singing vegetables, to 20 foot high dinosaurs chewing artificial food, to personalities out of history. In The American Adventure, a replica of Benjamin Franklin climbs a set of stairs to visit Thomas Jefferson.

EPCOT projects incorporate advanced environmental planning and urban design concepts throughout the 28,000 acres of Walt Disney World.

Pricing

Beginning in October 1982, the pricing structure shown in Exhibit 3 was established. A central purpose of the three-day passes for $35 was to enable adults to spend time at both EPCOT Center and the Magic Kingdom. The basic premise is that adults will be the major participants at EPCOT Center.

BEYOND 1982

Science fiction author and futurist Ray Bradbury, who provided concepts for designing Spaceship Earth, proposed that "The function of Epcot is to excite people to potentials, and to be as accurate as possible—not to educate fully, but to be on the rim of educating, so that when you leave, your life is changed forever." He suggested that being made an educable human being by the excitement generated by a visit to EPCOT Center would stimulate people to solve the world's problems. According to oral history at Walt Disney Produc-

Exhibit 3

PRICES FOR MAGIC KINGDOM AND EPCOT CENTER*

	ADULT	JUNIOR	CHILD
1-day admission†	$ 15	$14	$12
3-day World pass	35	33	28
4-day World pass	45	42	46
6-day World pass	60	56	48
Season pass	100	93	80

*Special prices are available for Walt Disney World Village guests, participants, and Magic Kingdom Club guests.
†Magic Kingdom or EPCOT Center.

tions, Walt preferred this version of the mission: "To entertain and hope people learn rather than teach and hope they are entertained."

The success of this newest Disney venture will help to ensure overall earnings wholesomeness for the corporation, a bottom line to be bolstered further when Tokyo Disneyland, built altogether on $500 million investment by Japanese sponsors, begins paying its American namesake royalties of 5 to 10 percent on revenues. Although a relatively modest contribution to Disney's total corporate fortunes, another consideration remains: Will success imply openings for other "franchised" operations elsewhere?

> As our Epcot Center slogan says, "The 21st century begins on October 1, 1982." It is a slogan that applies to Walt Disney Productions as a whole. We are on the threshold of a new beginning for the company as we broaden our base for expansion with the openings of Epcot Center and Tokyo Disneyland, our entry into pay cable TV and revitalized motion picture production.[2]

Your Task:

Advise Walt Disney Productions.

1. Do you believe the goals are modest—to attract at least 2 million additional visitors annually to the 28,000-acre complex and to entice at least 60 percent of visitors to the Magic Kingdom to spend an average of 1.5 days at EPCOT Center? (This translates into 8 million new admissions beyond the current 12 million admissions to the Magic Kingdom.) Discuss the impact of possible market saturation of such enterprises and the effects of the economy on travel and tourism.
2. Is it reasonable to expect most of those who visit the Magic Kingdom to add EPCOT Center to their tour? What would you recommend the organization do to promote this "total immersion"?
3. If you were asked to recommend the most desirable market target, or targets, what assumptions would you use? For example, do you agree with some that most business at EPCOT will come from adults who did not succumb to the mystique of Mickey Mouse and company? If you do agree, how might this tie in with the four-year-long decline in attendance at the Magic Kingdom?
4. Orlando International Airport officials apparently believed Disney's forecasts, announcing in November 1982 that they expected passenger traffic at their facility to increase by 30 percent in 1983, primarily because of EPCOT Center. What is your appraisal of these expectations?
5. In your opinion, what pricing strategy is implied in Exhibit 3? What is your reaction to this schedule? What would you recommend for Disney executives to consider over the next three to five years in evaluating the price structure?

[2] *1981 Annual Report*, p. 3.

6. At current price-earnings ratios and dividend payouts, would you invest in Walt Disney Productions? Analysts in 1982 made estimates of how much EPCOT Center might add to Disney's net income in 1983, ranging from $10 million to $35 million. October, traditionally Disney's worst month, was not considered to be a valid predictor of traffic.

7. Based on your inferences from this case study and adding ideas gleaned from other sources, including your own personal experience and observations, articulate a corporate mission statement for Walt Disney Productions.

DELOREAN MOTOR COMPANY[1]

"The reasonable man adapts himself to the world; the unreasonable one persists in trying to adapt the world to himself. Therefore all progress depends upon the unreasonable man." Thus wrote eccentric British playwright George Bernard Shaw in *Man and Superman.* John Zachary DeLorean was called by detractors unreasonable, visionary, rebellious, and even eccentric. Some thought him outrageous, starting an automobile manufacturing company from scratch after leaving one of the highest-paying and most prestigious jobs in the auto industry only two years previously, concluding a phase in his career during which he had often tried to recast the world of giant business to his own specifications, determining eventually that the system was intractable. Many likened him to a Horatio Alger zealot, possessed of an indomitable pioneering spirit and supreme self-confidence.

ENGINEER, MANAGER, MAVERICK, ENTREPRENEUR

John Z. DeLorean (JZD) was widely lionized, in industry and in society as well. Some of this deference extended into such realms in 1981–1982 as liquor ad-

[1]The final draft of this case study was written in May, 1982.

vertisements, one of which, for a well-known brand of Scotch, began with the headline: "One Out of Every 100 New Businesses Succeeds. Here's to Those Who Take the Odds."

Exhibit 1

PHOTOGRAPH OF JOHN Z. DELOREAN, 1982

Source: DMC corporate public relations photograph.

DeLorean startled the business world in 1973 when, at age 48, he resigned his position as group vice president of North American Car and Truck Operations at General Motors. At the time of leaving the auto giant, he was considered, both within and outside corporate walls, to be a leading candidate for the presidency of General Motors, understandable speculation, for his rise in the automotive industry had been meteoric. After receiving a bachelor's degree from Lawrence Institute of Technology and a master's degree from the Chrysler Institute, he joined Packard in 1952 as a member of that company's engineering team, and in 1956, at age 31, he was named head of research and development. Later that year he left the ailing automaker to take a position as director of advanced engineering with GM's Pontiac Division, subsequently contributing the wide track concept and the Grand Prix, a new "personal luxury car" based on GM's intermediate chassis. The Grand Prix spawned other GM derivatives, the Chevrolet Monte Carlo and Oldsmobile Cutlass. These "A Specials," so-termed because they shared the same special version of GM's "A" body, were the company's largest selling body style until redesigned for the 1978 model year. During his tenure at GM, DeLorean was awarded some 44 patents for technological innovations such as the recessed windshield wiper and the hidden radio antenna.

In 1965 JZD was named general manager of Pontiac and a vice president of General Motors, the youngest man ever to head a GM Division. By the time he was tapped for larger responsibilities as head of Chevrolet in 1969, Pontiac's U.S. market share had climbed from its 1958 level of almost 5 percent to more than 9 percent.

DeLorean was given the helm of Chevrolet—at age 44, the youngest man to hold that position—with the mission to reverse a seven-year trend of declining profits. He reorganized the division's unwieldy management structure, increased manufacturing efficiency, improved car quality, and revitalized advertising. By 1971 dealer profits had increased over 400 percent, the corporation's earnings were up even more, and Chevrolet became the first nameplate in the world to sell more than 3 million cars and trucks in a single year. The outstanding sales records set at both Pontiac and Chevrolet are still standing.

In 1972 DeLorean was appointed group vice president in charge of GM's American car and truck operations. With the presidency in sight, just six months later he left the auto colossus. Always the "unreasonable man," an individualist in both his private and professional life, DeLorean had become progressively disenchanted with the way America's automotive industry functioned and, most significantly, with the kind of product the industry was offering the public. "Simply put," DeLorean said, "I wanted to build cars the way I wanted to build them, and the system at General Motors just didn't allow for that. I was primarily concerned with two problems endemic in the auto industry in this country: the annual model change that made a purchaser's car obsolete long before it was worn out and the fact that cars wore out too soon." DeLorean's solution was what he called the "ethical" car, a vehicle that would spit in the eye of traditional annual model restyling and that would not rust, corrode, and collapse around its owner in two or three years.

With the concept of such a car in mind, DeLorean took his leave from the General Motors hierarchy in April 1973, allowing his auto idea to gestate for a year while serving as president of the National Alliance of Businessmen, an organization devoted to finding jobs for disadvantaged Americans, a cause JZD had championed during his GM days.

BIRTH OF DELOREAN MOTOR COMPANY

The first steps toward bringing his dream to fruition were taken when he formed the John Z. DeLorean Company in 1974, certainly not the most propitious time to bring a new car to market. The first OPEC oil embargo created an upheaval in Detroit as the major makers scrambled to bring their products into line with the demands of a radically changing world. Moreover, there had not been a successful car company start-up in the United States since Walter P. Chrysler formed the Chrysler Car Co. in 1926.

DeLorean's strategy, however, was not to confront established producers head on. GM, Ford, Chrysler, American Motors, and imports had the products, production capability, organization, and money to adapt to the market's demands. DeLorean chose to aim his car at a segment of the automotive market that has historically been relatively immune to both economic cycles and petroleum supply and cost—the higher-priced specialty market. Specifically, he intended to produce a limited-production sports car that, although expensive, would adhere to his definition of the ethical car.

To obtain funds for the early development, DeLorean formed the DeLorean Sports Car Partnership; additional capital was obtained through forming the DeLorean Research Limited Partnership. Finally, the DeLorean Motor Company was established as the basic operational entity in the enterprise. As his automobile took shape on the drawing board, he began canvassing the United States for well-established auto dealers interested in becoming part of the organization. Each joining dealer bought a minimum of $25,000 of DeLorean stock and agreed to purchase between 50 and 150 cars in the first two years of production, to stock $6,000 worth of spare parts, to erect a $3,000 sign, and to invest $1,000 in special tools. Over 340 dealers were sufficiently impressed with JZD's concept and track record to ante up the necessary capital outlays.

Initially, DeLorean approached various states as well as the federal government to secure the additional financial backing needed to get the program off the ground. When these attempts proved unsuccessful, he turned his attention to opportunities offered overseas, finally settling on Northern Ireland as a site for the manufacturing subsidiary, DeLorean Motor Cars Ltd. A series of 1982 business periodical advertisements informed readers: "Figures just released by the U.S. Department of Commerce confirm that return on investment in the Republic of Ireland is over 30% . . . twice the European Common Market average," which placed Ireland as a profitable industrial location at the top of the roster of European countries. On Ireland's list of overseas investors, the United States was number one at the beginning of the 1980s, accounting for just over half of all such sources. Some of the firms mentioned in Ireland Industrial Development Authority's *1980 Annual Report* are 3M Company, Milton Bradley, Johnson & Johnson, Apple Computer, Sunbeam, Black &

Decker, Fieldcrest, Nike, and True Temper—all had operations there. Ireland's incentives included a 10 percent corporation tax, nonrepayable capital grants, completely subsidized training grants for workers in new industries, low-cost loan financing, R&D grants up to 50 percent, advance factories, and an assortment of after-care advisory services.[2]

The British government proved to be an agreeable partner, advancing nearly $200 million to the project.

THE DELOREAN MOTOR CAR

In January 1981, the Dunmurry plant came onstream, its first output destined to receive favorable attention from auto experts and enthusiasts. Some called it an honest-to-goodness sports/GT car; others predicted that the DeLorean would become a cult car, a status symbol of individualists; most agreed it was handsomely styled and fun to drive.

With a body styled by Giorgio Giugiaro and an overhead-cam V-6 sourced from the manufacturing consortium of Peugeot-Renault-Volvo, the DeLorean did have a strong GT pedigree. But it was said by corporate marketing to be "a car that offers more than exotic styling and sports car performance." It also offered outstanding economy for a car in its class. The stainless steel exterior was immune to corrosion, and, echoing DeLorean's concern when he left GM, styling changes would not be an annual event. The introductory announcement was made by DeLorean: "The DeLorean offers a long list of standard features typically extra cost on other cars: air conditioning, leather seats, tilt and telescoping steering wheel, stereo sound system, complete instrumentation, electric windows, power brakes, etc. And something not available anywhere else: gullwing doors. When it comes to exterior color, however, the DeLorean is like a precious metal version of Henry Ford's black Model T: "any color you like, as long as it's the silvery hue of stainless steel."

Some thought DeLorean fastidious and a perfectionist, citing his dissatisfaction with the problem of smudgy fingerprints lingering grubbily on the stainless steel skin. A polymer chemical treatment was devised to solve that imperfection. Another anecdote: In late 1981 JZD sent 30 of his Irish workers from Belfast to the company's California quality-assurance center for indoctrination in the kind of precision body fitting the boss expected to see.

PRODUCT DESCRIPTION

The DMC is pictured in Exhibit 2. Exhibit 3 outlines the vehicle's product characteristics for the 1981–1982 production runs.

---

[2]Industrial Development Authority Ireland, *1980 Annual Report.* We wish to thank Declan Collins, vice president, IDA Ireland, for providing this literature.

GOVERNMENT REGULATIONS

Government standards for safety, fuel economy, emissions, and product warranty are applicable to all autos sold in the United States and additional, more stringent standards for emissions prevail in California. The DeLorean was meeting all currently applicable standards into mid-1982. Regulations specify that passenger automobiles must boost average fuel economy from 22.0 miles per gallon in the 1981 model year to 27.5 miles per gallon for 1985 and thereafter. Both Congress and the Department of Transportation have considered standards after 1985, but none had been established by mid-1982. Failure to meet the standard for a given year results in imposition of a fine for each vehicle of $5 for each tenth of a mile per gallon by which the fleet falls short of the standard.

Exhibit 2

THE DELOREAN MOTOR CAR

Source: DMC corporate public relations photograph.

Exhibit 3

THE DELOREAN SPORTS CAR NEWS RELEASE—1981

BELFAST—From the moment of its first public appearance the De-Lorean has been a design success. Its carefully crafted lines, from the pen of Ital Design's Giugiaro, broke new styling ground in the world of high-performance automobiles. But there's more to the DeLorean than sleek Italian styling, sweeping expanses of glass, and lustrous stainless steel.

The heart of the DeLorean is the 2.85 liter (174 cid) overhead-cam V-6 engine that nestles within the rear wishbone of the chassis. The engine faces the rear with the five-speed manual or three-speed automatic transaxle extending toward the front of the car. The engine's heads and block are cast in aluminum alloy.

The engine is fed by a Bosch K Jetronic mechanical fuel injection system that produces 130 SAE net horsepower at 5500 rpm and 162 foot pounds of torque at 2750 rpm. That's good enough for 0–60 clockings in the 9–10 second range and a top speed of approximately 125 mph.

But straight-line performance isn't the total DeLorean story. The Renault five-speed manual has a top gear ratio of 0.821:1, which at cruise has the V-6 loafing along well down in the rpm range, and that in turn means some very impressive fuel economy figures: 19 mpg, city; 29.4 mpg, highway.

Handling, of course, is a vital part of any high-performance sports car, and DeLorean's engineers, in concert with Lotus, have developed a suspension system that has given the DeLorean excellent handling characteristics. The independent front suspension has parallel unequal-length upper and lower control arms, coil springs, shock absorbers, and an anti-roll bar. The independent rear suspension has trailing arms with upper and lower unequal-length parallel, transverse control arms; coil springs; and shock absorbers. All this is connected to the driver by a sensitive and quick-responding rack-and-pinion steering system.

The best suspension bits and pieces in the world, however, are just so much metal until they're hooked to the wheels and tires that make it all work. At the front, the DeLorean has 6" × 14" alloy wheels wearing 195/60HR-14 Goodyear NCT steel radial tires. The rear wheels are larger, 8" × 15" and carry 235/60/HR-15 rubber. The Goodyear NCTs (neutral contour tires) represent the latest high-performance tire technology from Goodyear and have been specially designed for the DeLorean. The distinctive tread pattern was derived directly from Goodyear Formula 1 racing tires.

Four-wheel disc brakes, manufactured by Lucas-Girling, provide the stopping power. They're located outboard with 10" front and 10.5" rear

Exhibit 3 (Cont.)

discs. The braking force has been carefully biased front-to-rear to ensure maximum control in emergency situations.

The work force at DeLorean Motor Cars Limited, the manufacturing arm of the DeLorean Motor Company, now numbers almost 3000. In October 1978 the plant site in the small town of Dunmurry, just outside of Belfast in Northern Ireland, was nothing more than an undeveloped green field. In less than two-and-a-half years that green field was turned into the most modern car manufacturing facility in the world with nearly 700,000 square feet under roof. The plant can produce 30,000 cars a year without expansion. In 1982, based on planned production of 25,000 cars, DeLorean will export some $500,000,000 worth of products, making it the largest exporter in Northern Ireland.

The first shipment of DeLoreans landed at the port of Long Beach in California in mid-May, and distribution to dealerships began shortly thereafter. The new DeLorean is also arriving through a port of entry in Wilmington, Delaware.

The company has established quality-assurance centers at three locations: Bridgewater, New Jersey; Troy, Michigan; and Santa Ana, California. At the QACs each car undergoes a thorough inspection to ensure it meets the company's high standards before it is shipped on to a dealership.

Although U.S. sales have always been the top priority, the company is thinking of establishing distributorships in other countries.

Source: DMC corporate public relations.

MARKET REACTIONS AND BUYER PROFILES

Car and Driver comparison tested the DeLorean against higher-priced Porsche 911SC and Ferrari 308 GTSi and lower-priced Datsun 280-ZX Turbo and Chevrolet Corvette.[3] The newcomer received good marks. Also, DeLorean's car was being compared by some auto buffs with the Mercedes-Benz 300SL gullwing coupe produced in 1955, selling at $6,800 new, which in 1982 was cited as worth over $100,000. Clearly, some early buyers of the DMC reportedly were thinking not just about the thrills of being the first in their communities to drive it, but also were contemplating its value as a longer-term investment that would appreciate in value.

A DeLorean marketing official expressed a desire for better understand-

[3]*Car and Driver*, December 1981, pp. 39–47.

ing of purchasers with a statement and a question, followed by a tentative answer: "The car is designed to appeal to a multitude of buyers, from owners of Cadillac Sevilles to Porsche 924 turbos. The question still remains—what kind of person would spend $26,000 and up for this car? We have partially answered that question by examing profiles of early customers. Specifically, DeLorean buyers are well educated males, have incomes in the range of $50,000 and up, are successful in business—typically company presidents or owners of their own firms—and are risk-takers."

Earlier in the process of product design, while serious structural changes could still be made, the prototype DeLorean was shown to selected samples of shopping center customers. Mostly, reactions were favorable, and a majority thought the car would be more expensive than the company's targeted price of $20,000 to $25,000. A mail survey also revealed a great deal about the potential DeLorean customer who had already made a deposit on the promise of near-term delivery. These, and matched samples of respondents with comparable demographic characteristics, reacted favorably to the prospect of owning a DeLorean automobile. Most who were favorably disposed wanted (1) value for the money, (2) a car useful for daily driving, not just weekend jaunts, and (3) a car that was unique and attention getting.

EXPANDING DISTRIBUTION

Management was considering expanding sales efforts to Canada, Europe (Austria, Belgium, France, Germany, Italy, Luxembourg, The Netherlands, Switzerland, and the United Kingdom), and the Middle East (Bahrain, Kuwait, Lebanon, Qatar, Saudi Arabia, and the United Arab Emirates) in 1982. The distribution structure would probably be a single distributor in each country, with a dealer network strategically located throughout each country selected. DeLorean Limited planned to provide related services, such as processing vehicles through customs, providing technical training, and maintaining parts inventories. It was anticipated that the distributors appointed by DeLorean Limited would also be handling a complementary line of automobiles, with dealerships and support facilities in place.

PRODUCT LINE EXPANSION PLANS AND THE U.S. MARKET

The two-seat DeLorean was to be only the beginning. DeLorean's dream—and the future of his company—depended on further incursions into the upper-priced automotive market. That future included the planned introduction in 1982 of a twin-turbo, twin-intercooler version of the car. DeLorean planned to introduce in 1985 a sedan to compete in the Mercedes and BMW market. Some features would be derived from the sedan's sports car progenitor—stainless steel skin, rear engine, gullwing doors, and perhaps the lowest coefficient of drag of any car ever manufactured in volume.

The most important concentration for U.S. automakers had traditionally been the standard sedan, the family automobile, although it was rapidly becoming less standard, giving way to downsizing and other styling and technical changes. Still, sheer market volume placed it at the top of the heap of Detroit's revenue producers. The 1960s and 1970s brought sweeping changes in American consumers' purchasing behavior. A car with its chief claim that of occupying the "ugly" positions came into being, along with an array of other economy cars and an assortment of high-priced upscale vehicles from Europe. Market segmentation became an auto industry watchword in the mid-1970s, and thinking smaller in the United States was dictated by fuel crises and destructive competition of foreign imports, notably those from Japan. U.S. Goliaths were succumbing to the foreign Davids' attacks.

Downsizing and weight-shaving technology, sleeker aerodynamics in body contours, and engineering innovations in suspension systems, engines, and other underneath parts of the vehicle became part of U.S. automakers' efforts to recapture a position as Americans' preferred modes of transportation. Such was the competitive direction to serve the majority of car buyers who were looking for four- to five-passenger cars. Customers for the most part were turning to some combination of price, comfort, safety, and economy. The penchant for economy, however, began to diminish as gasoline prices held steady in late 1981 and 1982, supplies appearing to be plentiful. And fuel efficiency in many big cars was steadily improving.

ADVERTISING AND PUBLICITY—1981

Publicity for JZD's newcomer was provided quickly and plentifully by America's media, particularly in newspapers and periodicals; television news programs highlighted the first boatload of DMCs arriving at Long Beach and the arrival of the first cars at various dealerships. For its advertising agency, DeLorean selected Avrett, Free and Fischer, the agency that created campaigns for, among others, Contac's "tiny time pills" and Meow Mix cat food commercials with the fleet-footed "dancing" feline. Agreement was reached to launch paid mass media promotion for the new car using "The DeLorean. Live the Dream" as headline. One of the print ads is shown in Exhibit 4. The first television campaign was launched during the U.S. Open Tennis Championship in the fall of 1981, 30-second spots in a seashore setting, gulls flying overhead, DMC doors swinging up by themselves, and a driverless car racing along the wet sand.

Exhibit 4

"LIVE THE DREAM" ADVERTISEMENT

Your eyes skim the sleek, sensuous stainless steel body, and all your senses tell you, "I've got to have it!"

The counterbalanced gull-wing doors rise effortlessly, beckoning you inside.

The soft leather seat in the cockpit fits you like it was made for your body.

You turn the key. The light alloy V-6 comes to life instantly.

The De Lorean. Surely one of the most awaited automobiles in automotive history.

It all began with one man's vision of the perfect personal luxury car. Built for long life, it employs the latest space-age materials.

Of course, everyone stares as you drive by. Sure, they're a little envious. That's expected. After all, you're the one Living The Dream.

Start living it today at a dealer near you.

THE DE LOREAN. LIVE THE DREAM.

A dealer commitment as unique as the car itself. There are 345 De Lorean dealers located throughout the United States. Each one is a stockholder in the De Lorean Motor Company. This commitment results in a unique relationship which will provide De Lorean owners with a superb standard of service.

For the dealer nearest you, call toll free 800-447-4700, in Ill., 800-322-4400. ᗡᗰᑕ
DE LOREAN MOTOR COMPANY

© DE LOREAN MOTOR COMPANY 1981

PRODUCTION NOTES—1981

Some of the money advanced to the company as loans would become outright grants—not required to be paid back—if certain numbers of employees were hired within a specified period of time. The total of 2,000 employees, scheduled to be met after five years of production, was realized in the fall of 1981. Although it was not mandated by the British government, the DeLorean facility at Dunmurry maintained a policy of 50:50 hiring ratio between Protestants and Catholics.

Some Ulster businesses were willing to join forces with the new auto venture; some were not.

> *"Those who did take a chance on DeLorean are on the pig's back now."* *That's the verdict of one Ulster businessman who is enjoying the snowball effect of supplying the controversial car plant which is now getting into top gear. . . . How have Ulster manufacturers responded to this challenge on their own doorstep? Their reaction has been mixed apparently, perhaps reflecting the divided opinions on the project's long-term prospects of success. And the fainthearted do not have the makings of true entrepreneurs. . . . The challenge to local industry is still open to takers. For those prepared to work at them, there are still some opportunities at the end of the DeLorean rainbow.*[4]

MARKETING AND FINANCIAL SITUATION IN 1982

In the last half of 1981, some 4,600 DMC cars were sold, with net profit of $3.7 million reported for the quarter ending August 31. "And we expect a lot of black ink in 1982," said DeLorean. By the end of 1981, the firm had spent $217 million, including $137 million in loans and investments provided by government agencies of Northern Ireland, $52 million borrowed from banks, and approximately $8 million from dealers and others, and it was seeking further funding.

Break-even for the Belfast facility was estimated to be 10,000 cars annually, and Northern Ireland officials were working to reduce the break-even point to 7,000 vehicles by introducing efficiencies in manufacturing costs and creating overhead savings. At the start of 1982, the company was producing 80 cars a day—a yearly rate of 20,000—with plans to increase production up to 120 units daily.

Quests for additional funding were unsuccessful in early 1982, following postponement of plans to offer the public 2,250,000 shares of a new company, DeLorean Motors Holding Company, at $12.50 a share, to raise equity capital. This offering was scheduled for late summer 1981, when total new car sales in

[4]*Belfast Telegraph*, November 26, 1981, np.

the United States had declined from the previous dismal levels of sales in 1979 and 1980. The four major U.S. automakers reported 1980 aggregate losses totaling over $4 billion, with the slide continuing albeit at a decreased rate in 1981. Aggressiveness of the multinationals—for example, BMW, Fuji Heavy Industries (Subaru), Honda, Datsun, Toyota, and Volkswagen—added to the fiercely competitive environment.

Britain's Conservative government refused to add to the grants, loans, and guarantees advanced to the Belfast company over the period 1977 to 1981 and, along with the U.S. staff, was looking for investors willing to put up some $75 million. DeLorean, who remained in control of the New York companies, which continued buying and distributing cars made in Belfast, reportedly intended to invest $5 million of personal assets as a supplement to other sources.

One economy measure was in progress when the casewriter revisited DeLorean's New York headquarters in May 1982—employees were completing the move from DMC's 43rd floor, 280 Park Avenue offices, to the less expensive 35th floor, accompanied by a staff reduction from 30 to 15 people in the executive offices. Such cost controls at corporate level were seen by the staff as evidence of intent to cut back on some of the frills, although there was no indication that John DeLorean had changed his view that to sell a quality product one should be in classy surroundings.

The Appendix provides a summary of selected passages from management's discussion and analysis of financial conditions and operations results.

Your Task:

Key issues and decisions facing DeLorean Motor Company management in mid-1982 were several. If you had been advising DeLorean *in mid-1982,* how would you have addressed these questions:[5]

1. Would changing U.S. demographics bode well for DeLorean's future? Early predictions based on the 1980 Census called for a 10 percent growth in the 25- to 54-year age bracket, a group accounting for most of the auto industry's sales.
2. Would the company's operating results improve or deteriorate over the next several years, and what impact would this have on pricing flexibility?
3. What would be the impact of worldwide inflation on DeLorean's costs? If inflation continued rising in the United Kingdom, what would happen to operating margins and pricing policies?
4. How could the company get a better fix on who the competitors are and how prospective purchasers view the DMC against others' cars? Who will major competitors be for the remainder of the 1980s?
5. Given all relevant factors in forecasting, and suspending judgments about

[5]DeLorean presents a unique task section due to the ethical issues of the case which have come to the fore during the well-publicized DeLorean scandal. Students are to assume the identity of a consultant to DeLorean *in mid-1982.*

the company based on recent adverse publicity, what is the best approach
for such a company to use estimating potential and forecasting sales?

6. Is the promotional campaign as presently conceived, adequate for the next
    two or three years? What is the best media plan for the company to
    follow?
7. Is the product life cycle a useful construct for DeLorean Motor Company
    decision makers to use in thinking about product design, promotion, and
    pricing?
8. How can dealers be included in developing warranty fulfillment procedures
    and promotional plans for the company, and how can the company
    collaborate with them to reinforce the focus on customer satisfactions?
9. Finally, what are the odds that John Zachary DeLorean can succeed where
    others—for example, Kaiser-Frazer, Tucker, and Bricklin—failed? What
    strategies will ensure success?[6]

[6]In this particular case all of us are aware of the unhappy outcome. However, for our purposes here, we think the DeLorean case offers a splendid opportunity to deconstruct marketing strategies that the *reasonable* individual may well have considered for this particular company, or one like it, in mid-1982. Students are cautioned to approach the task section with this in mind.

Appendix

MANAGEMENT'S DISCUSSION AND ANALYSIS OF FINANCIAL CONDITION AND RESULTS OF OPERATIONS

CURRENT FINANCIAL POSITION

From commencement of the DeLorean enterprise through the end of fiscal 1980, the Company obtained approximately $178.6 million of financing. These funds were used for research and development for the DeLorean, the construction of Limited's manufacturing facility in Northern Ireland, the establishment of a distribution network, and working capital. Approximately $150 million was supplied by agencies of the Government of Northern Ireland in the form of grants, long-term loans, and equity investments. Of this amount, approximately $15.5 million was expended by DRLP, and approximately $3.4 million was expended by a research and development limited partnership (DeLorean Sports Car Partnership), which interests therein were exchanged for the Company's preferred stock, and approximately $8.2 million and $1.3 million was realized from the proceeds of the sale of the Company's common stock to DeLorean automobile dealers and other investors, respectively.

Due primarily to delays in production experienced in May 1981 as a result of political unrest in Northern Ireland, Limited required additional working capital loans, and in May requested, and in June and July re-

Appendix (Cont.)

ceived, from DOC an additional guaranty facility for up to 7 million pounds ($13.02 million) in additional working capital loans.

In May 1981, the Company completed a financing agreement with the Bank of America, whereby the Bank is providing transit financing covering shipment of automobiles and parts from Northern Ireland to the United States. The agreement provided for up to $33 million of credit facilities payable at various dates not later than October 31, 1981 for vehicles and December 31, 1981 for parts. While Motor hopes to extend the Agreement, it has no commitments for an extension, and if the Agreement is not extended or replaced and the Bank of America elects to discontinue financing on a shipment by shipment basis, Motor would not have sufficient funds to finance its inventory.

In addition, Limited's agreement with a major supplier of components permits Limited to purchase components on extended payment terms, subject to the continuing availability of export financing and approval from French Government export authorities, thereby providing Limited with significant amounts of working capital. There can be no assurance that such French export financing will continue, and if it does not continue, the Company would have need for significant working capital.

Based on present production and shipping schedules and existing dealer purchase commitments, the Company does not anticipate that it will require additional working capital financing arrangements in the short term, assuming that the DOC guaranteed working capital loans referred to above (which are due December 31, 1981 and transit financing (referred to above) are extended or replaced. There can be no assurance that present production and shipping schedules will be met or that the working loans and transit financing will be extended or replaced.

During the quarter ended August 31, 1981, the Company determined that additional grants for capital expenditures were available from the Government of Northern Ireland in excess of those already received. Such grants are at a rate of 30 percent of qualified expenditures and relate to capital expenditures which are in excess of those covered by 50 percent grants.

The Company estimates that its capital expenditures through the end of fiscal 1982 for the Sedan and homologation programs plus the cost of an engine development program will be approximately $41 million.

The development of the Sedan, from design through initial commercial production, is at present estimated to cost approximately $80 million in 1981 dollars, of which the Company plans to expend approximately $19 million by the end of fiscal 1982. As of the date hereof, the Company has no funds available, or commitments therefore from outside sources, for the Sedan program, although the Company intends to negotiate for

Appendix (Cont.)

financing of the Sedan project with NIDA and DOC. There can be no assurance that the Company will be able to obtain the required funds.

The total cost of the homologation program is currently projected to be approximately $4 million, of which approximately $2 million is estimated to be expended by the end of fiscal 1982. The Company expects to expend on engine development for fuel economy, emissions, and performance improvements approximately $20 million through the end of fiscal year 1982. As of the date hereof, the Company has no funds available or commitments therefore from outside sources for the homologation and engine development programs. The costs of the engine development program after fiscal 1982 cannot now be predicted with accuracy because they will depend on the future regulatory and competitive environments for the DeLorean, as well as on whether any product changes are made by the manufacturer in the engines supplied for the DeLorean. The Company believes, however, that such future costs are likely to continue to be substantial.

RESULTS OF OPERATIONS—1980 and 1981

In June the Company began to sell vehicles to dealers and accordingly is no longer considered a development stage enterprise. Since June the Company has recorded revenues from the sale of vehicles and parts of $25,656,612 and gross profit of $5,228,172. Sales to dealers totalled 1,084 vehicles as follows: June, 320; July, 256; and August, 508.

The Company has established three Quality Assurance Centers in the United States which perform vehicle inspection and preparation prior to delivery to dealers. The cost of these centers is part of cost of sales and totalled $2,442,965 for the three months ended August 31, 1981 and was comprised of $696,945 in June, $745,865 in July, and $1,000,155 in August, with costs per vehicle sold $2,178 in June, $2,914 in July, and $1,969 in August. The Company believes the cost per vehicle will decline from the levels experienced during the start-up of distribution operations.

The increase in research and development expense of $4,065,227 for the nine-month period ended August 31, 1981 compared to August 31, 1980 is a result of higher preproduction costs, final staging, and testing of facilities and equipment during the phase immediately preceding commercial production. The decrease of $5,389,995 for the quarter ended August 31, 1981 compared to August 31, 1980 reflects a reduction in the need for research and development activities during commercial production.

Selling, general, and administrative expenses increased for both the

Appendix (Cont.)

three months and the nine months ended August 31, 1981 compared to the same periods in 1980 due to the finalization of the parts and automobile distribution networks and dealer training together with the marketing of the car.

During February and August of 1981, Limited reached the 1,000 and 1,500 employee levels, respectively, which resulted in the conversion for financial statement purposes of long-term loans of £6,500,000 ($14,332,500) and £3,250,000 ($6,045,000) to deferred grants. These grants are being amortized as related employment costs are expensed.

Capital grants for the construction of the manufacturing facility and production equipment also are amortized into income in 1981 as related capital assets are depreciated. The amortization of all grants for the three months and nine months of fiscal 1981 was $3,061,250 and $6,138,650, respectively.

Source: Company Form 10-K, 1982.

case

13

DEMOCRATIC SOCIALIST REPUBLIC OF SRI LANKA

600,000 acres of Ceylon tea gardens? Yes siree! . . . and 1000 miles of sun-drenched beaches, 400 varieties of exotic birds and butterflies, 2,500-year-old cities, medieval frescoes, modern hotels . . . and mountains carpeted with tea. In short, the best of Asia in one, friendly, English-speaking island country. With 25,300 square miles of unusual, un-spoiled, undiscovered beauty, we may be the last paradise on earth.[1]

Situated on the seaways between East and West, and endowed with con-siderable natural wealth, this compact, pear-shaped land mass was often a vic-tim of invaders from China, India, and the Arabian coasts and in modern history, the Europeans. In the fifteenth century, the Portuguese were attract-ed by spice trading and dominated the small country until supplanted by the Dutch in 1640. In 1796 the British arrived and spent 20 years consolidating their position before annexing the Kandyan kingdom in 1815.

---

[1]Sri Lanka Tourist Bureau, 1982 media promotion.

BACKGROUND

Sri Lanka's (formerly Ceylon) program of economic reforms implemented five years earlier continued in 1982, given renewed impetus with the election of President Junius Jayewardene who was swept into office on a wave of economic discontent in 1977. The 76-year-old president was viewed favorably by the West, the World Bank, and other institutions that had favored his loosening the government controls on industry and commerce. Unquestionably, as President Jayewardene began his new seven-year term on October 21, 1982, with a time of reflection at the White Palace on the Indian Ocean, he was contemplating ways and means of attracting outside investment to provide further boosts to Sri Lanka's economy.

After assuming independence from the British Empire and becoming a full-fledged Commonwealth member in 1948, the country began its trip down the long road of social development. Postindependence politics featured a seesaw shifting of power between two main parties, accompanied by the highly vocal presence of leftist parties. An armed insurrection was spawned by the Marxists in 1971, and after order was restored, a declared state of emergency in the country remained in effect until February 1977. A new constitution was written in 1972. Successive governments pursued generous social welfare policies, diverting a large share of available resources to free education and medical care, free and subsidized food, and subsidized energy and transportation services. The literacy rate was 85 percent in 1982, life expectancy had risen to 67 years, the infant mortality rate had slowed dramatically, and population growth had slowed. Living standards for average citizens in Sri Lanka in the emerging 1980s were substantially better than those in most of the neighboring countries of South Asia.

However, economic growth into the late 1970s did not match progress made in improving distribution of income. Social programs stimulated consumption at the expense of domestic savings and investment. Nationalization and the creation of state corporations expanded the public sector, diminishing investment in the relatively more efficient private sector. Although foreign capital was officially welcomed, such investment was slow to come because of uncertainty over the specter of further nationalization.

Further economic impact came from stagnation of world prices for Sri Lanka's principal export products—tea, rubber, and coconut—and the rapid increase in petroleum prices after 1973. Efforts to increase production of food and agricultural exports were additionally hampered by droughts, declining commodity prices, a rising tax burden on exports, and generally low returns to producers. Overall economic policy was programmed toward keeping consumer prices low, which directly affected producer incentive. By 1977, unemployment had risen to 20 percent of the labor force.

A NEW GOVERNMENT[2]

In mid-1977, with the advent of Mr. Jayewardene's government, programs were initiated to unify and float the exchange rate; to remove exchange controls on imports; to liberalize import licensing; to eliminate government import monopolies; to lift more price controls; to guarantee prices for certain agriculture commodities; to reduce consumer subsidies on rice, sugar, flour, and petroleum products; to increase interest rates to stimulate savings; and to encourage foreign and domestic investment.

The government has concentrated on three major programs to meet its medium-term development goals and to provide sources of quick employment: (1) acceleration of the Mahaweli Ganga irrigation/resettlement/hydroelectric scheme, (2) an urban renewal and housing program, and (3) a Free Trade Zone (FTZ) north of Colombo, the capital city. In 1982, the government was attempting to estimate how much of the Mahaweli Ganga project could be completed by 1985; work had progressed slowly since the program's inception. Plans were to have started construction of 100,000 houses by 1984 under the urban renewal and housing programs. A new parliamentary building and two administrative buildings were also planned. The first FTZ or Investment Promotion Zone (IPZ) was set by the Greater Colombo Economic Commission on a 500-acre tract contiguous to the international airport, about 18 miles north of the capital. By early 1981, formal agreements had been signed for 64 projects; some 23 factories were in production and exporting, and 5 more were in trial production. Total employment was approaching 11,000.

On a sour note, inflation was increasing once more in the early 1980s, estimated to be more than 20 percent in 1982, and the Consumer Price Index was up proportionally, 25 percent by some estimates. Real wages declined in 1980 and 1981, and unemployment was gradually declining, estimated at 15 percent in 1981. An estimated 50,000 Sri Lankans were working in Middle Eastern nations in early 1981.

PROMOTING THE FTZ

After hanging out the welcome sign to foreign investors, seeking to attract capital, technical and management know-how, and knowledge of markets to expand production for export, a series of investment promotion missions was

[2]Portions adapted from U.S. Department of State, *Background Notes, Sri Lanka* (Washington, D.C.: Government Printing Office, April 1980); and U.S. Department of Commerce, International Trade Administration, *Foreign Economic Trends and Their Implications for the United States, Sri Lanka*, (Washington, D.C.: Government Printing Office, August 1981).

undertaken to several countries, including the United States. As of 1981, U.S. direct investment in Sri Lanka was estimated at $7 million. In May 1980, a U.S. government–sponsored investment mission, led by the Overseas Private Investment Corporation, visited the country, and during 1981 an increasing number of American corporations sent representatives to explore opportunities for establishing manufacturing facilities. Several saw it as a viable alternative to locating additional facilities in Europe, but some were apprehensive about power availability, noting that Sri Lanka began to face energy shortages in the late 1970s.

Sri Lanka and the United States have experienced problems over political factors. American economic aid to the country was stopped from 1953 to 1956 because of Ceylon's trading with the People's Republic of China, and again in 1963 assistance was halted when the Ceylonese government failed to pay compensation for the expropriation of two U.S. oil companies' distribution facilities; aid was renewed in 1965 when a reimbursement agreement was signed. Since 1971, when the United States, along with other nations, responded positively to the government's call for support during the insurgency, relations have steadily improved.

In descending order, Sri Lanka's major import sources in 1981 were Japan, Saudi Arabia, the United Kingdom, Iraq, India, Singapore, the United States, the People's Republic of China, Hong Kong, Australia, and Canada. Also in descending order, major export destinations were the United States, the United Kingdom, West Germany, China, Saudi Arabia, Pakistan, Japan, Iran, South Africa, Taiwan, and Australia.

OBJECTIVES OF THE NEW INDUSTRIAL POLICY[3]

Official directives regarding the "new industrial policy" were coalesced into the list presented in Exhibit 1.

GREATER COLOMBO ECONOMIC COMMISSION (GCEC)[4]

GCEC was established to manage the Investment Promotion Zones within Sri Lanka; it is a five-member body headed by a director general, who reports to

[3]"Sri Lanka's Industrial Policy," Ministry of Industries and Scientific Affairs, C. Cyril Mathew, minister, and A. A. Justin Dias, secretary, 1980, via U.S. Department of State Sri Lanka desk officer.
[4]Ibid.

President Jayewardene. IPZ is designed to provide the infrastructure, such as land, power, water, and roadways and to maintain close liaison with public sector organizations, such as transport, communications, clearance of imported cargo, and shipment of export cargo to provide efficient support services.

Exhibit 1

OBJECTIVES OF THE NEW INDUSTRIAL POLICY

1. To make maximum use of indigenous raw materials and other natural resources.
2. To enable widespread employment opportunities to the maximum extent possible, by a choice of appropriate technology and providing the maximum level of productivity.
3. To locate industries as much as possible in rural areas where the majority of the people live, also taking into account the provision of infrastructure, raw material availability, and markets for the finished goods.
4. To foster economic and social progress by enabling the masses of the population to participate in the process of industrialization and enabling them to share directly in the benefits of such industrialization.
5. To establish machinery for the control of industries by society to ensure that no monopolistic industrial concentration would take place that could exploit both the worker as well as the consumer.
6. To give equal opportunities to the private and public sectors to enable rapid progress and expansion.
7. To ensure that public sector institutions are commercially viable. The government will not subsidize any losses except where it is considered a national priority.
8. To make sure that public sector institutions maintain as low a level of prices as possible, consistent with commercial profitability and efficient management, so as not to cast any burden on the consumer.
9. To encourage industrial research to enable domestic fabrication of machinery and equipment and enable an increase in productivity.
10. To foster research, enabling the lower and more efficient utilization of energy dependent on imported fuels and promotion of greater utilization of energy sources available within the country.
11. To reduce the gap that exists between management and employees in industry, both in the public and private sectors, by enabling employees in industries to purchase shares in the institutions where they are employed. This would provide a greater motivation for employees to contribute toward the development of these enterprises.
12. To establish employees councils to provide effective worker participation in management.

As a second IPZ of 211 acres was being established some 12 miles northeast of Colombo, the ministry articulated some of the main features of its investment promotion package (Exhibit 2).

Exhibit 2

IPZ INVESTMENT PROMOTION PACKAGE ELEMENTS

1. Guaranteed foreign investments by the Sri Lanka Constitution
2. A tax holiday of up to 10 years and a further concessionary tax period of up to 15 years
3. Double taxation relief with major countries of the world
4. No limits on equity holdings of foreign investors
5. Free transfer of shares within or outside Sri Lanka
6. No tax or exchange control on such transfers
7. Dividends of nonresident shareholders exempt from any taxes and remittances of such dividends exempt from exchange control
8. No import duty on machinery, equipment, construction materials, and raw materials
9. Such imports and exports exempt from normal import control and exchange control procedures
10. Transfer of capital and proceeds of liquidation exempt from exchange control

---

Your Task:

1. As they seek the status of a full-fledged commercial state, advise officials of the Sri Lankan Ministry of Industries and Scientific Affairs on developing a program to attract foreign investment. Consider how they might package their "product," evaluate their pricing terms, and recommend the design elements of a promotional program for three different countries: the United States, Japan, and India. How would you rate these three as potential candidates for participation in Sri Lanka's Free Trade Zone program?

2. The daughter of a well-known American political figure has asked your advice about what products her firm might consider for export to Sri Lanka. Her firm and its subsidiaries handle products ranging from foodstuffs to heavy machinery. Your first comments are to be speculative—to provide suggestions for her to investigate—and not conclusive at this point.

3. You have been retained by a U.S. manufacturer of electronic devices, a Fortune 500 firm, to evaluate the desirability of Sri Lanka as a location for the company's planned facilities, a $5 million to $10 million plant that will produce a new product expected to be the bellwether of an expanding line of similar items. Initial employment is expected to be 250 to 300 people in assembly operations, 25 electrical engineers, and 12 middle- and upper-level managers. What is your advice? How should the manufacturer proceed?

MIGHTY DOG

Carnation Company, with 1981 net sales of $3.354 billion, produces and markets a number of different dry and canned pet foods for both dogs and cats; principal domestic labels are Friskies, Mighty Dog, Buffet, Bright Eyes, Fish Ahoy, Com 'N Get It, and Chef's Blend, all registered trademarks. In 1980 Carnation introduced Fancy Feast, an "ultragourmet" cat food in small single-serving cans in upstate New York and has gradually expanded that product's distribution, aimed at "hard-core, devoted" cat owners who prefer buying the best available products for their pets. With Fancy Feast, Carnation hoped to parallel the success of its premium canned dog food, Mighty Dog, which had earned one of the dominant positions in its target market segments. Introduced in 1973, Mighty Dog's share of the U.S. gourmet canned dog food market was slightly over 16 percent in 1981. Continued favorable buyer response to both the single-serving 6.5-ounce can and gains by the recently introduced 12.5-ounce size made possible the gourmet product's favorable performance.

THE OVERALL PET FOOD MARKET

Canned pet food group product manager, Miguel Osborne, discussed sales trends for pet food sales in food stores: "In 1975, total pet food dollar sales were estimated to be $2.4 billion, of which cat food accounted for $723 million and dog food $1,675 million; in 1980, the total had risen to $3.6 billion, with dog food amounting to $2,394 million; this year [1981] we expect overall pet food sales to rise by about 10 percent, dog food accounting for roughly 8 percent of the total dollar increase. Canned brands, if our estimates prove out, will increase about 5 percent over last year."

Growing at double-digit rates in the 1960s and 1970s, the pet food business then was considered a prime opportunity. New products were rapidly absorbed. In the 1980s, however, as some brands were expanding while others were shrinking, a leveling off, or maturity, had occurred. Several uncontrollable forces contributed to this situation: new household formations were increasing by 1 to 2 percent annually, there was a recessionary climate, and generic products were emerging as important factors in pet food sales. Estimates varied, but several sources reported a market share of about 8 percent for private-label and generic products as 1981 drew to a close. Compared with branded products, generics were considered by the major pet food marketers and by "hard-core" pet owners to be of inferior quality. Some manufacturers believed that an economic recovery would lead to declines in generic market shares and a resurgence in advertised brands.

In late 1981, a major producer, Ralston Purina, launched a brand priced between generics and Purina Dog Chow, its flagship brand.[1] The product was Mainstay, which in 1980 was heralded as "new proprietary technology . . . unique food nugget [containing] meat and bone meal and vegetable flavored particles."[2] The company expressed pleasure at Mainstay's market acceptance.

THE GOURMET SHARE

"In 1980, gourmet canned dog food accounted for 13 percent of total pet food dollar sales and an estimated 20 percent of all dog food sales," Osborne observed. "We're primarily competing against four other majors—Liggett Group's Alpo, Mars' Kal Kan, General Foods' Cycle, and Quaker Oats' Ken 'L Ration Tender Chunks—with our two brands, Mighty Dog and Friskies Dinners. Liggett is leader with a 29 percent share; we are next with 23 percent total for our two, 16 percent for Mighty Dog and 7 percent for Friskies; Mars posted a 17 percent share; General Foods came in with 10 percent; and Quaker Oats launched its canned version of the Ken 'L Ration Tender Chunks brand, achieving a 6 percent share of case volume. Those are the 1980 figures as we have them; I doubt there will be any dramatic shifts this year. However, we have programmed Mighty Dog's activities to earn a boost of three-tenths of a point, and in 1982 we project a share of 17.8 percent, about 9.4 million cases. That means an increase of 1.4 share points—plus 9 percent—and a 9 percent boost in total cases."

[1]Richard Kreisman, "Purina Goes After Generics," *Advertising Age*, November 23, 1981, p. 1.

[2]Ralston Purina Company, *1980 Annual Report*, p. 8.

PRODUCT ATTRIBUTES

Canned dog food products may be divided into three basic groups:

1. Flavored: less than 25 percent meat
2. Dinner: at least 25 percent meat
3. Pure meat: at least 95 percent meat

The first two categories are mostly water, cereal, and meat by-products—percentages in that order. Mighty Dog was the only leading brand containing "pure meat" products.

Gourmet lines differ among themselves in flavor varieties and in appearance. Mighty Dog has its own extraordinary features: a unique, pure beef variety, with no by-products; unique, single-serving 6.5-ounce can; and selling at a premium price within its category. "Those differences are real," stated Osborne, "but pet owners perceive few differences between gourmet brands in taste, appearance, and nutrition. Nonetheless, many buyers do perceive Mighty Dog and Alpo as having superior pure beef ingredients. Our current advertising communicates the point that 'no other brand has pure beef,' which has reinforced consumer perceptions of our exclusivity."

Comparing cost per pound, canned dog food is slightly more expensive than dry dog food, but less expensive than semimoist formulations. However, on a per feeding basis, gourmet canned dog food costs approximately four times as much as dry dog food, and Mighty Dog had the highest price per pound—an average of 96 cents—within the canned category in 1981. Carnation considered this premium price justifiable because of the brand's single-serving 6.5-ounce can and the product's high-quality ingredients (see Exhibit 1).

PROSPECTS AND PURCHASING DECISIONS

"We are fairly certain," Osborne commented, "that Mighty Dog's prime prospects are all gourmet canned dog food users (59 percent of all canned), but we can also count on some penetration in secondary prospect markets made up of people who are regular or maintenance (41 percent of all canned), semimoist (6 percent of all dog food), and dry dog food purchasers (63 percent of all dog food). Our data show that almost 55 percent of all dog owners vary their dog's diet by feeding multiple types of products, so gourmet competes with maintenance, semimoist, and dry dog food."

As indicated by market research, Mighty Dog's buyers were principally women, ages 25 to 54, who were working at either full-time or part-time paid jobs, who were at least high school graduates, in households reporting $15,000 or more income, and residing in high-population-density counties in northeastern, southern, and western regions of the United States. Sales data patterns revealed no seasonality.

Additionally, research indicated that the gourmet product is used primarily as a main meal for the pet, but it is also mixed with dry dog food by almost

Exhibit 1

MIGHTY DOG PRINT ADVERTISEMENT

"Do you know the difference between beef and beef hash?"

"That's the Mighty Dog Difference!"

"Surprisingly enough, many dog lovers like yourself don't seem to know the difference between Mighty Dog® Beef for Dogs, and other brands like Alpo, Kal-Kan, Cycle, and so forth. The difference is like the difference between beef and beef hash.

"While Mighty Dog Beef is pure beef, like a steak, those others combine meat with other ingredients, like hash. Ingredients like meat by-products and soy flour can make up to 75% of their weight.

"Check the ingredient list on your present dog food, and compare it to Mighty Dog's. You'll find that, although it may say "beef" on the front of the label, only Mighty Dog lists beef as its *number one ingredient.*

"That's the Mighty Dog difference, and speaking for dogs everywhere, I would say it's a mighty big difference."

half of the pet owners. An estimated 3 out of 4 canine connoiseurs enjoying the product weigh less than 30 pounds; about 3 out of 10 weigh less than 10 pounds. The overall dog population tips the scales as follows: almost 6 in 10 less than 25 pounds and 1 in 5 less than 12 pounds.

POSITIONING

Gourmet canned dog food is positioned in the mass media primarily on the basis of taste, nutrition, and quality ingredients. In developing Mighty Dog's marketing plan for 1982, Carnation's staff summarized its appraisal and expectation of competitors' positioning strategies as shown in Exhibit 2.

Exhibit 2

MAJOR COMPETITIVE BRANDS' POSITIONING/COMMUNICATION, 1981

BRAND	STRATEGY	REASON WHY
Alpo	Taste and nutrition/ quality	Dogs love the taste of beef/meat.
Mighty Dog	Taste and quality/ ingredients	Only one brand has pure beef.
Kal Kan	Taste and nutrition	Makes dogs healthy and look good.
Cycle	Nutrition	As dogs change, so do their nutritional needs.
KLR Tender Chunks	Taste and quality	No ordinary canned dog food.

PSYCHOLOGICAL DIMENSIONS

Dog's friendship to humankind is legendary. Tales of heroism abound. Carnation studies consistently reflect consumers' feelings that their dogs:

1. Are members of the family
2. Want variety in their meals
3. Usually will not eat dry food without water, broth, or some wet food

Owners are likely to see beef as the "gold standard" for taste and nutrition and to believe that dry foods provide exercise for gums, while cleaning and sharpening the dog's teeth.

"Our preferred strategy is to reinforce in mass media the frequently heard comment, 'Mighty Dog is the best dog food I can feed my dog,' to promote our advantage of being the only leading canned dog food with pure beef. That's the heart of our creative strategy—going with the strength of uniqueness," Osborne remarked. "Also, in our messages, we must stick with the basic proven themes of a convenient single-serving can, the branding iron as the brand's trademark, and a reassurance of taste that's preferred by dogs."

PROMOTION

Most brands concentrate an overwhelming proportion of advertising dollars in television, mostly network, roughly 25 percent daytime, 55 percent nighttime; about 13 percent in spot television. Print, mainly consumer promotion, gets about 8 percent of the total budget for advertising. Miguel Osborne ranked the spenders, "Alpo is top spender, followed by Ken 'L Ration Tender Chunks, and Kal Kan. Mighty Dog and Cycle outlays in 1980 were at comparable levels. Generally in the industry, canned products' budgets increased while expenditures for dry dog foods dropped about 10 percent."

The major gourmet marketers used couponing, sweepstakes, refunds, premiums, and sampling. An estimated one-fourth of this category's volume was bought on deal terms. "All major brands are dealing in the range of 72 cents to $1.00 a case," Osborne said, "except Tender Chunks, which deals consistently at over $1.00 and sells the industry high of 70 percent on deals." For an example of a planned special consumer offer for Mighty Dog, see Exhibit 3. Another special offer that proved attractive to dog lovers was the 1983 Mighty Dog Calendar premium, which was to be made available in exchange for 4 labels plus $1.00 or free for 30 labels.

"In our promotional budgets," Osborne related, "we spent more on deals than on advertising in 1980, but we reversed that proportion in 1981, and in 1982 we will continue holding that mix—a ratio of approximately 6 to 4, advertising to deals. And we expect to achieve record high volume and share levels in 1982 by maintaining a strong level of advertising behind our proven pure-beef creative strategy and through well-paced and solid consumer-oriented promotional programs. Our principal media target group will be females in families with children and household incomes at $25,000 or more, using television and print to provide national coverage. Major emphasis? We'll go for the opportunity markets."

Your Task:

Assume that Miguel Osborne has engaged you to advise him on strategy and tactics for 1983 through 1985 and to apprise him of what you consider to be the central strategic issues facing (1) the pet food industry in general and (2) the gourmet canned dog food category in particular. Based on your conclusions about threats and opportunities, and Carnation's and Mighty Dog's strengths and weaknesses, present your studied judgments in terms of the four Ps—product, price, promotion, and placement—taking into account the forces of competition, market demographics, sociocultural changes, regulation, and the economic climate.

Exhibit 3

MIGHTY DOG PLANNED DISCOUNT OFFER

case
15

NATIONAL SPORTING GOODS ASSOCIATION

During inflation, recession, and shifting life-styles of the late 1970s and early 1980s, Americans changed their buying habits, postponing new car purchases, putting off buying new wardrobes, and making the old furniture last a couple of years longer than usual. Business slumps and layoffs contributed to a lessening propensity to buy as consumers turned penurious. As buyers adjusted to an economy dramatically altered from a decade earlier, U.S. Department of Commerce data revealed increased spending for housing, utilities, and health and decreased spending for clothing, food and drink, and household expenses. The overall savings rate of after-tax income continued declining while families attempted to maintain their current standard of living.

In the leisure-time markets, some products and services suffered dramatic declines while others enjoyed expanding revenues and profits. Like their European counterparts who cling tenaciously to periodic holidays as means of recreating their motivational steam, North Americans also seemed reluctant to sacrifice their avocations, and so the sporting goods field appeared to be at least slightly recession resistant. Still, with family take-home pay often running several percentage points behind inflation, many consumers were forced to reassess alternatives for their disposable and discretionary income. Yet zeal for pursuit of the good life was not severely disrupted by bottom-line realities.

NSGA President James L. Faltinek, who holds a doctorate in administration from the University of Wisconsin, commented on competitive elements and other factors exerting pressure on sales of sporting goods:

"On a television show recently it was reported that Americans in the past year poured $8 billion worth of quarters into Asteroids, an electronic video game, and that didn't include the others—Space Invaders and Break-Out and the like—that line the bowling alleys, restaurants, and arcades throughout the country.

"That figure—$8 billion—is approximately two-thirds the amount spent during that period on sporting goods in the United States. Computer games represent just one more competitor for the consumers' disposable or leisure dollar.

"One conclusion is this: we at NSGA must undertake joint ventures with other associations in our field to promote sales of sporting goods. I think we are all on the same team, competing for that ever scarcer consumer dollar, and one of my personal goals is to develop closer cooperation among all of us who want to support more effectively the goals that our members hold in common."

An example of interassociation collaboration—focusing on the question of returned goods policies and procedures, a major issue in sporting goods retailing and manufacturing, and a great concern to NSGA—occurred in 1981. Sources of the conflict were manufacturers, who wanted to protect themselves against possible retailer abuse of their returned-goods policies, and retailers, who contended that manufacturers sometimes made it difficult for them to send back merchandise. In a series of discussions between NSGA and the Sporting Goods Manufacturers Association (SGMA), a model returned-goods form was devised to help streamline procedures for retailers and producers. Other associations—Ski Industries America (SIA), American Fishing Tackle Manufacturers Association (AFTMA), Sporting Goods Agents Association (SGAA), National Shooting Sports Foundation (NSSF), and the National Association of Sporting Goods Wholesalers (NASGW)—were invited to contribute their ideas to the form's first draft. In October, at their Fall Market, a merchandise show, in Anaheim, California, NSGA's board approved the form. Initial response from members was favorable. Faltinek and his staff had coordinated this effort from inception to conclusion.

THE MARKET: 1981

Director of Information and Research Thomas Doyle reflected on 1981's results and offered observations on 1982.

"No one will describe 1981 as a star-spangled year. However, the industry didn't fall apart in spite of a rather poor economy. It looks like the sporting goods market eked out a 3 percent increase in retail dollar volume over 1980. Sales of general sporting goods were about $11.68 billion this year. Lackluster is probably the best way to describe 1981, but it did have some bright spots. A few categories—archery, exercise, fishing tackle—outpaced inflation. All showed gains of 10 percent or more at retail.

"For 1982, exercise equipment is forecasted to show the strongest growth, approximately 15 percent, but again, overall sales of sporting goods products will be at around 5 percent, according to this study.[1]

"One trend we're reflecting in the current report is sales of sport footwear; in prior reports, shoe sales were included in various sport categories. Sales of these products amounted to about $1.8 billion in 1980, up 3 percent over 1979, at retail. The gym shoes/sneakers group jumped 16 percent in unit sales and 33 percent in dollars.

"If we look at the top 10 product categories for 1978 through 1981, it seems highly likely these same groups will be the 1982 and 1983 leaders, also. The top 10 will be athletic and sport clothing, team sport equipment, sport footwear, firearms equipment, exercise equipment, skiing equipment, fishing tackle, camping equipment, and golf equipment.

"All our members are continually making merchandising and inventory decisions for the coming year. So statistics, coupled with operating and other data in our sales and cost studies, are proving to be valuable to sporting goods dealers who belong to NSGA. And this information helps our association plan ways to serve our membership better."

Clearly, competition and economic conditions—inflation, recession, stagflation, or whatever sobriquet economists and politicians attach to circumstances surrounding income and spending—directly affect the fortunes of sporting goods makers and sellers. None is immune to these so-called "external influences," although some suffer the consequences and others reap the rewards to greater or lesser degrees, depending on their specialties and locations and management skills.

As 1982 advanced to center stage, some 4,600 sporting goods retailers, who operate 10,000 stores, were members of National Sporting Goods Association, which had recently relocated from its property on North Michigan Avenue in Chicago to leased space in nearby Mount Prospect, Illinois. Supplier—called "associate"—members numbered about 2,600. Other members were classified as wholesaler, agent, or personal, all together accounting for a small percentage of total membership.

Numerous segments comprise the sporting goods retailing marketplace:

Mass Merchandisers. Department stores, such as Sears, Penney's, and Montgomery Ward, and discount stores, such as K-Mart, Zayre, and Target.

Sporting Goods Stores. General, or full-line, retailers; specialty stores, such as ski shops and gun shops; and pro shops, retail operations attached to a sport facility such as a golf course or a bowling alley.

[1]*The Sporting Goods Market in 1982*, a survey and statistical report, prepared by Irwin Broh and Associates, Des Plaines, Illinois, for National Sporting Goods Association; 80,000 U.S. families were studied.

Other Retail. High-fashion department stores such as Saks and Neiman-Marcus; direct mail, such as L. L. Bean, Orvis, and Eddie Bauer; catalog show-rooms—Service Merchandise is an example; toy stores—Toys "R" Us is an example of this classification; drugstores, such as Osco, Walgreen's, and Skagg's; hardware stores, for example, Tru Value and Coast-to-Coast; and military base and post exchanges.

Based on estimates from the 1977 U.S. Census of Retail, there were about 14,490 sporting goods retail firms in the United States; of this number, some 7,865 (54 percent) were general sporting goods stores and 6,625 (46 percent) were specialty shops. NSGA members are primarily in general and specialty businesses, the most active groups in the association. Other retailers apparently joined just for benefits of the information provided.

Doyle expressed some frustration about inability of his data system to segment membership by style of retailing (full-line and specialty); by dominant products in the stores' product mixes (tennis shop, golf shop, tennis/ski, fishing/hunting, and so on); and by annual retail sales volume. Developing this analytic and reporting capability, he conjectured, would enable NSGA to target products and services for specific groups of members. The association prospect mailing list was also heterogeneous.

"Our 1982 study has been useful in developing new services, but we find that sometimes the store owners have difficulty clarifying what products and services they need from us. In May, for example, we did a telephone survey of 70 members and found that, unaided, 7 of these suggested services NSGA might develop for them. However, when asked to rate 10 existing services, several—the magazine, the buying guide, and a manufacturers' directory—came out high; the insurance program fared poorly. Overall, only 3 of the 70 named a product or service for which they might be willing to pay.

"We did a focus group in April and got some valuable information to help improve our annual Cost-of-Doing-Business Survey. That was very useful."

THE NATIONAL SPORTING GOODS ASSOCIATION—A PROFILE

One of the 10 biggest retail trade associations in the United States, NSGA is first in both total membership and budget in the entire industry. Other groups—SGMA, AFTMA, SIA, NASGW, and SGAA—sponsor events competitive to NSGA's trade shows, not to mention 15 regional trade shows arranged by sporting goods agents and 30 specialized shows. An example of competitive impact that dents NSGA's revenues was the introduction in 1974 of a trade show, under the banner of manufacturers of shooting sports equipment, that led to a loss of approximately 300 exhibitors and considerable revenues for the NSGA convention held later that year.

NSGA's mission—outlined in its bylaws—is to develop, improve, and promote the business of retailers and other members of the sporting goods industry; to further the business interests of and promote friendly relationships among its members; to study ways and means of improving business methods; to establish trade standards; and to compile and distribute to its members statistics and information regarding the industry. In association promotional literature, these statements of purpose sometimes are reduced: "to help sell more sporting goods, through the retailer, at a profit." While senior management professed consensus on these general notions, it was not clear that middle management and support staff clearly perceived this mission.

Faltinek expressed senior management's view of the mission and pride in NSGA's accomplishments: "The National Sporting Goods Association has been a leader in the industry for over 53 years, and as we move through the present economic uncertainty, NSGA has strengthened its commitment to help our members meet these times, to survive and prosper. All of our traditional services have been updated to become even more cost effective and useful for our members. Our educational seminars, led by experts, have been well received; NSGA's information center helps members get answers to almost anything they wish to know about the sporting goods business; and our special resource and guide books and the improved *Sports Retailer* magazine continue to offer ways of improving the state-of-the-art of sports retailing management. Now, more than ever, our members depend upon us for support."

The association's products and services are designed to help members reduce operating expenses—insurance programs, directory of toll-free telephone numbers of industry suppliers, discount on Master Card and VISA credit cards, and freight auditing service—and to provide information for more effective and efficient operations—educational programs, "Cost-of-Doing-Business Survey," buying guide, and information center publications. Smaller sporting goods stores are the principal users; few of the offerings are geared to larger retailers and specialty stores. While some books are a decade old, and their style and appearance dated, the contents of most are considered by NSGA staff to be excellent. According to department heads, whether or not the rate of sales of those publications warranted expenses of graphic and other updating is debatable.

Faltinek puts it this way: "Our long-range goal, as I see it, is to provide a mix of products and services to help retailers be more profitable. The short-range goal is to increase our membership base and the number of products and services offered to members. I'd like to see us add 800 new members by March 31 and to retain present membership at a rate of 90 percent. From the financial perspective, improved liquidity is a critical short-term goal. With the move from North Michigan Avenue, a major portion of our assets is no longer tied up in real estate, so we will be able to take more risks and do more R&D than previously—these require a substantial investment of money as well as time."

Until 1978, the association relied principally upon six full-time or part-time field representatives to identify prospective members, who were contacted only infrequently or not at all because of time limitations and an inclination to call on members instead of contacting prospects. In 1981, the field sales team was reduced to two representatives. Other sources of identifying new members were trade show lists of buyers, telephone books from the hundred largest U.S. cities, and the Dun & Bradstreet reporting services. The association's marketing was not centralized; rather, responsibility for products and services was spread over various departments.

The NSGA membership brochure outlines activities sponsored and products and services offered. Exhibit 1 describes trade shows; Exhibit 2, *Sports Retailer* magazine; Exhibit 3, other exclusive publications of NSGA; Exhibit 4, research data available to members; Exhibit 5, educational seminars; and Exhibit 6, what each type of member receives. These, in effect, constitute the Association's "product," pricing for which, as given in Exhibit 7, depends upon the category of membership. From 1970 until 1981, retailer membership dues were $60, raised to the new minimum of $75, and ranging up to $225, effective 1982. Retailer sales volume determined dues assessment.

Retailer membership accounted for slightly less than 6 percent of NSGA income in 1982, while according to the American Society of Association Executives (ASAE), associations with budgets comparable with NSGA's derived about 50 percent of their income from membership dues. Services purchased by both members and nonmembers contributed slightly less than 2 percent of association income, compared with approximately 14 percent of income from services and products for associations of similar size. In 1981 NSGA began reviewing its products and services with a view toward analyzing whether or not a more substantial contribution to income could be realized with new or improved offerings.

Periodically, the association conducts special membership drives, with offers attached to the front cover of a copy of *Sports Retailer* sent free of charge to a list of potential members and headlined: "If you act today, you can receive a year's subscription to *Sports Retailer* magazine, *plus* all of NSGA's Services & Benefits at 50% *off* regular membership dues."

Pricing was seen as important in attracting new members and in planning educational programs. For example, seminars with fees of $165 early in 1981 drew few registrants; seminars later in the year with fees of $95 to $125 drew 15 to 20 enrollments; a one-day seminar with a $35 fee, held in conjunction with the association's fall trade show, drew 40 participants. Membership survey data indicated members often expressed interest in various seminars providing they were "close" to the members' locations.

Three internal vehicles—the monthly magazine, the bimonthly newsletter, and direct-mail pieces—were the principal means of contacting members with news and offers about products and services. External advertising promoted the trade shows because it was judged that the level of participation in these events justified the expense of additional advertising. Because of the industry visibility and importance of NSGA trade shows and because of the asso-

Exhibit 1

TRADE SHOWS

The National Sporting Goods Association sponsors the largest and most effective sporting goods trade shows in the Western Hemisphere. The NSGA Convention and Show, held annually in the beginning of February, attracts approximately 1,600 U.S. and world-wide exhibitors. For the convenience of the buyers and exhibitors, product exhibit areas are organized by category: Camping, Hunting, Fishing, Winter and Water Sports, Physical Fitness and Exercise Equipment, Active Sportswear, Tennis and Racquetball, Trophies and Awards and Heat Applied Graphics on one floor; and Athletic Clothing, Equipment and General Sporting Goods on two floors.

Over 45,000 industry members attended the Annual NSGA Convention and Show. Highlights of the four day Show include the Industry Breakfast Meeting, Educational and Product Seminars and twice daily fashion shows.

NSGA's second major trade show in the United States is the NSGA Fall Market, held annually for industry members.

The Fall Market is a full-line sporting goods show featuring Camping, Fishing, Water Sports, Athletic Clothing, Equipment, General Sporting Goods, Tennis and Racquetball, and Trophies and Awards. Educational and Product Seminars are also held during the three day Market.

Both the Annual NSGA Convention and Show and the Annual NSGA Fall Market serve manufacturers, importers and manufacturers' agents, as well as meeting the buying needs of wholesalers and retailers. There is no charge for registration for either Show for members of NSGA and no charge for preregistration.

Source: Excerpted from NSGA membership brochure, 1982, with permission.

Exhibit 2

SPORTS RETAILER MAGAZINE

Sports Retailer (formerly **Selling Sporting Goods**) is the official publication of the NSGA, mailed monthly to members as part of their membership benefit package. Nonmembers must pay $30 annually for 12 issues of the slick, glossy, full-color publication, which is edited in the interests of the **Sports Retailer.**
Every issue includes

An in-depth look at a segment of the sporting goods industry, like **Sportlook,** a fashion/footwear prospectus, including stories on private labeling, fitting women athletes, and franchises

Current news of the volatile sporting goods industry, both on the local level and the national level, including a "Washington Update"

Helpful columns on retail management, inventory control, costs of doing business, computerization, store planning, team distributors, and agents

Sections on merchandising, marketing, and advertising—the best in the industry

Exclusive industry market research reports, based on interviews with 40,000 families

The latest new product information, catalog offerings, and point-of-purchase ideas

Interviews with key industry people

A monthly look at a successful retailer and what made him that way

Sports Retailer competes graphically with the best of the business press, because it competes with many publications for the time and attention of the sports retailer. It's a "quick read," yet it provides the nitty-gritty, how-to-do-it information retail management needs.
Merely one idea in any single issue of **Sports Retailer** can pay for your membership in NSGA. SR is a tangible benefit—one you can use and enjoy 12 months a year.

Source: Excerpted from NSGA membership brochure, 1982, with permission.

Exhibit 3

PUBLICATIONS

The National Sporting Goods Association offers a wide and varied list of publications in addition to **Sports Retailer** magazine, **Bottom Lines,** the **Buying Guide,** and the **Cost-of-Doing-Business** survey. A complete list follows. These publications can be purchased by NSGA members at reduced prices. For pricing information, contact the Membership Services Department at NSGA.

Store Design: Planning for Profit

Management and Merchandising for the Smaller Retailer

The Retail Profit Wheel: How It Turns

Retail Advertising: A Basic Guide, 158 pp.

A Guide for Outside Sporting Goods Salesmen, 78 pp.

Complying with Federal Wage-Hour Law & Regulations, 58 pp.

A System of Simplified Inventory Control, 66 pp.

Federal Fair Employment Practice Laws: A Survival Guide for Retailers, 32 pp.

Banking for the Non-Banker, 58 pp.

Starting and Managing a Small Business of Your Own, 96 pp.

Universal Vendor Marking Code Book, 55 pp.

The **Product Knowledge Fact Booklets** provide descriptive information on 22 separate topics from "Archery" to "Water Sports," as written by a former sporting goods buyer. These useful booklets can save hours of time by introducing new employees to the products you carry. Booklets range from 16 to 108 pages each.

NSGA's annual **Buying Guide** is a reference manual of sporting goods and services. The **Buying Guide** categorizes the products of sport-

Exhibit 3 (Cont.)

ing goods manufacturers under specific headings by general sport classification. The major sections in the Buying Guide are Sporting Goods
Industry Suppliers, which includes manufacturers' street addresses and
telephone numbers and lists key personnel; the Product Index and loca-
tor, which lists each manufacturer or source, showing city and state under
each product heading; the Brand Name Index; a directory of sporting
goods associations and institutions that serve the industry; and a directory
of NSGA Member Manufacturers' Representatives and the lines they represent. The annual NSGA, **Buying Guide** is a timesaver for the sporting
goods industry. It lists suppliers for 70 major categories of sporting goods
products broken down into 1,200 subcategories representing more than
3,600 manufacturers.

NSGA's memo to management, the bimonthly **Bottom Lines,** keeps
retailers and manufacturers on top of the latest in the industry and in the
nation. **Bottom Lines** contains all the up-to-date news on the sporting
goods industry . . . sales figures, trends, government developments, plus
upcoming NSGA events. **Bottom Lines** is free with your NSGA membership.

Show Business Report is a newsletter for associate members. It is
published every six to eight weeks, containing updates on NSGA's Trade
Shows: booth availability, hotel reservation information, directory listing
and advertising deadlines, and other pertinent information for trade show
exhibitors and potential exhibitors. **Show Business Report** is free with
your associate membership.

Source: Excerpted from NSGA membership brochure, 1982, with permission.

---

ciation's unique research, trade periodicals provide frequent publicity, and
national business publications outside the industry often cite statistical releases. Membership signup was promoted by direct mail only.

Sports Retailer was given not just a new name in 1981, but also new
graphics and a revised editorial positioning as a management-oriented periodical. An independent research study of reader preference showed NSGA's key
print voice to be a close second to the leader, *Sporting Goods Dealer,* an 81-
year-old trade magazine and the first in the sporting goods industry. A continuing slide in number of advertising pages in *Sports Retailer* had slowed over
the previous three years and a turnaround seemed imminent, even though
Sports Retailer's circulation was less than that of its competitors. *Sports Retail-*

Exhibit 4

RESEARCH—INFORMATION

The National Sporting Goods Association prepares two major research reports—one for its retailer (regular) members ("Cost-of-Doing-Business Survey"), the other for manufacturer (associate) members ("The Sporting Goods Market"). Because of its scope and regional demographics, larger retailers often make use of "The Sporting Goods Market."

COST-OF-DOING-BUSINESS SURVEY

This survey covers important financial and cost aspects of a retail sporting goods operation—sales, inventory levels and turns, markups, income before taxes, and profitability. It provides sales and inventory analysis, operating expense analysis, financial ratio analysis, and balance sheet ratio analysis—all important numbers to determine how you are doing compared with the average sporting goods store.

THE SPORTING GOODS MARKET

This consumer research, based on interviews with 80,00 U.S. families, reports sporting goods sales by product category with key descriptions of consumers—age, income, region of the country, and so on. This research allows you to look at long-term trends in various sport categories—information important in choosing to expand or contract departments, identifying regional preferences, and much more.

The NSGA Information Center, a new service to members of the Association, is prepared to respond to retailer members' questions quickly and efficiently. The Center has materials to provide information on

Brand names

Company names, addresses, phone numbers

Suppliers of offbeat or unusual products

RN and WPL textile identification numbers

Statistics on the sporting goods industry

Specific aspects of retail operation

Industry-related trade and consumer associations

Exhibit 4 (Cont.)

The Information Center has gathered trade show directories, magazines, books, newspaper clippings—materials to assist you in your store operation. The Information Center, professionally staffed to answer your needs, frees you to spend more time running your business.

The Information Center is investigating the types of resources it should possess to be most useful for NSGA members. These will be added as the Center expands to meet retailer needs more effectively.

Source: Excerpted from NSGA membership brochure, 1982, with permission.

Exhibit 5

EDUCATIONAL SEMINARS

To meet the marketing and merchandising challenges of the 1980s, something new was needed—an ongoing educational program that would keep NSGA members in tune with the rapidly changing times and the volatile economy. In response to a mandate from NSGA membership, the Education Department was created in 1980 for the express purpose of offering educational opportunities to NSGA members and to the entire sporting goods industry.

The new Education Department has created programs geared toward the sporting goods retailer, held regionally as well as nationally, with subject matter ranging from the latest electronic retailing methods to "How To" motivate and train sales personnel and from store security methods to "How To" market, merchandise, and sell specialty sporting items. There is a constant search for new and pertinent subject matter that will assist NSGA members in learning the latest retailing methods to help them increase profits.

Regional seminars are held in major cities around the country where there is a large concentration of retailers. Considerations such as employee down time, travel expenses, and total overall seminar costs are taken seriously by the Education Department so that the best is offered with the least expense and inconvenience.

"AT-SHOW" SEMINARS

At both the NSGA Fall Market (October in Anaheim, California) and the NSGA Annual Convention and Show (February in Chicago) seminars are an integral part of the trade shows. "At-Show" seminars are held daily,

Exhibit 5 (Cont.)

where and when members of the industry gather. Hundreds of retailers and manufacturers have walked away from the "At-Show" seminars with fresh, new business ideas.

NSGA MANAGEMENT CONFERENCE

Each year the Association holds the Management Conference in a different location—a four-day gathering of industry leaders—both retailers and manufacturers—through a common sharing of business knowledge. The speakers at the Management Conference are often the most successful members of the industry, willing to share their expertise with other outstanding leaders. Management from all across the United States attend this conference year after year to polish up their skills, making this event one of the most beneficial experiences of the business year.

Source: Excerpted from NSGA membership brochure, 1982, with permission.

Exhibit 6

MEMBERSHIP BENEFITS

As a **Regular Member** of the National Sporting Goods Association, you will receive the following benefits on a **no-charge** basis:

>   Free registration and preregistration at NSGA's trade shows
>   Subscription to **Sports Retailer** magazine (12 issues per year)
>   NSGA's memo to management, **Bottom Lines** (6 or more issues per year)
>   The Cost-of-Doing-Business survey
>   The NSGA Buying Guide
>   Unlimited use of NSGA's Information Center
>   Representation in Washington, D.C., by an NSGA "watch-dog" service

And available to a **Regular Member** at special **low** rates are

>   The Annual Sporting Goods Market survey
>   NSGA publications, including 22 product knowledge booklets (see complete list in "Publications" section)
>   Low-cost group term and comprehensive medical insurance
>   Worker's compensation insurance available through the Dodson Insurance Company in 31 states
>   Product liability insurance
>   Master Card/VISA program with Harris Trust Bank of Chicago

Exhibit 6 (Cont.)

Freight auditing service
Attendance at all NSGA educational seminars at special membership registration
     fees
Attendance at NSGA's management conference at special membership fees
Reduced travel rates by special arrangement

As an **Associate Member** of the National Sporting Goods Association, you will receive the following benefits on a **no-charge** basis:

The right to exhibit at NSGA's trade shows
Subscription to **Sports Retailer** magazine (12 issues per year)
NSGA's memo to management, **Bottom Lines** (6 or more issues per year)
Show Business Report (6 or more issues per year)
Unlimited use of NSGA's Information Center
The Annual Sporting Goods Market survey

And available to an **Associate Member** at special **low** rates are

NSGA publications (see complete list in "Publications" section)
Low-cost group term life and comprehensive medical insurance
Worker's compensation insurance, available in 31 states through the Dodson Insur-
     ance Group
Product liability insurance
Freight auditing service
Attendance at all NSGA educational seminars at special membership fees
Attendance at NSGA's management conference at special membership fees
Reduced travel rates by special arrangement

As a **Sustaining Regular** or **Sustaining Associate Member** of the National Sporting Goods Association, you will receive the following **additional** benefits on a **no-charge** basis:

Membership in **Sports Foundation,** a nonprofit organization that encourages the
     development of recreation programs and resources
Invitation to a special NSGA function at the February Convention & Show (for sus-
     taining regular members only)
The Annual Sporting Goods Market survey
Special badge recognition at NSGA's trade shows

And available to **Sustaining Regular** or **Sustaining Associate Members** are

Additional subscriptions to **Sports Retailer** magazine for your employees at a special
     discount rate

Source: Excerpted from NSGA membership brochure, 1982, with permission.

Exhibit 7

1982 MEMBERSHIP CATEGORIES

REGULAR MEMBERSHIP

For sporting goods retailers, annual dues are based on total gross annual sales. Includes all items listed under "benefits" in Exhibit 6 (membership benefits).

GROUP	SALES VOLUME	DUES
1	Up to $299,000	$75 per year
2	$300,000 to $649,000	$100 per year, plus one additional year's subscription to *Sports Retailer* magazine
3	$650,000 to $999,000	$150 per year plus one additional service package*
4	$1,000,000 and over	$225 per year plus two additional service packages

ASSOCIATE MEMBERSHIP

For manufacturers and suppliers. Includes all items listed under "benefits" in Exhibit 6.

$150 annual dues, plus additional $50 annually for foreign membership except Canada

SUSTAINING REGULAR AND ASSOCIATE MEMBERSHIP

Includes all items listed under "benefits" in Exhibit 6.

$50 annual dues above regular and associate membership dues

PERSONAL MEMBERSHIP

Available only to employees of members. Dues include subscription to **Sports Retailer** magazine and personal membership card.

$25 annual dues

Exhibit 7 (Cont.)

PERSONAL AGENT MEMBERSHIP

For individual agents. Includes a subscription to **Sports Retailer** plus eligibility for NSGA's insurance programs and a personal membership card.

$25 annual dues

---

*A service package consists of *Sports Retailer* magazine (12 issues), *Bottom Lines* (newsletter, 6 or more issues a year), the NSGA Buying Guide, and the "Cost-of-Doing-Business Survey."

---

er and other industry magazines suffered advertising declines in 1981. Another publication, *Sporting Goods Business,* offered increasingly tough competition to all other contenders.

MEMBER AND BOARD PROFILES

In addition to the Association's sporting goods retailer members, who operate an estimated 10,000 stores, sporting goods departments of many major retail chains are Association members, although these chains are not included in the estimate of number of stores operated by members. In a study conducted in

---

Exhibit 8

AFFILIATION OF NSGA BOARD OF DIRECTORS

Charles E. Caravati, past chairman, Dixie Sporting Goods Co., Inc., Richmond, Virginia
Robert E. P. Cherry, chairman, Cherry's Sporting Goods, Geneseo, Illinois
David N. Sington, vice chairman, Fred Sington, Inc., Huntsville, Alabama
Robert S. Boyer, treasurer, Doak Walker Sports Center, Inc., Dallas, Texas
Harvey H. Fox, Anderson's Sporting Goods, Inc., Salem, Oregon
Jerry Gart, Gart Brothers Sporting Goods Co., Denver, Colorado
Willis K. 'Kep' Harding, Kep Harding's Sport Shop, Inc., Lincoln, Nebraska
Steven C. Hauff, Dakota Sports, Inc., Sioux Falls, South Dakota
Robert Kislin, Bob Kislin's, Inc., Toms River, New Jersey
David L. Pieffer, Tuffy Brooks Sporting Goods, Dayton, Ohio
Ron Weston, Sam Manson Sporting Goods, Ltd., Hamilton, Ontario
John Cook, The Athletic House, Inc., Knoxville, Tennessee
Howard Willis, Willis Sporting Goods, Reseda, California

the fall of 1980, 72 percent of NSGA retailer members operated one store, 16 percent operated two, and 12 percent three stores or more. Approximately 49 percent had estimated 1980 retail sales volume of $300,000 or less.[2] The majority of sporting goods businesses affiliated with the Association are of entrepreneurial origin. Supplier members, unlike retailer members, have no voting power; these associate members are permitted to exhibit at NSGA trade shows.

Exhibit 8 indicates the affiliation and geographical dispersion of NSGA's board of directors, and Exhibit 9 represents the 1981–1982 chairman's interest in communicating with members.

[2]"Deciding NSGA's Future: A Survey of the Membership," September 1980.

Exhibit 9

WE NEED TO HEAR FROM YOU

This is my first opportunity as Chairman of the NSGA Board of Directors to talk with many of you. My purpose for this brief message is to open the lines of communication between the membership and the NSGA Board and staff.

For me, it's an honor to serve on the Board. During my 5 years on the Board, I have come to know my fellow board members. They are smart businessmen with the ability to look beyond the moment and see the big picture.

Also during this time, I have come to know the NSGA staff. They are sincere, hardworking people who, on a daily basis, serve the needs of the membership.

Both the Board and the staff want to know how they can better serve you. You and I know no matter how well a job is done, there is always the possibility to do it better.

But we need to hear from you. We need to know what your problems are so we may develop programs that can help you and your fellow retailers solve these problems.

I'm asking you to get in touch with the director in your district. These men are listed on this page. They are interested in knowing more about you and your business.

As a director, I get too little input. It's understandable; we are all busy running our stores. Picking up the phone or jotting a note takes time out of our active days.

But one of the things NSGA can do for you is help you save time and money. We can also help you make money. Anyone who has ever attended one of the fine NSGA seminars knows he learned more from the seminar that the price of admission. Seminars are only one of NSGA's services.

Contact your district director, your NSGA fieldman or call the NSGA member service department in Chicago. You may find NSGA offers services you weren't aware of. This can only help you because you now pay for many of these services with your membership dues.

Along with communicating with staff and directors you can do another thing to make the Association better. Convince non-member retailers in your area to join NSGA. This isn't a difficult task. Tell them only one way the Association has helped you. Or put them in touch with a director of the NSGA member service staff.

The more members NSGA has, the more services the Association can offer and still keep dues reasonable.

As good as it is, NSGA can improve. But we need and welcome your help. Tell us what we're doing right. Tell us what we're doing wrong. Tell us how we can better serve you.

Source: Charles E. Caravati, "Across the Board," column in *Sports Retailer,* April 1981, p. 10.

CENTRALITY OF TRADE SHOWS

NSGA sponsors two major trade shows; the largest U.S. sporting goods trade show, held at McCormick Place in Chicago each year drew 1,520 exhibitors and 19,328 buyers in 1980. At the annual Anaheim, California, trade show in 1980, 720 exhibitors participated. Exhibit 10 indicates the association's continuing emphasis on trade shows.

Faltinek has acknowledged the effect of inflationary prices on trade show

---

Exhibit 10

WHAT I LEARNED AT SIA

I'd like to start out my column this month with a thank you. This is the beginning of my second year as chief executive of the NSGA. During the past year, I've learned a great deal about the sporting goods industry. But I could not have gained as much knowledge without the generous help of many of you. Thank you very much.

It's no surprise that one area of concentration for me has been tradeshows. Fortunately, I had extensive background in trade shows and conventions before joining NSGA. And, NSGA has the most capable staff in the industry in this area. So my task has been to learn more about the NSGA tradeshows per se and to discover ways to make our shows better. By better, I mean more effective for both exhibitors and buyers.

While we have a time-tested and professional tradeshow staff at NSGA, it is sometimes necessary to observe what others are doing with their tradeshows. This way we can compare our shows, discover what they do better and integrate these things into our shows. Frankly, we get calls throughout the year from show managers who also want to learn from us. It is a sharing atmosphere.

Last month Paul Prince, NSGA manager of trade shows, and I attended both the SIA Ski Show and the SCA Snow Show in Las Vegas. We were impressed by many things these shows had to offer.

There is no question the Ski Show is well-run. It is a quality show with quality buyers. SIA has established buyer criteria designed to keep marginal people out of the show. Show management charges a $250 guest fee. Manufacturers make the rules that govern themselves. This is a major difference between manufacturers and retailers.

Exhibits at the show are not only large but exceedingly well-done. Each exhibitor has areas where his salespeople and the buyer can go to talk business. Many exhibitors put on fashion shows which were in excellent taste as well as highly entertaining. Exhibitors are out after the business, and in some cases, they have spared no expense to make a sale.

More than just the attendees benefit from this show. SIA, like NSGA, plows the profits from the show back into the industry. A majority of the many shows in our industry do not do this.

Traffic at this year's Ski Show was unfortunately but understandably light. The industry is coming off two bad winters. January's snowfall in the Sierras and Rockies proved too little, too late. The lackluster economy hasn't helped matters either. Manufacturers report retailers are very much in arrears.

Retailers at the show were extremely cautious, according to exhibitors I spoke with. Their open-to-buys were reportedly smaller than previous years.

Although a few exhibitors feel six days is too long for a show, many retailers do not. Typically, buyers spend the first three days walking the show and the last three placing their orders.

The Snow Show offers a full line of exhibitors the majority of whom are in the outdoor sports.

While many feel NSGA already dominates the trade show business in our industry, we intend to improve our show even more in '81 and '82. Size is secondary to quality. In the future, NSGA will incorporate many of the show policies which work so well for SIA.

Source: President James Faltinek, "On the Line," column in *Sports Retailer*, April 1981, p. 6.

attendance: "The one thing escalating faster than the national debt is hotel rates. Those who attend our shows are vocal about it and it definitely affects our attendance. The trade show staff and I have negotiated hard with many of the hotels serving attendees of our Chicago show. And our results are better than those negotiators involved in the baseball strike.

"Several hotels have agreed to hold the line and a few have even agreed to lower rates from those charged during the 1981 February show. One concession from several is a flat rate on the double/twin room. Starting with the 1982 show we will book rooms in five new hotels that have guaranteed a $50 single rate and a $60 twin/double rate.

"Another big component of show costs is airline fares. But by careful shopping we can usually get bargains. For the 1981 fall show, American Airlines is offering special fares for those attending the NSGA Fall Market.

"For the Chicago show we are offering complete packages that will include air fare, hotel, some meals, and airport transfers for as little as $300. We are working through the same travel agency that worked with NSGA on our European Trade Mission."

ORGANIZATIONAL STRUCTURE

According to American Society of Association Executives data, the average staff size for associations with a budget the size of NSGA's was 72; NSGA's staff numbered 40. Major departments were trade shows, 5 persons; publications, 7; education and business development, 3; research and information, 2; and membership fulfillment, 4. Operations and support personnel made up the balance. Exhibit 11 provides an overview of NSGA departments, the heads of which report to the president.

LEGISLATIVE WATCH

A significant and uncontrollable influence on the fortunes of sporting goods manufacturers and retailers is regulatory activity, which receives continual attention from NSGA leadership. To illustrate some of these points of interest, Exhibit 12 contains excerpts from 1981 editions of the association magazine.

TRENDS AFFECTING NSGA

In the early 1980s there was a marked increase in sporting goods merchandising by department stores and discount chains; franchising continued to grow;

Exhibit 11

OVERVIEW OF STAFF DEPARTMENTS AND MANAGERS

Department of Education and Business Development

Headed by senior staff person Don Oker. Plans seminar programs and responsible for recruiting new members for NSGA. Ruth Leigh is public relations manager.

Department of Membership Services

Manager Ken Baldwin's main job is to develop member services and to monitor existing ones such as the insurance plan, worker's compensation, and freight auditing. Heads NSGA's Athletic Team Distributor Division and serves as secretary of the joint NSGA/SGMA (Sporting Goods Manufacturing Association) Returned Goods Policy Committee and the Industry Hall of Fame Committee.

Department of Trade Shows

Robert J. Youngblood, over 30 years with NSGA, is vice president and director of this department. Produces two of the world's largest trade shows, drawing almost 70,000 registrants annually and 2,500 exhibitors. Paul Prince, manager of trade shows, is the associate member's primary contact when placing space reservations for shows; he coordinates exhibitors' on-site activities as well.

Department of Information and Research

Thomas B. Doyle directs this department, which was created in 1980 with two main tasks: to generate statistics on sales and costs in the industry and enhance information services offered to members. He formerly was associate publisher of **Selling Sporting Goods,** which evolved into **Sports Retailer.**

Department of Communications

Headed by John O'Neill, this department produces 400-page NSGA Buying Guide and other publications, including **Sporting Retailer.**

Exhibit 12

EXCERPTS FROM ARTICLES ON LEGISLATIVE DEVELOPMENTS

"PENTAGON GIVES NOD TO THE 9 MM." The Pentagon has finally de-cided to phase out the standard Colt .45 pistols and replace them with a metric-gauge, 9 mm model weapon now standard in NATO countries. . . . Gun dealers and gun-selling retailers are nervous about the effect of (pos-sible) dumping Army surplus weapons on the market. . . . Also . . . Ameri-can manufacturers fear it (contract for 9 mm weapon manufacturing) will be awarded to a European manufacturer already geared for metric weap-ons building. . . . Yet another fear is that the Pentagon will decide to go metric on its other standard weapons and create more havoc for manufac-turers and the marketplace. (October 1981, p. 10)

"REGULATIONS ON THE HIT LIST." Under the management of Vice Pres-ident Bush, the Reagan administration is examining the possibility of eas-ing certain government regulations, [one] requiring colleges and universities to spend comparable amounts on men's and women's sports programs, known also as Title IX. . . . Retailers and team dealers may have reason for concern . . . if schools return to their old discriminatory ways, retailers and team dealers may lose some of their previously expanding girl's and women's market. (October 1981, p. 10)

"CLEAN WATER, AIR ACTS ON DECK." There is talk of easing up on the requirements of these laws . . . to save cost for businesses which release pollutants into the air and water. In addition to the environmental groups, fishing and outdoor sports associations are joining together to help protect the . . . Acts. (April 1981, p. 7)

"CPSC, KAWASAKI MOVE TO CORRECT SNOWMOBILE SAFETY PROB-LEM." Following reports of serious injuries involving snowmobile drive tracks, a $3–4 million program has been announced by the U.S. Consumer Product Safety Commission and Kawasaki Motors Corp. (USA). Although the company denies any failure on its part to report potential problems . . . CPSC has exacted a $90,000 fine . . . alleging . . . such a failure. . . . the company has voluntarily instituted a recall program through June of this year of its 1978–79 Invader and Intruder model snowmobiles. (April 1981)

"TOUGH GUN LAWS, CRIME STATISTICS DON'T MATCH." A recent study by the National Rifle Association finds that major metropolitan areas with the toughest gun laws also lead the nation in their rates of violent crime. Boston heads the list of the most "violent" cities, followed by New York, Baltimore, Washington, D.C., and Cleveland. All of these cities have strict licensing, registration requirements, mandatory sentences for crimes with guns and/or outright bans on private gun ownership. . . . firearm in-volvement in murder declined from 67.9 percent in 1974 to 62.4 percent

Exhibit 12 (Cont.)

in 1980. Additionally, handgun involvement in murder has fallen from 54
percent in 1974 to 50 percent in 1980 . . . despite the influx of more than
13 million new handguns into the U.S. during this same time period. (November 1981)
"SAGEBRUSH REBELLION—STATE'S RIGHTS ISSUE OR ANOTHER LAND
GRAB SCHEME?" Historically, says Arizona Governor Bruce Babbit, state
control has meant land is given over to special interests. Hunters, fishermen and conservationists have spoken through opinion polls and member
organizations to demand careful examination of (Secretary of the Interior
James Watt's and others') efforts to hand land management over to the
states. There has been such controversy around Watt and his anticonser-
vationist policies that it doesn't look like there will be much action on land
turnover in the immediate future. (September 1981)

Source: "Inside Washington," monthly page in *Sports Retailer*, various 1981 issues.

---

and the emergence of regional and national sporting goods chains, along with
development of buying syndicates, was evident. Independent full-line and specialty sporting goods stores account for approximately 50 percent of retail
sporting goods sales; the other half is sold by retail units outside the primary
market to which the Association sells its services. A useful distinction between
the two groups is that of size—the full-line and specialty shops are smaller and
the other group is composed of larger entities.

Franchising burgeoned with the advent of specialty athletic footwear
groups, such as Athlete's Foot (now numbering over 400 stores), which began
operations in 1972. Some services formerly offered only by a trade association
are now provided by franchisers, and it is in footwear and softgoods that NSGA
management feels it has been weakest in offering support services for retailers.

Chains such as Herman's World of Sporting Goods (a division of W. R.
Grace & Company) dominate some markets; thus far, NSGA has offered less in
the way of financial and marketing knowledge and ideas for such giants than
the large corporations can provide for themselves internally.

The two major buying syndicates—retailers banded together for economies of quantity purchasing—have a total membership of some 260 stores,
about half of which do over $1,000,000 in business, the others reporting sales
of $500,000 to $1,000,000 annually. Both buying groups strongly support
NSGA's activities, and one group requires its participants to hold membership
in the association. Some of these groups' services compete with NSGA's.

Exhibit 13

ASSUMPTIONS AND IMPLICATIONS PERTAINING TO EXTERNAL FACTORS

DEMOGRAPHIC-ECONOMIC TRENDS AND IMPLICATIONS

DEMOGRAPHIC-ECONOMIC TRENDS	IMPLICATIONS
1. Decreased discretionary income	1. Less money is available for sporting goods products.
2. High interest rates	2. Retailers seeking to start new stores or expand present ones will find the costs prohibitively high. Also restricts facility development, critical to the growth of many sports.
3. Cuts in local school budgets	3. School districts are reducing or eliminating athletic programs.
4. Both household partners working	4. Amount of time is limited. Discretionary income is used for eating out and buying other services.

SOCIOCULTURAL TRENDS AND IMPLICATIONS

SOCIOCULTURAL TRENDS	IMPLICATIONS
1. Growth in individual sports participation	1. Educators are placing greater stress on "lifetime" sports.
2. Extended schooling	2. Students at all age levels are among the greatest consumers of sporting goods.
3. New place of women in America	3. Women are participating in many sport-society activities previously considered male domain.
4. Growing interest in physical fitness	4. Jogging, weight lifting, tennis, racquetball, and health clubs are manifestations.
5. Adoption of a more leisurely "life-style"	5. This shift makes sport footwear and clothing acceptable modes of dress in nonsport situations.

POLITICAL-LEGAL TRENDS AND IMPLICATIONS

POLITICAL-LEGAL TRENDS	IMPLICATIONS
1. Growing product liability	1. Retailers are moving away from certain high-risk sports products (e.g., football helmets).

Exhibit 13 (Cont.)

2. Cutback in federal money to support

3. Opening of federal lands for development of energy resources

2. Significant money for sports programs, specific school programs, and products will be unavailable to major buyers.

3. There is a potential loss of land and water for fishing, hunting, backpacking, and camping activities.

TECHNOLOGICAL TRENDS AND IMPLICATIONS

TECHNOLOGICAL TRENDS	IMPLICATIONS
1. Increased use of electronic games as recreation	1. More choices are available for children and young adults who could participate in sport activities.
2. Tie of computer technology to fitness equipment	2. New products graphically or digitally measure body response to certain types of exercise.
3. New materials for traditional sport	3. Changing materials create improved products (e.g., graphite tennis racquets). Such products usually carry significant status appeal.

Exhibit 13 outlines the implications of demographic-economic, sociocultural, political-legal, and technological trends bearing upon NSGA's policies and strategies.[3]

GAZING INTO THE CRYSTAL BALL

As Jim Faltinek, his staff, and the NSGA board pondered the future, it was evident that a number of unresolved items must appear on future agendas: (1) What should be done about products and services that were providing inadequate income (retail members paid only for educational programs and publications)? (2) How can a suitable balance be achieved between expanding products and services and increasing the membership base? (3) How can the membership base be broadened? (4) What actions should be taken with regard to existing products and services, some of which may be outdated? (5) How can we evaluate the fairness and adequacy of pricing policies and practices? (6)

[3]From NSGA internal documents.

Are we correct in targeting primarily to small and general sporting goods stores? (7) What is an appropriate procedure to budget for new product-service research and development? (8) How can we effectively organize for conducting marketing's functions in NSGA?

Your Task:

Advise NSGA management.

case
16

CITIZENS BANK & TRUST

BACKGROUND

Citizens Bank & Trust (CBT), the largest bank in its region and one of the second hundred largest banks in the United States,[1] serves some 250 banks with balances representing about 10 percent of its net deposits. In the 1970s, automated teller machines were installed by most affiliates in its holding company, and experiments were conducted with point-of-sale devices, telephone bill paying, and in-home banking terminals. Agribusiness is important to CBT—its livestock loans are far larger than those of any other bank in the state, with direct and correspondent participation loans covering about half the state's feeder cattle business.

In September 1975, a rural bank president approached CBT's correspondent division to request computerized record-keeping services for ranchers and farmers. "I think we can sell at least 500 in our market," he said, "because most of my customers don't have accurate bookkeeping. They need it." He pointed out banks in other states offered such a program, so implementing a similar effort at CBT would probably be "low-cost and practically risk-free."

Later that month several CBT officers debated the feasibility of selling

[1]*American Banker,* March 6, 1981, p. 56.

such a service to correspondent institutions and directly to their own customers. Introducing it promised several potential benefits:

1. CBT will be first with an automated bookkeeping service, enhancing its image as a full-service bank and leader in electronic technology.
2. Bank income and profit will increase.
3. Users will tend to become exclusive customers since all their financial data will be processed through the program.
4. New customers will develop other banking relationships with CBT.
5. Cash flow and other information will provide valuable reference data for other departments in the bank.
6. It will reduce excess capacity in the new computer.

A correspondent division officer said, "This looks promising. All we have to do now is analyze profit potential and have our computer experts put it together."

The next week in a meeting attended by CBT officers and the correspondent bank president who had first suggested the idea, all agreed to strive for operational simplicity, concluding that "the primary target market is the rancher or farmer who does not have time and ability to maintain adequate financial records." There was a brief discussion of trade press articles about banks with comparable services encountering costly data-retrieval operations, customer training, programming field service, and package updating—these cast some doubt on the simplicity concept in basic system design and created concern over profitability. Primary responsibility for the proposed service was given to the Commercial Division.

EXPLORING MARKET POTENTIAL

Each CBT division usually performs it own marketing tasks, for example, the Correspondent Division handles marketing matters related to its customers and the Commercial Division manages its marketing activities. These line functions are supported by Corporate Advertising and receive market data from the bank's economist and from periodic research conducted either by the advertising agency or outside suppliers. Sales training by outside consultants is scheduled as needed for tellers, commercial loan officers, and other public contact staff. Marketing task teams and planning committees are commonplace.

Directed by Jack Alvarez, research was undertaken to determine the structure needed in the service and to estimate market acceptance. The memorandum in Exhibit 1 was then sent to the CBT officer responsible for screening new service ideas in the Commercial Division:

Exhibit 1

ALVAREZ MEMORANDUM

March 13, 1976

TO: Melissa Heilbronner
          Commercial Division
FROM: Jack Alvarez
          Systems and Programming, Commercial

We have completed the preliminary study on Farm Accounting after evaluating costs and functions of similar systems, and we have a preliminary
design to fit farmers as well as small businesses and individuals.

I suggest meeting with representatives from Operations, Business Development, Commercial Lending, Correspondent Banks, E.D.P. Servicing, Accounting, Auditing, and Systems and Programming to discuss whether we
make or buy a system, how to market it, what time and cost are involved,
and how to price it. With your approval I will arrange the meeting this
week.

Exhibit 2 summarizes the preliminary design referred to by Alvarez.

Exhibit 2

PRELIMINARY SYSTEM DESIGN
AGRICULTURAL-PERSONAL-BUSINESS ACCOUNTING SYSTEM

PURPOSE:

To develop a computer processing system that will provide a customer of
this bank or its correspondents with a detailed accounting method utilizing regular bank checking account transactions to produce a monthly report of expenditures and income. Such reports are to be usable by the
customer for budget control, tax purposes, and business management,
providing a more sophisticated method of record keeping. The report data
will also be available for the banker in making credit decisions.

Exhibit 2 (Cont.)

SCOPE:

The system is conceived to handle three specific types of accounts:

> **Agricultural:** A set of two-digit codes, 1 to 99, will designate fixed categories of expenditures and income to align with farm tax reporting. Some selectivity of categories will be provided to allow for differences in operations.
>
> **Personal:** A set of two-digit codes, 1 to 99, will designate fixed categories of expenditures and income to align with personal income tax reporting.
>
> **Business:** A set of two-digit codes, 1 to 99, will be available for customers to assign categories. Customers may also designate points in the range of categories where totals and subtotals are required.

A special product task team appointed to guide the project decided to develop the service not only for correspondent banks and commercial accounts but also for other customers. Alvarez recommended added emphasis on proprietorships, small corporations, and upscale professionals. He discovered computerized bookkeeping services were generally cumbersome, featured card entry, and provided no reporting format flexibility. At its March 17 meeting, the task force agreed to the objective of program flexibility and established tasks and responsibilities indicated by Exhibit 3.

Exhibit 3

TASK TEAM MEMORANDUM TO FILE

Representatives from Business Development, Correspondent Banking, Accounting, Auditing, Operations, Commercial Loans, and Data Processing met today to discuss preliminary study results for the accounting package. We concurred in the decision to develop detailed systems specifications, to analyze costs, and to study market potential.

CBT Systems programming people will design the product. Accounting, work management and systems will develop cost data. Business Development and Correspondent Bank departments will study market potential.

SYSTEM DESIGN RESPONSIBILITY

Systems and Programming Division Supervisor Robert Cox was appointed project leader, although neither he nor Alvarez believed demand sufficient to warrant resources needed to build a system. The design work was assigned to programmer Helen Lefkowicz; Alvarez initiated a telephone survey of bank customers. Respondents indicated "strong interest in the concept." Several accountants in medium- and large-sized businesses stated that the service could be a useful supplement to their existing accounting systems. Over a dozen certified public accountants told Alvarez it could replace numerous trivial, time-consuming bookkeeping chores and help them close books more efficiently. Shifting from the stance of an unbeliever after several such conversations, Alvarez decided potential existed after all; his positive attitude coupled with similar reactions to their own queries transformed Lefkowicz and Cox from doubters into supporters. Both felt that their CBT package could avoid the flaws of similar programs.

In May, the team said no sales forecast could be made without further market analysis. Helen Lefkowicz's design work continued based on her ideas, on earlier notes from the task force group, and with occasional guidance from Cox. Citing negative statements about system deficiencies from customers testing it, a task group participant stated, "Our market research has been done the hard way. So the product isn't perfect—we do have a handle on what needs doing, so let's push on to refine and sell it." This was the consensus—implement the service in a full-scale effort and modify it from time to time as customers complain. Meanwhile, progress was reflected in a memo (Exhibit 4) from Cox.

Exhibit 4

MEMO FROM COX TO FILE—PROCESSING AND PRICING

1. Two deposit slips will be required of the customer. Classification—99 are available—will be left to customer choice. Adjustment forms will be required of customers desiring to correct entries and summary accounts.
2. Bank clerks will prepare a card for each check. Two items on a check will require two cards. The system will be suitable for businesses with up to 96 account codes, leaving numbers 97 to 99 reserved for bank use.
3. Charge for the service will include set-up, monthly minimum, and transaction fee. Correspondence banks will be charged a mimimum for each account, plus fee for entry items depending upon whether entries are encoded in advance. Pricing will be based on estimated average costs of operating the service for a variety of accounts.

TASKS AND ASSIGNMENTS AT CBT

Enthusiastic about specifications, the task group agreed to urge executive committee approval. Assignments included:

Barkley Duncan, senior vice president, take the proposal to senior management and help name the service

---

Exhibit 5

BOOK-KEEPER COMPLETION SCHEDULE

July 18   Cost projection
July 28   Brochures and forms order, final operating systems checkout, advertising
                        artwork
August 11   Run descriptions
September 15   Programming manuals, system test compilation
September 29   Analyze test results, produce samples, specific accounts, agribusiness
November 1   Pilot run

> Nicole Paget, corporate advertising, collaborate with the house advertising agency
> in designing a brochure on how to use the service
> Robert Cox, refine software

Planners expected development costs to be about $20,000 of which $4,000 had been spent in studies and design; nobody anticipated exceeding budget estimates. Deadlines for full-scale introduction shifted from November to January to allow time for pilot testing, system redesign, brochure development, and name choosing. Everyone left the meeting in an optimistic frame of mind, and the following week CBT's Executive Committee gave the go-ahead. A naming contest among employees led to the sobriquet "Book-Keeper," to convey the idea of books kept for subscribers.

Exhibit 5 indicates the time-and-task schedule for the new offspring.

PROMOTION PLANNING

During the summer, Donald Pierson, assistant cashier and member of the original planning group, assumed, along with Nicole Paget, Book-Keeper marketing responsibilities, including advertising and other nonpersonal communication. By mid-September, literature, forms, brochures, posters, and media advertising were designed. Envelope stuffers, lobby posters, radio spots, selective personal selling, and intensive cross-selling by tellers and other public contact staff were principal promotion elements. An advertisement was set for the December *American Medical Association Journal,* and stuffers were prepared for the bank lobby pigeonhole display and November's statement envelopes.

PRICING

Cost and income projections, based on forecasted 500 active accounts, are presented in Exhibit 6.

Exhibit 6

PROJECTED COST AND INCOME FOR AN AVERAGE ACCOUNT*

SET-UP FEE, INITIATION

Estimated $20,000 development costs to be amortized in	
3 years (1,000 new accounts, retaining 500 for 3 years)	$20.00
Initial supplies (forms, materials, etc.)	5.00
Initial account maintenance (consultation and customizing)	5.00
Total initial account set-up fee	$30.00

RECURRING COST AND INCOME PER ACCOUNT

Basic operating cost (includes check printing)	$6.50
Computer set-up	1.50
Estimated $8,000 advertising per year to sustain	
500 accounts; assess 10% to active accounts	1.60
E.D.P. servicing (10% of one person's time for each	
correspondent bank)	.40
Total cost per average account	$10.00
50% markup on costs	5.00
Total charge to customer	$15.00

*Based on average account with 63 chargeable entries.

EMPLOYEE TRAINING AND PROSPECT SEMINARS

The Systems and Programming Division held training sessions for bookkeeping, data processing, commercial, teller, and other selected employees. Nicole Paget wrote detailed instructions for business development and correspondent bank division staff who were asked to take responsibility for five accounts each during the pilot operation; she also assembled a color slide presentation portraying major features. This slide program was shown initially to an audience of about 100 CPAs; all received handbooks to help explain the service to their customers. Numerous small groups of potential users, CPAs, and attorneys attended briefing sessions, and Small Business Administration requested a special showing for the Senior Corps of Retired Executives. Generally, the slide presentation proved an effective medium for conveying Book-Keeper's essentials.

MARKET RESPONSE

By year-end, about 100 customers used Book-Keeper, with increasing numbers showing interest. Exhibit 7 is a letter of inquiry from a correspondent banker; Exhibit 8 is the response. Exhibit 9 is a letter of inquiry from a physician; Exhibit 10 is the response.

Exhibit 7

INQUIRY FROM CORRESPONDENT BANKER

November 1, 1976

Mr. Jeremy Bothwell
President
Citizens Bank & Trust

Dear Mr. Bothwell:

It has been called to my attention that your bank is now offering a new service called "Book-Keeper," and I want to obtain the mechanics and any other information. We feel it may definitely have some application in this part of the banking world.

We realize that you are not involved in this area, and if you will be kind enough to pass this inquiry on to the proper person or department, we would be very grateful.

Your truly,

Vice President and Cashier

Exhibit 8

RESPONSE TO CORRESPONDENT INQUIRY

November 7, 1976

Dear_____

In reply to your letter of November 1 to Jerry Bothwell, I am happy to provide you with the following information on our new record-keeping service.

Exhibit 8 (Cont.)

After reviewing several systems, we decided that this banking service had definite appeal but felt that a broader, more flexible program was needed. Thus, Book-Keeper was developed by this Bank, and we are sure you will find it to be the most flexible record-keeping service available in the country today.

Book-Keeper has been programmed for our computers in COBOL language. Input is from actual checks or substitute documents via magnetic ink going directly to a magnetic tape. We have 99 possible classifications plus 10 internal totals that can be used in reports to the customer.

Every customer chooses specific classifications and totals at any time during use of the service. Two reports are provided each customer monthly, a Detail Report and a Summary Report. The Detail Report lists every individual entry for audit trail purposes while the Summary Report provides, by classification, monthly as well as year-to-date totals expressed both as dollars and percentages.

Since announcing this service a few weeks ago, response has been very gratifying from both customers and noncustomers. Internally, we have had terrific enthusiasm from our staff as it is not often in this highly competitive business of ours that you have an opportunity to market an exclusive new banking service!

We have a system package available for sale at a price of $7,500, which includes the program, copies of all of our forms, a geographical exclusive for one year, training time at CBT, and, of course, any program changes or improvements that we might develop.

I am enclosing our sales brochure as well as a blank copy of a Detail Report and a complete copy of a Summary Report.

Again, please keep in mind that on the Summary Report it might be for a business instead of an individual, and customers dictate titles of every classification they want reported as well as the totals and their placement. After reviewing the enclosed information, please feel free to call me with any questions you might have. We appreciate your interest, and I look forward to hearing from you soon.

Sincerely,

Donald Pierson II, Assistant Cashier

Exhibit 9

PHYSICIAN'S LETTER OF INQUIRY

May 8, 1977

Citizens Bank & Trust
Business Development Department

Dear Sirs:

I should like Book-Keeper information, including some idea of cost. Presently, I have two accounts: a personal one at the Citizens, which has an average of about 4 credits and 30 debits a month; and a business account elsewhere, which has an average of about 4 credits and 15 debits a month. I should like to combine these into a single account, if the system is sophisticated enough for each to be separately reported.

Sincerely,

Exhibit 10

RESPONSE TO PHYSICIAN

May 11, 1977

Dear Doctor_____:

In accordance with your request, I am happy to provide you with details on Book-Keeper, offered exclusively by Citizens Bank & Trust. This product is designed primarily to report cash flow through your checking account by the coding of checks and deposit slips. We have up to 99 numbers available, to which you may assign any particular classification title you desire. Also, you may assign up to 10 totals, which can be sums or differences, placed and titled at your discretion.

I would suggest you consult your previous tax returns to establish the classifications of income and expense.

Exhibit 10 (Cont.)

The monthly Summary and Detail Reports provide a monthly as well as year-to-date accumulative totals. These reports will accompany your regular bank statement.

The one-time set-up fee is $30, with monthly charges depending on usage. Multiple entries of income or expense can be coded on all checks and deposit slips. Any style of check or deposit can be used with Book-Keeper with the simple addition of the "T Bar." Your checks will cost you no more than they have in the past. I expect your monthly charges would be about $15.00.

I have enclosed a sample of the Summary Report and a brochure for your perusal.

Please call me should you have any additional questions on this service, as we will be most happy to answer them for you.

Sincerely,

James B. Thompson
Assistant Vice President

EVENTS 1977 TO 1981

Users in fall 1977 were uniformly enthusiastic, and according to a CBT officer, word-of-mouth influence was selling many new accounts. A perceived gain for CBT: half the Book-Keeper clients were new customers who established account relationships to get the service. Business development staff were pleased to have a broad-appeal new banking service offered by no other local bank. A calling officer asserted, "With market potential good, and the price OK, Book-Keeper will be profitable in two or three years. It's already profitable on a direct-cost basis, but 500 accounts are needed to recoup R & D outlays."

When Donald Pierson resigned his position as assistant cashier to join another bank in summer 1977, management trainee Sam Levine was placed in charge of Book-Keeper, reporting to the head of data processing. In spring 1978, Levine, who had hoped to work into a marketing position at CBT, decided to return to college for the final year of his undergraduate degree; he was replaced in early summer by John Drakeford who had extensive background in data processing. A fledgling entrepreneur, Drakeford was beginning to get firsthand knowledge of small business inasmuch as he and his wife had just acquired a retail franchise outlet in a local shopping center.

Drakeford reviewed what he had learned in a few hours about Book-Keeper. "I believe it's a marketable service, inexpensive to the customer and low-cost to the bank; a profitmaker if we can just build those 500 accounts. We now have about 200 Book-Keepers running—two-thirds direct with us and the remainder at 11 correspondent banks. Customers like the service and recommend it to their friends. I speculate cancellations are people moving from the area, which means that they will sever their bank connections here, anyway. Our ad agency people are going to analyze this for us as soon as they finish updating this year's marketing plan.

"Pierson was a Book-Keeper booster, but after he resigned people lost interest. New accounts people don't know much about it and don't try to sell it. The loan people could make better use of information in Book-Keeper to work with potential borrowers who use it, but they prefer to do their own investigations. We don't have a full-fledged marketing department, so it looks like it's going to be my show."

Total 1978 advertising consisted of promotion stuffers in a lobby pigeon-hole display alongside some 20-odd other promotional folders. A summary listing of CBT's services inadvertently failed to mention Book-Keeper.

Drakeford commented, "Only one CBT employee has a Book-Keeper contract. We haven't tried to sell bank employees on it." Asked how the bank handled requests for Book-Keeper information, "The inquirer is referred to me. It takes at least 15 minutes to explain; I use the 'Personal Guide to Book-Keeper.' This brochure costs about $2.50, so I give it only to high-potential prospects. If the person wants set-up advice, I provide a 'classification assignment' form and explain the format of typical accounts. I suggest the prospect work up classifications with a CPA or whoever does the tax work. A person can examine checks for two or three months and determine categories to use. Classifying takes two or three hours, and I think many potential customers are lost at this stage.

"Back to this subject of bank employees using Book-Keeper—they get free checking accounts, and I think maybe they would resent paying fees for any bank service. So I proposed we waive set-up charges to get employees started, but the idea didn't fly.

"Levine tried the direct approach to physician customers sending individually signed letters and promotional material to 75 physicians, followed by a telephone call in a few days. This yielded two Book-Keeper customers. Letters won't do it."

Just prior to resigning, Sam Levine had listed Book-Keeper projects and tasks he wanted to start (see Exhibits 11 and 12).

Exhibit 11

LEVINE MEMO TO FILE

1. Improve and make Book-Keeper more useful to existing customers and usable by more types of potential customers.
2. Prepare a summary version of "Your Personal Guide to Book-Keeper," which would cost far less than the expensive brochure and could be given to **all** potential customers.
3. Develop sales literature explaining why an individual needs the service.
4. Provide customers with a folder for Book-Keeper summary sheets.

Drakeford devoted his immediate attention toward the ranked priorities in Exhibit 12.

Exhibit 12

DRAKEFORD MEMO TO FILE—BOOK-KEEPER TASKS

1. Get New Accounts Division personnel selling Book-Keeper.
2. Prepare typical account classifications for professions that are and will be using the service.
3. Contact recently signed new accounts to get their reactions.
4. Prepare a marketing plan to get the service into the profit column. Include correspondent banks in the plan.

Between 1977 and 1979, 4,000 brochures were mailed, and personal selling was directed toward professional people and merchants in local shopping centers. Small business owners who liked the idea of Book-Keeper expressed need of a trial balance in the printout, but the press of other matters at CBT prevented revising the system. Further, systems analysts thought a ledger-type system would increase prices and cause the service to lose simplicity—a cardinal characteristic of Book-Keeper—and might sabotage its future.

John Drakeford was assigned to rewrite the bank's mortgage loan package, and Book-Keeper responsibility was delegated to an EDP staff sales representative, Nancy Reese. When Drakeford resigned from CBT in midsummer 1979 to accept an EDP position in a petroleum company and after Ms. Reese moved up to a supervisory job and could no longer devote time to Book-Keeper, nobody was in charge of the service for a few months. From 1980 to 1981, each of three management trainees managed the service for three- to four-month intervals.

In 1981, correspondent banks accounted for 30 percent of customers using Book-Keeper, eight of these with the correspondent banker who initially contacted CBT about the service.

Tables 1 and 2 show a summary of accounts 1976 to 1981. A surge of new users tends to occur toward year-end, presumably because of sudden desires to maintain better income tax records. Account turnover is high relative to other CBT services.

Table 1

SUMMARY OF CBT BOOK-KEEPER ACCOUNTS BY TYPE: NUMBER OF ACCOUNTS, ESTABLISHED 1976–1980 AND ACTIVE 1981

	NUMBER OF ACCOUNTS ESTABLISHED					1981 ACTIVE ACCOUNTS	
Type of Client	1976	1977	1978	1979	1980	Total	Percentage
Professions	20	43	31	18	8	30	20%
Financial	18	42	27	14	5	25	17
Personal	20	45	10	0	1	20	13
Service	6	7	15	3	3	18	12
Marketing	2	9	12	7	2	15	10
Agribusiness	10	15	17	13	6	10	7
Real Estate	9	12	4	1	1	10	7
Manufacturing	8	12	4	5	3	8	5
Retail	5	6	4	5	3	8	5
Other	3	5	4	1	3	6	4
Total	101	196	128	67	35	150	100%
Cumulative	—	297	425	492	527		

Table 2

ACTIVE BOOK-KEEPER ACCOUNTS, GOAL VERSUS ACTUAL, 1977–1981

YEAR	GOAL	ACTUAL	% OF GOAL ATTAINMENT
1977	200	152	76%
1978	300	267	89
1979	400	204	51
1980	500	164	33
1981	600	150	25

Your Task:

1. Based upon the situation described, to what extent is the marketing concept being applied at CBT?
2. Going back to the beginning of the case, what else could CBT do to examine the feasibility of Book-Keeper?
3. Again going back in time, if there is sufficient evidence to warrant a full-fledged market introduction of Book-Keeper, what major factors ought to be considered in pricing the service?
4. What procedure would you recommend to introduce a new idea into the bank's line of services?
5. In your opinion, where does new product planning fit in the bank's overall plan? How should CBT organize for such processes?
6. Assuming that a major contribution to bank profitability can be made by an astute marketing person who understands EDP, how can CBT organize to capitalize on this synergism?

PIPES AND TOBACCOS UNLIMITED

Jerome Carlson puffed thoughtfully on a new meerschaum pipe and talked about his transformation from English teacher to businessman: "I opened Pipes and Tobaccos Unlimited (PTU) in 1976. This is not my first business enterprise, but it is the first I've owned outright." Mr. Carlson formerly taught college English and speech and then became manager of a high school friend's restaurant. There he went through a learning process of setting up and opening a new business. After an unfortunate mudslide, during which time he learned that business and old friends sometimes do not mix well, he left the business and worked in commercial art and furniture restoration before taking a high school teaching position. "After six months," he said, "I knew that I had to be my own boss, and I made the decision to go into business. But I didn't have an idea of what business."

Carlson spent considerable time doing research and reading before he settled on the idea of a pipe shop. Confident of his ability to succeed through hard work (he had learned many lessons in marketing from the restaurant experience), he borrowed the funds from a local bank, assigning as collateral the equity in his house.

CHOOSING AN ADDRESS

"My first decision concerned location. It takes a population of roughly 100,000 to support a pipe and tobacco store. I looked at several locations: the west side, downtown, some bedroom suburbs, and the east side. The west side seemed stagnant. The downtown was dead and had major competition. The Southwest Mall, while aesthetically appealing, was too far out of the way to draw major business. An indoor mall seemed preferable to an outdoor entrance. This criterion drew me to look at two other centers, one of which was in a rundown condition and generally unappealing. But the east side was growing; it had the indoor mall I was looking for, the weekend shopper traffic was heavy, and space was available."

Exhibit 1

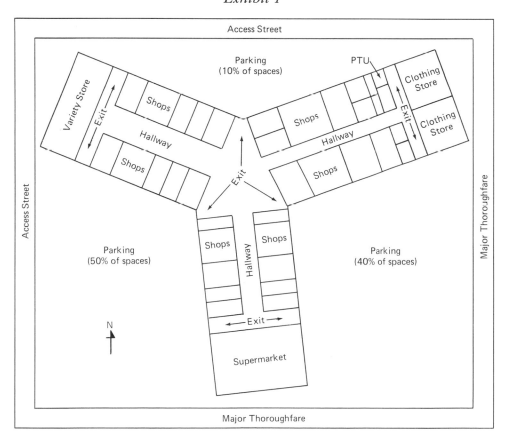

The site in the mall presented some problems. It was out of the way along an exit corridor on a low-traffic entrance. Parking immediately outside the exit was limited (Exhibit 1). Most pedestrians entered the mall through the south end, and, following a typical shopping flow through the mall, few potential customers passed the store. Carlson was aware of the problem, realizing it would cause some difficulties. "Through hard work and building a regular clientele," he stated, "I knew I could overcome that problem."

PRODUCT CLASS AND STORE CLASS

The teacher-turned-entrepreneur talked about the customers: "A large portion of the shop's clientele are avid pipe smokers. Many are collectors. All desire quality and uniqueness. A considerable amount of our business comes from impulse buying, so we stock many unique items aimed at this market. Much of our business during holiday periods is for gifts. Many of these shoppers don't necessarily know what they are looking for, but go through the mall, shop by shop."

PRODUCT LINES AND SERVICE

Pipes and Tobaccos Unlimited is a full-line store, but the bulk of its receipts comes from sales of pipes and tobaccos. Mr. Carlson carries a complete line of accessories and, having a penchant for the fine arts, sculpture, and reading, stocks a range of other items such as sculptures, paintings, and books. Exhibit 2 lists the major stock items.

When the store was first stocked, Carlson concentrated almost exclusively on lower-priced contemporary and hand-carved selections. "With only $7,000 start-up capital, I was limited somewhat in the kind of inventory we could afford. I was wary of being able to move expensive, unique stock. Most pipes sold in the $10 to $15 range." As the clientele developed, however, he realized there was a demand for these items, and he slowly expanded the selection. In 1983, pipes in stock ranged from $10 to several hundred dollars. The displays became segmented, offering sections of less expensive pipes as well as high-priced pipes for collectors.

The shop also expanded from handling strictly national brand pipes into dealer-branded pipes. As the ability to carry larger inventory grew, Carlson found that he could purchase pipes by the gross from name producers, have them stamped with PTU's brand name, and sell them at very reasonable prices. He was purchasing these pipes at less than half the cost of national brands, and the quality was comparable. Consequently, price-conscious shoppers could find quality at a savings.

PTU tobacco selections were primarily dealer brands. The owner hand-

Exhibit 2

PTU'S MAJOR STOCK ITEMS

Pipes
    Freehand carved
    Contemporary briars
    Meerschaums
        Contemporary
        Hand-carved
    Imports
    Pipe kits for do-it-yourselfers

Tobaccos
    Dealer brands
    High-quality imports, branded
    Cigars
    Cigarettes

Accessories
    Lighters
    Pipe tools
    Ash trays
    Humidors
    Pouches
    Other unique accessories

Other
    Theme items
    Books
    Pictures
    Sculptures
    Novelties

selected stock tobaccos and made his own blends. Each blend was given a catchy name related to famous pipe-smoking figures in history and literature, for example, "McArthur's Mix," "Knapp's Sack," and "Wild Woolf's." In addition, the shop carried a range of high-quality—and priced accordingly—imported and branded tobaccos. A range of top-of-the-line imported cigars was also carried by the store.

The owner discussed inventory control with the case writer: "I use a detailed running sales analysis to determine what items to stock. Each item in the store is tracked for sales performance. There are 80 suppliers pushing their products, so I have to be careful. I track what the customers are buying and follow their dictates. Through conversations with them, I get a feel for new items that will sell. There are also a few sales representatives I trust in selecting new items, but many of them are simply pushing products. I place most weight on customers' wants and needs when making stock decisions."

In addition to pipes, tobaccos, and accessories, Carlson offered related services as well. He remarked, "A large portion of pipe sales are layaways. With values of $200 to $300 on many pipes, customers are often unable to pay in full when they see something they like. Since most of these pipes are one-of-a-kind in terms of their qualities and design, once the item is gone, the chances of finding an identical replacement are often nonexistent. Doing layaways enables the store to ring up considerable business in the expensive lines.

"The store also repairs pipes, a service that doesn't make a lot of money, but it helps to promote a total package by providing continued product service. Smokers often develop strong affection for a favorite old pipe. The repair service we've contracted with is highly dependable and is often able to restore damaged pipes."

STORE ORGANIZATION

The interior of the store was constructed totally by hand by Mr. Carlson, who created a rustic, casual atmosphere conducive to his selling style. Display cases are partly rough unfinished woods. Wall displays are rough-cut frames with canvas backing. Toward the rear of the store there is a tobacco bar with stools; the bar is reminiscent of the old general store with its pot-bellied stove and cracker barrel. In place of the cracker barrel, there are samples of various tobacco blends that customers are invited to test smoke. There are rough-cut tables with felt tops, two hand-made counters, and an antique cabinet in which rare pipes are kept. Carlson said, "As an antitheft measure, every space that can hold a pipe is filled. When a space is empty, we know someone has removed the pipe, for some reason. This policy also ensures maximum use of display area." Signs in the store are of rough-cut timber with lettering burned into the wood. A teapot, table, and rocking chair embellish the "country" atmosphere.

But efficiency is the key to PTU's merchandising layout. As Carlson described it, "The shop is small by most standards, yet we have been able to display a large selection of merchandise in its limited space. You'll note that displays are arranged by segments into various pipe, tobacco, and accessory classes; by price range; and by variety. Customers do not have to search far to find what they are looking for. Since many collectors stop by regularly looking for new inventory, we mark new stock clearly so customers can locate it immediately."

PERSONAL SELLING

From the very beginning, Carlson knew that personal selling had to be a big factor if the shop was to become successful. "The location was not prime, and we had little money for mass selling. Therefore, we had to made a maximum impression on each customer to promote return sales. From the earliest days my role as a salesman was to help the customer make a selection. I take great care to learn the tastes and needs of each customer and to offer selections that met those needs." He also used his considerable technical knowledge of the products in advising customers. Carlson related his sales philosophy: "I subscribe to the casual sales approach and make full use of the tobacco bar to encourage customers to sit and chat. Growth has enabled me to hire more sales people, and each one has been selected from the customers. All are pipe lovers and have the expertise to provide help to customers just like themselves.

"When I go to pipe shows, or make pipe selections, I use our salespeople to help make selections and to become involved in the buying process. It does no good to stock items the sales people will not push."

The sales people seemed to take pride in the store and to desire its success and expansion. "They care for the store in the same way they would their own," Carlson exclaimed, "and this loyalty has enabled me to spend more time on the behind-the-scenes business and less time watching over the store. They are paid a straight salary of $4.50 to $5.25 and hour and also receive medical benefits and holiday season bonuses. Of course, medical doesn't mean much to the retired military sales people." Carlson's store is located in an area heavily populated by retired military.

ADVERTISING

Mr. Carlson had little use for some forms of advertising, having tried radio spots and newspaper ads, usually getting only a $10 return for a $100 layout. He did his own radio spots, which usually ran during sports programs.

Some forms of advertising, however, proved effective. One-line ads in the *Thrifty Nickel* often brought response. His theory was that people picked up the free *Thrifty Nickel* only to read the want ads. He believes that people are "often resistant to commercial advertising." *Thrifty Nickel* remains a relatively inexpensive medium and enjoys extensive distribution within his target market area.

Mailed fliers seem to be the most effective form of advertising for PTU. Carlson periodically solicits the addresses of customers and has compiled a mailing list. Working from this file, he has sent occasional product news and informed customers of specials. "I know every dime spent is going to a pipe smoker," he reasons. Dollar-for-dollar, I would rather spend extra money to give promotional items to my customers than pay for an additional radio spot. For example, when a customer buys a pipe, he gets a special pack of matches bearing PTU's logo. We offer free tobacco for different-sized purchases, and we give away pipe cleaners."

There have been exceptions. "We have found that business is good enough around some key holidays to pay for mass advertising—for Father's Day and Christmas in particular. What I wish I'd done, at the outset, was to borrow $3,000 extra and blitz the media to let people know we were in town. Mass media might have helped us to do more than $33,000 gross sales that first year. A lot of our business has been by word-of-mouth or people accidentally finding the store. Very slow!"

Carlson also has found cooperative promotion with other merchants in the mall ineffective. "When there have been big mall promotions," he said, "PTU has had some of its worst days. Here again, location has played a significant role. Action in the mall on special promotion days is in the main halls. I've been unhappy about this because our promotion dollar helps other merchants but rarely ourselves."

GROWTH AND COMPETITION

The business experienced steady growth in its first six years, going from gross sales of $33,000 its first year, to $65,000 the next, $95,000 the third year, $128,250 the fourth year, $179,550 in the fifth year, and $260,400 in the sixth year. The sales expense-sales ratio remained constant over the six-year period. From $260,400 in the sixth year, Carlson hoped for $350,00 in year seven.

The growth PTU experienced has not gone unnoticed. Heathcliff's Tobacco Shop, a downtown store, announced expansion into a new shopping center 1 mile away from Pipes and Tobaccos Unlimited. This competitor has priced comparable goods lower than Carlson, who eyes the competition as a new challenge to his imagination. In Carlson's words, "It would be difficult for any store to top our selection without carrying huge inventory. We hold the edge in store image. Price competition, however, could damage us with some customers. I am aware that Heathcliff's has an edge in sales of high-grade cigars. To combat this, we are building a large walk-in humidor to stock volumes of high-grade imported cigars. We also plan on carrying other exotic consumables such as rare teas that cannot be found in grocery stores."

PRICING

PTU's markups ranged from 10 percent on certain products to almost 300 percent on some. "A handful of stock doesn't cover its own cost," said Carlson; "however it is essential in completing the product line. Other items have large markups to carry the load for items that do not pay. We pay close attention to keeping prices competitive. Some items have low competition in the city and are marked up to a greater extent. This enables us to keep other stock with low markups so we can compete favorably.

"Dealer brands also help to carry the load. The custom blends have very little competition at present. Because of volume purchases of high-grade tobacco bases, we can blend tobaccos at relatively low cost, use a large markup, and still be competitive. The uniqueness and quality of the blends enable us to carry a relatively high price on them. The store has a fairly large customer franchise for blends.

"The same philosophy holds for dealer-branded pipes. We carefully select good-quality producers, buy in volume at low cost, and use a relatively large, 200 percent-plus markup. And the customer gets a good-quality pipe that is still very price competitive. In general, our merchandise averages a 35 percent markup. We aim to meet competition, coming in at the average market price."

Concluding on a note of optimism, Carlson said he felt lucky: "I've found a business I truly enjoy, selling things that customers are willing to exert special effort to find and to make sacrifices to buy. For much of what our customers want, they are not willing to accept substitutes, for either the national brand products or our special blends. We have a unique product assortment, our sales people know pipes and tobaccos, and nobody gives better service. Still, with only 120,000 population in this part of the city, even though there are 250,000 citywide, I'm concerned about the impact Heathcliff's might have on our business. One bright spot I can think of—their mall is about one-third the size of ours, which means we will still be more convenient, even though Heathcliff's will have two locations."

A 1982 shopping center patronage study, sponsored by a local daily newspaper, indicated that Carlson's mall had been visited by 21 percent of surveyed shoppers during the previous 30 days; the center in which Heathcliff's was located had been visited by 14 percent of those interviewed. The same report, borrowing from others' forecasts, predicted that population growth in the eastern area of the city would be two to three times that of other areas. Regular patrons of the mall where PTU is located had larger incomes, were older, and had attained higher levels of formal education than had regular customers of most other malls.

Your Task:

Jerome Carlson has retained you as a retailing consultant to help him develop a strategy for the next five years and a specific plan for the coming year, when his competitor will move into its second site.

1. Advise him on the priorities you think he should consider.
2. Is Pipes and Tobaccos Unlimited a specialty or a convenience store, and are the goods sold in the shopping classification, as Mr. Carlson implied? Based on your answer, what are the implications for PTU's merchandising planning?
3. Does Mr. Carlson need to improve his customer information system? If so, in what ways? What information, if any, does he need that is not now being collected, and how could he use it in decision making and planning?

case
18

THE CHINOOK BOOKSHOP

This is a happy tale about two young people who fell in love with each other and later with an idea, and a dream that came true.[1]

On Tejon Street in downtown Colorado Springs, across from Acacia Park, stands "one of America's finest bookstores," The Chinook. It is a friendly oasis for book lovers and browsers, but it never could be described as a "shoppe." Although its handsome carved wood doors afford two entries from the street side and it goes back hundreds of feet deep inside, in spirit it is far more than just a large bookstore.

Here, let's back up a bit—to 1958 when the bookstore was only in the springtime of its promise, coming to life as the spiritual brainchild of an ambitious young couple. From Dick Noyes, who was hearing a different beat from that marched to by his successful midwestern forefathers, came drive and creativity and experience with the technicalities of the book trade; from his wife Judy came a charm and different kind of creativity that earlier had expressed itself in journalism and broadcasting. The two shared equally a love for literature and books and the world of ideas.

Richard Hall Noyes, born in 1930, was the child of solid citizens of that solid satellite of Chicago—Evanston, Illinois. Dick had an older sister and was

[1]Adapted from "CHINOOK: Promise of Spring—Twenty-Nine Years of Bookselling on Tejon Street 1959–1979," a promotional booklet by Marshall Sprague.

the middle of three brothers. As he competed within the family, he grew up aggressive, rebellious, and determined to be a free spirit. His family thought of him as impractical and artistic. At Wesleyan University, he was an average student until his senior year when courses in philosophy and religion motivated him to hard work and high marks. But his ideas for his own future were hazy; he thought of becoming a painter or writer or of pursuing his childhood fantasy and going West to be a cowboy or a forest ranger.

During his junior year at Wesleyan, Dick accepted a blind date, arranged by one of his fraternity brothers, with a sophomore from Vassar. Judy Mitchell was from a New Haven, Connecticut, family that had moved to Jacksonville Beach, Florida, where she went through school. She was a bookish child who learned to read before kindergarten and from then on read everything she could get her hands on—from *Honeybunch* to the Brontës. All during her high school years, Judy worked as a columnist and feature writer for the *Ocean Beach Reporter* and as writer and broadcaster for radio station WJVB. At graduation, her senior class voted her "most likely to succeed," and she entered Vassar, class of 1953. Then came the blind date: on a January morning she stepped bravely off the bus in her 1950's uniform of tweed skirt, white sweater with pearls, and Capezio flats. She was met by a blue-eyed fellow, slender and wiry in white bucks, button-down shirt, and pressed khakis.

Judy and Dick became engaged while she was a senior at Vassar. Dick was drafted soon after his graduation in 1952 and sent off for Army service in the Far East. After her own graduation, Judy became an Army civilian employee and, with the help of her roommate's father, a strategically placed colonel, had herself assigned to Tokyo, where Dick just happened to be teaching in the Army Intelligence School. They were married there in October 1953. They loved life in Japan, but when their tours and Army paychecks ended in the fall of 1954, they moved to the Noyes's family home in Evanston where Dick began job hunting. He had a clear idea only of what he did *not* want to do.

Then, by chance, Dick heard of a year-long, one-at-a-time training program at Rand McNally, the Chicago book publishers. The starting pay was a modest $250 a month. The training program was thorough—offset, letterpress, bindery, makeup, editing, promotion—and Dick went at it for all he was worth. After his training, Rand McNally offered him a textbook, maps, and globes sales territory out West. They chose headquarters in Denver, which Dick had known from his boyhood summers at Cheley Camp in Estes Park and the Ferrington Carpenter ranch at Hayden.

Dick was away selling books most of the time, roaming by car over the mountain reaches of Idaho, Colorado, Wyoming, and Utah, and Judy played the patient mother to their two daughters, missing the stimulation of her academic and newpaper/radio years. But Dick was getting raises, offers of a prime sales territory in California, and hints of an executive future in Chicago. He was "top salesman of the year" in the Education Division.

Late one Friday afternoon in Dick's hotel room in Salt Lake City the phone rang. It was Judy. She was sick of being alone with the two babies—they'd gotten married to be together, not apart. Dick paused, thinking—for half a minute. Then he said, "There's a Denver plane leaving here in an hour. I'll fly home for the weekend. Get a sitter and we'll have dinner tonight at the Ship's Tavern." They reached a decision that left them elated. Dick had learned plenty about the book trade during his time with Rand McNally and proved he knew how to sell books. They would open their own bookstore. And he knew just the place—Colorado Springs.

SELECTING A LOCATION

They picked the name of the shop from the text of a book they'd just read, A. B. Guthrie's *These Thousand Hills*, in which Guthrie described those warm winds that melt the snow in minutes and end the gray bleakness of winters in the western high country—"Chinook . . . Promise of Spring." (See the appendix for the Chinook bookmark.)

With the advice of a lawyer, Morton McGinley, their first friend in Colorado Springs, and the help of a realtor, Roy Hackathorn, they got an FHA loan and bought a house on Arcturus Drive in Skyway Park. More help came from Harold Dillon, the Random House "rep" in Denver, although Dillon tended to regard all bookstores as dubious ventures and asked Dick why he didn't take up something sound like trash collecting.

Through that fall of 1958, Dick and Judy toiled among the packing crates, writing publishers, and pumping bookseller friends for guidance—friends Dick had met on his Rand McNally trips. Judy wrote to Bennett Cerf, the *Saturday Review* punster and columnist, who responded kindly with tips about joining the American Booksellers and how to apply for trade information.

Dick and Judy tramped the downtown for weeks to find a proper place for their bookstore. They decided finally on the soon-to-be-vacated Lee's Boys Store space at 208½ North Tejon Street. (Lee's was moving next door to the south.) Dillon was not sold on the location, particularly the fractional number, 208½, an address that he found demeaning. "Sounds like a popcorn stand," he said. But it fronted on Acacia Park with its elderly shuffleboard players and its benches where, Dick reasoned, people relaxing in the sun might wander over to the shop. There also was a lot of walk-by traffic, with downtown businesspeople, lawyers, and bankers walking from their offices for lunch at Ruth's Oven or the El Paso Club.

Dick was admiring and polite when he called on the city's two long-established bookstores—his main competition. Both of them impressed him in their way. Edith Farnsworth's on Kiowa Street and Their Book Shop on South Tejon had been around since 1924. Dick introduced himself to Edith Farnsworth, a stately lady born in Colorado Springs and held in high regard by the community. Marshall and Anne Cross had bought Their Book Shop in 1949 from Carol

Truax, an exuberant personality who spent her time directing the city's cultural affairs. Dick found the Cross's shop attractive but judged it to be poorly placed, too far from the downtown area. Both bookstores, he was told, had a stranglehold on what was called "the carriage trade." In addition, Bob's Books on Pikes Peak Avenue and the old Levine's, downstairs in Wilbur's (where Bryan and Scott Jewelers is now), claimed the rest of the new book market, with the knowledgeable veteran rare books dealer, Henry Clausen, then as now taking care of the demand for used and out-of-print books.

At the same time, Dick was studying the biggest problem—where to find the $25,000 that he felt he needed to get the store started. He was reluctant to ask his family for money, but there seemed no alternative since bookstores historically were the worst of risks. Dick's mistaken notion that the family might have reservations about his future was useful. When he finally approached them for the loan, he had spend most of his free time preparing an elaborate 32-page prospectus designed to overcome any hesitations. It covered the plans in detail, and it turned the trick.

"This prospectus," Dick had written, "is the outcome of almost a year's serious thought, a careful study of material recommended by many hours with booksellers, the American Booksellers Association, and the U.S. Department of Commerce. . . . I believe that several of our ideas are new and noteworthy and that in time the shop will be unique among bookstores in the west."

He went on to explain their choice of Colorado Springs for its prosperity and rapid growth brought on by its military installations and the resplendent and just-opened Air Force Academy (September 1958), its high education level, its existing bookstores, its cultural and transportation facilities, the cost of a three-bedroom house, and its many other demographics in detail.

Dick discussed what he deemed to be the proper size of their store, 2,000 square feet. He stressed plans for "an extensive collection of *good* children's books" with Judy setting it up (eventually becoming nationally known in this subject area). They would begin by stocking all the ABA's "basic book list," Western Americana, in particular, and maps, globes, and greeting cards. Sidelines would include ceramics, jewelry, art objects, egg cups, "and a few imported toys in excellent taste." Most of these sidelines—especially the egg cups—were dropped without regret later on.

Dick estimated first-year sales of $40,000, based on the study. The first-year opening inventory of books would cost $15,000 with other expenses of $13,000. For his salary, Dick would draw $300 a month. Judy, working four hours a day, would receive $80 a month. His Rand McNally–earned bonus would cover the secondhand car and other initial expenses.

Plans for setting up the store moved along through the late winter months of 1959. The February 9 issue of *Publisher's Weekly,* the "Bible of the booksellers," carried the first announcement that the Chinook Bookshop was a-borning, bringing a flock of publishers' reps to the Noyes home. Walt Wilson, teacher of art at the Fountain Valley School, and by now a friend, took on the job of designing the interior. When the old Skyway Cut-a-Corner market closed, Dick picked up discarded counters and cases and adapted them for use at 208½ North Tejon.

As Judy remembered later, " Ours was pretty much a do-it-yourself operation. Dick was good at carpentry and enjoyed it. I did a bit of everything, especially planning the big central counter, the paperwork, the inventory system, and such. We were like children with their tinkertoys. We had to learn by trial and error how the pieces went together to get the effect we wanted, but learning was marvelous fun."

Early in the spring, Jane Emery, then working at Edith Farnsworth's, turned up at a party at Patty and Walt Wilson's home. Jane, an Easterner with an academic background in social sciences, had just returned to the Springs with her writer-teacher husband Charles Emery, Jr., after several years in New York. The Noyes-Emery rapport was immediate. For some time Dick had been keeping his eye on the progress of a new kind of book, paperbacks. He had a talk with Jane about this in the Wilson's kitchen, and she agreed with him that a paperback boom seemed at the threshold.

They asked Jane to consider becoming the Chinook's first full-time employee. Jane went to work organizing a paperback department and helping in the selection of hardbacks for the planned opening of the store in June. Soon the Noyes garage was jammed with some of the $15,000 worth of books that would comprise the Chinook's initial inventory.

And so the great day of the opening, Monday, June 15, 1959, came at last. The first Chinook ad appeared in the *Colorado Springs Gazette-Telegraph* on Sunday, June 14. It was Judy's effort, displaying even then her characteristic lightness of touch. "Chinook?" the ad inquired. "What is it? An Indian tribe? A kind of salmon? A warm welcome wind?" She continued. "At The Chinook Bookshop you will find the finest selection of maps and globes from Chicago to the Coast . . . and a few surprises." On that same Sunday, Stanton Peckham, the distinguished book reviewer for *The Denver Post,* noted in his book column: "Here's a chinook we hope has a long and glorious future."

Judy and Dick and Jane can remember very little about what happened at that hectic opening. Invitations had been sent to friends, Colorado College people, and other likely customers. "We were so dazed and worn out getting everything ready," Jane says, "yes, and apprehensive. Suppose nobody showed up?" But the turn-out was good, and Jane recalls selling her first book, Irma Rombauer's *Joy of Cooking.* She hurried in triumph to the inventory control file, got the Rombauer card, crossed out the figure "1" and wrote "0," initiating the first reorder.

GROWING PAINS AND PROMOTION

The going was rough for Noyes & Company through The Chinook's first two years. There never seemed to be enough money coming in, and there was a lot going out. Even the free coffee for the browsing customers was a drain. Dick,

Judy, and Jane Emery were all things to the store—janitors, gift-wrappers, un-packers of incoming and outgoing books, bank runners with the day's receipts. Many hours were spent discussing new books with the publishers' reps. During the first summer, Dick had supper alone from 4:30 to 5:30 at Ruth's Oven nearby, and then he would return to keep the store open until 9 P.M. hoping to catch a sale from some tourist wandering along North Tejon. He reminisces now, "It's neat to open a bookstore when you're in your late twenties; you can work 15-hour days and still have energy left for the kids."

Each day brought its lessons. To guard against suspected shoplifters, Dick would call out "Dust those books up front, Judy, please." Theft never was much of a problem, in spite of the store's meandering layout, but Jane learned about confidence games when a smartly dressed woman ordered $500 worth of books to be sent to a college library in Kansas and then "borrowed" $10 for lunch—"How silly of me, left my purse at the hotel." She never returned, of course, and there was no such Kansas college.

Rough going or not, Dick was more than a little pleased at the end of the first year to be able to report to his father total sales of $65,000 as against $40,000 he had predicted in his prospectus. And 1959 was not just a lucky year. Thereafter, year after year, sales at The Chinook would increase from 20 to 25 percent annually with a proportionate increase in the size of the staff as it edged toward an eventual 20 people with the annual average inventory of books rising from the first year's $15,000 to over $200,000 at cost, with approx-imately 40,000 book titles and annual sales well in excess of $1,000,000.

How to explain such progress?

In Judy's words, "A key element was the hard work and devotion of the staff, their love of what they were doing, their pride in The Chinook, and their ability to work in harmony as a team. All of them were ardent readers who could pass their knowledge along to a customer wanting to know something about what he was buying. None of them objected—not much, anyhow—to Dick's attention to the tedious details of the trade that he had learned when he was with Rand McNally: the ins and outs of publishers' policies, tight systems and controls, and fast reordering and follow-up."

The shop's brief statement of policy begins: "The Chinook is intentionally an informal place, dedicated to the belief that its staff is the cream of the crop. For this reason extensively spelled-out do's and don'ts are unnecessary." Dick and Judy flinch at the title "clerk"; there are professional booksellers, not "clerks," at The Chinook. Over the years staff members have come and gone, but the turnover has been modest. As of now the average is over 10 years on the job for the floor sales staffers.

Among Dick's ideas was his stress on proper display. Publishers hired art-ists and printers to produce book jackets that would catch the eye. So he made it a rule that as many books as possible be placed face-out, in full view.

Walter Wilson contributed an idea for the store's Tejon Street window that followed the jacket display idea. He suggested a piquant character later referred to as "The Invisible Man" (or woman), a figure in the front window suggested by bits of dress, spectacles, a hat, shoes, and a book—all suspended by wire, with a slogan on a poster, usually with some sort of pun. Dick created the figures, and Judy was responsible for the puns.

One window showed the invisible man sitting on a log, "Stumped for a book to read." Another depicted a Cripple Creek miner and the slogan, "A gold mine of a book—it's loded." The sign accompanying the figure of a hiker: "To Thoreau-ly enjoy the fall, pack in mountains of good reading." A cowboy: "Quit horsing around! Wither it rains or snows, it's a cinch for all good chaps to hitch up to the wide range of brand-new reading in The Chinook stable." During the 1960s, a springtime theme had an invisible lady in a flutter of butterflies and the slogan, "It's a breeze to get high on books." Sue Ormes suggested one of the most popular windows, used every January, which has "The Invisible Man" with a broom, with discarded gift wrappings piled high, "Sweeping into the New Year." Friends and neighbors of the Noyeses contribute garbage bags filled with their Christmas wrap after the holiday every year. Hundreds of pedestrians make it a habit to walk by the bookshop to see if there is a new window with a horrible pun. In passing, they stop, of course, to look over the many new books piled around the invisible figure. Dick finally decided to pass along the responsibility for the physical creation of the window display to multitalented Karen Engel, who has been in charge of the shop displays since 1974.

Some things happened by accident. Dick built for $50 a playhouse at home for daughters Catherine and Stephanie. They and the neighbor kids were so entranced by it that he built another, also for $50, in a corner of the bookstore. A pair of large Steiff chimpanzees lived in the two-story house, and children customers were soon asking their parents to "take me to the store with the monkey house." Young parents who once played themselves in the house are now bringing in another generation, parking them with the monkeys while they take their time finding books to buy.

Another factor in The Chinook's growth was the closing of its two major competitors, Edith Farnsworth's and Their Book Shop. Most of the customers of those two established stores then switched their business to The Chinook.

In 1961, the third Noyes child, Matthew, was born. By now, The Chinook and its coffee corner had become a hangout for kindred book-loving spirits. Among them was a small young woman in very high heels and a big droopy hat named Nancy Wood who had a wild desire to be a writer. Nancy was editing an FM radio station weekly filled with local chitchat. One day she asked Judy to write a column on current books. The response to the column was surprisingly good. When Nancy's publication folded, Judy decided to keep on with the column as a promotional giveaway under the title "Currents from The Chinook."

The first "Currents" was a single page mailed out to regular customers at Christmas time. The time arrived when it had grown to six pages and thousands of words of copy. The demand for it grew until the Noyes found themselves mailing it to 6,000 people, some of whom wrote in from all over the world asking for copies and ordering books. The publication gave Judy a chance to develop the talent she had shown in Florida as a teenaged journalist. "Currents" is fast-paced, brightly written, informative, and amusing. It lists the bestsellers but gives considerable space to the books of regional interest and those by local authors.

All these activities advanced The Chinook upward, but paramount was the creativity of the Noyes themselves and their total fascination with the art of selling books. From the start Dick had believed that a bookstore's success derived from promoting books to the nonaddicted reader. He did not mind purveying the obvious bestsellers, of course. But what pleased him most was to see hard-hats or mechanics or any other sort of "unbookish" person wander into the store to buy hunting and fishing maps and then stop to look at books in the do-it-yourself section or to examine the rows of books on cooking or gardening or auto mechanics.

It was to lure such people who may never have read a book for fun to discover the joy of reading that Dick and Judy had decided to stock all kinds of books. There would be books on rock n'roll, veterinary medicine, judo, ancient Greek, taxidermy, science fiction, and the occult—the list is endless. They did not care how exotic a book might be, or that it might take a while to sell. Sooner or later somebody would come across *Finding Your Way with Clay* or *Be Bold with Bananas,* clutch it in triumph, march up to the sales counter, and leave to spread the word that The Chinook was just what Dick and Judy had hoped it would be, "the one place you can find everything."[2]

Dick and Judy marked The Chinook's tenth year in 1969 when annual sales were nearing half a million dollars by leasing the store next door to the north, which had been occupied by John Eastham's Whickerbill Gift Shop, which itself moved up one space. With architect Clifford Nakata (who a year later designed the Noyes's new home) in charge, they tore out a wall, moved a sales counter to its present central position, installed elaborately carved Spanish doors at the two entrances, and surrounded The Invisible Man with a decade of best bestsellers, including the two best in 1959, *Dr. Zhivago* and *Exodus.*

The expansion increased The Chinook's space from 2,500 to 5,300 square feet. Reporting their tenth birthday in *Publisher's Weekly,* Judy wrote: "Drippity-drop-drop was the sound of the very un-Colorado-like weather. Puh-*wop* was the promising refrain of champagne corks being popped inside The Chinook for the several hundred people dropping in for the festivities."

---

[2]See Jeff Blyskal, "Dalton, Walden, and the Amazing Money Machine," *Forbes,* January 18, 1982, an article about the "democratization" of book buying. "To be blunt about it, books are no longer bought just to be read but, like any other consumer item, to be owned, to be looked at, to be given as presents. Not surprisingly, picture books, sex books and cookbooks are major products. In an age of cable television and video cassettes, people may not necessarily be spending more time reading books, but they are spending more money buying books." (p. 47).

Dick was a bit irritable that day having just given up smoking, but he did manage a smile when Harold Dillon, the dean of Rocky Mountain publishers' reps, congratulated him on the enlargement with its change of address from the demeaning 208½ to 210 North Tejon. "Never thought you'd make it," Dillon said, "but I couldn't be happier to have been wrong."

NATIONAL PROFESSIONAL INVOLVEMENT

Soon after joining the American Booksellers Association (ABA) the Noyeses supported the regional book scene by attending the first meeting in Denver of the Colorado Booksellers Association where they met Pyke Johnson, Jr., managing editor of Doubleday & Company and others of the larger book world, many of whom would become personal as well as professional friends.

The ABA has a membership of 4,500 bookstores from every state and of some 1,500 publishers who supply bookstores with the 450,000 books in print and the 40,000 or so new books published each year. Its board of directors conducts a maze of projects: the *American Bookseller* magazine, the massive and often revised *Manual of Bookselling*, a Booksellers School with annual workships, an ABA newswire, and the selection and donation every four years of 500 books to the White House family library. Its 5 standing and 10 special committees address every conceivable aspect of moving books from the nation's stores to the reader.

This swirl of activity comes into sharp focus at the ABA's annual convention headquarters in a hotel in Washington, D.C., or New York or Boston or Los Angeles or Chicago. Thousands of booksellers attend the exhibits, the ABA program of work sessions, banquets, and parties. Reporters, camera operators, and radio and TV people frequent the scene along with the publishers, the bestselling and most flamboyant of authors (James Michener, perhaps, or Irving Wallace), or celebrity authors such as Vincent Price and Lauren Bacall.

It can be suspected that back in 1959, Dick began to think that he, the unknown owner of an embryo bookstore far out in the unregarded West, might some day become active on the board of the ABA. At any rate, Dick and Judy were present at the ABA conventions of the 1960s, giving trade talks and discussing the problems of booksellers far from the eastern scene.

The Chinook's name was gradually getting to be known in ABA circles through Judy's informative articles for *Publisher's Weekly.* Jane Emery and Dick also wrote about the store. One of Judy's most popular articles explained how to put humor into bookstore ads to make sure that they are read.

Her use of puns with "The Invisible Man" was helpful in writing these ads; some were inspired by regular repartee with Dick's father, a veteran punster. One Chinook ad for a local theater group showed an actor ducking rotten eggs and the line "Sure we're egging you on. We want you to make Chinook part of your scene." Another had a parent eating a wormy apple and the line

"The best way to worm your way into Dad's affections: choose an a-peeling new book from Chinook for Father's Day." The picture of an angry editor had the line "If the editor finds your work ode-ious, remember things could be verse. Come to The Chinook and be a-mused. Inspiration like you never meta-phor."

In the spring of 1965, Dick and Judy had a pleasant surprise—a phone call from Joseph Duffy, then executive director of the ABA, in Denver at a re-gional booksellers' meeting with Igor Kropotkin, then president of the ABA and head of Scribner's Bookstore in New York City. Duffy asked casually if the two of them could come down to Colorado Springs to see The Chinook about which they had heard so much. Duffy spoke of his special interest in The Chi-nook's inventory control.

Soon after the important visitors arrived, as Dick stood with them at the big main sales counter explaining his systems, a stressed sales staffer came waltzing up to the inventory control file remarking loudly and irritably, "Damn it, I can't find a *thing* in these stupid files."

Even so the two ABA big guns must have been impressed by what they saw at Chinook. A few months later Dick received word of his nomination as a director of ABA. From that time on, Dick delegated more and more of the store's operation to the staff as he advanced steadily in the ABA hierarchy, from third to second to first vice president and chairman of standing commit-tees and as a member of the faculty of the national Booksellers School.

Dick came to the ABA board with a strong conviction of the need to re-structure the whole operation to reduce the traditional emphasis on the con-cerns of Eastern booksellers, to broaden the geographical representation, and to develop the abilities of the younger segment of the membership. One of Dick's major contributions as a director was his rewriting of the ABA bylaws in the early 1970s. The excellence of his work in this difficult matter seems to have been rewarded in April 1974 by his election as president of the ABA, one of the youngest and the first of the booksellers from the Rocky Mountain re-gion to hold that office.

By coincidence, Dick's term of office involved greater responsibilities than more recent presidents had faced. One of his two years in office coincid-ed with celebration of the ABA's Diamond Jubilee, its seventy-fifth year. The convention took place in New York with a then record attendance of over 8,000 booksellers and book publishers and authors from all over the world.

AN EXPANDING REPUTATION

With a pleasant exhaustion, the Noyeses survived those four May days of that Diamond Jubilee of Dick's presidency: the entertaining, speaking assignments, press interviews, and attending autographing sessions with celebrities. Less wearing were the more intimate parties in New York's finest restaurants and enjoying the awe inspired by their two-story penthouse suite atop the Hilton assigned to them by the ABA.

One effect of Dick's presidency was to bathe The Chinook in a tide of admiring comment, which became by repetition almost a cliché in book circles. An article in the ABA's *American Bookseller* concluded "and today The Chinook's owners are among the best-known booksellers in the country." In a *Publisher's Weekly* article, "An Interview with Richard Noyes," Lila Freilicher wrote, "ABA's president is a perfectionist who, not surprisingly, runs one of the best bookshops in the country." In August 1975, *Town and Country* published an article about Colorado Springs by Patricia Linden who wrote of Dick, "He is the owner of Colorado Springs' far-famed Chinook Bookshop which sells a staggering $700,000 worth of hard- and soft-covered literature on every conceivable subject and has been called 'the best bookshop in the U.S.A.' "

Recently, Pyke Johnson, Jr., a senior editor of Doubleday, who was born in Denver, commenting on the store's twentieth anniversary, wrote, "I have always said that The Chinook was the best bookstore in the United States. At the beginning I might have been bragging a little in the way of a native son. But now I know that, by any standard, or for any reason, this statement is correct. I honor all the people at Chinook who have made it so; I am proud to consider them my friends."

In November 1977, Dick received the Intellectual Freedom Award given by the eight-state Mountain Plains Library Association. He had appeared many times in defense of the freedom-to-read in public hearings both in Colorado Springs and Denver. A co-founder of the Colorado Media Coalition, his impact in censorship matters derived from years as an ardent supporter of First Amendment rights.

In March 1978 Dick was one of two Booksellers members of a delegation sponsored by the U.S. State Department sent to Nigeria to acquaint the booksellers there with American distribution and marketing methods. In October he was chosen as part of a delegation requested by the British government to conduct seminars in London and Oxford on American bookselling and publishing procedures. In March 1979 Dick was one of two booksellers appointed by the Center of the Book of the Library of Congress to a committee of 100 authors, publishers, librarians, and others of the book world wishing to promote more widespread reading in the United States. Judy and Dick Noyes have taught the bookselling section of the Denver University Publishing Institute each summer since its inception in 1976.

Judy, meantime, was becoming known for her enthusiasm and expertise in selling children's books. Her reviews of new children's books appeared in *The New York Times* and *Publisher's Weekly,* and she was a founder of the liaison committee formed between the American Booksellers Association and the Children's Book Council to get better communications established between children's booksellers and editor/publishers.

THE CHINOOK STAFF'S ASSIGNMENTS

Dick and Judy enjoy their staff, now numbering 20, all of whom share their fascination with books and delight in a camaraderie rare in any business. Customers often comment on this atmosphere of fun and good nature in the midst of obvious busyness. Jane Emery recalls that Edith Farnsworth had told her "the most fun you'll have is the initial setting up of the store." But that's not how it turned out at all, says Jane. "It's been fun right along."

Francie Armstrong, who has assisted in the management of the paperback department for 15 years, agrees that the lighthearted atmosphere has been a major appeal for customers and staff, too. And Francie has a theory as to why such competent people come and remain at Chinook: "We are part of a team, but there is also a great feeling of individual respect and freedom." She also stresses the dedication and quality of the service. "The people on this staff will knock themselves out to get books for customers." That this service is appreciated is reflected in the many thank-you letters The Chinook special-order department receives from grateful customers.

Phyllis Zell's skill as head of special orders and out-of-print book finder has brought her queries and customers from all over the world. With the help of Mark Burski, she processes at least 200 special orders a week for Colorado Springs customers, not to mention the out-of-town and institutional business. Anne Cross, a Coloradoan who knows the town inside and out and was co-owner of Their Book Shop, is another longtimer (over 11 years). Carol Williams has been Chinook's prized keeper of the books for over a decade and is now assisted by Glenda Oldcrag, Wanda Jeavons, and Kim Mersman. Claudia Castle, who *insisted* upon working at The Chinook following her graduation from Mount Holyoke in 1970, now serves as the shop's "memory bank" for authors and titles.

Dick has always had a particular feeling for the kids who started as janitors after school and then worked up to better things their junior or senior year in high school. Lance Selkirk was the first, followed among others by the Koller and Garner Brothers, Jim Dunn, and recently Dave Kosley and Scott Chambers. The shipping room group, long the only male bastion at the Chinook was integrated finally and happily by three stalwarts, Sharon Sprague, Karen Engel, and Kathryn Redman.

So, what of the future? "We'll see," says Dick. "There has been pressure from many advisor-friends to expand—to branch The Chinook into a regional minichain. Dick and Judy see that as an option, but not a very agreeable one. The three Noyes children—Catherine N. Boddington, now 26 and a graduate of Bennington College; Stephanie, 25, a graduate of St. Lawrence University; and Matthew, 17, an undergraduate at Wesleyan University—have worked at the bookshop, and there is always the possibility of a second generation to carry on.

One thing is certain: Dick and Judy and the staff are fiercely independent booksellers who are dedicated to excellence and are determined that the present-day Chinook will never change its style, personality, and its belief in complete, personal service. They believe that The Chinook is a unique, personal place, selling "a commodity created to meet the needs of people seeking knowledge, wisdom, and pleasure."

The Appendix presents additional information related to the case study.

Your Task:

Advise Dick and Judy Noyes. From your viewpoint, what are the strengths and weaknesses of their operation? Give them your ideas of opportunities and threats in their industry and marketplace. What would you recommend they do to enhance their firm's performance over the next five years especially since B. Dalton Books, the national chain, is rapidly making inroads into their geographical area?

Appendix

RICHARD NOYES'S PHILOSOPHY OF SELLING

These three statements come from Dick's notes on selling, used in teaching courses mentioned in the narrative:

1. The average book on successful selling actually assumes that the customer does not want or need the product, is basically pretty ignorant, and must be coerced into buying. This is their premise, and the specific advice they give obviously is based on it. Almost always these sales technique manuals imply a basic lack of integrity (a hucksterism) that may be appropriate for the life insurance salesman but certainly has no place in retail bookselling. The good bookstore should work for long-range, repeat business—there's no room for the hard sell, the one-night-stand sort of thing.

2. Never make a casual recommendation—if it's way off base, your store has probably lost that customer. Highly personal recommendations can be difficult, especially if the customer doesn't give you much to go on. If there's quite a void of information, attack from the flanks. What has the person read recently and enjoyed? If the book is a gift, find out the profession of the recipient, or his or her age, hobbies, attitudes, etc.—it's amazing how much you can piece together once you get the hang of

Appendix (Cont.)

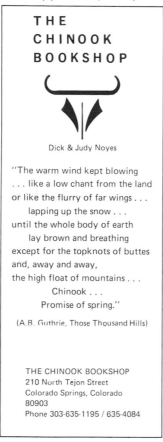

THE
CHINOOK
BOOKSHOP

Dick & Judy Noyes

"The warm wind kept blowing
. . . like a low chant from the land
or like the flurry of far wings . . .
    lapping up the snow . . .
until the whole body of earth
    lay brown and breathing
except for the topknots of buttes
and, away and away,
the high float of mountains . . .
        Chinook . . .
    Promise of spring."

(A.B. Guthrie, Those Thousand Hills)

THE CHINOOK BOOKSHOP
210 North Tejon Street
Colorado Springs, Colorado
80903
Phone 303-635-1195 / 635-4084

it. . . . You sincerely want that person to like that book; it's your recommendation, and if correct it's awfully good for business.

3. Your ad in the telephone directory is your least expensive, most effective advertising. Surely your store's telephone salesmanship deserves prime consideration.

FROM AMERICAN BOOKSELLERS ASSOCIATION

Permission has been granted by American Booksellers Association (the casewriters are especially grateful to Allan Marshall for his cooperation) to reprint in this portion of the appendix parts of "ABA Bookstore Financial Profile," the results of an ABA study, published in 1981 by American Booksellers Association. The key findings presented here are very similar to the conclusions reached in a similar ABA study of booksellers, published in 1977.

Appendix (Cont.)

1. The key findings of this report, in other words, confirm what everyone has been saying. The erosion of profitability in bookstores over the past four years has been measured and found to be alarming. Relief has come from some publishers through improved terms. Whether it came early enough or is adequate enough to help booksellers pull themselves out of the red will be the key finding of the next survey.[1]

2. Meanwhile, we asked respondents to this survey to share with other booksellers the methods they have found practical in reducing costs and improving profits. All but 20 stores replied to this question, which indicates that the vast majority are trying to control their own destiny. Of the 300 respondents,

158 have eliminated nonproductive categories of books
149 are ordering more from wholesalers to cut transportation costs
148 have made greater use of delayed dating plans on invoices
122 have cut back on the amount of advertising
121 are ordering more from publishers to increase discounts
116 are ordering less frequently to cut transportation costs and increase discounts
96 have eliminated special services or have instituted a charge for those formerly offered for free
90 have reduced staff
78 have added sidelines
55 responded to the "Other" category (explained below)
50 have increased emphasis on an area of specialization
44 have added used books to the merchandise mix
33 have reduced the number of hours the store is open
28 have added nonbook services
24 have reduced or eliminated owners' or employee benefits
14 have reduced the size of the store to cut back on overhead

Of the 55 stores who responded to the "Other" category, 22 offered the following specifics:

5 stores are ordering more carefully
9 stores are improving their inventory control and stock-turn performance
2 stores have relocated to reduce rent
2 stores are tightening up on budgets
4 stores have increased their co-op advertising

3. **Average Years of Operation and Average Hours Open.** If any single table confirms preconceived notions about bookstores, it is the one that follows, which shows that the larger stores have been in opera-

---

[1] "ABA Bookstore Financial Profile," p. 1.

Appendix (Cont.)

tion for more years than the smaller ones. The larger a store becomes, the more hours it is open per week as well. Neither years of operation nor hours open, however, have any apparent effect on profitability. Indeed, it appears that the most profitable stores have been in operation the shortest time, which may confirm the theory that management becomes lax after the eighth year of operation. The fact that the least profitable stores have been in business for nearly 10 years might also confirm the theory that some stores are run as a hobby rather than as a means of supporting the owner.[2]

	NUMBER OF STORES	AVERAGE YEARS OPEN	AVERAGE HOURS OPEN (per week)
Single store respondents			
Less than $50,000	20	3.5	49.7
$50,000 to $100,000	36	8.1	48.4
$100,000 to $150,000	29	9.2	54.0
$150,000 to $300,000	44	10.6	58.8
$300,000 to $500,000	16	22.5	59.0
Over $500,000	13	31.6	64.0
Multiple-store respondents	39	16.4	64.0
All stores	197	12.1	55.5
Stores in the top 25% profit range	36	7.6	54.1
Stores in the middle 50% profit range	102	14.4	56.6
Stores in the bottom 25% profit range	31	9.8	53.3

4. **Sales per Square Foot of Occupied Space.** The highest sales per square foot, as the following bar graph demonstrates, does not necessarily yield the highest gross profit, which is dictated by the overall factors affecting profitability. But the bar graph does demonstrate dramatically that the relationship between nonselling and selling space has a direct relationship to profitability among the responding stores.[3]

5. **Sales per Full-Time Employee.** The ratio of sales per employee to total sales measures employee productivity and is generally considered a good guide to the efficiency of a retail business. There is almost no correlation between the figures given by respondents in 1977 and 1981 due to a marked difference in method of reporting. Sales per employee increase as sales volume increases, but this is not necessarily because each

[2]Ibid., p. 6; as reported by 169 stores with annual sales totaling $51,645,316.
[3]Ibid., p. 8.

Appendix (Cont.)

SALES PER SQUARE FOOT OF OCCUPIED SPACE

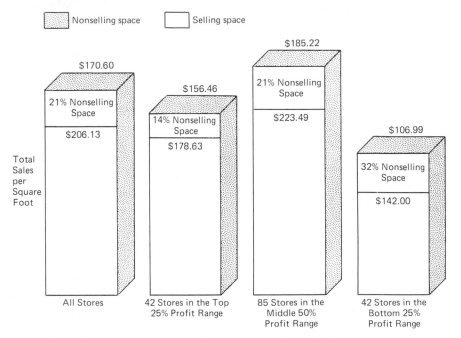

employee in a larger store employs better sales techniques: larger inventories attract more browsing and create more impulse buying.

	AVERAGE	MID RANGE
33 stores in the top 25% profit range	$45,516	$34,656–56,277
119 stores in the middle 50% profit range	61,855	39,090–66,523
32 stores in the bottom 25% profit range	45,233	27,447–54,266

The highest sales per employee does not necessarily result in the highest profitability, however, as the table demonstrates. The most profitable and least profitable stores in this sample reported virtually identical sales per employee.[4]

6. **Financial Profile, 1981.**[5] The following table shows both the average and the median profit and loss statements for 179 stores with annual sales totaling $48,185,364. All data in this section of the survey are based on the identical store sample.

In the table an "adjusted net profit" entry appears as the bottom

[4]Ibid., p. 9; as reported by 184 stores with annual sales totaling $48,364,614.
[5]Ibid., p. 17.

	33 STORES IN TOP 25% PROFIT RANGE WITH ANNUAL SALES TOTALING $4,546,963: Percent of Sales		116 STORES IN MIDDLE 50% PROFIT RANGE WITH ANNUAL SALES TOTALING $38,855,035: Percent of Sales		30 STORES IN BOTTOM 25% PROFIT RANGE WITH ANNUAL SALES TOTALING $4,783,366: Percent of Sales		ALL STORES (179 STORES WITH ANNUAL SALES TOTALING $48,185,364): Percent of Sales	
	Average	Median	Average	Median	Average	Median	Average	Median
Total sales	100.0%	100.0%	100.0%	100.0%	100.0%	100.0%	100.0%	100.0%
Less: Cost of goods sold	61.4	60.5	65.1	65.3	66.7	69.4	64.9	65.7
Gross margin	38.6	39.2	34.9	34.9	33.3	30.5	35.1	34.6
Less expenses:								
Payroll expense (total)	12.7	9.8	16.2	14.4	19.3	19.8	16.2	16.3
Owners' compensation	3.9	5.4	2.5	7.2	2.4	—	2.4	7.5
Wages: employees	8.4	5.0	13.3	10.1	15.6	15.4	13.2	10.0
Employee benefits	.4	.8	.4	.7	1.2	.8	.6	1.0
Data processing payroll	—	—	—	—	.1	—	.1	—
Occupancy expense (total)	7.7	7.6	6.6	6.5	6.3	10.0	6.6	7.8
Rent, mortgage, or building depreciation	5.4	5.1	5.0	4.7	4.5	7.5	4.4	5.4
Real estate taxes and insurance	.6	.6	.5	1.0	.4	1.1	.5	1.3
Utilities	1.0	1.0	.7	1.4	.8	1.8	.7	1.6
Repair, maintenance, cleaning	.7	.7	.4	.7	.5	.6	1.1	1.0
Advertising	1.7	1.8	1.8	1.7	1.8	2.8	1.8	2.2
Telephone/communications	.4	.6	.3	.7	.6	.9	.4	.9
Professional services	.3	.5	.3	.7	.7	1.2	.4	1.2
Stationery and supplies	—	—	.3	.5	.4	—	.3	.7
Data processing exclusive of payroll								
Depreciation	.9	1.0	.3	.5	.4	1.9	.3	.7
Travel and entertainment	.4	.9	.7	1.4	1.5	1.3	.9	1.7
Insurance	.5	.8	.2	.8	.8	1.2	.3	1.2
Credit card service charges	.3	.3	.2	.6	.8	.5	.3	1.1
Dues and subscriptions	.3	—	.3	.5	.3	.5	.3	.5
Miscellaneous office expense and postage	.4	.7	.3	.9	.2	—	.2	.7
Taxes	.4	.8	.2	.6	.1	.6	.3	1.0
All other operating expense	1.1	1.4	1.2	1.8	2.3	2.3	1.3	2.4
Total operating expenses	27.1%	27.6%	29.2%	32.0%	36.1%	37.0%	29.8%	32.0%
Operating income (loss)	11.5	12.9	5.7	3.1	(2.8)	(7.8)	5.3	2.4
Other income	.4	—	.4	.7	.5	—	.2	1.8
Other expense	.7	.7	.6	1.2	.5	—	.6	1.4
Net income (loss) before taxes	11.2	12.2	5.5	2.6	(2.8)	(8.6)	4.9	2.3
Less: Allowance for unreported owners' earnings	(3.6)		(3.8)		(3.3)		(4.0)	
Adjusted net profit	7.6		1.7				.9	

Appendix (Cont.)

line. The adjusted profit results from the inclusion after "net income before taxes" of an allowance for owners' earnings in instances where stores did not report such earnings under the "owners' compensation" entry in the Payroll Expense section of the questionnaire. The rate used in making these adjustments is a composite derived from actual owners' compensation in each size or profitability group.

The resulting adjusted net profit more truly reflects the profitability (or lack thereof) of the reporting stores. For further confirmation of this point, see the table illustrating "Total dollars available to owner" later in the survey.

7. Summary [6]

Once again, the financial survey has proven that controlling expenses rather than simply increasing gross margin is the key to profitable bookselling. But it has also shown the difficulty of controlling expenses under recent economic conditions, even in the most profitable stores.

The survey was completed before the effects of publishers' changing terms could have an impact in the bookstores. It is hoped that the next survey will show a better economic future for independent booksellers. If it does, it will be not only because terms have improved, but because booksellers have continued vigilantly to control expenses as well.

Booksellers in the lower sales groups should find some encouragement in the fact that size alone does not guarantee a reasonable profit. A reasonable profit on a small operation, however, is not necessarily a living wage.

[6]Ibid., p. 25.

case
19

EARLY WINTERS LTD

In the *New 1982 Catalog,* Early Winters Ltd (EW) covered its 92 four-color pages with "new and exciting outdoor items," including such products as wool/rayon gloves "knit by native women in the households of Hazar-Jat and Paghman," live llamas ("aficionados say 'yamas,'" the parenthetical admonition reminds the reader), and "Omnipotent," the forerunner of which launched the company over a decade earlier.

President Bill Nicolai recalled, "Peter Williamson, who is now EW's corporate treasurer, and I were camped miles from the nearest road when a sudden winter storm destroyed our tent. After hiking for days through the brush over rugged terrain to civilization and barely surviving, we decided that the Picket Range of the North Cascades called for a good tent, something better than anything then on the market. That's when we designed and constructed the first Omnipotent, basically the same one we offer today. There was good publicity when this product accompanied climbers in the first winter ascent of Mt. Everest."

COMPANY OVERVIEW

A few milestones of the youthful firm are listed in Exhibit 1. "It was easy getting accustomed to more cash flow and not living hand to mouth," the president commented, "but for a time we couldn't take care of the orders that were coming in. Our first mailer for the Gore-Tex fabric tent was nothing but a cover letter and a black-and-white mailer, with a certificate offering $20 off the selling price and a money-back guarantee card, not very different from what we are saying today—'you must be satisfied or we'll refund your money.'" Exhibit 2 is a typical letter included in each catalog.

Exhibit 1

SELECTED EARLY WINTERS LTD MILESTONES

1971 Nearly fatal accident leads to concept of Omnipotent.

1972 Nicolai produced 13 tents the first year, in a friend's basement.

Tent purchased by Bill Edwards, who later became EW's vice president of product operations.

First brochure designed by Ron Zimmerman, now vice president of marketing.

1973 Retail store opened by EW.

1974 Two additional sewing machine operators hired; one of these, Pat Salvador, is now sewing manager.

Company produced 300 Omnipotents.

1975 EW and Gore-Tex fabric discovered each other.

1976 EW's Light Dimension tent, the first outdoor application of Gore-Tex, a waterproof, breathable fabric, was introduced on May 1.

Company rented fifth floor of Prefontaine Building to manufacture tents.

First EW mail-order catalog was published in December; Gore-Tex rainwear and the Sleep Inn were introduced.

1977 Product lines were broadened; sales of $750,000 were achieved.

1978 First EW full-color catalog was printed; sales of $2.3 million were recorded.

1979 Acquired a Wang VS computer for mailing list and customer sales information, followed by inventory system and customer service inquiry and backorder system; sales of $5.2 million were recorded.

1980 Appointed a fulfillment manager, Steve Costie, and introduced Silver Lining garments; sales of $8 million were recorded.

1981 In July, EW was employing 115 and processing 750 orders daily; sales of $10 million were achieved.

1982 EW was employing 175 and was processing over 1,000 orders a day; sales of $13 million were achieved.

Exhibit 2

GUARANTEE LETTER IN 1982 CATALOG

Dear Friend,

It's easy for me to rave about Early Winters products. I take the stuff out. I use it, I wear it, I test it.

Exhibit 2 (Cont.)

I want to be sure you know that you can, too.

Too many people, I'm afraid, take our guarantee with a grain of salt. They balk at sweating up the socks or taking the tent out in hard weather. Or maybe they keep something not because they like it, but because they got it dirty.

You don't have to keep it "new" in order to get your refund or exchange. You can use our products under any conditions for a full month.

I believe in the things we offer and I want you to know how well they perform. Your order tells us that you'd like to try something. You have 30 days to decide if you want to keep it. Please, make use of the time!

Then, if you don't like it, just shake out the dirt and send it back. You won't get any argument from us. If you're not happy with it, we don't want you to keep it.

So if something in these pages sounds like it fits your needs, give it a try. **Really** give it a try—for a month from the day it arrives.

Sincerely,
Bill Nicolai, President

P.S.   If you think a friend of yours might enjoy receiving our catalog, just fill out the postcard across from page 18. We'll send one out, with your compliments.

"That guarantee keeps us on our toes," Nicolai reported, "and, yes, we do get back a fair amount of products. Then we dispose of that merchandise; it's not a total loss for the company. A lot of good product development data comes from those returns, too; often we take an item out of the line if too many come back for refunds."

Nicolai was mentioned in the first sentence of a 1981 article that named Early Winters Ltd number 38 in a list of 100 fastest-growing privately held companies in the United States.[1] Management claimed to want to control growth more closely from 1982 to 1985 than previously, to improve stability, and, as Nicolai said, "to build up equity because from the beginning we have been totally self-financed. Also, slower growth will enable our middle management to spend time developing their skills. I'd like to see us have just a little breathing space so we can consolidate, reflect, and do a better job of planning. Approaching Christmas, our payroll is 140 people; usually there are about 120." In 1982, the payroll stood at 200 for the Christmas rush.

[1]Bradford W. Ketchum, Jr., "The Inc. Private 100," *Inc.*, December 1981, pp. 35–37.

TURNING A HOBBY INTO A BUSINESS

"So what I did," Nicolai declared, "was to turn a hobby into my source of income. It might have been different if Seattle hadn't been in such an economic slump during that period, but as it was I couldn't get a job. So this was partly necessity."

The first piece of advertising was a brochure prepared by Zimmerman, who remembered his experience in mail order: "I had a small mail-order business in junior high and high school, selling fishing tackle that I made in my parents' recreation room. Since that wasn't a wealth of experience, you could say that Bill and I are self-taught; we've learned by doing. And the pay was terrific—we paid ourselves $2.50 an hour during the first couple of years, and we couldn't always make that payroll. Five of us were working at EW then, and total annual sales in 1974–1975 had reached only about $100,000."

"Another lucky occurrence," Nicolai joined in, "was in 1975 when Gore-Tex was looking for someone to use its fabric, somebody to try it. They contacted us because we were making tents, a product they thought would be very good made with Gore-Tex. They were right, and they came to us at just the right time. Up to that point, we had only the one tent and in just one design. This was just what we needed to provide the big push—to get us at least above the poverty level of income. Making something less specialized and at a lower price than the Omnipotent would greatly broaden our appeal in the marketplace."

"Our first product enjoyed a fine reputation," Zimmerman hastened to add, "but it wasn't something that a typical backpacker would buy. And we knew there were a lot more of the weekend backpackers out there than the highly skilled people who had been buying the tent we started with. The new lightweight tent—simple and quick to set up and to take down—weighed just 3 pounds. Its problem was that it condensed badly on the inside. Fortunately, Gore-Tex solved that problem and saved the day for Early Winter when we introduced it on May 1, 1976—a significant day for the company, because it was an instant success. Our sales multiplied sixfold practically overnight. That's when we rented the fifth floor of the Prefontaine Building and set about feverishly filling orders."

"Our retail store was very important to us, too," Nicolai remarked, "because then it accounted for about half our total sales volume. I think we developed a good local following because people could buy things from us that they couldn't get at the traditional sporting goods retailer."

POSITIONING AND PROMOTION STRATEGY

Using an insert in its 1982 catalog, EW continued to promote that uniqueness: "Most items are unique and available only from us. Don't expect to find most of the items in this catalog on the racks at your local sporting goods store. Early Winter's tents, parkas, and Gore-Tex fabric clothing are designed, manufactured, and sold only by us." Promoting this limited availability was EW's principal way of positioning itself against competitors.

Nicolai recollected that the first mailing was 7,000 pieces, with an initial response of $70,000 in orders, roughly six times the amount on the books when the mailer went out. "We covered the wall with those orders," he grimaced, "three walls floor-to-ceiling, covered with backorders. So what's the problem? Primarily it was this: the summer camping season was upon us and we had to keep customers happy, to keep them from canceling the orders, while waiting for their tents. I'm not sure how many we lost—maybe 10 percent, all told— even though some had to wait several weeks."

The 7,000 pieces were sent to a mailing list gained from small space ads promoting the Omnipotent. "Those customers," according to Zimmerman, "were different from the previous ones and really went for that $195 price. We stepped up the frequency of space advertisements, especially in such specialty outdoor magazines as *Backpacker, Outside,* and *Adventure Travel.* There were others, but these were the main ones that we used at that time. Then came our first catalog in 1976, all 32 glorious black-and-white pages of it."

"That one went to over 15,000 names," Nicolai said. "The problem was we were a little late. It was a Christmas mailing that wasn't dropped until about December 10. This was mainly because . . ."

Zimmerman interrupted, "Mainly because I was doing the entire project—product research, copywriting, typesetting . . . everything except actually running the press. It didn't get out on schedule. By the way, that catalog was reprinted, running the total to about 40,000—15,000 initially and 25,000 over the following nine months. This enabled us to capitalize on a big advantage— so far, nobody else was using the Gore-Tex technology. Then, in 1978, we started doing two catalogs a year. At first it was merely reprinting the original catalog, and Bill and I were still doing the whole thing ourselves. We still had difficulties making the mailing schedule on time, and we had to prepare that Christmas catalog in July or August, along with the spring catalog, in order to manufacture and buy the merchandise to be sold."

In 1982, Zimmerman, Nicolai, and their staff continued doing copywriting, typesetting, paste-ups, and layouts in-house; a Portland freelancer handled the photography.

Ron Zimmerman said EW's average order size varied between $53 and $55 in 1982, from a list of over 500,000 names, with about 180,000 customers buying at least once. "I must admit, that high annual growth rate was beyond our wildest dreams. That's why we went into electronic data processing—to handle that volume efficiently. That adds an element of control that's indispensable to a direct marketing company like ours. And we are adding to the list, partly by exchanging lists with competitors such as Eddie Bauer, L. L.

Bean, and others. We're creating new customers from their lists, and they find ours to be productive for them. We are concerned that lists may burn out, too, so we're watching that factor closely."

EW's marketing staff stated that the company's customers were, on the average, 34 years of age with a combined household income annually of $32,000. "I would call them an upscale audience," Zimmerman related, "very interested in the outdoor life. What we're trying to do is mature with them, to change the company as they change, to anticipate their needs. So far we've done just a little formal research to study who our customers are—mainly relying on letters and phone conversations. But we are considering some focus groups and additional questionnaire mailings, mainly to find out why we have been so successful. We know that what we're doing is working, but we don't always know exactly why. I expect this sort of quandary faces most firms our size."

Nicolai discussed other advantages of the computerized system at EW: "With EDP as part of the management team, we can plan targeted marketing as a specific part of total strategy. Now it will be possible to find out a lot about current customers, such as what the demographics are, what they've bought from us previously and how often they've ordered, how much it cost us to attract them, and what the profitability is for each segment of our various markets. Then, there is the possibility of improving our forecasting techniques—critical in these days when reducing inventories can add substantially to profits. But our biggest advantage has already been realized, which was escaping from that manual backroom operation that created slowdowns when business was good.

"Pinpointing where customers live is relatively easy—we know, for example, right now that they are approximately split between metropolitan and nonmetropolitan areas, that 35 percent are in West Coast and Mountain states, 47 percent are in the Midwest and Northeast, and 18 percent are in the South. This year, we have mailed upwards of 3 million catalogs, mostly around Christmas and early summer, but some are being mailed every month. I'd say we send about 10,000 each month in response to requests."

"We're thinking about an 800 number," Zimmerman commented, "that would help us give better service to customers. About 20 percent of total orders come in by phone now. And we are always thinking about adding new and unusual items. But we have no intention of attempting to compete with the L. L. Beans of this world—those positions in the market are effectively filled. We plan on sticking to our present strategy."

Your Task:

1. Evaluate Nicolai and Zimmerman's present strategy.
2. As a consultant to Early Winters Ltd , you have been called in for a goal-setting session. What key points need to be addressed given that Nicolai and Zimmerman appear to be sold on their present strategy?

SPRINGVILLE Y/USO

In 1869 the first YMCA in the country opened its gymnasium, with old cannonballs, weighing from 18 to 80 pounds, serving as exercise weights. These gyms were called "halls of health." Several decades later, the Springville YMCA opened its doors, commencing a history that by 1980 amounted to some 60 years of service to civilian and military sectors of the city. The Springville Y/USO (Y and USO) combined the YMCA, YWCA, and the USO, and after functioning for many years in a general-purpose building, moved into new quarters in 1973. The city's population was 281,000.

Throughout the 1970s, Springville grew rapidly in population and geographic area, so that the 1973 building was pressing capacity soon after opening. Area population had grown to 350,000 by 1979. Membership in YMCA-YWCA organizations increased rapidly, and programs, services, and staff also greatly expanded. USO usage remained stable, however.

Because the Y was feeling the pinch of overutilization, and hearing an increasing volume of complaints from its members about these problems, its board of directors agreed to gather data to decide an issue it had discussed for a number of years: whether it was time to plan seriously for construction of a second facility. The board instructed Executive Director Robert Ryerson to contract with a professional consulting firm to gather data on whether and under what conditions the Y should open a second facility.

BACKGROUND

With its founding in 1871, the city became known for its scenic topography, healthful climate, cultural and learning activities, and tourist attractions; around these its early economy developed. Semiarid and remote from metropolitan centers, there was little agriculture and industry in the earlier decades. In the 1880s and 1890s a series of important developments—rich mineral strikes, railroad construction, new hotels—accelerated mining and tourist activities, and, consequently, population growth. Some local industry producing brick, tile, lumber, and pottery began. By World War I mining declined as general economic and population growth diminished.

World War II brought a turn toward large-scale military activity and the establishment of several installations over a 20-year period, including the U.S. Air Force Academy, which opened in 1958. While government employment dominated the city in the late 1970s, indications were that the industrial sector, principally electronics and related businesses, would flourish in the next two decades. The city's accelerating population growth fell back to a level of 2 to 3 percent annually between 1975 and 1981, appearing to stabilize at about 2.5 percent, with most new construction activity—single-family and multifamily dwellings and shopping centers—occurring in the northeast suburbs.

Springville's sports consciousness was heightened when the U.S. Olympic Committee decided to locate there and to construct its training center on property formerly occupied by a U.S. Air Force headquarters group. Also located in Springville were the Amateur Basketball Association, U.S. Field Hockey Association, National Archery Association, Professional Rodeo Cowboys Association, U.S. Cycling Federation, U.S. International Skating Association, U.S. Modern Pentathlon and Biathlon Association, U.S. Volleyball Association, and U.S. Athletic Association. Other such groups were investigating the area as a location for their headquarters.

ORGANIZATIONAL STRUCTURE

Although the Y is a worldwide organization, each local unit is autonomous in programs, administration, and finances. The Y belongs to a federation of 1,800 Ys divided into six regional districts, with a national council that meets biannually. The local Y/USO pays 3 percent of certain portions of its income to support the national and regional staff. As general director, appointed in 1979, Kent Johnson devotes full time to local operations and employs professional staff needed to run the institution's programs and nonprofessional staff who provide support functions. The Y's board carries out its functions through a number of committees, subcommittees, and task groups. Exhibit 1 portrays the

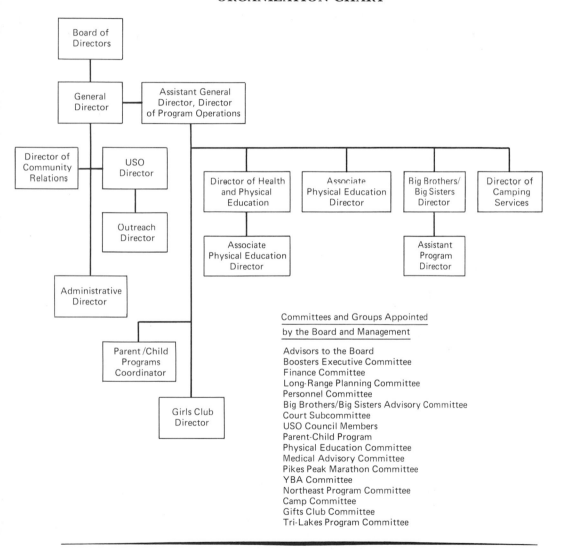

Exhibit 1

SPRINGVILLE Y/USO PROFESSIONAL STAFF ORGANIZATION CHART

Board of Directors

General Director

Assistant General Director, Director of Program Operations

Director of Community Relations

USO Director

Outreach Director

Director of Health and Physical Education

Associate Physical Education Director

Big Brothers/ Big Sisters Director

Director of Camping Services

Associate Physical Education Director

Assistant Program Director

Administrative Director

Parent/Child Programs Coordinator

Girls Club Director

Committees and Groups Appointed by the Board and Management

Advisors to the Board
Boosters Executive Committee
Finance Committee
Long-Range Planning Committee
Personnel Committee
Big Brothers/Big Sisters Advisory Committee
Court Subcommittee
USO Council Members
Parent-Child Program
Physical Education Committee
Medical Advisory Committee
Pikes Peak Marathon Committee
YBA Committee
Northeast Program Committee
Camp Committee
Gifts Club Committee
Tri-Lakes Program Committee

265-person organization—65 full-time salaried, including 14 professional staff, and 200 part-time hourly workers.

FINANCIAL PROFILE

Exhibit 2 compares selected financial highlights for 1977 through 1981. Although the Y usually came through each year with a balanced budget, a principal goal of board and management was to improve the financial picture in the 1980s, to ensure the future growth and stability of the Y, and to gear up for the capital contributions campaign that would have to be mounted if expansion appeared to be necessary and feasible. Exhibit 3 draws some financial comparisons between the Springville Y and other YMCAs in the United States with a budget size of $700,000 to $2,200,000. The board was pleased with the local Y's relative performance.

Exhibit 2

Y/USO SELECTED SOURCES AND USES OF FUNDS, 1977–1981
(in thousands)

	1977	1978	1979*	1980	1981
Sources					
Fees from programs	$ 243.6	$ 256.9	$ 329.3	$ 372.9	$ 445.7
Memberships	436.1	544.5	600.6	726.4	784.3
United Way	—	—	—	224.7	251.7
Contributions	242.1†	291.7†	317.2†	86.0	99.4
Sales of products and services	31.2	31.6	40.3	44.0	37.9
Investments and rentals	72.2	81.0	85.4	65.7	66.0
Miscellaneous	0.8	0.8	0.8	21.0	57.2
	$1,026.0	$1,206.5	$1,373.6	$1,540.7	$1,742.2
Uses					
Salaries	$ 508.7	$ 570.1	$ 673.4	$ 815.9	$ 846.6
Benefits and taxes	58.0	63.1	77.8	95.9	99.4
Occupancy/equipment	228.3	274.4	313.4	366.9	386.8
Building and equipment	—	—	—	46.0	34.3
Program costs	94.8	127.7	113.8	191.7	223.2
Supplies and cost of sales	109.4	137.5	159.9	75.7	67.9
Legal insurance and dues	26.7	33.7	35.2	26.8	40.3
Miscellaneous and dues	—	—	—	17.6	43.6
	$1,025.9	$1,206.5	$1,373.5	$1,540.6	$1,742.1

*Reconstructed estimates in some categories.
†Including United Way allocation for USO and other programs.

Exhibit 3

Y/USO BUDGET RATIOS COMPARED
WITH OTHER Ys', 1980

	Y/USO	OTHER Ys*
Total payroll as % of total expenses	53%	56%
Benefits and taxes as % of total expenses	6	7
Program income as % of total revenues	24	31
Membership dues as % of total revenues	47	27
Contributions as % of total revenues	20†	20

*Percentages estimated from National Council data.
†Recombining United Way and other contributions.

PROGRAM SMORGASBORD

"Monday Morning Memo" is a weekly Y newsletter mailed to members notifying them of special programs, appealing for volunteers, and providing news of recent events. Exhibit 4 illustrates several briefs taken from various editions of the "Memo."

Exhibit 4

EXCERPTS FROM "MONDAY MORNING MEMO"

"GO TO DISNEYLAND!" Kids 12 to 14 years old are going to have a fantastic time on the Y's Ninth Annual Disneyland Caravan, June 22–July 2. They'll visit the Grand Canyon, San Diego Zoo, and lots of other great spots along the way. Cost is $330 for Y members, $350 for nonmembers. Call for your youngster's reservation today!

"CHRISTMAS FUN CLUB." A recreation program for kids in 1st through 6th grades, will be offered at the Y December 21–24 and December 28–31. Swimming, gymnastics, crafts, and field trips will keep youngsters busy from 8:30 A.M.–4:30 P.M. Bus pick up and drop off is available at Fremont, Keller, Rudy, Carver, and Penrose schools. Cost is $6 per day for Y members and $8 for nonmembers. Parents who provide their own transportation can deduct $2 from the daily fee. Register at the Y.

"FROM THE ART DEPARTMENT." The winnners of the 1981 Christmas Coloring Contest are Sarah DeJong, 1–2-year-old age group; John Tau-

Exhibit 4 (Cont.)

sam from the 3–4-year-old group; and Sarah Zeidler in the 5-year-old category. Capturing the best of show title was Stephanie Keller.

"GIRLS' CLUB MEMBERS." Enjoy a tour of the world without leaving the Y! It's International Month for their 250 members, and so far they have learned to prepare egg rolls and tortillas with salsa. Tomorrow's agenda has them learning Japanese songs and the meaning of Mikado play. On the 17th, a Vietnamese Y employee will show 2nd graders how to prepare a special dish, and on the 18th Spanish dancers from Palmer High School will be at the Y to perform and teach their dances.

"SAY HELLO TO THE DENVER BRONCOS AND A GREAT SUMMER AT Y CAMP!" Youngsters and parents (and all other Bronco fans) are invited to meet and visit with Denver Bronco starting linebacker Larry Evans this Wednesday afternoon from 4–5:30 P.M. Larry will be our special guest during the Y's "All Aboard for Camp" party in the lobby. We'll have balloons, some special prizes, and a drawing for a free Y Youth Summer Membership. And, of course, we'll be helping youngsters register for either the Y's Camp Shady Brook special holiday session, other summer sessions, or Y Day Camp. Kids 7–15, friends, and parents are all invited to Meet-a-Bronco-on-Your-Way-to-Camp!

"IF YOU THINK A DAY IS FUN." Try an overnighter at the Y. Boys and girls 7 years and older can join us this Friday night from 7:30 on to 8:30 Saturday morning for fun, swimming, games, and a tasty breakfast. Only $7.50 for members, $10.00 for nonmembers. Proceeds go to the Junior and Senior Leaders Club. Call Nadine for details; then bring sleeping bag, swimsuit, towel, and a friend!

"CLOWNING AROUND, ACTING CRAZY, AND WALKING TALL." Your kids can really learn to do these things well in the Y's Circus Skills, Youth Theater, and Youth Modeling classes. All offered this summer at the Y, all fun and well instructed. Call Jennifer for details, 471-9790, and help your youngster to a fun summer.

"JOIN US FOR A ONE-DAY SKI TRIP." Ski at Winter Park on Monday, February 15. A comfortable coach will depart the Y at (yawn) 5:30 A.M. and will return at approximately 7:00 P.M. The cost includes the price of a lift ticket. Youth under 12 years: $20 for Y members, $22 for nonmembers; adults: $31 for Y members, $33 for nonmembers. Phone the Y for senior citizen rates.

"A MOUNTAIN-TOP EXPERIENCE." This is what the Y's High Altitude Training Camp is! If you're into fitness, you'll want to be in one of three special sessions of training held at beautiful Catamount Ranch. Teens will

Exhibit 4 (Cont.)

have a special week this year August 1–7, with adults (over 18) scheduled for August 8–14 and 15–21. Top-caliber runners and fitness pros from across the nation will be instructing. Come join us! Call Marge for details, 471-9790.

"HOW'S YOUR BLOOD PRESSURE?" Remember to come in and let us check it any Tuesday in May from 10:00 A.M. to 2:00 P.M. Takes just a minute . . . to help guarantee healthy years!

"KEEPING SAFE: A CHILD'S RIGHT." The Big Brothers and Sisters organization will sponsor a seminar for parents on child molestation, its definition, what you should know, and what to do if you suspect something unusual. The seminar will be held on Wednesday, January 20 at 5:30 P.M. at the Y. Dick Brown, a counselor with the Victim Services Bureau, will present the informal talk. Interested parents should register for the seminars by calling, 471-9790, ext. 222.

"WEDNESDAY IS TACO DAY." Join us in the Y's Salad Bar. Open from 11:30–2:00 P.M., Monday through Friday, it's the convenient place to grab a healthful lunch at the salad bar or pick up a taco. All menu items, including baked goods, are prepared daily in the Y's kitchen. Open to all.

"WOMEN'S WINTER WEEKEND." Join us February 27 and 28 at the Y's Catamount Ranch. For women of all ages for two days of sharing, outdoor exercise, great dining, informal talks, and warm chatter in comfortable surroundings. For details, pick up a brochure at the Y. Open to members and nonmembers.

"LAKE PLACID WAS OK." But wait till you behold the 1982 Rocky Mountain Senior Winter Games! March 8–10 at Winter Park seniors 55 and over will be participating in ice skating, speed skating, and cross-country and downhill skiing events with a fun social to warm up the nights. If you'd like to participate as an entrant or a helper, contact Lorrie Bensik at 471-6640.

"RACQUETBALL FANS." Come join the fun this summer at the Y. Y members now have a discounted fee during special hours and minitournaments have been scheduled for the weekends. Call Marge Carter or Jim Asleson for details, 471-9790.

"FOR PARENTS AND KIDS, TOO." The Y's Indian Guide/Princess/Maiden program offers something every family could use more of . . . time together. Sign up for the 1982–1983 program and you'll be guaranteeing your family of many meaningful hours of fun and fellowship that can help build a lifetime of family happiness.

Besides the weekly mailer, seasonal catalogs also were mailed to members and to various organizations in the city. These pieces usually were 16 to 20 pages of 100 or so listings of programs and classes, "something for everyone." For example, the spring 1982 mailer, in addition to schedules of facility hours and availability by age and activity categories, announced the Y's corporate goals and the 1982 annual membership fees and described over 100 programs and activities, such as diving instruction, youth ballet, Mexican folk dancing for youth, diapergym, fitness classes for youth and adults, gymnastics, racquetball lessons, ski clinics, theater class, weight training, special parties and celebrations, drawing, ceramics, Christian fellowship hour, and cooking classes.

Anticipating an expanded role in the city's northeast area, brochure mailers heralded an assortment of programs, activities, and classes in several neighborhoods scheduled for 1982. New offerings targeted to the younger families residing in those sections included, for example, Lamaze childbirth sessions, roller skating, and an Easter egg hunt. Discount coupons printed on the mailers offered get-acquainted fees for new customers.

PROPOSED GOALS FOR 1980-1985

As Robert Ryerson resigned the Y/USO's general director's post in 1979, management and the board of directors were drafting the institution's planning targets for the next five years, an activity in which Ryerson's replacement, Kent Johnson, then serving as assistant general director, had participated from the beginning. Exhibit 5 contains selected passages from the planning document published that summer.

Planners distinguished goals—somewhat general statements forming a "planning umbrella" for the organization, and ordinarily with a time span of from two to five years—from objectives, which were defined as "specifically measurable statements of attainable outcomes within the framework of operational goals, with a time span of one year or less." Fiscal responsibility and future developments were two of the primary planning topics.

Exhibit 5

SELECTED PASSAGES FROM 1979 PLANNING DOCUMENT

STATEMENT OF PURPOSE

The purpose of the Springville Y/USO is that of establishing and maintaining a fellowship of individuals and families of all faiths and helping its members develop Christian character and build a Christian society

Exhibit 5 (Cont.)

through activities and services that contribute to spiritual, intellectual, physical, and social growth.

INTERPRETATIVE STATEMENT

The Y seeks to help its members:

> Develop self-confidence and self-respect and an appreciation of their own worth as individuals
>
> Develop a faith for daily living based upon the teachings of Jesus, that they may all achieve their highest potential as children of God
>
> Grow as responsible members of their families and as citizens of their communities
>
> Appreciate that health of mind and body is a sacred gift and that physical fitness and mental well-being are conditions to be achieved and maintained
>
> Recognize the worth of all persons and work for interracial and intergroup understanding
>
> Develop a sense of world-mindedness and work for world understanding
>
> Develop their capabilities for leadership and use them responsibly in their own groups and community life

Source: Springville Y/USO, "Proposed Corporate Goals for 1980–1985 and Objectives for 1980," Summer 1979.

In 1981, spokespersons enunciated a set of 13 goals for the decade (Exhibit 6). Some planning guidelines set forth in 1978–1979 were reaffirmed, while marketing (item 6) and program expansion (item 7) were new additions, and financial administration/development (item 11) was modified to recognize unmet needs for physical fitness facilities and programs through the community. During the period in which these goals were being articulated, a creeping commitment to expansion into the northeast portion of the city similarly evolved. "All the signals," Johnson reported to a midyear board meeting, "appear to be highly positive for this long-considered expansion."

Exhibit 6

Y/USO CORPORATE GOALS FOR 1980–1990

1. **Youth.** To develop the foundation for adulthood through youth programs stressing values education.
2. **Family.** To develop and conduct programs that strengthen the traditional family structure as well as deal with the unique needs of all family units, both traditional and untraditional.

Exhibit 6 (Cont.)

3. **Physical Fitness.**To provide a holistic approach to wellness for all ages and populations of the community.
4. **Physical Education and Recreation.**To provide opportunities for all ages to learn new skills, improve skill levels, enjoy healthful physical activities, and provide for worthy use of leisure time.
5. **Program Evaluation.** To structure an ongoing evaluation system to ensure optimum facility usage, program participation, and program validity.
6. **Marketing.** To keep the community continually apprised of Y/USO programs, membership benefits, and volunteer opportunities through a well-structured, cost-effective public relations program.
7. **Program Expansion.** To answer the demands of the community by providing services on a year-round basis that are accessible to different population centers.
8. **Facilities.** To ensure that all existing Y/USO facilities adhere to a total use concept to achieve maximum utilization by all members and expand as necessary to meet growing needs.
9. **Personnel, Lay.** To maintain a strong lay structure of dedicated, involved volunteers, committee people, and board members who actively support the Y/USO organization and its goals.
10. **Personnel, Staff.** To recruit and maintain well-qualified staff members who are dedicated to a high level of quality in Y/USO programs and facilities.
11. **Financial Administration/Development.** To pursue sound fiscal administration and a comprehensive financial development program to expand to meet the needs of a growing community.
12. **Relationships to National Organizations.** To participate actively and meet all qualifications necessary to maintain membership in the National YMCA, Big Brothers/Big Sisters, and USO.
13. **International Understanding.** To develop and conduct programs to increase international awareness, and understanding and to promote world peace.

PRESENT AND FUTURE: COMPETITION AND PRICING

For two reasons—one, to examine the parameters of a price increase being considered for the downtown facility, and, two, to assess potential pricing strategies for the proposed new facility—management analyzed 1979 membership rates for competing firms in the for-profit sector. Exhibit 7 reviews pricing for competitors, and Exhibit 8 reports results of 1979 membership rates from Ys in other cities; Exhibit 9 shows Springville's fees for 1982. Three Nautilus Fitness Centers, the Lynmar Racquet Club, the Point Athletic Club, and several health spas were located in the northeast/north sector of the community in 1982.

Exhibit 7

COMPETITIVE RATE COMPARISON

NAUTILUS FITNESS CENTER

Memberships for persons over 12 years old. Open 24 hours a day, 7 days a week. Coed sauna, steam with eucalyptus, whirlpool and swimming pool 20' × 40', massage $7 for 30 minutes. Free nursery, free ballet, jazz, exercise, and beginning karate classes. Separate weight rooms for men and women.

Fee structure:

One-year membership	$210 one individual $120 for each additional family member Ex.: family of 4, $570.00
Two-year membership	$300 one individual $200 for the second family member and $180 for each additional family member Ex.: family of 4, $860 or $430 a year
VIP two-year membership	$400 one individual (renewable for $70 a year thereafter) $250 for the second family member $200 for any other family member Ex.: family of 4, $1,050 or $525 a year

After two years renewable at $70 a year for one individual and additional family member fees
Ex.: family of 4, $395 a year

EUROPEAN HEALTH SPA

Memberships for men/women 18 and over. Great number of weight machines (similar to Nautilus); sauna, steam, inhalation room with eucalyptus, whirlpool, ice pool, swimming pool 20' × 46', sun lamp rooms. Nursery is 50 cents an hour; massage is $7 for 30 minutes.

Ladies day: Monday, Wednesday.
Men's day: Tuesday, Thursday, Saturday until 2 P.M.
Coed day: Friday, Saturday after 2 P.M., Sunday 10–6

Fee structure:

Matinee	6 months, $119 12 months, $250
Bronze	12 months, $340

Exhibit 7 (Cont.)

Silver   18 months, $435 ($290 a year)
Gold   18 months, $595 ($396 a year)
                        Additional family members over 18, 50% reduction
                        At end of 18 months, renewable for $200 a year
                        $100-a-year renewal fee if you join on first visit

EXECUTIVE PARK ATHLETIC CLUB

Recreation facility specializing in handball/racquetball and gymnastics. Hours are 6 A.M. to 10 P.M. Monday through Friday and 9 A.M. to 6 P.M. Saturday and Sunday. Separate men's and women's carpeted locker rooms with sauna and whirlpool. Ten handball/racquetball courts, elevated carpeted running track, pro shop and weight room. A restaurant is located off the main lobby.

Fee structure:

Annual Fitness Membership with No Monthly Dues

Single	$150 annual fee
Couple	$275 annual fee
Child (under 18 years or with a parent)	$ 60
Junior/student (without a parent membership)	$125

The fitness memberships pay hourly court fees of $2.50 per hour regular time and $3.50 per hour prime time (6–8 A.M., 11–1 P.M., 4–8 P.M.)

Regular Full Facility Membership with No Court Fees

	One-Time Initiation Fee	Monthly Dues
Single	$150	$38
Couple	200	55
Junior/student	50	23 (no 4 to 8 P.M. M-F courts)

Gymnastics programs are available at an extra cost.

Fee schedule:

    1 class, 1 day per week: $15.00
    1 class, 2 days per week: $20.00
    1 class, 3 days per week: $24.00
    1 class, 4 days per week: $29.00

EPAC members, $2.00 off; additional children, $2.00 off.

Exhibit 7 (Cont.)

GLORIA STEVENS FIGURE SALON

Women over 18 years, $25 introductory fee for 6 weeks' membership plan.

> 6 months, $152
> 12 months, $305

Exercise classes conducted every hour. Open 8 A.M. to 8 P.M. Monday through Friday, 8 A.M. to 2 P.M., Saturday. No sauna, whirlpool, or showers. Exercise machines, slant boards, dumbbells.

LYNMAR RACQUET CLUB

Membership is currently 900 persons; cut off will be at 1,200. Deluxe facilities including lounge with fireplace, covered swimming pool, eight indoor tennis courts, four outdoor tennis courts, three racquetball courts, separate sauna, whirlpool for men and women, nursery (75¢ an hour), pro shop, weight room.

Plans include 11 Nautilus weight machines to be installed within four months and four new racquetball courts to be built by fall of 1980.

Fee structure:

Type	One-Time Initiation Fee	Monthly Dues
Family	$250	$30
Husband/wife	200	24
Individual	150	18
Junior (under 18)	100	11

Extra charge for tennis and racquetball courts.

Tennis	Racquetball
Prime time, $9 per hour, 5 to 10 P.M.	Prime time, $4 per hour, 5 to 8 P.M.
Regular time, $7 per hour	Regular time, $3 per hour

FOREST EDGE RACQUETBALL CLUB, LTD.

Breaking ground October 1979. Plans call for two racquetball/handball courts. Fitness center will have exercise machines and weights, whirlpool, towel service and lockers, lounge with T.V.

Exhibit 7 (Cont.)

Fee Schedule:

Full Facility Membership (No Court Fees—Unlimited Use)

	Initiation Fee	Monthly Dues
Junior (13 to 18 years)	$ 40.00	$15.00
Individual (19 and over)	75.00	25.00
Couple	100.00	35.00
Family (3 to 4)	125.00	45.00
Family (5 or more)	150.00	55.00

Fee Schedule:

Fitness Membership
(Court Fees Extra: Prime, $4 per Hour, Regular, $3 per Hour)

Junior (13 to 18 years)	$ 26.00	$10.00
Individual	50.00	17.00
Couple	66.00	23.00
Family (3 to 4)	83.00	30.00
Family (5 or more)	100.00	36.00

Dependents 19 and over may not be included in a family membership.

Court fees for general public use are regular time, $4 per hour; prime time, $5 per hour.

A MARKET STUDY IN 1978

During the summer term, 1978, three students in a local university's marketing research class conducted a study of 150 households in the city's northeast area, using personal interviews with respondents who were chosen using a random cluster sampling technique. Impetus for this project came from the Y's executive director, Robert Ryerson, who wished to explore potential for a Y program and facility to serve that sector's rapidly increasing population. Selected key conclusions, excerpted from the team's report, are presented in Exhibit 10. The students concluded that theirs was an "extremely small sample of the total northeast area" and that "further research in the area must be done before intelligent management decisions can be made." Their "gut feeling" supported locating a facility in the survey area, and they all agreed that the "present location of the Y is a detrimental factor affecting use by the northeast residents."

MEETINGS BETWEEN Y MANAGEMENT
AND PROSPECTIVE CONSULTANTS

On May 15, 1979, Robert Ryerson and Assistant Director Kent Johnson met with local market research consultants, and, after reviewing the board's deliberations and desires, Ryerson said intuition told him a second facility surely was needed. But what he and the board wanted were concrete data, not only to confirm or to reject their own judgment but also to present to outsiders, especially prospective donors and fund-raisers, to generate public support for the new venture should such an effort be undertaken.

"We need to know whether the public, including Y members, really wants us to build a second major facility," he said. "But much more information is needed as well," he added, "such as where it should be located and what specific programs, activities, and facilities should be offered." Then he explained how the Y had significantly expanded its variety of activities, programs, and services in recent years, and how the majority of the non-Y public did not recognize the broadened role of the Y in the community. He pointed out that the Y tried to serve not only a full range of the public's sports and recreational needs but that it also offered extensive educational, cultural, crafts, personal development, health, and other programs—everything from prenatal classes to senior citizens' programs. Looking at the current alphabetical list of Y program offerings, Ryerson smiled and said, "Everything, if not from A to Z, at least from aquatics and adult handicap classes to yoga and youth theaterworks."

Ryerson said there was a whole other set of questions regarding financial matters that he would like answered. There were two types of financial questions. The first included issues such as what would be the construction and operating costs of the new facility, what fees should be charged, and what would be the break-even points.

The other set of financial questions related to alternatives for funding construction. Ryerson wondered how responsive the community might be to a formal fund-raising solicitation by a professional organization and what might be the other alternatives for financing the large capital construction project.

The day after their first meeting with Y management, the consultants drafted a proposed outline of what they understood the Y needed and what they thought their team could do. This outline provided a discussion agenda for the next meeting of managers and researchers.

A week later, the four met again. The researchers began by noting again the tentative nature of their proposal, the need to refine the topics and the process before a firm schedule and consulting fee could be established, and the issue of recognizing and trying to resolve the "everything depends on everything else" problem. An example of the complex and reverse cause-and-effect relationship, they pointed out, was that reliable costs and prices necessary for a

Exhibit 8

1979 MEMBERSHIP RATE SURVEY

MEMBERSHIP CLASSIFICATION	DENVER CENTRAL	OMAHA CENTRAL*	LINCOLN CENTRAL	OKLAHOMA CITY CENTRAL	WICHITA CENTRAL	SPRINGVILLE Y/USO
Youth	$15 (0 to 12) $30 (3 to 17)	—	$60 (6 to 17)	$15 (6 to 14) very limited program	—	$45 (7 to 17)
Student	$90 (18 to 22) (full-time students)	—	—	$40 (15 to 17) $90 (18 to 29) (student)	$68 (18 up) (full-time students)	$75 (full-time students)
Young adult, male and female	—	$80 (15 to 22)	—	—	—	$102 (18 to 24)
Adult male	$155 (over 18)	$145 (over 18)	$120 (over 18)	$175 towel service	$110 (over 18)	$117 (over 25)
Adult female	$150 (over 18)	$145	$120	$175 towel service	$110	$117
Basic	—	$70 ($1.50–$2.00 extra each visit	$12 (6 to 17) $18 (18 up) $24 family plus daily-use fee of 50 cents under 18 and $2 over 18	—	$15 (plus $3 a day, 18 and over)	—

	Col 1	Col 2	Col 3	Col 4	Col 5	Col 6
Family	$235	$195	$198	$330 (husband/wife) $360 (2 children)	$175	$195 regular $126 special
Senior citizen	$85	$75	—	—	—	$75
Businessmen's and women's (not fitness centers)	$255 (men only, sauna and steam)	—	—	—	—	—
Men's fitness center	$335	$295	$246	$295	$325 or $530 (deluxe including 110 massages)	$285
Women's fitness center	—	$240	$189	—	—	$261
Men's fitness and family	—	$340	$300	$450, plus youth or student fee	—	$369
Women's fitness and family	—	$290	$267	—	—	$345
Family fitness center	—	$490	$369	—	—	$462
Nonmember day pass	$3.50	$4 regular, $8 fitness center	$4 regular, $5 fitness center	$4 regular, $10 fitness center	$5 regular	$3 regular, $6 fitness center
Military pass	—	—	—	—	—	$1 and $3
Military family	—	—	—	—	—	$141

*Building fund included in fee ranging from $5 to $25 per year.

263

Exhibit 9

1982 ANNUAL MEMBERSHIP FEES

MEMBERSHIP CATEGORY/AGES	RATES	ACW* DOWN	ACW MONTHLY
Youth	$ 48	$ 9.00	$ 4.50
Young adult, 18 to 24	117	20.50	10.25
Adult, 25 and up	144	25.00	12.50
Student, military, rank of E5 and below	84	15.00	7.50
Senior citizen, 65 and up	81	14.50	7.25
Family, parents and all children under 18	240	41.00	20.50
Military family, rank of E5 and below	156	27.00	13.50
Single-parent family	153	26.50	13.25
Men's fitness center, 18 and up	366	62.00	31.00
Women's fitness center, 18 and up	336	57.00	28.50
Family fitness center	594	100.00	50.00
Men's fitness center and family	474	80.00	40.00
Women's fitness center and family	444	75.00	37.50

*Automatic check withdrawal. Increases over the 1980 rates averaged close to 10%, ranging from 4% for a military family membership to an 18% increase for the men's fitness center.

Exhibit 10

SELECTED CONCLUSIONS, ADAPTED FROM THE 1978 STUDY

. . . there is a significant demand for a facility such as the YMCA in the northeast area.

. . . 69% indicated they would be willing to support a facility on a membership basis if it offered activities they would use.

. . . many of the activities children were involved in were more inclined toward the types of programs that the YMCA offers or could offer.

. . . their ideal facility would be one within 15 minutes of their homes.

. . . a significant number of people would . . . support a facility if fees were similar to the YMCA's current rates.

. . . 75% planned to remain in the northeast area for at least the next five years.

. . . top 10 preferred activities of respondents (108 answering this question) were swimming (52% expressed this as one of their preferences), tennis (23%), skating (9%), hiking and camping (9%), dance (7%), running (6%), basketball (5%), racquetball (4%), skiing (4%), and arts and crafts (4%).

Source: Marketing research study in conjunction with the Springville YMCA, summer 1978.

valid break-even analysis could not be available until the size and cost of the facility were known. Yet the size of the facility depended on probable user demand, which could not be known until completion of the market survey, which, in turn, required some assumptions about prices.

Ryerson said that from the Y's standpoint, a major point to keep in mind was the Y's limited budget. He said that as a nonprofit community service organization with limited funds, the Y knew that it had to be content with a research study that might not be the most scientifically perfect or the best that money could buy. In reviewing the long list of topics in the consulting group's tentative proposal, he concluded that the cost of doing them all would exceed what the Y could afford to spend.

It became apparent that first and primary research contribution should focus on researching market demand and that financial analysis and fund-raising matters ought to be postponed. The rest of the meeting was spent refining market research aspects of the proposal.

Johnson said he would like to see two other issues addressed by the research study. First was whether the Y should begin "outreach programming" in the near future, and well before a new facility might be constructed. By this he meant the Y could take some of its programs and staff out to areas of the city far away from its downtown building. This would require renting or borrowing outlying facilities. "This is usually the first step in a Y expansion to a second location," Johnson explained.

What he would like to know was (1) whether the public would want and use outreach programming and (2) which specific types of programs and activities would be desired. For example, would the Y have to rent a large facility like a high school gymnasium or swimming pool, or would people out in mostly residential areas want family-type activities such as father-son "Indian Guides," cooking classes, and so on?

The second thing Johnson wanted in the study was feedback on the Y's service and image in the community. "We never have had such an extensive survey of both Y members and nonmembers as this study promises," he observed, "and it would be a shame not to use the opportunity to find out how we are doing, how we are perceived." Admitting that an image analysis was not part of the original and primary purpose of the market study, he wondered if it could be incorporated.

Extensive discussion then ensued about the relevant geographic market. If a new facility were built, in what general area of the city should it be located—northeast, northwest, southeast, southwest?

Ryerson pointed out that he had talked with a number of the city's leading developers, some of whom were members of the board of directors, and they all confirmed Ryerson's intuition that the major locus of new development should be northeasterly.

The research group, which had consulted with the economic development department of the local chamber of commerce, studying the city's growth patterns, agreed that the major growth forces converged toward the northeast. Private developers and the city's planning officials confirmed this judgment. Ryerson said that money and time would be saved if the research effort assumed that any new facility would be located in the northeast, so it was agreed to proceed on that assumption.

The 90-minute meeting ended with the plan to put in writing a refined proposal incorporating the issues discussed.

CONSULTANTS' PROPOSAL

A few days later, the consulting team met to consider and draft the proposal to the Y. They quickly agreed that the project was feasible and worth bidding on. Two had served on the Y board; one had been on the design committee for the 1973 building. All knew a large number of local business and community leaders, including those most knowledgeable about and supportive of the Y. One member of the team, a young woman academic, was interested in seeing that the questionnaire and focus groups addressed the special needs of working women. And while all viewed this project as a professional business agreement, they also were personally interested in helping "their" Y as a community service. Therefore, they agreed to do the study for $7,000, about one-third their usual fee for such studies.

Y BRANCH FACILITY FEASIBILITY STUDY, 1980

Presented in August 1980, the consultants' report, some 300 pages in length, including computer printout appendices, came up with three major conclusions:

1. There is strong demand from Y and non-Y members for a second, full-scale facility in northeast Springville.
2. There is strong demand also for immediate outreach programming even before a new facility might be built.
3. Because of its facility, staff, and programs, the Y enjoys an outstanding image and reputation in our community.

The report followed with these recommendations:

1. Begin immediate communitywide programming, especially in the northeast area, following the specific program requests enumerated in this report.
2. Begin immediate planning for the construction of a second building in the northeast section, carefully considering the specifics as to facilities and location described in this report.
3. Improve the Y's service by building on strengths that are apparent and responding to the dissatisfactions enumerated in this report.

The Appendix contains selected narrative and key figures from the consultants' report.

DECISION POINT, 1980

As he and the board considered results and recommendations of the study, Johnson offered several observations: "It isn't unusual for a community to have more than one Y facility in operation, and most communities this size probably have two or three buildings. If we decide to build another unit, I expect it will include a swimming pool, a gymnasium, racquetball courts, and office space."

When queried about facility size and utilization, he speculated: "It will be at least half the size of the current one, which was built 10 years ago, and hopefully will have an outdoor area or be located near a park. Here (downtown) we are packed to overflowing and, when we think of expanding, we want to look at an area where we can serve the family most. That's what made us look to the residential area to the northeast. About 17 percent of present membership is made up of those residents, but the highest population density of young families is in that area, and, if we really want to have an impact on the families, we need to go there."

Y programs in the northeast were held in churches, schools, a bowling alley, a skating rink, and other rented accommodations. "We know the people want us out there. The question is, how much will it cost to build another facility and can we raise that much money? Those are the two issues to be analyzed. Soon we'll have a representative of the national YMCA visit here to help us evaluate those critical questions. We'll tell him what sorts of programs we plan to offer in the northeast area, and he'll tell us how much space we need and how much it will cost."

Given that circumstances favored taking the next steps of deciding whether to build and what programs were most desirable, resolving the capital funding barrier loomed as a significant undertaking. "We've invited a professional fund-raising organization to visit us in the spring [1981] to see how much money can be raised for construction. Then, we anticipate a final decision to be made in June by the Y's board of directors."

IMPLEMENTING THE DECISION, 1981-1982

During the fall of 1981 an agreement was reached between the Y and Junior Achievement (JA) to undertake jointly the capital funding campaign for a building to be shared by the two entities. After deciding to commence a program to raise $2 million in donations in January 1982, the Y/USO board president reported in the local press, "The money will be combined with a recent $1.75 million foundation (a local, philanthropic institution) gift to build a 47,000-square-foot structure to house both organizations." The press conference buzzed with comments about the current recession, or as some called it, "depression," and many questions were asked about probabilities of success in such an environment. "We are very optimistic that the city's residents will rally to this cause," the JA president said, "because we have here two organizations that have served this city well and will continue to serve the needs of youth and families in the future."

The Y/USO president talked of plans to include a large gymnasium, a swimming pool of a size similar to that in the downtown facility, four locker rooms, and handball/racquetball courts. The Y/USO would occupy 39,000 square feet, with the remaining 8,000 square feet for JA, which would have five meeting rooms, a shop, a materials area, and office space.

"More than 30,000 persons are using the downtown Y/USO annually," the Y/USO president continued, "while JA provides economic and career education to 3,500 youngsters each year. And 60 percent of our client populations, for the Y and JA combined, live in the northeastern section of the city." Two well-known local leaders, one from the civilian and one from the military, were appointed to head the six-month capital campaign.

Fund-raising handout materials were prepared to explain in question-and-answer format the nature of the Y and JA, and reasons for the solicitation. "The purpose of Junior Achievement," read one paragraph, "and its five major programs is: To provide practical and realistic education and experience in the private enterprise economic system." And the handout contained endorsements by James H. Rosenfield, president of the CBS Television Network; Frank Cary, chairman of IBM Corporation; and David T. Kearns, president of Xerox Corporation. JA's activities were programmed to serve high school students. Efforts were targeted toward large corporate and foundation gifts as well as toward smaller givers: "A Sack of Nails =$1.00; A Stack of Bricks = $5.00; Some Building Boards = $10.00; and Concrete for a Foundation = $25.00," proclaimed the outside of the contribution envelope. Signifying the joining together of these two service organizations was the logo shown in Exhibit 11.

Exhibit 11

LOGO FOR Y/JA FUND-RAISING PROGRAM, 1982

Y/JA Development Campaign

ADDING NAUTILUS EQUIPMENT
AT THE DOWNTOWN Y

In 1982, three Nautilus Fitness Centers were operating—in the north/north-east residential sections—and one was scheduled for a fall opening downtown. Lynmar Racquet Club and Point Athletic Club were enjoying growth in total number of members, and numerous women's spas, while not flourishing, continued to attract new customers through special promotional campaigns. Plans were made by Y management to add Nautilus equipment, a decision based upon members' favorable reactions to a December 1981 survey.

Your Task:

1. Evaluate the process and decision for selecting the consultants. Is an "outsider" or "insider" usually best?
2. What do you think of the decision to restrict the geographical area of the new facility and of the survey sample to the northeast quadrant of the city, even before any formal research was done? How do you know when to trust your management experience or intuition, and when you need to hire outside researchers, to come up with the right decisions?
3. If you were conducting this study, how would you make the best use of focus group interviews? Whom would you select to interview, and what questions would you ask?
4. For a market research project like this, which type of interview method is best—personal survey, telephone survey, mail survey? Why? What are the relative advantages and disadvantages of each in the case of Springville Y/USO?
5. By what methods could you obtain a random, representative sample of interviewees in the chosen geographic area? How would your methods vary according to whether you had a generous or minuscule budget?
6. What questions would you ask and how would you word them, to learn people's preferences for the types of facilities and programs to provide in the second, new Y?
7. How would you word questions that would reveal people's preferences regarding location and transportation?
8. If you wanted to survey the recreation activities and interests of people, what questions would you ask and how would you word them?
9. What specific questions would you ask to develop demographic profiles of your respondents?
10. Do you think it would be important to learn whether families would use one Y, and if so which one, or both Ys? How would you test for this?
11. If you wanted to survey the image, reputation, and service of an organization like the Y, as perceived by both members and nonmembers, what specific questions would you include in the questionnaire?
12. What coaching should be given to door-to-door interviewers to assure complete, unbiased, and efficient interviews?
13. What things might the interviewer say or do in first approaching a respondent to avoid rejection?
14. Evaluate management's approach to and use of the research in this case study.

Appendix

EXCERPTS FROM CONSULTANTS' REPORT

RESEARCH METHODOLOGY

Questionnaire Design

Choosing the precise questions, phrases, and words must be done with an eye on not only what the fundamental objectives are, but also on how the interviews will be conducted and by whom and on how the answers will be tabulated, arrayed, and compared, whether by machine processing or manually.

Two focus groups of 8 to 10 persons each were formed. Participants were chosen from a cross section of northeast residents who were interested in and knowledgeable about the Y, either as active Y members or as experts aware of our community's development and the Y's role therein. The purposes of meeting with the focus groups were to get their outsider's views of (1) the study's ultimate objectives that had been developed up to that point, (2) what issues might have been overlooked, (3) what impact the study might make on the community, and (4) what and how communitywide developments should influence the study—all for the general purpose of learning how the Y, through this study, could improve its service to the community. Many specific research idea improvements resulted, with the overwhelming general conclusion that time and circumstances mandated serious consideration of constructing a second Y facility. Almost four hours of audio tapes were made of the two meetings, and these were given to Mr. Johnson.

The next step was drafting the first questionnaire and discussing it with Mr. Johnson and his staff. A second version and yet a third followed; then, there was another evaluation meeting with Y management. After the fourth version was completed, it was given as a pretest interview to a dozen people. The fourth draft was also evaluated by another professional market research specialist from the local college. Then, the fifth and final draft of the in-person questionnaire was completed.

The next three steps included (1) redoing the questionnaire for mail and telephone surveys, (2) choosing the sample interviewees, and (3) hiring and training interviewers. All three steps were undertaken simultaneously.

The Sample

Three sample groups were chosen:

Appendix (Cont.)

1. 248 households for personal interviews
2. 65 Y members for mail questionnaires
3. 56 Y members for telephone interviews

Concentration of interview households was in city ZIP codes 17 and 18; other ZIPs included were 07, 08, 09, 15, and 19.

Statistical reliability is based upon the sample of 248, even though these were not entirely randomly chosen. To illustrate, if 80 percent of these heads of household respond "yes" to a certain question, then the standard error of that 80 percent figure is plus or minus 2.5 percent, or one standard error; thus, one can say that we would be 67 percent certain that the "true" percentage lies within plus or minus 2.5 points of 80 percent, that is, between 77.5 percent and 82.5 percent. Using the two standard error bound, or 5 percent, one could say that the odds are 20 to 1 that the true percentage is between 75 percent and 85 percent. Strict randomness was not observed because replacement households were sometimes chosen for not-at-homes and refusals.

Collecting The Data

Difficulty, time, and expense of conducting interviews decline in order from personal, to telephone, to mail interviews.

Twenty-six door-to-door interviews were first conducted by us personally to understand and interpret both the process and the responses encountered by the hired interviewers. We also handled all the mail questionnaires.

Three interviewers were hired and trained to conduct the bulk of personal and telephone interviews. Each had either prior professional interview experience or substantial academic background. Their special preparation for this project consisted of touring the Y building with a staff member, studying the questionnaire, giving test interviews, and participating in training sessions with us. They were provided with a set of written instructions and a packet of nine materials.

The interviewers, supervised on a daily basis, were directed to contact a random sample of five households in about a five-square-block area carefully selected by judgmental sampling. They were coached to seek a balance of factors such as sex, single-family versus multifamily residences, day versus night, and weekday versus weekend interviews.

For every interview completed, it was necessary, on the average, to approach about four different residences. On the assumption that the reasons people gave for declining interviews might provide further community comment on the Y, the interviewers filled out a worksheet documenting the households contacted but refusing interviews.

Appendix (Cont.)

The average personal and telephone interview lasted about 30 minutes.

The 369 families surveyed resided on approximately 300 different streets throughout the northeast quadrant of the city.

Data Analysis

Some parts of the study, particularly those relating to near-term Y programming, were manually tabulated and reported to management as the data were collected, because of the immediate need to begin outreach programming. All the final numerical data were computer-tabulated using the Statistical Package for the Social Sciences, a group of programs developed over the past 10 years by social science researchers, computer scientists, and statisticians. The availability of this data modification, file handling, data description tool simplified considerably the analytic work.

ANALYSIS OF RESPONSES

Introduction

The Y's management will find the lengthy appendix detail behind the summary findings in this section helpful for various purposes beyond this study's focus and extending over a long time. The Y can best judge, in light of its needs and purposes, how best to summarize and organize this secondary material. The lode of raw data is deep and rich—and it is all in the appendices. We will keep the computer program and input deck, and if the Y should want future assistance in processing data, we will be glad to accommodate it.

This section summarizes and analyzes the major interview results. It follows in sequence the questions on the forms. The responses reported here come primarily from the computer printouts, but also occasionally from the open-ended questions. Major findings are stressed, with some of the less relevant background material grouped together and summarized briefly.

Personal Interviews Analysis—Community At Large

ZIP Code Distribution. Residences of people interviewed in person were distributed throughout the northeast quadrant of the city, with major concentration within a strip along but mostly north and east of Academy Boulevard.

Interviewee Gender. Female interviewees accounted for 69 per-

Appendix (Cont.)

cent of the sample, males 28 percent, and couples 3 percent. Although we did sample at various times of the day and evening, weekdays and weekends, interviewers found that females most often answered the door and gave the interview information on behalf of the family.

Demographic Data Concerning Children in Household. Of the households interviewed, 56 percent of the families reported one or more boys under age 18 living at home, while 49 percent reported one or more girls. Less than half of the sample population indicated that no children lived at home. Many of the childless households were those of retired persons.

Only 10 to 15 percent of the households reported having children who attended year-round schools. We assume, therefore, that demands for children's programming center on after-school and summer programming for the greater majority of households.

Family Recreation Activities. Families were asked to report their present recreational activities, so that the Y might know more about the recreational profile of people it seeks to serve. The five most frequently mentioned activities were swimming, fishing, camping, skiing and tennis (tied), and hiking, in that order. A ranking of 23 activities is in Table 1.

Membership and Y Use in Personal Interview Sample. Under 9 percent of the 248 households included in the personal interview sample claimed to have a Y member; over half these members used the downtown Y three or more times each week.

Of the group with Y memberships, most maintained either single or family memberships, not fitness center memberships. Interestingly, half the total random sample indicated that a fitness center would be a desirable feature of a new Y facility. Approximately 74 percent of all respondents were unfamiliar with the downtown Y facility, citing their newness to Springville, the inconvenient distance of the Y from their homes, the expense of using the Y, and lack of time as reasons for their unfamiliarity. Slightly over a quarter of the interviewees had had experience with the Y during the last three years, mainly through their children's involvement in such Y programming as basketball, camp, or swimming.

Interviewees were also queried about other club memberships; one-third responded in the affirmative that they maintained other club memberships, chief among them the Peterson Field facility, an indication of the heavy military population of the northeast area of the city. Nautilus came in as the second most heavily used additional club with many interviewees praising the Nautilus equipment and the relatively low annual fee.

Prefacility Y Programming in Northeast. Y management and board members expressed interest in gauging response to Y prefacility programming in advance of possible Y construction in northeast Springville, that is, the feasibility of offering swimming lessons, fitness classes, or

Appendix (Cont.)

Table 1

FAMILY RECREATIONAL ACTIVITIES
$(n = 248)$

ACTIVITIES	NUMBER OF MENTIONS	RANK ORDER
Arts and crafts	84	(6)
Baseball/softball	57	(12)
Basketball	56	(13)
Bowling	80	(7)
Camping	103	(3)
Climbing	19	(18)
Dance	43	(16)
Fishing	114	(2)
Football	40	(17)
Golfing	78	(8)
Handball	11	(19)
Hiking	88	(5)
Hunting	54	(15)
Ice hockey	5	(20)
Physical conditioning	71	(10)
Racquetball	58	(11)
Running	73	(9)
Skating	71	(10)
Skiing	94	(4)
Soccer	55	(14)
Swimming	161	(1)
Tennis	94	(4)
Volleyball	24	(19)
Other (see Appendix A for complete listing)		

any of a host of program possibilities under the auspices of the Y, housed in a northeast educational or recreational facility. Interviewees expressed overwhelming approval of such programming, with 83 percent responding affirmatively to the idea. Individual open exercise and organized group exercise and sports programs surfaced as the major program preferences. These were followed closely by learn-to-swim programs and weight-loss classes (Table 2).

It is not surprising that individual preferences for programming clustered around physical fitness types of activities because this general category of programming emerged as an important choice for 66 percent of those interviewed, followed by adult programs (62 percent), individual programs (55 percent), family programs (50 percent), children's programs (48 percent), arts and crafts (45 percent), and educational programs (36 percent). A significant comment from many families: "Our family is in-

Appendix (Cont.)

Table 2

PREFACILITY PROGRAMMING PREFERENCES
$(n = 248)$

PROGRAMMING PREFERENCES	NUMBER OF MENTIONS	RANK ORDER
Dance	72	(9)
Day care	43	(15)
Elderly, special programs	29	(18)
Exercise (group) and sports programs	113	(2)
Exercise (individual) and sports programs	142	(1)
Gymnastics	88	(7)
Parent-child togetherness programs (including singles)	75	(8)
Physical fitness programs, specialized (e.g., cardiovascular)	92	(5)
Preschool educational	32	(17)
Self-defense/martial arts	67	(10)
Single parent-child programs	21	(19)
Smoking clinics	46	(14)
Sports conditioning programs	41	(16)
Stress management	59	(11)
Swim programs (adults and children)	112	(3)
Swim and gym (preschool)	58	(12)
Weight-loss classes	102	(4)
Year round student programs (break periods)	56	(13)
Youth sports leagues	89	(6)
Other (see Appendix F for complete listing)		

volved in so many activities now, we hardly need more ways of organizing our lives."

Reaction to Projected Y Facility. With 238 interviewees, or 96 percent of the random sample, applauding the idea of constructing a new Y, the personal interview segment indicates strong support of a new facility. Most significant, not 1 person out of 248 disapproved of the idea. The numerous expressions of excitement in the "comments" section of this question reinforce the community's enthusiasm for the prospect of a new facility.

Significant differences of opinion occurred only when people were asked to indicate those features and amenities of a new Y that might be important to **their** families.

Predictably, a large swimming pool, gymnasium, weight room, tennis courts, arts and crafts area, racquetball courts, and an indoor track were mentioned by a large number of those interviewed. A surprising number of individuals mentioned sauna and whirlpool followed closely by

Appendix (Cont.)

a youth game room as desirable amenities for their families. Most of the people we talked to were familiar with the fitness center concept. About 58 percent favored a fitness center component in the new Y, and 109 of the 143 who mentioned a fitness center believed that such a center should be restricted to adult use (Table 3).

Location and Transportation Preferences. Possibly because issues of energy and automobile use have been a major national issue during 1979 and 1980, the people who consented to the personal interview were most eager to share their perceptions of where a projected Y should be located and what sorts of transportation issues loomed large in their individual family situations. The location and transportation preference section of the interview is one segment in which the verbatim answers proved more telling than the tabular data (Tables 4 and 5).

Mention of Springville's busiest thoroughfare, Academy Boulevard, produced extremely negative responses among the interviewees, even those who registered responses of "unimportant" at the suggestion of an

Table 3

FACILITIES PREFERRED IN PROJECTED NORTHEAST Y
(*n* = 248)

FACILITY	NUMBER EXPRESSING PREFERENCE	% OF TOTAL SAMPLE	RANK ORDER
Arts and crafts area	117	47%	(6)
Child care center	77	31	(13)
Fitness center	143	58	(3)
Gymnasium	164	66	(2)
Health food/snack area	75	30	(14)
Racquetball/handball courts	115	46	(7)
Running path (outdoor)	87	35	(11)
Sauna	107	43	(9)
Steamroom	62	25	(15)
Swimming pool (large)	224	90	(1)
Swimming pool (warm, small)	80	32	(12)
Tennis courts (outdoor)	123	50	(5)
Track (indoor)	107	43	(9)
Track (paved, outdoor)	47	19	(16)
Weight room	138	56	(4)
Whirlpool	108	44	(8)
Youth game room	94	38	(10)
Other (see Appendix A for full listing of suggestions)			

Appendix (Cont.)

Table 4

LOCATION
($n = 248$)

Location Description	IMPORTANT		UNIMPORTANT	
	Number	% of Total	Number	% of Total
Near a park	150	61%	98	39%
Near Academy Boulevard	92	37	56	63
Near College Parkway	51	21	197	79
Near major shopping center	36	15	212	85

Table 5

TRANSPORTATION

Type of Transportation	YES		NO	
	Number	% of Total	Number	% of Total
Need bicycle access	198	80%	50	20%
Bus	198	80	50	20

Academy Boulevard location for the projected Y. Many of these people seemed to take the existence of the street as an unpleasant but inevitable fact of life. However, almost every person who mentioned Academy as a potentiallly acceptable location stipulated that a new Y must be located on his or her side of this busy thoroughfare because of safety factors. "Academy is a death trap" was not an untypical comment.

A majority of people commented on access for bicyclists and pedestrians. Because many women not employed outside the home were interviewed, we received myriad comments about the difficulty of chaufferring children to and from a distant facility. Although 80 percent of the sample indicated a need for public transportation access, most complained that bus service was inadequate in the northeast section of town.

Supervised Children's Programs. In this category 28 percent of the households favored summer day camps, 27 percent after-school programs, 22 percent year-round school vacation activities, and 20 percent day care for young children. Approximately one out of every five households interviewed was open to a more desirable child care or youth supervision program than was currently available . Those who spoke of the need for supervised children's programs were working parents, many of these working mothers, and often single parents. However, fees and transportation arrangements both ranked high on the list of these families' concerns.

Appendix (Cont.)

Pricing and Membership. After interviewees were given an opportunity to peruse a partial list of current monthly fees at the Y, 209 persons—84 percent of the total random sample—endorsed the present fee structure. Eleven percent judged the structure too high, and 5 percent said it was low for what one gets in the present Y membership package.

Although the pricing and membership question proved to be one of the more sensitive interview areas, with many individuals pausing to comment on the state of the economy and their personal financial situations, 53 percent of the total sample said they would join, 32 percent were undecided, and 15 percent said they would not join if a new Y were constructed in the northeast part of town. Many of the undecided interviewees, while endorsing the idea of a new Y, expressed concern about their personal budgets. A majority of those who responded negatively suggested that their family's recreational needs were well served by either military or existing park and recreation facilities.

The 21 Y members included in the random sample were questioned about continued use of the downtown Y should a northeastern Y materialize; 5 said they would discontinue using the present facility, 2 said they would continue using the downtown facility only, 9 said they would join both, and 3 said they would want different types of memberships. Proximity of the downtown Y to the workplace was cited as the chief reason for maintaining their downtown Y membership even if a new Y were built in their part of town.

Demographic Profile of Personal Interviewees. The random sample reflects a relatively mobile population; 53 percent reported living in Springville more than five years but only 31 percent at their present residence. In this relatively new and rapidly growing section of the city, 29 percent had resided in their present dwelling for less than one year. When asked whether they expected to be in Springville for the next five years, 84 percent of the sample answered affirmatively.

Our random sample appears consistent for U.S. Census Bureau data for the Springville Standard Metropolitan Statistical Area. The age group occurring most frequently (the mode) was in the 26- to 35-year-old segment.

Although very few of those interviewed represented what sociologists term the "professions"—law, medicine, engineering, and the like— 53 percent of the families reported a total annual household income of $25,000 or above. Of families interviewed in the random sample, 20 percent reported a military retiree member of the household. A majority of retirees in the sample, all military, were currently working in civilian occupations, several in a self-employed capacity.

Eight and a half percent of respondents were military, and 21 per-

Appendix (Cont.)

cent of their spouses were military. Twelve percent were single and 88 percent married.

Community Image of the Y. Over 200 people responded when asked what was the first thought that comes to their mind about the Y. Even though many people had limited firsthand knowledge of the Y—its location, programs, personnel, history, or projected plans—impressions of the institution were uniformly positive. "A great place to get in shape!" "Keeps the kids out of trouble!" "Fantastic program!" suggest repeated variations of positive comments.

The Y is viewed as a good place to exercise, with a fine facility, serving children especially well. The Y is seen as responsive to community needs; it has generated predominantly positive feelings, even in those persons who have not had direct contact with it.

The few negative comments about the Y's image centered upon its downtown location, its crowded conditions, and the presence of "undesirable elements" in the Y.

Respondents frequently used this opportunity to urge the construction of a second facility.

Mail/Telephone Interviews Analysis—Y Members

Family Recreation Activities. The five most frequently mentioned recreational activities of Y family members are, in order, swimming, racquetball, running, camping, and hiking (Table 6). The recreational profile of Y members differs somewhat from that of the community-at-large, as can be seen by comparing the ranking of 23 family activities in Tables 6 and 1.

Profile of Y Member Activity. Consistent with our community's high mobility, about 46 percent of respondents have belonged to the Y less than two years and more than 84 percent for five years or less.

By far, the largest percentage of respondents—53 percent—held family memberships, and the next largest was single memberships—27 percent. Surprisingly, while only 8 percent held fitness center memberships, 56 percent said they wanted a fitness center in the new facility.

Seventy-one percent had attended Y programs in the last three years. The most frequently attended classes have been swimming lessons, swimming, lifeline, and arts and crafts.

Twenty-two percent of respondents belonged to other clubs, less than the 34 percent of the community-at-large interviewees who belonged to other clubs. The most used other clubs were, in order, Nautilus, Air Force Academy, Racquet Club, Lynmar, and Executive Park.

Prefacility Programming in Northeast. Interestingly, a somewhat

Appendix (Cont.)

Table 6

**FAMILY RECREATIONAL ACTIVITIES OF Y
MEMBERS**

$(n = 121)$

ACTIVITIES	NUMBER OF MENTIONS	RANK ORDER
Arts and crafts	15	(15)
Baseball/softball	16	(14)
Basketball	27	(10)
Bowling	31	(9)
Camping	49	(4)
Climbing	3	(21)
Dance	10	(18)
Fishing	37	(8)
Football	9	(19)
Golfing	19	(13)
Handball	6	(20)
Hiking	47	(5)
Hunting	13	(17)
Ice hockey	1	(22)
Physical conditioning	44	(6)
Racquetball	61	(2)
Running	57	(3)
Skating	26	(11)
Skiing	49	(4)
Soccer	24	(12)
Swimming	78	(1)
Tennis	43	(7)
Volleyball	14	(16)
Other (see Appendix A for full listing)		

smaller percentage of Y members than the community-at-large approve community outreach programming before a new facility is built—75 percent and 83 percent, respectively. Still only 7 percent disapprove.

The great majority of comments solicited for this question said favorable things like "Great idea," "Get going," and "The community really needs it."

Asked to choose among six general types of prefacility programming they desired, respondents selected, in order, physical fitness, adult programs, children's programs, family programs, educational programs, and art and crafts.

To gain more detailed programming suggestions, interviewees were asked to choose among 19 specific programs. The first five choices were, in order, individual exercise and sports programs, group exercise and

Appendix (Cont.)

sports programs, adult and children swim programs, specialized physical fitness programs, and gymnastics.

Reaction to Projected Y Facility in Northeast Springville. An overwhelming majority of respondents approve the building of a second facility in northeast Springville—90 percent. Only 3 percent disapprove.

The five facilities most desired in a new facility are, in order, large swimming pool, gymnasium, indoor track, racquetball/handball courts, and weight room. The ranking of respondents' desires for 17 facilities is in Table 7. Some differences in preferences between Y members and the community-at-large show up, with the former preferring more than the latter an outdoor running path and indoor track. But the community-at-large desires, more than Y members, arts and crafts and a fitness center.

The appropriateness of a fitness center in a new neighborhood Y is an important consideration, for which the study's findings can be summarized this way: 58 percent of the community-at-large favors a fitness center and ranks it third among 17 types of facilities; fifty-six percent of

Table 7

FACILITIES PREFERRED IN PROJECTED
NORTHEAST Y
$(n = 121)$

FACILITY	NUMBER EXPRESSING PREFERENCE	RANK ORDER
Arts and crafts area	47	(14)
Child care center	35	(15)
Fitness center	68	(8)
Gymnasium	91	(2)
Health food/snack area	52	(12)
Racquetball/handball courts	86	(4)
Running path (outdoor)	71	(6)
Sauna	58	(10)
Steamroom	47	(14)
Swimming pool (large)	103	(1)
Swimming pool (warm, small)	55	(11)
Tenis courts (outdoor)	63	(9)
Track (indoor)	87	(3)
Track (paved, outdoor)	47	(14)
Weight room	72	(5)
Whirlpool	70	(7)
Youth game room	49	(13)
Other (see Appendix A for full listing of suggestions)		

Appendix (Cont.)

Y-member respondents favor it and rank it eighth. However, it should be noted that only 8 percent of the same Y respondents now have a fitness center membership, and 9 percent have combination memberships, some of which surely include the fitness center. Seventy-six percent of the personal interviewees who want a fitness center think it should be for adults only, while 66 percent of Y member respondents think so.

Pricing and Membership. About current Y fees, 83 percent said they were about right, 9 percent said high, and 8 percent said low. A number of margin comments were made to the effect that most fees were reasonable except for the high price for fitness centers.

To the question whether they would join the new Y, 71 percent said yes, 14 percent said no, and 15 percent said maybe. The majority of comments was that the decision to join would most depend on the new facility's proximity to their home.

Asked how they would alter their membership and what kind of joint membership policy would be desirable, if a new facility were built, 52 percent would want full membership in both facilities and 23 percent would discontinue using the downtown Y. The great majority of comments was that one parent, working downtown, would want a single membership downtown, but the family, especially for children, would want a family or children's membership in the new branch.

Overall Impressions/Evaluation of Y. The first thought about the Y that comes to members' minds is extremely favorable. Typical phrases were "excellent facility," "good place," "a positive feeling." Out of 112 responses to this question, only two were definitely negative.

About a dozen members said their overall favorable impression was marred only by overcrowded conditions.

The three things members like most, and they were chosen about equally, are facilities, staff, and programs. More specifically, the following were most frequently cited: friendliness of staff, pool, racquetball courts, cleanliness, and variety of programs.

The three things members dislike most are overcrowding (especially racquetball courts), location, and inadequate parking, in that order. Also frequently mentioned were inadequately supervised children running too freely, unhelpful staff especially at front desk during busy times, excessive privileges given nonmembers, and thefts.

Overwhelmingly, members urged that the best single improvement the Y could make would be to build the second new facility.

COMPASSION INTERNATIONAL

VISIT TO COMBASE

It was early morning in the sprawling Bolivian city of Cochabamba, and already families were lined up in front of the entrance to COMBASE (Commission for Evangelical Social Action in Bolivia) headquarters. As I walked through the compound with Compassion staff workers, we passed mothers holding crying babies and children chasing one another. Another activity-filled workday was about to begin.

Like so many Third World countries, Bolivia has tremendous needs, even though the government has made great strides in recent years. In some areas, as many as 50 percent of the children die before age 5. Malnutrition and diseases are common among the survivors. Many school children are so weakened and nauseated from lack of good nutrition that they cannot study.

COMBASE is made up of about 60 Bolivian churches that cooperate with Compassion to meet the physical and spiritual needs of more than 2,000 Compassion-sponsored children as well as other Bolivians in need.[1]

[1]Stephen Sorenson, "A Busy Day at COMBASE," *Compassion*, January–February 1982, p. 3.

BACKGROUND

Compassion International's mission, as proclaimed on the stone-and-brass sign in front of the headquarters building is "Caring for Children and Families in the Name of Jesus." Compassion began in 1952 during the Korean Conflict when Everett Swanson, Compassion's founder, visited Korea and was moved by the plight of thousands of homeless orphan children roaming the streets, struggling to survive. Upon returning to the United States, he initiated the program that was to become the present-day Compassion International. For 16 years, all efforts were concentrated in Korea, helping to support orphans and abandoned children in institutions. Then, in 1968, the organization expanded into India and Indonesia, working primarily with children of widows and poverty-stricken families.

COMPASSION'S WORK[2]

When asked which was the greatest commandment, Jesus replied: "Love the Lord your God with all your heart and with all your soul and with all your mind." This is the first and greatest commandment. And the second is like it: "Love your neighbor as yourself."

The central purpose of Compassion is to help channel practical assistance and personal caring to children of poverty living in the neediest areas of the world. Who are these children of poverty? They are children

Who are hungry and malnourished

Who live in unspeakable conditions, who have no bed of their own, who are victims of insect and rodent bites

Who do not have shoes or decent clothes to wear, a sweater or coat to keep them warm, a blanket to cover them

Who remain illiterate because there are no teachers, no books, and no money for school fees and supplies

Who have no doctor or health care worker, little medicine, and few adequate treatment centers within reach

Who have no playgrounds, no safe place to play, few toys; who have to work, and who are often robbed of their childhood

Worldwide, 1.2 billion children suffer serious deprivation. In many areas, as many as 50 percent actually die before their fifth birthday.

Compassion ministers to children, families, and communities who find themselves in desperate need.

[2]Based on annual report, June 30, 1980, p. 3.

CONTINUING SORENSON'S COMBASE VISIT

Stephen Sorenson's narrative of a visit to Bolivia afforded the starting point for this case study. To provide a snapshot of Compassion's philosophy and service, his observations are continued here:

"As I entered the building, Paul Stubbs, regional director for Compassion, introduced me to Linda Erickson, a nurse in charge of the pediatrics section who would show me around.

" 'Here on the first floor,' Linda said, 'we treat sponsored children ages 15 and up—and their parents—in a general medical clinic on an outpatient basis. Complete records of vaccinations, dental work, and appointments for each patient are kept in a statistical room.'

"She then led me through a fully stocked pharmacy where prescriptions given out by COMBASE's four doctors are filled and through a first-aid room where immediate treatment is available.

"Linda introduced me to Dr. Hernan Quiroz, who cares for Compassion-sponsored children 15 years of age or older.

" 'I've been here 10 years,' the doctor stated. 'I've had opportunities to work in other places, but I feel called to help poor children, and I want to be where the Lord wants me.'

" 'How do you feel about Compassion's program?' I asked.

" 'The best way to help these children,' he quickly responded, 'is to give them medical care, food staples, clothing, and school supplies. Since children represent our country's future, health is very important. These children will be future leaders.'

"Dr. Quiroz then explained how he directly helps children. 'I routinely examine normal Compassion children every six months. If they have problems, then I may see them every two or three months. Anytime they are sick they can come and be examined for free; we charge low fees for medicine. My staff and I also work with COMBASE social workers to assist malnourished children. If we see such physical signs as hair loss, skin changes, or sores in their mouths, we send a note to their social workers and place the children in COMBASE's Meals Program. As a result, we've seen positive growth in Compassion children.'

"On the second floor we visited the social work department. A pretty Spanish girl in her twenties named Christina explained, 'There are six social workers and one supervisor. Each of us is responsible for between 300 and 400 sponsored children in our designated zones. We maintain our own records and visit homes to answer questions that come from Compassion headquarters or to solve problems the families are having. If a mother or child misses a monthly meeting, we check that out, too.'

" 'Why are you working at COMBASE?' Linda asked.

" 'My main purpose is to teach the Word of God to the children so they really learn it,' Christina answered. 'I also like to teach mothers how to better care for their families.'

"A short while later, we joined the other Compassion staff and entered a large room where a monthly meeting for children and adults was starting.

" 'We hold 40 meetings like this a month,' Linda whispered to me.

"After singing a chorus, the mothers and children sat down, and a mother prayed for God's blessing on the meeting. A boy and a girl sang a song in the Ketchua language for us, and a young boy played a song on a homemade charango.

"After Paul Stubbs said a few words, a social worker taught a Bible lesson based on John 20.

" 'Themes and verses for the meetings are set up a year in advance,' Linda told me, 'and every meeting has a Bible lesson in it. Each social worker holds about seven meetings a month, and about 50 children attend each meeting. The mothers and children are required to attend regularly.'

"After the Bible lesson, the mothers and children memorized Bible verses and watched a puppet show put on by the social workers. 'You need more protein than just what's in bread,' the puppets emphasized. 'You need meat and milk, not just chocolate and ice cream. Eat proteins so you'll be handsome like us.' After the laughter subsided, the final business began.

"The first mother and son were called up to the front, where a clerk behind a table looked at the child's identification card, checked his name off an attendance list, and looked at the letter the boy had written to his sponsor. At this time, the child also received a letter from his sponsor. Each child must write to his sponsor at least every three months.

"A second clerk then examined the boy's Sunday school attendance card and medical record card to ensure the child was regularly attending Sunday school and maintaining his medical appointment schedules. After verifying that everything was in order, the clerk gave him a special ticket entitling him to pick up his support money in the form of material goods at the COMBASE store.

"After lunch, Linda and I walked up to the third floor, where a modern laboratory, dental clinic, and pediatric clinic are located. A continual stream of people passed us, and others waited patiently on benches placed against the walls.

" 'Six dentists work here,' Linda said as we entered the dental clinic. A young girl seated in one of the two dental chairs squirmed as a dentist examined her teeth.

"Linda continued, 'The dentists work different shifts and usually see 20 patients a day. They clean teen, remove teeth, fix cavities, and take X rays just like most dentists do. Compassion-related children only pay half what other patients do.'

"After walking down another hallway, we entered the laboratory. 'This,' Linda said proudly, 'serves all COMBASE patients. The lab staff does blood tests, stool tests to see if patients have parasites, urine tests, and so on for the various departments and clinics.'

"Suddenly a handsome man walked up to me and shook my hand. 'This is Dr. Delphin Carvenas,' Linda told me. 'He's our full-time biochemist who works in hematology, biochemistry, and microbiology.'

"I then asked her to ask the doctor why he is working at COMBASE and helping Compassion-sponsored children.

" 'My own professional ethic is to help the poor people,' he commented, 'and it is the poor people who come to COMBASE.'

" 'What's left?' I asked, as Linda and I started down another corridor.

" 'Now we're going to pediatrics,' she said, 'which I coordinate. We have divided the clinic into two parts: sick child and well child.'

" 'What's the difference between them?' I asked.

" 'The term "well child" is a stumbler,' Linda said seriously, lowering her voice, 'because we don't have many completely well children. To us, a well child is one who doesn't have a contagious disease, an infection or fever, or serious malnutrition. We treat about 40 well children a day here, and many other sick children.'

"Stretched out on a table was a young child whose stomach was enlarged. I couldn't help remembering the medical care I had always received while growing up. 'What are the common illnesses?' I asked.

" 'They vary with the seasons,' Linda said, sitting down in her small office. 'Right now we're going into winter, so we see many upper respiratory infections, bronchitis, and pneumonia. In the summer, we see typhoid fever, diarrhea, and intestinal disease. All year long we treat parasite-related problems and chagas—little organisms that multiply in the bloodstream and cause premature heart attacks.'

" 'Do you give vaccinations to every child?'

" 'We vaccinate children up to age 3 for polio, diphtheria, whooping cough, tetanus, and tuberculosis,' Linda continued, 'and the children's parents pay 2 pesos per vaccination. That's less than 10 cents. In the clinic, we also perform regular physical examinations, send children to the lab for lab work or to the dentist, give health talks to mothers who attend monthly meetings, and give growth and development examinations to children up to age 5 to make sure they're developing normal physical and mental skills. We treat quite a few children, considering there are more than 2,000 sponsored children and also their brothers and sisters.'

"As I stood up to leave, I asked Linda what the most rewarding part of her work was.

" 'When I see a mother doing what we teach her to do,' she replied. 'The mothers are learning to help themselves and to care for their children. For example, more children are drinking boiled water instead of the polluted water stored in barrels outside their homes.'

"After we parted, I went downstairs to visit the COMBASE store, where sponsored children purchase essential food, clothing, and school supplies with the tickets Compassion workers give them during the monthly meetings. No money changes hands.

"As I watched, a girl presented her identification card and ticket, and a man behind the counter checked the support list. He then automatically gave her such essentials as shoes, food, and school supplies and a receipt showing how much each item cost. Because she had credit left over after the essentials were purchased, the girl was allowed to choose two notebooks, and she signed a receipt showing she had received the supplies. She and her mother then walked away, and another child stepped up to the window.

"Tired, having experienced COMBASE's schedule for a day, I walked outside and watched families come and go. I saw hope on the mother's faces as they brought their children out.

" 'What a priceless privilege for them,' I thought. 'Their children can be examined by doctors for free, and the medicines from the pharmacy are affordable. And through the store, children receive essentials they never would receive otherwise if it weren't for sponsorship support.

"Now I'm back in the United States and have easy access to qualified doctors and medicine. But I haven't forgotten the sponsored children who receive regular Bible teaching and important care through COMBASE. Although the needs are great, COMBASE is able to communicate effectively God's love in action to children and families because Compassion sponsors are reaching out in practical ways in the name of Jesus Christ," wrote Sorenson.

CHILD SPONSORSHIP

More than 56,000 children were receiving monthly assistance through the one-to-one sponsorship program. Each needy child was linked with his or her own sponsor, who sends $18 a month to provide for such basic needs as food, clothing, school fees, books and supplies, and Biblical training.[3] A sponsor may correspond with his or her sponsored child, provide special gifts, and is encouraged to pray for the child. Many sponsor more than one child; one woman was sponsoring 100 boys and girls in 1981. Sponsors can discontinue sponsorship at any time.

Exhibit 1 is a count of sponsored children from 1952 to 1981. Exhibit 2 lists totals by countries of residence.

Compassion's work was managed by 74 staff people in the U.S. headquarters; overseas staff included 17 expatriates and 93 national workers, in addition to many national pastors, church leaders, and Western missionaries who assist-

---

[3]In May 1982, this sponsorship figure was increased to $21.

Exhibit 1

COMPASSION-SPONSORED CHILDREN, 1952–1981

YEAR	NUMBER OF SPONSORED CHILDREN
1952	35
1953	105
1954	140
1955	210
1956	360
1957	480
1958	720
1959	2,000
1960	3,500
1961	6,200
1962	10,000
1963	12,700
1964	13,800
1965	14,600
1966	15,400
1967	16,700
1968	17,400
1969	16,800
1970	16,355
1971	15,938
1972	15,658
1973	18,970
1974	23,348
1975	26,360
1976	30,993
1977	34,284
1978	40,645
1979	46,517
1980	55,108
1981	56,562

ed in supervising individual projects. Exhibit 3 shows Compassion's 1981 organizational structure.

As an indication of growth, Sorenson reviewed these figures: "At the end of 1978, Compassion had 867 projects; then we added 195 new ones from October 1979 to October 1980, bring the total to 1,062 around the world. The number in each country changes constantly due to such factors as political changes, combining projects, and so on."

Exhibit 2

WHERE SPONSORED CHILDREN LIVE*

COUNTRY	SPONSORED CHILDREN	PERCENTAGE[†]
Belize	173	.31%
Bolivia	2,310	4.19
Brazil	37	.07
Burma	2,349	4.26
Colombia	2,150	3.90
Dominican Republic	3,381	6.14
Ecuador	61	.11
El Salvador	1,653	3.00
Fiji	250	.45
Guatemala	588	1.06
Haiti	14,173	25.72
Honduras	26	.04
Hong Kong	650	1.17
India	6,411	11.63
Indonesia	8,247	14.97
Jamaica	42	.08
Korea	5,481	9.95
Liberia	45	.08
Malaysia	257	.47
Mexico	25	.05
Nicaragua	175	.32
Paraguay	43	.08
Peru	11	.02
Philippines	3,129	5.68
Rwanda	1,842	3.34
Singapore	76	.14
Thailand	1,023	1.86
Uganda	315	.57
United States	160	.29
Venezuela	13	.02
	55,096	

*As of January 31, 1981.
[†]Rounded figures.

Exhibit 3

COMPASSION'S 1981 FORMAL ORGANIZATIONAL STRUCTURE

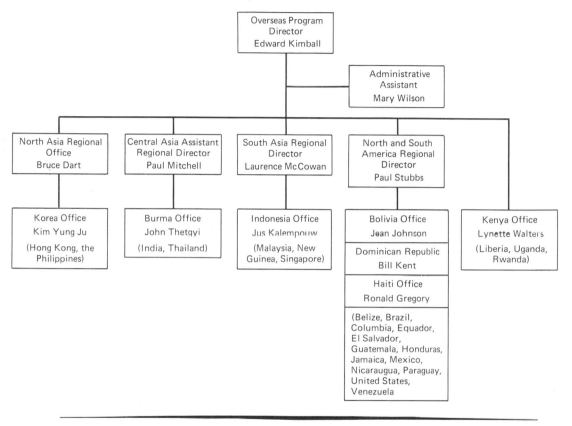

MEALS SPONSORSHIP

Compassion was also involved in a meals sponsorship program, in which a sponsor paid $5.00 a month to provide one hungry child with at least 20 nourishing meals a month. This type of sponsorship was not emphasized heavily. It resembled child sponsorship in certain respects. A meals sponsor received a packet describing the specific project where his or her monthly support check was sent and also received photographs and updated quarterly reports. Like child sponsors, meals sponsors received Compassion's bimonthly magazine free, and the following groups regularly received brochures describing the meals sponsorship program: sponsors who canceled their child sponsorship, people who asked for a "no money" packet to see if they wanted to sponsor a child, people who asked for information about Compassion, and small donors who could not afford to sponsor a child. As of June 30, 1981, 2,600 children were receiving meals each school day.

Compassion receives many contributions from friends who are not assigned to a specific project. These funds are used by field staff in areas where the need is greatest.

TYPES OF PROJECTS[4]

Compassion's projects are classified into four major groups: Family Helper Projects, School and Hostel Projects, Children's Homes, and Special Care Centers. See Exhibit 4 for percentages of sponsored children by group, for selected years.

Family Helper

In this type of project, Compassion staff members and cooperating groups and individuals help children whose families are too poor to care for the children's basic needs and education. This helps prevent abandonment by keeping the children within the family unit. In many cases, the children's mothers are widows or their fathers have abandoned the families or suffered crippling injuries. The sponsorship funds help the children pay for such essentials as food, clothing, school fees and supplies, and medical care. The funds are channeled through the projects' center—in many cases, a local church or mission group.

School and Hostel

With more than 400 primary schools involved in school projects, Compassion clearly emphasizes the importance of education and Bible teaching. Many poverty-stricken children who live in areas where primary education is either unavailable or unaffordable benefit from child sponsorship. They have the opportunity to attend school regularly because the tuition and related school fees are paid. All the children in schools and hostels—as in all other projects—receive Bible training, school supplies, and clothing. Many of them also receive school uniforms and hot lunches according to their needs. In some countries, children attend government schools. In other countries, children attend church or mission-operated schools.

Hostels provide bilingual instruction for tribal children who, because they cannot speak the national language, are ineligible to enter public schools

[4]Adapted from Compassion's literature, 1981.

Exhibit 4

PERCENTAGES OF SPONSORED CHILDREN BY GROUPS, SELECTED YEARS 1976–1981

	DEC. 30, 1976	1978	JUNE 30, 1980	FEB. 30, 1981
Homes	23.2%	37.3%	5.9%	5.2%
Family helper plans	51.0	50.3	42.2	41.5
Schools and hostels	24.0	10.8	50.9	52.4
Special care centers	1.8	1.4	1.0	.9

and also provide room and board for children who live too far from school to go home after school.

Children's Homes

Although the emphasis on this type of project has diminished, some children who are abandoned or orphaned are cared for in homes where they receive food, clothing, shelter, and other elements of daily care.

Special Care Centers

These centers provide specialized treatment, education, and care for physically and mentally handicapped children. Sponsorship support meets their needs while they are in mission hospitals, clinics, and/or special training schools.

SPECIAL FUNDS[5]

Compassion programs are designed to help children, families, and communities develop their potential in the way God intended. The following programs are helping to remove some of the barriers that prevent this development:

Education Assistance

Deserving youngsters receive the necessary fees for middle school, high school, Bible school, or vocational schools. Additionally, funds are available to provide desks, books, blackboards, teacher training, and so on for schools in needy areas.

[5]Adapted from *1980 Annual Report,* p. 7.

Medical Assistance

Support is provided for destitute children who need surgery, hospital care, braces, or other costly medical treatment they otherwise would be unable to obtain.

Community Development

Compassion works with local governments and national Christian leaders to help deprived communities improve living conditions and develop their own resources and skills; it also supports programs to improve health and nutrition, to help provide clean water, and to encourage vocational training. Compassion carefully works through Christian leaders within the community who recognize the importance of spiritual needs as well as the physical ones. Compassion's programs help deprived communities improve living conditions and develop their own resources and skills.

Emergency Relief

Special care is provided for victims of famine, floods, hurricanes, war, or other extreme circumstances who are involved in the child sponsorship program.

COOPERATING GROUPS AND INSTITUTIONS

Compassion's field staff cooperates with missionaries, national pastors and church associations, and indigenous Christian leaders associated with numerous missions (Exhibit 5).

Compassion, U.S.A., cooperates closely with three agencies in its family: Compassion of Australia, Compassion of Canada, and TEAR Fund/Great Britain. Each of these evangelical agencies is autonomous, with its own board of directors and executive staff. Compassion, U.S.A., administers child care projects overseas for these agencies, although each is responsible for its own fund raising and home office administration. Exhibit 6 provides a financial summary for the U.S. agency.

COMPASSION'S FUTURE

Stephen Sorenson offered several observations concerning Compassion's present status and future directions: "We have a reputation for responsible, Bible-based child care and needy-family assistance, and because of Compassion's responsible use of funds, the Better Business Bureau's Philanthropic Advisory Service has given the institution a very high rating. This is not an endorsement

Exhibit 5

COOPERATING MISSIONS, AGENCIES, AND NATIONAL CHURCHES

FOREIGN MISSIONS

Action International Ministries
American Baptist Churches of U.S.A.
Anglican Mission of Great Britian
Assemblies of God
Australian Baptist
Bible and Medical Missionary
    Fellowship, U.S.A.
Bibles for the World
Christian and Missionary Alliance
Christian Brethren
Christian Deaf Fellowship
Christian Missions in Many Lands
Church of God (Cleveland)
Church of God of Prophecy
Church of the Nazarene
Conservative Baptist
Evangelical Mennonite Church
Free Methodist Church
Latin American Mission
Missionary Church
OMS International, Inc.
Plymouth Brethren
Protestant Episcopal Church of U.S.A.
Salvation Army
Scheiffelin Leprosy Research and
    Training Center
Sepik Christian Akademies
Spanish Evangelical Literature
    Fellowship
Sudan Interior Mission
The Evangelical Alliance Mission
Unevangelized Fields Mission
United Brethren
Wesleyan Church
World Gospel Mission
Worldteam
Worldwide Evangelization Crusade

NATIONAL CHURCH ORGANIZATIONS

Andhra Evangelical Lutheran Church
Bangkok Evangelical Fellowship of
    Thailand
Burma Anglican Church
Burma Baptist Convention
Burma Methodist Church
Burma Presbyterian Church
Christian Medical College Hospital,
    Vellore
Church of South India
COMBASE (Bolivia Commission of
    Evangelicals for Social Action)
Convention of Baptist Churches of
    Northern Circars
Episcopal Church of Brazil
Evangelical Church of India
Evangelical Free Church of Burma
Evangelical Pentecostals
Evangelical Western Center for
    Children
Full Gospel Church (Bangkok)
Galilea Baptist Church (Nicaragua)
Guatemala Evangelical Ministries
India Pentecostal Church
Interamerican Church (Ecuador)
Interamerican Evangelical Church
    (Colombia)
Liberian Christian Assemblies
Metropolitan Church Association
    (India)
Pentecostal Church of Indonesia
Philippine Assemblies of God
Philippine Baptist Church
Prince of Peace Church
Thailand Baptist Missionary
    Fellowship
The Gospel Church (Fiji)
United Methodist Church of Malaysia

of our work but an appraisal of funds use. Compassion also is a member of the Evangelical Council for Financial Accountability. We have excellent relations with evangelical missions, national church organizations, foreign governments and their agencies, and organizations similar to ours. (See Appendix A for a summary of some organizations similar to Compassion.)

Exhibit 6

FINANCIAL SUMMARY FOR THE U.S. AGENCY, JUNE 30, 1980*

Expended for program ministries		
Direct grants for children and projects	$5,852,319	
Field and project supervision	561,122	
Sponsor services	179,306	
Total program	$6,592,747	75.4%
Funds for future ministries	383,948	4.4
Expended for supporting services		
Administration	938,735	10.7
Fund-raising	828,138	9.5
Total supporting	$1,766,873	20.2%
Total U.S.	$8,743,568	100.0%

*These figures reflect U.S. income and expense only.

"Nevertheless, we are not well known among the general public. Also, we have done little promotion through the press to improve visibility with various target publics. This is my feeling. We must take steps to overcome a number of deficiencies in presenting our story to sponsors and prospects. These are our objectives, as I view them." (See Exhibit 7.)

Appendix B summarizes Compassion's strengths and weaknesses as viewed by Sorenson.

PROMOTIONAL FACTORS

Sorenson's reflections on Compassion's promotion covered mass media and direct mail. He noted that Compassion's advertising program has done very well in recent years. Procurement cost per sponsor was $57.52—an increase of $8.44 per sponsor over the 1978–1979 cost—due to inflation that has particularly affected the magazine advertisements and direct-mail efforts. (See Exhibit 8, a summary of new sponsors, based on February 1981 figures.)

"Compassion has effectively used TV to gain sponsors for many years, and it is important to understand our use of television," emphasized Sorenson. Starting with a Dale Evans special, Compassion developed several others, including "Pat Boone Presents Compassion Children," "Pat Boone and the Little Ones," "Faces of Compassion," "Faces with Pat Boone," "Children of the Third World," and the new television show titled "Children: The World's Most Valuable Resource," which was developed and released in 1981.

Exhibit 7

COMPASSION'S KEY OBJECTIVES FOR THE 1980s

1. To continue to develop effective child development programs that will meet the needs of needy children and their families. This involves helping each child learn
   a. What it means to be a Christian in word and deed
   b. How to maintain a healthy body
   c. How to develop as a responsible member of his family, church, and community
   d. How to be self-supporting and in turn to share with others in need
2. To expand existing child development programs creatively
3. To increase the number of sponsors, thereby increasing revenue and the overall ministry
4. To even more effectively manage the organization's operations as they dramatically expand while continuing to treat sponsors, donors, and the like, on a personalized basis
5. To maintain its strong evangelical emphasis at a time when many similar child development programs are not
6. To keep overhead costs as low as possible so that Compassion can continue to direct the highest percentages of the sponsorship dollar into programs directly benefiting needy children and families
7. To continue to attract high caliber employees who are dedicated to Compassion's goals while at the same time being committed to family, God, and personal relationships
8. To increase its visibility and credibility in the eyes of its various publics
9. To put into practice daily Biblical principles and look to God for direction
10. To continue to maintain excellent relations with its cooperating agencies, missions, national churches, and so on. This means designing into every program a sense of cooperation and an opportunity for national church leaders to participate.

An agency in California, in cooperation with Compassion's director of communications, purchased television time. After time was purchased, the communications department was sent a schedule of stations, times, and costs, so an administrative assistant could keep track of telephone response to each viewing.

Sorenson outlined to the case writer the method of handling responses. When an interested individual calls the toll-free number in response to a show, a contract service answers the telephone, asks specific questions, and records the information. The call is then keyed into the CRT unit. Later, Compassion receives important data, such as name, address, and source; the ZIP codes reveal which stations generated the calls. Since Compassion's show is aired at many different times across the country and hundreds of calls may come in

Exhibit 8

SUMMARY OF NEW SPONSORS, 1978–1979 to 1980–1981

SOURCE	1978–1979	1979–1980	1980–1981*
Television	2,600	2,555	4,490
Magazines	1,190	1,519	1,437
Concerts	108	327	472
Compassion magazine	216	353	273
Direct mail	1,255	654	413
Referrals	303	261	512
Current sponsors	166	152	239
Miscellaneous	338	347	437
Subtotal	6,176	6,168	8,273
Great Britain	869	2,024	1,278
Canada	843	1,440	365
Australia	279	495	564
Total	8,167	10,127	10,480

*Eight months of 1980–1981 fiscal year.

within a half-hour period, the answering service is required. Sorenson feels that presently there is no effective way to set up an in-house telephone answering system.

The Assignments Department sends out "no money" packets to the potential sponsors, with instructions to return the packets within 10 days if they do not wish to sponsor a child. When a person sends in a check and requests to sponsor a child, this "money sponsor" will then be assigned a child.

"Direct mail," Sorenson explained, "is an important medium for us." On a regular basis, the Communications Department sends out direct-mail appeals, for such funds as the education fund and the medical fund. New lists must be developed and promotion pieces designed to attract people who have never heard about Compassion. Much emphasis has been placed on sponsors, who could resent high-pressure tactics. Although the mailings are carefully evaluated as to their tone and content in relation to the whole mailing program, Compassion exercises care to ensure that sponsors already sacrificing should not feel pressured to sacrifice more.

Compassion continues to advertise regularly in magazines, but increasing costs are proving to be a detriment. The average cost to gain one magazine-related sponsor in the 18 months ended in June 1980 was $42.22, and those costs have continued to climb. (See Exhibit 9.)

Content and appeal of advertisements are represented in Exhibits 10 and 11, which appeared in *Compassion* (September–October 1982), a special thirtieth anniversary issue.

Exhibit 9

1979–1980 MAGAZINE ADVERTISING
(18 months ending June 1980)

MAGAZINE	SPONSORS	COST TO DATE	COST PER SPONSOR
Campus Life	451	$10,481.44	$23.24
Christian Herald	32	1,986.70	62.08
Christian Life	172	10,673.23	62.05
Christian Reader	136	7,119.68	52.35
Charisma	32	2,253.25	70.41
Christianity Today	162	5,581.08	34.45
Evangelizing Today's Child	1	277.10	277.10
Logos Journal	51	4,703.95	29.04
Moody Monthly	645	18,499.33	28.68
Saturday Evening	47	3,069.57	65.31
Today's Christian Woman	45	645.57	14.35
TV Guide	256	20,408.59	79.72
Total	2,030	$85,699.48	$42.22

Compassion magazine is published bimonthly and, according to Sorenson, has proved an effective means of informing existing sponsors. But in spite of the fact that the magazine's circulation has increased from about 49,000 in the fall of 1980 to a 1981 figure of some 67,000, he stated that Compassion needs to evaluate critically its entire format. "In my opinion, other similar organizations are publishing nicer magazines that contain more information and interesting articles for sponsors. Now might be a good time to conduct this review, since we will be seeking a replacement for the present editor who retires later this year."[6]

THE SPONSOR PUBLIC

To the general populace, Compassion may not be viewed as being very different from similar organizations, and Sorenson speculated that his organization's sponsors probably differ little, if at all, from those contributing to other such organizations. Exhibit 12 is a profile of Compassion's sponsors, based on a study conducted by an outside marketing research firm.

Although the sponsor survey was completed in 1981, Sorenson believes that his organization should do another in 1982 so the Compassion staff members can spot trends among the types of people who are becoming sponsors.

[6]Sorenson assumed editorship of the magazine effective with the September–October 1982 issue.

Exhibit 10

COMPASSION MAGAZINE ADVERTISEMENT

Exhibit 11

COMPASSION MAGAZINE ADVERTISEMENT

You Can Become
A Meals Sponsor
for Just $5.00 a Month!

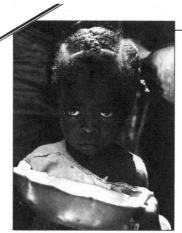

Give a Hungry Child
a Meal Each Day

In India, Haiti and other poor countries, many little children come to school without any breakfast or lunch. Their weakness and hunger make it impossible for them to learn. Tragically, many actually die because their weakened bodies cannot recover from simple childhood diseases.

As a COMPASSION Meals Sponsor, you can provide a nourishing meal each school day for one hungry child. Amazingly, the cost is just $5 a month.

Although you are not assigned to one specific child, you are assigned to a specific project, such as a needy primary school or Christian center. You'll receive a project description as well as periodic photos and reports telling about individual children in your project.

Begin today! You can help *transform* the health and well-being of at least one malnourished child.

☐ Yes, I will be a Meals Sponsor for _____ hungry child(ren) at $5 a month for each child. Please assign me to a specific project and send my Meals Sponsorship packet today. I wish to send my support ( ) Monthly ( ) Quarterly ( ) Annually.
My first check is enclosed in the amount of $ _____.
☐ Enclosed is a special gift of $ _____ to help feed hungry children.

Name _____

Address _____

City _____

State _____ Zip _____

Gifts are tax-deductible. Make checks payable to: COMPASSION, 3955 Cragwood Drive, Box 7000, Colorado Springs, Colorado 80933.

CM0982

Exhibit 12

PROFILE OF COMPASSION SPONSORS, 1981

Age of sponsors	Approximately two-thirds of new sponsors are under 41 years of age.
Income of sponsors	More than two-thirds of all sponsors have incomes under $25,000.
Educational background	One-third of all sponsors have a college degree.
Religious preference	One-third of all sponsors are Baptist or Methodist. Thirteen percent said they were "nondenominational; 7 percent were Roman Catholic.
Motivation	More than one-third of all sponsors first heard of Compassion through a television special. More than one-third learned about Compassion through advertisements.
Christian emphasis	Eighty percent of every age group sampled believe that every child should learn about Jesus Christ and attend Sunday school regularly.
Compassion program	Approximately one-third feel they get too much mail from Compassion office; 87 percent believe Compassion is efficient in providing assistance for their children.
Correspondence/child	In spite of the fact that we have many questions about child's correspondence, 80 percent of current sponsors say they would sponsor if they did not receive letters from the child; only 56 percent of former sponsors agreed to this. Forty-seven percent feel they *do* hear often enough from their children, 86 percent of sponsors say letters are meaningful and satisfying, and 83 percent appreciate the opportunity to write to the child.

Commenting on cancellations and delinquencies, Sorenson indicated a need to monitor these rising trends carefully, a problem faced by similar organizations. Actually, Compassion's percentage of cancellations is lower than that for many similar organizations. But with faltering economic conditions in the United States, he expects there may be an acceleration of delinquencies and cancellations. "I believe we must look at the quality of service—and the contact with sponsors—we are providing and figure out ways they can be improved. For example, we recently revised the letters sent to delinquent supporters so ultimate cancellations will be reduced. We believe regular child letters are also a key factor in reducing sponsor dissatisfaction." Sorenson hopes that data processing printouts, once the new computer system is fully operational, will help to identify overdue child correspondence early enough to correct the problem quickly. Cancellations have ranged from 15 to 20 percent monthly and the delinquency rate from 5 to 10 percent.

Referring to response by telephone, Sorenson commented on his idea to hire someone for that responsibility: "The telephone can be an effective approach for the Correspondence Department to use in communicating with sponsors. I believe we need a full-time person to do this and to help with written correspondence. This will supplement our traditional methods of follow-up. With a little experimenting we can decide how effective the approach might be and how best to use it."

Appendix C summarizes Sorenson's proposal for a telephone specialist, indicating qualifications, training, a suggested approach for testing the position, and a list of principal responsibilities for the person hired.

Sorenson explained that Compassion had conducted a telephone calling campaign to see if the approach would help retain delinquent sponsors. The caller was given a list of 150 names, drawn at random by data processing, who would otherwise receive a final reminder. A script was developed, and the caller spent nine hours telephoning 150 individuals.

The final results indicated that 18 had already sent checks; 27 wanted to continue sponsorship; 2 indicated intent to cancel; 3 were uncertain about sponsorship; 50 could not be located; 12 numbers were unpublished; 15 people could not be reached because they were absent when called; 13 were not reached at all after three attempts; and 10 had already made up their minds to cancel. "Keeping in mind the small sample used, we concluded this approach was not feasible," finished Sorenson. Telephone numbers for sponsors are not asked for currently because the computer system does not have room to store them, but the new system will have the capacity.

THE FUTURE

"Thinking further about our approach to promoting what Compassion does," Sorenson summarized, "most of us are convinced that we must employ better ways to relate to various publics—church, college, missions, donors, deferred giving, the press—and the general public that will, of course, be influenced by how we deal with the other publics."

Your Task:

Advise Compassion International.

Appendix A

OVERVIEW OF COMPETITIVE ORGANIZATIONS SIMILAR TO COMPASSION

SAVE THE CHILDREN

Founded in 1932. Primary emphasis on hot-lunch program for children in Appalachia. Sponsorship program developed later to help feed, clothe, and provide school supplies for needy youngsters. Began overseas operations in 1939 to aid war refugees. Recently began self-help development projects to encourage people in entire communities to improve their own living standards and futures of their children. Member of American Council of Voluntary Agencies for Foreign Service, Private Agencies Collaborating Together, and International Council of Voluntary Agencies. Registered with consulting status with United National Economic and Social Council.

FOSTER PARENTS PLAN

Founded in 1937 to aid children caught up in the Spanish Civil War. Present approaches have evolved into programs comparable in many ways to those of Compassion International.

CHRISTIAN CHILDREN'S FUND

Begun in 1938 to help needy children in China. Program similar to Compassion's in some respects, but does not highly stress biblical teaching in its projects.

WORLD RELIEF CORPORATION

The international relief and development arm of the National Association of Evangelicals, designed to help in refugee relief and development, disaster relief, and self-help development. Active in 43 countries. Has no child sponsorship program.

CHRISTIAN NATIONALS EVANGELISM COMMISSION, INC.

Started by two Indian doctors to aid villagers in their home area. No child sponsorship program.

Appendix A (Cont.)

WORLD CONCERN

Provides emergency relief aid for needy individuals, participates in long-term development, but has no sponsorship program. Does collaborate with a number of overseas agencies.

FOOD FOR THE HUNGRY

Does have a sponsorship program, but primary emphasis is on relief and a student volunteer "Hunger Corps" that assists in relief and development efforts.

WORLD VISION INTERNATIONAL

Well-known organization reportedly sponsoring some 300,000 children in 50 countries. Also emphasizes emergency aid and a self-reliance program.

Appendix B

SUMMARY OF COMPASSION'S STRENGTHS AND WEAKNESSES*

Strengths

Sound financial management.

Experienced senior staff members at headquarters and in the field who are highly skilled in technical, human, and conceptual aspects of the work; who are highly motivated; who work well as a team and/or individually; who meet regularly to discuss important policies, progress, problems, and so on; and who are committed to the organization's goals and objectives.

Vision for the future that allows the organization to take advantage of opportunities and anticipate problems.

A proven track record in the eyes of important individuals, groups, agencies, and organizations cooperating with Compassion in various ways.

Effective relations with key individuals, groups, agencies, and organizations that benefit all aspects of Compassion's work.

The desire to continually improve, to learn, to reach out in new areas.

The recognition that God's blessing is important to the organization's work.

Appendix B (Cont.)

A new headquarters that will allow the organization to manage new programs and absorb tremendous growth in future years.

Loyal sponsors and donors who believe in Compassion's work/ministry and will sacrifice to further its goals and objectives.

Weaknesses

A system of management that, although it is working well now, will need to be adapted so that other management techniques can be used. For example, executive leadership will need to begin choosing middle managers who can take charge of certain areas and report to executive staff.

An inadequate computer system (that will be replaced in the fall of 1982).

Not enough thought concerning all the ramifications of tremendous sponsorship growth and the dramatic need for volunteer assistance.

Overdependence on the use of television to attract new sponsors. Currently, this is not a problem.

Lack of a written, cohesive promotional plan in the Communication Department that will be able effectively to guide future decisions regarding approaches, new personnel, new target publics, and the overall emphases of the department and its current staff.

Lack of regular, in-depth meetings by communications staff members to plan new directions, discuss issues and problems, and in general grow together as a more effective team.

Too little contact with certain publics, such as deferred givers, churches, and college students. More traveling needs to be done to reach certain publics.

*From Stephen Sorenson's perspective.

Appendix C

PROPOSAL FOR TELEPHONE SPECIALIST

Position	Compassion Telephone Specialist, Correspondence Department.
Objective	To use the telephone in those areas where we believe it would be the most effective tool to allow us to more effectively communicate with and meet the needs of our sponsors so as to reduce the number of cancellations we receive each month. The telephone would be one of the approaches used by the Correspondence Department to meet its objective.

Appendix C (Cont.)

Personnel	To hire one full-time person to do the majority of the telephoning for the Correspondence Department and to help with the written correspondence work.
Hours	To have person work part of the time during the day and part of the time in the evening. We would work toward a W/Th/F 7:00–3:30 and M/Tu 12:00–8:30 schedule.
Qualifications	To hire a person who has the qualifications and experience necessary to minister effectively to the needs of our sponsors. Person should have a good telephone voice and a warm personality. Should enjoy using the telephone. Should be able to pick up facts quickly and to handle negative responses from sponsors in a positive way. Have ability to communicate effectively verbally and in writing. Must be able to keep accurate records and to be able to issue follow-up reports. (Personnel from the Communications Department will use a telephone role-playing exercise with applicants as part of the screening process.)
Training	To have this person report to the Correspondence Department supervisor and to handle the regular dictation work of the department. This is done to prepare the new employee for the role of telephone specialist. New employee will receive the necessary orientation to the work of the other departments to gain a background to enable this person to answer questions of sponsors intelligently. Training period would be 4 to 6 weeks.
Equipment	New employee will need a phone and dictation equipment to record conversations or to dictate follow-up letters. Dictation equipment will be used by person to help with other work in the department.
Scope of project	When trained, new employee will spend 6 hours a day handling telephone needs. The rest of person's time will be used in doing the other work in the department. The success of the telephoning will be the determining factor as to how much of the employee's time will be used in the telephone specialist role. If very successful, this will become a full-time job. (Personnel from the Communications Department will help evaluate trainee's performance by critiquing how well the person actually handled various sponsor problems over the telephone.)
Test areas	For several categories test samples will be set up. Half the people will be called and half will only receive a letter with the results monitored. After three months, our phone calling will be reviewed. Categories that are successful will be expanded. Those not successful will be deleted from the program. New categories can be added at this time.
Initial telephone responsibilities	1. Incoming calls not directed to another employee in the Correspondence Department 2. Angry sponsors 3. Special problems that require dialogue 4. Follow-up or those replies from sponsors we are still waiting on

Appendix C (Cont.)

5. Sponsors showing any confusion or irritation about the substitute child offered to them
6. Follow-up on no money requests that have not been responded to
7. Certain categories of departures
8. Cancellations and subrejects because person is angry or those with no reason or a vague reason
9. New sponsor follow-up (see how sponsorship is going after 2 to 4 months)

case
22

SEMESTER AT SEA

In October 1877 the Woodruff Scientific Expedition departed New York City on an around-the-world voyage on the steamship *Ontario*.[1] Composed of 400 students and a faculty of experienced teachers, the expedition was to travel as a floating college that would land at interesting points en route for short excursions. "It will afford a rare opportunity for young students to see the world and at the same time pursue their studies in science under the most pleasant and favorable auspices," according to the written purposes set forth by its sponsors. This was the first on-record floating university.

The 1920s saw another effort in the floating university concept of providing "an adventure in education" and "a quest for knowledge about our world" as well as "a preparation for active life." In this endeavor, with New York University as the sponsoring institution, faculty and students were to carry out their studies and social life "with mutual sympathy in an eager investigation of the meaning of ideas and the importance of varied civilizations today." The idea was that participants through world travel would forge lasting friendships with people of other cultures. The 1928 voyage, which took approximately nine months, drew mainly women students. Similar attempts in the 1930s, however, were generally unsuccessful.

[1] "Around the World," *Harper's Weekly*, September 1, 1877, pp. 689–690.

The University of Seven Seas aboard Holland-America Lines vessels had its embryonic beginnings and was operated as a private venture in the early 1960s. Interest was lively enough for the operators to begin looking around for a way in which the floating university concept could be practically implemented. A few alumni of previous voyages as well as a group of businessmen from Whittier, California, were among the interested people who saw potential in this type of contained international experience during the 1960s. They approached Chapman College, a church-related liberal arts institution, in an attempt to get the school to take on the shipboard education program, such as it was, and to develop it into a nationally recognized project. After debating at length the pros and cons of such a program, Chapman College decided in the mid-1960s to undertake the project.

Chapman College first developed a University of Seven Seas division—named after the vessel that carried the students—headed up by a staff employed by the school. In these early days, the voyages were comparatively long including 19 or 20 ports and a variety of itineraries—Mediterranean, Latin American, European, and around the world via several routes. The major problem with the Seven Seas program was generating a sufficient number of applications to ensure a qualified and motivated student body. (This remains a major obstacle for Semester at Sea today.) When S.S. *Seven Seas* was no longer the ship for the program, the S.S. *Ryndam* was provided and the name of the program was changed to "World Campus Afloat," still under the auspices of Chapman College in its Division of International Studies. Several people at Chapman had been assuming responsibility for the program. The Vice President for Academic Affairs of Chapman M. A. Griffiths needed a more permanent staff to provide continuity for planning and to manage the shipboard operation. Lloyd Lewan served on the administrative side in the late 1960s and early 1970s. Griffiths and Lewan are the only executives from those days remaining with the program in the 1980s, Lloyd Lewan as director of academic affairs.

Holland-America Lines offered the program a ship on a contractual basis for two academic semesters each year and in 1969 chose to discontinue the arrangement. Lewan and others were dispatched by Griffiths to evaluate other ships to find a new home for the World Campus Afloat program. Just when options seemed to be running out, Orient Overseas Line, one of many companies owned by shipping magnate C. Y. Tung (deceased 1982) of Hong Kong, called the World Campus Afloat office and invited key administrators to Long Beach where the S.S. *Oriental Esmeralda* was docked C. Y. Tung was present at the first meeting and expressed great interest in a United Nations University concept and shipboard education generally. Several months after the meeting, a representative of Orient Overseas Line called unexpectedly to announce, "We have a ship for you." The people at World Campus Afloat were surprised to learn that Mr. Tung had purchased R.M.S. *Queen Elizabeth I,* one of the largest passenger ships ever built. Mr. Tung had the *QEI* moved from its moorings in Ft. Lauderdale and taken back to Hong Kong for extensive repairs and refurbishing. After considerable investment and effort, she was redesignated *Seawise University*, after C. Y. Tung and was about to be used as the principal World Campus Afloat when a fire destroyed the vessel in Hong Kong harbor.

Because Mr. Tung had committed himself to providing a vessel for shipboard education, he continued to look for a ship and purchased the S.S. *Atlantic*, renaming it S.S. *Universe Campus*. The ship, refurbished in Baltimore and ready for students in the fall of 1971, was offered to Chapman College on a special contractual basis, with academic control remaining in Chapman College. This relationship continued until 1975 when Chapman discontinued the program. In the midst of campus politics, the World Campus Afloat program was forced to depart from Chapman.

With the program went Griffiths, Lewan, and John Tymitz who had been with the program since 1973. With C. Y. Tung's encouragement, the nonprofit, tax-exempt Institute for Shipboard Education (ISE) was formed, and in 1976 an educational affiliation was formed with the University of Colorado. Semester at Sea (SAS), the new name of the endeavor, had found a new academic home. The University of Colorado assumed the role of academic sponsor and agreed to provide academic sponsorship of the program. The Seawise Foundation provided a ship, the S.S. *Universe Campus*. The three-way structure embraced the university, the private foundation, and the private corporation. The legal and financial responsibility fell to the Institute for Shipboard Education, the academic responsibility to the university, and the responsibility of providing the ship to the Seawise Foundation.

The agreement between the ISE and the University of Colorado ended with the conclusion of the fall 1980 semester voyage, whereupon the University of Pittsburgh assumed academic sponsorship.

The Institute continues to attract students from the University of Colorado community; indeed, a large number of students each voyage hail from the University of Colorado. The SAS program presently has a long-term contract with the University of Pittsburgh. Interestingly, Dean Amos from the University of Pittsburgh, a supporter of SAS coming to Pitt, was among the participants of the 1928 around-the-world voyage that developed the original concept of the floating university. So there seemed to be a sense of arriving full circle as SAS settled in at the University of Pittsburgh.

A few states typically contribute many names to the Semester at Sea roster. Almost 100 came from California and 90 from Colorado (54 of these from the University of Colorado), with 37 states represented on the fall 1982 voyage, which had an overall enrollment of about 400 students.

THE ORGANIZATION

The Institute for Shipboard Education has an executive director whose primary responsibility it is to oversee the overall direction of the Institute—with specific responsibility for marketing, recruiting, development, and institutional relationships. An ongoing task is that of developing associations with member institutions for shipboard education; there were over 40 institutional members in 1982. There are no costs or financial privileges attached to membership in the association. However, a concerted effort is made to recruit faculty and students from the membership institutions. The association has a separate board elected from membership institutions. The role of the board is essentially advisory and supportive. The director of academic affairs serves as the chief institutional representative at the University of Pittsburgh and as the chief planning officer of ISE. He is assisted by Max Brandt in planning and development. Both the director of administrative affairs and the executive director are based at University of Pittsburgh.

Field recruiters, strategically located, travel extensively on behalf of Semester at Sea and are housed at Chapman College, the University of Colorado, and the University of Pittsburgh. Small offices are maintained in New Jersey and in Boston, each with a full-time representative/recruiter. From these offices emanate the major recruiting efforts.

The SAS program pays Pittsburgh per unit hour of academic credit generated. The University of Pittsburgh, for its part, provides an academic dean, an assistant to the dean, and a librarian for each voyage. The academic dean, who is appointed at least a year in advance, works with ISE to prepare for the voyage—the overall program, field activities, faculty selection, and core courses. Dr. Lewan credits planning and quality of personnel with "the substantial improvement in the academic quality of the program" that has occurred at Pittsburgh since 1981. Student demographics have changed somewhat with the SAS move East, although upper-middle-class students remain the nucleus of the program because of the cost, ranging from $8,200 to $9,400 for a single semester's room, board, tuition, and passage.

BUDGETING

No financial obligation is connected to the university component of the project. ISE assumes all legal and financial responsibilities. The shipping line quotes a per diem rate per student to ISE, 40 free positions are allotted for faculty and staff in addition to the 30 work/study positions at half-fare allocated to each voyage, and adult passengers who make their arrangements through ISE also fall under the per diem rate. ISE pays about 75 percent of the fees received to the shipping line, leaving 25 percent to cover ISE expenses of operation at headquarters and on voyages and to pay credit hour fees to the university. The in-port trips are practically a break-even proposition for SAS. The university is currently paid between $16 and $18 per credit. In 1982, to operate the S.S. *Universe* cost about $31,500 daily, depending upon the type of passenger and the type of service delivered. Variables are length of stay in a

Exhibit 1

MR. C. Y. TUNG AND SEMESTER AT SEA

SHIPMATES

A Newsletter for Alumni of Shipboard Education

Spring, 1982, No. 13

SAS Mourns the Passing of A Friend

Mr. C.Y. TUNG
1910–1982

Mr. C.Y. Tung Dies at 71 in Hong Kong

Mr. C.Y. Tung, Chairman of the Board of Directors of the Institute for Shipboard Education, died suddenly in Hong Kong on April 14. Mr. Tung was 71.

Mr. Tung has been associated with shipboard education since 1971, when he purchased the *Queen Elizabeth I* to become a floating world university. When the *Q.E.I* burned in Hong Kong harbor, Mr. Tung purchased the *S.S. Universe*, which has served as the home of Semester at Sea since that time.

C.Y., as he was known to his many friends, was one of the largest shipowners, with a world-wide shipping empire of tankers and container ships. But he found the time to devote to shipboard education, which was his favorite enterprise. In an interview some time ago, he stated, "I have learned that there is a link between ships and education. Ships not only can carry oil to meet energy needs, but also can be used as a center of learning to implement improved understanding among nations."

Mr. Tung visited the Semester at Sea many times, and each time made a hit with the students. His enthusiasm for the educational process seemed to be sensed by the students, and each time he appeared he was given an overwhelming student reception.

The Semester at Sea program, which has become firmly established at the University of Pittsburgh, is expected to continue without interruption. Plans are already under way to utilize the ship year around for educational purposes.

Memorial Scholarship Fund Established

Shipmates is setting up a special scholarship fund, in memory of C.Y. Tung's great contribution to shipboard education. Mr. Tung not only provided the ship which we use, he often underwrote it, and additionally provided scholarships for students from Asia and South America. We invite your contributions to this fund, which will be utilized for funding deserving students who could not otherwise afford to participate in Semester at Sea. Use the enclosed reply envelope.

Exhibit 1 (Cont.)

Executive Staff of the Institute for Shipboard Education with Captain Yen and Mr. C.Y. Tung aboard the S.S. Universe in March, 1982, during the annual shipboard conference.

Vision of a Shipowner: "Ships Carry Ideas"

Shipboard education is a very delicate undertaking and requires the bringing together of three important elements. At the hub is a great university, which provides the academic foundation which will guarantee that the program is sound, and which makes it acceptable among other academic institutions. This responsibility has been assumed by the University of Pittsburgh. Second, it requires a solid administrative structure which can bring together twice a year all of the resources necessary to make such a complicated project viable. This is the role of the Institute for Shipboard Education.

But paramount to the concept is a shipowner of vision who can see the vital role which international education can play in the world today, and who is willing to make a ship available for that purpose. C.Y. Tung was this kind of enlightened individual, and more. Not content with providing a ship, he became actively involved with the concept as an active participant. He served as Chairman of the Board of the Institute. He regularly became involved with the annual shipboard conferences, at which he acted as host. C.Y. enjoyed these conferences immensely. He worked to keep up the in-

terest of the United Nations in the concept, and personally provided scholarships to Asian and Latin American students through the Seawise Foundation. In the midst of all of his other projects and responsibilities, he always had time for the concept.

Why should a busy shipowner devote such time to a project which, at best, just paid for itself, and many times required a subsidy? Part of the explanation lies in the Chinese respect for learning and scholarship. But mostly it came from a recognition that all things are related, and in the constant quest for understanding among nations, all available means must be used. His special contribution to this quest was a ship. Ships, he would say, not only carry cargo, they carry ideas. He understood the great role which ships had played in history, as transmitters of new ideas, of cultural diffusion, and as a means of fostering mutual understanding among nations. As a shipowner, he felt that he should bring his special knowledge of shipping in the service of global education, and this became his mission. It was this sense of mission which motivated him to buy the Queen Elizabeth I and convert it into a world-circling university.

And it was this sense of mission which prompted him to buy the Atlantic for Semester at Sea, converting it into the S.S. Universe when the Queen Elizabeth I met its untimely death by fire.

C.Y., in spite of his many other accomplishments, liked to describe himself as an educator. And those of us in education were proud to have him as a colleague. He had a nimble mind, a mastery of fine detail, and a broad grasp of concepts. He was interested in all areas of education. In addition to I.S.E., he was a Trustee of the International Council on Education for Teaching, and served on the Board of the Hoover Institution.

C.Y. made an unparalleled contribution to world understanding through ships. The thousands of students who participated in Semester at Sea and those who will participate in the future owe him a great debt of gratitude.

C.Y. Tung was truly a rare individual, and those of us who knew him shall miss him.

– Staff of the
Institute for Shipboard Education

port, cost of fuel, and expense attached to docking in a given port. Given that the ship burned 90 tons of fuel when running at 16 knots, fuel costs alone in 1982 were about $15,500 daily.

To use the ship in a cost-efficient manner, the early 1980's schedules included two 100-day SAS cruises each year, with five or six two-week cruises in the summer to Alaska chartered to another agency. The Institute was exploring in 1983 the feasibility of operating the ship year-round, adding undergraduate sailings, adult programs, graduate programs, conferences, and other programming that would give the Institute responsibility for the ship 340 days a year, thus enhancing its financial control and management efficiency. In short, the off-season use of the ship has a direct bearing on the financial situation of the Institute and the SAS program.

The administrators of Semester at Sea had envisioned the S.S. *Universe* serving the program well for another three to five years. Yet the long-term planning of ISE must include thinking of another ship to serve the program's expanding needs. Mr. C. Y. Tung's death in April 1982 was a tragic loss to Semester at Sea, for it was largely through his good offices that the program has been able to endure. See Exhibit 1 for a story that appeared in the SAS newsletter.

All ISE programs have the possibility of academic credit being awarded: Semester at Sea with its accredited program available to qualified students at accredited institutions of higher education; the Voyages of Discovery program, which offers optional credit; and the World Explorer Cruises, which offer the possibility of credit through the University of Pittsburgh for graduate credit and through the University of California, Irvine, for extension credit. Lloyd Lewan emphasizes the role of the Institute as a "broker," coordinating all involved institutions.

Semester at Sea by virtue of its focus upon "the general improvement of international education and overseas study within higher education" has established networks with a number of other organizations interested in the concept: the American Universities International Field Staff, general shipboard conferences, and the organizational contacts of the University of Pittsburgh and its Center for International Studies, which houses SAS. Another major source of contacts occurs through the vast logistical apparatus of travel agents, suppliers, international contacts, and other connections that are part of every SAS voyage. The Institute has helped develop written planning criteria to achieve SAS goals, an example of which is found in Exhibit 2.

Exhibit 2

CRITERIA FOR ACHIEVING SAS CURRICULAR GOALS

To achieve the Semester at Sea goals and objectives, curriculum is developed along the following lines:

1. Selection of disciplines that can be adapted and profit from the global setting.
2. Selection of standard University of Pittsburgh courses that fit within the selected disciplines and that can be taught "to the itinerary."

Exhibit 2 (Cont.)

3. Development of special courses in the disciplines that can be designed around the unique opportunities presented by the mobile concept.
4. Development and offering of an interdisciplinary core course that draws upon the human and physical resources aboard the ship and in the areas to which the ship travels. This course is oriented to global concerns, such as human rights, population and food distribution, energy, economic development, and so on.
5. Development of in-country programs that will support the courses offered aboard ship. To be included are discussions with local experts, briefings such as U.S. State Department, observation and directed study, student-to-student contact, and organized and independent travel within the host country.
6. Creation of a true learning environment aboard ship by
   a. Fostering conditions and creating an environment in which faculty-student, faculty-faculty, and student-student intellectual dialogue may take place.
   b. Utilization of audio, film, and TV for augmentation of the academic program.
   c. Providing means through which students and faculty can explore the global dimension, beyond the limits of the academic program.
   d. Providing means through which the academic community can learn the practical essentials of factual data about the host countries prior to arrival.
7. Provide library support specifically tailored to the courses offered and areas visited.

STUDENTS AND CURRICULUM

Semester at Sea, a unique program in global education, is designed to provide one special international semester in a student's college career. Credits earned on Semester at Sea meet the usual standards for transfer back to a student's home institution. Typically, more than 50 courses are offered in the disciplines of anthropology, art history, biology, business, communications, economics, ethnomusicology, geography, geology, history, international studies, journalism, literature, philosophy and religion, political science, psychology, sociology, and theater and dance. Both lower-division and upper-division courses are offered. SAS offers many courses to enhance experiences in the various ports visited by the students. Exhibit 3 provides a cross section of representative courses, adapted from the 1982 catalog.

Classes meet daily, except Sunday, while at sea, and provide the number of contact hours students would find at their home campuses. Faculty are drawn from major universities in the United States, augmented by selected

Exhibit 3

SELECTED SAS COURSES, 1982

Anth. 177 (3)—Modern Society and Culture

Using ethnographic writings and films from the societies we will visit, as well as from the United States, the course will explore the prevailing features of contemporary cultures and their variations. Modernization will be examined as a process, and will be looked at from several theoretical viewpoints. The goal of the course is to provide the student with an appreciation of the factors that shape contemporary cultures and the impact that these factors have on individuals' lives.

Cas 165 (3)—Marine Ecology

This course will consist of lectures while at sea and field trips in certain ports. It will consider the geological, chemical, physical, and biological characteristics of the marine environment and the various ecosystems that operate in the sea. Detailed studies will be made of the ecology of the open ocean, the sea floor, coral reefs, mangrove swamps, rocky shores, sandy beaches, mudflats, and estuaries. Special emphasis will be made on various tropical seas such as the Indian Ocean and the Red Sea.

Economics 153 (3)—Development Economics

The process by which countries attempt to improve the standards of living of their people is examined by means of an analytical framework, combining economic, demographic, cultural, and political elements, with special emphasis on conditions and trends of the countries to be visited. The role and activities of the World Bank, the Asian Development Bank, and the International Monetary Fund in aiding the economic development efforts of underdeveloped countries are reviewed, and prospects for economic progress in the future worldwide are assessed.

Music 86 (3)—Music of the Whole Earth

This introductory course takes a comparative approach to the study of music on a worldwide basis. The focus will be on the relationship between musical sound systems, distribution of musical instruments, aesthetic standards, and the functions of music in the societies we visit. Emphasis will be on listening to and discussing representative examples of recorded music and observing in-port performances.

Exhibit 3 (Cont.)

Political Science 30 (3)—Comparative Politics

This is an introductory course in comparative politics designed to acquaint students not previously concerned with developing countries with that type of state and with the methods and concepts political scientists have developed to analyze developing policies in a systematic manner. Focus will be on Asia and the Middle East. Attention will be given to traditional political cultures, nationalism, political integration, political structures, group theory, modes of recruitment, tension between tradition and modernity, and implications of planned socioeconomic change.

Religious Studies 30 (3)—Religion in Asia

This course surveys the nature and role of religion in three major Asian societies—China, Japan, and India. It explores the influence of religion historically and currently with familiarity gained in several movements: Buddhism (Indian and Japanese), Confucianism, Taoism, Shintoism, Advaita, and Bhakti Hinduism.

---

area experts who serve as interport and in-port lecturers. A recent voyage drew faculty from the University of Southern California, the University of Colorado, Penn State University, Columbia University, Brown University, the University of Hawaii, and the University of Pittsburgh. Typically, 20 faculty and 20 support staff are hired for each voyage, which serves 400 to 500 students and adult passengers.

The in-country field experiences, both formal and informal, are an essential part of the academic program. Included in the formal program are a number of standard activities—for example, a visit to a university, a U.S. embassy briefing, an ethnic music program, a visit to a factory, or an art museum—many of these are related to specific courses and are faculty led. In addition, a number of optional programs are offered in each port. These programs, which often take the student away from the port city to sites of historical and cultural interest are not included in the tuition and must be paid for separately. These might include visits to mainland China or to central India, for example. Exhibit 4 provides some examples of field program activities. Many students choose to engage in individual projects, independent travel within the country, or special programs such as the home stays, which are encouraged in some of the host countries.

Semester at Sea must consider economies of scale—a voyage that carries 500 students clearly is more cost effective than is a voyage with only 350. Yet, students who wish to apply for admission to Semester at Sea must be in good standing at their home institutions; those with grade-point averages below 2.5

Exhibit 4

EXAMPLES OF FIELD PROGRAM ACTIVITIES, FALL 1982

Kobe, Japan

A briefing by a member of the U.S. State Department, discussing the current political, social, and economic structure and relations between the United States and Japan.

Nara and Kyoto

Overnight trip by bus to Nara, ancient capital of Japan. Visit Todaiji Temple, with the world's largest wooden structure containing the largest bronze Buddha; Kasuga Shrine with its 3,000 stone and bronze lanterns, Deer Park, and Horyuji Temple. Lunch in Nara. Stay in Japanese-style hotel in Kyoto. In Kyoto visit; Toji Temple, Kyoto National Museum, Golden Pavilion, Sanjusangendo Hall with its 1001 statues, and Kijomizu Temple. All meals included.

Beijing

Travel from Hong Kong by train to Guangzhou and then by air to Beijing, the capital of the People's Republic of China and one of the world's great historic cities. The tour will include Tian An Men Square, the Forbidden City with its many imperial museums, the Great Wall, and the Summer Palace, the Temple of Heaven, and visits to a people's commune and a university. Four nights will be spent in Beijing, with return to Hong Kong by air via Guangzhou.

Sri Lanka Village

Officials from the Sarvodaya movement, an organization that promotes community self-help based upon Asian religious and philosophical concepts, will host participants on a tour of their headquarters outside Colombo and a nearby village where their ideas are put into practice. At the headquarters, participants will be treated to a vegetarian lunch and have an opportunity to see an orphanage, a batik factory, and various workshops. Most of the time will be spent at a village where a model schoolhouse and various projects will be observed.

Bombay: Special Arrival Session

This special session with guest lecturers and students from the University of Bombay will take place as the lengthy customs and immigration proce-

Exhibit 4 (Cont.)

dures are being conducted. A diplomatic briefing, lectures, and cultural events will take place simultaneously. Cultural events will include a special Indian welcoming ceremony, a Hindu religious ceremony, and a performance of traditional music. Each session will be attended by students from the University of Bombay who will interact both in group discussions and on a personal level with members of our community.

Haifa, Israel

This tour covers most of the important historical places and landmarks in Israel. First day see Haifa, Mt. Carmel, Nazareth, Cana, Tiberias, Tabgha Capernaum, pass Mount of Beatitudes, Sea of Galilee, Jordan River, and Wadi Ara, with dinner and overnight in Tel Aviv. Next day tour of Jerusalem and Bethlehem, returning to Tel Aviv for dinner and overnight. Third day visit Dead Sea, Masada, and Beersheba, with overnight in Tel Aviv. Final morning for leisure swimming and shopping before returning to ship via Netanya and Caesarea.

Cairo and Luxor

A three-day trip to Cairo and the historically significant sites of Luxor—the Temple of Luxor, the Karnak Temples, the Valley of the Queens, and the Valley of the Kings, including King Tut Ank Amon's [Tutankhamen's] tomb. First day to Cairo, where you will be on your own until departing on an afternoon flight to Luxor for dinner and overnight. Next day sightseeing in Luxor and late afternoon flight to Cairo for dinner and overnight. Morning of third day free to see Cairo on your own, departing at 1 P.M. for Alexandria. Lunch on first and last day not included. All other meals and hotels included.

Thebes and Delphi

A one-day trip inland to Delphi, famed in ancient times for its magnificent Temple of Apollo and the oracle, one of the oldest in Greece. With Mt. Kirphis looming behind it like a great wall, Delphi stands as if isolated from the rest of the world. Many other ruins of archeological interest will be viewed and some excellent pieces from the Archaic and Classical periods will be seen at the Museum in Delphi. Dinner will be provided.

are evaluated case by case. Students not in college at the time of application must meet the admissions standards of the University of Pittsburgh and "must demonstrate a serious academic intent in taking the voyage."

Past participants in SAS voyages frequently speak of the experience in the language of those who have been through a religious experience. "It has changed my life," stated Michelle Tschudy, a University of Colorado student majoring in international relations. Alums keep in touch through *Shipmates,* a newsletter for alumni of Shipboard Education (see Exhibit 1).

Through this newsletter, members of the alumni group keep in touch with each other about personal news, which often has an international cast. One student writes that he is living in Taipei, Taiwan, where he is associated with a magazine, another that he has accepted a teaching position in the Republic of China. A woman employed by International Field Studies invites Shipmates to visit her in the Bahamas. Many alumni write in about their international careers. Diane Martin Livingston, a 1968 alumna, writes, "it is my voyage halfway around the world on the S.S. *Ryndam,* 1968–69, that helped me synthesize and focus my ideas. I think that the students that are drawn to this program are self-reliant, adventurous, truth-seeking wanderers from all walks of life and many diverse cultures." A student who hopes to return to India as a missionary writes in about her future plans. Peggy Shull, who went on two voyages, tells about her employment as a travel agent specializing in student travel: "The ship experience made travel a true necessity for me. It also gave me a unique and diversified experience that I put to use in the travel field. I try to pass on to my clients the excitement I first felt on the ship." Often students accept, even seek out, public speaking assignments to recount their experiences on Semester at Sea. Students seem to feel a heightened sense of responsibility for spaceship Earth as a result of the SAS experience.

MARKETING

The Institute develops brochures for recruiting purposes, one of three direct advertising expenditures, which takes about 5 percent of ISE's budget. This publication is its major informational and image piece, complete with an attractive photograph of the ship and an itinerary (see Exhibit 5). Those who inquire about the SAS program are sent that brochure. Lewan observed, "What money we have for marketing is spent on the printing of brochures, scholarships, the salaries and expenses of the four recruiters, and mailings. We send out 200 to 500 of the brochures each week. Lewan estimated that it takes over 20,000 inquiries and 1,100 applications to produce one voyage of 400 to 500 students. Semester at Sea recognizes that students, faculty, and staff perform a major recruiting and promotional service. "Because of the importance of the experience," Lewan commented, "the personal selling effort of a past SAS participant is one of the most effective selling strategies available to the program;

Exhibit 5

REPRESENTATIVE ITINERARIES
FROM SAS MAJOR BROCHURE

PLANNED SEMESTER AT SEA ITINERARIES, 1983 (subject to modification)	
Spring 1983 January 26–May 6	Fall 1983 September 8–December 18
Ft. Lauderdale, Florida	Seattle, Washington
Cadiz, Spain	Kobe, Japan
Piraeus, Greece	Pusan, South Korea
Alexandria, Egypt	Keelung, Taiwan
Haifa, Israel	Hong Kong*
Bombay, India	Jakarta, Indonesia
Colombo, Sri Lanka	Colombo, Sri Lanka
Manila, Philippines	Bombay, India
Hong Kong*	Haifa, Israel
Keelung, Taiwan	Alexandria, Egypt
Kobe, Japan	Piraeus, Greece
Yorohama, Japan	Casablanca, Morocco
San Francisco, California	Ft. Lauderdale, Florida

*Optional pay trips are planned to Peking, Shanghai, Guilin, and Canton in the People's Republic of China.

indeed, the personal contact is essential." During the final week of the 100-day voyage, the administration makes it a practice to share information about plans for future voyages with students, faculty, and staff. "The quality and the future of the program are largely determined by the alumni of this organization," he remarked. Certainly the frequent reunions scheduled to bring "S.A.S. Alums," "Shippies," and "Friends of S.A.S." together underscore the faith that the Institute places in its alumni. Their perceptions emphasize key selling points in SAS promotional literature.

The recruiting effort is concentrated upon campuses that have generated SAS students in the past. The international market, however, looms as a challenge for the future. Currently, the international students who sail with the ship are mostly on C. Y. Tung scholarships—three to nine each voyage—while the U.S. student profile of the typical SAS voyager, because of the high per student cost, is dominated by percentages of students from affluent families who attend the so-called "play" universities.

Advertisements for Semester at Sea are placed in student newspapers of schools whose students have enrolled in SAS previously. The Institute credits its success in recruiting students to carefully targeted publicity. ISE looks toward the computerization of alumni and student files to recruit and market more effectively and to analyze the demographics of their market.

Semester at Sea has recently begun to market the program to special interest groups: teachers on sabbatical, adults, and postbaccalaureate students.

MANAGEMENT OF SEMESTER AT SEA

The first step in the planning process of an SAS voyage is the selection of an itinerary, a process that begins two years in advance. Next comes the appointment of the academic dean by the University of Pittsburgh who will work with the director of academic planning to develop the voyage. Identifying and hiring a core program coordinator is central to the curricular planning, for around the core the remainder of the curriculum revolves. The core is a carefully orchestrated series of lectures, readings, and discussions on pivotal global issues. In spring of 1982 the course entitled "Ecopolitics and the New World Order," involved students in the discussion and study of topics such as global birth control or wealth control; environmental integrity or industrial growth; food supply and global distribution; and the control of technology and Third World growth among other foci. An assistant to the academic dean is hired who will be responsible for registration and field programs related to the faculty.

The development of curriculum precedes the search for faculty, which concentrates on four major areas: the social sciences, the humanities, international business, and the marine sciences and other sciences with field components. The curricular pattern is approved by the University of Pittsburgh; work is presently going on to develop particular strengths in these four areas as they relate to international studies and the Semester at Sea itinerary. The recruiting of faculty is approximately a six-month process. The idea here is to assemble a heterogeneous faculty of people whose experiences and teaching backgrounds complement each other's and mesh harmoniously with the particular itinerary of the voyage. The University of Pittsburgh has final approval on all faculty appointments.

The faculty are responsible for developing their own syllabi and also the field programs that they are asked to lead in relation to their own courses. The Institute, as a resource office, is prepared to offer advice and comment on programs and syllabi generated by new faculty. Other practica are developed through the Institute office with guidance from the director of field planning.

Video tapes, library books, supplies, visas, Telex traffic, interport lecturers, the ordering of buses—all this is handled through the ISE office. In recruiting interport lecturers, the central concern is to book people who are knowledgeable both politically and geographically about a given area and who will be available in an informal way to talk to students and faculty on a one-to-one basis in the common areas of the ship as well as in the classroom situation.

Staff members serve as resident directors, audiovisual personnel, secretaries, and administrative personnel, as differentiated from faculty whose responsibilities are restricted to teaching and interacting. "Maintaining peace and order and tranquility; dwelling on the positive rather than the negative are extremely important in a living situation in which 500 people are on a 500 foot long ship," according to Lewan who considers staff support crucial to the success of the voyage.

The executive dean functions in a capacity as the "mayor of the city," while the academic dean is roughly equivalent to the chancellor of the university in this short-lived community. Theoretically, the executive dean takes care of the safety, the personnel, the atmosphere, and the logistics of shipboard life, while the academic dean attends to academic issues and to the support of faculty. Legally, the ship's captain is in command; however, he defers to the administration for university matters. A good working relationship between the academic and executive deans is of paramount importance in this city of primarily college-age individuals.

Faculty are often presenting new material, and teaching with an itinerary in mind rather than only a syllabus—a situation that requires very different teaching skills from those demanded on a land campus. "This is one of the toughest teaching assignments in higher education," in Dean Lewan's analysis, "but can be a good professional experience if teachers are willing to grow and to be open." Perhaps most difficult of all for many teachers is that they are not only teaching students but are living with them. It is almost impossible to separate one's personal life from the professional tasks.

The role of the deans is to provide an environment conducive to academic work and to a healthy social life. The dexterity with which they handle their assignments has a substantial ripple effect upon the spirit of each individual voyage and the perceptions the students take away with them of shipboard education. Establishing credibility can be a significantly more precarious undertaking for faculty and administrators than in traditional institutional settings. ISE administrators are very familiar with the delicate organizational balance; it has been their task to communicate this to the constantly changing personnel of the program through the years who are unfamiliar with the shipboard experience. Other elements contributing to the uniqueness of the organization aboard ship are the Chinese crew, often unfamiliar with American ways, and the various, frequently conflicting, constituencies on board (e.g., faculty, students, and adult passengers), and the instant-campus aspect of the community. Of paramount concern to ISE, however, is that every person who leaves the ship at the end of the voyage becomes an alumnus or alumna who will speak of his or her experience. Moreover, the Institute bears legal and financial responsibility. Sometimes, a trip is not without disastrous moments and tragedies, such as when a female student fell to her death while descending a pyramid on the fall 1980 voyage.

FUTURE OF SEMESTER AT SEA

Although often compared erroneously with a study abroad program that gives students a long-term experience in one cultural setting, Semester at Sea is clear about its goals, among them to introduce students, in a comparative, introductory way, to several cultures, to extend their liberal arts curriculum through first hand observation, and to enrich their understanding of and concern about world issues.

ISE believes that the economy will remain prosperous enough to support young people and adults' continued participation in Semester at Sea. However, as the program moves further into the 1980s, there is some concern on the part of people at the Institute that SAS will suffer if the economy falters over the long term.

The Institute officials feel sanguine about the commitment of Pitt to the program and about its new location in the East, which provides access to a different and expanded market of students. Increasingly, students are being drawn from a wider variety of colleges and universities, including the more prestigious institutions.

The Institute itself, headed by four academic administrators who have worked together over a period of years, is characterized by rapport and interchangeability of roles. This is important since one of these four is on board during each voyage, serving as executive dean. During the next year the Institute plans to move its major headquarters to the University of Pittsburgh from California. With the death of C. Y. Tung, his successor and oldest son, Mr. C. H. Tung, has pledged his full support to the concept of shipboard education.

Considerable attention is now going toward the enhancement of the SAS image, to present the shipboard learning experience as "a laudable academic program." Because of increased emphasis on the academic content since the program moved to Pittsburgh, Semester at Sea hopes to find increased acceptance among many and varied institutions. Through broader acceptance of the SAS concept and the intellectual integrity of the program, the Institute hopes to realize greater success in recruiting good students for the voyages.

Perhaps the most difficult task for the 1980s is the recruitment of international students, which means that scholarship money must be developed to attract them—particularly those from the Third World.

Currently Semester at Sea is beginning to participate in empirical projects aboard the ship in connection with agencies with international objectives—for example, the 1980 project in which a drug to help control dysentery was tested on volunteer students. The results could have worldwide implications. The Institute is interested in involving students in data collection for projects initiated by numerous agencies. Concluded Dr. Lewan, "The whole educational spectrum is available to us, particularly since we have a fixed itinerary and a relatively stable curriculum." With a twinkle in his eyes, Lewan suggested that the ultimate dream is an institute modeled on ISE in several countries, both developed and developing so that "Shipping can become a viable university concept for the interaction of students who must solve the issues facing their generation, recognizing the reality of interdependence of all nations."

Lewan, while acknowledging the imperfections and problems of Semester at Sea, believes that the ISE program plays a vital role in preparing its students, some 900 of them each year, to face the realities ahead in the twenty-first century.

Your Task:

Advise the University of Pittsburgh and Semester at Sea about marketing strategies for the program. If you were called in as a consultant, what recommendations would you make concerning SAS organization and plans for continuation and expansion?

NATIONAL REVENUE CORPORATION

BACKGROUND

Mr. Schultz, 29 years old, is founder and sole owner of the National Revenue Corporation, a Columbus, Ohio, debt collection agency that [he] started [at age 22] with a $5,000 investment in 1973.[1]

Pleased though he usually was to be in the spotlight of public notice, especially in such prestigious periodicals as *The New York Times*, Richard D. Schultz, National Revenue Corporation's president, did not appreciate the sobriquet "collection agency" being attached to his organization. Leaning back for a rare moment of quiet reflection in his recently constructed $5 million building, he explained, "We are a preventive maintenance cash flow management company. If a business uses our system, it will never use a collection agency. Today's complex economy requires a different form of collection apparatus.

"The average collection agency, and there are about 5,000 of them in this country, has 8 employees. National Revenue Corporation employs over 1,000. Size is important because with all of our sophisticated software equipment and

[1]Edwin McDowell, "Making It: Bosses Under 40," *The New York Times*, Business and Finance, March 30, 1980.

an effective top-management team, we have significant advantages over the small and outmoded firms."

When in the Columbus headquarter's complex, Schultz oversees his company's operations from a horseshoe-shaped marble desk in an elegant office, but he is usually moving about the capacious room, pausing momentarily in front of the marble fireplace, then shifting to the spacious windows, punctuating with a smile and a flourish of the index finger points on a favorite topic:

"We can design a program for a client that costs less than internal collection efforts. We charge fixed fees and not percentages, as traditional collection agencies do. And we guarantee results, or the client pays us nothing. What's the core of our success? It's NRC's ability to solve the three main objections companies usually have to hiring outside collection services. First, collection agencies are expensive, with typical fees running from 20 percent up to as high as 55 percent. Second, recovery rates for those agencies are poor. Third, and this is critical, companies don't want to alienate their customers. That's it. We're economical, we get results, and we protect the client company's image with debtors."

Upon graduation from Eastern Michigan University and prior to entering law school, Mr. Schultz worked for a collection agency. At the end of a few weeks he was earning more in commissions than the income of an attorney whom he had served earlier on as a law clerk. When his bosses ignored the newcomer's suggestions for marketing a system based on fees for services performed, not unlike a law firm, Schultz applied the untried notion to launch his own corporation, which in 1982 boasted some 60,000 clients, including about 10,000 banks and financial institutions, and had branched out into credit insurance through acquiring the Manchester Life Insurance Company of St. Louis. Offering an insight into his success, Richard Schultz claimed a major influence on his motivation was marrying Marva, who was Miss Majorette of America and National Baton Twirling Association national champion in 1974. They met in 1973 aboard a flight to Columbus as she was returning home after a personal appearance in Las Vegas and he from a business meeting in St. Louis. "That," he said, "was one of the turning points in my life."

The firm's 54,000-square-foot office structure, which features a heliport and other business and social luxuries, including a remarkable collection of fine art, was outgrown by the burgeoning enterprise soon after moving in. "We take great pride in our corporate headquarters," Schultz wrote, "because it was planned, built, furnished, and decorated with a particular ideal in mind. It represents the realization of our thinking about what the environment of the workplace should be and so seldom is. Men and women have needs on the job that require more than just conventional space and facilities. These are needs of the spirit and the eye. The enjoyment of beauty should not be restricted to after working hours."[2] The National Revenue Corporation center is

---

[2]Internal publication, 1981.

the command post of its nationwide business network, an environment in which the company's capabilities are presented to visitors with grace and beauty, in Schultz's words, "A building symbolic of the organization's stature in the financial services industry." One item in the constantly changing art collection is a statue of Mr. Schultz, a bronze sculpture by Joel Hurst, commissioned by NRC's 1977 sales management team and presented to the president in 1979.

There's no need to apologize for enjoying an expensive life-style," Schultz declared, "not if you earn it as those of us at NRC do." The Schultz's 20-acre estate near Columbus includes an indoor Olympic-size swimming pool that is part of the family room and sunken tennis courts. The president is an avid pilot, but on business trips leaves flying the corporate-owned jet to the command of a more experienced captain than himself. A leased helicopter ferries prospective customers to and from the company's heliport.

REGULATORY AND ECONOMIC ENVIRONMENT

Schultz believes that the collection industry's abusers led to justifiable public resentment, brought on the considerable interest of governmental bodies, statewide and national, and led to the Fair Credit Reporting Act as well as the Federal Trade Commission's "Guides Against Deception in the Collection of Delinquent Accounts." States passed licensing laws for collection agencies and began to limit the remedies available to credit grantors and third-party collectors. "During those years, from 1965 onward, consumerism was at an all-time peak," Schultz said, "with more consumer-oriented legislation regulating our industry than in the previous 50 years."

For varying reasons, and in different stages of exigency, businesses and individuals were increasingly filing for bankruptcy in the late 1970s and early 1980s. Record numbers of people walked away from their debts. A sharp rise in personal bankruptcies occurred after passage of the Bankruptcy Reform Act of 1978 (from 1898 until 1978, the bankruptcy code was virtually unchanged), which, among other provisions, permitted individuals to keep an equity interest of $7,500 in a home and up to $7,000 in such basic personal possessions as autos, clothing, and life insurance policies. In the aftermath of what many considered to be a direct result of the 1978 act, states began moving to limit exceptions. Nationwide, bankruptcies rose to about 457,000 in 1981, an 11 percent increase over 1980 and 2.5 times the number occurring in the last full year before the new federal law took effect. Some argued, however, that recession conditions obscured the extent of the 1978 law's impact on such dramatic increases.

Consumer debt rose 6.5 percent in 1981 over 1980 and appeared headed for yet another plateau in mid-1982. This new credit was heralded by some Federal Reserve Board and other analysts as a promising sign for the U.S.

economy, assuming that increases in consumer debt indicated a spirit of optimism about the economy as opposed to less hopeful times when pessimistic consumers are likely to concentrate on paying off debts. In 1982, revolving credit outstanding, which included store and bank credit cards, increased along with other levels of household credit. Federal agencies estimated 1982 second quarter consumer debt to be over $328 billion.

THE NRC APPROACH TO MARKETS

"About 65 percent of our business comes from companies unable to collect debts owed by other firms," Marketing Vice President Frank McCormick commented, "with the remainder involving individuals delinquent on payments ranging from charge cards to auto loans. When we do our job well, it benefits the entire economy because when people don't pay their bills, it increases the cost of doing business, causes interest rates to go up, and slows the economy."

"The greatest influence on the ability to collect past-due accounts is time. When an account is in arrears, the creditor's accounting department typically sends out invoice notices stamped 'past due' or increases the frequency of statements. This procedure is later reinforced by telephone calls. The results, however, are not good. According to U.S. Department of Commerce studies, these efforts lose 50 percent of their effectiveness within 60 to 90 days and become almost totally ineffective beyond that point."[3]

"As common sense would tell you," the enthusiastic Schultz commented in his article, "the easiest debts to collect are the ones that are the most recent. I have built NRC on that premise. Most companies that try for several months to collect a bill decide, in desperation, to turn it over to collection agencies that take a fee of up to 50 percent for individuals' bills and up to a third for those owed by companies. Those agencies are lucky to get 20 percent of what is turned over to them for collection. NRC's batting average is also about .200 on the long-overdue, or salvage category, of accounts, but up to .800 on those turned over to the company while in the first eight weeks."

NRC offers assistance at almost every stage of the cash flow cycle, serving in a consultative and in a third-party capacity, including giving advice on credit granting, providing invoicing service, establishing accounts receivable processing management, offering collection or preventive maintenance cash flow management, and aiding in litigation procedures, including forwarding and follow-up through an attorney network. As the decade of the 1980s began, NRC had assigned accounts with a total value in excess of $100 million and expected earnings of $5 million in 1980.

[3]Richard D. Schultz, "Preventive Maintenance: New Key to Cash Flow Management," *Financial Executive*, October 1980, reprint.

Exhibit 1

BENEFITS PROVIDED CLIENTS BY NRC

1. We charge an unusually low one-time fixed fee to collect any account, regardless of age, size, or debtor location.
2. We offer a 100 percent guarantee on the results to our users.
3. There are never any percentage charges on accounts submitted.
4. Service will be completed within 120 days upon receipt of account.
5. All payments are made directly to you.
6. You maintain 100 percent control of your accounts at all times.
7. A complete debtor profile is available that details specifics about the debtor and strengthens personal contact and collection strategy.
8. A concerted effort will be made to personally contact and discuss the account with the debtor when needed.
9. At your discretion, NRC will arrange for decisive court action when needed.
10. Your reputation and goodwill are maintained at all times.
11. Our services may be used on any retail or commercial account as well as any bogus check.
12. At your option, an audit notice will precede the efforts of NRC on any accounts desired.
13. Western Union mailgrams, with business reply money pouches, are available on accounts for speed, impact, and immediate response, as needed.
14. Personal progress reports from the collection officers create a teamwork atmosphere and maximize communication and efficiency.
15. A complete, monthly computerized activity report gives you an accurate picture of your accounts' standings.
16. Face-to-face debtor interrogation and demand for payment is available when needed.
17. Before litigation, asset, income, personal property, and court record search reports can be compiled for you to aid the suit decision.

Exhibit 1 is a list of benefits contained in a brochure, "Your Alternative Collection Source," mailed by NRC to prospects.

Frank McCormick pointed out: "National Revenue Corporation guarantees 100 percent collection or we will handle another account for free, repeating this process up to three times if necessary. Besides that, the client gets a moneyback guarantee. This is one of the important differences between the way our preventive maintenance works and the way collection agencies handle these problems." The marketing vice president highlighted fee differences between his and other firms, comparing NRC's charge of $6.25 to $600, based on the magnitude of the account collected, the sizable percentages assessed by competitors, and, most important, the types of services rendered.

RECRUITING THE FIELD FORCE

As company operations grew in complexity, recruiting of consultants changed considerably from the earlier days when Schultz could easily convince a prospective sales representative to join NRC by demonstrating in the field how simple it was to earn commissions totaling $1,000 in a single day. He thought his age to be an advantage: "Because I'd appear to be just a kid, not yet dry behind the ears, and ordinary, the prospective salesperson would think if I could make that much money he certainly could." NRC placed no ceilings on representatives' earnings, emphasizing instead unlimited earning opportunity for ambitious people. Reportedly, NRC consultants often earn in the six figures.

A brochure presented to new sales recruits declared:

> *Consumer indebtedness accounts for only 10% of the 3½ trillion dollar credit industry! Commercial and industrial indebtedness is NRC's primary marketplace. When times are good, creditors grant more liberally and more accounts receivable are created. These in turn generate more delinquent accounts. When times are bad, debtors and debtor firms neglect obligations and cash flow importance increases even more. Up or down, boom or bust, NRC serves a constant need! It's an inflation-proof, recession-proof industry.[4]*

For planning purposes, NRC's marketing staff estimated that there were over 30,000 prospects for every 1,000,000 population, proclaiming in the new-hire brochure that NRC "is the largest firm in the industry," but, even so, that "the surface has only been scratched. Therefore, today, even though you are joining the industry leader, you are still getting in on the ground floor."

Appendix A contains other excerpts from the new employee handout, including the introductory letter from Richard Schultz and concluding with the statement of commitment required of those undertaking a sales consultant's career with the company.

McCormick stated: "To an extent we are in the financial education business; our representatives are well-trained executive consultants who teach customers how to control write-offs throughout the process, from granting the initial credit to the least desirable alternative, which we help them avoid, of going into litigation. At the same time, we assist the debtor in maintaining a good credit rating by facing and discharging obligations. That, too, is a training progress that helps everyone involved."

The marketing vice president talked of NRC's hunt for consultant talent: "We recognize the client's public goodwill as an invaluable asset that must be

---

[4]NRC publication, "Questions and Answers About Your Career Path," 1981, presented to newly hired sales representatives.

preserved. We protect that goodwill with methods that are effective without being harsh, procedures always tailored to each client's specific needs. That's why we must have only the best qualified professional personnel, all of whom are carefully selected by in-depth testing. Each person is prepared by extensive training and in-service education to handle collections in a way that will not jeopardize a grantor's reputation. More often than not, we arrange for payment that gives the client the needed cash flow and at the same time often salvages the seller-buyer relationship for future business. It's expensive for a client to attract a customer, and he can't afford to have some insensitive third party destroy that asset."

TRAINING AND CAREER PATHS

Initial training of field sales force recruits commences in Columbus, consisting of an "intensified orientation" providing industry and product knowledge with emphasis on sales applications, skills, and techniques (see Appendix A). The corporate marketing communications program has been designed to provide the staff with an ongoing flow of sales aids and information.

In addition to the Columbus educational programs, NRC provides training schools at various locations around the country. Richard Schultz has been the featured speaker in this program intended both for new recruits and for representatives who have already attended the four-day initial training school but who want to upgrade their skills. Emphasis continues to be on supplementing, not supplanting, the headquarter's sessions.

Additional seminars and management development programs are offered for those who qualify and aspire to advance in the company. The initial opportunity for promotion to field trainer is a position offered to those who demonstrate "consistency" in their productivity and adherence to corporate policies and procedures. Such opportunities often become available during the first six months with NRC. Promotion from trainer to territorial development manager depends on group productivity. Other opportunities for advancement exist at area, district, and regional levels. The firm follows a policy of promoting mostly from within the organization. Exhibit 2 illustrates these responsibility levels and indicates the company's compensation plan. For example, a sales representative receives 20 percent of the total fee charged clients; as corporate field trainer, 5 percent is added to that base, for a total of 25 percent for one's own sales, including override. A region representative is paid 40 percent of his or her own clients' fees, besides a 5 percent override on all fees in that region. A corporate regional vice president receives salary compensation plus incentives in the form of profit-sharing and various bonuses.

A corporate sales manual for the field force had been developed in 1981. Chapter 1 provides background on the industry and NRC's position in it; Chapter 2 deals with prospecting; and Chapter 3 covers the essential facets of

Exhibit 2

NRC CAREER PATH AND COMPENSATION PROGRAM

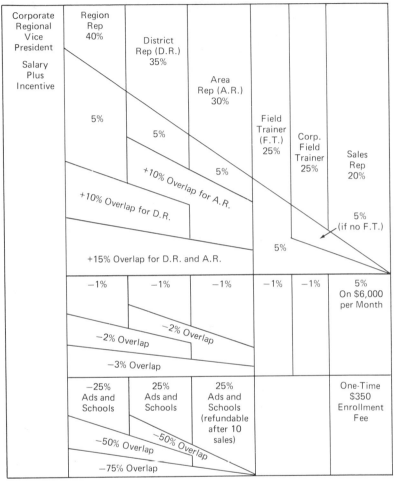

giving an effective presentation. These three were the first of several chapters to be included as NRC marketing continued its efforts to help the field consultants hone their abilities and improve productivity.

LEAD GENERATION AND PROMOTION

A change in the firm's program for generating leads, the lifeblood of NRC's field force, was announced in 1981:

On May 1, 1981, NRC will initiate the most ambitious lead-generation program in our eight-year history. An intensive research effort within the Marketing Department over the last year has provided input that will vastly update our lead-generation capability ... it is a directed effort program.

Directed—because the pool of leads selected for distribution (projected to total nearly 1.5 million by the end of this year) are determined beforehand to be in markets which have high levels of need for our service. Directed—because each prospect will have been exposed to high-visibility ads selectively placed in the premier publications and trade journals of their industry.

Directed—because each prospect will have received a direct-mail piece reinforcing that ad and preconditioning the fact that you will be calling on them to help them become our clients

Each lead will be accompanied by a comprehensive profile (business synoptic) of the company and an overview of their industry. Each lead will detail the following information: business name and address, SIC code, decision maker's name and title, business description, sales volume, number of employees, number of locations, year established, headquarter's location.

You will also receive that industry's average for bad debt expense, days sales outstanding, write-offs, collection period, and customer base. [5]

The article states that each sales force subscriber would receive 30 to 40 of these leads each week, initially distributed by region managers and district managers, later to be assigned to area managers after the program was refined. Representatives were to be sold the leads for a fee of $0.85 each, whereas the fee had been $10.00.

Appendix B contains the text of a National Revenue Corporation mailer containing a perforated response card, which emphasizes the company's preventive maintenance cash flow management approach to working with clients.

Appendix C is illustrative of specialized mailings, this one in the lawn care industry. The tab for NRC's promotional mailings in 1981 often ran to $25,000 monthly.

NEW PRODUCT DEVELOPMENT

Schultz has been particularly excited about a new insurance product he plans to market. "It's similar to mortgage insurance for homes," he reasons. "The

[5]*NRC Update,* Vol. I, Issue I (April 1981), pp. 2–3.

program features advantages for the consumer, the banker, and the automobile dealer. For example, a consumer walks in to buy an $8,000 car and has, let's say, a trade-in worth $2,000 in equity. With 5 percent down, the buyer could squeeze the $400 out of the equity and walk out with a check for $1,600 for the difference. This offers all the benefits of a lease plan plus the additional benefits of equity to the owner. And the loans would be totally insured under our program, eliminating the need for banks to reserve money to cover auto loans." The president sees this plan as a potent propellant for company growth, expressing hope that it will become as commonplace as BankAmericard and Mastercard.

Your Task:

Advise the corporate officers about strengths and weaknesses and opportunities and threats (a SWOT analysis) for the remainder of the decade.

Appendix A

EXCERPTS FROM "QUESTIONS AND ANSWERS ABOUT YOUR CAREER PATH"

A Message from the President . . .

Please accept my warmest congratulations on your acceptance to National Revenue Corporation's nationwide network of Executive Consultants. I am proud to welcome you as a new representative for the nation's leading cash flow management corporation.

Operating on a base of services designed exclusively to meet the pressing needs of America's credit grantors, you will soon discover the challenge and rewards that the role of an Executive Consultant affords.

Working in side-by-side consultation with business leaders throughout your community, you'll perform an instrumental role in shaping their understanding of credit as a tool that will enhance their business future. Through the services of National Revenue Corporation, you will help them realize their most sought after objectives: Profits and Growth.

You are to be commended for having taken your first step along a very rewarding Career Path. Because this is a beginning, I am certain that you and your family have a number of questions about our organizaton and your role within it.

Appendix A (Cont.)

This brochure is provided to answer those questions and to once again review the material covered in your personal interview.

In conclusion, let me personally assure you that National Revenue Corporation is committed to provide all assistance necessary in your career development to ensure that you too will realize your most sought after goals and objectives.

Cordially,

Richard D. Schultz
President

Source: NRC 1981 publication.

Q: *What is National Revenue's market penetration to date?*
A: *National Revenue Corporation is the largest firm in the industry with over 60,000 business and professional clients nationwide. However, since there are over 30,000 prospects for every 1,000,000 population, you can see that the surface has only been scratched.*
Therefore, today, even though you are joining the industry leader, you are still getting in on the ground floor.
Q: *How will my prospects be generated?*
A: *A major portion of your initial training school is devoted to new business generation. National Revenue will provide leads from our direct-mail programs, national advertising, and trade association endorsements. However, the majority of your prospects will be self-generated utilizing the techniques taught in the training schools. Then experience and proficiency in executing telephone techniques and referral gathering will result in a virtually unlimited supply of new business generation. The types of business on which you focus in your area will be to a large extent under your control; however, guidance and assistance will be provided from your management structure.*

THE POSITION AND RESPONSIBILITY OF AN NRC EXECUTIVE CONSULTANT

Q: *What will my initial position encompass as an NRC Executive Consultant?*

Appendix A (Cont.)

A: *As an Executive Consultant, your primary objectives will be to develop your professional marketing and sales skills.*

These skills will include consultative selling techniques designed to develop your business and client base through service to your customers.

Arranging for the proper implementation of NRC's services will maximize the profit and growth potential that properly granted credit offers in today's marketplace. The value of your efficiency in providing NRC's services to collect overdue accounts and keep cash flow on a current basis will accrue benefits for your clients, benefits for your clients' customers, and benefits to the American economy.

Providing these benefits through professional consultative selling is where your responsibilities end. All debtor servicing is handled at our National Account Servicing Center in Columbus, Ohio. The Sales Administration Department and your Sales Management Team will provide the support necessary to execute proficiently your career development.

Q: *What are the benefits and responsibilities of an Independent Contractor relationship with NRC?*

A: *As an NRC consultant, your Independent Contractor relationship is in many ways tantamount to having a franchise or having the benefits of having a franchise without a fee. There will be no tax deductions taken from your weekly paychecks, so you will enjoy full commissions on all reorders of your own protected client base. There are no set territorial responsibilities until you advance to management, and leads can be pursued outside of your management structures territory almost anywhere in the country (even when you are on a vacation) by simply following established procedures for coordinating this activity.*

Paperwork requirements on your weekly activities are minimal, and opportunities exist for each representative's spouse to make significant contributions to the growth of your business should participation be desired. Though an Independent Contractor, you will receive all of the support and benefits offered in any employer/employee relationship. There is no investment required and total assistance is provided in all areas to assure your success. New products and sales tools are constantly being developed and made available as part of the ongoing Headquarters support that supplements the assistance provided through your sales management structure. There is no requirement for an office or secretary at the consultant level, so expenses are minimal. All services are provided from National Revenue's Headquarters, so, the only servicing responsibilities you have at all, are to your clients in the form of consulting with them in ways they can maximize the benefits of each of the programs you will be offering to facilitate reorders.

A Comprehensive Major Medical Plan is made available to all consultants at low group rates arranged by NRC. In addition, you will enjoy the benefits of our elaborate Incentive Awards Program that provides bonus-

Appendix A (Cont.)

es in every form. There are trips to Hawaii, savings bonds, new Lincolns/ Cadillacs, and an exclusive merchandise catalog providing thousands of other gifts when you qualify. Qualifications are published in an annual Bonus and Incentive Brochure that will be provided at your Initial Training School.

However, along with the opportunity to run for the sun goes high expectations that require a strong self-starting initiative of those who are accepted. Since this is a career where rewards are multiplied in direct relation to the efforts put forth, a full-time commitment is expected from each applicant. There are no exceptions. This responsibility of a full-time commitment will be especially emphasized during your first few weeks in the field. Our entire organization places tremendous importance upon immediate sales success and achievement, as well as earnings and advancement potential. Therefore, the full-time commitment to an all-out effort immediately will benefit those few applicants who are better suited for other careers through quick discovery. Consistent, professional, personal discipline in adhering to NRC's corporate policies and selling procedures will assure the achievement of your earnings and advancement potential.

Since expenses are minimal as an Independent Contractor and commission checks (including those from re-orders and payments from invoiced clients) are mailed weekly, there is no need for operating capital requirements. Executive Consultants enjoy the flexibility of determining their own sales schedules. However, success requires a strong 40-hour 5-day-a-week minimum effort. But, since the majority of our prospects and clients are only available from 7:30A.M. to 5:30P.M., and travel is only necessary as you desire, representatives are generally unencumbered on weeknights and weekends. Consequently, NRC's representatives have more time for personal pursuits than do those of related professions. As your business builds and client base matures, your efforts will pay off in more ways than just exceptional earnings. The services you provide often become more important to many credit grantors in achieving profit objectives than the services of their accountant or attorney. One can feel a certain pride in contributing to their community in such an important way. This sense of satisfaction is often the ultimate reward for many.

Above all, the preeminent benefit provided by NRC is an ongoing commitment to excellence. That attitude manifests itself in quality services for you to offer your clients and a progressive development program that continually ensures the services you offer will be the finest value available from any source. For monitoring purposes NRC provides a constant stream of communications to you and your clients through computerized and personal progress reports. NRC's complete business support program includes research and development responsibility to ensure the constant improvements in each product line you'll offer. This enables you as a rep-

Appendix A (Cont.)

resentative to devote your full-time efforts to new business development so that your annual earnings are maximized. Additional corporate support will be provided in the form of association endorsements and ongoing lead assignment programs that focus on key account development. This corporate emphasis on prospecting assistance enhances your business development efforts in providing the most unique guaranteed service available to America's credit grantors.

It bears repeating that NRC is never adversely affected by economic trends. When times are bad, financial officers are more sensitive to the importance of cash flow management and demand for our service is heightened. When times are good, credit is extended more liberally, accounts receivable are generated at a faster pace, and, again, the markets demand for our services escalates.

This opportunity for unlimited earnings and growth has consistently rewarded those who've put forth the necessary effort and commitment with substantial six-figure annual incomes!

Q: *What is required to develop a successful business in my new career?*

A: *A full-time, enthusiastic, persistent commitment to National Revenue Corporation's proven program for success will provide a career path capable of accomplishing any goal or objective. NRC will bear the responsibility of ensuring your success and consistently fulfill that responsibility in the years ahead, if you will simply make your best professional effort to follow and implement this proven program.*

Most find that the willingness to take action (even in making the initial decision to change careers) is the highest hurdle to overcome. Those that do soon begin realizing personal goals and enjoying a winning attitude.

CAREER PATH SUPPORT AND DEVELOPMENT

Q: *What kind of training and support will I receive to assure that I get off to a fast start?*

A: *Your initial training will begin with a three-day school at National Revenue Corporation's Headquarters in Columbus, Ohio. This intensified orientation provides in-depth industry and product knowledge with an emphasis on sales applications, skills and techniques.*

Then a special follow-up program offered through the field management structure will be responsible for providing additional training in accordance with a detailed installation program.

Q: *Is there an ongoing support program to ensure my continued progress and development?*

A: *In addition to the very comprehensive training tapes and support materials provided initially, our extensive Corporate Marketing Communica-*

Appendix A (Cont.)

tions program will provide you with a consistent stream of new selling tools, informative newsletters, and training information designed to ensure the progressive growth of your business. This ongoing corporate support will also include trade association endorsements, national advertising, and public relations campaigns. Local seminars will keep you abreast of the latest developments in NRC's products, policies, and procedures. In addition, a series of biweekly sales meetings and region workshops will provide personal assistance in your sales skills development and orient you to local centers of influence and prospects' needs. As you progress along your NRC Career Path, you will have an opportunity to participate in Advanced Training Seminars as well as management development training if you have appropriate backgrounds and/or aspirations.

Throughout your career growth as an Executive Consultant and in our sales management programs, we will provide comprehensive instruction and support. Your time, efforts, and talents are assets we value and appreciate. NRC will do everything possible every step of the way to help you develop your potential for success in marketing our products.

Q: What are the opportunities for growth and development?

A: National Revenue Corporation is a dynamic corporation creating new and exciting opportunities every day. Because of the size and scope of our marketplace, there are literally hundreds of management opportunities available. Your initial opportunity for promotion will be to the Field Trainer level. This rewarding and important position is offered to those who have demonstrated consistency in their productivity and adherence to corporate policies and procedures. Promotion opportunities often become available to those who qualify within only three to six months. Promotion from trainer to territorial development level responsibility comes as a result of group productivity achievement and demonstrated consistency. Quite frankly, not all Executive Consultants want management, and it isn't an essential ingredient for extremely high incomes. However, lucrative and demanding opportunities exist at the area, district, and region levels of the corporation for those whose experience or aspirations are acclimated to careers in management. Our growing corporate staff throughout the country is promoted from within in most cases. Consequently, a diverse selection of Career Path opportunities exist, assuring an exciting future for everyone associated with our organization.

QUALIFICATIONS AND ENROLLMENT

Q: What qualifications do I need to be considered for an association with NRC?

A: A proven track record in a professional sales or marketing environment is

Appendix A (Cont.)

the best qualifier. The experience or ability to deal at the executive level with business in your communities in a professional manner is mandatory. Although rare, NRC managers sometimes accept an applicant with little selling experience if they have been successful in the past, working in an organized, high-energy level environment.

The main criteria for Executive Consultants, however, is the ability and desire to make a full-time commitment to their career. NRC will not consider part-time representatives.

Q: *How do I get started?*

A: *You are already started if you are reading this brochure. To follow through, first, an interview and/or orientation meeting should have already been arranged to see the NRC story on film and review your profile application. Your NRC Representative's Agreement will be provided at your interview. Most important, a reservation form must be filled out by your manager to reserve a place for you in an upcoming NRC Training School. This form must be submitted to the Training & Manpower Development Department along with your enrollment fee and signed Representative's Agreement. Upon receipt, your manager will provide you with the necessary training materials to prepare for your Initial Training School. A date should be set with your manager to review your presentation prior to school attendance.*

Q: *What preparations are necessary prior to my Initial Training School?*

A: *Since the Initial Training School may well be the three most important days of your career, we ask that you make the following preparations in order to receive the maximum benefits from each session:*

1. In order to formally register for the school, we must have your completed Profile Form, your **signed** Representative's Agreement, the Enrollment Fee, and a recent photograph. If for any reason these items have not already been forwarded to the Home Office, please have them ready when you arrive for your Training School.

2. Plan to arrive at the designated host facility between 5 P.M. and 10 P.M. on the day prior to the school's initial session. While attending the school we ask that you dress for all sessions in a manner befitting professional salespersons attending a formal sales meeting. The school's final session will conclude at 5:30 P.M. on the third day, so reservations for departing flights should be made no earlier than 6:15 P.M.

3. All meals will be hosted by NRC from breakfast on your first day of training to lunch on the last day. Breakfast each day will be at your hotel (the exact location will be announced at check-in and registration). All other meals will be served in the dining facility at the Home Office. Double-occupancy lodging expenses will be covered by NRC (excluding charges to your room for room service, telephone calls, and other incidental expenses.)

4. Travel costs will be assumed by you; however, upon completion of your first $5,000 in sales receipts you will be promptly reimbursed 50 percent of this expense.

5. In order to maximize your learning during your Initial Training School you

Appendix A (Cont.)

must have a high level of knowledge of the NRC "basic" sales presentation prior to your arrival. Your manager will provide you with the materials necessary to learn the presentation. It is essential that you study it thoroughly prior to your departure because modifications to the presentation for the various product lines will be provided in the school.

6. At the school you will participate in a workshop that will enable you to send direct-mail prospecting materials to prospects in your selling area. Therefore, you need to **bring** to school a list of potential prospects in your sales area: Yellow Pages, Chamber of Commerce directories, and so on are adequate.

CONSULTANT/MANAGER COMMITMENT

STATEMENT OF COMMITMENT

As you begin your new career as an Executive Consultant for National Revenue Corporation, we pledge to you we will provide the best sales tools, products, and services in the industry. We expect in return specific commitments from you before we invest in your training. The following are some specific commitments we ask you to affirm with your signature -- plus commitments to you from the field manager who is working with you.

Richard D. Schultz
President

Executive Consultant Commitments

1. I will make every effort to learn my presentation before attending the training school.

2. I will start work full-time within___days after completion of the training school.

3. I will master the complete presentation and all options within one (1) week after the training school.

4. I will work with and learn how to use all sales tools.

5. I will participate with my field manager on my field training program and help set specific production goals for me.

6. I will sell the service properly and in accordance with the Fixed Fee Philosophy.

7. I will maintain contact with my field manager and cooperate with his direction and efforts.

_____   _____
Signature   Date

Field Manager Commitments

1. I will provide the new Executive Consultant with the necessary materials to learn his presentation.

2. I will make every effort to be available to field train the new Executive Consultant in the first week after training school.

3. I will work with the new Executive Consultant in his first week to help him master his presentation through role play and other techniques.

4. I will assist the new Executive Consultant with learning how to prospect and use his sales tools most effectively.

5. I will ride with the new Executive Consultant in his first weeks several times to help him develop his sales technique and demonstrate how to make sales.

6. I will maintain regular communication and provide direction for the new Executive Consultant on a regular basis.

7. I will work with the new Executive Consultant to help him establish realistic production goals and meet them.

_____   _____
Signature   Date

NATIONAL REVENUE CORPORATION / 2323 Lake Club Drive / Box 13188 / Columbus, Ohio 43213 / (614) 864-3377

Appendix B

NRC CASH FLOW MAILER

Today more than ever American business depends on strong cash flow for its very survival. When accounts receivable (cash flow) dries up, its first impact is on growth. Funds are either not available or are overleveraged to finance profitable new products or ventures. Worse yet, when current expenses swell beyond cash on hand, borrowing becomes necessary to preserve your credit reputation—costing you interest rather than earning it for you. At this point a vicious cycle is created—a cycle that often has long-term repercussions on your cash flow and entire business system.

NATIONAL REVENUE GETS TO THE SOURCE OF CASH FLOW PROBLEMS

Cash flow is the lifeblood of any business. We know it . . . and so do you. NRC's work with major corporate executives across the nation has made one thing very clear about business's biggest cash flow problem—slow pays and bad debts: they're more easily prevented than cured. That's why professional business people watch their cash flow on a daily basis: to monitor their receivables current activities and to identify symptomatic trends. And it's the primary reason thousands of managers and chief executives have turned to our Executive Consultants and National Revenue Corporation as "The Precedent" for Preventive Maintenance Cash Flow Management in the 1980s.

EACH DOLLAR OF CASH FLOW IMPROVEMENT IS A DOLLAR OF PROFIT

Each dollar of bad-debt expense that is not written off is one more dollar that adds to your bottom line. Our preventive approach to cash flow management relies on the significance of that equation. Although anticipating write-offs may be a sound business practice, taking positive steps to prevent them from occurring is an even better one. National Revenue's "Preventive Maintenance Cash Flow Management Programs" are designed to achieve this very objective; elimination of your write-off loss and direct improvement of your profitability.

THE ALTERNATIVE COLLECTION SOURCE IN THE 1970s

In the early 1970s when National Revenue Corporation was founded, we prided ourselves on being "The Alternative Collection Source." In contrast to conventional agencies that charge 33 percent to 50 percent of what little they collected, National Revenue charged a low, economical, fixed fee that produced excellent results and preserved our client's image and

Appendix B (Cont.)

reputation. This unique approach has been acclaimed in business and trade press across the country and has earned us the confidence of over 60,000 businesses. But this was only the beginning.

THE PRECEDENT IN PREVENTIVE MAINTENANCE CASH FLOW MANAGEMENT FOR THE 1980s

Because we were more effective and economical than conventional sources, our position as "The Alternative Collection Source" became well established. Manufacturers, distributors, service companies, banks, credit unions, and retailers found that National Revenue returned their cash flow to a current basis—and did so more economically than their own internal efforts. As a result, we have encouraged clients to utilize this capability earlier in the accounts receivable cycle ... where our third-party credibility and sophisticated technology are even more effective. Relying on this cooperative approach, we cost effectively eliminate slow pays, past dues, and delinquencies, which establishes a **higher level of profitability!**

A NATIONWIDE NETWORK OF PROFESSIONAL EXECUTIVE CONSULTANTS

NRC's network of Executive Consultants is comprised of experienced professionals who possess the expertise to review your entire cash flow procedure from credit granting to collection. They concentrate on diagnosing the root causes of the problem—such as slow pays, delinquencies, and write-offs—information that will aid in establishing a receivables acceleration program and developing an effective prevention plan. The result—healthier cash flow—evident in the reduction of days sales outstanding and increased cash on hand.

ESTABLISH THE PRECEDENT FOR BOTTOM-LINE RESULTS

As we have grown in capability from collections to full accounts receivable servicing and management, our outlook has changed. Now, rather than just an alternative, we stand alone as "The Precedent" in our industry. Our Executive Consultants work with you to analyze your cash flow objectives as concerned partners, not isolated associates. It's a working relationship that produces bottom-line results—and we think you'll agree, that's the real precedent!

To get all the facts on "The Precedent," return the attached reply card.

Appendix C

LAWN CARE INDUSTRY MAILING

NATIONAL REVENUE CORPORATION

2323 LAKE CLUB DRIVE / P.O. BOX 13188 / COLUMBUS, OHIO 43213 / 614-864-3377

JAMES F. McCORMICK   Vice President,
                                                                                                  Marketing

CHEMLAWN	LAWN DOCTOR
PERF-A-LAWN	LEISURELAWN
TURFGARD	BAREFOOT GRASS

As a lawn care professional, you are familiar with the
companies I have listed because you share a great deal
in common with them.

> I point them out because I know you will
> be interested in a revolutionary idea they
> have adopted to <u>increase their profit-
> ability</u> -- without major investments.

That idea is the product of years of work by the National
Revenue Corporation. It is contained in our new "Lawn
Care Industry Cash Flow Acceleration" program -- an
approach to slow pays and delinquencies uniquely designed
to turn the accounts receivable of America's lawn care
professionals into immediate <u>cash</u>.

It is an approach developed through years of research
that revealed a major obstacle: lawn care companies tend
to view conventional collection agencies as expensive,
ineffective, and detrimental to their public image.

> But with average recovery ratios of less than
> 15%, average collection fees of 50%, and cus-
> tomers lost through crude collection methods --
> it is not hard to understand why you have de-
> veloped this opinion.

Nor is it hard to appreciate the fact that National
Revenue has successfully changed that same opinion in
a variety of <u>diverse markets</u> since our founding in 1971.
Our position as an alternative collection source was
established then and is maintained now by techniques
which continually return <u>the highest recovery ratios</u> in
the collection industry.

In fact, our <u>results</u> to date in the lawn care market have
been among our <u>most impressive</u> -- attributable in part to
the time we have been involved with the firms I mentioned
at the start of this letter.

You see, we've found that the more you work with a specific type of debtor - the more <u>effective</u> you become in
assessing their attitudes toward payment. And the more
successful you then become in <u>dealing swiftly and deci-
sively</u> with each individual case.

> In the final analysis, our success with your
> past due customers will be traced to primar-
> ily one factor -- we know from experience
> the stalling habits of lawn care slow pays.

(Next page, please)

Appendix C (Cont.)

(2)

For instance, we're aware that accounts are often dis-
puted; for a variety of reasons -- some valid others not.
And that discussing the debt with the debtor early in the
delinquency will often resolve the problem.

We recognize that a major problem associated with providing a professional service like a doctor or a dentist
is that you often get paid last. And that customers will
take advantage of the fact that a service cannot be re-
possessed -- correctly assuming their balance will probably be too small to litigate.

We're also familiar with the scam where customers receive
two or three applications, then switch companies; and so
on -- always keeping balances small enough that by just
being obstinate they might evade payment.

> We know all too well the problems you face.
> And we know full well how to solve them.

By tracking collection results we have obtained over the
years with our existing lawn care clients, we know the
stages at which delinquencies common to this industry are
most responsive. And based on that knowledge we have
tailored our collection techniques to address these unique
debtor profiles, to eliminate current delinquencies and
slow pays, and to establish and maintain cash flow on a
current basis.

The overwhelming success of our research, experimentation,
and experience in this market is fully incorporated in our
"Lawn Care Industry Cash Flow Acceleration" program.

I've taken the liberty of enclosing case histories for two
clients who've benefited from the program. These are only
excerpts from a brochure which details NRC's Lawn Care
Industry Cash Flow Acceleration Program.

If your objectives include converting receivables into cash
and write-offs into profits, while keeping cash flow current,
our Lawn Care Industry Cash Flow Acceleration Program can
make it happen. It's one of several market-specialized programs that have helped improve profitability, efficiency,
and productivity for our 60,000 commercial and retail customers nationwide. It can work for you, too.

Call us today toll free at 800-848-7590 (in Ohio call collect: 614-864-3377) or return the enclosed postage paid
reply card to my attention to receive your copy of our
"Lawn Care Cash Flow Acceleration Program" brochure at no
cost or obligation.

We look forward to the opportunity of working with you to
accelerate your cash flow economically and effectively while
preserving your fine reputation.

Sincerely,

James F. McCormick

James F. McCormick
Vice President-Marketing

P.S. Ask your NRC Executive Consultant when he calls for a
     complete presentation of our capabilities, including
     our new PLUS option for particularly troublesome accounts.

Appendix C (Cont.)

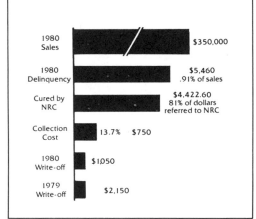

LAWN CARE CLIENT A

NRC has been working with this client for nearly four years. They have purchased three 100 account systems during that period. And, in fact, over one-third of their most recently installed systems had yet to be submitted when these figures were compiled.

1980 Sales	$350,000
1980 Delinquency	$5,460 .91% of sales
Cured by NRC	$4,422.60 81% of dollars referred to NRC
Collection Cost	13.7% $750
1980 Write-off	$1,050
1979 Write-off	$2,150

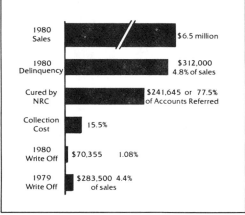

LAWN CARE CLIENT C

During 1980, total sales at this firm's eight branches exceeded $6.5 million dollars. Delinquencies for the year had reached $312,000 when they were turned over to National Revenue for collection in January. By March over $200,000 of that total had been recovered and another $40,000 had been resolved by settling disputes and correcting errors.

1980 Sales	$6.5 million
1980 Delinquency	$312,000 4.8% of sales
Cured by NRC	$241,645 or 77.5% of Accounts Referred
Collection Cost	15.5%
1980 Write Off	$70,355 1.08%
1979 Write Off	$283,500 4.4% of sales

Yes, I am very interested in receiving further details about National Revenue's "Lawn Care Industry Cash Flow Acceleration" program.

☐ Please forward complete details to me at the address below.

☐ Please have an NRC Executive Consultant arrange to meet with me personally to present a complete overview of your firm's capabilities.

Name _____

Title _____

Company _____

Address _____

Phone _____

case
24

OMEGA MEDICAL PRODUCTS

Omega Medical Products (OMP) is one of the top manufacturers of life support medical equipment and surgical pharmaceuticals. In fiscal year 1981 OMP recorded sales of $230 million (see Exhibit 1). Over the past three years, sales have been increasing at an annual rate of 18 percent. The company currently employs 175 sales representatives, including a separate sales force of 40 that handles the company's anesthesia line exclusively. As the result of a recent staff reorganization, a decision was made to realign the Sales and Marketing Department to meet the future goals of the company better.

Five years ago, Omega's president retired and the top position was filled by the executive vice president, Christopher John. Subsequently, several other major changes occurred in the executive staff hierarchy. The most important were the elimination of the executive vice president position and the creation of the position of vice president, marketing and sales. Reporting to the new vice president would be the current vice president of sales, service, and distribution; the vice president of international sales; the general manager of medical equipment marketing; the general manager of distribution, customer services, and gases; the director of market research and strategic planning; the director of communications; and the marketing manager of architectural products (see Exhibit 2).

The vice president of marketing and sales, destined to be one of the most

Exhibit 1

1981 SALES
(in thousands)

Patient care		$ 84,270
Anesthesia equipment	$40,100	
Anesthesia disposables	20,450	
Nursing products	13,720	
Infant care	10,000	
Respiratory therapy		40,418
Architectural products		35,980
Anesthesia (gases)		50,055
Other (government, OEM, service, military)		20,000
Total		$230,723

powerful positions at OMP, was ultimately filled by Earl Callahan. Callahan had previously held the top marketing job in a firm that manufactured medical products unrelated to those sold by Omega. Filling this position with an "outsider" generated noticeable discontent among several OMP executives who had considered top contenders. Shortly after he began work, Callahan was pressured by Christopher John to create a revised sales organization chart prior to Omega's new fiscal year, beginning July 1. After reviewing Omega's current organization charts, sales figures, and marketing plans for new products, Callahan realized that several major problems existed.

MARKETING ACTIVITIES

Omega's marketing function was divided into four separate product areas. The patient care group consisted of anesthesia equipment and disposables; nursing equipment; and infant care supplies. The anesthesia equipment and disposables line accounted for the greatest dollar volume, with 1981 sales of $60 million. With new products as the primary growth factor in the portable patient monitoring area, sales were expected to be $115 million by 1985. Product prices ranged from a few cents for disposables to several thousand dollars for equipment.

The respiratory therapy line accounted for $40 million of sales in 1981. The line had experienced only slight growth over the last few years but was expected to generate $58 million by 1985 with the introduction of one major new critical care ventilator, priced as high as $35,000 with all accessories. The prime market for this do-everything machine was the small- to medium-sized

Exhibit 2

ORGANIZATIONAL STRUCTURE

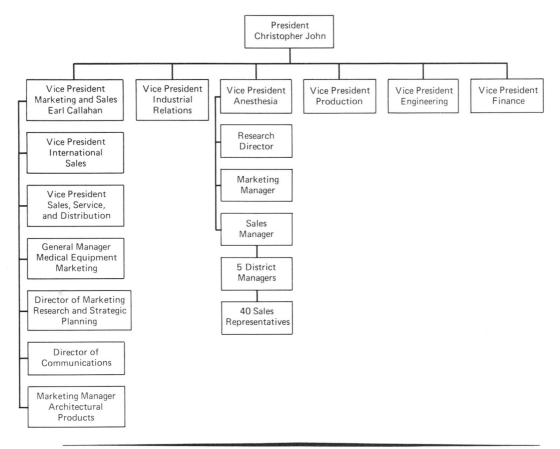

primary care hospital. Although Omega was the leader in the anesthesia field, it did not enjoy the same position in respiratory care. In fact, due to several major failures with new products during the last 10 to 15 years, the Omega name was still associated by many therapists with inferior quality, poor product design, and inadequate service.

The architectural product line, composed of pipelines and gas outlets, had sales of $36 million in 1981, while the anesthesia line (gases), sold by a separate sales organization, accounted for $50 million. The major product was a liquid that, when converted to gas, was used to anesthetize patients for surgery.

SALES ACTIVITIES

The general sales force, consisting of 135 representatives in the United States and Canada reporting to 16 district managers and 6 regional vice presidents (see Exhibit 3), were currently expected to call on four major departments in each hospital: operating room, recovery room, emergency room, and nursery. Additionally, they were expected to keep in contact with purchasing and, if one existed, with the biomedical engineering department. The latter, usually present only in larger hospitals, was often responsible for reviewing and testing potential new equipment. Biomedical engineers were becoming instrumental in the purchase of sophisticated electronic monitoring devices. Also, the sales force was expected to sell bulk oxygen and nitrous oxide as well as Omega's architectural product line equipment to new hospitals or those being remodeled. This required that they work very closely with architects and construction contractors, usually a very time-consuming endeavor, ranging from several months to over one year. The anesthesia sales force called on the anesthesia staff exclusively. Close and frequent contact was necessary in most cases. The sales force, all with chemical backgrounds, was expected to keep abreast of technological developments in the field. Some sales representatives were formerly anesthetists.

Although Omega's products covered a wide variety of medical applications and necessitated sales calls to many different departments, the general line sales force had, to date, handled the lines very well. Callahan felt that one primary reason they had done so well was that the majority of Omega's products were not particularly complicated and the sales force could be adequately trained by product managers when new products were introduced. Additionally, although Omega sold several thousand items, which realistically is a line much too broad for a sales representative to handle effectively, Callahan knew that many products sold with little or no sales effort because of the overall Omega reputation and strong dealer network. Most dealers handled low-cost, easy-to-sell products; some very large dealers sold high-priced equipment. Callahan projected, however, that the days of easy sales were numbered because many products planned for market introduction in the next five years were state-of-the-art electronic monitoring equipment. Most of these products were in the anesthesia line. Omega's lack of experience in the medical electronics field would require an intensive sales effort to enter the market profitably, as several formidable competitors controlled the market.

Unfortunately, it was generally known that as many as half of Omega's sales representatives did not have the training or experience to sell these kinds of products. In view of the need to deal with hospital biomedical engineers on a very technical level, in the long run, Callahan surmised, it would be better to use only sales personnel experienced in selling electronic equipment rather than attempt to train the entire force. Besides, he knew from personal conversations with the sales force that no more than 10 percent of the representa-

Exhibit 3

SALES ORGANIZATION

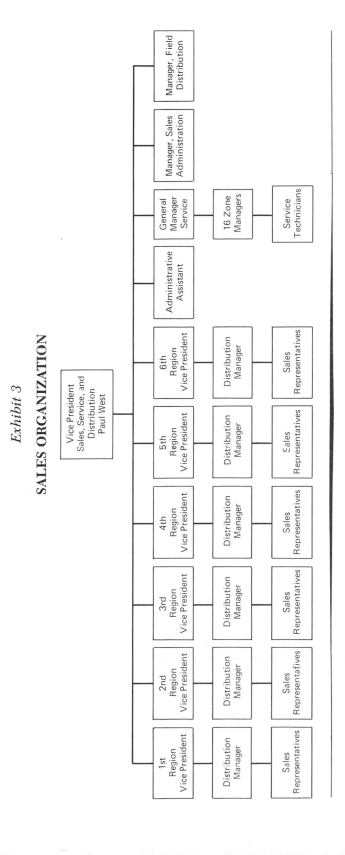

tives had an interest in learning about or selling the new equipment. Thus, he thought about augmenting the sales force with specialists able to provide technical assistance to sell portable patient monitoring equipment. However, since both general line and anesthesia sales representatives were calling on hospital personnel, he feared having third parties calling on the same personnel; this could be more confusing than advantageous.

OTHER INFORMATION

For a year, the marketing manager of respiratory care, Bill Griese, had been attempting to convince Callahan that, in spite of the line's history, real growth potential existed in respiratory therapy. Griese wanted the company to spend more time and money pursuing this market and he indicated to Callahan that to sell and service the products adequately, particularly the new critical care ventilator, the line should be handled by a separate sales force. Bill Griese argued that because most of Omega's products were in the anesthesia field, the representatives were spending a disproportionate amount of sales time in that area, thus perpetuating Omega's relatively poor sales and image in respiratory therapy.

Callahan knew that Jeff Hardy, marketing manager for patient care, would lobby for a separate sales group for anesthesia products since that line represents one-quarter of the company's sales. Apparently, this request had been made several times over the past five years. One proposal had included plans for the anesthesia (gases) sales force to also handle the anesthesia equipment because both were sold to the same department. Another proposal had called for a separate anesthesia equipment force altogether. Callahan was convinced that drugs and equipment required substantially different sales techniques and that one force could not adequately handle both; yet, he had reservations about two different representatives calling on the same customer, as was currently the case. On the other hand, Jeff Hardy's suggestion for a separate anesthesia equipment force might well result in substantially more sales time spent on respiratory products by the general line sales force.

ANESTHESIA SALES ORGANIZATION

Approximately 10 years ago, Omega's chemical research department discovered a revolutionary new drug (gas) to anesthetize patients safely for surgery. Following two years of testing for the Food and Drug Administration, the drug was approved and successfully introduced to the marketplace. It is currently used on 60 percent of all surgical patients, and it continues to capture market share. The drug has a very high gross margin, and in 1981, it had profits of $21 million on sales of $50 million. Its patent runs through 1990.

Exhibit 4

SALES COMPENSATION PLANS

	GENERAL LINE REPRESENTATIVES	ANESTHESIA REPRESENTATIVES
Base monthly salary, 1980	$1,500–1,850	$1,650–2,100
Commission on sales up to quota (percent)	1%	1%
Commission on sales over quota (percent)	2–5%	2–5%
Annual salary range, 1980	$24,200–35,800	$29,800–42,750
Average salary	$38,100	$42,000

To develop the surgical drug market fully and lead the marketing and sales activities, a vice presidential position was created at the time of discovery of the new drug. Ronald Hagen was hired for this position. He, in turn, put together a separate sales organization with 45 persons by 1981. Most of the sales representatives were hired away from pharmaceutical companies and thus demanded and were paid salaries and commissions somewhat above those paid to Omega's general line sales force (see Exhibit 4).

Hagen is very proud of his organization, believing that his sales representatives are a cut above the general line organization. Consequently, he wants no part of any plans to join the two forces. Besides, other new drugs are scheduled for introduction in the 1983–1984 period and will provide the drug sales group with a sufficient product load for several years into the future.

GENERAL LINE SALES ORGANIZATION

The general line sales organization, reporting to Paul West, consisted of 135 representatives, 16 district managers, and 6 regional vice presidents. The service department, also under West, consisted of a total of 172 technicians reporting to 16 zone managers. Also reporting to West were the manager of sales administration, the manager of field distribution, and an administrative assistant.

West was initially quite upset about the apparent demotion of his position as a result of the reorganization; he had reported directly to Christopher John before Callahan was hired. Knowing that further reorganization was imminent, West calculated that he would ultimately lose control of the service and distribution areas. Although this would narrow his responsibilities somewhat, West was not particularly concerned. In fact, because of the need to update both the service organization and the distribution organization to handle the new portable patient care monitoring products, those areas had been commanding a disproportionate amount of his time. West preferred to hire a general manager for service and distribution who would report to him and handle most of the responsibility in those two crucial areas. He intended to propose this to Callahan at an opportune moment.

In the meantime, West was most interested in studying the sales force reorganization and conveying his ideas to Callahan. Paul West had always been interested in developing a separate sales force for anesthesia equipment and disposables. He was persuaded that there was sufficient sales volume to support it, and he knew customers would be receptive to the extra attention and service. When selling this equipment, the representative called on the anesthesia staff, a group typically more difficult to deal with and more technically oriented than personnel from other hospital departments. Often the sale involved the hospital's biomedical engineers, a sales situation not true of Omega's other products. A separate force could be more intensively trained, according to West's calculations, thus ensuring better customer service.

Further, West was prepared to make a strong case for putting architectural products under the mandate of a small but specialized sales force. General line sales representatives tended to ignore architectural products because their sales consumed too much time and involved contact with nonhospital personnel.

If a separate anesthesia equipment force were developed, the remaining general line would be left with nursing, infant care, respiratory therapy, and architectural products. This seemed reasonable to West because many of these products were sold in the same hospital departments even though they were categorized in different product lines. West wanted to encourage dealers to handle more low-cost products, giving the general line sales force more time for other products.

The real problem with splitting out the anesthesia products, West thought, was that each group would remain responsible for the new portable patient monitoring equipment, but since each force would be responsible for a smaller number of the new products, sales people could be sufficiently trained to do this work. Most of the new portable patient monitoring equipment was in the anesthesia area, so the selection of this sales group must come from those with the most training and experience with electronics products. Additionally, West was insistent upon having "monitoring specialists" in both sales groups to handle all the products of their groups with emphasis on the new equipment. Specialists must be available for dual sales calls with their less informed colleagues.

At a recent convention, West briefly discussed his ideas with Tom Reinke, the western regional vice president and one of West's closest friends. Reinke had at one time worked for a company that manufactured sterilization equipment for hospitals. Following the development of a new, very sophisticated unit, Reinke's company had divided the sales organization into two groups. One handled the existing line, and the other group specialized in the new equipment. Reinke indicated that the sales force division proved disastrous, leading to duplicate sales calls, customer confusion, and increased expenses. The same problem would occur with West's monitoring specialists, cautioned Reinke. He recommended instead that Omega should hire more technically qualified personnel for the general line sales force. West left the convention somewhat less enthusiastic about his sales force proposal.

Your Task:

Advise Omega on these issues:

1. Should the sales force be reorganized by product line?
2. If OMP establishes three separate sales forces, including the anesthesia line, how should they be organized? Should there be specialization by product within groups?
3. Should the compensation system be changed?
4. What changes are in order for the sales, service, and distribution departments?
5. Should the proposed service department be organized along comparable product lines?
6. How should the reorganization be implemented?

case
25

JULIE RESEARCH
LABORATORIES

The Department of Defense needs to become a more demanding customer with regard to quality, performance, and price. . . . contractors . . . do not automatically provide quality goods and services at the lowest possible cost.[1]

As one who has attempted, and unsuccessfully thus far, to become a supplier of electronic technology to the U.S. Army Missile Command, Loebe Julie agrees with Admiral Rickover's assessment. The drama that began for Julie Research Laboratories (JRL) in 1974 had continued, without the promise of denouement, in 1982.

The seven-year dispute between the Army and Loebe Julie, the small businessman going out of business because of the battle, again has reached an impasse.[2]

Julie Research Laboratories has been spotlighted in numerous media—*Electronic Engineering Times, Federal Times, The New York Times, Daily*

---

[1] This excerpt from Admiral Rickover's address to the congressional Joint Economic Committee is reprinted from Hyman G. Rickover, "The Moral Responsibility of Business," *Technology Review*, May–June 1982, pp. 12–15, at p. 15. Copyright 1982.

[2] Eric Yoder, "Dying Firm Won't Bet on Army 'Horse Race,' " *Federal Times*, March 1, 1982.

Exhibit 1

JRL CARTOON/NARRATIVE BOOKLETS, 1980 AND 1981*

*Front Cover. The artist is Dick Hafer, who calls himself 'The Comics Commando,' Lanham, Maryland.

News, Washington Post, Electronic News, and others—and was featured on "60 Minutes" in December 1981, all this attention mostly a result of tireless effort by the beleaguered electronics engineer who once believed that benefits in cost and performance of superior equipment would be quickly recognized and such a system purchased by those needing its capabilities. How he discovered the error of this assumption is detailed in two "comic books" commissioned by the inventor, the first published in 1980, the second in 1981 (Exhibit 1). Each back cover provides JRL's telephone number and a plea for help, concluding with the statement, "By working together, we may be able to strengthen our country."

THE ESSENCE OF BOOK ONE

Prefacing Book One with "what you are about to read is true," the 44-page publication, plus four information-filled cover pages, was mailed to many, including such notables as Jimmy Carter, then president of the United States; Ronald Reagan, then Republican candidate for the presidency; James T. McIntyre, director, Office of Management and Budget; Congressman Ted Weiss, New York City; Lt. General Donald Keith, Army Chief of Staff for Research, Development, and Acquisition; A. Vernon Weaver, Jr., Small Business Administration; Senators Jacob Javits and Patrick Moynihan of New York; the Senate Armed Services Committee; Senator William Proxmire of Wisconsin; and a large selection of newspapers, magazines, and television news organizations. What follows are excerpts from Book One.

> *This story is about Julie Research Labs, one of a dwindling group of inventor-led high-technology research companies.*
> *What is a calibrator? . . . All types of instruments must be checked and adjusted—calibrated—precisely, or they won't work properly. Many test instruments are used to adjust these devices. But, what if the test instruments are not accurate?*

The dangers of inadequate calibration can be illustrated in a missile's guidance system: if the calibration device is not quite accurate, and if the test instrument is somewhat off, its error is added to that of the calibrator. Finally, if the guidance system of the missile is also in error, this factor compounds both the test and calibration errors. The consequences could be disastrous.

> *In 1974, the Army decided that they needed better calibration equipment and issued an R.F.P. (Request for Proposals).*
> *What Julie Labs offered is what the Army asked for: upgraded capability of 2,750 calibrations per year by each technician (up from 800); fully automated; savings of 22,000 hours per year at each installation; identi-*

cal service, regardless of the location or skill level of the technician; sub-stantially improved turnaround and data.

The booklet narrates how the Army "rejected our bid without even opening it," claiming that the bid allegedly arrived 4 hours and 57 minutes af-ter the hour of closing. JRL protested, illustrating that the Labs' bid was tele-graphed in before the deadline, but even with documentation, Loebe Julie said, "The Army refused to reconsider, even though the Western Union supervisor recorded the time our bid was TWX-d. All we got was the typical bureaucratic runaround." The booklet narrative reflects Mr. Julie's reaction that a sense of humor is his only escape, for the bid had arrived on time, although not at its final destination within the Pentagon. He pressed the case.

At last, the problems were over. The Army decided to reinstate our bid. A very strong proposal, comparing the Julie Labs' equipment with the com-petition, showing many advantages, was presented at a special meeting held with each bidder.

"The response we got," a frustrated Loebe Julie remembered, "was that they just couldn't understand how our equipment could possibly work and still be so superior to the others. We had a portable unit set up just outside the door, in the next office, and told them that in a few minutes we could prove that JRL's equipment could do all that we claimed it could. Besides, the final bids were dramatically different: PRD Electronics came in at about $1.12 mil-lion; RCA was $1.94 million; John Fluke bid $1.49 million; Hewlett-Packard's bid was $2.19 million; and Julie Research Labs offered to do what was required for $0.91 million. It's interesting that with such high-powered contestants, all contestants except the John Fluke Company were declared technically unac-ceptable. Fluke was declared the winner."

"Actually," Loebe Julie continued, "there were three different stories coming out of the Missile Command simultaneously. One report had it that the Army calibration program needed 5 automated calibration systems. The Mis-sile Command decided that any of the 5 bidders could get the contract by sub-mitting an acceptable proposal. Yet, before evaluating the first bid, word came down that they needed 95 automated calibration systems, but that only one U.S. bidder was qualified to supply these needs, meaning that the contract would be noncompetitive, sole-source purchase, and from the John Fluke Company. And believe it or not, at the same time it was stated by the Missile Command that 95 systems were needed and could be supplied by only one firm—Hewlett-Packard. So we went to the General Accounting Office with a formal protest. We got nowhere. GAO bowed to what they obviously thought was the superior technical judgment of the Army."

By that time, Julie suspected that attempting to operate within the sys-tem might not work for a small company with limited resources. Nevertheless,

Exhibit 2

BOOK ONE, JULIE RESEARCH LABORATORIES*

REJECTED AGAIN.

ABOUT THAT TIME, WE LEARNED THAT WHITE SANDS MISSILE RANGE HAD BEEN USING FOUR DIFFERENT AUTOMATED CALIBRATION SYSTEMS.* THEY WERE NOT PAYING FOR THEMSELVES, SO WE INVITED THEIR PEOPLE TO COME TO GRUMMAN & G.E. SPACE CENTER TO SEE OUR CALIBRATORS IN ACTION.

PLEASE, LET'S GO SEE THE EQUIPMENT. MAYBE THEY'LL HAVE A TREE THAT I CAN SEE.

U.S. ARMY WHITE SANDS MISSILE RANGE

BOB REIB, THE MILITARY COORDINATOR FOR "TECOM" (WHICH OVERSEES WHITE SANDS), IN HIS REPORT OF THE VISITS, STATED: "IT WAS OBVIOUS THAT THE JULIE RESEARCH LABS SYSTEM DID REPRESENT A SIGNIFICANT IMPROVEMENT OVER THE HEWLETT PACKARD 9213C AND JOHN FLUKE 7505/7510 SYSTEMS."*

* THESE WERE THE SYSTEMS BOUGHT BY "SOLE SOURCE" EARLIER.

Exhibit 2 (Cont.)

THE REPORT BY WHITE SANDS ALSO READ:

"IT WAS OBVIOUS THAT THE JRL SYSTEM WAS FAR EASIER TO PROGRAM THAN EITHER THE "TECOM" HEWLETT PACKARD OR JOHN FLUKE SYSTEMS."	"... IT WOULD APPEAR THAT 'TECOM' WOULD HAVE BEEN BETTER OFF WITH THE JRL SYSTEM IN THE PRODUCTION ENVIRONMENT."	'THE JRL 'LOCOST' SYSTEM IS MORE ECONOMICAL FOR AUTOMATED SUPPORT OF METERS THAN EITHER THE HEWLETT PACKARD 9123C OR JOHN FLUKE 7505/7510 AND SHOULD BE PURCHASED IN LIEU OF EITHER..."

SO, IN 1977, WE WERE
INVITED TO MOSCOW.

27

*Pp. 26–27.

Exhibit 3

BOOK ONE, JULIE RESEARCH LABORATORIES*

AFTER SAYING NO FOR 3 MONTHS, WE DECIDED TO GO...

DR. K. KRASNOV CHIEF OF DEPT., STATE COMMITTEE FOR STANDARDS OF THE COUNCIL OF MINISTERS OF THE U.S.S.R.

DR. M. ZEMELMAN CHIEF OF DEPT. ALL-UNION SCIENTIFIC RESEARCH INSTITUTE OF METROLOGICAL SERVICE

YURI TARBUU, DIRECTOR OF MENDELOV INSTITUTE OF METROLOGY

NIKOLAI RAMBIDI CHIEF OF DEPARTMENT ALL-UNION RESEARCH INSTITUTE OF METROLOGICAL SERVICE

OUR HERO

DR. ERNEST ZHURAVLJEV HEAD OF DEPARTMENT METROLOGY OF ELECTRONIC PROCESSES, ALL-UNION SCIENTIFIC RESEARCH INSTITUTE OF METROLOGY SERVICE

VADIM RAKHOVSKY CHIEF, DEPT. OF GAS DISCHARGES, METROLOGY & CORPUSCULAR DIAGNOSTIC, ALL-UNION INSTITUTE OF METROLOGICAL SCIENCE

THE **RUSSIANS** WANTED TO BUY OUR EQUIPMENT→

...WE ONLY WISH TO USE YOUR EQUIPMENT FOR PEACE.

YES... ONLY TO AUTOMATE DRESS-MAKING MACHINES

2B

Exhibit 3 (Cont.)

UPON ARRNING HOME, THE ORDER WAS TORN UP.

EVEN THOUGH OUR COMPETITORS **DO** SELL THEIR CALIBRATION EQUIPMENT TO THE RUSSIANS, WE DECIDED THAT **WE DIDN'T WANT TO.**

AFTER AN ATLANTA CONFERENCE, IN WHICH GENERALS SAMET, D'AMBROSIO AND HUNT SPOKE OF OUR POOR STATE OF READINESS, COMPARED TO THE RUSSIANS, AND ON OUR LAGGING TECHNOLOGY IN CRITICAL AREAS, WE WROTE TO GENERAL GUTHRIE, THE COMMANDER OF THE ARMY MATERIEL DEVELOPMENT & READINESS COMMAND.

29

*Pp. 28–29.

he decided to put the past aside and to prepare a new, unsolicited proposal for the U.S. Army Missile Command to illustrate JRL's superiority over its competition for the calibration needs outlined in the first R.F.P.

"We even added new features, such as graphics display that would allow less highly-trained personnel to operate the system. The Army sent back our proposal, saying in essence, 'No, thank you.' So we went to General Malley who was in charge of R&D at the Pentagon, who was very interested in our claim that we could do a calibration job normally taking 10 hours with other equipment in 25 minutes. The labs confirmed our claims, and further testing at other Army sites provided further proof that our LOCOST system was up to the tasks required. But listen to this: the office that prepared the report for General Malley gave inaccurate summaries of what happened, although the writer did admit our system worked as we said it would, and it cast doubts on JRL's cost benefits. We lost another round. Worse, all this took two months of valuable time."

Julie Labs pointed out 168 errors in the summary report, including Army logic that because it had been unable to solve the technical issues JRL claimed to have solved, it was not likely that the JRL claims were justified. Rejected again, Julie attempted another tack (Exhibit 2), and an expression of interest in JRL's work came from the Soviet Union (Exhibit 3).

"To no avail," Julie lamented, "and it was all absolutely inconsistent. General Guthrie met with us, and I began to think at that point that patriotism might be at least recognized if not rewarded, but a budget flunky said the Army had no money to buy calibration systems. Precisely at the time when they were advertising to buy 95 manual calibrators for $12 million. Unbelievable! Further, we contended that manually the Army would need not 95 but 150 pieces of equipment to do the job correctly.

"Meanwhile, using interviews and data gained through the Freedom of Information Act, we proved that the cost per calibration was $243 for the John Fluke Systems that were now in use by the Missile Center. This compared to $24 per calibration for the JRL LOCOST systems already in use and $21 for our proposed units. The best that in-use manual systems could do was $65 for each calibration. I maintain that these savings are indisputable! So the Army bought the 95 manual systems.

"In October 1979, we made one last attempt, making a proposal, using detailed, documented computer studies, to the assistant secretary of the Army, in which we showed savings of $200 million over the next 10 years. Again, the Army's response was negative, and again they used erroneous data and absolutely faulty logic to reject us. We can only hope that their missile work is less sloppy than their accounting work which was shot through with glaring mistakes."

These mistakes and a subsequent purchase were caricatured on page 37 of Book One (Exhibit 4).

And Exhibit 5 portrays the saga to June 18, 1980.

Exhibit 4

BOOK ONE, JULIE RESEARCH LABORATORIES*

WHILE SEVERAL MAJOR **ERRORS.** AND **FLAT-OUT UNTRUTHS** WERE POINTED OUT DURING THE MEETING, THE ARMY PERSONNEL **REFUSED** TO CORRECT ANYTHING!

WE CHALLENGED THEM TO SHOW THEIR PROOF TO US AND THEY WERE **UNABLE.**

NOW ooo

BACK WHEN GEN. GUTHRIE BOUGHT THE 95 SYSTEMS, WE TOLD HIM AND HIS QUALITY SUPERVISOR, THAT 150 WOULD BE NEEDED, RIGHT?

WELL, GUESS WHAT THEY ORDERED IN MAY OF 1980?

OH, NO!

RIGHT 97 MORE MANUAL CALIBRATION SYSTEMS!

*P. 37.

Exhibit 5

BOOK ONE, JULIE RESEARCH LABORATORIES*

ON JUNE 5, WE WROTE TO GEN. GUTHRIE, AND EXPLAINED OUR FEELINGS ABOUT THIS TURN OF EVENTS:

"Please meet with us to review the facts.... you can still stop the continuing 30-50¢ waste, out of every Army calibration dollar.... The is still time for you to stop this latest procurement, which will lock the Army into a wasteful $2,000 million calibration support system, from the year 1980 to the year 2000..., The obsolete and inefficient manual equipment now being procured, will again fail to provide the quality calibration support urgently needed by the Army's sophisticated weapons systems."

On June 18, 1980, Gen. Guthrie rejected our request, stating that the issues were carefully reviewed, but that the Army must purchase "mobile" calibration equipment, which, he assured us, is all "modern".

IN JULY, SEVERAL ITEMS OF THIS "MODERN" EQUIPMENT HAD TO BE DROPPED FROM THE PROCUREMENT, BECAUSE, AFTER 20 YEARS, THE MANUFACTURER WASN'T ABLE TO SUPPLY THEM.

Exhibit 5 (Cont.)

WHERE ARE WE NOW?

- THE ARMY'S LEVEL OF CALIBRATION QUALITY IS NO LONGER 95% (WHICH WE OFFER), OR EVEN THEIR OWN DEGRADED 85%. BECAUSE THE TIME FRAME FOR CALIBRATING HAS BEEN LENGTHENED, THE TRUE LEVEL IS A SCANDALOUS 64%!

- OVER HALF OF THE ARMY'S CALIBRATION FUNDS FOR THE REST OF THIS CENTURY IS BEING BLOWN ON SLOW, LOW-QUALITY, EXPENSIVE-TO-OPERATE, 1960-STYLE CALIBRATORS.

- STANDARDS ARE BEING FUDGED EVEN MORE. THE OFFICIAL "CALIBRATED" STICKER HAS BEEN SUPPLEMENTED BY ANOTHER STICKER THAT STATES THAT CALIBRATION IS NOT NECESSARY. 50% OF THE ARMY'S EQUIPMENT IS NOW OFFICIALLY NEGLECTED!

- IT HAS BEEN ESTIMATED THAT OUT OF EVERY 66 PIECES OF ARMY EQUIPMENT, ONLY 20 WILL BE WORKING IN TOLERANCE! WORST OF ALL: WHICH 20 ARE THE GOOD ONES?

*Pp. 38–39.

Exhibit 6

BOOK ONE, JULIE RESEARCH LABORATORIES*

Don't be misled by the humor in this booklet....

THE OUTCOME OF THIS WAY OF OPERATING BY THE ARMY MAY BE A

NATIONAL DISASTER!

THIS HIGH-HANDED PURCHASING APPROACH TO WEAPONS SUPPORT MAY AFFECT THE **ULTIMATE SURVIVAL** OF **YOU AND YOUR FAMILY** !

ARE YOU OUTRAGED ?

WE ARE OFFERING THE U.S. ARMY – (<u>YOUR</u> ARMY - SPENDING <u>YOUR</u> TAX DOLLARS) THE FOLLOWING THINGS....

1. SAVINGS OF 25 TO 40 % (400-600 MEN) ON <u>SCARCE</u> SKILLED MANPOWER NEEDS!

2. SAVINGS OF 31% (62 VANS) ON SPECIAL EXPENDABLE VAN REQUIREMENT !

3. SAVINGS OF 50% ($60 MILLION) ON START-UP EQUIPMENT & PERSONNEL COSTS!

4. SAVINGS OF 30% ($200 MILLION) ON LIFE-CYCLE (10-YEAR) TOTAL COST !

plus... BADLY NEEDED

QUALITY... WHICH PRESENT WEAPONS SUPPORT CALIBRATION SYSTEMS DO NOT HAVE.

Exhibit 6 (Cont.)

IN SUMMARY:

HERE IS WHAT IS BEING SAID ABOUT OUR EQUIPMENT...

- "... the JRL system did represent a significant improvement over the Hewlett Packard 9213C and John Fluke 7505/7510 systems"... "easier to program" ...."more economical for automated support of meters."

  From report by Bob Reib, U.S. Army, Aberdeen, TECOM, dated 22 MAR 78

- "One of the nicest systems I've ever used. If I had to do without it, it would cost me an additional four men."

  Roger Innes, Newport News Naval Shipyard

- "... the LOCOST system can adequately calibrate a large variety of TMDE in periods of less than 30 minutes each."

  From report by Elmer Rogers of the U.S. Army Harry Diamond Laboratory, to Commander, DARCOM, 22 Feb 77

- "LOCOST is the most valuable equipment I've seen in all my years in the calibration industry."

  Charles Weber, Grumman Aerospace Corp.

- "The best investment I ever made."

  Alex McCarovich, General Electric

- "The Julie system with one operator is doing the work previously done by two to three people manually." "Mr. Weber stated that the JULIE system has greater accuracy than other competing systems." "The claim of $12 per calibration is valid." "Downtime has been approximately 1% of on-line time." "G.E. anticipates a real reduction in personnel as a result of buying the system."

  Excerpted from report of JRL users interviewed by John Stolarick for DARCOM

41

*Pp. 40–41.

Mr. Julie posts an admonition near the conclusion of Book One: "Don't be misled by the humor in this booklet" (Exhibit 6).

THE EPIC CONTINUES IN BOOK TWO

During the casewriter's visit to JRL in the summer of 1982, Loebe Julie, administrative assistant and technician Pamela Spencer, and other employees were occupied in a variety of activities involved in supplying its automated test systems, calibration systems, and other equipment to some of the country's leading high-technology firms. That the company was keeping its head above water, given the expenses incurred by its leader in fighting the military monolith seemed a minor miracle, but Mr. Julie and his co-workers were a tenacious lot. Appendix A shows a financial summary presented by a CPA in June, 1981. Already in circulation was Book Two, from which selected quotations and pages are presented. Exhibit 7 reflects occurrences according to Loebe Julie after a story in the *Washington Post* recounting Julie's jousting with the powers of the Pentagon.

"Now the word had begun to spread rapidly," Julie recounted, "with over 300 newspapers running some version of our story. Hundreds of stations broadcast it as well, and I was on talk shows in many areas. General Guthrie even announced that he was organizing his own task force to look into the charges we had leveled."

According to JRL's president, "Subsequently, the Army awarded further contracts for millions of dollars worth of additional obsolete equipment. Finally, on July 22, 1980, three GAO Procurement Division investigators showed up here for a 2½-day visit. Skeptical upon arrival, they apparently left convinced that JRL could substantiate its claims. At a point almost a year later, the GAO audit investigators issued a summary report that clearly favored Julie (see Exhibit 8). Some observers began calling it "Julie-gate" and others talked of "stonewalling" between Army and White House. Loebe Julie, thought by some to be a latter-day Don Quixote tilting at windmills and by others to be the iconoclast needed for these times, but a man generally admired by all except his military detractors, continued what many feared was a hopeless battle to gain recognition for his firm and acceptance of its equipment by the U.S. Army.

Julie did reach several highly placed public figures. Senator William V. Roth, Jr., chairman of the Committee on Governmental Affairs, U.S. Senate, issued a statement, observing:

The Army's Inspector General makes three key findings:

Mr. Julie was not afforded a full and fair opportunity to compete on an equal footing with other suppliers of calibration equipment.

The principal reason for this was that Mr. Julie was too aggressive in his marketing techniques to suit the taste of Army procurement officials.

Some Army officials made statements in this case which were inaccurate, unproven, inconsistent, or open to misinterpretation.

In short, this is one of the most blatant cases I have seen of the "old-boy network" operating to freeze out a legitimate, innovative small business-man from competition for government contracts. In essence, what happened was that Mr. Julie tried to sell the Army a better mousetrap, but instead it was Mr. Julie who got it in the neck.[3]

As Senator Roth put it, the battle was "not yet over," but it was clear that this son of a Polish immigrant family, and a native of the Bronx, was bruised and less than ebullient about prospects of negotiating the military maze. At the same hearing, Senator Alfonse D'Amato of New York argued,

We must protect and encourage our innovative, high-technology small businesses. In order to have a strong national defense, we must have a strong defense industrial base. People like Loebe Julie are the foundation upon which this nation's economic and military future are built. His roar of outrage must be heard and heeded, or our future may be bleak indeed.[4]

In a cover letter dated April 8, 1982, the Army's Office of Legislative Liaison sent the latest Army report to Senator Roth. The 14-page summary included these comments:

Mr. Julie's allegations are addressed in detail, but the key issues he has raised can be summarized in three questions: (1) Has the Army handled this matter in a fair and objective manner? The answer to that question is yes. (2) Have all prospective participants in this test and the procurements associated with it been given a full and impartial opportunity to compete? The answer to that question is yes. (3) Has anyone in the Army and specifically anyone in the U.S. Army Missile Command rigged this test or the procurements associated with it to bias the result, restrict participation, favor the products of any prospective competitor or "get" Julie Research Labs? The answer to that question is no.[5]

[3]Statement of Senator William V. Roth, Jr., chairman, Senate Committee on Governmental Affairs, November 5, 1981, p. 2.

[4]"Introductory Statement by Senator Alfonse D'Amato Regarding Mr. Loebe Julie," November 5, 1981.

[5]JRL corporate files.

Exhibit 7

BOOK TWO, JULIE RESEARCH LABORATORIES*

AFTER 3 MONTHS AND MANY
REQUESTS, THE ARMY SENT
ITS OFFICIAL TASK FORCE RESPONSE....

THEY HAD EARLIER GIVEN GAO THEIR OFFICIAL RESPONSE
TO OUR PROTEST.

THAT'S NICE.... BUT THERE WAS ONE SMALL PROBLEM....,

THE ARMY GOT TRAPPED IN ITS OWN LIES, BY TELLING GAO & CONGRESS CONFLICTING STORIES!

Exhibit 7 (Cont.)

THE ARMY/GAO STORY	THE ARMY/CONGRESS STORY
1. THE MANUAL EQUIPMENT IN THE VAN CANNOT BE TOUCHED. IT'S ALL STANDARD. IF ANYTHING IS CHANGED, IT WOULD CAUSE TREMENDOUS LOGISTICS PROBLEMS.	1. THE JULIE BOOK SAYS THAT WE'RE STANDARDIZING ON OBSOLETE MANUAL EQUIPMENT ABSOLUTELY NOT!!! WE'RE ALWAYS UPDATING THE CONTENTS OF THE VAN, WHEN EVER ANYTHING BETTER COMES ALONG.
2. JULIE DOESN'T MAKE MANUAL EQUIPMENT.* EVERYONE UP TO THE ARMY SECRETARY HAS TOLD THEM THAT AMCC HAS NO REQUIREMENT FOR AUTOMATED EQUIPMENT WHATEVER!!!	2. WHY, WE'RE SO UP TO DATE THAT AMCC JUST RUSHED OUT AND BOUGHT 9 AUTOMATED SYSTEMS ....FROM JOHN FLUKE, OF COURSE. OF COURSE

* NOT TRUE

*Pp. 16–17.

17

Exhibit 8

BOOK TWO, JULIE RESEARCH LABORATORIES*

THEN ON APRIL 3, THE GAO ISSUED THEIR FORMAL, WRITTEN REPORT

(DON'T CONFUSE THIS WITH THE GAO PROTEST DIVISION DECISION ON OUR FORMAL PROTEST - STILL TO BE ISSUED.)

(1) "THE ARMY, CONTRARY TO WHAT IT HAS TOLD JRL, HAS BOTH LABORATORY AND FIELD REQUIREMENTS FOR AUTOMATED CALIBRATION EQUIPMENT."

(2) "THE ARMY'S TECHNICAL EVALUATIONS OF JRL'S EQUIPMENT APPEAR TO BE BASED ON SOME QUESTIONABLE CONCLUSIONS. AND ASSUMPTIONS AND LARGELY IGNORE FAVORABLE IMPRESSIONS BY ARMY REPRESENTATIVES WHO SAW THE EQUIPMENT IN OPERATION."

(3) "....OUR WORK HAS DISCLOSED THAT THE DEPARTMENTS OF DEFENSE AND THE ARMY NEED TO REEXAMINE THE FIELD ARMY REQUIREMENTS FOR CALIBRATION EQUIPMENT ---- TESTS SHOULD ESTABLISH THE MOST COST-EFFECTIVE EQUIPMENT THAT WILL SATISFY VALID ARMY REQUIREMENTS."

(4) "THE ARMY ELECTED TO DELETE FROM JRL'S PROPOSAL, COST SAVINGS ATTRIBUTED TO AN OSCILLOSCOPE AND A SIGNAL GENERATOR THAT JRL HAD NOT PRODUCED, BUT IT DID NOT REDUCE THE ASSOCIATED LEASE PRICE FOR THESE DELETED ITEMS FROM WHAT JRL HAD ORIGINALLY PROPOSED."

(5) "THE ARMY USED ONE WORKLOAD LEVEL TO DETERMINE THE NUMBER OF LOCOST SYSTEMS NEEDED AND A DIFFERENT WORKLOAD LEVEL TO DETERMINE THE MANUAL EQUIPMENT NEEDED."

Exhibit 8 (Cont.)

⑥ "ARMY TECHNICAL AND COST EVALUATIONS OF JRL EQUIPMENT WERE INCONSISTENT ---- DARCOM MAY HAVE UNDERSTATED PERFORMANCE CAPABILITIES OF THE "LOCOST" SYSTEM AND OVER STATED PERFORMANCE CAPABILITIES OF COMPETING SYSTEMS."

⑦ "THE [ARMY METROLOGY & CALIBRATION] CENTER DID NOT CONTACT JRL TO ---- ENSURE THAT IT UNDERSTOOD WHAT JRL HAS TO OFFER."

⑧ "THE ARMY'S ASSERTION THAT JRL'S LOCOST SYSTEM IS NOT UNIQUE OR NEW TO THE INDUSTRY NOR STATE OF THE ART IS INCONSISTENT WITH REPORTS FROM LOCOST SYSTEM OWNERS. THE REPORTS SUGGEST THAT THE LOCOST SYSTEM MAY INDEED OFFER ADVANTAGES BECAUSE OF SHORTER PROGRAMING TIME AND SIMPLER OPERATION. FOR EXAMPLE, WHITE SANDS MISSILE RANGE OFFICIALS REPORT THAT 100 PROGRAMS WERE DEVELOPED IN ABOUT 75 HOURS AND THAT AVERAGE PROGRAMER TRAINING TIME WAS 24 HOURS. ANOTHER LOCOST SYSTEM OWNER, AN AEROSPACE COMPANY, TOLD US THAT PROGRAMING PREPARATION TIME ON THE LOCOST SYSTEM RANGED FROM 15 MINUTES TO 1 HOUR WITH MOST PROGRAMS TAKING 30 MINUTES OR LESS. THIS COMPANY ALSO TOLD US THAT IT KNOWS OF NO OTHER COMMERCIAL OFF-THE-SHELF CALIBRATOR THAT WILL PERFORM AS WELL AS THE LOCOST SYSTEM."

31

Exhibit 8 (Cont.)

(9) "DARCOM WAS SKEPTICAL OF JRL's CLAIM THAT EQUIPMENT COULD BE PROGRAMED IN ABOUT 15 MINUTES BECAUSE THE ARMY'S EXPERIENCE WITH COMPETING SYSTEMS SHOWED AN AVERAGE REQUIREMENT OF 120 HOURS. REPRESENTATIVES OF HARRY DIAMOND LABORATORIES AND THE ARMY METROLOGY AND CALIBRATION CENTER, HOWEVER, HAD REPORTED OBSERVING PROGRAM PREPARATION FOR A SIMPLE TEST INSTRUMENT IN LESS THAN 3 MINUTES AND THE INSTRUMENT'S CALIBRATION IN ANOTHER 3 MINUTES. THE HARRY DIAMOND REPRESENTATIVES ALSO REPORTED THAT (1) THE LOCOST SYSTEM COULD CALIBRATE A VARIETY OF INSTRUMENTATION IN LESS THAN 30 MINUTES, AS JRL CLAIMED, (2) THE SIMPLICITY OF PROGRAMING AND USING THE SYSTEM WAS EVIDENT, AND (3) THE SYSTEM COULD PRODUCE SIGNIFICANT SAVINGS IN THEIR LABORATORY."

(10) "IN ADDITION, WE RECOMMEND THAT THE SECRETARY OF DEFENSE REQUIRE THAT AN INDEPENDENT HARDWARE DEMONSTRATION BE CONDUCTED TO ESTABLISH THE COST EFFECTIVENESS AND PRODUCTIVITY INCREASES THAT MAY BE ATTRIBUTED TO AUTOMATING THE FIELD ARMY CALIBRATION FUNCTIONS."

(11) "DURING OUR REVIEW, WE SAW SEVERAL ASPECTS OF THE ARMY METROLOGY AND CALIBRATION CENTER ACTIVITIES WHICH APPEAR TO WARRANT OUR FURTHER EXAMINATION. ACCORDINGLY, WE PLAN TO PURSUE THESE MATTERS IN A SEPARATE REVIEW TO BEGIN SHORTLY."

THE ABOVE QUOTES WERE ALL DRAWN FROM THE OFFICIAL GAO REPORT, SIGNED BY THE ACTING COMPTROLLER GENERAL OF THE U.S.

32

*Pp. 30–32.

"Yet the Army's own impartial Inspector General report came to exactly the opposite conclusions on November 4, 1981," Julie commented. "And nothing has improved. I've circled some of the key passages and phrases of the new report—all of them clearly contradicting that the Army is now 'open and above-board, and making extraordinary efforts to ensure objectivity throughout the evaluation process.' From the Army's newest report, it is patently obvious they are not."

Not seeing himself as an heroic crusader, soft-spoken Loebe Julie did admit that being at war with the U.S. Army was not his first foray into matters of ethics in his profession and into waste and abuse in government. Appendix B outlines six of the activities in which he has been engaged since 1962.

Appendix C provides a biographical overview of this man who claimed to have invented the better mousetrap, but who could not seem to crack the network leading to contracts with the Army. Not only did the prospective customers refuse to recognize the equipment as a valid answer to their needs, but they seemed to be intent on ignoring inventor Julie and, according to some observers, mousetrapping him in the process.

Returning for a moment to Admiral Rickover,

> ... *we need to create, by actions rather than words, an environment in which those in the Defense Department can operate efficiently and obtain from industry needed goods and services at minimum cost to the taxpayer.*[6]

To which businessman/scientist Loebe Julie responded wearily, "Amen. Easier said than done, certainly, but something else is certain," according to JRL's president, "getting rid of arrogance and foolishness in the procurement echelons is a step in the right direction."

Your Task:

Analyze the JRL events from 1974 to 1982, focusing on key circumstances and incidents as described in the case study. If you had been in Mr. Julie's shoes, what, if anything, might you have done differently? Now, as we peer into the future, present to Loebe Julie conclusions and recommendations based on your studied judgments. In the light of Loebe Julie's odyssey in confrontation with his military adversaries, do you encourage the private sector to try to effect changes such as those sought by this intrepid entrepreneur? What strategies, in your opinion, are feasible?

---

[6]Rickover, "The Moral Responsibility of Business, p. 13.

Appendix A

JRL FINANCIAL STATEMENTS,
DECEMBER 31, 1980

BALANCE SHEET
(UNAUDITED)

ASSETS

Current Assets	
Cash	$110,474
Cash, Dreyfus Liquid Assets	152,762
Accounts receivable:	
Trade, net of $22,178 allowance for	
uncollectible accounts	192,929
Prepaid expenses	4,575
Inventories	76,542
Total current assets	537,282
Property, Plant, and Equipment, at cost	
Machinery and equipment	96,261
Furniture and fixtures	15,869
Leasehold improvements	5,371
	117,501
Less: Accumulated depreciation and amortization	97,544
Property, plant, and equipment, net	19,957
Total assets	$557,239

LIABILITIES AND STOCKHOLDERS' EQUITY

Current Liabilities	
Accounts payable	$ 25,670
Accrued taxes and expenses	170,261
Loan payable, officer	41,534
Total current liabilities	237,465
Other Liabilities	
Reserve for retirement bonus	9,000
Total other liabilities	246,465
Stockholders' Equity	
Common Stock:	
Par value $1.00 per share; authorized	
600,000 shares, issued 442,497 shares	442,497
Capital surplus	154,582
Retained earnings (deficit)	(153,382)
	443,697
Less: Treasury Stock, at cost (24,983 shares)	132,923
Total stockholders' equity	310,774
Total liabilities and stockholders' equity	$557,239

STATEMENT OF INCOME
(UNAUDITED)

Sales	$1,410,352
Cost of goods sold	926,735
Gross profit	483,617
Selling and administrative expense	404,400
Net income	$ 79,217
Average number of shares outstanding	417,514
Net income per share	$0.19

SCHEDULE OF COST OF GOODS SOLD

Inventory, beginning	$ 262,972
Purchases	355,635
Labor, production	264,899
	883,506
Less: Inventory, Ending	76,542
Prime cost	806,964
Manufacturing overhead	
Engineering fees	31,778
Rent and utilities	56,156
Factory supplies	19,201
Maintenance and repairs	2,668
Plant protection	3,708
Depreciation, machinery and equipment	1,744
Outside services	4,516
Total manufacturing overhead	119,771
Cost of goods sold	$ 926,735

SCHEDULE OF SELLING AND ADMINISTRATIVE EXPENSE

Sales salaries	$ 22,010
Commissions	3,010
Advertising	13,529
Auto expense	892
Travel and entertaining	11,924
Officers' salaries	63,693
Office salaries	42,476
Telephone and telegraph	19,721
Office expense	4,595
Insurance	18,673
Interest	110,198
Legal and accounting	13,261
Dues and subscriptions	11,227
Supplies and general expense	15,153
Hospitalization insurance	2,449
Postage	3,560
Payroll and miscellaneous taxes	34,238
Stock registration	2,170
Shipping and freight out	8,781
Depreciation and amortization	1,094
New York State and City corporation taxes	1,746
Total	$ 404,400

Source: Company records.

Appendix B

SUMMARY OF JULIE PRO BONO ACTIVITIES
(For current activities, see V and VI)

I. Special study on Industrial Utilization of Gifted Engineering Graduates (1962)—
There is evidence that new, creative engineering talent underachieves in American large business. The intent of this study was to improve the fit between corporate management and unrecognized engineering "geniuses."

II. Special Award Program for Gifted Engineering Undergraduates (1964–1967)—
The special study disclosed that several identifiable engineering school mechanisms transform bright, enthusiastic, young Edisons into grey flannel engineering administrators. The Julie program rewarded concentrated, creative, engineering work instead of social-political activities as an encouragement to fledgling engineering innovators.

III. Committee on Ethical Practices in Precision Measurement (1965)—
Science, technology, and industry are critically dependent on accurate observations and measurements. The validity of these measurements depends on the integrity of the measurement practices (procedures) and of the measurement practitioners. Standards of ethical practice and a code of ethics are nonexistent in this critically important field and should be established.

IV. Tier 2 Committee on DOD Procurement (1975–1978)—
The U.S. government's neglect, waste, and abuse of American inventive talent (Goddard et al.) is destroying new innovator/producers and will destroy U.S. world leadership in science, technology, and industry. Improvements in the system can readily be made and are most urgently required.

V. Committee Against Waste and Abuse in Government Procurement (1981)—
Outgrowth of IV. The government's continuing failure to act to correct its own procurement abuses is not only wasteful but is a major cause of the decline of U.S. leadership in science, technology, and industry. This new committee is result (rather than study) oriented and has already singled out the likeliest targets of opportunity in the government for reform and improvement. The specific reform projects are practical, long overdue and if properly selected and pursued can produce major results in a short time span. The committee is admittedly undertaking an extremely arduous task. Nevertheless, with this high challenge comes an extraordinary opportunity to benefit the whole of the United States and its citizens.

VI. American Calibration Association (1981)—
Outgrowth of III. The continued absence of uniform, ethical standards of practice in measurement and calibration,* and the continued lack of official accreditation of U.S. calibration laboratories has caused serious quality problems in the U.S. national measurement system. In a close parallel to the earlier days of medical practice, careless and invalid (quack) practice can easily outadvertise and undercut careful and legitimate practice. There is an urgent need for a national calibration organization, analogous to the American Medical Association, to monitor and maintain legitimate standards of practice for U.S. measurement and calibration.

*Calibration consists of measurements accompanied by an official label or certificate, implying that the measurements were valid.

Source: Company files.

Appendix C

BIOGRAPHY—LOEBE JULIE

Loebe Julie is President and Chief Engineer of Julie Research Laboratories, Inc., which he founded in 1954 to do development work on computerized fire control systems. He received a Bachelor's degree in Electrical Engineering in 1941 from the City College of New York and a Master's degree in Mathematics in 1948 from New York University.

Mr. Julie is best known for his pioneering work in the development of ultraprecision components, instruments, and systems designed to increase the accuracy and speed of DC and low-frequency test and measurement for the standards and calibration laboratory. He has received 40 patents for his work in this field and is recognized as the originator of a large number of innovative 1 ppm standards, instruments, and systems. These include the Evanohm resistance standard (1955), the air bath EMF standard (1957), the Kelvin-Varley divider standard (1957), as well as a number of resistance bridge and potentiometer standards (1955–1965), voltage current and gyrocalibrator standards (1958–1963), and highly sophisticated manual and automated calibration systems (1958–1978). The Julie-Ratio Bridge is included in the IEEE Standard Code for Resistance Measurements.

Since 1975, Mr. Julie has been campaigning for recognition by the D.O.D. of the importance of small, high-technology companies in advancing U.S. technological strength and reducing wasteful government procurements of obsolete, labor-intensive, manual calibration systems.

Mr. Julie is an active member of PMA and NCSL and has served as a member of the Advisory Committee of the IEEE. He has also served as president of the New York section and as publications chairman of PMA and has taught, lectured, and written extensively, in the United States and abroad, on new developments and methodology in precision measurement.

Source: Company files.

case
26

MARY KAY COSMETICS, INC.

BACKGROUND OF THE COMPANY

A proliferation of products and a change of partners that might dazzle a square dance caller have characterized the cosmetics industry in the late 1970s and the 1980s. Witness Eli Lilly's purchase of Elizabeth Arden, Squibb's acquisition of Lanvin-Charles of Ritz, Pfizer's take-over of Coty, Norton Simon's of Max Factor, Colgate-Palmolive's of Helena Rubenstein, not to mention British-American Tobacco's gobbling up Germaine Monteil.

Accompanying the change of corporate identities there has been a distinct shift in management styles as practiced in cosmetics concerns. The "flair and flamboyance" of the old school cosmetics moguls—the Revsons, Rubensteins, and Ardens of the industry—has been replaced by a new breed of management types. Charisma has given way to pragmatism. The new styles are diverse, however—as urbane, cool, and international as ITT-trained Revlon's chief executive, the Frenchman Michel Bergerac, or as fundamentalist, *nouveaux riches,* and Texas-grown as Mary Kay Ash, founder and driving force behind Mary Kay Cosmetics, Inc., whose pink Cadillac incentive plan for sales agents and skyrocketing corporate profits have made Mary Kay a legend in the highly competitive American cosmetics business.

In 1963 Mary Kay Ash, a much decorated veteran of in-home sales (Child

Psychology Bookshelf, Stanley Home Products, World Gift) founded Mary Kay Cosmetics, Inc., on $5,000 for product formulas, containers, and secondhand office equipment and on the belief that women could be sold on using a proven skin care regimen through an educational approach. Mary Kay Ash's expertise in the area of human motivation and in direct sales combined with son Richard Rogers's wizardry in finance and marketing catapulted the company from its humble Dallas beginnings to a major national cosmetics corporation. Exhibit 1 charts this growth pattern. By August 1976 Mary Kay Cosmetics was listed on the New York Stock Exchange.

Mary Kay Cosmetics consists of "a scientifically formulated line of skin products" that is presented to the user programmatically during home beauty shows with emphasis on Mary Kay's Five Steps to Beauty (Exhibit 2). Over 50 percent of the company's sales are derived from the basic skin care line. Skin, body, and hair care products in addition to cosmetics, toiletries, and fragrances compose the remainder of the relatively small Mary Kay line (Exhibit 3).

The company uses self-employed women billed as Beauty Consultants to introduce the products to customers in the home where customers sample the products and are instructed in their use. This deceptively simple format has resulted in dramatic growth in the company's sales and sales force since the beginning, when Mary Kay Cosmetics had only nine consultants. By 1981 net sales were $235.3 million, and about 150,000 consultants were selling the products (and one presumes faithfully using them). Exhibit 4 analyzes the productivity of the Mary Kay sales people. Major distribution centers in the United States assure rapid delivery of the products to the consultants who are able to provide the customers with their products without delay at the beauty show. Thus, there should never be a gap between ordering and receiving the product as there is in Avon's distribution method.

An oft-quoted management truism in the cosmetics industry is Michel Bergerac's conclusion that "every management mistake ends up in inventory." Mary Kay has addressed this concern and has avoided the pitfall through its unique distribution and operations systems. Charged with the task of instantaneously providing each consultant with the inventory she requires at the moment she requires it, Mary Kay has developed five domestic regional distribution centers, located in Atlanta; Chicago; Los Angeles; Piscataway, New Jersey; and the corporate warehouse in Dallas. Dallas is mission control for the company, where the products are manufactured and the orders received. The Marketing Department has instant access via computer to individual and unit sales. Manufacturing uses the data bank at Dallas to control inventory by forecasting and planning products' runs. On the microlevel, directors of sales units are only a toll-free call away from comprehensive information about the performance of their unit or of specific individuals.

In 1978 Mary Kay Cosmetics formed a sister company in Toronto that has evolved into one of Canada's largest cosmetic enterprises. As of 1971 and 1980, respectively, separate operations were launched in Australia and Argen-

Exhibit 1

MARY KAY GROWTH, 1971–1981

NET SALES
in millions

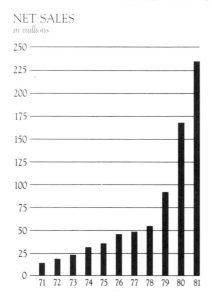

NET INCOME
in millions

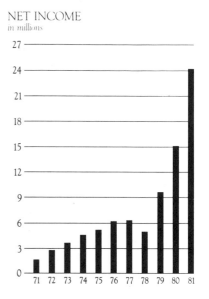

BEAUTY CONSULTANT GROWTH
in thousands

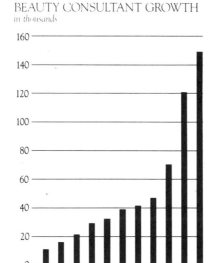

SALES DIRECTOR GROWTH
in hundreds

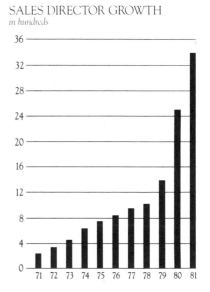

Source: Mary Kay Cosmetics, Inc., *1981 Annual Report*, p. 20.

Exhibit 2

THE FIVE STEPS TO BEAUTY

THE FIVE STEPS TO BEAUTY

MOVEMENT OF APPLICATION

Follow this movement of application when applying Cleansing Cream, Cleanser, Magic Masque, Skin Freshener, Night Cream or Moisturizer:

Always apply with the tips of the fingers. Beginning with the neckline, apply with upward and outward motion. Be sure to use the ring finger when working around the delicate tissue near the eyes. Remember to stroke delicately — don't massage.

1 CLEANSE

All of the Mary Kay cleansing products cleanse the skin deeply, thoroughly and gently, penetrating and loosening impurities and softening the skin.

Cleansing Cream Formula 1 and Formula 2 — Smooth on face and throat. Follow movement of application. Remove with warm, wet facial cloth.

Cleanser Formula 3 — Shake well. Apply thoroughly to face and throat. Lightly pat water on top of cleanser and follow movement of application, working cleanser into a foam. Splash skin with warm water and remove remainder with warm, wet facial cloth.

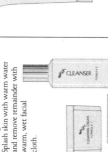

2 STIMULATE

Mary Kay Magic Masque® stimulates circulation, removes impurities and dead surface cells. Also brightens, refines and freshens the skin.

Magic Masque Formula 1 and Formula 2 — After cleansing, smooth on face and throat, avoiding eyes and mouth. Let dry for approximately 10 minutes. Soften and gently remove with warm, wet facial cloth. Apply Skin Freshener and allow to dry naturally. Use Magic Masque twice a week.

3 FRESHEN

Mary Kay Skin Freshener further stimulates circulation, makes pores appear smaller and removes any residue of previous products.

Skin Freshener Formula 1 and Formula 2 — Apply a few drops to clean cotton pad and gently smooth on face and throat. Avoid use in the immediate area of the eye. Allow to dry naturally. Always use Skin Freshener after Magic Masque.

4 LUBRICATE/MOISTURIZE

All of the Mary Kay moisturizing products help to smooth and condition the skin, working as a preventive measure against dryness.

Night Cream Formula 1 — After cleansing and freshening, moisten face and throat with warm water and gently apply a very small amount of Night Cream. Leave overnight.

Night Cream Formula 2 — After cleansing and freshening, gently smooth a small amount of Night Cream over face and throat. Leave overnight.

Moisturizer — After cleansing and freshening, gently smooth a thin film on the dry areas of the face.

5 PROTECT

Mary Kay's Day Radiance® provides daytime protection for the skin with a subtle tint of color that covers minor imperfections and gives a smooth, even toned finish to your complexion. Day Radiance is available in perfectly blended shades, ranging in color from the lightest to the darkest skin tones, including white and yellow shades for highlighting and correcting.

Day Radiance Formula 1 — Provides an emollient moisture base and luminous powder finish. Using fingertips, apply a thin film to a moistened face. When using Moisturizer under Day Radiance, do not moisten face.

Day Radiance Formula 2 — Water based product that provides a fresh sheen without shine. Shake well. Using fingertips, blend over a dry face with outward sweeping strokes.

Each morning, cleanse, freshen and protect.
Each evening, cleanse, freshen and lubricate/moisturize.
Twice a week, stimulate.

Source: Mary Kay, Inc., promotional literature.

387

Exhibit 3

ANALYSIS OF SALES BY PRODUCTS, 1977–1981

	1977	1978	1979	1980	1981
Skin care products for women	48%	50%	49%	52%	49%
Skin care products for men	2	1	1	2	1
Makeup items	21	21	26	22	26
Toiletry items for women	13	12	10	10	10
Toiletry items for men	2	3	2	2	2
Hair care	4	3	2	2	2
Accessories	10	10	10	10	10
Total	100%	100%	100%	100%	100%

Source: Mary Kay, Inc., *1981 Annual Report*, p. 21.

Exhibit 4

MARY KAY COSMETICS SALES ANALYSIS, 1970–1982E

YEAR	SALES (000)	NUMBER OF BEAUTY CONSULTANTS AND SALES DIRECTORS AT YEAR END	AVG. NO. OF BEAUTY CONSULTANTS AND SALES DIRECTORS	SALES BEAUTY CONSULTANT AND SALES DIRECTOR (Productivity)	YEAR-TO-YEAR INCREASES IN PRODUCTIVITY
1982E	$346,000	190,000	175,000	$1,980.0	3.4%
1981E	242,000	150,000	140,072	1,915.0	9.0
1980	166,938	120,145	94,982	1,757.6	11.5
1979	91,400	69,820	57,989	1,576.2	26.9
1978	53,746	46,158	43,282	1,241.7	0.7
1977	47,856	40,407	38,818	1,232.8	−3.4
1976	44,871	37,229	35,176	1,275.6	13.3
1975	34,947	33,123	31,042	1,125.8	−6.0
1974	30,215	28,961	25,234	1,197.4	1.4
1973	22,199	21,508	18,805	1,180.5	−3.1
1972	17,232	16,103	14,142	1,218.5	1.5
1971	12,367	12,181	10,299	1,200.7	7.2
1970	8,091	8,418	7,224	1,120.0	−6.3
Average annual growth					
1975–1980	36.7%	29.4%	25.1%	9.3%	
1970–1975	34.0	31.5	33.9	0.1	

Source: Mary Kay, Inc., data.

tina. The Argentine Mary Kay undertaking has run into difficulties because of international problems. During May 1982, in the midst of the dispute between Argentina and Britain over the Falkland Islands with sky-high inflation in Argentina, Mary Kay was forced to write off $1.5 million there in a reassessment of the value of the company's marketing unit in Argentina.

MARY KAY ASH'S PERSONAL STORY

Mary Kay Ash's personal story is a rags-to-riches success saga in the great American tradition, and it mirrors the stories of many of the company's beauty consultants. In her autobiography, the best selling *Mary Kay,* "the success story of America's most dynamic businesswoman," published by Harper & Row in 1981, Mary Kay tells of her life. In the company literature, this simple story is told and retold, and the lesson of self-discipline is underscored (Exhibit 5). Mary Kay Ash received the Horatio Alger Award from Dr. Norman Vincent Peale in 1978, and the company refers to Mrs. Ash's story as "a Horatio Alger Story."

THE BEAUTY CONSULTANT AND THE BEAUTY SHOW

The lifeblood of the Mary Kay organization is the beauty consultant and director force who have generated Mary Kay's phenomenal sales and following. Independent beauty consultants, who buy their own sample case and products, are organized into sales units led by a sales director. Mary Kay Ash believes the cash system has assured the health of the company. "At Mary Kay, our consultants and directors pay in advance for their merchandise with a cashier's check or money order—no personal checks."

> *It's impossible for a Consultant to run up a debt with the company. Therefore, we have few accounts receivable. We don't have the expense of collecting bad debts, and we pass the savings on in the form of higher commissions. This way, everyone benefits. Most financial people just marvel at it—it's unheard of for a company of our size.[1]*

Richard Rogers sums up the distribution plan this way: "Each Mary Kay consultant is an independent contractor. They are not employees of the company. Mary Kay serves as a wholesale house—freight in, freight out. The consultant buys directly from the company at wholesale prices and sells at retail prices. The difference is her profit."

[1]Mary Kay Ash, *Mary Kay* (New York: Harper & Row, 1981), p. 29.

Exhibit 5

MARY KAY—A HORATIO ALGER STORY

A CHILDHOOD FILLED WITH CHALLENGE

From a small Texas town to national prominence was not an easy journey. Mary Kay's success can largely be attributed to the discipline and independence she learned in her childhood.

The youngest of four children, she was born in the small town of Hot Wells, Texas, where her parents owned a hotel. When her father's health deteriorated and he became an invalid, the family moved to Houston so Mary Kay's mother could find work.

While her mother worked 14-hour days managing a restaurant, seven-year-old Mary Kay stayed home cleaning, cooking, and caring for her father.

Throughout those early years, Mary Kay's mother strongly influenced her daughter by encouraging her to excel in everything she did and told her over and over again, "You can do it." Whether in school or at home, Mary Kay wanted to be the best. Another lasting influence on her life has been her Christian faith. Her sincere convictions enabled her to express her love and affection toward those around her, and her faith has also been the cornerstone of her business success. Her basic philosophies are "God first, family second, career third," and the Golden Rule.

YOUNG ADULTHOOD

After finishing high school, Mary Kay married and had three children. Her husband was soon called away for World War II active duty, leaving Mary Kay with mounting financial problems. She worked as a secretary at a Baptist Church to help support the overwhelming cost of raising three children.

A postwar divorce left Mary Kay the lone support of her young family. With the same determination that brought her through her earlier years, Mary Kay became a dealer for Stanley Home Products, a direct sales party plan company. This job enabled her to earn a living and still spend time with her children.

After three weeks of work and average sales of only $7 worth of products per party, Mary Kay attended a sales convention. She sat in the back row and decided that she would one day be crowned "Queen of

Exhibit 5 (Cont.)

Sales." Upon sharing her goal with the president of the company, Frank Stanley Beveredge, he replied, "Somehow, I think you will."

Mary Kay triumphantly won the crown the following year and eventually moved to Dallas where she continued her 13-year career with Stanley Home Products. But this was only the beginning of Mary Kay's rise to success.

Later, upon joining World Gift, a company that sold decorative accessories, she quickly became National Training Director. In 1962, though, she experienced a personal ordeal that threatened her health and her career. She suffered from a rare form of paralysis on one side of her face, but after surgery and several months of hospitalization, she recovered completely.

THE COMPANY BEGINS

Upon her recovery and after her retirement from World Gift, Mary Kay remarried and began to think about starting her own direct sales company. She planned to run the sales division, while her husband acted as administrator. One month prior to the launching of the company, her husband had a heart attack and died. Mary Kay's three children joined their mother in the early days of the new venture. Today, Richard Rogers, her youngest son, is the president of Mary Kay Cosmetics, Inc.

Source: Mary Kay, Inc., promotional literature, 1981.

Although the beauty consultant is in business for herself—the point is stressed in the corporate literature that "she is not by herself." The director is available as a consultant and teacher to the beauty consultant to help her successfully present the all-important beauty show. An effective director, according to the company, can handle in embryo the problems of poor consultant performance and thus control turnover in the ranks.

Because the beauty consultant is not a cosmetologist, federal and state laws prohibit her from applying cosmetics to the faces of the five or six participants at each show. Rather, her task is to assist each woman who attends the session, usually held at the home of a voluntary hostess, to determine her skin type and to answer questions about the five steps of beauty process. "This is an effective teaching method. We don't sell—we teach!" emphasizes Mary Kay. "Polite persuasion" is the Mary Kay euphemism for selling. The hard sell is avoided, according to the literature.

In its *1981 Annual Report*, Mary Kay Cosmetics, Inc., shared with readers the philosophy of the beauty show.

> *The Beauty Show is our primary marketplace. Its importance cannot be overstated. Here the Consultant has undivided attention as she presents the entire line. She has ample time to give each guest personal attention. The customer learns valuable tips on skin care and grooming and, because she receives her order at the Show, puts the lessons into practice immediately.*

During the course of the two-hour beauty show, the consultant demonstrates, presents, persuades, collects, and delivers. (Exhibit 6 is the price list for Mary Kay products demonstrated in the beauty show). In addition to the sales activities implicit in the show, a consultant may recruit other consultants and arrange bookings for future shows at the demonstration. The person who agrees to host a show at her home "earns" Mary Kay products. Often if the consultant notes a potential customer's reluctance to purchase because of the cost, she may suggest that the woman earn products by hosting.

Exhibit 6

1982 MARY KAY PRICE LIST

ITEM	PRICE	✔
Complete Collection (as shown)	$71.00	
Basic Skin Care	39.00	
CLEANSE		
Cleansing Cream Formula 1, 4 oz.	6.50	
Cleansing Cream Formula 2, 4 oz.	6.50	
Cleanser Formula 3, 3.75 oz.	6.50	
STIMULATE		
Magic Masque Formula 1, 3 oz.	7.50	
Magic Masque Formula 2, 3 oz.	7.50	
FRESHEN		
Skin Freshener Formula 1, 5.75 oz.	7.50	
Skin Freshener Formula 2, 5.75 oz.	7.50	
LUBRICATE/MOISTURIZE		
Night Cream Formula 1, 4 oz.	12.00	
Night Cream Formula 2, 4 oz.	12.00	
Moisturizer, 2.8 oz.	12.00	
PROTECT		
Day Radiance Formula 1, .5 oz.	5.50	
Day Radiance Formula 2, 1 oz.	5.50	
☐ Ivory Beige ☐ Toasted Tan ☐ Light Beige ☐ Cinnamon ☐ Medium Beige ☐ Chestnut ☐ Warm Beige ☐ Coffee ☐ Suntan Beige ☐ White ☐ Suntan ☐ Yellow ☐ Honey Tan		
GLAMOUR COLLECTION		
Blush Rouge	4.00	
Eyeliner	5.00	
☐ Black ☐ Brown		

ITEM	PRICE	✔
Eyebrow Pencil	$ 3.00	
☐ Black ☐ Brown ☐ Auburn ☐ Charcoal ☐ Light Brown ☐ Blonde		
Mascara	5.50	
☐ Black ☐ Brown		
Lip and Eye Palette	14.50	
(Complete with 2 brushes)		
Lip Palette	12.50	
(Complete with lip brush)		
Eye Palette	12.50	
(Complete with eye brush)		
Retractable Lip or Eye Brush	2.00	
Lip or Eye Palette Refill	4.00	
Great Fashion Lip Color Shade Selections:		
☐ Pinks ☐ Plums ☐ Russets ☐ Reds ☐ Corals ☐ Spices		
Great Fashion Eye Shadow Shade Selections:		
☐ Blues ☐ Greens ☐ Browns ☐ Plums		
Blusher	8.50	
☐ Soft Pink/Soft Peach ☐ Tawny Rose/Tawny Amber ☐ Cinnamon/Mahogany		
Lip Liner Pencils	6.50	
☐ Raisin/Ripe Cherry		
Lip Gloss	4.50	
SPECIALIZED SKIN CARE		
Moisturizer, 2.8 oz.	12.00	
Facial/Under Makeup Sun Screen, 2.7 oz.	7.00	
Hand Cream, 2.8 oz.	5.50	

ITEM	PRICE	✔
BODY CARE		
Cleansing Gel, 8 oz.	$ 7.00	
Buffing Cream, 6 oz.	7.50	
Moisturizing Lotion, 8 oz.	6.50	
Sun Screening Lotion, 6 oz.	8.50	
BASIC HAIR CARE		
Shampoo for Normal/Dry Hair, 8 oz.	4.50	
Shampoo for Oily Hair, 8 oz.	4.50	
Protein Conditioner, 8 oz.	6.00	
Intense Conditioner, 3 oz.	7.00	
Non-Aerosol Hair Spray, 8 oz.	4.50	
FRAGRANCE BOUTIQUE		
Avenir Spray Cologne, 2 oz.	15.00	
Intrigue Spray Cologne, 1.75 oz.	10.00	
Facets Spray Cologne, 2 oz.	11.00	
Facets Cologne, 1 oz.	6.50	
Angelfire Spray Cologne, 1.75 oz.	12.00	
Exquisite Body Lotion, 8 oz.	6.50	
MEN'S PRODUCTS		
Mr. K Skin Care System	34.50	
Cleanser, 2.7 oz.	4.50	
Mask, 2.6 oz.	6.50	
Toner, 2.6 oz.	4.50	
Moisture Balm, 2.5 oz.	12.00	
Sun Screen, 2.7 oz.	7.00	
Mr. K Cologne, 3.75 oz.	9.50	
Mr. K Lotion, 3.4 oz.	4.50	
ReVeur After Shave Cologne, 3.75 oz.	10.00	

Source: Mary Kay, Inc., price list for beauty consultants.

To become a consultant a woman submits a signed beauty consultant agreement with a cashier's check or money order to Mary Kay Cosmetics. The pink beauty showcase is then shipped immediately to her from Dallas. Before she is a full-fledged consultant, a recruit must attend three beauty shows with an experienced consultant, book five beauty shows for her first week's activity, and attend training classes conducted by a director in her area. Because each Mary Kay show provides yet another opportunity to recruit beauty consultants into the company, to book future shows, and to establish reorder business, Mary Kay puts a premium on running a smooth and professional show. Mary Kay consultants are expected to present a well-groomed, Mary Kay–cosmeticized image and to dress in a manner consistent with Mary Kay Ash's personal philosophy of feminine attractiveness.

Mary Kay annual reports feature attractive models representing the consultants on their appointed rounds, dressed in tailored suits, tastefully manicured, coiffured, and made up, usually wearing soft, pastel blouses and Mary Kay jewelry (golden bumblebees and Mary Kay pins are sought-after prizes in the company). The ideal image of the consultant is that of the "dressed-for-success" career woman.

> *A career woman should dress in a businesslike manner. Personally, I'm opposed to wearing pants on the job. In fact, that's a company policy at Mary Kay (except in the manufacturing area). After all, we are in the business of helping women look more feminine and beautiful, so we feel very strongly that our Beauty Consultants should dress accordingly. We suggest they always wear dresses to Shows, rather than pants, and we emphasize well-groomed hair and nails. After all, can you imagine a woman with her hair up in curlers, wearing jeans, calling herself a Beauty Consultant—and trying to tell other women what they should be doing to look good? We're really selling femininity, so our dress code has to be ultra-feminine.[2]*

MOTIVATION—MARY KAY STYLE

Within the honeycomb of the sales unit—the basic organizational entity in Mary Kay, though it is not included in the company organization chart—the consultant receives weekly sales training and encouragement, sings Mary Kay booster songs, and applauds the successes of others. Personal vignettes are as legitimate in this revival-style gathering as is instruction in specific sales techniques. The professionalization program at Mary Kay also includes regional workshops, Jamborees (conducted by national sales directors), leader's conferences, and seminars. "The Seminar" is the "multimillion-dollar extravaganza"

[2]Ibid., p. 10.

staged each year at the Dallas Convention Center where thousands of Mary Kay consultants and directors converge for inspiration, entertainment, and education—Mary Kay style. It is in this immense convention forum that Mary Kay leaders are recognized publicly, where they share their own sagas of success with the audience. Here the Cadillacs, mink coats, diamond bumblebees, and other coveted Mary Kay status symbols are meted out to the deserving ones; and here women aspire to these material rewards by goal-setting activities for the coming year. Seminar classes, conducted by successful Mary Kay directors, teach the intricacies of sales technique, bookkeeping, leadership, customer service, and other skills necessary for Mary Kay entrepreneurship. In 1980 the special effects staff for the seminar arranged for the pink Buicks and Cadillacs to "float" phantomlike through mist onstage via a remote control process much to the delight of the assembled. Seminar showmanship has proven effective in creating the Mary Kay myths.

The company believes that tangible symbols of success motivate the Mary Kay women and serve to fuel the belief "that if they work hard enough—if they give of themselves—that they will be successful, personally and professionally." Vacation trips, prizes, contests, photographs of Mary Kay with members of the sales force, and constant praise are among the motivators the company has used with great success. In 1980, 311 sales directors earned more than $30,000; 98 earned more than $50,000. Almost 500 are designated as "Cadillac-status" directors. The highest-paid Mary Kay saleswomen are the national sales directors, a group of more than 39 women who began as consultants. They average more than $150,000 annually. Mary Kay Cosmetics gives a great deal of publicity to these star earners, for example, Helen McVoy who started back in the humbler days of the company and now earns $300,000 a year.

EARNINGS

A consultant is in business for herself and therefore her earnings are determined by her sales at retail. She purchases products from the company at a discount (up to 50 percent) from retail and her gross profit is the difference between her purchase price and the retail selling price that she herself determines.

In 1981 Mary Kay Cosmetics raised prices 16 percent and simultaneously upped the commission thresholds to increase productivity on a sustained basis. If the consultant wants to qualify for a 50 percent discount, she must order $1,000 of products at the suggested retail price. Previously an $800 order qualified her for a 50 percent discount. Selling $800 of merchandise currently entitles her to $360. Price hikes and the revised commission thresholds allow the consultant to increase her earnings if she manages to maintain her customer base. But there is no time to rest on her laurels, because the Mary Kay system is geared toward the sales woman who aggressively builds her business.

While it is relatively easy to become a Mary Kay consultant, the company demands considerably more of those women who wish to qualify as sales directors. The labor of the sales director is sweetened by the possibility of substantially increased financial rewards over the consultant status, however. Like the consultant, the sales director is self-employed. As the resident advisor for her unit, she supplies her people with inspiration, positive suggestions for improving sales performance, and business advice of all kinds. A carefully orchestrated program for the directors and a rigorous screening process that admits only those women who have met stringent performance standards in terms of volume sales and number of recruits assures that the directors will be an experienced, aggressive sales group. In 1982 the company numbered 3,500 directors. The director-in-qualification travels to Dallas (at her own expense, as is the case of travel arrangements for the entire Mary Kay sales force) to receive training in management of a sales unit.

The directors' commissions were revised upward in 1981 along with the consultants'. To receive the pink Cadillac ("those little pink jars mean little pink cars"), the director must maintain a wholesale volume of $12,000 per month. Under the previous commission scheme, the director earned 12 percent if her unit volume topped $6,000. After the revision, her unit needed to "politely persuade" customers to buy from $8,000 to $12,000 to receive 12 percent. Although the director currently gets only 11 percent on unit volume between $5,000 and $8,000, a 13 percent commission is now possible for the director on volume over $12,000. The director must maintain the momentum of her unit if she is to succeed. Simply put, success for consultants spells success for directors, and vice versa.

GROWTH OF THE COMPANY

Inside and outside of Mary Kay, declining recruitment of consultants was expected in the early 1980s, and the 50 percent growth rate experienced until 1980 was considered unsustainable. Anxiety that the company might reach an early saturation point due to its rapid growth has proved to be groundless, however, with 180,000 consultants projected by December 1982.

Cosmetics, along with beer and cigarettes, have generally been earmarked "recession-proof." Yet cosmetics unit sales in late 1981 and 1982 for Mary Kay and other companies did falter as disposable incomes declined in a recessionary environment. During this period Mary Kay Ash's autobiography went on sale. Her promotional tour to major U.S. cities to discuss her life, career, and company on television and radio provided unprecedented visibility for the Mary Kay message and gave recruitment a shot in the arm. The company spent an estimated $450,000 in television and other advertisements during this period (Exhibit 7).

THE MARY KAY PHILOSOPHY

At Mary Kay, attention to the family unit is central to company ideology. Mary Kay Ash often states the formula, "God first, family second, career third." Since most Mary Kay consultants have families, the organization realizes that enlisting family cooperation makes for happier, more successful Mary Kay salespersons. A husband who is unfavorably disposed to his wife's Mary Kay career, "who gets upset when she comes home an hour late from an evening beauty show" may be "disastrous" to the business. So Mary Kay consultants are urged early on to enlist the cooperation of husbands with tact and caring. At the seminar in Dallas each year, husbands participate in workshops led by experienced Mary Kay husbands designed to imbue them with "that Mary Kay enthusiasm" at best or at least to help them handle issues that sometimes arise in a Mary Kay household: ego crises that occur when a wife brings in more income than her spouse, household crises when a woman may not be on hand to perform all the "wifely" functions to which the family has become accustomed, readjustment problems for the family when the wife and mother may be away from home attending Mary Kay functions. To cheer those husbands left at home when wives are in Dallas, training to be directors, letters are dispatched to them from Mary Kay headquarters thanking them for the support they are giving to their wives' careers.

> *If you are a working woman, getting your husband involved is so important! It's always been my observation that* people will support that which they help to create. *When a woman goes to work, she must not only sell her husband on her career, but if she's wise, she'll find ways to get him involved. Once he's involved, she'll get his support. One area where many of our Beauty Consultants have gotten their husbands involved is in the bookkeeping and record-keeping that goes with any business. Many sales-oriented women don't especially like record keeping, so they welcome their husband's help in this area, and it's been our experience that most husbands enjoy keeping their wives' records.* [3]

To assist the woman in rendering the family the time that is theirs, and to Mary Kay Cosmetics its fair share, Mary Kay Ash advocates good time management. Since she has found that getting up at five in the morning gives her an additional workday each week, she urges consultants and directors to join her Five O'Clock Club: a routine of rising early each morning, using the early hours to dress, apply makeup, do household chores, and prepare to begin Mary Kay business-related activities by 8:30 A.M. The ideal consultant will stop for a half-hour lunch and stay with business until five in the evening. In the best of all possible Mary Kay worlds, a woman will earn enough to allow her to dele-

[3]Ibid., p. 72.

Exhibit 7

ADVERTISING FOR THE MARY KAY AUTOBIOGRAPHY
IN *PEOPLE MAGAZINE*

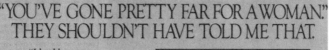

"YOU'VE GONE PRETTY FAR FOR A WOMAN."
THEY SHOULDN'T HAVE TOLD ME THAT.

"I had been a success in my field for more than 25 years. A promotion to a top executive position was long overdue. Instead, I was passed over again and again. Has that happened to you?

"Well, my response was to create an opportunity that would reward women for what they were really worth!

"My dream was to offer women not only a wonderful new Skin Care Program, but also an opportunity to prove how far we can go."

Today Mary Kay Cosmetics has more than 120,000 Beauty Consultants on three continents and our sales are in the hundreds of millions of dollars!

Now the Mary Kay story is available in a book.

It is a personal business history of a dream that happened when all the skeptics said it would fail.

"If you have ever been told you can't do something,

Yes, there really is a Mary Kay.
Portrait by Francesco Scavullo, June 1981.

my story will prove you can. I urge you to read it right away, and I hope it will open some closed doors and closed minds in your life."

It's available at your local bookstore. Or ask your Beauty Consultant how you can get a copy. If you don't have a Consultant, look in the Yellow Pages under Cosmetics/Retail. Or call toll-free (800) 527-6270.

gate many household duties to a housekeeper, the better to perform her sales duties. Getting organized, however, is key to the success of the woman who cannot afford a housekeeper:

> *I know many women do manage to wear all those hats, but it can certain-*
> *ly take its toll. In order to be effective in their careers and still be good*
> *wives and mothers, they must be organized. As a general rule, I have*
> *found that getting organized is one of the biggest problems working*

women have. And if a woman is trying to wear a great many hats and she isn't organized, she's operating under a tremendous handicap.[4]

A unique feature of the company is the flexibility built in for working mothers. Inherent in the company philosophy is the notion that women working as a team can cover for each other in case of family emergency. The beauty show will go on, but perhaps another consultant will carry on when a woman needs to care for a sick child or spouse, a procedure called "the dovetail system."

The Mary Kay organization becomes an extended family for its sales force, a bountiful maternal figure dispensing prizes of minks, diamonds, and Cadillacs to dutiful daughters. The nonhierarchical family atmosphere of the company promotes high morale, according to Mary Kay and upper-level staffers.

The personal touch—be it serving cookies mixed up by Mary Kay Ash with her own hands at company functions or sending Christmas, birthday, anniversary cards and condolence messages—underscores the familial concept of the organization and builds company loyalty. The allegiance of the sales force to the company, personified in Mary Kay Ash, surfaces in every aspect of the consultant's training. In problem solving, consultants are asked to think what Mary Kay herself "would do in your situation," much as if Mary Kay Ash were an exemplary, albeit absent, mother. Adopting Mary Kay Ash's personal routine as their own in many cases, consultants and directors are attached to Mary Kay by an umbilical cord of personal habit and life-style. Many of the sales force display photographs of Mary Kay in their workspaces at home.

SKIN CARE PRODUCTS AND MARY KAY

Mary Kay Cosmetics in 1963 had hit upon an idea whose time had come with its introduction of skin care products, now the staple of almost every major cosmetics house. The basic five-step skin care process includes cleansing, stimulating, freshening, moisturizing, and protecting the skin. The company suggests that the basic set not be broken as it is the centerpiece of the Mary Kay concept, that is, to teach people how to care for their skin.

The best reason to start a new company is that there is a need for what you have to offer, or that you're better than what is being offered. When we began, no cosmetic company was actually teaching skin care. All of them were just selling rouge or lipstick or new eye colors. No company was teaching women how to care for their skin. So we came into a market where there was a real need—and we filled it. Oddly enough, it's still true today that women are not knowledgeable about skin care, despite all

[4]Ibid., pp. 169–170.

the information on television, in magazines, and in newspapers. They buy a product here, there, and everywhere, but they don't have a coordinated program. We fill a void by helping women understand how to take care of their skin. So, if you want to start a successful business, you must offer something different or something better than what is available.[5]

In what is being called a "cosmetic revolution" by some, major cosmetics firms in the 1980s are taking scientific approaches to beauty. While the promise of cosmetics before the 1980s was one of glamor, the present appeal is made to the customer's consciousness that the scientific result of good skin care is healthy, younger-looking, cleaner skin. Advertising stresses the chemical properties of collagen, linoleic acid, and many more. Consumers are presumed, in such high-tech ads, to be conscientious about skin care and conversant with its sophisticated vocabulary replete with such terms as "cell renewal," "exfoliation," and "hydration."

This scientific approach began in the 1960s when Dr. Erno Lazlo introduced his pathbreaking line of skin care products to an enthusiastic public. Worship at the altars of Revlon's Eterna 27 and Clinique also began in the 1960s and has continued into the 1980s.

Scientific research in the 1950s set the stage for the cosmetic revolution, although Mary Kay Cosmetics maintains that the original recipe for its skin preparations emanated from a hide tanner in Texas.

From the 1950s to the 1970s, soluble collagen became available to cosmetic chemists at that time seeking a protein to be used in products to treat dry, flaking, aging skin.[6] Marketing research had demonstrated (and continues to reveal) that approximately 90 percent of American women perceive their most serious skin problem to be dry skin.

According to scientist Bernard Idson of Hoffman-La Roche, when it was understood that it is not oil but water that causes skin to be soft and flexible, cosmetic marketing shifted emphasis from total emolliency to the moisturizing qualities of various products. Idson and other researchers found that a water level of less than 10 percent in an individual's skin results in dried keratin, which causes lowered skin elasticity, a characteristic of sun-damaged, chapped, and aged skin.[7]

With over half its sales in the skin care area, Mary Kay finds itself in the 1980s heavily invested in the fastest-growing product category in cosmetics. Industry analysts project continued growth for skin care products, estimating in optimistic moments the general moisturizer market to number 100 million persons.

[5]Ibid., p. 120.

[6]See R. D. Todd and L. I. Biol, "Soluble Collagen: New Protein for Cosmetics," *Drug and Cosmetic Industry*, Vol. 117 (October 1975), pp. 50–52.

[7]See Bernard Idson, "Dry Skin Moisturizing and Emolliency," *Drug and Cosmetic Industry*, Vol. 117 (October 1975), pp. 43–45.

PSYCHOGRAPHICS, DEMOGRAPHICS, AND MARY KAY

Psychographic market segmentation stretches beyond the more traditional demographic and socioeconomic descriptors used to predict consumer behavior. Product psychographics are bound up with product promises, price-value perception, and the overall image of the product. Because of this relational posture, psychographic market segmentation is particularly applicable to the behavior of the cosmetics purchaser, who according to an old aphorism, is buying not only a product but hope. In a way, however, proponents of the scientific approach to marketing skin care are placing bets on a consumer's responding to demonstrations of empirical results and moving away from purchasing merely out of *hopes* that the product will deliver.

The last decade has seen a tremendous consumer responsiveness to computerized and education-oriented beauty programs (Clinique) and carefully orchestrated, scientific-based programs to control "age zones" (Charles of Ritz). According to those in the testing area at Ritz, their test methodology for the product Age-Zone Controller used 100 subjects and, according to Eileen Kregan, Director of Consumer Education for Charles of Ritz (1982), "consisted of making silicone skin replicas of the subject's outer eye area on the first, seventh, and fourteenth days of the test. To measure line reduction, light was passed through the positive skin replicas and a transparency was made. Direct

---

Exhibit 8

U.S. POPULATION PROJECTIONS BY AGE GROUP (BOTH SEXES)
(in millions)

Age Group	1970	1975	1980	1985	1990	COMPOUND % INCREASE (DECREASE) 1975 vs. 1970	1980 vs. 1975	1985 vs. 1980	1990 vs. 1985
15–19	19.3	21.0	20.6	18.0	16.8	1.7%	(0.4)%	(2.7)%	(1.4)%
20–24	17.2	19.2	20.9	20.5	18.0	2.3	1.7	(0.5)	(2.6)
25–29	13.7	16.9	18.9	20.6	20.2	4.3	2.3	1.7	(0.4)
30–34	11.6	14.0	17.2	19.3	20.9	3.8	4.2	2.3	1.6
35–39	11.2	11.6	14.0	17.3	19.3	0.6	3.8	4.9	2.2
40–44	12.0	11.2	11.7	14.1	17.3	(1.3)	0.9	3.8	4.1
45–49	12.1	11.8	11.0	11.5	13.9	(0.7)	(1.4)	0.9	3.8
50–54	11.2	12.0	11.7	10.9	11.4	1.4	1.4	(1.4)	0.9
55–59	10.0	10.5	11.4	11.1	10.4	1.0	1.7	(0.5)	(1.3)
60–64	8.7	9.2	9.8	10.6	10.4	1.1	1.3	1.6	(0.4)

Source: U.S. Department of Commerce, Bureau of Census, 1970, 1980, Series P-25, *Population Estimates and Projections.*

measurements were then made of the transparencies to determine what changes occurred in the length and number of age lines over a 14-day period." Advertising for the product will reflect the scientific findings.

Mary Kay relies much more heavily on the educational than on the high-tech approach with its customers. Quality control is a term that surfaces more often at Mary Kay than specific scientific terminology and vocabulary. The company envisions customers as interested more in the process of using the product than its specific theoretical underpinnings.

The demographic trends as projected by U.S. Census figures indicate that Mary Kay will continue to find an increasing number of women customers in the 25- to 44-year age group, a group May Kay has already targeted as one vitally interested in skin care. Projections call for the 63 million persons in the 25- to 44-year age group in 1980 to increase to 80 million in 1990. Although the teenage and early-twenties market is dwindling, this should not be problematic for Mary Kay since its products presently do not get high visibility among this group due to the beauty show method of sales.

Mary Kay Cosmetics sees many positive signals in the 1980 Census data (Exhibit 8). Constructing "the woman of the '80s," the company profiled a woman "in her mid-30s."

Her husband has a good job, but they could use extra income. They have one child.

She has completed some college and would like to return, part-time, for more. She is highly inclined to a job or career—both from economic necessity and from a desire to experience something new and to test her abilities.

The woman of the '80s has a new awareness of political affairs but, at the same time, is keenly aware of improving herself, physically, intellectually and professionally.

She wants to live life on **her** terms. She is interested in acquiring things and achieveing goals, but above these she places **experience**. She is not content to be a spectator. While she may admire the looks and figure of a fashion model, she would rather **be** one.

Even though she enjoys her homelife, she seeks to expand her world by finding a part-time job or full-time career. This new world makes her more aware of her appearance. She works hard to stay fit; she is nutrition-conscious; she cares deeply about how she looks—her wardrobe, her skin and her grooming.

To the ends of feeling and looking good, she has educated herself in the accoutrements of fitness and appearance. She is more conscious than her mother's generation about matters of sophistication, taste in clothing and cosmetic fashions.

She eagerly searches for products and services that satisfy her powerful sense of self and her need for self-improvement. She is a customer in the market for what Mary Kay has always offered. And now, more than ever, she is willing to try both our products and our career opportunity.

The inevitable meeting of Mary Kay and the woman of the '80s usually takes place at a Mary Kay beauty show.[8]

As Mary Kay Cosmetics looks to the 1990s, it sees a population in which 60 percent of all women will be working. Women working outside the home have clearly demonstrated that they spend more on cosmetics than do their counterparts in the home. One-third of all households will be composed of single persons, people who have discretionary income to spend on their own needs. Mary Kay sees great opportunities to convert a "middle-aged" population to skin care products. On another level, there will be a large middle-aged working female population from which to recruit the corps of Mary Kay consultants. That the number of women entering the labor force is tapering off (in 1980, 50 percent of the female population between ages 18 and 65 were working) does not appear to be of major concern to the company.

MARY KAY AND THE FOOD AND DRUG ADMINISTRATION

Inquiries made to the Food and Drug Administration (FDA) regarding the claims made by cosmetics companies for their products is a major escalating problem at the agency, which is receiving less funding than it says it needs to investigate. The FDA sustains the burden of proof in establishing that the claims made by cosmetics companies are misleading to the consumer. Although cosmetics companies, including Mary Kay, express concern about a climate of increased regulation, the FDA complains that "we are not in any position to challenge the cosmetics industry. It is a $12 billion industry being regulated by a handful of people at the FDA."

Until the 1970s, the government took a strong stance with regard to the regulation of cosmetics formulations. Consumer activism across the board in the 1970s resulted in more stringent regulation of the industry. The use of dyes, hexachlorophene, and mercury in cosmetics and toiletries sparked debates and engendered legislation on the appropriate labeling of cosmetics. Major regulatory requirements imposed on manufacturers included

[8]*1980 Annual Report*, p. 5.

Responsibility for the safety of the cosmetic being marketed

Responsibility for required testing to determine toxicity, irritation, and/or sensitivity to the product

Compliance should the FDA insist on further discretionary testing by an FDA-appointed, independent organization to verify the safety of ingredients

Mandatory labeling of cosmetic packages or containers with specific ingredients in order of predominance, although flavor and fragrance need only be indicated by the words "flavor" and "fragrance"

A waiting period of 20 days before the release of the new product after notification of the FDA

Reports of increased regulation hover over the industry, but the fact is, according to the *1982 U.S. Industrial Outlook,* that less than 1 percent of the FDA's budget goes toward regulation of the cosmetics industry. The FDA depends on voluntary programs for the reporting of product formulas and adverse effects, for example, the Cosmetic Ingredient Review (CIR), a screening and warning process to alert the industry to possible harmful effects of cosmetic ingredients.

Mary Kay's reaction to regulation has resulted in expansion of its laboratories, acquisition of capital equipment to support skin science, and development of contacts in the scientific fields of dermatology and skin science. "Regulatory agencies are responding to increased scientific information, ensuring a more complex environment in the '80s for our entire industry," the company reported to stockholders in 1981.

OF TOILETRIES AND COSMETICS

Increasingly the distinction drawn between toiletries and cosmetics is becoming a matter of semantics. Because they are higher priced, cosmetics theoretically are geared to the individual whereas toiletries at a lower unit price are targeted to the mass market. The mode of distribution of cosmetics—through department stores and drugstores on a franchise or semifranchise basis or through direct sales—differs from that of toiletries, which are found in mass marketing outlets. This distinction is beginning to blur as cosmetic houses begin limitedly to place lower-priced lines in grocery stores and discount houses, although it is doubtful that toothpaste will appear in department stores. More utilitarian in nature, toiletries, including shampoos, toothpastes, and deodorants because of their proletarian nature, occupy a more competitive marketing niche, one in which higher promotional advertising expenditures are the rule. Lipsticks, fragrance products, eye makeup, face makeup, and the treatment lines—the mainstays of cosmetics—tend to engender a strong brand-name loyalty if the product delivers, even though it may be less advertised than a toiletry. A satisfied Mary Kay customer, for instance, often will use no other brand of cosmetic, although she may use several brands of toothpaste. Mary Kay and other cosmetic companies are making strong bids to sell toilet-

Exhibit 9

TOTAL U.S. COSMETIC AND TOILETRY TRENDS IN MARY KAY'S RELEVANT MARKETS, 1970–1980*

YEAR	SALES MANUFACTURING (millions) PRICES	PRICE INCREASE (Decrease)	REAL SALES (Increase)	U.S. FEMALE POPULATION (millions)	COSMETIC AND TOILETRY SALES PER WOMAN† (Mfg. Prices)	REAL COSMETIC USE INDEX‡ (Per Capita)
1980	$3,950			113.6	$29.55	1.33
1979	3,653			112.7	27.55	1.36
1978	3,317			111.8	25.18	1.32
1977	3,040	$	$	110.9	23.29	1.20
1976	2,816			110.1	21.71	1.25
1975	2,476			109.2	19.27	1.19
1974	2,275			108.5	17.84	1.16
1973	2,110			107.7	16.62	1.15
1972	1,980			106.9	15.74	1.10
1971	1,875			106.0	15.06	1.04
1970	1,735			104.9	14.08	1.00

% Increase (decrease)

1980–1979	8.1%	10.1%	(2.1)%	0.8%	7.3%	(2.8)%
1979–1978	10.1	6.0	4.1	0.8	9.4	3.4
1978–1977	9.1	4.0	5.1	0.8	8.1	4.1
1977–1976	8.0	4.0	4.0	0.7	7.3	3.3
1976–1975	13.7	7.2	6.5	0.8	12.7	5.5
1975–1974	8.8	.4.6	4.2	0.6	8.0	3.4
1974–1973	7.8	6.4	1.4	0.7	7.3	0.9
1973–1972	6.7	0.0	6.7	0.8	5.6	5.6
1972–1971	5.4	(0.8)	6.2	0.9	4.5	5.1
1971–1970	8.1	2.5	5.6	1.0	6.9	4.4

Compound growth

1980 vs. 1970	9%			1%	8%	3%
1980 vs. 1975	10			1	9	3
1975 vs. 1970	7			1	6	3

*From sources believed reliable. Excludes toothpaste and other categories in which Mary Kay does not compete.
†Assumes 85% of U.S. cosmetics and toiletry industry sales of products Mary Kay sells are used by women.
‡Cosmetic and toiletry sales per woman minus price increases, indexed to 1970.
§Not available.

ries as cosmetics, especially in the hair care line, by marketing a cluster of such products as a hair care program with much the same educational approach found successful for the skin care line (Exhibit 9).

A common property to both cosmetics and toiletries is their appeal to the psyche of the user. No one would argue with the idea that people buy these products with the expectation that they will look and feel better after using them.

Analysts have concluded that one problem in capturing the potentially vast market for men's cosmetics is in breaking down the image that it is normal for a man to buy toiletries but somehow "abnormal" for him to purchase cosmetics. In recent years men appear to have been convinced that colognes are acceptable masculine cosmetic items. Mary Kay and other firms believe that growth in the men's cosmetic market will be slow and will probably begin with a skin care line accompanied by an educational process of some sort.

MARY KAY COSMETICS AND THE FUTURE

Returning to the familial theme at the end of her autobiography, Mary Kay reflects on the possibility of her retirement—if and when she can no longer present the glamorous, ageless public persona that people recognize through photographs such as the one taken by celebrity photographer Francesco Scavullo for the cover of her book. In passing she remarks that her mother's skin, even at age 87 "looked wonderful."

Looking toward the long term, Mary Kay Cosmetics purchased 176 acres of land in Dallas in June 1981 to pursue a major four-year expansion program to encompass production, distribution, and administrative facilities. Construction was set to start in October 1982 on the first of several manufacturing and distribution facilities.

> We're also so fortunate to have as president my son, Richard, who has filled in for me on many occasions and won the hearts of our people. He, one day, will not only fill his job as chief executive but mine as well, as motivator of our people.[9]

Exhibit 10 portrays the management team at Mary Kay Cosmetics.

The development strategy to see the company through a lengthier expansion period will call for construction as needed to support sales, to be financed from retained earnings. The leased 300,000-square-foot manufacturing facility allows Mary Kay Cosmetics to support $400 million in sales volume. The $12 million site development project, underway in 1982, was capitalized and also financed by internal cash flow and limited bank borrowing—a conservative fiscal strategy consistent with Mary Kay Ash's personal philosophy of paying cash rather than incurring heavy, long-term debts.

[9]Ash, *Mary Kay*, p. 205.

Exhibit 10

MARY KAY MANAGEMENT TEAM, 1982

Mary Kay Ash, Chairman of the Board

Richard Rogers, President. Co-founder of Mary Kay Cosmetics, Inc. Served as General Manager, Vice President. 1968 "Marketing Man of the Year" Award from North Texas Chapter of the American Marketing Association.

Gerald M. Allen, Vice President, Administration. Responsible for planning, organizing, and directing the delivery of administrative services to the beauty consultant and supervising a staff of sales promotion directors. Supervises company security, communications and word processing, sales administration and compensation programs. B.B.A., Arlington State College.

J. Eugene (Gene) Stubbs, Vice President, Finance, and Treasurer. Responsible for financial planning and accountable for company's financial assets and profitability objectives. Directs the treasury, controllership, and internal audit functions. Also responsible for all financial reporting. M.B.A., University of Texas; C.P.A.; B.B.A., Texas A & M University.

Richard C. Bartlett, Vice President, Marketing. Responsible for planning and implementing marketing strategy including incentive programs, education and development of consultants, special events and meetings, public relations, and market-related research. B.S., University of Florida.

Monty C. Barber, Vice President, Secretary, and General Counsel. Responsible for supervising activities prescribed by law and the company regulations, establishing legal policies, advising and rendering opinions, supervises the public affairs program. As corporate secretary, attends to administrative matters for the board, shareholder relations, consumer relations, and coordinates all contribution requests. J.D., University of Texas; B.B.A., University of Texas.

John Beasley, Group Vice President, Manufacturing. Responsible for planning, organizing, and evaluating all manufacturing decisions. Directs the development of the product line and ensures the quality of the products. B.A., Georgia Tech, Industrial Engineering National Merit Scholarship.

Phil Bostley, Vice President, Operations. Responsible for planning, directing, and coordinating the distribution of all Mary Kay cosmetics and sales

Exhibit 10 (Cont.)

aids through regional distribution centers. Also responsible for directing the forecasting of product mix, the maintenance of inventory levels and coordinating the company's data processing group. B.A., Penn State University, math and science.

Myra O. Barker, Ph.D., Vice President, Research and Product Development. Responsible for planning and directing skin technology, process technology, and product development. Directs regulatory and medical affairs and ensures product safety. Ph.D., Tulane University, biochemistry; B.S., University of Texas, chemistry.

Bruce C. Rudy, Ph.D., Vice President, Quality Assurance. Responsible for the procedures that assure the quality of raw materials in the product line. Controls the finished products certifying that they meet cosmetic, FDA and company standards. Plans and directs quality audits of all phases of product development, research, manufacture, and distribution. B.S., E. Stroudsburg State College; M.S., Clemson University; M.B.A., Columbia University; Ph.D., University of Georgia.

Pat Howard, Vice President, Manufacturing Operations. Responsible for manufacturing material control including purchasing, warehousing, production, planning, and international manufacturing. B.S., St. Mary's University; M.S., Texas A & M University.

Jack Dingler, Vice President, Controller. Responsible for all operating financial functions of the company, including expenditure review, to ensure the continuation of the company's sound financial position. B.B.A., University of Texas at Arlington, accounting; C.P.A.

William H. Randall, Director, Marketing Services. Responsible for marketing research, incentive program, visual communications, marketing publications, communications, and creative efforts. M.B.A., Harvard; B.A., Rutgers, economics.

Dean Meadors, Director, Public Relations. Responsible for all public relations activity. M.S., University of Illinois, advertising; B.S., University of Illinois, journalism.

Netta Jackson, Director, Product Service. Responsible for the marketing rationale for product development. Ensures that the company remains competitive in price and positioning. Active in sales force training. B.S.B.A., University of Arkansas, marketing.

Exhibit 10 (Cont.)

Michael C. Lunceford, Director, Public Affairs. Responsible for monitoring of local, state, and federal laws and regulations; community liaison with emphasis on corporate philanthropy. Master's program, Southern Methodist University, business administration; M.S., Southern Methodist University, public administration; B.B.A., East Texas State University, business administration, finance/economics.

Richard Rogers has publicly set the goal of $500 million in annual sales by 1990, emphasizing that 35 percent of the Mary Kay business is repeat sales to faithful customers. "As we grow, we're bringing our customer base forward," he states. His plan for growth reflects the guarded optimism of industry analysts. They predict that beauty products will rebound in the 1980s as the economy limps toward recovery. Most companies are placing their chips on moisturizing products, although many will continue diversification strategies, for example, Chesebrough-Ponds, a leader in the moisturizing business with Vaseline Intensive Care Lotion, but also a leader in spaghetti sauce, children's clothing, and casual footwear with the Ragu, Health-tex, and G. H. Bass brands. Meanwhile, Avon, Mary Kay's most look-alike competitor, continues to diversify. In 1982 Avon began peddling magazine subscriptions along with its vast cosmetic and costume jewelry lines. In a surprising 1979 move, Avon picked up Tiffany and Company, the preeminent jewelry concern.

Mary Kay intends to ride the moisturizing and skin care wave. Its Basic Skin Care Program will remain the staple product line. While other cosmetic companies (Avon and Bonne Bell, to name just two) are sponsoring women's running, bowling, and tennis competitions, Mary Kay Cosmetics will channel its energies into support of women working—for Mary Kay. An Avon piece of advertising copy reads, "At Avon, sports, health and beauty go naturally together." Mary Kay, however will continue to endorse a work and beauty ethic.

Introduced in 1982, the four-step Body Care Program seemed the next logical step for Mary Kay Cosmetics, a continuation of the company's appeal to the 25- to 44-year-old segment. Other major product constellations for the 1980s include Specialized Skin Care products (sun screen and hand cream), the Glamour Collection (cosmetics), and the Beauty Boutique, an array of bath and after-bath products. In keeping with the programmatic presentation pioneered in the Skin Care System, the company has developed a Basic Hair Care System, including shampoos, conditioner, and hair spray. Mary Kay Cosmetics hopes to nurture the presently minuscule market for the Mr. K. line of men's skin care products.

I've talked about how important it is for women to look good, but I think men care just as much about their appearance. However, unfortunately, often you'll see a man dressed in beautiful clothes, with good-looking shoes, an expensive briefcase, well-groomed hair, and manicured nails— but whose face could look so much better with a little help! A woman wouldn't look complete without her face made up. So why shouldn't a man do the same thing?[10]

As the company feels its way through the 1980s, it will accentuate quality control aspects ensured by a vigilant R&D policy. John Beasley, vice president of manufacturing, addressed this major concern in an interview, which appears as Appendix A. Also, see Appendix B, an excerpt from *U.S. Industrial Outlook.*

Because of the style of life that Mary Kay is selling along with the product—that of the independent, well-compensated, career-woman beauty consultant—the company has not been altogether successful in translating the Mary Kay concept into other, non–English-speaking, more patriarchal cultures. Mary Kay Cosmetics internally appears sanguine that "the philosophy of Mary Kay Cosmetics has proven well suited for women everywhere," but this remains a debatable area in places like Japan.

Mary Kay Ash has stated on many occasions that Mary Kay Cosmetics is "in the business of helping women create better self-images so that they will feel better about themselves." Whether she is invoking Ralph Waldo Emerson's "Nothing great was ever achieved without enthusiasm" or leading her devoted consultants and directors in a chorus of "That Mary Kay Enthusiasm," Mary Kay Ash, genius of direct sales motivation, thinks and dreams enthusiasm: "My own dream," she states in her autobiography, "is that Mary Kay Cosmetics will someday become the largest and best skin care company in the world."

Your Task:

Mary Kay Cosmetics has hired you as a consultant to review their current marketing strategy and to advise the company today about the direction in which they should be moving during the late 1980s and 1990s. In your analysis take into account the philosophy of the company, its declared mission, U.S. demographic and social trends, and the overall picture of the U.S. cosmetics industry.

[10]Ibid., pp. 130–131.

Appendix A

JOHN BEASLEY ON QUALITY CONTROL AND RELATED TOPICS*

Q: *How does the quality of Mary Kay products compare with others on the market?*

A: *We direct our research and development and all our efforts toward producing the finest products we can produce. We know what other companies are producing. We understand all major competitive concepts, formulas, and approaches. But our focus is on producing the best product for the Mary Kay system. You see, we have a different orientation from most cosmetic companies. We can't just produce a product for a particular market segment. Our skin care products are used in a teaching system, so we are systems oriented. Our products work together, they're modular, and there's a synergism between them.*

Q: *Wasn't Mary Kay a pioneer in teaching skin care?*

A: *Mary Kay, as a specialist in skin care, has set trends for the only product segment of the market that's really growing. In 1963, we began marketing a five-step program of skin care. In 1976, we started teaching the scientific basis of skin care to and through our beauty consultants who today number over 150,000. Now every major cosmetic company in the country is talking about the scientific basis of skin care.*

Q: *How did the new Body Care System happen?*

A: *We've always had products aimed at body skin. The idea evolved from what we had learned about facial skin care. Body skin is different from facial skin, yet there are functional needs that need to be addressed in a complementary way. Body care was a natural extension from the Mary Kay tradition of scientific skin care.*

Our Body Care products have been formulated according to the same high standards we use in skin care. We've tested them and used them ourselves. We've come up with a very, very high-quality system for an economical price.

Q: *What standards do you use internally for making product decisions?*

A.: *We came up with four factors that have to be included in every decision that is made from every level. Since we are a participative management organization, everybody has to know what the rules are, exactly what is*

---

*The following is an interview with John Beasley, vice president, Manufacturing Group for Mary Kay Cosmetics, Inc. Mr. Beasley has been with Mary Kay since September 1975 and is currently responsible for planning, organizing, and evaluating all U.S. and international manufacturing decisions. A major portion of his responsibility is quality assurance. The interview was conducted in May 1982 at Mary Kay's corporate headquarters in Dallas.

Appendix A (Cont.)

important. The first thing that has to be considered in every decision is quality . . . the impact on product quality. The second is service. Service to the beauty consultant and consumer.

The third thing that everybody has to take into account is the flexibility of the decision. What range does it work in? The fourth is the actual cost of the decision: total cost of capital investment, impact on cost of goods, and cash flow.

We teach all management and some hourly people to use the four criteria. I will not look at any proposal that doesn't address these four things—and the first thing I see has to be quality. Richard Rogers [president of Mary Kay] uses the saying "If it's worth doing, do it right." That is the kind of quality statement that underlines everything we do all day long. That's the way the company was founded.

Q: *You mentioned you are a "participative management organization." How does this work at Mary Kay?*

A: *You cannot get quality by having only one part of your company responsible for quality. The assumption that the better traditional organizations have made is that if you want to get something accomplished, you have to focus on it through a special part of your organization.*

Our assumption here is much different. Everybody is in charge of quality. The Research and Development Department is in charge of quality. The Marketing Department is in charge of quality. The Material Control Department is in charge of quality.

The actual "Quality Assurance" function serves as a measuring device. The quality audit measures how well we are matching our stated quality standards. These specifications are set in a type of committee process that starts in research and development and get approved right up through the CEO in final form. From there our job is to expand them backward, through all the maze of processing, all the way back to vendor level. It's very much like the idea behind the Japanese quality circles when you get everybody involved in focusing on quality. For example, in 1976 we gave everybody in the hourly (nonexempt) group an across-the-board pay increase, explaining that we were adding the quality inspection responsibility to their job. We said, "Part of your job is to make sure we always produce Mary Kay quality."

Q: *How did they respond to this?*

A: *Many of them consider quality to be the predominant part of their job. The people in the plant don't simply report a problem; they are actually the ones doing the rejecting. And most of them are very tough. They see things that you and I won't see because they have developed a whole different set of skills out there. We normally produce on only one shift, we*

Appendix A (Cont.)

hire special people, we evaluate them and reward them. Mary Kay was always, from the very beginning, attracted to people who are quality conscious. If you look around, you see a very consistent type of person in dress and quality standards. When new people come in from other companies, and we've had to do a good bit of recruiting because we've grown so fast, they usually come from companies that were more interested in cost as the first factor. Even top executives don't understand that quality is the first criterion. So we create a whole culture that reinforces our standards.

Q: *How many of the products Mary Kay sells are made in your own facilities?*

A: *We manufacture probably 99 percent of the products in house; and 100 percent is quality inspected here. The same quality standards apply internationally. In general, if they don't pass the same quality standards that we use here in the United States, they don't go to the consumer.*

Q: *How does your sales force respond to this?*

A: *The sales force is very, very conscious of the quality aspect. Sometimes there has been some disappointment when we've said, "We're sorry, we can't sell this product because it's not Mary Kay quality." But it's very important to the sales force that they be very proud of the products and systems they teach . . . and sell.*

Q: *What are your long-term goals for Mary Kay?*

A: *We want to be the finest teaching-oriented skin care company in the world with sales of $500 million by 1990. That's our corporate objective. It has been stated in our annual report, and everybody around here can quote it.*

Q: *How do you begin to meet that goal?*

A: *Research and development is the leading edge. Since 1975, Research and Development has grown from 1 Ph.D. and a technician to a staff of 47. We recruited Dr. Myra Barker to be our vice president of research and development. We go after the top 10 percent of the people in the country who have the skills that we're looking for and personal integrity. They don't come necessarily from the cosmetic industry. Many have come from the drug industry because we see cosmetics, especially skin care products, more like drugs than traditional glamor products.*

In addition, the Research and Development Department is in the forefront in developing new technology. We have a group that has been formed to do nothing but research how the skin relates to the rest of the body and how it relates to its environment. A very large part of the research and development budget, for example, is aimed at research all over the world. We're funding a research dermatologist in Wales who is

Appendix A (Cont.)

doing research into skin attribute measurement. We have grants in Eng-
land. When you came in, I was signing a purchase order that goes for a
research grant to Southwestern Medical School.

Q: *What types of tests are you doing?*

A: *There are many levels of testing and two major issues: one is safety, one is*
efficacy. We don't take risks with the consumer. Our products must meet
acceptable levels in terms of oral toxicity . . . sensitization . . . irritation.
We are having to stretch current technology in establishing some new
standards in the industry in the area of comedogenicity, the interaction
of the new product, the environment, and the skin-causing comedones
(acne).

We screen raw materials at the vendor level. If you get something that's
99 percent pure, it means it's 1 percent impure. In our business we're in-
terested in the 1 percent impure. We made substantial investments in
computerized instrumentation so that we can screen raw materials rou-
tinely for impurities.

Efficacy testing is also something that is fairly new. Cosmetic products
used to be a coverup, but now we're producing skin care products that are
functional. We need to measure how a product actually performs, but
we're having to develop the technology.

Q: *As vice president in charge of manufacturing, how do you challenge your*
departments?

A: *We have no negatives in terms of product quality, number one. We can't*
afford any big savings in quality. We have to be consistently above the
line in terms of the impact on the consumer. Consistently positive! Then
what we try to do is to raise that line to the top of the industry. We estab-
lish a consistent quality level, and then we figure out how to make that
better. That's our drive, our constant challenge. The quality standard has
never, ever been stagnant. We always strive to be the best we can be.

Appendix B

SUMMARY OF COSMETICS PROSPECTS FOR 1982
AND THE LONG TERM

Moderately priced products are expected to sell best, especially hair, skin, nail, and eye care products.

Fragrances will become more popular, especially among men, in the 1980s.

Ethnic cosmetic sales are expected to pick up.

Up to 45 percent of males in the population will use cosmetics by 1986.

Sun-screen agents that reportedly protect skin from damaging ultraviolet rays will be added to many skin care products to prevent premature aging, wrinkling, or cancer of the skin.

An estimated 65 percent of all cosmetics are purchased on impulse, although during recessionary periods consumers are most cost conscious.

The industry's principal target group of teenagers and young women is shrinking, although the "baby boom" generation is aging and is likely to spend money for beauty aids.

Among the present 20- to 35-year-old age group, there is a much larger lower-income sector.

Rising costs of raw materials and the high cost of research are the scourge of the cosmetics industry.

New products are essential for greater sales, yet new product introductions lag because of the decrease in research and development.

The skin care market, including moisturizers, sun-care creams, lotions, scrubs and cleansers, collagen and elastin protein rejuvenating agents, is growing and reached $2.5 billion in 1981 because of increased concern among consumers over aging skin, personal cleanliness, and the damaging effects of ultraviolet rays.

Hypoallergenic and fragrance-free products have been demonstrated to be most successful in the skin care market.

The hair preparations market increased to $2.2 billion in 1981 due to consumer interest in healthy looking hair and frequent shampoos by both men and women. Women frequently use cream rinse and hair conditioning products, although an untapped male market exists for such products. Hair spray remains popular with older women.

Industry shipments of cosmetics, toiletries, and fragrances were valued at $9.9 billion in 1981, only a 0.6 percent increase from 1980, as opposed to a 2.6 average annual increase from 1972 through 1981.

Source: 1982 U.S. Industrial Outlook.

TIME INC./SEAGRAM

The case for advertising frequency—and its effect on people's buying habits—receives a major boost in an exhaustive and groundbreaking study just completed by Jos. E. Seagram & Sons and Time Inc.[1]

Released to advertisers, agencies, and media in late 1982, "A Study of the Effectiveness of Advertising Frequency in Magazines" presented the results of an extensive study into the relationship of magazine advertising frequency and brand awareness, advertising recall, favorable brand rating, willingness to buy, and product use and purchase. Selected passages from the report have been extracted for this narrative.

BACKGROUND

Because of the complexity of the problem and the high costs involved, studies attempting to answer the question "How much frequency is enough?" have generally shied away from large-scale projects involving participating consumers. Ordinarily they have drawn on the results of experiments in behavior and

[1]"Major Study Details Ad Effect on Sales," *Advertising Age*, June 21, 1982, p. 1.

learning conducted by pioneer psychologists, have sought answers through manipulating mathematical models, or have taken other approaches that were financially and methodologically feasible and showed promise of providing operational findings. "Even fewer have examined the effect of frequency as it relates specifically to advertising in the print medium."[2]

Four characteristics set this study apart from previous ones:

1. **Scope.** This study extended over a 48-week period and generated findings from a base of 16,500 respondents and 132,000 data points.
2. **Design.** The design permitted control of all insertion frequency variables, without forced exposure, in a natural environment.
3. **Range of information.** This included both changes in attitudes and changes in behavior that resulted from changes in the frequency of "opportunities to see" advertising.
4. **Focus.** This was the first study ever to deal with the effects of frequency of advertising in magazines.[3]

HIGHLIGHTS OF THE STUDY[4]

Objective   To examine the relationship between "opportunities to see" advertising in print and advertising effectiveness, at predetermined levels of advertising frequency, and in a controlled "real-world environment."

Advertising Effectiveness Measures Evaluated   Brand awareness, advertising awareness, brand rating, willingness to buy, recent product use, and recent product purchase.

Advertising Frequency Levels Evaluated   Control group—no insertions; light frequency—one advertising insertion every four weeks of the study; moderate frequency—two advertising insertions every four weeks of the study; and heavy frequency—one advertising insertion each week of the study.

Design Criteria   Magazine advertisements studied were inserted in standard copies of *Sports Illustrated* and *Time*. These copies were then mailed in the usual fashion to known subscribers of these magazines.

Markets chosen were the state of Missouri and the city of Milwaukee.

Products studied were eight Seagram brands that had low usage in these markets. There was reasonable distribution of the test brands in the markets studied, assuring that should a consumer want to buy the brands, they would be available.

Another criterion was that no other advertising would be scheduled for these brands in the test markets during the course of the study. This assured

[2]Time Inc., "A Study of the Effectiveness of Advertising Frequency in Magazines," 1982.
[3]Ibid., p. 10.
[4]This section is adapted from ibid., pp. 15–17.

that the only advertising that could affect respondent attitudes and behavior toward the test brands was the advertising programmed in the study.

Experimental Design The experimental design was balanced both to ensure that each group of respondents was involved in some way in every brand and to permit matched comparisons for all test measures at all levels of frequency. To achieve these objectives, the respondent sample was divided into four groups, with each group receiving magazines containing ads for each brand at different controlled levels of frequency. As Exhibit 1 demonstrates, over the course of the study, for example, group 1 received magazines with no ads for brands A and E, 12 ads for brands B and F, 24 ads for brands C and G, and 48 ads for brands D and H. Similarly, each of the other groups received magazines with ads at different levels of frequency for each brand.

In analyzing the data, responses were pooled for each level of frequency. For example, to study the effects of every-week frequency (48 insertions), responses were pooled from group 1 for brands D and H, from group 2 for brands C and G, from group 3 for brands B and F, and from group 4 for brands A and E.

Sample and Response Subscriber lists were "cleansed" to ensure that no respondent received ads in both *Time* and *Sports Illustrated* even if subscribing to both. The duration was 48 weeks, with fieldwork completed between November 1979 and September 1980. The sample base was just over 21,000 with a 77 percent completion rate; 80 percent of the respondent base of approximately 16,500 were liquor users. Questionnaires were mailed weekly to subsamples of subscriber respondents, with no participant receiving more than one (see appendix for related questionnaire). Data were analyzed only for liquor users, and brands were weighted equally, so that results from larger

---

Exhibit 1

EXPERIMENTAL RESEARCH DESIGN MATRIX

Group	DESIGN							
1	0X	12X	24X	48X	0X	12X	24X	48X
2	12X	24X	48X	0X	12X	24X	48X	0X
3	24X	48X	0X	12X	24X	48X	0X	12X
4	48X	0X	12X	24X	48X	0X	12X	24X
	A	B	C	D	E	F	G	H
				BRAND				

brands did not distort the results from small brands for any measure. Ads were chosen by Joseph E. Seagram & Sons, Inc. and then were arranged in printing and binding so that, over the course of the project, each appeared an equal number of times in the front and the back of each magazine and an equal number of times facing right and facing left. Fieldwork data collection, tabulation, and editing were carried out by Lieberman Associates; curve fitting was prepared by Marketmath, Inc. (In this case study, we include only narrative, not graphs.)

MAJOR FINDINGS[5]

1. *Significant changes in consumer attitudes were apparent beginning with the first insertion.* It has been postulated that at least three ad exposures are required to make a significant impact on consumer attitudes.

Contrary to this assumption, the data show that, while reported levels of awareness of advertising built slowly, reported levels for such measures of attitude as brand awareness, favorable brand rating, and willingness to buy jumped sharply following the first "opportunity to see" advertising.

2. *Gains in reported levels of brand awareness and in favorable attitudes toward advertised brands were still being achieved at the end of the campaign.* Contrary to previously held theories, favorable effects resulting from "opportunity to see" advertising did not level off or drop in the later weeks of the study.

For some measures of attitude, reported increases did diminish briefly in the early weeks of the campaign following the initial jump. This may have occurred because these early ad exposures served to bring back to mind previously held attitudes based on experience.

For all attitude measures, the decline was temporary, and, in later weeks, a stable pattern of increase was established. This pattern of increase then remained constant for the duration of the campaign.

By contrast, the rate of increase in levels of awareness of advertising tended to flatten in the later weeks of the campaign.

3. *More frequent "opportunities to see" advertising resulted in higher average weekly gains in measures of attitude.* Study findings confirmed the assumption that greater advertised frequency (more opportunities to see advertising) produces greater advertising effect.

For all measurements, increased levels of exposure resulted in more favorable attitudes toward advertised brands.

4. *Changes in behavior as a result of frequent advertising were greater than changes in attitude.* For all brands, opportunities to see advertising re-

[5]This section is adapted from ibid., pp. 17–19.

sulted in greater increases in product use and purchase than in measures of awareness, favorable brand rating, and willingness to buy.

For example, at the heaviest frequency level, in an average week, brand awareness increased 36 percent, favorable brand rating gained 45 percent, willingness to buy increased 59 percent, recent reported product use rose 72 percent, and recent reported product purchase jumped 170 percent.

5. *It was more difficult to change attitudes toward "high-awareness" brands than it was to change attitudes toward "low-awareness" brands for the low-usage brands studied.* Although study findings showed that frequent advertising resulted in substantial gains in both awareness and favorable attitudes for all brands studied, they also revealed a distinct difference in the pattern and magnitude of increase between high- and low-awareness brands.

Increases were substantially greater for low-awareness brands than for high-awareness brands. The size of the increase reported for low-awareness brands also proved to be more sensitive to increases in advertising frequency. For both high- and low-awareness brands, gains were still being achieved at the end of the campaign. Also for both, the magnitude of change was greater for measures of behavior than for measures of attitude.

6. *Awareness of advertising may understate the effects of advertising.* Although awareness of advertising increased during the test, these increases did not consistently reflect changes in attitudes that resulted from the advertising.

For example, in an average week, 14 percent of respondents in the control group reported seeing advertising for high-awareness brands in the past four weeks. However, they were not exposed to any advertising for these brands in that period. At the same time, 75 percent of respondents in the high-frequency group reported seeing no advertising for these brands. This was despite the fact that they had opportunities to see 48 ads in the period.

More significant, changes reported for such measures of advertising effectiveness as brand awareness rose more rapidly than did awareness of advertising. This indicates that people are affected by advertising even when they claim they cannot recall having seen it.

In sum, the findings suggest that while awareness of advertising can provide some indication of consumer response to advertising, it is, at the same time, limited in its ability to reflect accurately the effectiveness of advertising.

CONCLUSIONS[6]

The study was designed specifically to explore the effects of frequent magazine advertising on attitudes and purchasing behavior.

The findings, however, also offer insights into the dynamics of advertising

[6]This section is adapted from ibid., pp. 19–21.

itself and provide clues that could have practical application in planning media strategies.

1. *Magazine advertising works.* At its most basic level, the study reaffirms the effectiveness of magazines as an advertising medium.

As the data demonstrate, "opportunities to see" advertising in magazines dramatically increase brand awareness. To an even greater degree, it produces favorable attitudes toward advertised brands and stimulates product purchase. This is true even when the people affected cannot recall having seen the advertising.

More important, gains in reported brand purchase are greater than gains in favorable brand rating. This seems to suggest that advertising in general and magazine advertising in particular may trigger changes in behavior without corresponding changes in attitude.

Several conclusions are also clear about the effects of increasing the frequency of opportunities to see advertising.

2. *More is better.* Although reported gains in the levels of response to study measurements are not always proportional to increases in opportunities to see advertising, the data show that greater frequency does result in greater advertising effect.

The relationship between increased frequency and increased advertising effect is particularly apparent for low-awareness brands.

3. *There are no fixed rules for effective frequency.* The data also indicate that no fixed, specific number of ads is necessary to change attitudes effectively. No minimum number appears to be required. The first ad produced a significant effect.

There is no maximum frequency level after which ads seem to lose effectiveness. Awareness and favorable attitude levels were still on the rise at the end of the 48-week study.

4. *"Low-awareness" brands benefit the most from heavy, sustained frequency.* Data seem to indicate that new brands or low-awareness brands might have the most to gain from frequent advertising.

This is perhaps true because consumers have no preconceived opinions of these brands and therefore have no deeply entrenched attitudes to overcome. Whatever the explanation, there appears to be a direct relationship between increasing frequency and increasing effectiveness. For low-awareness brands, more seems almost always to be better.

5. *For "high-awareness" brands studied, campaign duration appears to be important.* For high-awareness brands, the first ad produces a substantial increase in awareness and favorable attitude. This, in turn, is followed by a temporary fall back and a subsequent return to rising levels of awareness and favorable brand rating. This seems to suggest that a campaign of extended duration may be required to overcome entrenched attitudes toward these brands.

6. *Other observations.* In assessing the results of the study, it should be

emphasized that all products studied were low-usage brands that had not been advertised in the test markets for some time. The study did not examine the effect of frequency on heavily advertised, high-awareness, high-usage brands.

Therefore, no firm conclusions about the effect of frequency on established brands of this nature can be drawn from the findings. A cessation or reduction in advertising might harm such brands, however. If a leading brand were to lose acceptance as a result of a reduction in advertising, it would have difficulty regaining its position in the marketplace, the data suggest.

It should also be noted that the study findings represent only the minimal effects of advertising. First, a repeat purchase or a first purchase made by a respondent after the 48-week study period would not have shown up in the data. Second, liquor advertising, in general, is severely limited in its creative approach. Due to governmental and industry restrictions, benefits cannot be claimed, and it is forbidden to depict liquor consumption.

It is likely, therefore, that reported gains would have been greater had the ads studied been fewer. It is probable also that a study of longer duration would have revealed greater long-term changes in respondent attitudes and purchase patterns.

In addition, the insertion of as many as six liquor advertisements per issue also created a magazine environment with greater clutter than is usual. If, as some theorize, advertising effectiveness is diminished by clutter, then the effectiveness of the advertisements studied, particularly at the highest levels of frequency, was probably understated.

Director of research for Time Inc.'s magazine group, Robert Schreiber summed it up: "This study shows that advertising really works. Intuitively we have always believed this; now here is the evidence to back it up." Should advertisers and agencies be skeptical of the results because Time Inc., was a sponsor? "Absolutely not," rejoined Schreiber, "because the other partner in the pioneering venture was Seagram, which had no vested interest whatsoever in promoting the value of increased advertising. Further, the outside research agencies involved are noted for their integrity."

Your Task:

Comment on the value of this landmark study (1) to advertisers and (2) to media.

Appendix

QUESTIONNAIRE

This is an edited version of the questionnaire used in the Time Inc./ Seagram research. Response categories for products have been omitted to avoid identifying brands under study.

1. Which of the following beverages have you had in the past 4 weeks? (Check as many as apply.)

   ☐ Coffee   ☐ Soft drinks   ☐ Wine
   ☐ Tea   ☐ Beer   ☐ Liquor

2. Please check the brands of beer listed below you have ever heard of.
3. Please check the brands of wine listed below you have ever heard of. As an aid to help you answer the next few questions, we have enclosed pictures of the bottles of the next group of brands, about which we would like your opinion. When answering the following questions, please refer to these pictures.
4. Please check the brands of liquor listed below you have ever heard of.
5. Now, we would like you to give your overall impression of each brand listed below, based on any experience you have had or anything you have heard or read about each brand.

   To do this, please rate each brand by using the 0 to 10 scale shown here. The more favorable you feel about a brand, the higher you should rate it. The less favorable you feel about a brand, the lower you should rate it. A "0" rating means you feel the brand is one of the worst of its type and a "10" rating means you think it is one of the best of its type.

   For each brand, please circle how you yourself rate the brand, feeling free to use any number on the scale that best describes how you feel.
6. In column 1 below, please check the brands of liquor you yourself have ever used, at home or in a bar, cocktail lounge, or restaurant.
7. In column 2 below, check the brands of liquor you yourself have used in the past 3 months, at home or in a bar, cocktail lounge, or restaurant.
8. In column 3 below, please check the brands of liquor you yourself have used in the past 4 weeks, at home or in a bar, cocktail lounge, or restaurant.
9. Now, in column 1 below, please check the brands of liquor you bought a bottle(s) of in the past 3 months, for your own use, to serve to guests, or as a gift.
10. In column 2 below, please check the brands of liquor you bought a bottle(s) of in the past 4 weeks, for your own use, to serve to guests, or as a gift.
11. In the past 4 weeks, did you happen to go to a store to buy a bottle(s) of liquor, ask for one of the brands listed below (under Q. 12), and find that the store did not have that brand in stock?

    ☐ Yes   ☐ No

    If yes in Q. 11, answer Q. 12.

Appendix (Cont.)

12. Please check which, if any, of the following brands you asked for but found that the store did not have.

13. Suppose you were going out to buy some bottles of liquor today, for your own use, to serve to guests, or as a gift. For each brand listed below, please check how likely you would be to consider buying it. (For each brand listed, check one box on each line.)

14. Some people only have a cocktail or a drink of liquor at social gatherings or on special occasions, while other people find it relaxing to have a cocktail or liquor drink before meals or in the evening after work. Generally speaking, please check the statement below that comes closest to how often you yourself have a cocktail or liquor drink. (Check only one answer.)

☐ More than once a day
☐ Once a day
☐ Two or three times a week
☐ Once a week
☐ Two or three times a month
☐ Once a month
☐ Once every two months
☐ Two or three times a year or less often
☐ Never have a liquor drink

15. Please check how often you or someone else in your household serve cocktails or liquor drinks to guests in your home. (Check only one answer.)

☐ More than once a week
☐ Once a week
☐ Two or three times a month
☐ Once a month
☐ Once every two months
☐ Two or three times a year or less often
☐ Never serve a liquor drink

16. For each type of liquor listed below, please check whether or not you yourself happened to drink that type of liquor, either straight or in a mixed drink, in the past 6 months. (Please be sure to answer for each type of liquor.)
    For each type of liquor you have had in the past 6 months, answer Q. 17.

17. For each type of liquor you happened to drink in the past 6 months, please check the statement which comes closest to describing how often you had it. (Please give one answer for each type of liquor you drank in the past 6 months.)

18. For each type of liquor listed below, please check whether or not you or someone else in your household served it to guests in your home anytime in the past 6 months. (Please be sure to answer for each type of liquor.)
    For each type of liquor served to guests in past 6 months, answer Q. 19.

19. For each type of liquor served to guests in the past 6 months, please check the statement which best describes how often you served it. (Please give one answer for each type of liquor you served to guests in the past 6 months.)

Appendix (Cont.)

Question 18	Vodka	Cordial or Liqueur	Bourbon, Rye, Canadian or Blended Whiskey	Scotch
Have served in home to guests in past 6 months	☐	☐	☐	☐
Have not served to guests in past 6 months	☐	☐	☐	☐
Question 19				
More than once a week	☐	☐	☐	☐
Once a week	☐	☐	☐	☐
Two or three times a month	☐	☐	☐	☐
Once a month	☐	☐	☐	☐
Once every two months	☐	☐	☐	☐
Two or three times a year or less often	☐	☐	☐	☐
Never serve this type of liquor drink	☐	☐	☐	☐

20. In column I below, check the brands you recall noticing any advertising for in the past 3 months.

21. In column 2 below, check the brands you recall noticing any advertising for in the past 4 weeks.

Now, just a few questions for classification purposes:

22. What is your sex?
    ☐ Male   ☐ Female

23. What is your age?
    ☐ Under 25   ☐ 35–49   ☐ 65 or older
    ☐ 25–34   ☐ 50–64

24. What is the highest level of schooling attained?
    ☐ Grade school   ☐ Some high school
    ☐ Completed high school   ☐ Some postgraduate school
    ☐ Some college   ☐ Postgraduate degree
    ☐ Graduated college

25. Is the head of your household
    ☐ Employed full-time?   ☐ Not employed?
    ☐ Employed part-time?

26. Please check the category of employment
    ☐ Professional
    (such as doctor, attorney, teacher)
    ☐ Management/executive
    ☐ Own a small business
    ☐ Salesman
    ☐ Clerical (such as secretary, typist, clerk)
    ☐ Skilled trade/technician (such as farmer, truck driver, construction, machinist)
    ☐ General/labor
    (such as janitor, domestic, laborer)

Appendix (Cont.)

☐ Uniformed services
   (such as policeman, fireman, armed services)
☐ Retired
☐ Student

27. What do you estimate your total family income was in the past 12 months? (Please include income from all family members and all sources, such as wages, profits, dividends, rentals, etc.)

☐ Under $10,000   ☐ $35,000–$49,999
☐ $10,000–$14,999   ☐ $50,000–$74,999
☐ $15,000–$19,999   ☐ $75,000–$99,999
☐ $20,000–$24,999   ☐ $100,000 and over
☐ $25,000–$34,999

Source: "Major Study Details Ad Effect on Sales," pp. 52–54.

case
28

ADOLPH COORS COMPANY

Having risen from twelfth to fourth position between 1965 and 1969, dropping to fifth in 1975, then slipping to sixth place among the nation's brewers in 1982, Adolph Coors Company began to weigh alternatives for turning around shrinking sales. In the second quarter, shipments in the Coors 20-state marketing area were 3,056,000 barrels, a decline of 13 percent from the same period in 1981. As recently as the mid-1970s, the company had rationed its output among distributors without vigorously promoting the product.

BACKGROUND

Gateway to the gold fields, Saturday-night carousing spot for local cowboys, stopover for those intrepid souls crossing the Continental Divide, a way-off-Broadway arena where Buffalo Bill delighted crowds with his Wild West Shows—that is the Golden, Colorado, that was. Remnants of the Old West linger in this historic city—the Colorado Railroad Museum is a notable vestige—but today the old and new have merged. In the winter Golden is a crossroads for skiers and in the summer a curiosity for tourists. The Colorado School of Mines adds an educational flavor to the community of 9,800 population. The town's primary focal point, however, is a surreal complex of concrete, steel, copper, asphalt, and glass rooted firmly in the 5,600-foot-elevation canyon, shaded by its Castle Rock trademark. This is the Adolph Coors Company, in 1982 employing 3,500 people in Jefferson County, of which Golden is the county seat.

Immigrant entrepreneur Adolph Herman Joseph Coors, with partner Jacob Schueler, established a brewery in spring-laden Clear Creek Valley in 1873; in 1880, at age 33, Coors became sole owner. The company flourished until 1916 when Prohibition forced a shift to other endeavors—producing malted milk, near beer, skim milk crystals, sweet butter, and double rich cream—in order to survive. With repeal in 1933, 750 of some 1,600 U.S. breweries that had existed two decades earlier resumed production. Coors brewed 136,720 barrels of beer that year, reviving the dynasty founded on Rocky Mountain Spring Water.

Exhibit 1 is a narrative description of the business as reported to the Securities and Exchange Commission.

Exhibit 1

NARRATIVE DESCRIPTION OF THE BUSINESS*

The Company presently has one brewing facility, now the largest in the United States, and has achieved a high degree of vertical integration in brewing-related operations. Substantially all of the Company's malt requirements are produced in the Company's own malting facility. The Company pioneered the development of the two-piece aluminum can and manufactures all of its own aluminum can requirements. The Company's glass bottle manufacturing plant supplies substantially all of its own glass bottle requirements. The Company designs and constructs a majority of its own facilities. Approximately 1,100 engineers and construction workers are employed by the Company on a full-time basis for these purposes. The Company has provided for certain of its energy requirements through the development of its own natural gas reserves with associated gathering and transmission systems and through the acquisition and mining of coal reserves. In addition, the Company has acquired rights to sources of water for industrial uses and for use in its brewing process. The Company has its own waste treatment facility. The Company operates seven wholesale beer distribution outlets. During 1981, the Company's trucking subsidiary hauled approximately 8% of total beer shipments from the brewery.

The Company believes its technologically advanced brewing facility, coupled with the use of carefully selected raw materials, enables it to produce beer of a uniformly high quality. Coors is brewed using a natural fermentation process which does not require the use of additives. The

Exhibit 1 (Cont.)

Company brews and packages Coors under aseptic conditions which eliminates the need for heat pasteurization. The Company is committed to maintaining refrigerated temperatures throughout packaging and distribution operations because it believes that controlled temperature is the most essential factor in the preservation of fresh beer flavor. After being packaged at near freezing temperatures, Coors is loaded directly into insulated railcars or refrigerated trucks for immediate shipments to the Company's distributors. All distributors' warehouses are refrigerated to keep Coors at proper temperatures until it is delivered to retail accounts in refrigerated trucks. In addition, retailers are encouraged to keep Coors refrigerated until purchased by consumers. Distributors are responsible for maintaining proper rotation of Coors at their own expense if sale to consumers has not occurred within a time period prescribed by the Company. This rotation is required by the Company because it believes that the flavor qualities of Coors, as with any beer, diminish over time.

*Company's Form 10-K, December 2, 1981.

In the 1980s, with an estimated 100 breweries operating in the United States, merger and acquisition ferment dominated industry headlines. Some intended coalitions were presumably designed to face off against the tough competition of Anheuser-Busch and Miller, which together dominated over half of 1981 industry sales. Detroit-based, privately held Stroh Brewery acquired the Joseph Schlitz Brewing Company, making it third largest in the nation, a union with the ostensible purpose of reversing Schlitz's market share slide, but raising doubts from some quarters that the company could boost promotional expenditures and expand markets for Schlitz after servicing the debt to be incurred for acquiring the firm. In an attempt to form the world's fourth largest brewer, Pabst reportedly offered over $35 million for a 49 percent interest in Olympia Brewing, and Pabst itself was being viewed by G. Heileman Brewing Company as a purchase target. Brewers eyed expanding West Coast and Southwest markets as holding the greatest potential in the United States for expanding sales. Market share leaders in 1982 were Anheuser-Busch, Miller, Stroh/Schlitz, Heileman, Pabst/Olympia, and Coors, in descending order. The 10 largest U.S. producers dominated approximately 94 percent of the market.

New beers and market tests were widespread in 1982. As an example, Henry Winhard's Private Reserve, a Pabst Brewing Company (Portland-based) product, was expanding from its West Coast introduction to tests in the Midwest and East; this brand reported garnering substantial market shares when tested in western markets against Anheuser-Busch's Michelob. There was speculation that U.S. unemployment in the East had led to hard-core beer drinkers becoming more price-conscious, presaging in that region a negative impact on the premium-priced newcomer. Schlitz and Pabst were readying new light beer entries, and Budweiser Light was gaining acceptance in many markets, presumably cutting into Miller Brewing's Lite and the Coors Light segments. Superpremium Stroh Signature debuted in the spring, aiming, according to the advertisements, for the entrepreneurial individualist who is an independent thinker, likely to be a business maverick, definitely not a big-corporation executive type. In the Stroh broadcast advertisements, an announcer's voiceover linked the beer's quality to the Stroh family's 200 years of brewing experience. Coors's emphasis on Herman Joseph's 1868, the superpremium beer, and George Killian's Irish Red ale accelerated in postmarket test rollouts.

OFFICE OF THE PRESIDENT

Coors brothers Joe and Bill occupy side-by-side desks in an unimposing executive suite at the Golden headquarters. Absence of decorative trappings reflect informal relationships that the two corporate leaders were quick to say "put all of us here on a first-name basis." Coats and ties are scarce throughout the

---

Exhibit 2

LETTER TO SHAREHOLDERS

Adolph Coors Company takes great pride in the technological and brewing expertise that for 108 years has enabled us to make the finest beer possible. As we move forward through the 80s, this technological edge continues to apply to the beer business and has also taken us successfully into a number of related business endeavors. . . . However, our beer business, which continues to be the foundation of our company's strength and accounts for approximately 85 percent of consolidated net sales, had a disappointing year as we did not attain either profit or barrel sales objectives.

EARNINGS AND SALES

Net income for 1981 was $51,970,000 or $1.48 per share, down 20 percent from $64,977,000, or $1.86 per share, in 1980. This earnings decrease is attributed to a decline in beer shipments coupled with increased operating costs. . . .

Exhibit 2 (Cont.)

Record net sales were achieved in 1981 totaling $929,916,000, a 4.7 percent increase over $887,897,000 in 1980. The increase was due principally to higher beer selling prices and an increase in non-beer business sales.

Beer shipments were 13,261,000 barrels in 1981 compared to the record 13,779,000 barrels sold in 1980. This represented a 3.8 percent decrease in barrel sales while total industry sales increased approximately 2 percent. Our decrease in beer shipments during the year can be attributed to intense competitive pressures in our markets. We hope our expansion into new states will begin to offset those pressures.

PRODUCTS

The consumer acceptance of Coors Light continues to excite us. In only three years, Coors Light has made significant gains against competitive brands, moving to number one in many major markets. A quality beer, an effective marketing program, and a strong sales effort have made Coors Light a winner. Sales increased approximately 35 percent over last year.

We expanded the test market of Herman Joseph's 1868, our superpremium beer. Initial reception of this product in its test markets—including Dallas and Denver—has been encouraging. We are strengthening the marketing campaign for this product and will continue to measure its performance in test market situations.

In 1981 we began producing and test marketing George Killian's Irish Red ale. George Killian's has a unique color and taste which appeals to a broad spectrum of beer drinkers. Its success in selected test markets in California, Colorado and Kansas during the year led to the decision to roll out the product in major portions of our marketing area in 1982.

Quality beer of recognizable superiority remains our greatest strength. We are uncompromising in this area, and in 1981 efforts were expanded to seek new ways of improving the already high quality of our products.

EXPANSION

Mississippi, northern Louisiana, and central and western Tennessee were added to our marketing territory in 1981. Consumers have responded enthusiastically to the distribution of Coors products in these states. Competition in these areas is very intense, but we are confident that our new distributors will meet this challenge. While we look forward to ultimately distributing beer in additional states, we are currently intensifying efforts to regain growth trends in existing markets. . . .

Exhibit 2 (Cont.)

In 1981 the company completed the acquisition of 2,100 acres of land near Elkton, Virginia, which will be held as a site for a potential second brewery. This Virginia property satisfies our needs for water quality and availability, transportation needs and fuel sources. However, we have not made a decision to begin construction of a brewery on this property.

Research and project development costs totaled $16,848,000 in 1981 compared to $14,256,000 the year before. These expenditures included development of Herman Joseph's and George Killian's, in addition to new brewing and packaging techniques.

THE FUTURE

Meeting the challenges ahead isn't going to be easy. For the immediate future, we intend to move Coors back into the number one position in our sales territory. We remain confident that the expertise, dedication and determination of our people, along with the high quality of our products, will ensure that we will again achieve our long-standing tradition of not only meeting objectives but exceeding the goals we set for ourselves.

William K. Coors
Chairman and
Chief Executive Officer

Joseph Coors
President and
Chief Operating Officer

March 5, 1982

Source: 1981 Annual Report, pp. 2–3.

---

plant. "And when we call it the office of the president, we don't mean there's a consensus on everything. There are two of us here—before our brother died, there were three of us—and we often have conflicting opinions about how to run the organization," Bill Coors explained. It was easy to see how this friendly, attentive, and astute man could inspire confidence among managers, employees, and the public in general. At the casewriter's first interview, Bill Coors was preparing a speech to be given that day at a local civic organization luncheon, but he put the notes aside and gave full attention to the visitor.

Exhibit 2 contains selected paragraphs from the chairman and president's March 1982 letter to shareholders. The appendix presents an overview of Coors's sales and marketing, distribution, operations, and miscellaneous aspects of the company's and products' profiles.

SELECTED FINANCIAL DATA

Exhibit 3 presents selected financial features, consolidated for Coors Energy Company, an exploration program; Coors Food Products Company; Coors Container Company; Golden Recycle Company; and Coors Transportation Company.

In 1977 13,545,000 barrels were sold, with a dropoff to 12,824,000 in 1978. A continuing slide to 12,566,000 was experienced in 1979, followed by increases each of the next two years, and then another decline in 1982. Given trends during the first half of 1982, it was likely that sales would suffer even more in the year ending February 28, 1983.

In the five years from 1978 to 1982, company strategy was to increase advertising budgets, to bring out new brands, to expand distribution to additional states, and, in 1982, to make certain organizational changes for streamlining the marketing function and facilitating future changes in the corporate suite. While volume was boosted from 12,566,000 barrels in fiscal year 1978 to 12,912,000 in 1979 and 13,779,000 in 1980, operating income was reduced and profits suffered. In fiscal year 1981, net income was $52 million, down 20 percent from $65 million in 1980, a decrease attributable to declines in beer shipments coupled with steeper operating costs. Barrels sold declined 3.8 percent, and although net dollar sales for beer went up 3.9 percent, from $758 million to $788 million, operating income from beer dropped 26 percent, from approximately $87 million to $64 million. In California, its largest market, Coors commanded less than 20 percent of 1981 beer sales, down from 45 percent in 1976.

Exhibit 3

SELECTED FINANCIAL DATA, FISCAL YEARS ENDING
FEBRUARY 28, 1979–1982
(in thousands)

	1982	1981	1980	1979
Barrels sold (000s)	13,261	13,779	12,912	12,566
Net sales, beer business	$787,739	$758,017	$638,768	$549,448
Net sales, other businesses	142,177	129,880	101,736	75,356
	$929,916	$887,897	$740,504	$624,804
Operating income, beer	$ 64,100	$ 86,637	$ 97,951	$ 78,647
Operating income, other	7,997	10,953	9,882	6,905
Assets, beer business	754,108	703,623	649,692	605,301
Assets, other businesses	125,662	102,870	78,040	57,579
Assets, corporate	76,614	87,883	101,213	88,550
	$956,384	$894,385	$828,945	$751,610

MARKETING ORGANIZATION

The reins at Coors, which was over 75 percent family owned, were passing from one generation of the family, brothers William K. Coors, age 65 (who remained in the executive suite as chairman), and Joseph Coors, age 64, president, to Joe's sons, Peter H. Coors, age 35, and Jeffrey H. Coors, age 37, who in June 1982, were named division presidents. Thus, the two-generation administrative Zeitgeist was to be blended, with the younger team evolving into roles of strategic command. The four-man president's office was augmented by Robert A. Rechholtz, who came from Schlitz to Coors as senior vice president of marketing in late 1981 and was named to the post of executive vice president as the mid-1982 managerial changes were instituted.

Evident in the interaction of Peter and Jeffrey Coors and Robert Rechholtz was a camaraderie and mutual commitment to get the company on track to improved performance. In August 1982, the marketing organization appeared as represented in Exhibit 4. Not shown on the chart are seven Coors-owned distributors whose primary interactions were with the sales managers who handled personal selling for the 20 states.

In 1982 the vice president for brands' staff managed premium, light, George Killian, corporate advertising, and media. The director of market development's staff conducted market research, managed new product introductions, and was responsible for the marketing information system. The director of marketing services' group covered four support functions, including merchandising and sales promotion, special markets, special events and product publicity, and creative services. It was anticipated that the morphology of marketing's domain would remain essentially unchanged in the wake of upper-echelon alterations.

The company had experienced some turnover at vice-presidential levels when, in the fall of 1980, the marketing vice president, John Nichols, left after two years on the staff to become a Coors distributor in Nashville, and Fred Vierra, who had been vice president of sales for about the same period of time, resigned to join a cable television firm. Their departures coincided with intensified price promotion and related efforts by Anheuser-Busch and Miller.

Peter Coors reflected management's feelings regarding Robert Rechholtz: "Bob Rechholtz brings something to Coors I don't have—a lot of experience in consumer products marketing and the beer business. Neither his two guys, both of whom are very bright, nor I have the marketing experience to take on the challenge of this assignment. And he is a team player, our sort of person. At lunch recently, one of our people asked him how long it would take to fix things around Coors, and he responded he wasn't going to fix anything but that he and I and the staff would act in concert for the benefit of the company. He knows our industry and is quickly learning all he needs to know about Coors. He exceeds even my original expectations and is clearly dedicated to keeping this company in a leadership position."

Exhibit 4

COORS MARKETING ORGANIZATION, AUGUST 1982

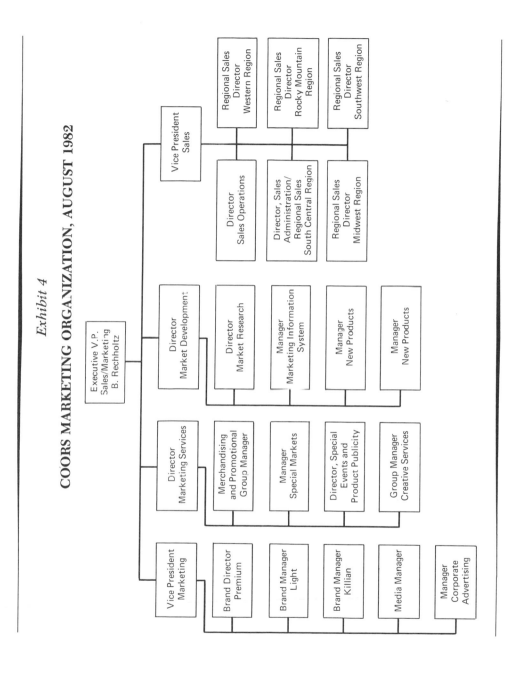

Selected points from Robert Rechholtz's background are summarized in Exhibit 5.

In early December 1981, shortly after joining Coors, Rechholtz noted: "My most important goal right now is to understand the company. I've been here just a few weeks, too little time to understand fully the policies, operating procedures, the key people's thinking, even what's up with my own marketing staff. At the moment we are conducting reviews of problems and opportunities, strengths, and weaknesses. This company is a believer in continually examining and, when necessary, redefining its corporate mission. I need to have a better grasp of our resource capabilities before I will feel comfortable doing much strategic planning. Who knows—we may have to change priorities. I can't say right now."

Rechholtz reflected on the qualities he appreciated most in the Coors presidential pair: "Bill and Joe represent an ideology I share—honest, tough, loyal. You only go around once in life, so you might as well get the most out of it, and the best thing in it for me is a challenge like this assignment. After four years in the beer business, I feel this is where I belong. Coors is in a position to

---

Exhibit 5

CONDENSED BIOGRAPHICAL SUMMARY FOR R. A. RECHHOLTZ

Robert A. Rechholtz is senior vice president, marketing, for Adolph Coors Company.

Mr. Rechholtz has a broad background in marketing and corporate development with several major packaged goods industries. Before joining Coors, he was senior vice president, marketing, for the Jos. Schlitz Brewing Company. He began his career in 1958 with Procter & Gamble in soap products advertising. He subsequently held marketing and planning positions with the R. J. Reynolds Tobacco Company, E. & J. Gallo Winery, and Ligget Group.

During his career, Rechholtz has been active in many professional organizations, including the Association of National Advertisers, the Tobacco Institute, and various state and national brewing associations. He has lectured widely at the college and professional levels. Publications include releases through ANA on new product development, budgeting, and advertising effectiveness.

R. Rechholtz was born in New York City. He is a 1958 graduate of the University of North Carolina, where he was elected to Phi Beta Kappa. He and his wife Caroline have three daughters, including an undergraduate at the University of Colorado.

---

meet its challenges and I'm excited about what the future holds for us. Coors is technically superior to all the others. They just can't make what we can. Ours is certainly a unique product, and my commission is to take care of and to build this franchise."

NEW PRODUCTS, STRATEGIES, AND PRICING

Various executives discussed new products, strategies, and pricing for Herman Joseph's 1868: "We've been in test market with Herman Joseph's two years now, since 1980," Peter Coors said, "an unusually long time, and mainly because results have been somewhat mixed. We started in Fresno, Sacramento, the Valley, San Diego, Phoenix, and Austin (Texas), thinking all those somewhat isolated markets would give us a good cross section. San Diego is especially good because of hitting the idea of a 'fuller-bodied beer.' In other words, we pushed what we thought consumers were telling us they wanted. And we priced at 10 to 25 cents above Michelob.

"Michelob is the premium market leader, and success for HJ means we have to take share away from them. Since they went to Michelob Light—and they did this because of a fear that customers would be eroded from Michelob by other brands—both Michelobs combined have 65 to 70 percent nationwide market share—around 10 million barrels—in this product category.

"Our campaigns for HJ and George Killian's are targeted at the young adult consumer group. We have realized high trial rates and high awareness, but consumers were saying, 'We've been drinking Michelob 10 years now and there's no need to change,' so repurchase rates were disappointing, not what we had expected. We modified the formulation for HJ from an 80 percent malt blend to a 70 percent blend and readjusted our pricing to be head-up with Michelob. Our initial strategy of indicating higher quality by a higher retail price was not successful.

"Then we ordered additional markets—the rest of Arizona, New Mexico, Midland-Odessa (Texas)—and saw some improvement, recently quite a bit of improvement. Dallas and Fort Worth results have been right on target, and we are getting closer to the formulation we want. Herman Joseph's is our first departure from identification with the Adolph Coors Company, so we didn't know what to expect close to home. But after adding Denver and the rest of the Colorado market, results have been excellent. We are very excited about it, and if we can translate that into other markets, we're going to be in good shape on this product.

"To get repeat purchasing, we're trying sweepstakes, using in-store, point-of-sale materials to influence buyers. But I must say that the jury is still out on HJ and Killian's. We don't have enough evidence yet to be completely confident that we should go full scale with the products as they are.

"Killian's has been handled differently from Herman Joseph's. We gave it heavy promotion at first and could see good spikes in two to three weeks, high sell-through at retail levels, then the curve would slide off when the distribution pipeline would fill up. Although we have had no direct retaliation on Killian's tests, Michelob came in with aggressive price competition in response to our Joseph's efforts. In some markets we've seen Michelob even lower-priced than Budweiser.

"We've taken Killian's into new test market areas so it wouldn't be confused with HJ. To begin with, we chose Santa Barbara-Monterey, and we also went into Wichita and western Kansas, along with southern Colorado. In those places our strategy has been to push more selectively in retail outlets and without heavy mass media. The sales curve is steadily increasing, new customers and repeat customers coming in to replace those who drop out.

"There are five states where we couldn't initially have a full rollout of these products. For example, Washington, where all beverages with alcohol content over 4 percent by weight must be sold through state liquor stores. We didn't want that hassle. In Nebraska, state law dictated we couldn't use 11-ounce containers. In Oklahoma and Utah, there are 3.2 laws; we can't sell in excess of 3.2 percent by weight alcohol in Utah and we can in Oklahoma, but Oklahoma has other restrictive laws. And we can't sell it as a draft product in Texas because it exceeds 4 percent by weight alcohol. Except for Nebraska, these difficulties have been solved.

"Killian's is unique; it has a purpose for being—a lot of color, flavor, uniqueness not in any other product brewed in this country. Herman Joseph's doesn't have that unique positioning that would make it more than just another superpremium beer."

Peter Coors asked and answered a question about volume. "Do I think we'll hit 20 million barrels in the mid-1980s? Perhaps, but I am not betting on it. Two critical forces have hit us. Miller Brewing Company has changed the ball game by applying cigarette marketing concepts, and Anheuser-Busch wouldn't be denied, coming back against the Philip Morris subsidiary with very heavy advertising guns. Miller then claimed to be shooting for number one spot in U.S. beer business by 1980, and Anheuser responded with a vengeance. We were late fighting back.

"Coors was perceived as America's fine light beer. Then Miller's Lite came out, leaving our main brand with a somewhat confused image. In 1978 we hit with Coors Light, a move that saved our bacon. The textbook says you shouldn't do a line extension when you have a failing brand, but we analyzed what was happening and decided to give our customers an alternative, which was fewer calories in the Coors brand name."

On Peter Coors's perceptions of immediate problems: "Our marketing staff's problem in the next couple of years is to find a positioning for Coors, our flagship brand, that will eliminate the erosion of that brand, to get it turned around, to get back into the growth mode. We still have a strong franchise of Coors loyalists, very strong in the younger segment, which portends well for the future. But what happens when they mature and become more serious beer drinkers? They may not see Coors as their sort of product.

"So, do we go to a male macho beer and lock horns with the others who have done that? Or do we go line extension? Is there a place for a Coors Stout or something else with our name on it? And, if so, how do we formulate it and promote it? In other words, how do we go about protecting our franchise?"

The vice president of marketing development discussed Herman Joseph's 1868: "It's no big secret what our target is—it's Michelob—and because Anheuser-Busch has been in the field for years, we're playing catch-up on superpremiums. During the initial test marketing in 1980, we decided to lighten the original recipe for this one.

"It's no secret that Coors has been a latecomer to this new products arena. This has been an important learning process for us, but it became obvious in the late 1970s that we couldn't stick to what we were doing and not bring out products to appeal to the various important segments, and still stay up with the front-runners.

"When our marketing research people quizzed Michelob drinkers about what they were looking for in a beer, they kept focusing on robustness. 'Robust' seemed to be the key word. But this tells you something about how such responses can be misleading. We brewed such a taste in the original formulation of Herman Joseph's, but soon decided that what beer drinkers were saying and what they were drinking were completely different. So, in the trials, the malt in the Coors superpremium entry was lightened. I liken it to the Edsel—what drivers said they wanted in a car didn't turn out to be their idea of a perfect automobile. What we are discovering all over again is that we have to put out a product that doesn't merely meet buyers' expectations but that exceeds them. Promotional positioning is critical.

"Positioning is a key dimension and so is price. When we're going after those market segments, we must have the right combination of ingredients and a price that tells consumers this is a unique brew. The industry defines superpremium on a price basis—it costs more than the others, at least a dollar more a six pack."

Another new entry from Coors, George Killian's Irish Red ale, is a darker, fuller-bodied drink than most, intended to capture some of the imported beer market. He continued: "In our George Killian's, we have duplicated the original bottle used in Ireland where this ale was brewed by one family for over a hundred years. In getting the special shape of the bottle, and to meet specifications for bottle height on the production line, the product turned out to be 11 ounces, an ounce less than competitors' products. We had some concern that the customers might think they were getting ripped off, but we've been right up front about it and it hasn't been a problem. This is an authentic product, authentically brewed.

"Killian's test results have been very favorable, even a higher response in some test markets than we anticipated. The reddish ale gets its color and taste from a longer-roasted malt, different hopping from the other Coors's products, fermentation at a higher temperature, and a higher alcohol content. One reason for more alcohol is that ales are required by law in some states to have more alcohol in them."

According to a Killian's assistant brand manager, 40 percent of superpremiums and imports were consumed by 18- to 24-year-olds, many buying impulsively. Bill Coors remarked, "Our consumer research showed that people drinking light beer didn't especially like it, but they thought it liked them."

"In looking back about 10 years, light beers and what we now call superpremiums weren't around," observed Robert Rechholtz, "but today, in 1982, they represent approximately 25 percent of the total beer market. Coors Light has been a bright spot for the company. This low-calorie beer's volume accounts for over one-fifth of our total sales; about a fourth of the volume has been cannibalized from other products. In this race it runs neck-and-neck with Miller's national leader, Lite, and now must compete in its key markets against Budweiser Light, which is being heavily promoted in two of Coors's key states, California and Texas. Both Miller and Anheuser are putting increased emphasis on regional marketing. And one of their clear-cut goals is to do battle with Coors in its traditional strongholds."

"I'm not familiar with how Bud Light is doing in the marketplace," related Bill Coors, "but it is watered-down Budweiser beer, not a thoroughly fermented-out beer, just diluted to the 100-calorie level to meet the qualification of being light beer. Our laboratory tests indicate that Michelob Light is nothing more than 3.2 Michelob. Dilution does cause a beer to lose some of the hop character, so they might have added a hop infusion to get the flavor back. The average beer," he explained, "has 160 calories per 12 ounces; a fully fermented-out beer of the same alcoholic strength has about 120 calories, but if you get below that you must cut it, and this is done by putting in more water. My obsession is to get all our beers right—that's what we've been doing during my 40-plus years in the company. There's always room for improvement, and perfecting the products we sell is my primary involvement in the company. But the time frame is years, not months. I'm glad to say we're getting about 25 percent of our volume from Coors Light, and that's because we're emphasizing the taste, not the calories. But it also accounts for some of the drop in market share of our other beers."

Rechholtz stated, "Coors is sold in market areas where about 40 percent of the U.S. population is located. We are in the right locations, but prefer the West over the East although competition out here is getting as bad as in the eastern states, and pricing has become a problem. This is unfortunate. Brewers have taken to pricing as an element of marketing strategy. Price-cutting simply means we are trading dollars with one another from promotion to promotion. Of course, it is a benefit to the consumer. Coors is meeting competition in price promotion but strives to maintain a strong price-value relationship. Our basic strategy is to maintain the quality image of Coors beers and to help sustain this to some extent through pricing, being at least head-up with Miller and Bud, for example. Average prices for Bud, regardless of posted price, are always less than for Coors, so Anheuser-Busch is buying share by pricing. Last winter it raised prices on all products. However, A–B is the price leader because it is the market leader."

In early fall, 1982, Anheuser-Busch announced its choice of Fort Collins as a future site for a $400 million brewery should it decide to build in Colorado, a decision to be made during 1983. Tentative plans called for operations to begin in 1986.[1]

OTHER COMPETITION

While the U.S. beer market's total growth has been approximately 3 percent a year, imported beers rose from an estimated .5 percent of the beer market in the early 1970s to approximately 7 times that share, or 3.5 percent by 1981 and 1982. Retailers generally liked the markup on six packs that sold to consumers at from $3.75 to $8.00, although turnover in some markets was slow. But as with some of the U.S. superpremiums, it was anticipated that economic conditions would have a negative impact on 1982–1983 import sales. To appeal to the highly segmented American beer markets, and flying in the face of recession conditions, a number of new, small breweries were starting up in the United States. Some industry experts believe these premium entries and the other high-priced brands will continue to sell well because they have become part of beer drinkers' changing lifestyles. These connoisseurs would prefer to sacrifice other amenities before their drinking pleasures, according to industry observers.

Import brands numbered about 210, most with minuscule sales; only a dozen or so had measurable market shares. Cartage costs affected pricing; some foreign brewers, therefore, were evaluating production locations in this hemisphere, where Mexican and Canadian producers have a significant advantage. Just as Michelob was directed toward upscale segments when it appeared in the 1960s, the imports and American higher-priced offerings went after the urban, educated, affluent male beer drinker. Herman Joseph's 1868 and George Killian's Irish Red were promoting in this milieu.

In 1980, wine surpassed distilled spirits in U.S. beverage consumption. Two decades earlier, Americans were consuming a half gallon of table wine per capita each year, compared to 30 gallons a person in the principal wine-drinking countries of Europe. Estimates in 1982 were that about 5 percent of U.S. wine drinkers accounted for more than half the wine sales. "The news that brewers must pay attention to," said a Coors market researcher, "is that

---

[1]"Colorado Update," a newsletter published by United Banks of Colorado, Inc., Summer–Fall 1982 edition.

Americans are learning the wine habit. Nobody holds the perception anymore that wine is for foreigners, rich folk and bums. And some wineries are attempting to follow in brewers' footsteps by offering so-called 'light' wines, another attempt to increase vintners' market penetration. Still, it may work," she continued. "Since the mid-seventies, consumption of light beer has almost doubled, while there has been only about a 20 percent increase in total beer sales. Forecasting the impact of wine sales on beer sales is difficult at best, but we know there is and will be an increasing impact on our business."

PROMOTION

Peter Coors commented on changing marketing practices: "Coors has been feeling growing pains the past few years. In 1978 a substantially changed marketing emphasis was implemented, with heavy expenditures in promotion both to support our expanding distribution efforts into other states and to ward off those who were encroaching on territory in which we were the leader. There were some gains, but success has been limited because of dramatically changing competitive situations and shifts in composition of the markets themselves. And our management has had some disagreements about marketing strategy, but all that is coming into clearer focus now.

"Our 1980 growth came from expanding into the eastern United States and good results from Light. Coors's national market share last year increased by about two-tenths of a percentage point to 7.8 percent, on a 7 percent rise in volume. Outlays in 1981 of $85 million for promotion was one of the highest per barrel allotments in the industry, but that will have to be reduced because of the drag on profits.

"For years our products were so popular we didn't have to put much effort into marketing. Our reputation was such that people even bootlegged it when traveling back to their homes in the eastern and midwestern states. The mystique was legendary. Anheuser and Miller forced us to change that philosophy. We had to respond when Coors's customers were persuaded to try Bud and Miller's. Some began to switch, often on a price basis. They were chipping away at us.

"We have two ad agencies—Ted Bates and Company in New York City, which came with us in 1979, and Foote, Cone and Belding, which came aboard in 1980. Bates does the premium, Light, and Herman Joseph's campaigns; Foote, Cone and Belding handles Killian's and the Coors's corporate account."

Coors's advertising rose from a relatively low 3 percent of 1977 sales to 11 percent of 1981 sales, which was a higher percentage than Anheuser-Busch spent on advertising. See Exhibit 6 for a summary of Coors's advertising outlays.

"Corporate advertising," Peter Coors mentioned, "is now marketing's

Exhibit 6

COORS'S ADVERTISING EXPENDITURES,
1977–1982 (est.)
(in thousands)

1977	$15,500
1978	33,500
1979	46,400
1980	66,800
1981	84,500
1982 (est.)	80,000

rather than public affairs' responsibility. We'll continue some of it, but all will be tied to brand advertising. For corporate advertising, TV is the wrong medium. In any metro area, the problem is different, depending on which part of the city you are in. We have to be selective, to do pinpoint targeting of messages, even down to the neighborhood level. There's no point telling everyone we're solving a problem because most may not even be aware there is a problem."

Bill Coors reviewed changes in strategy that occurred in 1980 and 1981: "Coors launched selling efforts in Arkansas in 1980, with initial consumer response above anticipated levels. Sales to military bases in the Pacific also started in 1980, beginning in Hawaii and Alaska, with Japan and Korea added later in the year. Greater exposure was created through substantially increased advertising, sponsorships, and special promotions, to position the flagship brand as a premium beer; to align it with major competitors, the name was changed from Coors Banquet to Coors Premium, and the package was given a more streamlined look."

Peter Coors explained that the company's emphasis on promoting professional sports had included pro skiing—the Coors American Pro Tour—but this effort was dropped, primarily because costs exceeded benefits. "Skiing is not a suitable spectator event and media don't provide the coverage this sport deserves. We are now sponsoring one of the best known international bicycle races, previously called The Red Zinger and formerly the property of Celestial Seasonings (see Case 6). This nine-day event, now the Coors International Bicycle Classic, starts and finishes here on our grounds. We have also become the primary sponsor of the U.S. Volleyball Association and are a major sponsor on the professional rodeo circuit. In 1980, Tom 'The Mongoose' McEwen was a drag racing representative for Coors, and professional golfer Lee Trevino continued his promotion of our products through exhibitions and personal appearances."

Anheuser-Busch's equation to strengthen its position as the world's top brewery appeared to be special events sponsorship plus national sports plus television and radio coverage equals beer drinkers, recognizing that those who drink the most beer are sports fans and avid radio listeners and television viewers. Estimates were that 70 percent of beer sales were made to 20 percent of the drinkers. Whereas at one time the St. Louis Cardinals baseball team was Anheuser-Busch's only sports connection, the company in 1982 had a tie to almost every pro and college team in the country through participation in radio and television coverage. Baseball, football, basketball, hockey, and soccer activity were in the Anheuser-Busch sponsorship portfolio, along with special ads on golf, tennis, rowing, cycling, and horse-racing broadcasts. In the period 1976 to 1982, Anheuser's sales of all beer products increased by an estimated 85 percent, or an average of roughly 14 percent a year, in an industry with an average annual sales increase of about 3 percent.

BILL COORS'S WELLNESS CAMPAIGN

Fat bottom lines and fit employees—both were stated goals of Bill Coors, who started the Coors Wellness Center to benefit workers, managers, and executives directly and the corporation indirectly. The center has an indoor track, individual and group exercise areas, fitness testing and evaluation facilities, locker rooms, and shower facilities. A 2½-mile jogging track was planned. Group exercise includes fitness and aerobic classes, treadmills, bicycle ergometers, rowing machines, and assorted weight equipment.

"Ten years ago I said that 95 percent of all illness is a result of life-style, preventable from within. More and more people now believe in the correctness of that view, although I was definitely a prophet without honor then. Just look at the cost of health services—10 percent of our GNP and escalating. It will overwhelm us if we don't move to change it. Granted, a lot of employees think of it as some form of window dressing, but the ones using the new center are very, very grateful for it. And as we get more into it, there will be incentives for wellness and disincentives for lack of it. We want to get our people to share the risks of abusing their bodies and to reap the rewards for treating them right. If someone smokes two packs a day and comes down with emphysema, it's not right to expect the company to pay for it. If an individual has high blood pressure and won't do anything about excess weight, then we shouldn't be held responsible. You'll note that I differentiate between wellness and athletics. Athletics might just focus on recreation, but a wellness emphasis embraces stress management, nutrition, alcohol abatement and smoking cessation, drug rehabilitation, and other aspects of health. A psychologist runs the wellness center, and another person is director of health services."

Institutions in other countries—Japan, Germany, and Sweden, for example—have been supporters of fitness programs, recognizing that healthy employees are absent less frequently and suffer fewer of the degenerative ills associated with modern industrial environments, especially in somewhat sedentary occupations. These afflictions include, among others, bad backs, high blood pressure, heart disease, and cancers of various sorts. Many U.S. companies now consider it a facet of enlightened self-interest to provide such professional support and facilities. "As for myself," continued Bill Coors, "I don't lift weights or do aerobic exercises and the like, but I do jog three miles a day. That is sufficient to keep in shape." In 1974, oldest in the group of businessmen by at least 10 years, he joined an Outward Bound–sponsored journey to climb Africa's Mount Kilimanjaro and, having done nothing to train specifically for the expedition, finished the 19,700-foot climb leading the younger crowd and seasoned guides.

FACING THE UNCONTROLLABLE FORCES IN COORS'S WORLD

There is no question about what Bill Coors saw as the single most critical uncontrollable influence facing Coors and the entire industry. He was emphatic: "Abuse of our product! Alcoholism! Alcohol abuse is an issue that will not die. The brewing industry was put out of business by this problem. Maybe 10 percent of drinkers abuse it, but what can we do about that? We can't change people's life-styles by advertising, by persuasion. Alcohol is a way of managing stress, just like overeating and other abuses. The American Medical Association says alcoholism is a disease, and if we just cut out the diseased tissue, the difficulty will disappear. How can they be so naïve as to treat the product as though it is the problem is beyond me. If that's the case, they should take away the aspirin, the Valium, and the antacids.

"Two practical reasons why they call it a disease: this decriminalizes it, that's one reason. The other is they can treat it and have the health insurance pay for it. We call these people neo-Prohibitionists because they would impose sanctions on our industry. Anyone with even an elementary understanding of our society's behavior patterns knows these kinds of restrictions simply will not work."

On the subject of a lingering boycott against Coors in California by union members, homosexuals, racial minorities, and women, Coors noted a substantial negative effect on the company's sales. Considered by corporate officers as fulminous outbursts, the disagreements began in 1977 when the AFL-CIO took issue with personnel policies, alleging discrimination against various groups. These actions led to what Bill Coors calls a "wronged company image, a bum rap." Efforts to combat the image-tarnishing assaults through using corporate advertising were halted in 1981 as the effect of the boycott waned, and the funds were applied to other promotions. Referring to the nature of this difficulty, Bill Coors concluded, "This is the first time I'm aware of in the annals of organized labor that unions have set out to destroy a company. And there's no truth, no validity to their accusations. Still, it will be a long haul for us to overcome the bad publicity created by their efforts."

Peter Coors commented on issues facing Coors: "The industry is consolidating rapidly, which means intensified competition as the result of a number of mergers and acquisitions. Of course, our major opponents are Anheuser-Busch and Miller.

"There is the issue of taxation—the excise tax is running at $9 a barrel, and there is some talk in Washington about doubling that figure, although I don't think that will happen soon. There is also discussion about no longer allowing deductibility of advertising expenses as a means of minimizing exposure of the public to alcohol advertising. It's not logical, but supporters of such a move believe it will help to prevent alcohol abuse.

"Then there is parcel legislation, state by state. Rather than seeing it done piecemeal, we prefer having it on a national, uniform basis; but state laws are proliferating. We follow the industry position on that—for example, to contest bottle legislation at any level—but I believe we would support a national law under certain circumstances. What isn't commonly recognized is that bottle legislation would be a disaster for retailers—none is equipped to handle all the inventory that such regulations would create. Problems associated with legislative controls are clearly demonstrated in several states."

Your Task:

Advise Coors management.

Appendix

MARKETING, DISTRIBUTION, AND PRODUCT INFORMATION

SALES AND MARKETING

Coors began selling beer east of the Mississippi River for the first time, expanding into Mississippi and western and central Tennessee. Northern Louisiana was also added in 1981. Coors Premium and Coors Light are now officially distributed in 20 states.

Advertising, sponsorships and consumer promotion efforts were expanded in 1981 to increase consumer awareness of all Coors products. Advertising expenditures were increased 27 percent over 1980 with emphasis on two major campaigns—"Taste the High Country" for Coors Pre-

Appendix (Cont.)

mium and "The Surprise Is How Good It Tastes" for Coors Light. Corporate image advertising was used in selected areas, and new ethnic advertising campaigns were introduced.

Herman Joseph's 1868 also received special marketing emphasis. The company refined its advertising campaign while broadening consumer awareness through product promotions. A unique advertising campaign for the test market introduction of George Killian's Irish Red ale was also developed. The Killian's commercials, filmed in Ireland, stress the uncompromising quality of the ale.

The company received positive visibility through its sponsorship of many professional sports in 1981. In only its second year, the Coors International Bicycle Classic became one of the premier bicycle races in the world. Coors is also a major corporate sponsor of rodeo. Commitments to motor sports in 1981 included sponsorship of the Caesar's Palace Grand Prix, drag racer Tom "The Mongoose" McEwen, the World Champion Coors Light Drag Boat and numerous off-road racing events.

The company, together with U.S. Tobacco, recently developed an amateur competitive snow skiing program—the Coors/Copenhagen/ Skoal Challenge series. This sponsorship is designed to reach the 1,000,000-plus weekend or recreational skiers in the Rocky Mountain area.

Marketing efforts on college campuses expanded as extensive intramural sports programs and a wide variety of other educational and social activities were sponsored. Also in 1981, through consumer promotions, Coors increased its advertising messages during peak beer consuming periods to stimulate product awareness and sales of all Coors products.

DISTRIBUTION

Coors Distributing Company operates seven company-owned distributorships. Through these distributorships, the company gains a better understanding of the beer distribution business. In turn, Coors is able to provide more comprehensive service to its 259 independent distributors. Coors products are shipped to the marketplace by rail and truck. Approximately 60 percent of the beer shipped from Golden in 1981 was by insulated rail cars. The remaining 40 percent was handled by Coors Transportation Company or other common carriers, all using refrigerated trailers.

Appendix (Cont.)

PACKAGING

Coors Container Company was merged into Adolph Coors Company in 1981. This strategic step solidifies Coors' management structure and provides greater efficiency within the combined organization.

Container operations produced approximately 2.9 billion 8-, 12- and 16-ounce cans for use by the brewery. In addition, the glass division supplied the brewery with approximately 90 percent of its bottle needs, including the new Coors longnecks. The company's paper converting plant produces a significant portion of the can wrappers and bottle carriers and labels used at the brewery. Major emphasis is given to packaging research and development as the company strives to maintain its high level of packaging quality while keeping costs down.

INGREDIENTS

Coors' commitment to using only the finest natural ingredients remains unchanged. Through agricultural research and development programs, the company strives to develop even better ingredients. Coors uses Pure Rocky Mountain Spring Water and only the highest-quality barley, cereal grains and domestic and foreign hops.

Coors continues an extensive barley research program aimed at developing new barley strains which produce beer with better taste, added flavor and more stability. Research and development efforts were also directed at new varieties of hops, seeking those that will provide the delicate subtle flavor and aroma required for Coors beer. Although the company buys 40 percent of its hops from Germany, researchers continue to test-grow European varieties of hops in Washington and Idaho, where the company's domestic hops are purchased.

BREWING PROCESS AND PACKAGING

In 1981 the brewery produced increased quantities of Coors Light and Herman Joseph's and introduced George Killian's. These products placed new demands on both brewing and packaging operations, which required modifications to existing facilities. Technological developments during the year led to product quality improvements as well as refinements in both brewing and packaging operations. In addition to new products, new packages such as the longneck bottle, Coors Light 12-pack, special holiday packages and the stainless steel keg caused dramatic changes in packaging operations.

Appendix (Cont.)

Coors brews the "Purest Beer in America" so it is not necessary for the company to heat pasteurize its products. Thus, the company eliminates 50 percent of the thermal energy required by other brewers.

The principal enemies of packaged beer are warm storage and age. Heat can adversely affect the taste of naturally brewed beer. An innovative distributor quality certification program established during 1981 ensures the time Coors products are in the marketplace is consistently the shortest in the industry. Brewery-fresh beer maintained under a carefully controlled distribution system will contribute significantly to the company's long-term success.

Coors, with its advanced brewing and packaging processes, continues to lead the industry in terms of technology, product quality and energy efficiency.

MAP OF COORS'S OPERATIONS AND FACILITIES

■ Coors Marketing Territory	◆ Ceramic Manufacturing Plants	● Company-owned Distributorships	✗ Rice Mill	▲ Paper Converting Plant
■ 1981 Expansion Areas	Benton, Arkansas El Cajon, California Golden, Colorado	Boise, Idaho Cedar Rapids, Iowa Denver, Colorado Omaha, Nebraska	Weiner, Arkansas □ Glass Bottle Manufacturing Plant	Boulder, Colorado ▽ Grain Elevators Burley, Idaho
★ Main Offices Golden, Colorado Largest single brewery and aluminum can manufacturing plant in the United States	Grand Junction, Colorado Hillsboro, Oregon Norman, Oklahoma Rio Claro, Brazil Singapore	Spokane, Washington St. Louis, Missouri Tustin, California	Wheat Ridge, Colorado	Delta, Colorado Huntley, Montana Longmont, Colorado Monte Vista, Colorado Worland, Wyoming

Appendix (Cont.)

FACTS AND FIGURES ABOUT COORS, 1980–1981

One barrel of beer = 31 gallons or 13.5 12-ounce cases.

Average capacity of a railcar is 7,200 cases of 12-ounce cans; of a truck trailer, it is 2,000 cases of 12-ounce cans.

An average of 60 insulated railcars leave the brewery each day (70 percent of beer is shipped by rail).

An average of 525 refrigerated truckloads leave the brewery each week (30 percent of beer is shipped by truck).

Packaging breakdown is 71 percent cans, 19 percent bottles, 10 percent kegs.

Coors Premium, like other American beers, is sold in two strengths, 3.6 percent and 3.2 percent alcohol by weight, depending on state laws. Twelve ounces of 3.6 beer contain 140 calories.

Coors Light, with 3.2 or 3.3 percent alcohol by weight, contains 104 calories per 12 ounces of 3.3 percent beer.

Herman Joseph's 1868, Coors's superpremium at 3.96 percent alcohol by weight, is currently being test marketed.

George Killian's Irish Red, an Irish ale brewed in Golden with 4.10 percent alcohol by weight, entered test markets in April.

Yeast, not an ingredient of beer; it is used as catalyst to convert sugars to alcohol and carbon dioxide.

Coors has the longest natural brewing process in the world: it takes about 60 days to brew, age, finish, and package Coors beer.

The sterile-fill method, pioneered in 1959, replaces traditional heat pasteurization. The process saves energy by eliminating heat, an enemy of beer flavor.

For maximum flavor retention, beer is refrigerated from packaging through transportation, distributor warehousing, and delivery. Retailers are encouraged to refrigerate Coors beer. If left unrefrigerated, beer will **not** spoil; however, at higher temperatures, flavor will deteriorate more quickly—this is true for all brands of beer.

Appendix (Cont.)

OTHER ASPECTS OF THE CORPORATION'S OPERATIONS

ENGINEERING AND CONSTRUCTION

The company's engineering and construction departments, which total approximately 1,100 employees, historically have devoted efforts to expansion of Coors brewing and container manufacturing facilities. To take advantage of business opportunities, utilizing the capabilities of this staff, the company decided to pursue actively external engineering and construction business. Several potential outside ventures are now under study.

COORS TRANSPORTATION COMPANY

Coors Transportation Company serves Adolph Coors Company in many ways. It continues to haul Coors beer to specific points within the 20-state market area. In addition, the company has refined a "back haul" system where other companies' products, such as produce and many consumer goods, are carried to maximize profits. Coors Transportation also has a special fleet of transport trucks to haul coal from the Keenesburg mine to the brewery's power plant.

GOLDEN RECYCLE COMPANY

Having completed its first full year as a subsidiary, Golden Recycle Company's objective is to ensure Coors will have sufficient raw materials to meet aluminum can production requirements. Golden Recycle Company has a number of programs which recover used aluminum beverage cans. These recycled cans are sent to aluminum suppliers to toll into can stock for use in manufacturing new cans. The company recovered over 106,000,000 pounds of aluminum in 1981, much of this coming from the over 300 recycling centers located at Coors independent distributorships in 20 states.

Golden Recycle has developed and produced a reverse vending machine called "CanBank," which pays out cash for used beverage cans. These units are being installed in many Denver supermarket parking lots.

Coors continues to support the philosophy that voluntary recycling is economically and environmentally sound. Its goal is to be the leader in beverage container recycling.

Appendix (Cont.)

COORS ENERGY COMPANY

Coors Energy Company made significant progress in 1981. This subsidiary's primary function was to develop coal and oil and gas properties for profit while it continued to supply the brewery with much of its fuel requirements. Continued exploratory drilling and field development programs in the Piceance Basin and the Denver-Julesburg Basin were successful, and operations began at the Keenesburg coal mine.

Ownership in oil and gas leasehold interests was increased to approximately 180,000 net acres. The added acreage was acquired in Colorado and Utah. In 1981 Coors operated or participated in drilling 31 net wells, primarily in the Piceance Basin. Approximately 16 billion cubic feet of natural gas were added to proved developed reserves, bringing total proved developed reserves to nearly 29 billion cubic feet of natural gas at year end. Sales contracts were completed which committed natural gas from 53,000 acres in the Piceance region. Several wells on this acreage have been completed and shut-in pending construction of a pipeline, which is expected to be completed early in 1982.

The company is contracting for a non-interrupted supply of natural gas to supplement its own natural gas production from the Wattenberg field, located 35 miles northeast of Golden. This contract will help assure a continued future supply of natural gas to Coors.

Coors Energy Company is also responsible for operation of the Keenesburg coal mine, 55 miles northeast of Denver, which began mining operations in 1981. Plans are to produce about 300,000 tons of coal in 1982 to meet brewery needs. With coal now supplying a majority of the brewery's fuel requirements, this source is expected to meet future steam needs for over 20 years.

Expansion of energy-related activities will continue in 1982. Increased natural gas production, greater output of coal, further drilling for oil and gas and additional acquisitions of leases on undeveloped acreage are expected. Coors Energy Company has now established a foundation that will strengthen its growth and profitability.

COORS PORCELAIN COMPANY

Coors Porcelain Company and its subsidiaries operate in five states and three foreign countries. Although several company operations performed

Appendix (Cont.)

well, overall 1981 was a disappointing year. The electronic ceramics business did not grow at the anticipated rate in 1981 due to competitive and economic pressures. However, when the worldwide economy improves, Coors Porcelain Company is positioned to experience a strong turnaround.

Coors ceramics are sold worldwide and are used in such diverse fields as energy, electronics, communications and data processing. Coors ceramics are also used at home in plumbing applications, kitchen appliances and television sets. Coors Porcelain Company is a technological leader in the ceramics industry and is constantly developing new products and improving the wear-resistance, strength and hardness of existing products. The company emphasizes research and development to keep pace with today's rapidly changing technology, while striving to meet the needs of its customers.

Two new wholly-owned Coors Porcelain Company subsidiaries were formed in 1981. Coors Biomedical Company, located in Lakewood, Colorado, develops and produces ceramic products for medical and dental applications. This market has the potential to become one of the fastest growing segments in the industry. Coors has developed a ceramic dental crown which has many advantages over those made of metal and has characteristics of an actual tooth. The company hopes to capture a large share of the $850,000,000 spent on dental restoration each year.

Coors Ceramics/U. K. Ltd., located in Glenrothes, Scotland, was formed early in 1981 to better serve the European ceramics market. This company will finish electronic and mechanical parts from ceramic blanks. Customers of Coors Ceramics/U. K. Ltd. include the electronics, automotive and fluid handling equipment industries.

COORS FOOD PRODUCTS COMPANY

Again in 1981, Coors Food Products Company showed improved sales and earnings. The company's rice mill in Weiner, Arkansas, had an excellent year as sales volume increased 23 percent over last year. Improved productivity and favorable market conditions, particularly in certain export markets, resulted in improved operating margins for the rice mill. New customers were obtained in both domestic and export markets. Packaging capacity has been significantly increased, which allows the mill to compete for a greater portion of the competitive packaged rice business.

Appendix (Cont.)

Research and development efforts focused on products made from brewery by-products. The company has developed Brewers Grain 28, a high-protein, high-fiber product with many commercial uses. Testing began on new products made from food grade brewer's yeast. These products have been well received in the expanding health food industry.

Cocomost blends, also made from brewer's yeast, are now being used in commercially produced food products. Coors Food Products Company is planning to build an edible yeast processing plant in 1982.

AMERICAN CENTER FOR OCCUPATIONAL HEALTH

The American Center for Occupational Health, Inc., was formed in 1980 as an answer to a vacuum on the American industrial health scene. The company provides hearing conservation programs and pulmonary testing to approximately 60 companies. It also provides support functions to organizations that are implementing and operating in-house occupational health programs.

case
29

L. L. BEAN, INC.

Maine—a state of remarkable contrasts—is 350 miles long, has a 2,500-mile shoreline, is populated by a million residents, endures some of the hardest winters in North America, is a place where one must go up north to get Down East, provides extraordinary panoramas for Columbus Day leaf-viewers, offers seafood to the world market, and justifiably boasts of its residents' propensity for industriousness. A state of mind as well as a political entity, its inhabitants fervently espouse cherished basic values of self-reliance and honesty. Visitors are likely to be pleasantly surprised at discovering not the stereotypical taciturnity reflected in humorists' interpretations but, rather, a genuine outgoing demeanor of helpful friendliness. And if, after checking in at Yarmouth's Down-East Village, one asks the distance to Freeport, the innkeeper may well answer, "Oh, L. L. Bean's! Less than a 10-minute drive up Route 1." Freeport is the home of L. L. Bean, a company with a worldwide reputation for quality and integrity, a character that is quite compatible with Maine's.

Why is this company so well known nationally? What is its primary theme? "Simple," according to Leon Arthur Gorman, L. L. Bean president. "Sell good merchandise, at a reasonable profit, and treat your customers like human beings."

Observed Mr. Gorman,

Exhibit 1

L. L. BEAN SALES AND TRANSACTIONS, SELECTED YEARS, 1967–1981

	1967	1970	1975	1980	1981
L. L. Bean sales (000s)	$4,755	$9,933	$29,500	$121,545	$172,349
Store sales (000s)	$951	$1,987	$5,932	$20,524	$16,172
Store transactions*	76,851	130,511	184,859	668,690	792,701
Sales per square foot†	$7,000	$8,000	$11,000	$26,000	$28,200

*Number of transactions.
†Approximations.

The most important legacy of "L. L.'s" genius was the power of his personality. It transcended the buying and selling of products. His personal charisma based on "down home" honesty, a true love for the outdoors, and a genuine enthusiasm for people, inspired all who worked for him and attracted a fanatic loyalty among his customers. He'd established an image that was as broad in its appeal and as enduring in its acceptance as any in marketing history.[1]

This philosophy was the guiding premise of Mr. Gorman's grandfather, the late Leon Leonwood Bean. After seven decades of doing business, the company reported 1981 sales of over $172 million (Exhibit 1), about 85 percent from orders by mail and telephone. The remainder was sold through the 60,000-square-foot retail shop on Freeport's Main Street, which, as many campers, hunters, fishermen, and other outdoors people know, is open around-the-clock every day of the year. Many who take the two-hour drive to Freeport from Boston are not necessarily devotees of outdoor living, but simply enjoy the experience of visiting the store—a New England landmark—and buying products that fit their suburban and city life-styles.

Declaring that "We can all assert our individuality—there's no need to dress like everyone else," Roger Horchow, recognized internationally as an arbiter of good taste, has expressed a fondness for L. L. Bean dress shirts and an aversion to cultlike emblematic paraphernalia (possibly alluding to makers' initials, reptiles, and such).[2] This direct marketer is one of many repeat patrons. Another who touted the Maine merchant on national television is the "Today" show's raconteur and sometime weather forecaster, Willard Scott, a relatively

[1]From address delivered by Mr. Gorman at a July 7, 1981 meeting of The Newcomen Society in North America, Brunswick, Maine, at which the speaker was guest of honor.

[2]Discussion with the casewriter. Horchow is the creator of the Horchow Collection, mailer of some 22 million catalogs annually to customers and prospects all over the world, and author, with Patricia Louden, of *Living in Style*, New York: Rawsen, Wade Publishers, 1981.

recent convert to the Bean-booster coterie. Bean public affairs spokesman Kilton Andrew said, "We enjoyed our visit with Willard just as he relished his first trip to L. L. Bean's. And we were very pleased to be mentioned on the 'Today' show. This is publicity we couldn't buy. A terrific testimonial!"

ORIGIN OF THE COMPANY:
"OUTDOOR SPORTING SPECIALTIES SINCE 1912"

Since the days of Nimrod (although biblical history is mute on this assumption), hunters have complained of cold and wet feet. When Mr. Bean decided in 1912 to solve this problem, he experimented with wedding a pair of regular leather boot uppers to rubber galoshes, the sewing feat performed by an accommodating cobbler in the shoe manufacturing town of Freeport. The resulting footwear was an improvement over leather, and after favorable first blush reactions from several hunting companions for whom he made the boots, next came a test of the mail-order channel of distribution that seemed to work for the likes of Sears, Roebuck and Company and Montgomery Ward, then the largest retailers in America. Bean got the mailing address of Maine hunting license buyers and notified them in a mailed three-page brochure, "You cannot expect success hunting deer or moose if your feet are not properly dressed. The Maine Hunting Shoe is designed by a hunter who has tramped the Maine woods for the past 18 years. We guarantee them to give perfect satisfaction in every way." But success was short-lived when 90 of the first 100 pairs he sold came back after bottoms and tops ripped loose from each other. So he borrowed more money and solved the manufacturing problem, using triple stitching and better materials. "Today," remarked Gorman, "we still get back about 12 out of every 100 pairs of shoes we sell, but mostly because they don't fit quite right. Footwear remains the most difficult item to sell by mail."

The latter-day version of that 1912 combination, still headlined with its registered trademark, "Bean's Maine Hunting Shoe," appeared in four versions on page 48 of the early autumn 1982 catalog, and a fifth version, a three eyelet "GumShoe" model, was on the cover. Priced at $36.75, the GumShoe was promoted for canoeing, yard work, campus, or after-ski wear. The tallest version, a direct descendant of Mr. Bean's first model, sold for $66.50. A glance at page 49 of this catalog reveals yet a sixth sibling, Bean's rubber moccasin, differentiated by its moccasin-style collar and a cut somewhat lower than that of the GumShoe (price: $33.75, postage paid). Altogether, 200,000 pairs of the line were sold in 1981.

The unconditional guarantee still holds, even for those who guess their size wrong for the style of shoe ordered. Whether in the several catalogs published each year, or in *The New Yorker, The Wall Street Journal,* and other periodicals in which the ads appear, the offer for all products is universal: "All are guaranteed to be 100% satisfactory or your money back."

Leon Gorman speculated that he was fortunate not having had any experience specifically related to the business when he assumed the helm in 1967: "The only business principles I could learn were those L. L. had practiced for 50 years: deep-rooted beliefs in practical, tested products for outdoors people and in giving complete customer satisfaction were accepted by me as the only way to run a business. His catalog production methods, his style of writing copy, his advertising techniques for getting new customers, and his conservative financing became the basis of my business education. I was deeply influenced by his strong personality and fundamental honesty. I absorbed as much from him as I could, I studied the old catalogs, talked with the long-time employees and vendors, got seriously involved in hunting, fishing, and our other outdoor product areas, and took many evening business courses at the University of Maine in Portland."

Gorman fondly recounts the milestones of Bean's history:

"Word-of-mouth advertising and customer satisfaction were critical to L. L.'s way of thinking. 'We consider our customers a part of our organization,' he stated in his catalog, 'and want them to feel free to make any criticism they see fit in regard to our merchandise or service.' To hear that one of his products was failing was a genuine shock to his system. He'd charge around the factory trying to find an explanation. Then he'd write the customer, return his money, enclose a gift, invite him fishing, or do anything to make the matter right. That customer had put his trust in L. L.'s catalog and was a real person to L. L.

"You ask what our return policy is today," Mr. Gorman continued, "Well, there isn't one. Do we lose money on it, say, when we repair a damaged item? Or when we enclose a check to repay the customer for postage costs? I'm not sure, but I hope we don't. What I do know is this: when you do your best to take care of a customer's request or to handle a complaint, that person is with you for life. One order after another. This company wouldn't have it any other way."

Twenty-five percent of all customer returns arrive at the company with no reason given; 50 percent are simple sizing problems—too large or too small; of the remaining 25 percent, reasons include damage in shipping, delays, quality, a color not consistent with the catalog description, or parts missing. All told, about 9.5 percent of all sales come back as returns, less than half the industry average. Only about one-half of 1 percent come back because of claimed defects—in other words, approximately 5 items for each 1,000 shipped.

ORGANIZATION STRUCTURE AND HUMAN RESOURCES

In growth situations, it is common to encounter numerous crises, including human relations issues. The president observed: "We overhauled our personnel policies, increasing compensation to levels that were more than competitive in our area and included an equitable job rating system and a companywide performance bonus. We began to attract and retain better people. In 1961, for example, the average age of our employees was over 60; in 1975 it was in the forties. We added pension, savings, and group life insurance programs. Also, we implemented professional training courses for supervisors. Working conditions and communications improved, and the momentum of growth provided abundant opportunities for individual advancement.

"Like many companies, we had been reluctant to bring in outside talent; one reason was we didn't know if we could afford it or not, and we were worried it might disrupt our organization. Hiring Bill End as our marketing director proved conclusively that we couldn't afford to be without the best people if we were to continue growing. And if they like the outdoors, as Bill did, they'd get along fine at L. L. Bean. In 1961, I was the only college graduate in our management staff; now we have 66 college graduates, 15 of them MBAs."

William End was a 26-year-old group product manager at the Gillette Company in Boston—a job he took after graduating from the Harvard Business School—when hired by Leon Gorman. All officers reporting to the president (Exhibit 2) had been hired since 1975.

The company had come a long way from its original clapboard building to the contemporary, well-landscaped corporate headquarters on Casco Street that management moved into in early fall 1982.

An organizational study was implemented in the summer of 1981. According to the president, "Fifteen or twenty years ago, when our staff numbered about 150 people, it was fairly easy to know how things were going. Problems could be addressed quickly. But with our current size of 964 permanent and 737 seasonal employees, and being spread over five buildings on three different sites, keeping a finger on the pulse is very difficult. Our formal attitude survey conducted last summer measured individual job satisfaction; we discussed the results at feedback meetings last fall. Our morale is quite superior, we share a pride in the company, and we identify with our products and our customers. There is high commitment to quality. By and large, we like our jobs, our compensation, and our working relationships with each other. Further, we are optimistic about the future.

"But there are some things needing attention, such as problems with our job evaluation system and our pay structure. Advancement opportunities aren't seen as being what they should be, and some of our management practices aren't sufficiently sensitive to our human needs. Some of our jobs are boring. Upward communication needs improvement. Many of us don't know what others in the company are doing, and some of us don't seem to care. We are all working together on improvement programs; all of us should take responsibility for everyone's overall job satisfaction. It's a cooperative effort."

Temporary workers, hired at Christmas, may evolve into full-time employees. Because of the excellent benefits, including profit sharing and a hefty 20 percent bonus check at the end of the year, people want to get on at L. L. Bean as permanent employees. The company has a record of promoting from

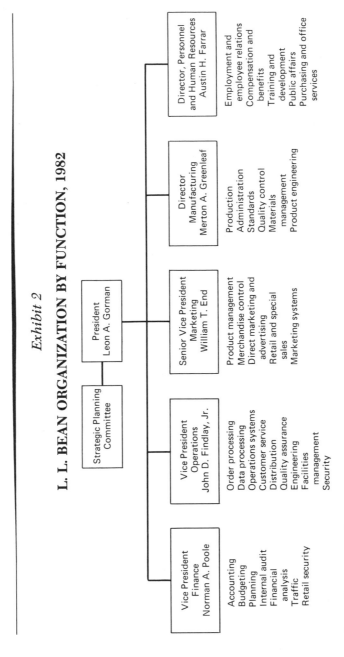

Exhibit 2

L. L. BEAN ORGANIZATION BY FUNCTION, 1982

Strategic Planning Committee

President
Leon A. Gorman

Vice President
Finance
Norman A. Poole

Accounting
Budgeting
Planning
Internal audit
Financial
   analysis
Traffic
Retail security

Vice President
Operations
John D. Findlay, Jr.

Order processing
Data processing
Operations systems
Customer service
Distribution
Quality assurance
Engineering
Facilities
   management
Security

Senior Vice President
Marketing
William T. End

Product management
Merchandise control
Direct marketing and
   advertising
Retail and special
   sales
Marketing systems

Director
Manufacturing
Merton A. Greenleaf

Production
Administration
Standards
Quality control
Materials
   management
Product engineering

Director, Personnel
and Human Resources
Austin H. Farrar

Employment and
   employee relations
Compensation and
   benefits
Training and
   development
Public affairs
Purchasing and office
   services

Source: Company records.

within. All employees are allowed a one-third price discount off all products sold by Bean.

Concern for employees is apparent even to visitors. A well-promoted employee fitness program is considered a benefit. In his introduction to *The L. L. Bean Guide to the Outdoors,* Gorman wrote: "Preparedness (for outdoor activities) also means staying in reasonably good physical shape. You can cover a lot more ground and put up with more extreme conditions if you've got strong legs and healthy lungs. Many of us at L. L. Bean jog, skip rope, ride bicycles, or play racquet sports to stay active when we're not outdoors. L. L. used to walk briskly back and forth to work in order to exercise his legs. Fitness adds to your outdoor experiences just as both add to your life. L. L. lived to be 94, sound of mind and body, and enjoyed every minute of it."

Programs of physical activity are supplemented by courses in nutrition, stress management, weight control, and how-to-stop-smoking clinics. During a visit by the casewriters in October 1982, 500 employees attended an orientation for their new indoor exercise facility. To use the circuit-weight system, many employees logged in at 6:00 A.M. on opening day. A professional trainer was added to the staff to manage the facility, to design programs, and to provide individual consultation.

Despite the relative magnitude of the operation, those who had been around since before L. L. Bean died say a family atmosphere still prevails—informality reigns. Most employees address their chief executive by his first name, with a Down East accent that merges the two syllables virtually into one—Lee'-un. The working atmosphere around all the Bean locations seems to reflect Mr. Gorman's demeanor—relaxed and friendly, with an evident pride in greeting visitors and attending to customers' needs, both in person and on the telephone. Casual, indeed, but unmistakably professional.

GROWTH, 1967–1982

Although characteristically self-effacing ("My grandfather always had a soft spot for unemployed relatives and so put me on the payroll at $80 a week in 1961"), Gorman has been accorded major share of the credit by competitors and others who have followed the company's progress for taking the organization beyond the entrepreneurial stage to successful expansion. Following his assuming the presidency when L. L. Bean died at age 94 in 1967, the company achieved a 25 percent compounded growth rate from 1967 to 1975 and an average return on equity of 30 percent between 1975 and 1980.

Are these high-performance ratios likely to continue? And would such growth be desirable? As management pondered such questions, Norman A. Poole, named vice president of finance in 1981, calculated a trendline projection indicating a potential sales level of $350 million by 1985, producing, based on existing ratios, a net income on the order of $20 million, sustaining the recent return on equity of about 30 percent.

Pointing out the necessity of close collaboration between finance and marketing, Poole, whose experience includes both Sears and Spiegel, discussed strategies to enhance cash flow: "A gap we began bridging this fall [1982] is handling the cash management system. For instance, by sending in our credit card orders on a daily basis, rather than biweekly, we will maximize cash available for investment. Speeding up this flow will become even more important should we ever decide to install a toll-free 800 number. Phone orders already amount to almost 30 percent of catalog sales and, incidentally, average 23 percent higher than mail orders. A toll-free number would result in a huge jump in phone orders."

The financial vice president's responsibilities also encompass coordination of strategic planning and serving on the strategic planning committee.

"Most of the work must be done by the members of the planning committee. We are completing the first cycle of the process this fall, but it is very difficult implementing a long-range plan when we are so busy dealing with rapid expansion," commented Poole.

Poole expressed the belief that L. L. Bean would continue to grow at rates in excess of industry averages for the foreseeable future. Admitting that he is "bullish" on the prospects for healthy economic growth in the overall economy during the 1980s, he blamed problems facing big business on bad decisions focused on growth for growth's sake and their inability to understand the nature of the small businesses they have acquired. "This, combined with too much government, has compounded the seriousness of problems we all face today," he observed.

"We've identified the quality measurements that are important in guiding our company, and knowing who we are will help us maintain a perspective of maturity and good judgment. As time passes, we must face the issue of how we can grow without going into debt and of what happens when growth slows. Meanwhile, there is plenty to occupy our immediate attention.

"We must do a better job of developing cost accounting measures in manufacturing. Better forms of insurance coverage will be evaluated. Store security is being improved. We will pay close attention to improving investment of saving plan and other funds. We will work to improve accuracy control in inventory reporting procedures. Those are just some of the immediate concerns we are working on. In all of this, an encouraging aspect at L. L. Bean is how closely managers work with each other to improve company performance."

THE L. L. BEAN CUSTOMER PROFILE

According to a 1980 company-sponsored marketing study, L. L. Bean's "average" customer was over 35 years of age, highly educated, in upper-income brackets, and lived in the eastern United States. Customers were mostly either "satisfied" or "very satisfied" with the company's products, considering them to be high quality and reasonably priced. Delivery time was also favorably perceived. These survey results reconfirmed management's conviction that there was no need to attempt to reposition the company through changing products, advertising themes, and service. Plans for the mid-1980s were to circulate more catalogs both to new prospect and existing customer target segments. Rented mailing lists were expected to yield enough potentially valuable names for mailing about 5 million catalogs in 1982. "Renting lists costs us about $50 per thousand names," Bill End said, "so one of my concerns is whether we can continue buying new lists and gaining new customers without paying for unprofitable duplication of prospective names."

Orders placed by women increased from 25 percent of the orders in 1976 to over 50 percent in 1982. The under-35 segment also increased, from 31 percent to 42 percent in the same period. The 55-and-over group accounted for 29 percent of the orders in 1977 and 23 percent in 1982. Some insiders believe that women's apparel represents one of the best growth opportunities for L. L. Bean, but there is concern about uniqueness of the Bean image that gives them pause when thinking about shifting more toward feminine appeals and products.

Average mail-order size in 1980 was approximately $45 with credit card orders, 23 percent greater than cash; telephone orders averaged $55, and again credit card orders ran about 23 percent above cash orders. Mail and telephone combined produced average order sizes of just over $46. Transactions in the retail store averaged $34, with credit card purchases more than twice the average of cash.

The contents of Eddie Bauer (Seattle) and Lands' End Direct Merchants' (Dodgeville, Wisconsin) catalogs bear a resemblance to L. L. Bean's and have been considered, along with a few others, to be direct competitors to the Freeport establishment. Bauer—mailing a 100-page Christmas catalog in 1982—around for 60 years is, according to management, the number one competitor. Talbots, located in Massachusetts, has been a competitor in the women's apparel business, but its catalogs used to carry some items for men, with a general emphasis on name brands manufactured by other suppliers. For example, the Talbots November 1982 34-pager featured footwear (on page 17) resembling somewhat L. L. Bean's moccasin and models wearing fashions by such makers as Adrianna Papell, Jacques Levine, Ciao, and Gordon of Philadelphia; 4 pages were devoted to men's apparel. In fall 1983 Talbots discontinued menswear.

Focus group interviews conducted by L. L. Bean in Washington, D.C., and Dallas among noncustomers of both Bean and Lands' End reveal that the majority of participants (who were shown the two firms' catalogs) have strong preferences for either one catalog or the other. Those preferring Bean's mentioned better quality merchandise as their main reason, while those opting for Lands' End did so on the basis of its clothing being more fashionable. Land's

End appealed more to women under 35, while Bean's catalog was seen as more suitable for the older men's segment. Lands' End was perceived as being for "less serious" buyers who casually enjoy the outdoors. Bill End commented that L. L. Bean, taking postage and handling charges into account, is ordinarily 5 percent lower in price than Bauer, Lands' End, and Talbots.

PRODUCT MANAGEMENT

Basic product groups that L. L. Bean originated remain its foundation in the 1980s. Gorman explained: "What he staked out, we continue today: outdoors apparel and footwear for men and women; hunting, fishing, camping, canoeing, and winter sports equipment; and casual apparel, footwear, and camp furnishings. Everything else has had to be consistent with the Maine Hunting Shoe—quality and value."

Long before turmoil erupted in many companies when the consumer movement of the 1960s began, L. L. Bean, Inc., already paid close attention to customers' needs expressed in letters, on the phone, and in the retail store. The president commented on product development: "In all of our product groups, people wanted lighter weight, longer wear, extra comfort, more safety, higher performance, and easier care and maintenance. Item by item we reviewed our product lines and tried to enhance them with those features that the new outdoors person wanted. It was an incremental process with hundreds of relatively minor decisions being made. Our product lines were systematically brought up to date. Today we continue this process of rigorous ongoing reviews of our products, making evolutionary improvements whenever appropriate."

Dealing with over 400 vendors for upwards of 83 percent of all products sold (42 percent under direct contract to L. L. Bean, 23 percent private label, and 18 percent name-brand merchandise), product managers—buyers—regularly visit vendors' facilities to discuss product developments and technologies. "Working closely with suppliers has cemented long-term mutually productive relationships," observed Charlie Kessler, manager of product development. "The philosophy is what it was in L. L. Bean's day, that time outdoors is too valuable to be wasted with faulty apparel and equipment that doesn't function as it is supposed to." The company implemented a formal quality-assurance department in 1977. In 1982, over 30 people worked in it, using a full range of testing facilities, systematically inspecting every incoming shipment to ensure that product specifications were adhered to.

Ned Kitchel, of Bean's product management team, talked about the company's concept of value: "Inherent value is what we look for in each of our products—that is, does it have worth, in and of itself? Our customers aren't after candy bars; they don't want a quick fix. When they look through our catalog, they've got to see products that are solid, utilitarian, and not overbuilt. Fireplace gloves are a good example of a product with an industrial application but that can be merchandised to consumers for personal use. Also, every item has to be suitably priced; even one product out of line on price might lead a customer to conclude that we price everything that way."

Kitchel's ideas were amplified by the apparel product manager, Ron Campo: "Although some of our competitors may approximate or meet Bean's quality standards, few if any offer the overall merchandise value when the pricing equation is considered in conjunction with the perceived quality level. Our pricing integrity has been built on adherence to margin levels that are consistently—in many instances dramatically—below industry levels. By setting margin levels in the 40 to 45 percent area, L. L. Bean has maintained a favorable competitive pricing profile. Given the nature of products we sell, industry margin levels, on the other hand, average 'keystone plus'—approximately 52 to 55 percent—particularly in the women's wear lines."

As an example of how products are developed at L. L. Bean, the footwear product manager, Jim Jennings, recounted the history of the recently added Bean's Western Boot: "Eighteen months ago [1979 to 1980], this boot hadn't even been considered, but people in the shoe industry kept saying: 'The western boot thing's getting real strong,' which meant it had become fashionable, just like mediumweight hiking boots were several years ago. Demand for hiking boots went through the ceiling, not from backpackers but from buyers who wanted the backpacking look.

"I didn't think the western boot suited our image, yet we couldn't ignore the pattern. I noticed at various trade shows that it was making inroads even among the more conservative companies. So I contacted Mason Shoe, a company we hadn't dealt with before but wanted to get to know. They made one up for us and stamped the L. L. Bean name on it. I set it on my desk so passersby could see it, then sat back and waited. Charlie Kessler picked it up and didn't laugh—he liked it. When I hesitantly said, 'Charlie, we should have one of those in the catalog,' he told me to go ahead and develop it. Mason said they wouldn't be able to fill their existing orders and produce the kind of quality boot we wanted so I went to Red Wing Shoe. They gave us a product that met our quality and price standards, so we introduced the first Bean's Western Boot in the fall, 1981 catalog. Sales have justified the product."

Jennings had worked as a shoe buyer for Sears for 12 years before joining L. L. Bean. "Contrary to the Bean approach," he said, "Sears starts with a firm price and then designs in the features to meet that price and cover necessary margins. We begin with features and quality and then talk about price."

Regarding the occasional failure of products to sell at forecasted levels, Kitchel said: "This problem is greater for us than for much of our competition. Unlike Eddie Bauer, as an example, which has several retail stores where slow-moving merchandise can be marked down and sold at discount, we have only the one store in Freeport, and no matter what we do, there's a limited amount of merchandise that can be channeled through it.[3] Eastern Mountain Sports, for example, can take 10,000 pair of skis that don't sell in their catalog or in their East Coast stores and ship them to Denver or Minneapolis/St. Paul. We don't have that option, so the incentive is just that much greater for our product managers to take prodigious care and to consider all the variables."

On the other hand, when sales levels are higher than expected, product managers are responsible for anticipating the impact on personnel and production time at the mill, availability of raw materials in sufficient quantities and on time, and other considerations related to adequate stocks and profitability.

L. L. Bean Guide to the Outdoors,[4] first published in 1942, is considered by management to be a useful supplement to the catalog by providing ideas on various items especially to help the person who has little outdoors experience to choose between products. Says Leon: "How is one to know that a Thinsulate parka might suit him better than one insulated with down or that an ABS canoe might make better sense for his purposes than one built of fiberglass?

"Of course, our customers love visiting the retail store because they can draw on the experience and expert advice of our sales clerks. This is a service our catalog can't provide directly. There's simply not enough space to explain what we think, as L .L did, that our products are the best for the use intended, to describe all the field testing we've done, and to give the technical perspective within which we make our recommendations. The book helps us communicate this."

In preparing the 1981 version of the *Guide,* the review process became cumbersome—with first-draft reading and subsequent suggestions and comments by Gorman, End, former camping product manager Roger Poor, and product management director Charlie Kessler—so Bruce Willard, assistant product manager for apparel, was assigned the additional duty of acting as liaison between L. L. Bean and Random House, the publisher, and the primary author, outdoor winter and Maine guide Bill Riviere. Bruce Willard graduated from Middlebury College, where he majored in American literature, and attended the prestigious Breadloaf (Vermont) writers' conference. In his day-to-day contact with vendors and other members of the product management team, Willard was in a good position to coordinate the profusion of information and advice coming from many sources.

Willard discussed the process: "Product testing has been the backbone for descriptive information in the *Guide.* Much of the initial data were provided by our suppliers such as Eureka, Mad River, and Danner—all provided a

---

[3]The 1982 Eddie Bauer holiday catalog listed 22 U.S. (9 in the West, the others in the Midwest, North Central, and East) and 3 Canadian stores. Talbots listed 27 stores in its 1982 holiday book: 7 in Massachusetts, 6 in Connecticut, and 14 located in 9 other eastern states.

[4]1981; Random House, September $15.50 postage paid, in L. L. Bean's Christmas 1982 catalog, p. 101.

great deal of sound testimony based on their own research and testing. The North Face, makers of high-quality outerwear and backpacking gear, are especially well-known for their extensive field testing on expeditions to the remotest parts of the world. Their designers were particularly helpful. What we did was to pick experts for reading and helping revise certain parts; for example, we had a meteorologist review the chapter on weather."

L. L. Bean exhibits an intensity of product testing efforts that includes continuous feedback from experience-based evaluations of employees, friends, and customers. Decades ago, L. L. Bean stated in the catalog that he personally used and tested every item sold. Continuing this approach, current decisions are still made largely on the basis of whether the decision makers personally find a product to be useful, durable, and practical.

Kessler explained that because of the background research done for the *Guide*, Willard's responsibilities expanded to include coordination of field testing contracted with individuals and organizations throughout the country. "The importance of the information we receive from these people accelerates with the rapid development of new theories and concepts." Kessler said, "particularly as the variety of rugged and special uses to which our products are subjected continued to proliferate. That constantly changing state of the marketplace is one reason why the book embraces generic descriptions of clothing and gear, rather than referring to specific products by name."

"Using this approach," said Willard as he picked up on this theme, "we concentrate on the important concepts and theories which underlie, for example, how to keep warm in wet, cold weather; we avoid listing every available brand of effective clothing—and the associated risk of becoming outdated as new technology emerges. One interesting and, I think, intriguing theory of the vapor-barrier principle was omitted from the book because product management concluded that the jury is still out on this one. But if further study and field testing prove the theory's value, it will be discussed in later editions."

He emphasized theoretical evaluation because L. L. Bean deals with many suppliers, and considering the likely impact of any book with the Bean name attached, close attention was paid to being objective and even-handed, although diplomacy does not diminish the quality of the finished volume.

"The old books that addressed the problems fairly are still relevant today. Horace Kephart's *Camping and Woodcraft*, first published in 1917, is now in its thirtieth printing—most of the principles in it are still applicable, just like the layering method of dressing for cold weather, or as L. L. Bean described it in the first *Guide*, the 'onionization' technique. Now, as then, wool is one of the best insulators, even though several new lightweight synthetic fibers have become available. We have probably covered the greatest scope of activities and products in one book since Kephart, and I've enjoyed being a part-time product manager and part-time research editor in helping put together the new edition. Response has been so positive that a second printing, after a 125,000 first run, has become necessary."

REACHING CUSTOMERS AND PROSPECTS—MAIL
AND RETAIL STORE

Circulation in 1980 included distribution of approximately 10.8 million catalogs to a group identified as "L. L. Bean Buyers," 3.5 million to L. L. Bean "Best Customers," 3 million to those who responded to advertisements, primarily in periodicals, 4.7 million to purchased lists, and 4.6 million to prospects derived from master file inquiries, customer referrals, and buyers at the retail store. Important sources of 660,000 new customers in 1980 included all of these, plus gift recipients, and a large number, approaching 280,000, of unidentified origin. These "unknowns" could be former customers appearing on the mailing list under new names or addresses, those using plain stationery in ordering, or those ordering without using preprinted labels. Mr. End is convinced that about half of these "unknowns" were new buyers.

Sales in 1982, expected to be about 50 times greater than those 15 years ago, were derived from sophisticated handling of lists, "house lists," which are files of previous customers, purchased lists chosen from over 50,000 business and customers mailing list selections, and the distribution of four-color catalogs ranging in size from 64 to 136 pages and filled with products appealing to deer hunters and preppies alike. All models are Bean employees. There are six basic catalogs plus variations in size and contents. L. L. Bean was mailing 1 million catalogs in 1967 when Gorman took over; the mailing in 1982 was expected to be 45 million, sent to about 24 million names, some customers receiving several full-coverage and minicatalogs.

Catalog strategy was augmented when Leon Gorman increased the firm's advertising budget in the late 1960s, spending in outdoor books such as *Field & Stream, Outdoor Life,* and *Sports Afield* and in other magazines. *The New Yorker* turned out to be one of the best lead generators of all, along with another inquiry producer, *The New York Review of Books.* A typical Bean advertisement appears in Exhibit 3.

Bean's customers are responsible for referring many potential buyers. When an order is shipped, Bean encloses a request that customers supply additional names and addresses of people who might be interested in the catalog.

Discussing how his programs to expand catalog distribution were mainly an extension, but more sophisticated, of what his grandfather used to do, Gorman has explained the principle of list generation: "L. L. was obsessed with building his mailing list and for years put most of his profits into advertising. He placed hundreds of small ads in the outdoor magazines promoting his 'free' catalog. He developed a unique coding system to evaluate the responses. His inquirers became customers. John Gould, the famous Maine writer and Freeport native said, 'If you drop in just to shake his hand, you get home to find his catalog in your mail box.'"

As might be expected, hunters and fishermen are no longer undisputed mainstays of company business. Still, there is understandable reluctance on the

Exhibit 3

L. L. BEAN AD, OCTOBER 1982

L.L.Bean®
Outdoor Sporting Specialties

Corduroy Chinos

Same comfortable pattern as our popular Chino Pants. Full cut, yet neat in appearance. Durable medium weight corduroy is 84% cotton and 16% polyester. Machine Wash. Two front, two rear pockets, 1¾" belt loops. "Easy alter" waistband can be expanded 1½". Colors: Tan. Navy. Brown. Even waist sizes: 30 to 44. Inseam: 29", 31" and 33". An exceptional value. 2815W, Navy Corduroy Chino. 2816W, Tan Corduroy Chino. 2852W, Brown Corduroy Chino. **$19.00 ppd.**

Chamois Cloth Shirt
(For Men, Women & Children)

Mr. Bean's favorite hunting and fishing shirt. Well made from a 7 oz. cotton flannel, thickly napped on both sides. Warm, wind-resistant and comfortable to wear. Machine Wash. Colors: Navy. Bright Red. Tan. Green. Slate Blue. Ivory. Men's Regular sizes: 14½ to 20. 1611W, **$18.25 ppd.** Men's Long sizes: 15 to 19. 1612W, **$19.25 ppd.** Women's sizes: 6 to 20. 4311W, **$18.25 ppd.** Children's sizes: 8 to 18. (No Ivory) 4335W, **$17.00 ppd.**

Lined Moosehide Slippers
(For Men, Women and Children)

Fully lined with warm acrylic pile. Genuine Moosehide is thick and long-wearing, yet supple and soft. Moccasin construction with adjustable rawhide laces for comfort and fit. Color: Moosehide Tan. Whole sizes, medium width. Men's sizes: 7 to 13. 3636W, **$17.75 ppd.** Women's sizes: 5 to 10. 4893W, **$15.75 ppd.** Children's sizes: 10 to 13; 1 to 4. 4895W, **$13.75 ppd.**

Flannel Sheets

Take the chill out of getting in bed on cool evenings. Made of a tightly woven, softly napped flannelette fabric. Whipstitched ends. Cut generously to allow for normal shrinkage. Machine Wash and Dry.

Solid Color Flannel Sheets. 50% cotton/50% polyester. Colors: Blue. Pink. Gold. Camel. White. 7681W Twin Size, **$11.00 ppd.** 7682W Double Size, **$12.50 ppd.** 7683W Queen Size, **$15.00 ppd.** 7464W King Size, **$19.00 ppd.**

Striped Flannel Sheets. Slightly heavier weight blend of 80% cotton/20% polyester. Not available in White or King Size. Colors: Blue. Pink. Gold. Camel. All with natural background. 7481W Twin Size, **$11.50 ppd.** 7488W Double Size, **$13.00 ppd.** 7489W Queen Size (No Pink), **$16.00 ppd.**

FREE Winter Catalog

72 pages of cold weather favorites from L. L. Bean. Quality apparel and footwear for men, women and children. Snowshoeing, cross country skiing and hiking gear. Wood burning accessories. Casual home furnishings. Our 70th year.

Item #	Qty.	Color	Size	Description	Price

Please Ship Postage Paid   100% Guarantee

Add 5% Maine Sales Tax on Shipments to Maine Addresses   TOTAL

☐ Check Enclosed   ☐ VISA   ☐ MasterCard®   ☐ American Express

Card No. _____ Expires _____

☐ **SEND FREE WINTER CATALOG**

Name _____
Address _____
City _____ State _____ Zip _____

L. L. Bean, Inc., 881 Casco St., Freeport, ME 04033

Source: Advertisement which appeared in various publications.

part of management to reduce space allotted to camping gear in favor of, say, women's apparel. Expanding the number of catalog pages and the overall inventory of items carried in stock would have considerable financial impact. Considered to be extremely critical was what might happen to the Bean image if such trade-offs were made to move away from a predominantly hard-core outdoor position in the public's mind. Company market studies were quite clear on one point: few see Bean as a purveyor of trendy goods.

The most aggressive enlargement of Bean's mailing list commenced in 1975 when Bill End was hired as director of marketing, just a year after the company organized a customer service program to maintain its reputation for service although undergoing dramatic expansion. While taking as many as 10,000 telephone calls and handling, with personal replies, 6,000 letters in a busy week, the order-fulfillment error rate hovers at around 2 percent or slightly less, unusually low in the direct-response marketing field. Customer service telephones are answered around the clock.

In the Freeport retail outlet, even the skeptic is immediately impressed by knowledgeable and unfailingly patient sales clerks who seem genuinely to enjoy helping customers learn the products and make their choices. The affable retail store manager is Bob Felle, hired in April 1979 as assistant store manager in charge of operations and promoted to the top position in February 1981, filling a position vacated the previous year. His background includes an MBA degree in marketing earned at Michigan State University and several years as an exchange officer in the U.S. Navy. He joined L. L. Bean from the Brunswick Naval Air Station where he oversaw a $7.5-million-per-year exchange program. He explained some of the remodeling and other changes taking place: "We have set up the camping department in the midst of the tents and boats where customers have instant access to expert advice. There is a full view of the outside—so our outdoorsman doesn't get claustrophobia shopping in here."

From the outside, approaching customers peering in the window can see the contemporary styling and the array of products in a well-lighted interior. "We are expanding the selling area all the way back to the far end of the building; backup stock, stored there now, will be taken to the warehouse." Upstairs on the second floor is a new receiving operations area, with a new and modern loading dock to accommodate deliveries. On the third floor is a vastly expanded men's clothing department, housewares, a spacious shoe department, and an enlarged book department.

New light-stained wood fixtures brighten the interior, although a rustic decor maintains throughout. "We realized from our volume over the past couple of summers that we were going to have to do something or we just weren't going to be able to fit all those people in, so we went ahead with renovations last summer despite the impact of summer crowds. The whole project was much bigger than anticipated, but we have everything under control now. Employees like it and so do customers."

ELECTRONIC DATA PROCESSING

Growth came not without hazards threatening customer service. Mr. Gorman expressed concern over problems arising from rapid sales expansion: "Sales were outstripping our operations capabilities. We needed to catch up in the 'back end' of our business. In 1969, with the help of consultants, we converted our mailing list from a hand-typed operation into a computerized system. In 1970 we moved our manufacturing operation to rented space in a modern building also located in Freeport. We mechanized our order entry system and our inventory management system. In 1974 we bought the building, installed our own computer, and built a new 110,000-square-foot distribution facility on the adjacent property. In 1975, another consultant reorganized our customer service department to provide more timely and efficient responses to our many customer requests for product information and delivery status." (See Appendix A for a chronological review of implementing electronic data processing at L. L. Bean.) Computer operations in the company continue 24 hours daily.

Bean concentrates on customer service at the front end, when the order is received. The order fulfillment goal is to have in stock 90 percent of all items ordered, but with rapid growth, the percentage has fallen slightly below that level in some recent seasons.

"It is easier to get fast turnaround when we had only 250,000 to 300,000 customers and $4 million or $5 million in sales," said Gorman. "Today we carry 80,000 items, and product lines don't stay the same year after year as they used to 10 to 15 years ago."

In 1982 the company had the capability of opening and sorting 35,000 mail orders a day and could fill and ship over 35,000 orders a day. The goal was to get orders processed, filled, and shipped within 48 hours of receipt, but no longer than 72 hours except under very unusual circumstances.

In the warehouse stock area, product pickers (order fillers) go about their task industriously. The picking is done from computerized compilations. Fifty percent of orders are single-item orders, so the picking system devised by Bean involves clusters of the same item picked off the shelves, later to be merged into single orders. Warehouse operations span two 8-hour shifts daily in the storage area of 310,000 square feet of floor space and 33-foot ceilings, stacked with goods in bins accessed by forklift trucks. Planning was underway in fall of 1982 for erecting additional distribution facilities to come onstream in 1984 and 1985.

MANUFACTURING

Adding a 72,000-square-foot manufacuring building in 1979 tripled production capacity. The president expressed an opinion that "Each incremental increase in volume allows us to put more quality and relevance into our product line, to price our products more competitively, and to increase the efficiency of our service and the satisfaction of our customers." Despite its modernity, the factory presents mixtures of new and old—machines are abundantly evident but a good deal of the work is still done by hand. Two hundred employees make footwear and rebuild boots sent in by customers, and all take pride in the idea that the company provides repair service for everything it makes and sells.

Responding to a question about his department's role, the director of manufacturing, Mert Greenleaf, affirmed: "Manufacturing contributes favorably to the overall profitability. We must compete with outside vendors to produce products of a quality to carry the L. L. Bean label, and I'm justifiably proud of our workers who make those products."

Noting that Bean's manufacturing employees earn higher wages and benefits than do their counterparts in other companies' plants, he continued: "Even so, we compete successfully, keeping costs at an acceptable level, which is difficult when one considers that about 225 different items make up our three major product categories. Here is the Orvis (a Vermont mail-order company) catalog with one page devoted entirely to three different handsewns and a gumshoe—all made here, even though they don't identify them as Bean's products. This is fill-in production that helps to level out some of our normal pattern of ups and downs in demand."

The director noted that modern management techniques have helped in a great many ways: "In the past five years, since adding our standards department and product engineer position, we've increased labor efficiency from 65 percent to 95 percent, and we're going for 100 percent in attempts to increase productivity. Four years ago we were turning out 900 units of specialities (briefcases, wood carriers, boat and tote bags, etc.), 240 handsewn shoes, and 300 Maine Hunting Shoes daily. Compare those figures with our 1982 daily average of 2,500 specialty units, 900 handsewns, and 720 Maine Hunting Shoes."

Video equipment is presently being used for production training, new fume-and-dust collection technology has been added, and methods time measurement has been implemented, along with experimentation to reduce noise levels in the factory.

Greenleaf concluded with the following observation: "My interests center around the three prime concerns of our management team: quality, competitive pricing, and timely delivery. And we have a common long-range interest: where we're going to be five years from now. We must improve our strategies to handle growth."

As if to underscore Greenleaf's assessment, over the manufacturing area hangs a huge sign: TOMORROW IS YOUR BEST REASON FOR QUALITY TODAY.

MANAGING THE FUTURE

The Direct Mail Marketing Association (DMMA) has 2,700 member companies, which account for an estimated 60 percent of the total of goods and services sold through direct marketing methods. Sales volume in the entire field was expected to reach $125 billion to $130 billion in 1982, or about 4 percent of the nation's GNP, some $40 billion (4 percent of U.S. retail sales) from the catalogs. According to DMMA, 72 million adult males and females—roughly 46 percent of the total adult population—placed mail orders in 1981. Telemarketing and cable TV have become popular with several direct marketers as electronic technology and sales techniques are increasingly integrated.

Upwards of 15,000 businesses reportedly used mail order in 1981 to sell their products; mail-order sales were estimated to be growing at a rate of 15 percent annually, whereas the retailing industry generally was growing at about 7 percent. Acquisitions of mail marketing companies became prevalent as, for example, ITT bought Burpee Seed Company and General Mills purchased, among others, Talbots and Eddie Bauer.

Commenting on the environment's impact upon mail marketing business, Gorman reviewed some factors contributing to its growth: "Women entering the work force in large numbers have less time for conventional retail shopping. High gasoline prices and lack of informed sales clerks discourage trips to shopping centers. Shopping by catalogs with detailed product descriptions appears more convenient and credit cards and the telephone further enhance buying by mail. Catalogs could reach national markets that will support the highly specialized product lines increasingly in demand by selective consumers. People seem to be returning to the 'old-time' values, and traditional products with intrinsic value are becoming fashionable once again."

Mail order in the early 1980s yielded an average profit after taxes of 7 percent as compared with about 2.5 percent for companies in traditional retailing and 5.4 percent for those in manufacturing. Further, results in the direct marketing business were easy to measure against expenditures for promotions, primarily because mail-order sales could be linked directly to the number of catalogs mailed. DMMA actually calls upon the measurability factor to define the field as "an interactive system of marketing that uses one or more advertising media to effect a measurable response and/or transaction at any location."[5] In November 1982, DMMA's board recommended changing its name, deleting "Mail," to Direct Marketing Association—a sign of the times.

Bill End echoed the business advantages of direct marketing, but he was troubled by a major disadvantage—unpredictability of the United States Postal Service. "Postal rate increases, coming as they do every two or three years, have great impact on our profits, mainly because we ship our products postage

[5]*DMMA Fact Book*, 1981.

prepaid, but at the front end because we rely on the mails to deliver our millions of catalogs. Since 1975, costs of printing and mailing our fall catalogs have increased by 15 percent to 20 percent a year. One way we've saved is by having R. R. Donnelley and Sons take over our catalog printing; before that we had worked with a small local printer until it became impossible for that firm to take care of our needs."

L. L. Bean's management team enjoys deliberating about the future; uncertainty only heightens the team's anticipation of alternatives open to the company to capitalize on existing opportunities, continue its enviable performance record, and absorb the future shock of unexpected significant events. Management realizes the danger, while perhaps basking in the glow of success built on solid foundations of good business practices, of losing clarity of vision and strength of purpose. They harbor few illusions about L. L. Bean's strengths and weaknesses and the opportunities and threats facing them over the next few years.

Several questions seem cogent to them in strategic planning:

1. In what ways, if at all, should they expand?
2. Besides strengthening their position in their current geographic segments, should they consider publishing specialized catalogs for particular market segments based on sex, income, and other demographic variables? What variables should be included in their "model" of the marketplace?
3. Whatever expansion routes they choose, what considerations should be given to saturation of the existing customer base and diminishing returns from rented lists?
4. How can Bean supplement, expedite, and make simpler the ordering process? What considerations should be given to an 800 telephone number, for example?
5. Does it make sense to expand the retail operation into other cities, into shopping malls, or possibly into franchised sections of existing department stores? (The company has received several requests from retailers in recent years to expand in this manner.)
6. Should economics be sought by manufacturing more of their own products, and would this justify expansion of facilities?
7. Since other countries' citizens purchase through mail order, what opportunities exist for developing Bean's international presence? For example, West Germany and England have enjoyed relatively high per capita sales through direct-response marketing channels.
8. What allowances should be made for effects wrought by the shape of the overall economy? Has serving relatively upscale segments of the market buffered the company from the effects of economic slumps?
9. Because most business is done in the fall months, creating a considerable burden on the company's policy of fast turnaround and high accuracy, can this cycle be smoothed by distributing the orders received more evenly throughout the year?
10. Of paramount concern is whether or not the essential nature of the business can be altered without harming the L. L. Bean image.
11. How might other objectives—growth and improved profitability, for example—be attained without diluting product quality and efficiency of service?

12. Are circumstances likely to arise that might lead management and shareholders to undertake equity financing?

Your Task:

The L. L. Bean management team has requested that you advise them on these matters. Are there additional salient issues you believe Messrs. Gorman, End, Findlay, Poole, Greenleaf, Farrar (and others) ought to address in coping with change and managing the future? If so, please outline these and make any suggestions regarding them that you think would be of value to the strategic planning committee.

Appendix

EDP—CHRONOLOGICAL REVIEW*

Over the past dozen years, data processing at Bean's has grown from four Flex-o-writers (keypunch machines that punch data onto paper tape) to a computer complex whose equipment rents for over $1 million per year.

In October 1969, Flex-o-writers from Singer were introduced to L. L. Bean, the primary purpose being to replace the typing of catalog labels by putting the customer names and addresses on the computer. This was accomplished through a local bank. The initial effort included converting the manual file of about 750,000 records and then keying the name, address, and order value and source code for all orders and inquiries to update the file. Priscilla Leavitt was in charge of order processing, while Jane Brewer led the group responsibilities for the mailing list. Nancy Marston was hired for her experience with Flex-o-writers.

Except for the increase in the number of Flex-o-writers (to 14) needed to accommodate the volume growth, things remained pretty much unchanged until 1974. Enter our first computer—an IBM System 3/10. An inventory file was established and order sets were printed from the computer using data prepared on the 3742 key-to-diskette machines, which are still our primary input media today. The keyers were led by Sylvia Estabrook and the order writers/coders by Berla Allen. We also ran mailing labels on this computer (we had just reached 1 million names on our masterfile) and tried to run accounts receivable using CRTs that were in the offices located at the store. The computer was not fast enough, and the accounts receivable were backlogged almost two months as Lee Surace (then manager of accounting) can attest.

So in 1975, we brought in our first real computer, an IBM 370/115.

Appendix (Cont.)

Horace Gower joined us to lead the conversion to the new machine. During 1975 we added a physical inventory system and brought our mailing list in house. We also began the design of a full order processing system.

The year 1976 was a big one for data processing. We upgraded the computer again (which we have done every year except one) and began the implementation of an order processing system with Pam Allen and Shari Chaney doing much of the early work. Information must be accurate to be useful, so we introduced our first edit program—if the data were not valid and logical, they were rejected and rekeyed. This seems so necessary in hindsight but caused many discussions at the time, especially since we would be adding 10 to 15 percent to the keying load. We also sent our list processing work to Figi so we could concentrate on other priorities.

In 1977 we automated backorders! No longer did we use rulers to measure backorders. No longer was the manual status board in the warehouse needed for checking each order prior to sorting for picking. We now could ensure shipping the oldest backorder first when merchandise arrived. We also could distinguish between demand (what the customer wanted) and sales (what we shipped). All the monetary systems relating to customer orders were also incorporated at this time including refunds, accounts receivable, and credit card billing.

The year 1978 represented the beginning of on-line corrections for order processing and the first financial package—general ledger (which included budgeting).

In 1979, another big year, the inventory planning system (item forecasting), which required over 5 man-years of effort, was implemented. This was our largest effort to date and required a lot of support from the merchandising people and especially Dick Leslie. We also implemented a batch picking system to analyze the orders and sort them into the most efficient picking sequence for the distribution center. Accounts payable was implemented as well.

In 1980 we introduced the manifest shipping system, the customer service inquiry system, and the store system to support the new cash registers. The customer service system had a significant impact on the computer as an order is kept on file for 30 days after disposition. This means a file of $1\frac{1}{2}$ million orders (about 1 billion characters) during peak.

In 1981, the department made a major commitment to designing computer systems to support the Advertising and Direct Marketing department activities. In conjunction with the Marketing Systems Department initial anlaysis and design, work was started on a system to report how well our direct-mail and advertising programs were doing. A system to track the movement of batches of orders through the picking and packing operations in the warehouse was also implemented in the fall of

Appendix (Cont.)

1981, and the old physical inventory system and accounts receivable systems were written.

In the near future, we will be completing our largest project ever—an entirely new mailing list system. This project, which will require a total effort of 8 to 10 man-years, is scheduled for initial implementation during the spring of 1983. This system will be the Cadillac of the industry and should allow us to continue refining our mailing strategies. At the same time, we are working on an automated personnel system and a manufacturing resources planning system. Both of these will utilize programs purchased from other companies.

Our programming staff has grown from 1 person to 25, with over half being recruited and trained from within L. L. Bean. Our operations staff now numbers almost 20 people. We are fortunate that we have been able to attract and retain good people. The data processing profession has a turnover rate in excess of 20 percent and we have been able to keep ours to less than 2 percent.

This fall [1982] we will be printing 8 million lines per day. This will be comprised of 50,000 to 60,000 order sets and nearly 2,000 copies of reports to be distributed throughout the company each day of the week. To accomplish this, the computer will be run 24 hours a day, 7 days a week. The amount of processing that will take place is staggering when you consider that our computers together can perform 2 million instructions per second!

Continual hardware growth has been necessary to keep pace with the company's volume growth and our own applications growth as outlined. Our current system includes an IBM 4341 with 8 million bytes of memory (with a second computer scheduled for this fall), 12 billion bytes of on line storage (disk), 12 tape drives, and a large terminal network that will soon support over 100 terminals. The total budget for data processing for 1982 approaches $2.5 million. Big dollars to be sure, but think about some of the applications and what the alternatives would be without our computers.

Source: Company files, 1982 document. Written by Kilt Andrew, Public Affairs.

case
30

APPLE COMPUTER INC.

HELLO, I'M YOUR INFORMATIVE AND INEXPENSIVE ELECTRON-IC COMPANION. LINK YOUR MIND WITH MY MICROPROCESSOR AND LET US MAKE TIMELY DECISIONS TOGETHER.[1]

MAKE BREAD WITH AN APPLE. EVEN IF YOUR COMPANY HAS A BIG COMPUTER SYSTEM, YOU COULD PROBABLY DO YOUR JOB BETTERFASTERSMARTER WITH AN APPLE ... SITTING ON YOUR DESK.[2]

MY NAME IS REVEREND APPLE.... GROOM, WHAT'S YOUR NAME?[3]

Apple Computer Inc., hasn't given its blessing to the computer marriages, but a spokesperson has said, "It's good to have divinity on your side." Reputedly the world's first ordained computer, the Apple II's human co-pastor

---

[1] Opening conversational gambit on an Apple II.

[2] Excerpt from fall 1981 Apple Computer Inc., advertisement.

[3] Marilyn Chase, "Do You Take This Input to Be Your Lawfully Wedded Interface?" *The Wall Street Journal,* July 28, 1981, p. 29.

in a California church used his electronic helper "to get people interested in marriage, the church, and God," offering the programmed ceremony free along with marriage counseling by a warm-blooded being for the lucky couple.

Personal computer-craze cartoons abound. For example, a boy stares incredulously at a book, a gift just handed to him by someone who looks suspiciously like a harried mother, and asks how it can be full of information since it doesn't even have a display screen.[4] Another lists on a house-for-sale sign features that include 9 rooms, 3 baths, and 2 computer terminals.[5] The third example, a cover cartoon, portrays a psychoanalyst fingering a lap-held keyboard and asking the couch occupant to tell him when the urge first struck to buy a home computer.[6]

CORPORATE BACKGROUND

Widely acknowledged as the leader in the personal computer arena, Apple Computer Inc., was founded in 1976 by 21-year-old Steve Jobs, whose private goal was to make computer capability widely accessible—not unlike Henry Ford's desire to provide automobiles for the masses, and by Steve Wozniak, both college dropout design engineers.

> *Basically, Steve Wozniak and I invented the Apple because we wanted a personal computer. Not only couldn't we afford the computers that were on the market, those computers were impractical for us to use. We needed a Volkswagen. . . . After we launched the Apple in 1976, all our friends wanted one.*[7]

Jobs likened the Apple offspring's contribution to human efficiency to the IBM Selectric typewriter, the calculator, the Xerox copying machine, and advanced telephone systems.

The youthful entrepreneurs used $1,300 from the sale of a Volkswagen to assemble their first prototype. Both Steves wanted to avoid a threatening name, one smacking of high technology, and Jobs was a fruitarian, so the corporate name "Apple" sounded appropriate. The unspoken corporate motto might well have been, "Don't trust any computer you can't lift."

After meeting in the garage of a mutual friend, Jobs and Wozniak's friendship evolved into the partnership that became Apple Computer Inc., primarily by the happenstance of assembling computers for friends, not realizing that they were on to something that could be a leading-edge effort in mak-

[4]*The Wall Street Journal*, n.d.
[5]*The New Yorker*, July 26, 1982, p. 33.
[6]*Forbes*, August 2, 1982, front outside cover.
[7]Fall 1981, corporate advertisement.

ing computers available to the masses. Before forming the company, Wozniak worked as a technician at Hewlett-Packard and Jobs was employed developing video games at Atari. Apple II was designed for the most part by fall 1976, using 4K dynamic random access memories (RAMs), which no other firm used at the time. As Jobs put it, "Going out with a product based on dynamic memories was untried; fortunately, we didn't know how risky it was." According to the chairman, Commodore saw the Apple II and immediately made overtures to acquire the fledgling firm, which would have transformed Apple II to Commodore I. The partners wanted reliable manufacturers who could build a total package for them, so they visited familiar haunts. "Atari couldn't get involved because of a heavy commitment, quite correctly, to developing their games, and Hewlett-Packard, which was working on the HP-85 at that time, was dubious of our abilities, I'm convinced, because we didn't have electrical engineering or computer science degrees."

ADVENT OF PERSONAL COMPUTING

What is a personal computer (PC)? It is an extension of the microprocessor, a computer on a chip, developed by Intel Corp. in the early 1970s and in those earlier years bought principally by hobbyists. Unlike their predecessors, units of the 1980s became total systems, including input keyboards, video readout monitors, and software found at laboratory benches, in manufacturing plants, on executive side tables, and in schools and private dwellings.

The PC industry grew from nothing in 1975 to an estimated $1.5 billion plus in 1981 and was forecasted by industry specialists to continue an annual growth of from 40 to 50 percent through the mid-1980s. Stock prices of such firms as Apple, Tandy, and Commodore soared. Apple went on the market at $22 a share in 1980, and traded over the counter at $25 in August 1981, or roughly 100 times earnings, definitely a glamour stock. In November 1982, prices hovered in the area of $30, having risen from $11 earlier in the year.

Apple's first units, small, simple, and relatively inexpensive, were designed for consumer use, not for business and scientific applications, but after add-on small-disk memory was introduced in 1978, many software authors started developing Apple programs for business. One, a general-purpose financial analysis program, is credited with giving Apple a year's lead time over competitors, making it the top banana in the business PC bunch.

According to various sources at the company's Cupertino, California, headquarters, independent software vendors were thought to spend a large proportion, possibly more than half, of their time on Apple software. The April 1982 issue of *BYTE* had no fewer than 11 pages of ads from companies promoting products to boost Apple II's performance. Rather than a hardware race, software technology was seen as the desirable focus to help buyers increase the usefulness of their machines.

As research and development proceeded rapidly, Apple III was announced in May 1980, finally making a full-fledged debut in March 1981. Initially technical problems had led to customer complaints that were covered by a policy of outright exchange. Both software and hardware came in for varied and widespread criticism as users bombarded Apple management with queries and grievances. It was rumored that the new units were about to be replaced by improved hardware and operating systems, but management denied this, predicting a 10-year life span for Apple III.

Operating mostly in leased facilities, manufacturing operations consisted of purchase, assembly, and test of materials and components used in Apple products. Facilities were located in Dallas; Cupertino, San Jose, and Los Angeles, California; County Cork, Ireland; and Singapore.

Purchases of personal computers for home use were at first disappointing; still, leading producers continued to emphasize these markets while consumer analysts warned that sales to these segments would not be sensational until the hardware and software were designed to serve the needs of household users. Home computers can be entertaining and educational and might even prove useful as information and transaction devices. One writer, whose personal computer was an Apple II, described dialing into a central network to view an airline schedule and suggested numerous other potential dimensions of what he called "home computer bulletin boards," speculating that students would have access to information comparable to the complete Library of Congress and that mail would be instantaneous.[8]

As electronic hobbyists' purchases dwindled in the late 1970s and early 1980s, manufacturers started eyeing the 80 million U.S. households, stressing fun and educational aspects. Predictions were that one of every four American homes would have a computer by the late 1980s. Planners spoke of two or three in every home and one atop every businessperson's desk. Speedups in automation, including PCs, were to affect directly the jobs of some 9 million managers and 14 million professionals in American industry.[9] Small computers were expected to be information processing building blocks in this changing structure.

CULTIVATING EDUCATIONAL MARKETS

In 1979, Apple helped to create the nonprofit Foundation for the Advancement of Computer-Aided Education with the goal of furthering efforts of software authors. In 1980, Atari and Texas Instruments sponsored software

---

[8]Neil Shapiro, "Now Your Home Computer Can Call Other Computers on the Telephone," *Popular Mechanics*, February 1981, p. 130.

[9]"The Speedup in Automation," Special Report in *Business Week*, August 3, 1981, pp. 58–67.

writing contests. About this time, Tandy launched collaborative efforts with textbook publishers to enrich educational software. Most microprocessor makers hoped that expanded use in schools would stimulate computer sales in the home market. Educators claimed that poor software, frustrated users, and attempts at electronic humor in response to users' errors were insulting deterrents to students, although youngsters were said to approach the keyboard enthusiastically and to become comfortable quickly when exposed to computers.

Far below expectations, 1980 shipments of 50,000 microcomputers to schools were predicted by many to rise to some 250,000 units annually over a five-year period. Sales to schools in 1981 were estimated at $150 million. The shrinking cost of computer power was credited with the sudden popularity of school computers. C. Gregory Smith, director of educational marketing at Apple, expressed conviction that not only were schools sold on computers but they also were more likely than business buyers to make repeat purchases. That computer literacy would become a survival skill equal in importance to reading, writing, and arithmetic was not in doubt in the Apple hierarchy.

Engineering and business students at many colleges and universities opted for their own computers—individual units either owned or leased—partly because of the difficulties encountered gaining access to the institution's central devices. Several schools began leasing computers and telephone modems so students could have remote access to the larger processors on campus. Some colleges—for example, Stevens Institute of Technology in Hoboken, New Jersey—required that a student studying science, systems analysis, management, and other computer-intensive courses in 1982 own a microprocessor. Quite apart from relieving demand for the institutions's scarce terminals, schools taking this approach expected it to encourage students to become more familiar with and dependent upon computers, to treat them as an integral part of their intellectual support systems.

Donating an Apple II computer to some 83,000 public elementary and secondary schools in the United States seems a laudable and easily attainable goal, one that could be accomplished simply by management fiat. Not so, however, particularly when the would-be contributor posed a condition: boosting the ceiling on the annual amount of such a donation to 30 percent of its taxable income from 10 percent, the existing maximum. Without success Apple lobbied for a change permitting it to "further the cause of computer literacy in the nation's public schools," an attempt rejected by the House Ways and Means Committee.

New hope came in September 1982, as the House passed part of a temporary tax break giving the proposed program a boost.[10] The legislation (323 for and 62 against) would permit computer manufacturers to donate computers to

---

[10]"Apple Clears Hurdle on Its Plan to Send Computers to Class," *The Wall Street Journal,* September 23, 1982, p. 31.

public schools and to receive the favorable tax treatment reserved for donations of scientific equipment to universities. Congressional tax analysts estimated the tax break to be worth about $36 million in fiscal years 1982 and 1983 for Apple or for any others who wished to make such contributions. The Senate was yet to consider a similar bill. Apple executives thought the bill would stimulate computer education and, in turn, the computer industry; Treasury Department spokespersons opposed the idea on grounds that tax law should not be used to form social policy.

TOP-LEVEL ORGANIZATIONAL CHANGES

In early 1981, Apple Computer Inc., restructured its management team, naming former vice president of marketing, then chairman, A. C. Markkula, Jr., 39 years old, to the post of president and chief executive officer to concentrate on day-to-day operations of the company; Markkula was succeeded in the chairmanship by former Vice Chairman Jobs. Michael Scott, age 38, shifted from the position of president/CEO to the role of vice chairman, in charge of long-range business growth planning, and in 1982 left the company.

Self-taught computer engineer Stephen Wozniak programmed himself out of the Apple family portrait when he decided to seek gratification beyond the corporate agenda. Following an airplane wreck and a five-week loss of memory, he took a leave of absence from the company and enrolled at the University of California-Berkeley, under an assumed name, to take undergraduate computer science courses he had dropped out of for lack of interest 11 years previously.[11] The wizard—"Woz" to his friends—promoted a new-kind-of-unity rock concert at which 200,000 Californians and others showed up to hear music and relate to a philosophy pushing "us" instead of "me." At 32, with an estate thought to be over $50 million, Wozniak was said to be out approximately $3 million unless subsequent film and album revenues would cover his expenditures.[12]

FINANCIAL HIGHLIGHTS

As unemployment hovered around 10.4 percent in October 1982, and many industries were in the doldrums, the microcomputer marketers enjoyed continued increases in sales and profits. "One reason," CEO Markkula pointed out, "is that a recession prompts many companies to invest in products that

[11]Paul Ciotti, "California Magazine," in the *Denver Post,* August 1, 1982, p. D-1.
[12]Rom Morganthau, David R. Friendly, and William Cook, "A Wizard called 'Woz'," *Newsweek,* September 20, 1982, p. 69.

will boost productivity. That perspective has helped our sales not just here but also in Europe and England." Apple estimated that its profits rose 70 percent on sales gains of 80 percent in the fourth quarter ending in September. For its fiscal year, earnings were up more than 50 percent on a revenue increase of almost 75 percent. Exhibit 1 provides a review of selected financial statistics.

Cash flow was consistently healthy at Apple, partly because the company encouraged its 1,400 North American and 1,600 international dealers and distributors to pay in full for shipments within two weeks, while Apple generally took up to six weeks to pay its own suppliers.

Markkula was pleased with the company's financial shape, pointing to return on equity of 28 percent, return on assets of 20 percent, and return on investment of 33 percent. The balance sheet at the end of fiscal 1982 also revealed about $150 million in cash and equivalents and negligible debt, stellar performance from a company in existence only five years. There was talk around the company of breaking into the *Fortune* 500 list.

Exhibit 1

SELECTED APPLE FINANCIAL STATISTICS, FISCAL YEARS SEPTEMBER 30, 1977–1982
(in millions, rounded)

	1977	1978	1979	1980	1981	1982
Net Sales	$0.8	$7.9	$48	$117	$335	$583
R&D expenses	NA	0.6	4	7	21	38
Marketing expenses	NA	1.3	4	12	46	32
Net income	0.4	0.8	5	12	39	61

NA – Not available.
Notes: Net sales increases were not greatly affected by price changes.

Net income in 1981 was increased principally by improved gross margins and higher interest income, partially offset by increased marketing (increased advertising and other promotion costs and expansion of the distribution system) and general and administrative expenses (resulting mainly from foreign exchange losses, which were included in G&A expenses in 1981). Interest income in 1981 of $11.7 million was over 10 times the previous year's, resulting from investment in short-term securities of the proceeds from Apple's common stock offering in December 1980.

Apple paid no cash dividends, choosing to reinvest earnings to finance growth.

During the first quarter, a one-time, after-tax charge of $700,000 was accrued for an extra week's vacation awarded to employees as the company exceeded $100 million in quarterly sales for the first time.

A common stock issue of 2,600,000 shares was subscribed in 1981. Apple's 13 officers and directors own approximately 25 million of the company's almost 58 million common shares outstanding; Jobs has over 7.5 million, Markkula over 7 million, and Wozniak over 4 million, the three totaling almost a third of all shares.

FACING THE COMPETITION

Digital Equipment Corporation

After a winter of discontent that saw IBM storm down the field and a surge by Tandy and Commodore, 1982 was the season for Digital's challenge in the personal computer wars. Months earlier the company had moved into office automation. The acknowledged leader in superminicomputers—machines offering the performance of larger mainframe systems for a mini's price—presumably was counting on a strong position in information processing at major companies to give it a needed competitive edge. Digital bought advertisements in a few trade magazines in early summer and ran announcement-type ads in selected business periodicals. Observers concluded that this campaign was intended to reach the company's existing markets, not to cultivate awareness and interest in the much wider market already penetrated by the microprocessor pioneers and believed that Digital looked to the new line as an aid to sustain its high growth rate. However, insiders expected that the company would concentrate on sales to professionals and small businesses in an attempt to gain a share of the crowded $2.5 billion microcomputer markets. Meanwhile, by 1982 Digital had had three years of experience operating its chain of retail stores, computer shops intended to eliminate computer fear, to communicate benefits information in a friendly atmosphere, and to be flexible in how its systems were presented to the public. The overall goal was to keep prospects from being intimidated.

Osborne Computer Corporation

Fall 1982 brought an advertising headline "the best holiday offer your career ever had," showing a picture of the unit followed by "The Osborne Personal Business Computer. $1795. dBASE II Data Base Software. Free." Most of the body copy promoted available software packages. The pre-Christmas theme (the free offer was to end December 24) announced "the best buy in a personal computer just got better."

Commodore International

An enviable stock performance record reflected this company's second-generation system's success. Entering the market in 1976 by purchasing MOS Technology to get a supply of calculator chips, CI benefited serendipitously from the acquired firm's research and development in microprocessor technology. The principal result of that development was named PET (personal electronic transactor) and was merchandised primarily in Europe simply because there was less competition there than in the United States. Calling themselves "the American Japanese," Commodore's strategy became that of offering a processor that could emulate those made by others, offering it at a price under $1,000, compared with prices of four times that for competitors' models. The rallying cry from Commodore was "A real computer for the price of a toy," while insisting that this computer went beyond games to teach computing skills to users. "The Commodore 64. Only $595. What nobody else can give you at twice the price," showing a picture of a user's hands, a keyboard, and color graphics, covered one side of a two-page advertisement. The opposite page showed how favorably Commodore 64 compared with Apple II ($1,530), IBM ($1,565), TRS-80 III ($999), and Atari 800 ($899). Commodore was apparently "coming home" to make its mark against entrenched microprocessor makers.

Tandy Corporation

Industry sources estimated that Tandy's 25 percent of the PC market in 1981 had declined to 24 percent in 1982. Tandy distributed through its chain of about 8,000 Radio Shack outlets, 200 of which sold only personal computers. Its TRS-80 and Apple were the most common stand-alone computers used by managers. Tandy widely advertised low prices ranging from $250 for a hand-held computer to a $10,000 system for small businesses. Science and science-fiction author Isaac Asimov was spokesman for Radio Shack's TRS-80, announcing in 1982 a price of $399.95 for the color computer. A 1981 survey reported that businesses typically spent about $9,460 for a computer system, while hobbyists' outlays averaged $1,574.[13] Factors delaying proliferation of executive desk-top computers reportedly included lack of communication software and physical design as well as resistance from entrenched data processing departments in the larger firms.[14]

Texas Instruments

Lessons learned in selling hand-held calculators were apparently being used by Texas Instruments in slashing the price of its entry in the home computer field. The offer was a $100 rebate to customers buying the 99-4A computer. The predecessor 99-4 system came on the market in 1979 at about $1,000, the 4A was introduced in 1981 at $525, and the 1982 list price was pegged at $299.50. Comedian Bill Cosby was spokesman for TI's home computer.

[13]Small Business section, *The Wall Street Journal,* July 6, 1981, p. 17.
[14]"Microcomputers Invade the Executive Suite," *Computer Decisions,* February 1981, p. 70.

Sinclair and Timex

"Under $200," advertised Sinclair Research Ltd. for its ZX80, describing it as a complete and powerful full-function computer that matched or surpassed other computers costing "many times more." The 1981 brochures proclaimed, "You simply take it out of the box, connect it to your TV, and turn it on. . . . With the manual in your hand, you'll be running programs in an hour. Within a week, you'll be writing complex programs with confidence." The company announced a 30-day moneyback guarantee and a 90-day limited warranty along with its national service-by-mail facility. After Timex acquired the computer maker, Timex Sinclair's 1000 became an update of the ZX series and was called "the first ready-to-go personal computer for under $100" (actually $99.95), aimed at the consumer market. Should the machine become available where Timex watches were distributed, 100,000 retail outlets might display and sell the ZX 1000. Some analysts recommended that the leaders should carefully observe the progress of this efficient and low-priced product, claiming it could well provide a substantial impetus for the personal computers revolution. The assumption was that introducing neophytes to computers with low-priced units could provide a reservoir of demand for trading up to units such as those made by Apple.

IBM

In all its years of successful EDP product introductions, IBM avoided growing slovenly or complacent, even though the giant firm was not always the undisputed leader in new products. With its large war chest of R&D and promotional funds and an eye for where much of the present, and probably a considerable portion of the future, seemed to lie, the company's riposte in microprocessors made its mark in this burgeoning field, eliminating the downside risk of ignoring the opportunities and sharing in the upside potential after parrying opponents' lunges. IBM personal computers were distributed through 150 ComputerLand stores and at Sears Business Systems Centers, as well as at IBM product centers that sold and serviced the system. October 1982 demand for its systems exceeded supply, as the company announced anticipated output of 15,000 machines each month. While prophets of gloom heralded IBM's entry as a severe blow to competitive hardware precursors, many observers considered it yet another good omen for the booming business of software, an industry based on writing those coded sets of instructions that provide maps for computers to follow in processing data. As with all other entrants, IBM's success in PC markets would depend heavily on availability of software to drive the systems. With an estimated 5,000-plus software producers in the United States alone, competition was strong, and after details of

IBM's configuration became available, conversion work in software supply houses became a major priority.

In an amicable mood, an Apple ad campaign in 1981 forthrightly greeted the newcomer: "Welcome, IBM. Seriously. . . . to the most exciting and important marketplace since the computer revolution began 35 years ago. . . .When we invented the first personal computer system, we estimated that over 140 million people worldwide could justify the purchase of one, if only they understood its benefits. Next year alone, we project that well over one million will come to that understanding. . . . We look forward to responsible competition in the massive effort to distribute this American technology to the world. . . . what we are doing is increasing social capital by enhancing individual productivity. Welcome to the task."

Using mass media to address the general public about its personal computer, IBM's fall 1982 advertisements pushed such product features as non-glare screen (easy on the eyes), 80 characters a line (with upper- and lower-case letters for a quick and easy read), flexibility of moving components about (the keyboard could be placed on one's lap and the user could rest his or her feet on the desk or elsewhere), and user memory expandable up to 256K, with 40K of permanent memory. Friendliness to users was claimed; BASIC language and high-resolution color graphics on the user's own TV set were mentioned as IBM invited shoppers to look around and compare theirs with others. The action imperative asked readers and viewers to visit an authorized IBM Personal Computer dealer, promising an address, along with other information, at an 800 number. And the competitive price was mentioned: "The quality, power and performance of the IBM Personal Computer are what you'd expect from IBM. The price isn't."[15] One headline announced: "30 years of computer experience: $1,565 and up."

On television, IBM employed a "humanizing" approach to hawking its machines by claiming they "are warm and friendly and okay to touch." The Chaplin-like figure attempting to understand a computer's intricacies, and finally emerging triumphant, presumably was meant to persuade the reluctant that microprocessing could be conquered.

Meanwhile, Dick Cavett was acting as spokesman for Apple, and Tandy planned to show some at-home, family sorts of applications for its machines during the 1982 fall football broadcasts, but the NFL strike altered those intentions. All three producers pushed utilitarian simplicity.

---

[15]Early in 1982, IBM announced standardizing its typewriter line, cutting prices on some models and offering volume discounts for the first time. In late 1982, American Express Company sent a special mailer to cardholders announcing availability of the Selectric III, through American Express, at the going price, equal payments over 20 months, and no interest charges.

Hewlett-Packard

HP announced its desk-top model, designed to compete with the IBM Personal Computer and Apple III, in late winter 1982. This producer of precision electronics, with annual sales of over $4 billion, fired promotional salvos headlining HP-87 maximum memory of 544K, analytic software including the CP/M module, and the read-only-memory-based operating system that put built-in BASIC to work for the user. "We're building power, friendliness and reliability . . ." announced the body copy, with the tag line, "It's very good at what you do." HP's program library offered only two games in contrast to the dozens provided by competitive producers. One of HP's advertisements used the headline: "The personal computer comes of age." Perhaps the idea was old or useless by this time, but Apple ran no promotion welcoming Hewlett-Packard to the field of front-runners. Moving rapidly, in late summer, the company unveiled HP-75, its 26-ounce, battery-operated machine set to retail at $995. HP sources indicated the easily portable unit was intended to provide a transition between pocket calculators and desk-top computers.

Xerox

A formidable entry was Xerox, going for a total system configuration by promoting integrated office automation products—including a microcomputer doubling as low-cost word processor—and threatening to vie for the anticipated largesse ready to be harvested in homes across the land.

Other competitors were expected to emerge, particularly since the capital gains tax, which was cut to 40 percent (from 50 percent) in 1978, favored high-technology entrepreneurs ready, with this added incentive, to start new businesses in the data processing field.

MARKET SHARES AND DISTRIBUTION

Based on several sources, it was estimated in mid-1982 that personal computer sales were shared as follows: Apple and Tandy/Radio Shack combined dominating almost half the market, with the market shares of 24 percent each; next came Commodore at 9 percent; Nippon Electric Company with 6 percent; Hewlett-Packard and IBM at 5 percent each; Osborne accounting for 3 percent; and others, including Xerox, Digital Equipment, Texas Instruments, and perhaps 20 smaller producers sharing the remainder.

Estimates varied widely, but it was conjectured that stores were the channel of distribution for about 60 percent of desk-top computers purchased in 1982, while mail order accounted for 15 to 20 percent and direct sales 10 to 15 percent, the remainder being sold by other means.

Except for Tandy and Texas Instruments' units, personal computers were available at computer stores; and Texas Instruments sold through department stores and catalogs. Struggling for display space was a way of life, and marketing became extremely vital to PC sales. Such firms as Sears reportedly planned to carry no more than four brands in 1983, all chosen according to what seems logical for the most customers. The chain's 26 business retail centers stocked IBM, Osborne, and Vector Graphics systems in 1982. A Sears manager rejected the idea that this limited array hindered customers' choices: "Most suppliers are merely assemblers of components by other firms that provide the same components for many manufacturers, so it is difficult when you look inside the case to tell them all apart." MOS Technology, Zilog, Inc., and Intel Corporation were the leading processor designers.

Apple's retail dealers were asked by the company, in November 1981, to sign an amended dealer contract to prohibit telephone and mail-order sales of its products under penalty of losing dealership status. The rationale was simple: success depends on customer satisfaction, which, in turn, depends on dealers providing support services to users. Although some mail-order firms were discounting prices, Apple management said that this was not the issue, maintaining that its effort to eliminate mail-order sales was legal and in line with the company's philosophy of adequately serving customers' postpurchase needs. Filing a suit to block the company from enforcing the new policy, a group of mail-order distributors accused Apple of bowing to pressure from full-service dealers by attempting to fix prices and restrain trade.

A long-standing central buying agreement with a Minneapolis-based retail chain was renewed for 1983. Team Central, entering its sixth year of association with Apple, is a franchiser of approximately 90 retail stores that sell general consumer products in medium-sized and smaller markets nationwide.[16]

"We're happy the negotiations are complete and look forward to another strong selling year with the Team organization," announced Gene Carter, Apple vice president of sales. "Team provides Apple with an important presence in secondary and tertiary markets."

Gary Thorne, Team executive vice president of sales and marketing, said his company's strategy in 1983 would be to emphasize personal computer sales through its franchisees. "The pervasiveness of personal computers and Team's importance in the markets we serve make the Apple line an exciting part of our sales thrust in the coming year."

Earlier in the year, Apple ended a similar agreement with Computer-Land Corp., to help achieve geographic control of new franchisees.

---

[16]Based on corporate press release, August 12, 1982.

APPLE'S DIRECT ATTACK

In February 1982 Apple's offensive included this campaign: "NOW THAT YOU'VE SEEN THEIR FIRST GENERATION, TAKE A LOOK AT OUR THIRD," making the comparison shown in Exhibit 2. Highlights of claims for the Apple III are shown in Exhibit 3.

Promoting its third generation, Apple announced: "The only thing we didn't build into the Apple III is obsolescence." The new product was available at over 1,000 dealers in the United States and Canada, all offering technical support.

In contrast to some Apple advertisements that were hard-hitting and directly confrontational, others were somewhat whimsical, appealing to specific market segments. Consider these headlines: "Grow Corn with an Apple," targeted to the agribusiness segment, pushing its more than 1,000 full-service dealers as the contact point for farmers desiring to aid their decision making; "E. F. Hutton simplifies life with Apples," attempted to persuade life insurance agents to have an Apple to help ensure their futures; "Make bread with an Apple," a third-party testimony about Apple's role at Pepperidge Farm; "Baked Apple," described how a fire-damaged Apple, *"mirabile dictu,"* still worked when brought into one of the nearly 1,000 Apple dealers with complete service centers, where everything would be "well done"; and a fourth quarter 1982 ad listed 1,100 Apple-compatible computer programs.

> *Consumer awareness and brand recognition are prerequisites to long-term success in a marketplace of intensifying competition. Apple has been known for its marketing emphasis, with a resultant identity that we consider memorable and strong. Awareness of Apple, according to market surveys, rose from approximately 10 percent at the beginning of 1981 to nearly 80 percent at year-end.[17]*

Apple also launched Apple Expo—a dealer trade seminar, trade show, and public exposition—in major U.S. cities and created extensive merchandising aids and dealer training programs.

> *[Apple's] marketing emphasis in the past two years has been on the business, professional and managerial segment, which today accounts for approximately 40 percent of revenues. . . . Ultimately, the greatest demand for personal computers will come from a broader spectrum.[18]*

Apple supported the advertising campaigns of retail dealers with reimbursements of up to 3 percent of their dollar purchases from the company for

[17] *1981 Annual Report*, p. 3.
[18] Ibid., p. 3.

Exhibit 2

APPLE'S COMPARISON OF ITS FEATURES WITH THOSE OF SELECTED COMPETITORS

	XEROX 820	HEWLETT-PACKARD 125, MODEL 10	IBM PERSONAL COMPUTER	APPLE III
Standard memory	64K	64K	64K	128K
Maximum memory when fully configured*	64K	64K	192K	256K
Expandability	No expansion slots	No expansion slots	No extra expansion slots in fully configured* 192K system	4 extra expansion slots in fully configured* 256K system
Diskette storage (per drive)	92K	256K	160K	140K
Mass storage (per drive)	—	1.16 megabyte floppy disk	—	5 megabyte hard disk
Display graphics capability	High resolution, B/W	High resolution, B/W	High resolution, B/W or 4-color (color requires additional card)	High resolution, B/W or 16-color
Software available	Word processing	Word processing	Word processing	Prod processing
	SuperCalc®	VisiCalc® 125	VisiCalc®	VisiCalc® III
	—	Business graphics	—	Business graphics
	—	Data base management	—	Data base management
	Communications	Communications	Communications	Communications
	—	—	—	Apple II software library
	CP/M® library	CP/M® library	CP/M® 86 programs	CP/M® library (Spring 1982)

*"Fully configured" means that the system includes, at a minimum, monitor, printer, two disk drives, and RS-232 communicator.

Note: Based on manufacturer's information available as of December 1981.

Exhibit 3

CLAIMS FOR APPLE III, 1982

Dollar for dollar, the most powerful personal computer.

Up to 256K of usable internal memory.

New software packages exclusively for the Apple III, including VisiCalc III.

Apple Writer III software—professional word processing capability—for less than the price of most word processors.

Apple business graphics—plots, graphs, bars or pie charts in 16 high-resolution colors or 16 gray scales.

Mail list manager lets you store nearly 1,000 names on one disk.

Access III communications software: access to mainframe computers.

Apple III can run thousands of Apple II programs . . . soon . . . thousands of CP/M programs. More available software than any other personal computer.

ProFile, a new hard-disk option. With this addition, Apple III can store over 1,200 pages of text (5 million bytes of information). Enables you to handle problems once reserved for big computers.

---

actual advertising expenses incurred and provided there was compliance with standards set by Apple. At its own expense, Apple provided demonstration models, brochures, and point-of-sale posters and conducted sales seminars to assist dealers. Corporate expenditures for product advertising accelerated from $573,000 in 1978, to $2 million in 1979, $4.5 million in 1980, $6.4 million in 1981, and an estimated $26 million in 1982. Internal estimates were, as Apple continued fending off those who would challenge its industry leadership, that advertising expenditures would remain in the interval of 4 to 5 percent of sales.

SUMMER OF 1982 LEGAL ISSUES[19]

Imitators of good ideas seemed to come out of the woodwork as Apple's executives lost count of look-alikes. In July 1982 the company filed a number of lawsuits overseas, notably in Taiwan, Hong Kong, and New Zealand, in an ongoing effort to stop the manufacture and export of bogus Apple II personal computers. Investigations continued in Japan, Singapore, and Australia.

In Taipei, Taiwan, Apolo brought a civil action under Taiwan's copyright laws against Sunrise Computer, maker of the "Apolo II" computer, an Apple

[19]Based primarily on corporate memoranda, July–August 1982.

copy.[20] As a first step in this action in accordance with Taiwanese law, Apple seized as evidence several Apolo computers during a surprise raid on a Sunrise facility in Taipei. Apple planned to press similar charges against another Taiwanese manufacturer. The government of Taiwan, according to the company, was collaborating with Apple to help prevent export of Apple II copies.

In Hong Kong, Apple filed a civil action under local patent laws against a small manufacturer selling Apple II copies, a number of which were seized as evidence in a surprise raid similar to the one in Taiwan. Sales and purchase records of the company were also seized. Because its patents and copyrights were enforceable in Hong Kong, Apple expected to halt all manufacturing and selling of copies there.

In New Zealand, Apple obtained an injunction against Orbit Electronics, which was passing off "Orange" computers from an unknown Taiwanese manufacturer as Apple II computers.

Apple registered its trademarks and copyrights with U.S. Customs authorities and expected that bogus Apple products would be confiscated by the U.S. government at the port of entry. On August 19, Apple announced that the U.S. Customs Service had begun detaining and seizing imitations of the Apple II personal computer. "All copies seized will be destroyed," a company spokesperson reported. "The imitations originated in Taiwan and Hong Kong. The company will take whatever action is necessary to prevent unlawful reproductions of its products from being imported and sold in the United States and abroad."

On August 16, 1982, Apple reported asking the U.S. District Court of eastern Pennsylvania in Philadelphia to reconsider its denial made on August 2 of a preliminary injunction in Apple's lawsuit against Franklin Computer Corporation.

On the same day as the district court denial, the Third Circuit Court of Appeals in Philadelphia issued its opinion in the *Williams Electronics, Inc.* v. *Artic International, Inc.* case involving similar issues. The circuit court, Apple believes, decided some of the key issues that the district judge in the Apple case felt were open questions. Specifically, the circuit court found that U.S. copyright statutes cover object code stored in a computer's read-only-memory (ROM) components.

On May 13, Apple sued Franklin for "patent infringement, copyright infringement, unfair competition, and misappropriation," charging Franklin with copying Apple's diskette- and ROM-form computer programs. Apple sought preliminary and permanent injunctions against the manufacture or sale of Franklin products. A company report claimed, "Copying the programs en-

---

[20]During a trip to the Orient, the casewriters were made aware of Taiwanese-assembled microprocessors closely resembling Apple II selling at prices below U.S. $300, and in the shadow of a major Hong Kong shopping complex, counterfeit computers very much like Apple II regularly sold at 60 percent less than local retail for the U.S.-made counterpart and could be bargained down on slow days.

abled Franklin to produce a computer known as the ACE 100 which can run programs available for the Apple II personal computer."

TOWARD NEW HORIZONS

Chairman Stephen Jobs summarized his view of the corporate mission: "Apple is dedicated to making the personal computer not only indispensable, but understandable." Indications are that the company that invented the personal computer, specializing in nothing else, had just about mastered the delicate balance of technology and customer need in its stated intent to bring "computer power to all the people." Like IBM, Apple has been characterized by restlessness, change, and an absence of complacency, as management spanned the gap between the conflicting aphorisms "haste makes waste" and "those who hesitate are lost."

Speaking with schoolchildren, operating as part of management's information systems, performing as factory servomechanism controllers, translating foreign languages for tourists, playing "Dungeons and Dragons," handling bank-at-home and in-home shopping transactions—the list of potential applications seems endless. In the words of Chairman Jobs, "There are 140 million people in the world who could justify buying a personal computer, if they could only see the benefits to be derived from it."

As the year ended, President and Chief Executive Officer Mike Markkula and his staff were grappling with such crucial issues as product distribution, long-term product strategy, dealer relations, software development, pricing and promotional strategies, and a variety of issues that ordinarily confront rapidly growing organizations.

Your Task:

1. Address Mike Markkula's concerns:
   a. Product distribution—how is Apple doing so far? As you perceive the future, what alternatives should the management team be considering?
   b. Dealer relations—assess the immediate issues broached by the dealers who accused Apple of wrongdoing. Depending upon how you see the outcome, who stands to lose in this conflict?
   c. What might the company do to enhance dealer relations toward improving effectiveness of channels of distribution?
   d. Assess the company's current activities in software development—from the case and from what you read in external literature.
   e. Compare Apple's pricing strategies, as you infer them, with those of competitors. Given changing competitive circumstances, will present practices be sufficient later on?
   f. Is 4 to 5 percent of sales sufficient for advertising? Explain how you would go about setting the promotional budget. If the advertising

manager asked you to suggest a model for him to use in estimating the returns from advertising, how would you respond?

    g. Given the CEO's statements and Chairman Jobs's expectations about future markets, assess Apple's product strategy.

2. Assuming that the president might like to contemplate additional ideas, advise him and the strategic planning committee.

3. Summarize the company's key strengths and weaknesses.

4. Summarize the significant threats and opportunities facing Apple.

5. Overall, what is your prognosis for the microprocessor business in (a) North America, (b) Europe, and (c) Third World countries?

6. Is dramatic shakeout imminent in this industry?

7. Would you invest in Apple stock?

8. Would you work for the company?

BELL LABS/THE WRITER'S WORKBENCH

After first finding one's way out of Newark International Airport's perplexing maze of streets and then negotiating the New Jersey Turnpike, which at times resembles a stock car raceway, the passage is pleasant through wooded countryside to Piscataway, where yet another network of odd turns and doubling back faces those in search of Bell's leased buildings at Number 6 Corporate Place, situated in an industrial park. Inside, a series of corridors is punctuated by modest offices, each, except for those occupied by a manager or supervisor, populated by two or more bright, curious, and inventive people. Ph.D.s abound. The escorted guest is likely to observe congeniality laced with an underlying tension born of constructive impatience.

Considerable ferment had begun in early 1982 in the wake of the consent decree with great expectancy about opportunities offered by change and some apprehension on the part of those who wondered what directions corporate restructuring might take and how their futures would be affected.

THE WINDS OF CHANGE

Commenting on the restructuring of the Bell System, C. L. Brown, chairman of the board, American Telephone & Telegraph Company, spoke on new competitive directions:

In short, I believe that 1980 was in a number of significant ways Year One of the Bell System's future. It was a year in which we redefined the scope of our business and raised our marketing horizons. No longer do we perceive that our business will be limited to telephone or, for that matter, telecommunications. Ours is the business of information handling, the knowledge business.

And the market we seek to serve is global. The technology of the Information Age is ours. Indeed it was Bell System technology that very largely brought it into being. And it is Bell System technology that positions us to fulfill its opportunities. . . . But we have even greater strength than our technology: Bell System people. It is not only their skills but their spirit that makes our business great—and will keep it great.[1]

Bell's business philosophy and R&D directions were reflected in this comment:

The Bell System continued in 1980 to invest heavily in the technology of the future, spending nearly $1.4 billion for research and development work performed by Bell Laboratories and Western Electric.

But technology alone is not sufficient to guarantee success in the marketplace of the future. Technology will have to be matched to the needs and opportunities of the market.[2]

POSTCONSENT DECREE, 1982

In early 1982, Chairman Brown referred to the antitrust action:

As 1981 drew to a close . . . the government antitrust trial was approaching its conclusion. . . . Clearly it was the time to act, time to put uncertainties behind us and to begin reshaping the Bell System's structure and operations to match the requirements of a new era. . . . In the year's unsettled economic circumstances, we improved earnings. We also improved service—not only in terms of the quality of service we provided but in the technological and marketing response we demonstrated in meeting customer needs. . . . For the sixth consecutive year, earnings per share and net income were higher than the year before."[3]

[1]American Telephone & Telegraph Company, *1980 Annual Report.*
[2]Ibid., p. 11.
[3]American Telephone & Telegraph Company, *1981 Annual Report*, p. 2

SELECTED FINANCIAL DATA

The selected financial data presented in Exhibit 1 are based on consolidated accounts of American Telephone & Telegraph Company and its subsidiaries: the Bell telephone operating companies, the Western Electric Company, and Bell Laboratories.

Business services provided 52 percent of Bell System operating revenues in 1981, while residence services contributed 41 percent. Together they accounted for $6.9 billion of the year's $7.4 billion growth in operating revenues. Total expenses amounted to $52.3 billion, an increase of 14.5 percent over those in 1980. Employment costs were $21.4 billion, interest costs $4.4 billion, operating taxes $8.6 billion, and depreciation expenses $7.9 billion. Despite renewed recession and large depreciation increases not fully recovered through repricing, earnings per share were $8.55, up from $8.17 in 1980. The dividend rate was raised to $5.40, the company's eighth increase in 10 years.

HISTORICAL OVERVIEW OF BELL LABS

Exhibit 2 outlines a few historical milestones for Bell Laboratories.

Bell's scientists are accustomed to honors—in 1982 seven had received the Nobel Prize in Physics. In 1979, Bell staff originated some 5,000 technical talks and publications and received over 70 scientific and engineering awards.

Exhibit 1

AT&T SELECTED FINANCIAL DATA, 1977–1981
(in millions)

	1977	1978	1979	1980	1981
Total revenues	$ 37,003	$41,744	$46,183	$51,755	$59,229
Total expenses	32,537	36,482	40,528	45,697	52,341
Net income	$ 4,466	$ 5,262	$ 5,655	$ 6,058	$ 6,888
Preferred dividends	184	164	156	150	146
Earnings per common share	$6.84	$7.73	$8.01	$8.17	$8.55
Average shares outstanding (000s)	625,878	659,843	686,109	723,516	788,178
Total assets	$ 93,677	$103,025	$113,444	$125,553	$137,750*
Long- and intermediate-term debt	$32,305	$34,203	$37,168	$41,255	$43,877
Dividends per common share	$4.20	$4.60	$5.00	$5.00	$5.40

*Includes cash of $282.9 million and temporary cash investments of $1,775.5 million. Drafts outstanding amounted to $795.8 million.

Exhibit 2

SELECTED BELL LABS HISTORICAL HIGHLIGHTS

1876   The telephone was invented by Alexander Graham Bell.

1880   American Bell Telephone Company was organized, technical work was performed by Electrical and Patent Department, and the first Bell System research and development unit was instituted.

1882   Western Electric officially became the manufacturing unit of the Bell System.

1885   American Telephone & Telegraph Company was organized.

1941   First occupancy of Murray Hill, N.J., laboratory occurred. Staff size was 4,455 in July 1981.

1975   Bell Labs opened new major location at Piscataway, New Jersey, for work on computer-based information and operations systems. Staff size 1,865 in July 1981.

1979   Ian M. Ross succeeded William O. Baker as Bell Labs president.

The 325 patents awarded in 1980 brought the total number of Bell Labs patents to more than 19,000.

BELL LABS STAFFING, FUNDING AND RESEARCH EMPHASES:

Altogether there were 19 Bell Labs locations, 11 of these in New Jersey, employing 16,050 in 1981. For all locations in the United States, Bell Labs's roster listed 22,000 employees as both staff size and facilities were expanded. Over 3,000 had Ph.D. degrees, about 5,000 master's degrees, and some 4,000 bachelor's degrees.

To help employees maintain skills and keep abreast of new technologies, the company expanded its education programs, including a new marketing course for technical managers. The computer science curriculum was restructured to help technical staff members increase their expertise in this field.

Personnel assignments by primary and major classifications are summarized in Exhibit 3.

The sustaining financial support from AT&T, Western Electric, and the operating companies of the Bell System enables Bell Labs to serve technological needs of the information marketplace. Exhibit 4 portrays sources of income and cost of work by technical areas.

Linking software and hardware is an ongoing enterprise at Bell Labs, especially developing programs for extremely high-volume, high-reliability, real-

Exhibit 3

1980 PERSONNEL CLASSIFICATIONS, BELL LABS

PRIMARY CLASSIFICATION		MAJOR CLASSIFICATION	
Finance and general services	22.4%	Member of technical staff	41.8%
Software and processor technologies	11.6	Clerical and general	15.2
		Senior technical associate and technical associate	14.8
Customer services	11.3		
Operations systems and network planning	11.2	Member of administrative group	8.1
		Associate member of technical staff	7.4
Switching systems	11.1	Other support staff	12.3
Electronics technology	10.9	Legal and other patent staff	0.4
Transmission systems	7.9		
Research	6.8		
Personnel and public relations	4.0		
Military systems	1.6		
Legal and patent	1.2		

Source: Bell Labs 1980, corporate publication, 1981.

time systems, such as those used in switching. Company scientists are also delving into operations systems—software packages that supervise an array of computer-controlled business functions—and are leaders in creating portable software programs to operate on computers of different types and manufacture. The Bell Labs UNIX[4] system, to be discussed in a later section, has become a widely used operating system in education, industry, and government.

As an example of Bell's interest in home information, a project was undertaken jointly by AT&T, Southern Bell, and Viewdata Corporation (a Knight-Ridder Newspapers subsidiary), in which Bell Labs software controlled an experimental home information system being tested in Coral Gables, Florida, with 160 families using special color TV screens and Bell Labs-developed terminal equipment to access displays of more than 15,000 frames of news, information, and entertainment. In collaboration with CBS, AT&T prepared to start a seven-month Videotex system test in New Jersey in fall 1982, with the television network providing the information content and AT&T the host computer facilities, telecommunications lines, and home terminals.

[4]UNIX is a trademark of Bell Labs.

Exhibit 4

SOURCES AND USES OF BELL LABS INCOME, 1980*

SOURCES OF INCOME		USES OF INCOME	
Western Electric Primarily for specific development and design	50.2%	Operations systems and network planning	20.3%
For national defense	3.0	Electronics technology	17.1
AT&T Primarily for research and systems engineering	34.9	Customer services	15.7
		Switching systems	14.8
		Transmission systems	11.8
Operating companies For business information systems programs	11.9	Research	9.9
		Software and processor technologies	6.8
		Military systems	2.8
		Legal and patent	0.8

*1980 expenditures were approximately 1.3 billion.

Source: 1981 Annual Report.

MARKETING IN THE BELL SYSTEM

Elsewhere in the *1981 Annual Report* additional comments on marketing appeared:

> *Intelligent marketing now guides and unifies our efforts in every aspect of the management of our business—an approach increasingly apparent to and welcomed by our customers. About half of all the management people hired in 1981 filled marketing and sales support assignments.*
>
> *We intend to market all our services vigorously, including those subject to traditional regulation as well as those which would be offered in a detariffed or deregulated part of the business....*
>
> *To ensure the professional development of our business sales people, we have instituted a certification program for Bell System Account Executives and an evaluation and development program for sales managers. We opened a national sales training center, the first of its kind in the Bell System. We also introduced a new incentive pay plan, similar to plans used by other companies to attract and motivate their sales forces.* [5]

[5] *1981 Annual Report*, p. 18.

AT&T watchers are legion, and most economists and others who attempt to evaluate the actions and future of the corporate giant concur that the agreement reached between the Justice Department and the company will open new product avenues in the race for communications dollars, but few proclaim any inside knowledge of how many of these opportunities the firm will pursue. Will it be computer, cable, electronic advertising, office information, home information services? Apparently nobody claims access to an unclouded crystal ball in forecasting the timing of such events.

> *K. W. Weihe, advertising director-business at AT&T, said ... that although the company was always developing new products it was hard to plan ahead because Bell didn't know when those products would be permitted to enter the market.*[6]

Many observers and some AT&T staff members aver that competitors can take a long-range view as to when their products are introduced, and by what processes and under what kinds of marketing efforts they wish to organize, but government so affects the AT&T program that the company simply does not know when its presence in various markets will or can be established.

THE PRESIDENT'S PHILOSOPHY

Ian M. Ross, president of Bell Labs, observed that

> *The key to market leadership in the Information Age is the mastery of certain fundamental technologies, especially microelectronics, software systems, digital systems and ... photonics. The technology of the Information Age was born at Bell Laboratories. As it matured from promise to reality, many others contributed to its growth and now compete vigorously with us in providing innovative products and services for home and office. Once we faced a stable market in which we could systematically introduce new technology. Now market windows and discrete customer preferences increasingly shape the nature of our work.*
>
> *Ultimately, ... our performance depends on our people. A significant part of the Bell System's enviable record of productivity improvement can be traced to ingenious innovations, large and small, developed by dedicated Bell Labs people. In 1980, for the third year in a row, we managed a program of record hiring of technical staff to meet the rapidly growing needs of Western Electric and the Bell Operating Companies ... our foremost priority is to maintain a strong sense of community and a*

[6]*Advertising Age,* January 18, 1982, pp. 2, 84.

*climate in which individual contributions are encouraged and appreciat-
ed.[7]*

THE BIRTHPLACE OF WRITER'S WORKBENCH

The Writer's Workbench system first evolved in the minds of staff members
assigned to the Human Performance Engineering Department at Bell Labs in
Piscataway, New Jersey. Exhibit 5 provides an overview of the department's
mission.

THE WRITER'S WORKBENCH TEAM

The "team" comprises individuals of diverse backgrounds and interests, including, among others, computer science, experimental psychology, English,

[7]*Bell Labs, 1980,* corporate publicity literature.

Exhibit 5

OVERVIEW OF HUMAN PERFORMANCE
ENGINEERING DEPARTMENT

The Human Performance Engineering Department serves as a centralized
resource center for human factors support in the development of computer-based systems.... Most members of the department majored in psychology. However, since much of the department's work involves
computer-based systems, we also attract people who have had course
work and interest in computer science.

The work of the department is carried out on two levels. At one level, direct support is provided for the human performance aspects of particular
developmental projects. This work includes consultation and the collection of empirical data on the most important design questions. At the second level, work of a more general nature is carried out, leading to generic
solutions to problems that arise repeatedly in the system design. Projects
are identified and priorities established for this work on the basis of experience at the first level of effort. This ensures that the more general work is
timely and meets real needs.

Source: Bell Labs internal document.

---

cognitive psychology, educational psychology, and computational linguistics. Larry Frase, a member involved in behavioral applications in office automation, commented: "I'm convinced that behavioral science can contribute significantly to software invention and design, to developing information handling technology among staff and management. I'm trying to encourage closer contact among behavioral science, computer science, and various product design and marketing groups. I'd like to see new courses made available to us on software marketing and others that expand behavioral science training."

Regarding the origin and usefulness of Writer's Workbench to Bell Labs, Paul Turner, director of Human Performance Engineering, observed: "It was developed for in-house applications, like virtually all other software invented here. The Bell System spends about $100 million annually preparing and publishing technical documents. Considerable effort is devoted to reviewing and revising. The Workbench not only speeds up this process and makes it more accurate, but it also adds a great deal to readability. The proofreading and prose analysis programs alone are useful supplements to human writing and editing."

THE PRODUCT

Before describing Writer's Workbench, some background on the UNIX system under which it runs will be useful.

UNIX Operating System Overview

The time-sharing UNIX operating system offers users a combination of flexibility and sophistication usually found only in larger computer software packages. It was designed in 1969 by K. Thompson of Bell Labs for use with Digital Equipment Corporation's PDP-7 computers; versions for PDP-11 machines were produced in 1971. Since then, it has undergone continual improvements. By 1980, more than 800 UNIX systems had been licensed to universities, over 400 to industrial and government organizations, about 1,100 had been installed by Bell for its own uses, and half a dozen commercial software houses were offering products based on the UNIX system under license from AT&T. Because it is a time-sharing system, a number of users can perform different operations on the computer, simultaneously communicating with the UNIX system through teletypewriters.

First applied at Bell Labs to computer research, text editing, and document preparation, UNIX systems are now aided by a collection of convenient programs, originally called the "Programmer's Workbench," to develop software for other hardware ranging in size from microcomputers to very large units. One version, written in 1981 for IBM 370 computers, brought the convenience of the UNIX system to relatively powerful machines.

AT&T supplies no maintenance to users outside of the Bell System. However, some licensees throughout the country distribute and support the system under a special agreement, which includes the provision that the marketing licensee can only make binary, or object code, licenses available. AT&T provides source code for its licensees. While some of the support licensees have added facilities to the basic UNIX system and have renamed the total product, the heart of the offering is still a disk-oriented, time-sharing operating system that features multiprogramming, device independence, and access method independence.

One variation of the UNIX system is "XENIX," produced and distributed by Microsoft, Inc., for 16-bit hardware. Microsoft claimed in its promotion, "Whether you're developing multi-tasking, multi-user, or networked systems, the XENIX operating system helps you get the most from your 16-bit product." Microsoft's staff reportedly expected XENIX to become the de facto standard operating system for 16-bit microprocessor-based systems. Single-copy XENIX was offered in 1982 through distributors, and multicopies through original equipment manufacturers. Seattle-based Microsoft was well regarded by its customers and respected by its competitors for excellent products and service follow-through.

In 1982 the UNIX system was priced at about $300 to colleges and universities and upwards of $20,000 to commercial buyers.

WRITER'S WORKBENCH DESCRIPTION[8]

The Writer's Workbench analyzes prose documents, suggests improvements, and assists in editing by performing several text analyses and providing correct usage information. The programs can be divided into three major areas: (1) proofreading, (2) stylistic analysis, and (3) on-line information about English usage and Writer's Workbench programs. Users can obtain either extended editorial comments or brief summaries and can select different standards of comparison. The programs detect features that characterize poor writing, as defined by writing experts, including errors in punctuation and spelling, split infinitives, overly long sentences, awkward phrases, and passive sentences. They provide alternate views of the text as aids to editing, organizing, and rewriting. Some programs offer users on-line help in selecting the appropriate word and finding correct spellings.

Nina Macdonald observed, "Most of us overlook errors when we edit a paper, especially our own. Although a computer does not overlook errors it is programmed to find, algorithms for judging complex language are imperfect. Our programs provide a means of computer-person collaboration to improve

---

[8]For all this section, we drew extensively from papers and information provided by members of the Writer's Workbench team.

text rapidly and thoroughly. Once potential errors are identified, a human editor decides which changes to make."

"That's correct," added Patricia Gingrich; "the programs supplement, they do not replace, human judgment. As the Writer's Workbench programs are enhanced and augmented by others, authors will be able to avail themselves of additional aids. The programs are tools." She outlined major assumptions underlying the programs.

They should:

1. Supplement and support human editing, not replace it
2. Adjust their evaluations for different types of readers
3. Deliver editorial comments in ordinary language
4. Explain their evaluations (for novice users, especially) when requested to do so
5. Give experienced users the option of receiving summary data rather than full editorial comments
6. Allow users to tailor the Workbench environment to their own needs (for instance, by adding or deleting items that programs search for)

Exhibit 6, which outlines key aspects of the software, is excerpted from a paper prepared by Nina H. Macdonald, Lawrence T. Frase, Patricia S. Gingrich, and Stacey A. Keenan.[9]

IN THE LIMELIGHT

An article on Writer's Workbench began in this fashion:

Writers, rejoice. The bellowing editor and his axe-like pencil may soon join the ranks of blacksmiths, beatniks, slide rules, and vacuum tubes. At Bell Laboratories in New Jersey, scientists, linguists, and psychologists have developed a computerized editor, a sort of Lou Grant on a chip. In the blink of a screen, a set of 32 integrated computer programs will display a breakdown of what is wrong with an author's text. The breakdown of the writer's ego is sure to follow.[10]

Writer's Workbench developers fed it two passages from familiar literature. Lincoln's "Gettysburg Address" received a readability (years of education required to comprehend) score of 10.8, with a program comment that the average sentence length of 26.7 words is very high and a recommendation

---

[9]This paper, "The Writer's Workbench: Computer Aids for Text Analysis," was accepted for publication in the *IEEE Transactions on Communication*, Special Issue on Communications in the Automated Office, January 1982.

[10]Natalie Angier, "Bell's Lettres," *Discover*, © Time Inc., July 1981, pp. 78–79.

Exhibit 6

PROFILE AND SELECTED ASPECTS
OF THE WRITER'S WORKBENCH

The programs can be divided into three major areas:

1. Proofreading
2. Stylistic analysis
3. On-line reference information on English usage and on Writer's Workbench programs.

Additional programs provide information on other topics, such as the text's conceptual level and organization.

PROOFREADING: PROOFR

PROOFR invokes five separate programs. These can each be run individually, but they are more conveniently run as a package (to take advantage of their interactive capabilities not available when run alone). [See Appendix to this case study for example PROOFR output.]

Spelling: SPELLWWB

The UNIX system has long had a spelling checker, based on a 30,000-word dictionary. It allows users to have their own dictionary of additional, specialized words and can be personally tailored to fit individual needs. Another program, SPELLTELL, helps to ascertain the correct spelling. The file can be updated.

Punctuation: PUNCT

In searching for simple punctuation errors, this program prints the original line and its correction and moves commas and periods to the left of double quotes and semicolons and colons to the right, for example. Other examples are capitalizing the first letter of sentences and warning of unbalanced double or single quotation marks or parentheses.
It enforces only straightforward rules, not those that require subtle judgments, such as deciding whether a comma or semicolon is the appropriate punctuation mark. It follows accepted standards of American English usage.

Exhibit 6 (Cont.)

Consecutive Occurrences of Same Word: DOUBLE

This program locates consecutive occurrences of the same word, which can appear on different lines, a type of error difficult for human proofreaders to detect.

Faulty Phrasing: DICTION, SUGGEST

These programs search for phrases that have been classified as poor by writing experts. Latest version of the dictionary also contains some phrases that may reflect a sexual bias. The programs print sentences containing such phrases, surrounding the phrases with stars and brackets: *[]*. The SUGGEST program recommends substitution phrases for those flagged by DICTION. (**Note:** Because DICTION does not use contextual cues when searching for pattern matches, it will sometimes flag phrases for which the recommended alternative is unreasonable. For example, DICTION will flag the phrase "provided that" in the sentence, "Joe provided that book and May this one." SUGGEST will recommend that "if" be used as an alternative, which is incorrect. By understanding the program's limitations, the user can reject unreasonable suggestions.)

Split Infinitives: SPLITINF

SPLITINF uses the **parts** program to find infinitives that are split by adverbs, by far the most common type of split infinitive, as in "to quickly decide." SPLITRULES can be summoned to print grammatical information about split infinitives, if the user needs a refresher.

STYLISTIC ANALYSES

Tabular Stylistic Information: STYLE

STYLE provides information about stylistic features of a text, based on a parts of speech analysis. It reports readability indices, information on the average lengths of the words and sentences, the distribution of sentence lengths, the grammatical types of sentences used (e.g., simple and complex), the percentage of verbs in the passive voice, the percentage of nouns that are nominalizations, and number of sentences that begin with expletives.

Exhibit 6 (Cont.)

Interpreted Stylistic Analysis: PROSE

PROSE provides the STYLE statistics and an interpretation as well, describing the user's text against a set of standards in a two- to three-page output in English. [See Appendix to this case study for example PROSE output.] Several sets of standards are provided, since texts are written for different types of readers and for different purposes. Users select the set of standards to be used in the interpretation of their text. Additional standards can be created in the file by the user.

PROSE explains the difficulties and recommends solutions to improve the text.

For experienced users, there is another option: extensive explanations can be avoided by selecting the short-output option, which produces an abbreviated list of comments rather than the two- to three-page output. [An example is provided in the Appendix at the end of this case study.]

Stylistic Problems in Context: FINDBE

FINDBE takes the idea that one way to improve text is to locate all the forms of "to be" and to try to rewrite them. Forms of "to be" should be minimized because they occur with the passive voice (e.g., "The ball **was** hit by the boy"), with many constructions using nominalizations (e.g., "this book is a description of . . ."), and of course, with expletives, which are considered wordy by stylists (e.g., "There **are** 63 paragraphs in this text"). FINDBE underlines and capitalizes all forms of "to be." This turns out to be a useful way of looking at the first draft of a paper.

Descriptive Information About Use of Words: WORDUSE

This program gives a brief description of correct use of over 300 English words and phrases that are commonly confused (e.g., affect/effect and cite/site/sight). It also flags frequently misused words such as "comprise," "due to," and "which."

Finding Correct Spelling: SPELLTELL

If someone doesn't know the first few letters of a word, he or she may not be able to look it up in a dictionary. SPELLTELL provides the correct spelling given **any** correct part of the word, whether it occurs at the beginning, in the middle, or at the end of the word.

Exhibit 6 (Cont.)

Program Information: WWBINFO and WWBHELP

These provide on-line information about the programs.

Judging Organization: ORG

Without a parser for English or any way of interpreting the meaning of a text, our programs cannot provide feedback on the content or organization. ORG formats the text and provides an abstract of the paper so the writer can see overall structure of the paper.

Sexist Language: SEXIST

A variant of the DICTION program, SEXIST is a dictionary of about 100 possibly sexist words and phrases, including old Bell System titles that have been updated, such as "frameman," now replaced by "framewirer." A table of substitutions is printed.

Checking Text Abstractness: ABST

ABST checks the percentage of words in the text that also occur on a list of words rated as abstract in psychological research. When this percentage is over 2.3 percent, the program suggests that concrete examples be introduced to make the document more understandable.

---

that the writer rephrase the most important ideas in simple sentences. From Charles Dickens's *A Tale of Two Cities,*

> *It was the best of times, it was the worst of times, it was the age of wisdom, it was the age of foolishness, it was the epoch of belief, it was the epoch of incredulity, it was the season of Light, it was the season of Darkness, it was the spring of hope, it was the winter of despair, we had everything before us, we had nothing before us, we were all going direct to Heaven, we were all going direct the other way—in short, the period was so far like the present period, that some of its noisiest authorities insisted on its being received, for good or for evil, in the superlative degree of comparison only.*

Writer's Workbench computed a bizarre readability score of 46.1 for this passage, concluding that "sentences this long are frequently lists, which will be easier to follow if you convert them into list format." Based on the program's recommendations, the revised version was as follows:

> *The times were the best and worst, wise and foolish. The era was one of belief and disbelief, light and darkness, hope and despair. Before us lay everything and nothing. We were all going direct to heaven or straight to hell. The period was so much like today that its loudest critics could describe it only in superlatives.*

Examining all this, *Discover's* verdict was that "the Workbench may be a boon to scientists, but will be of little use to the Dickenses of the future."

Also in 1981, Nina Macdonald and Lorinda Cherry were guests on the "Today" show in a five-minute interview and demonstration of Writer's Workbench, other publicity appeared in various periodicals, and Workbench developers presented numerous papers inside the company and at professional meetings throughout the nation and in foreign countries.

GRAVEMAN APPOINTED

Richard Graveman was placed in charge of the program's development activities in July 1981. "There is a fantastic group of dedicated people here. Perhaps you didn't know that originally Writer's Workbench was not ordered by management, but was done on the developers' own time. That's how committed they were to the concept of sophisticated computer-aided text editing. As of this past summer all projects are authorized, thanks to some outside notice of Writer's Workbench potential by people from other sections of the company and to the enthusiastic leadership of Paul Turner who believes in what we are doing." Graveman's eyes lit up as he discussed the talents of his co-workers and his satisfaction with the new assignment.

ENGLISH COMPOSITION FIELD EXPERIMENT

Shortly after joining the Writer's Workbench project, Graveman helped to conclude arrangements for two professors at Colorado State University (CSU) to use the Writer's Workbench programs in their English composition classes.

Charles R. Smith (Ph.D., Princeton University, 1972) and Kathleen E. Kiefer (Ph.D., Ohio State University, 1979) were the principal investigators working in collaboration with other colleagues, including Thomas McCall, who was responsible for all software, operating systems, applications, and hardware at CSU. Mr. McCall had managed implementation of a universitywide office automation system at CSU and believed that text-editing programs would be useful adjuncts.

Asked how they and Bell Labs got together in the first place, Smith recalled that he first saw a word processing system with text editor, printer, and dictionary in the office of an engineering faculty member of CSU and was motivated to explore further the notion of using such a set-up for teaching composition. Costs—of hardware and software—seemed formidable, but the appearance of a new and powerful microcomputer supporting six terminals reduced the costs of hardware, and Dr. Rosemary Whitaker, chair of the CSU Department of English, learned that Bell Laboratories had developed a little publicized package of programs for textual analysis. Nina Macdonald then sent photocopies of papers she and her colleagues had delivered in April 1980 that explained how the Workbench could help isolate writing errors and could teach writers to correct their own work before producing final copy. Interest spurred, Smith and Kiefer initiated the events leading to an agreement with Bell Labs.

Conversations with Professors Smith and Kiefer were punctuated by their eagerness. "We English teachers," Smith commented, "had pretty much resigned ourselves to declining writing skills with little hope of solution. Writer's Workbench held promise of saving the next generation of American college students from deficiencies so common to current ones." Kiefer concurred, "We believe these programs could revolutionize the way composition is taught. The programs concerned with style are especially helpful." By early 1982, the English Department had spent $45,000 for hardware, including two terminals and a small computer, and had requested additional funding, a total of $200,000 to expand the activity. Both teachers thought the series of existing and envisioned programs would teach most of the editing skills that students lacked, allowing composition instructors more time to focus on the central problems of writing—support, ideas, and organization—rather than editing for surface errors.

"And Writer's Workbench is appropriate not only for colleges," added Professor Kiefer, "but also for high schools. We would like to begin teacher training workshops, perhaps as early as the summer of 1983."

Their project promised to be practical and feasible in teaching composition at all levels. Computers with editing software could offer applications in journalism, copy editing, business writing, teaching foreign languages, preparing legal documents—whenever formal writing was necessary.

Exhibit 7 summarizes selected ideas from a working paper by Smith and Kiefer regarding benefits for teachers and students.

Professor Smith offered the idea that "Computers seem to introduce a certain magic often missing from these classes that require such great investments of time and energy by both teachers and students. Students enjoy touching the center-title key and seeing the title zip automatically to the center. They watch in awe as the automatic printer spews forth a perfectly typed essay at 55 characters per second. Even I get caught up in the excitment."

The objectives of CSU's English Department's 1981–1982 project to col-

Exhibit 7

WRITER'S WORKBENCH VALUE FOR TEACHERS AND STUDENTS

VALUE FOR THE TEACHER

Rather than editing for surface errors (the chief drain on teachers' time and energy), teachers will be able to focus on the central problems of writing, namely, support, ideas, and organization, and so will spend their grading time more profitably.

Some secondary teachers may be able to assign more essays than they now dare simply because surface editing will no longer be so necessary. Students will no longer view the composition teacher as focusing on trivial matters of style and punctuation.

For the first time, a student can be interrupted at that most crucial stage between the last draft and the final copy and so discover errors shortly after they occur rather than a week or more later after the teacher has marked them.

Students correct all errors flagged by the computer, not merely see them marked with a red pencil.

Teachers read perfectly typed copy, even with margins justified left and right should they so desire.

VALUE FOR THE STUDENT

Because the programs flag real as well as potential weaknesses and because users must choose either original versions or one or more suggested versions, students will learn that they make choices when they write, that good writing is often a matter of goods and betters, not absolutes.

Whether the teacher has the time, knowledge, or inclination, the student can get reliable criticism of the surface of his or her written work and can learn on his or her own to avoid wordy expressions, faulty usage patterns, and mechanical problems.

Once programmed, the computer, unlike teachers, never misses, never nods; as a result, the student has a discreet, ever-present teacher constantly making suggestions and asking questions to think about.

The student can make corrections in private before a teacher has seen and marked the error.

Exhibit 7 (Cont.)

Students will be learning as they prepare final copy, not merely typing. The speed of the automatic printer will allow students to type, edit, and print their essays in about the same time as they now spend preparing final copy on their own typewriters at home.

By making extra terminals available, students can continue to benefit from composition instruction throughout their college careers, not just in a formal composition class.

Teachers in other areas—no longer plagued by hundreds of surface errors—may once again assign the term papers formerly so common in university classes of all kinds.

If the instructor requires revision of organization and content, the student can return to the computer terminal, call up the computer record of the essay, make changes and additions, review the editing programs, and again have completed copy ready for marking less than a minute after activating the printer.

The programs address only the specific problems of individual students in their own work.

---

lect data on students' and teachers' reaction to computerized text editing are summarized in Exhibit 8.

To collect the data mentioned, Smith and Kiefer organized two experimental sections using the computer, balanced by two control sections using the same textbook and syllabus. In the spring of 1982, plans proceeded to enlarge the number of sections participating. Their hopes for continued research included preparing and testing, on a small scale, software that would more directly address the composing and editing problems of high school and poorly prepared college students. Proceeding with these plans was contingent upon continued approval of Bell Laboratories. The professors hoped to reach college teachers at national conventions in 1982 and through national publications such as *College Composition and Communication* and *College English*. There would also be sharing—sessions with high school teachers at state meetings—and tentative plans were being laid for state high school English teacher training workshops.

Asked why CSU was chosen as the experimental vehicle, Graveman responded: "There are several reasons, including the aggressiveness of the two instructors who sought us out. CSU has a stable research program. They're innovative in getting grants and acquiring talent. Writing composition is an important part of their English Department, not just a chore to be done with

---

Exhibit 8

FIRST SEMESTER OBJECTIVES OF THE CSU EXPERIMENT

In the first semester we will test:

1. Whether students editing their papers with Bell's programs improve in editing skills
2. Whether students using computers show more positive attitudes toward writing at the end of the composition course
3. Whether students using computer programs use them less by the end of the semester, that is, whether students, after editing several papers at the terminal, learn to edit their work before they begin to type the final copy
4. Whether students using computers learn to write better than those students taught in the traditional way

---

distaste. Forty faculty there teach composition and at least three consider it to be their primary research interest. Kiefer and Smith are interested in the mechanized aids and have interests closely aligned with ours. Then, too, the school's computer center is professionally run by full-time staff, not a hodge-podge mix of part-time employees. They are cooperative and pleasant people, professionally competent, who will demand a lot of us and, in turn, will give a lot back. It's an excellent arrangement, the kind you dream about but often fall short of."

USER RESPONSE AND VALIDITY TESTS

Response to the programs at Bell was explored in a 1981 random sample of 63 program users. The data in Exhibit 9 show that most users think the documentation and program output were clear, the programs did not miss much, and they were likely to find things the writer would not. Further, using the programs apparently did not lengthen the time users spent on documents. Finally, a significant proportion of users believed the programs improved their writing skills.

Evidence was building that the programs were useful, that they did what they were intended to do, and that they possibily affected the editing and writing skills of people who used them.

Some hoped that the trends toward office automation systems, with word processing devices at their core, would make Writer's Workbench sales to businesses possible. Word processors came into their own in the early 1980s. In a series of advertisements, Isaac Asimov, billed simply as a science and science-fiction author, proclaimed, "You Don't Have to Write as Much as I Do to Ap-

---

Exhibit 9

**PROPORTION AGREEMENT WITH STATEMENTS EVALUATING
CHARACTERISTICS OF WRITER'S WORKBENCH**

OPINION STATEMENT	PROPORTION (n)	PROBABILITY*
Program explanations are clear	.84 (63)	.001
Supporting documentation is clear	.92 (53)	.001
Workbench improves writing skills	.56 (54)	.02
Programs do not miss problems	.64 (47)	.05
Programs detect problems writers miss[†]	.90 (50)	.01
Programs do not slow writing activities[‡]	.90 (58)	.001
Programs useful for technical and nontechnical material	.80 (35)	.001

*Probabilities determined by binominal test. Expected proportion is 50, except where indicated otherwise.

[†]Expected proportion is 40.
[‡]Expected proportion is 60.

Source: Lawrence T. Frase, Nina H. Macdonald, Patricia S. Gingrich, Stacey A. Keenan, and James L. Collymore, "Computer Aids for Text Assessment and Writing Instruction," *NSPI Journal*, November 1981, p. 21.

---

preciate a Radio Shack TRS-80 Word Processor," and *Time* featured pictures of former President Jimmy Carter, "Sesame Street" consultant Christopher Cerf, and novelist Stanley Elkin all sitting at their word processor keyboards, involved in "plugged-in prose."[11] Meanwhile a Writer's Workbench technician was developing word processing system applications of Writer's Workbench in various Bell Labs offices in New Jersey.

COMPETITION

Text processing software programs appeared in the mid-1970s, providing users with a basic array of specialized text manipulation capabilities and requiring a large mainframe for operation. In the early 1980s, these products evolved into more flexible tools with broader applications, supportable on different types of data processing equipment. Writer's Workbench progenitors believed that this segment of the software industry, in a transitional phase beyond late development and early growth and just before rapid takeoff, was worth pursuing aggressively.

In 1981 and 1982, there were over 100 text processing vendors, ranging in size from diversifed industry giants—IBM, Digital Equipment Corporation, and Hewlett-Packard, for example—to software developers and vendors gen-

---

[11]*Time*, August 10, 1981, p. 68.

erating annual sales of as little as $100,000. Atex and other larger software houses promoted their services with expensive brochures, well-planned sales consultation, and follow-on maintenance and support. Lesser purveyors relied chiefly on free publicity releases in software publications; sent out photocopies of product descriptions, claims, and prices; and offered scant backup for users.

Attempts to find products competitive to Writer's Workbench in early 1982 revealed a handful of similar programs but with fewer diagnostic capabilities. Selected examples were IBM's EPISTLE and Displaywriter (only the latter was being sold to the public), SCRIPSIT, and Writer's Companion.

IBM's planned EPISTLE (Evaluation Preparation and Interpretation System for Text and Language Entities) was the closest of any to the Bell programs; although claims were that it could detect agreement errors, computing time was thought to be greater than that for Writer's Workbench. EPISTLE provided in-house services for IBM administrators and authors in critiquing natural language text; developers reportedly expected soon to implement "a variety of syntactically-based stylistic evaluations." The long-term focus appears to be on a variety of applications for satisfying the needs of middle-level managers.[12] The IBM Displaywriter system could point out spelling errors, with the aid of a 50,000-word dictionary, at up to 1,000 words a minute and in 11 different languages. This program allowed users to edit, revise, change format, do math, merge, and file on line.

Radio Shack's TRS-80's SCRIPSIT word processing software permitted text writing and editing on the video screen and provided a familiarization course, on audio cassette, to get the user started. It advertised a 100,000-word English dictionary program that could proofread text for errors.

Aspen Software Company called its text editor Writer's Companion, heralding it as a "total word processing system" with full-screen editing; complete text formatting capability; a proofreader spelling checker with a 38,000-word dictionary; and a typo, style, and grammar checker with its GRAMMATIK program. The firm also stated that the command structure was logical and simple to learn and that it would run on CP/M & 8086, TRS-80 Mod I/III, and TRS-80 Mod II. The price ranged up to about $400 for all the options. *InfoWorld's* December 7, 1981 software report card rated GRAMMATIK excellent on performance, ease of use, and error handling but only fair on documentation.

Writer's Workbench program components—PROOFR, PROSE, and others—and the possible addition of new programs presented to users a package clearly superior to those available in early 1982.

Your Task:

Advise Bell Labs on steps to take in marketing Writer's Workbench.

[12]Lance A. Miller, George E. Heirdorn, and Karen Jensen, "Text Critiquing with the EPISTLE System: An Author's Aid to Better Syntax," paper presented at the National Computer Conference, 1981.

Appendix

INPUT TO AND OUTPUT FROM THE PROOFR PROGRAM

Input: Our report, "The Basic Fundamentals of Computations Complexity", is enclosed. Please send any recommended changes at your earliest convenience. thanks.

PROOFR   ******************* SPELLING ********************
Output:

Possible spelling errors in examplefile are

                computatonal   recomended

If any of these words is spelled correctly, later type
                spelladd word1 word2 . . . wordn

to have them added to your spelldict file.

**************** PUNCTUATION *****************

The punctuation in examplefile is first described.
                2 double quotes and 0 single quotes
                        0 apostrophes
                0 left parentheses and 0 right ones

The program next prints any sentence that it thinks is incorrectly punctuated and follows it by its correction.

line 1
OLD: Our report, "The Basic Fundamentals of Computations Complexity",
NEW: Our report, "The Basic Fundamentals of Computational Complexity,"
line 3
OLD: earliest convenience. thanks.
NEW: earliest convenience. Thanks.

For more information about punctuation rules, type

                        punctrules

****************DOUBLE WORDS ****************

For file examplefile

                No double words found

**************** WORD CHOICE *****************

Sentences with possible wordy or misused phrases are listed next, followed by suggested revisions.

Appendix (Cont.)

beginning line 1 examplefile

> Our report, "The *[Basic Fundamentals]* of Computational Complexity", is enclosed.

beginning line 2 examplefile
Please send any recommended changes *[at your earliest convenience]*.

file examplefile number of lines 3, number of phrases found 2

---------------------- Table of Substitutions ----------------------

PHRASE   SUBSTITUTION

at your earliest convenience: use "soon" for "at your earliest convenience"
basic fundamentals: use "fundamentals" for basic fundamentals

*************** SPLIT INFINITIVES ****************

For file examplefile:

> No split infinitives found

Source: "The Writer's Workbench: Computer Aids for Text Analysis," *IEEE Transactions on Communications,* Vol. COM-30, no. 1, January 1982.

ABBREVIATED OUTPUT VERSION EXAMPLE

SHORT WWB OUTPUT

The WWB command with the "-s" flag produces a shortened version of the PROOFR and PROSE outputs.

$ wwb -s example
—SPELLWWB for example—

DWRC	Lizell	reproted
Gertsch	al	

ABBREVIATED OUTPUT VERSION EXAMPLE *(Cont.)*

—PUNCT for example—
0 double quotes and 0 single quotes
0 apostrophes
1 left parentheses and 1 right ones
line 12
OLD: of rodent attack to cables. later Lizell et. al. ran tests
NEW: of rodent attack to cables. Later Lizell et al. ran tests

—DOUBLE for example—
and and appears beginning line 19

—DICTION for example—
beginning line 17 example
P Since the early studies of gopher-resistant materials, a large *[number of]* new wire, cable, and designs have been developed and and many new materials are available.

beginning line 21 example
The Denver Wildlife and Research Center (DWRC) and the Bell Telephone Laboratories decided to *[join together]* to *[try and]* determine the gopher resistance of the new designs.

beginning line 24 example
The *[man power]* for the experiments came from both DWRC and BTL; Bell prepared the test samples, took photographs after exposure to gophers, and evaluated the engineering implications of the results, and the DWRC designed and conducted the exposure test and rated the damage to the samples.

beginning line 35 example
The gophers were not separated *[as to]* size or sex.

file example: number of lines 41 number of phrases found 5

—SPLIT for example—
Possible split infinitives:

to repeatedly chew

ABBREVIATED OUTPUT VERSION EXAMPLE *(Cont.)*

BECAUSE YOUR TEXT IS SHORT (< 2000 WORDS & < 100 SEN-
TENCES), THE FOLLOWING ANALYSIS MAY BE MISLEADING.

Compared to TMs.

Reading grade level—12; Good
Variation—Too many short, simple sentences—subordinate.
Passives—29%: High
Nominalizations—1%: Good
Don't forget the styl.tmp file

$

SECTION OF PROSE OUTPUT

SENTENCE STRUCTURE

Passives. This text contains a much higher percentage of passive verbs
(44 percent) than is common in good documents of this type (22 percent).
A sentence is in the passive voice when its grammatical subject is the re-
ceiver of the action.

PASSIVE: The ball was hit by the boy.

When the doer of the action in a sentence is the subject, the sentence is
in the active voice.

ACTIVE: The boy hit the ball.

The passive voice is sometimes needed

    1.   To emphasize the object of the sentence
    2.   To vary the rhythm of the text
    3.   To avoid naming an unimportant actor

EXAMPLE: The appropriations were approved.

Although passive sentences are sometimes needed, psychological
research has shown that they are harder to comprehend than active sentences. Because of this, you should transform as many of your passives to

SECTION OF PROSE OUTPUT *(Cont.)*

actives as possible. You can use the STYLE program to find all your sentences with passive verbs in them by typing the following command when this program is finished.

style -p filename

Nominalizations.

You have appropriately limited your nominalizations (nouns made from verbs, e.g., "description").

case

32

DELTA AIR LINES

Early April is a natural festival of visual and olfactory delights in Georgia. Stands of fragrant pines and species of desiduous trees abound, here and there accented by clusters of dogwood trees blossoming in riots of pink or white bracts that emerge each year about Eastertime, when Southern air is redolent of nature's finest perfumes. However, these groves and other bucolic vistas belie the energy generated by tensions and activities inside Delta's headquarters, just a few minutes away from Atlanta's Hartsfield International Airport. The company's two major office structures face each other across the center drive, the second building only recently finished, a 133,440-square-foot, five-story operations center housing consumer affairs, stockholder relations, public affairs, simulator flight training, flight control, and communications departments.

Airline equities, for a time growth stocks with glamor, were largely ignored in the early 1980s by investors and viewed with no little scorn by securities analysts. The 1970s, which saw price controls, OPEC's 10-fold increase in petroleum prices, a recession called the worst since the 1930s, double-digit inflation, out-of-sight interest rates, deregulation of the airline industry, and, with scarcely any warning, fare price warfare border-to-border and coast-to-coast, were devastating. No airline escaped the impact, but while none was unscathed, some weathered the storms better than others. Delta Air Lines, although scarred, had retained its fiscal and market health, not to mention its substantial organizational strengths.

HISTORICAL BACKGROUND

In calendar year 1981, Delta's rank among U.S. carriers was first in domestic enplaned passengers, second in system enplaned passengers, and sixth in system revenue passenger miles; in the world it was third in enplaned passengers and eighth in revenue passenger miles.

Delta Air Lines was born as a crop-dusting operation in Georgia in 1924, moving shortly thereafter to Louisiana, and soon introducing single-engine passenger service between Dallas and Jackson, Mississippi. Its aircraft flew at the then incredible speed of 90 miles per hour. Exhibit 1 indicates a few milestones in the company's annals.

A turning point for Delta came when its coverage expanded dramatically in 1953. Another important event took place in 1959 when jet service, using DC-8s, was begun, followed in 1960 by the Convair 880 and in 1965 by DC-9 service. Delta was the first airline to operate all three of the new-generation wide-body jets—the Boeing 747 (in the fleet from 1970 to 1977); the DC-10 (1972 to 1975); and the L-1011 TriStar, added in 1973.

Boeing's 767-200 was to be the world's first airliner designed since fuel prices started their steep climb in the early 1970s, as well as its first all-new

---

Exhibit 1

HIGHLIGHTS OF DELTA'S HISTORY, 1924–1979

1924	Huff Daland Dusters operating in Macon, Georgia, moved to Monroe, Louisiana (primary origin of the later name Delta, referring to the Mississippi River Delta), in 1925.
1929	Delta Air Service was instituted for passengers, financed by southern capital.
1930	Name was changed to Delta Air Corporation. Reliance upon U.S. Post Office Department contracts was heavy.
1945	Routes were extended to Chicago and Miami; name became Delta Air Lines.
1953	Company merged with Chicago and Southern Air Lines.
1961	Delta became transcontinental with award of route from Dallas/Fort Worth to five California points and Las Vegas.
1972	Delta merged with Northeast Airlines.
1978	Service from Atlanta to London was inaugurated.
1979	Service from Atlanta to Frankfurt was added.

Source: Corporate records.

airliner since the 747 was manufactured in 1978. United Airlines was to have the first five of these new planes in July 1982; Delta planned to welcome the new jet to its fleet in December 1982, with passenger flights set for February 1983. The airplane was designed to seat 178 in coach and 24 in first class. Airbus Industrie of Europe announced plans to deliver the A310 comparable to the 767 in size, range, and price shortly thereafter. Boeing had twice as many orders as Airbus.

In the late 1920s, when Huff Daland Dusters became Delta Air Service, the improvement of aircraft technology combined with the adventurousness of a few brave souls made air passenger travel possible. As of 1980 and 1981, by industry estimates, 65 percent of Americans over 18 years of age had flown on a commercial airline, and about one-fourth of all adult Americans took an air trip in 1981, averaging approximately three round trips each. Personal and pleasure trips in the early 1980s increased rapidly, estimated in various studies at about 45 to 50 percent of total air travel; the majority of these travelers were women. The remainder, or 50 to 55 percent, of the trips were for business; women accounted for about one-fifth of these.

For the fiscal year ended June 30, 1982, Delta's scheduled passenger service accounted for approximately 93 percent of the company's revenues. Freight, mail, and express services were 5 percent, and other sources, 2 percent. See Exhibit 2 for a comparison of 1981 and 1982.

Exhibit 2

OPERATING REVENUES (in thousands) BY MAJOR CATEGORIES, 1981–1982

	1982		1981		
	Amount (000)	% of Total	% Change	% of Total	% Change
Scheduled passengers	$3,352,173	93.0%	$3,287,511	93.1%	
Freight and express	167,699	4.5	156,355	4.0	2%
Mail	62,928	1.5	57,076	2.0	7
Charter	1,264		1,766		10
Other, net	33,489	1.0	30,618	1.0	−28
Total	$3,617,523	100.0%	$3,533,326	100.0%	9

Source: 1982 Annual Report, p. 5; percentages are rounded.

DELTA'S BUSINESS

Delta Air Lines, a certified major air carrier, provides scheduled air transportation for passengers, freight, and mail over a network of routes throughout the United States and abroad. As of June 1982, the company served 82 domestic cities in 32 states and the District of Columbia; operations extended to every major region, except Alaska and Hawaii, and included Nassau, Bahamas; Bermuda; Montreal, Canada; London, England; Puerto Rico; and Frankfurt, Federal Republic of Germany.

An important characteristic of Delta's route system, the gathering and distribution complex (the "hub") in Atlanta, the nation's busiest airport and location of the corporation's principal offices, connected passengers from cities throughout the South with flights to and from other cities (the "spokes") such as Boston, Chicago, Dallas/Fort Worth, Los Angeles, New York, and Washington, D.C. Smaller hub-spoke networks operated in Boston, Cincinnati, Dallas/Fort Worth, and Memphis.

The hackneyed expression, "If you want to get to heaven, you'll have to change planes in Atlanta," takes on the ring of truth for onlookers observing the 10 major daily changeover periods directed by Delta. What seems awesome to the uninitiated is that all this traffic—70 percent of passengers arriving in Delta's complex in 1982 connected with other flights to their ultimate destinations—appears to be handled with such calmness, but definitely not insouciance. Only occasionally, usually during inclement weather, does efficiency collapse and turmoil ensue. Seldom is Delta stymied by these disturbances.

Some air travel buffs and industry pundits say that Braniff invented the hub-spoke concept in Dallas; still, few would deny that Delta has developed the idea. Examination of system route maps shows that Eastern's closely resembles Delta's, with a giant hub at Atlanta, and Delta-like feeder routes to connecting cities. Statistics in 1981 indicated that Eastern had acquired about 40 percent of Hartsfield International's boardings.

PERSONNEL IN 1982

The airline's ability to perfect its hub-and-spoke techniques was attributed by management partly to freedom from union restrictions. Although Delta's pilots and dispatchers were organized, they represented only about 12 percent of the total work force, leaving considerable flexibility to arrange schedules and assign work duties. Comparing this advantage to heavily unionized Eastern, Delta served essentially the same route with 5,000 fewer employees.

"Does this mean that Delta's employees are underpaid?" the rhetorical question came from an operations supervisor. Her answer was negative, because Delta's labor costs were among the highest in the industry. Delta anticipated and topped other wage-and-benefit contracts negotiated by industry unions. The answer, some believed, must lie in the unique *esprit de corps* of Delta employees whose productivity was the envy of many competitors. In response to a pay raise of 8.5 percent, announced by management in 1982 despite severe declines in net earnings, employees decided to pledge 2.5 percent of their coming year's pay to buy Delta a Boeing 767 as a gift of appreciation. Delta already had 20 Boeing 767s on order.

In 50 years of operation, Delta had never suffered a strike. In the words of David Garrett, president and chief executive officer, "We strongly feel that the needs of an employee should be met by the company, and our communications must be open at all levels in the organization. Our basic philosophy is that we are all in this together, and I don't want to sound corny, but it really is 'one for all and all for one.'" Another contributor to employee morale and confidence was Delta's policy of promoting from within. Corporate personnel files usually held upwards of 200,000 applications for employment at any given time, none over six months old. Total personnel in the Delta system numbered close to 38,000 in 1982, including 1,600 temporary and part-time employees. An overview of number of employees and years of experience is presented in Exhibit 3.

Exhibit 3

NUMBER OF EMPLOYEES AND YEARS OF EXPERIENCE, FISCAL 1968–1981

Year	Number of Employees	YEAR-END FISCAL 1981 Years of Experience	YEAR-END FISCAL 1981 Number of Employees
1981	38,559	45 to 50	1
1980	36,883	40 to 44	42
1979	36,546	35 to 39	393
1978	32,801	30 to 34	553
1977	29,665	25 to 29	1,233
1976	28,695	20 to 24	2,953
1975	27,800	15 to 19	4,340
1974	27,600	10 to 14	9,203
1973	27,500	5 to 9	6,720
1972	21,300	Less than 5	
1971	20,800	Under 1	2,549
1970	20,500	Total	38,559
1969	18,700		
1968	16,500		

Source: Company records.

Reflecting upon the traumatic events of 1981 and 1982, President and CEO David Garrett reported,

> When the Company had to reduce its schedules, temporary and seasonal personnel were removed from the payroll a few weeks sooner than normal. The number of authorized leaves of absence in certain job categories was increased, and a few people were temporarily reassigned to other jobs. However, Delta continued its policy of stable employment for its permanent personnel. This policy has proven to be very beneficial to the Company over the years, and we expect that this will be the case again. When the economy improves, Delta will be able to take immediate advantage of increased traffic demand because its family of highly trained and dedicated personnel remains intact.[1]

FINANCIAL PERFORMANCE PROFILE

A consolidated operations summary appears as Exhibit 4, fiscal years ending June 30. In his review of fiscal 1982, Garrett related a gloomy perspective:

> Throughout the year, the national economy continued in a recession. High interest rates, caused largely by the government's anti-inflation efforts and by large federal budget deficits, severely impacted many of the nation's largest industries, especially those which depend heavily on credit. The national unemployment level reached its highest point since the 1930s. These factors had a depressing effect on traffic demand, and Delta's revenue passenger miles declined 4% for the second consecutive year. This loss of traffic was offset by a 6% increase in the passenger mile yield, and passenger revenues rose 2%.
>
> Passenger fares were continually changing throughout the year. Four basic fare increases were taken by the industry during the year, all of which Delta matched. These increases, plus the carryover effect of increases taken in fiscal 1981, should have resulted in a significant increase in the passenger mile yield. However, throughout much of the year the industry was plagued with an unprecedented level of fare discounting. Several carriers, seeking a competitive advantage or attempting to solve pressing cash flow problems, initiated a number of uneconomic deep discount fares, many of which were largely unrestricted. This resulted in a confusing array of fares, many of which have no relationship to costs or distance traveled. While we strongly disagree with the discount fare policies of these carriers, it was in the Company's best interests

[1]1982 Annual Report, p. 2.

Exhibit 4

CONSOLIDATED SUMMARY OF OPERATIONS FISCAL 1973–1982
(in thousands, except per share figures)

	1973	1974	1975	1976	1977	1978	1979	1980	1981	1982
Operating revenues										
Passenger	$ 962,558	$1,124,759	$1,271,720	$1,406,417	$1,575,642	$1,861,100	$2,213,024	$2,733,820	$3,287,511	$3,352,173
Cargo	76,323	86,685	85,388	100,626	114,800	153,233	167,904	190,490	213,431	230,597
Other, net	10,818	15,683	19,922	21,899	29,203	36,578	46,918	32,650	32,384	34,753
Total operating revenues	1,049,699	1,227,127	1,377,030	1,528,942	1,719,645	2,050,911	2,427,846	2,956,960	3,533,326	3,617,523
Operating expenses	928,940	1,070,043	1,282,000	1,411,333	1,578,464	1,845,816	2,218,814	2,864,323	3,359,132	3,625,679
Operating income (loss)	$ 120,759	$ 157,084	$ 95,030	$ 117,609	$ 141,181	$ 205,095	$ 209,032	$ 92,637	$ 174,194	$ (8,156)
Interest expense, net†	(9,463)	(17,465)	(31,281)	(31,387)	(23,061)	(17,313)	(9,461)	(11,062)	(7,596)	(22,284)
Miscellaneous income, net	292	3,088	2,297	2,284	4,825	7,640	9,069	10,687	19,917	11,280
Gain on disposition of flight equipment	4,653	18,607	7,944	7,680	29,403	32,689	20,514	36,091	30,078	1,570
Realized and unrealized gain (loss) on foreign currency translation	—	—	5,855	13,357	2,699	(3,339)	(7,110)	(3,735)	6,227	2,385
Income (loss) before income taxes	$ 116,241	$ 161,314	$ 79,845	$ 109,543	$ 155,047	$ 224,772	$ 222,044	$ 124,618	$ 222,820	$ (15,205)
Income taxes credited (provided)	(56,736)	(78,953)	(39,324)	(53,949)	(76,362)	(109,296)	(104,429)	(54,433)	(101,447)	9,652
Amortization of investment tax credits	6,490	8,288	11,359	14,613	13,695	15,651	19,129	22,973	25,101	26,367
Net income	$ 65,995	$ 90,649	$ 51,880	$ 70,207	$ 92,380	$ 131,127	$ 136,744	$ 93,158	$ 146,474	$ 20,814
Net income per share†	$1.66	$2.28	$1.30	$1.77	$2.32	$3.30	$3.44	$2.34	$3.68	$0.52
Dividends paid	$9,925	$11,926	$11,928	$11,928	$13,916	$14,911	$20,875	$23,857	$27,832	$37,773
Dividends paid per share†	$0.25	$0.30	$0.30	$0.30	$0.35	$0.38	$0.53	$0.60	$0.70	$0.95
†Has been reduced by interest capitalized of	$6,345	$10,810	$6,099	$3,247	$2,922	$4,794	$6,717	$10,790	$15,539	$38,154
Other Financial and Statistical Data										
Long-term debt	$168,000	$345,119	$390,437	$350,968	$237,497	$167,331	$125,483	$147,901	$198,411	$362,774
Stockholders' equity	364,553	443,826	483,833	542,112	620,583	736,799	852,668	921,969	1,040,611	1,023,651
Stockholders' equity per share†	$9.17	$11.16	$12.17	$13.63	$15.61	$18.53	$21.44	$23.19	$26.17	$25.75
Shares of common stock outstanding†	39,761,154	39,761,154	39,761,154	39,761,154	39,761,154	39,761,154	39,761,154	39,761,154	39,761,154	39,761,154
Revenue passengers enplaned	23,702,870	25,565,208	25,831,631	27,996,665	28,811,966	33,007,670	39,360,368	39,713,904	36,743,214	34,169,927
Available seat miles (000)	27,958,095	28,417,679	29,497,234	30,389,761	32,614,260	35,135,046	39,826,891	43,217,372	45,428,277	45,154,885
Revenue passenger miles (000)	14,449,748	15,445,891	15,916,860	17,621,247	18,042,339	20,825,722	25,518,520	26,171,197	25,192,531	24,284,804
Passenger load factor	51.68%	54.35%	53.96%	57.98%	55.32%	59.27%	64.07%	60.56%	55.46%	53.78%
Breakeven load factor	45.20%	46.76%	49.93%	53.14%	50.36%	52.74%	58.02%	58.51%	52.52%	53.91%
Available ton miles (000)	3,515,285	3,847,226	4,030,116	4,145,183	4,478,038	4,743,778	5,357,995	5,748,143	6,037,476	5,937,817
Revenue ton miles (000)	1,711,229	1,800,400	1,822,574	2,034,848	2,113,798	2,426,265	2,916,585	2,934,375	2,845,425	2,773,337
Passenger revenue per passenger mile	6.66¢	7.28¢	7.99¢	7.98¢	8.73¢	8.94¢	8.67¢	10.45¢	13.05¢	13.80¢
Operating expenses per available seat mile	3.32¢	3.77¢	4.35¢	4.64¢	4.84¢	5.25¢	5.57¢	6.63¢	7.39¢	8.03¢
Operating expenses per available ton mile	24.35¢	27.81¢	31.81¢	34.05¢	35.25¢	38.91¢	41.41¢	49.83¢	55.64¢	61.06¢

†Adjusted for 2-for-1 stock split distributed December 1, 1981.

in the longer term to match many of those uneconomic fares rather than lose a substantial amount of traffic to our competitors. As could be expected under these conditions, the percentage of revenue passenger miles flown on discount fares increased from 60% in fiscal 1981 to 69% in 1982, causing the increase in the yield to be much lower than the combined total of the basic fare increases taken during the year.[2]

Delta's Richard Maurer, vice chairman, commented on the company's second quarterly loss in 25 years: "In the last quarter of 1957, Delta lost about $70,000, not a giant sum by any standard, but unwelcome, nevertheless. From then until now, we have been profitable. Then came our fiscal third quarter [ending March 31, 1982] in which we lost about $18 million on revenues of just over $881 million. This is even more unsettling when we compare it to profits of $28 million in the same period last year, when sales were also $881 million. How could it happen when our passenger traffic was up about 2 percent? Easy to explain that: about three-fourths of our passenger miles were on discount tickets. Actually, it was more like 72 percent, and that compares with 57 percent same time last year.

"It isn't just Delta. When the figures are in, we'll see most of our competitors in the same boat. We did expect some drop, but not this much because a lot of help was expected from continued lower fuel prices; fuel outlays account for roughly 32 percent of our operating expenses.

"Our nine-month loss has been modest—we're in a lot better shape than most—and we definitely expect a turnaround this quarter. The factor that could thwart us is continued deep-fare cutting."

Exhibit 5 compares operations results for fiscal 1981 and 1982 in selected major categories expressed in thousands (except per share figures).

Exhibit 6, adapted from "Forbes 500," compares sales figures and rankings for Delta and selected competitors.

In profit rankings, Boeing was number 43, down from position 31 in 1980, and Delta was 217, up from position 320 in 1980. All the other airlines were missing from the 1981 roster of top 500 companies, measured by amount of profit.

Delta's fiscal 1982 net income plummeted 86 percent to $20.8 million in a year beset by the recession, the PATCO strike's disruption of flight schedules, Braniff's bankruptcy, and record financial losses by a number of airlines. Nevertheless, Delta's plans were implemented without interruption. Nonstop service was added between 28 new city pairs, including inaugural service into Pittsburgh, Amarillo, and Lubbock. Delta suspended service to Evansville, Indiana, and Burlington, Vermont. It accepted five new Lockheed L-1011-1 aircraft and one new Boeing B-727-200 and purchased two that had been leased. Three Douglas DC-8-61s were converted to DC-8-71s with advanced engines plus other major modifications. As the operations center was being completed

[2]Ibid., p. 2.

Exhibit 5

COMPARISON OF 1981 AND 1982 OPERATIONS RESULTS
(in thousands)

	1982	1981	% CHANGE
Operating revenues	$ 3,617,523	$ 3,533,326	2%
Operating expenses	3,625,679	3,359,132	8
Net income	20,814	146,474	−86
Earnings per share	$0.52	$3.68	−86
Dividends per share	0.95	0.70	36
Revenue passengers enplaned	34,169,927	36,743,214	−7
Available seat miles	45,154,885	45,428,277	−1
Revenue passenger miles (000)	24,284,804	25,192,531	−4
Passenger load factor	53.78%	55.46%	−3
Break-even passenger load factor	53.91%	52.52%	3

Source: 1982 Annual Report, p. 1.

Exhibit 6

EXCERPTS FROM THE MAY 10, 1982 FORBES SALES 500
(in thousands)

Company	1981 Sales	% Change Over 1980	RANK 1981	RANK 1980
Boeing (supplier of airplanes)	$9,788,000	3.8%	44	40
Trans World Airlines	5,265,000	4.9	103	96
United Airlines	5,141,000	2.0	108	95
American Airlines	4,109,000	7.5	147	141
Pan Am World Airways	3,979,000	−5.5	158	134
Eastern Air Lines	3,727,000	8.0	162	161
Delta Airlines	3,533,000	19.5	169	200

Source: Forbes, May 10, 1982, p. 208; these data are at pp. 216–226.

in Atlanta, Delta occupied new and expanded terminal facilities in a number
of cities. This summary appeared in the 1982 annual report:

> During fiscal 1982, Delta added three new cities to its domestic route sys-
> tem, occupying new terminal facilities in Pittsburgh, Amarillo and Lub-
> bock. Soon after the end of the year, the Company secured terminal

facilities in Oklahoma City to support new service which began in August 1982. During the fiscal year, Delta occupied new or expanded airport facilities in Orlando, Cincinnati, San Francisco, Charlotte, Raleigh-Durham, New Orleans, and Baton Rouge. Reservations offices in Knoxville and Cincinnati moved into expanded facilities to allow for future growth.

In July 1981, the Company began construction of a 230,000 square foot passenger terminal building at LaGuardia Airport in New York City. This new facility, which will accommodate all current and planned future Delta aircraft, is scheduled for completion early in fiscal 1984. The Company is planning a similar terminal building at Chicago's O'Hare Field, and construction is expected to begin early in fiscal 1983 for occupancy in the September 1984 quarter.

The expansion of Delta's maintenance and overhaul base at Hartsfield Atlanta International Airport continued on schedule during the year. Subsequent to the end of the year, Delta began construction on a new maintenance hangar at Tampa International Airport. Upon completion of the 125,000 square foot hangar and support shops, the current maintenance facility at Miami International Airport will be closed. During fiscal 1983, Delta will begin a major expansion of its Dallas/Fort Worth maintenance base which will double the size of the existing facility. All three maintenance facility projects are scheduled for completion during fiscal 1984.[3]

Although Delta's capital expenditures were approximately $1.2 billion in fiscal 1981 and $511 million in 1982, its debt-to-equity ratio was one of the lowest in the airline industry, 20 percent in 1981 and 35 percent in 1982, while some competitors' ratios were 2-to-1 and higher.

Early in fiscal 1982, stockholders approved increasing authorized shares of common stock to 100,000,000 along with a 2-for-1 stock split. Company officials and the board believed these actions would broaden the market for common shares, improve their marketability, and increase the number of shareholders. All told, Delta hoped that this would enhance its flexibility in responding to business needs and opportunities, including financing investments and possibly acquiring other companies.

Delta's move to develop another hub-spoke complex at Dallas/Fort Worth represented a major commitment of resources, a marketing strategy that would require replication of many features of the firm's Atlanta base. No airline in the country was in better shape for such outlays and changes in its established network. But Dallas/Fort Worth was an environment characterized by hostility that flared between American Airlines, which had a profitable 1981 following substantial losses in 1980, and Braniff:

[3]Ibid., p. 6.

Mr. Crandall [American's president] fortified American's growing repu-
tation around Dallas as a corporate villain by casually saying it would
suit him to see beleaguered Braniff "go out of business" so American
could start competing with "healthier airlines" that aren't prone to cut
fares "out of desperation."[4]

Based in Dallas about 50 years, Braniff was considered "hometown folks" by
Dallasites, whereas American had moved its headquarters there in 1979, challenging competitors by methodically opening new routes in a market-share-
seeking slugfest.

Delta, with its primary history rooted in the South, could be seen as less
of an intruder, or possibly even welcomed because of its reputation for sound
operations and good public relations. As one competitor commented to the
casewriter, "Delta Airlines is committed to its passengers and practices good
citizenship in every city and town where it does business. They don't let running their airline to make profits stand in the way of being nice. They've
earned the respect of their competitors."

Delta occupied mostly leased buildings in 1982. Its principal offices and
maintenance base were at Hartsfield Atlanta International Airport on realty
owned by the City of Atlanta, under long-term leases. Delta had constructed
various buildings and facilities on portions of this property and owned a number of radio transmitting and receiving sites and a fuel farm.

In June 1980, Delta sold its 67-acre Greenbriar office complex in southwest Atlanta and leased it back from the new owner, with options to renew up
to 19 years. Greenbriar housed Delta's finance division, including the computer center.

Ticket counter space and operating areas were leased, generally for periods of from 5 to 30 years, rents based on fixed charges per square foot of occupied floor space, with provisions for periodic adjustment of rates. Airport
leases provided for the nonexclusive use of ramps and runways; landing fees
were based on schedules and type of aircraft. Delta also leased downtown ticket and reservations offices in the major cities it served; these leases normally
were for shorter terms than the airport leases.

Exhibit 7 provides an overview of the company's aircraft commitments
and options at June 30, 1982.

The orders for 60 Boeing B-757-200 aircraft included 30 that were subject to reconfirmation by Delta. Three DC-8-61s were reengined in fiscal 1982
and 10 were scheduled for the same treatment in 1983 and 1984. Planned future expenditures for aircraft (excluding those on option) and engine commitments are summarized in Exhibit 8.

Almost $1.2 billion was committed beyond 1987. As of late 1982, Delta
anticipated financing most of these commitments with internally generated

---

[4]"American Airlines Gets a 'Bad-Guy' Image in Dallas from Its Harsh Attacks on Braniff,"
The Wall Street Journal, March 12, 1982, p. 27. Reprinted by permission of *The Wall Street Journal*, © Dow Jones & Company, Inc., 1982. All Rights Reserved.

Exhibit 7

DELTA'S FLEET AND PURCHASE COMMITMENTS FOR AIRCRAFT

AIRCRAFT TYPE	CURRENT FLEET	ORDERS	OPTIONS	CAPACITY	AVERAGE FLEET AGE, YEARS, APPROXIMATE
L-1011-1/200	37	4	—	293	3
L-1011-500	3	—	—	244	2
B-727-200	129	—	—	137	6
B-757-200	—	60	10	—	—
B-767-200	—	20	22	210	—
DC-9-32	36	—	—	88	12
DC-8-61/71	13	—	—	198	12
Total	218	84	32		

Source: Corporate records.

Exhibit 8

FUTURE EXPENDITURE COMMITMENTS, 1983–1987

YEAR	AMOUNT (millions)
1983	$550
1984	356
1985	496
1986	416
1987	297

funds, augmented by intermediate-term loans. As indicated in a 1980 article, "Delta is the youngest airline of all where it really counts—the age of its airplanes—and both it and the unprepossessing Garrett are on the make."[5]

In military aircraft three factors—speed, payload, and range—are major considerations and reasons for the propeller-driven aircraft's decline since World War II. Propellers could not provide the thrust needed for combat aircraft operations, nor could they match the jet engine's ability to drive airliners at high subsonic speeds. However, the propeller was being revisited, according to a Delta news release:

[5]Harold Sencker, "Delta Is Ready," *Forbes,* September 15,1980, pp. 81–85.

> *The propeller is experiencing reawakened interest, at least as a research target. The reason is that the turbine-driven propeller has inherently better fuel consumption than the jet or turbo-fan engine. That was a negligible factor in the days before the OPEC oil price rampage, when fuel cost 10 to 12 cents a gallon. Now the price is over $1.00 a gallon and surveys indicate that it may double in the next decade. Rising fuel cost is the biggest single problem confronting the financially-harried airlines, who might be persuaded to take a new look at the propeller—if it could provide the measure of speed and comfort to which the jetliner passengers have become accustomed.[6]*

This article speculated that unlike the turboprop aircraft designed in the 1950s (e.g., Lockheed's Hercules and Electra), the proposed new aircraft would have advanced technology propellers that would allow cruise speeds and levels of cabin comfort comparable to modern turbofan "jet" planes. Such aircraft could bring 15 to 20 percent savings in fuel consumption, according to Delta engineers.

Exhibit 9 shows Delta's jet fuel costs and consumption for fiscal years 1977 through 1982. For the first time since 1973, fuel prices in 1982 did not rise at a double-digit rate; the increase was 4 percent.

Upward fuel price pressures during fiscal year 1981 were caused by two events: decontrol of domestic crude by President Reagan in January and the price increases instituted by OPEC ministers at their Bali meeting in December, events that triggered significant surges from January to April 1981. Mar-

[6]*Delta Digest,* January 1982, p. 10

Exhibit 9

DELTA'S JET FUEL COSTS AND CONSUMPTION, FISCAL 1977–1982

Year	FUEL CONSUMPTION In Millions of Gallons	In Millions of Dollars	Average Price per Gallon	As a % of Operating Expenses
1977	949.4	$ 316.5	33.34¢	20.0%
1978	1,029.6	382.2	37.12	20.7
1979	1,144.8	475.7	41.55	21.4
1980	1,141.9	857.2	75.07	29.9
1981	1,118.3	1,070.1	95.68	31.9
1982	1,078.4	1,078.0	99.97	30.0

Source: Corporate records.

ket resistance to the higher prices took effect and caused prices to decline slightly in May and June, with continued easing into 1982 as prices appeared to stabilize and supplies became readily available.

DELTA'S PASSENGER MILES AND PROFITS, 1972 to 1981

Airlines must file reams of reports to the Civil Aeronautics Board, data that become public domain; it is relatively simple, therefore, for competitors to keep track of each other. Exhibit 10, which reflects some of the data that must be reported regularly, covers Delta's load factors, revenue passenger miles, operating profit, and net income for calendar years 1972 through 1981.

Exhibit 11 depicts distribution of Delta's passenger traffic, 1973 through 1982, by type of fare.

CARGO SERVICE

The company offered a standard array of cargo shipment services. Air freight was the base, with local pickup and delivery and air/truck service available throughout the United States. The container program offered containerization

Exhibit 10

DELTA AIR LINES, INC.
TRAFFIC AND FINANCIAL DATA
(system scheduled services)

CALENDAR YEAR	LOAD FACTOR	REVENUE PASSENGER MILES (000)	OPERATING PROFIT (000)	NET INCOME (000)
1972	50.46%	13,536,187	$101,150	$ 48,855
1973	51.25	15,022,048	123,677	74,993
1974	56.70	16,127,706	164,621	87,344
1975	55.83	16,460,463	70,861	37,385
1976	55.61	17,623,433	127,750	84,149
1977	56.92	19,119,652	175,457	116,564
1978	62.13	23,332,254	216,163	137,375
1979	62.68	26,113,015	123,703	103,602
1980	58.92	24,245,068	164,179	130,470
1981	53.26	24,245,068	86,535	91,640

Source: CAB, *Form 41s*, Schedule T-1(a).

Exhibit 11

DISTRIBUTION OF PASSENGER TRAFFIC BY FARE TYPE, 1973–1982
(REVENUE PASSENGER MILES IN BILLIONS)

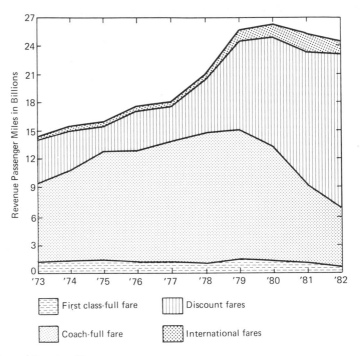

Source: *1982 Annual Report*, p. 11

rates to customers, with discounts for high-density shipments. Air Express, the first individual airline air express service, permitted any size or weight shipment within air freight service limits; space was guaranteed on both originating and connecting flights. A newer service, "DASH," introduced in 1981, offered same-day delivery for small packages, an over-the-counter arrangement with a flight guarantee (see Exhibit 12). Delta flights also carried U.S. mail.

Revenue figures were not available for public release, but Anthony McKinnon, Delta's vice-president of marketing, pointed out that this is "close to being a cost-free extra, with very little incremental expense to offer it."

While Delta pinned modest profit hopes on its DASH product, United Air Lines was headlined in one periodical as the "lone airline to dent overnight cargo area."

Exhibit 12

EXCERPTS FROM DELTA'S DASH PROMOTIONAL BROCHURE

DASH, Delta's expedited small package service, comes to the rescue when your package must reach its destination in a matter of hours. You can ship via DASH to any of Delta's domestic cities and their more than 5,000 adjacent communities, most of the time with same-day delivery. And Delta flights carry DASH shipments to places outside the United States—to Montreal, Nassau, Bermuda, London, and Frankfurt.

Almost any package with dimensions not exceeding 90 inches (length plus width plus height) and weight not exceeding 50 pounds, can use DASH. Charges for domestic shipments up to 50 pounds generally are $40 per shipment. For an additional $20, we will accept shipments up to 70 pounds. Call your Delta DASH office for further rate information.

Just take your parcel to the airport passenger ticket counter 30 minutes or more before the scheduled departure time of the flight you want your package to ride. Or you can take it to the Air Cargo Terminal counter 60 minutes or more before departure. The parcel can be picked up at the DASH claim area in the destination city 30 minutes after the flight's arrival.

You can request expedited pick-up or delivery for DASH packages in any domestic Delta city for a very reasonable additional charge. Just call toll free (800) 638-7333, and we'll make the arrangements. For London pick-up and delivery, ask about Delta's DASH-PAK service in the U.K.

There's an excellent chance that Delta can arrange for expedited small package service to the destination you desire. Besides the many Delta destinations available, Delta provides you with an expanded number of cities through our interline agreements with . . . other airlines.

Don't forget the DASH guarantee! With DASH you get the fastest small package service available plus Delta's guarantee: We will send your shipment on the flight you specify or we will refund a portion of the charges.*

    *Subject to certain tariff provisions.

United Airlines . . . committed to spend $13 million on advertising and promotion this year for United Air Express. . . . Executives say the overnight package delivery business [alone] currently racks up $2 million a year in sales and is growing at a 20% clip.[7]

[7]*Advertising Age*, March 1, 1982, pp. 39–40.

The article went on to state that American, Trans World Airlines, Delta, and Eastern were "watching" United's program with interest, but continued offering the more expensive, same-day, airport-to-airport package delivery programs. There was a potential competitive hazard not directly related to United's flying competitors: the risk of alienating cargo companies that use United Aircraft to supplement their own operations. This risk reportedly was discounted by the newly appointed vice president of United Air Express.

NEW WAVE COMPETITION

People Express CEO Donald Burr was quoted to the effect that:

> Before deregulation, the airline industry was run by the lawyers. Those who worked for the airlines petitioned those who worked for the CAB. Meanwhile, airline management forgot how to compete.
>
> Burr doesn't intend to let People forget how to compete. The two-year-old airline's headquarters, at Newark's old North Terminal, is furnished in the style favored by more prosperous county jails. People's passengers carry their own luggage (unless they want to pay $3 a bag) and pay 50 cents for in-flight coffee.[8]

Burr, who served as president of National Aviation Corporation, a closed-end investment firm specializing in airline and aerospace stocks in the early 1970s and did a stint in top management at Texas International Airlines, started cut-rate People Express in early 1980, with $5 million of venture capital, later in the year raising $23 million in a public stock offering, and then, in 1981, borrowing $58 million from Bank of America and four New Jersey banks. While getting capital together for entry into the extremely tough airlines business was considerably more difficult than easing through four mazes in a Pacman game, Burr seemed to have mastered the process in record time.

People picked up 14 10-year-old 737-100 jets from Lufthansa for less than $5 million each; new, the airplanes would have cost about $13 million each. After rearranging internal space to increase capacity by approximately one-third, flights began April 30, 1981. They lost money, estimated by observers at up to $10 million including start-up costs, while earning revenues of over $38 million, all in nine months ending December 31, 1981. Officers predicted that the airline would make money in 1982.

> People is the busiest airline at Newark Airport, with 72 departures and landings a day ... it made a profit in December, its eighth month of flying—about $500,000 on revenues of $9 million by Fortune estimates.[9]

[8]*Forbes*, May 10, 1982, p. 182.
[9]Peter Nulty, "A Champ of Cheap Airlines," *Fortune*, March 22, 1982, pp. 127–34.

AIRLINE INDUSTRY PROFITS

Headlines proclaiming losses abounded in April 1982, among them

> *PAN AM HAS LOSS ON OPERATIONS OF $100.1 MILLION[10]*
> *UNITED AIRLINES HAS RECORD LOSS IN FIRST QUARTER[11]*
> *EASTERN AIR HAD 1ST PERIOD LOSS OF $51.4 MILLION[12]*

Eastern's net income had been $4.1 million for the same period the previous year. With the airline industry in recession, the company's ratio of debt to equity was said by some analysts to be too high, making it, in the eyes of funds suppliers, an inadequate credit risk at a time when new generation aircraft were needed to stay competitive.

> *Many of the shareholders [at the April 28, 1981 meeting of owners and management] were union members who wore large yellow buttons on which the figure 3.5% was crossed out by a red line. The message referred to Eastern's five-year "variable earnings program," which it wants extended for another five years when it expires July 4. The machinists strongly oppose this. Under this program, Eastern's 37,700 employees donate 3.5% of their wages to the company when it falls short of profit goals.[13]*

Meeting the profit goals meant that workers would receive increments of 3.5% in their wages. Earlier in the year, Eastern pilots and nonunion white-collar workers had approved extension of the plan, which Eastern officials claimed would save the airline $97 million in 1980–1981 wages.

BRANIFF'S BID FOR SURVIVAL

Although Braniff International Corporation gladly anticipated the much needed $30 million cash inflow from leasing most of its South American routes to Eastern Airlines in late April 1982, including the upfront payment by Eastern of $11 million, there remained the necessity of quick moves to restructure some $733 million of debt owed 39 private lenders. The agreement was to be in effect for only 15 months while the CAB was to decide whether to approve the full six-year lease contract. In the bargain Eastern was to hire Braniff's 400 South American–based flight attendants, a move calculated to hasten approval by the foreign governments involved. By this arrangement, Braniff would be

[10]*The Wall Street Journal*, April 28, 1982, p. 10. Reprinted by permission of *The Wall Street Journal*, © Dow Jones & Company, Inc., 1982. All Rights Reserved.
[11]Ibid., p. 22
[12]Ibid., p. 56.
[13]Ibid.

able to reduce its payroll, sell eight aging aircraft, and close down maintenance facilities in New York and Miami.

A big advantage was that Braniff could shift from concentration on just surviving to consideration of more strategic concerns in marketing planning. Competitors speculated that fare structures would be the first element to come under scrutiny and that changes would likely be made in the company's simplified, single-class fare structure that offered fliers passage for one-third to one-half less than standard coach fares. Braniff officials hoped to reduce its 9,000-employee work force by 20 to 25 percent.

REGULATORY ASPECTS

Despite passage of the Airline Deregulation Act of 1978, the air transportation industry remained subject to extensive federal regulation. Under the Federal Aviation Act of 1958, as amended, the Civil Aeronautics Board, the Federal Aviation Administration, and the National Transportation Safety Board continued to exercise regulatory authority over air carriers. The CAB was concerned with regulation of economic, fair trade, consumer protection, and antitrust matters. The FAA regulated flying operations generally, including personnel, aircraft, maintenance, and other technical matters. The NTSB investigated accidents and recommended improved safety standards.

In the post-deregulation transition, Delta's tariff section in the marketing planning department was busier than ever. The volume of competitive filings had increased greatly. Prior to 1978, the office handled less than 200 pages of tariff filings each day, mostly minor adjustments to current fares, and the staff had 30 days' notice, which was usually sufficient time to analyze and plan competitive responses. In 1982, the section was receiving an average of 1,000 pages of competitive tariff filings each day, most of which were to be implemented on 24 hours' notice. Anyone using the *Official Airline Guide* knows how quickly listings become outdated, many of them inaccurate at publication time. Carriers were given more flexibility in route scheduling and fare setting than five years previously, but government-related paperwork became more onerous than ever. The following notes pertaining to regulatory matters appeared in the 1982 Annual Report:

> *In economic matters, the various steps toward full deregulation in domestic air transportation continued to unfold under the 1978 Airline Deregulation Act, but efforts also emerged in Congress both to speed the effort along and to reverse or slow down the process. Most of these attempts to change the present deregulation law have thus far been unsuccessful, although some efforts are still being made to increase the protection for airline employees against possibly adverse effects of deregulation and of various transactions between air carriers. Delta and most*

other major air carriers oppose these efforts as contrary to the basic intent and objective of deregulation and, indeed, believe that even some of the labor protective provisions which were built into the 1978 Airline Deregulation Act are excessive, illegal and perhaps unconstitutional.

Rate and fare regulation, for all intents and purposes, will terminate entirely in domestic air transportation beginning on January 1, 1983. As with other aspects of economic regulation, however, extensive rate and fare regulation continues to exist in international markets, administered both by this country and by foreign governments. [14]

PRICE WARFARE IN THE "FRIENDLY SKIES"

Delta's *1980 Annual Report* included the following comments on marketing:

In fiscal 1980, while other carriers relied heavily on discount coupons, games, lotteries, and various other giveaway promotions, Delta chose to invest its marketing resources in lasting improvements in its customer services. The company completed the automation of all its ticket offices and began a program to automate certain travel agencies. Improvements were made in Delta's automated reservations system. New and more efficient communications systems were added to Delta's reservations offices. Additional ticket offices were added at locations convenient to customers in major cities across the country.

During the coming year, a computerized fare system will be introduced which will quickly calculate fares for the most difficult and involved itinerary and produce for the customer a printed report showing each flight, date and fare for each planned trip. [15]

In its 1981 *Annual Report*, these comments appeared:

Late in fiscal 1980, the Civil Aeronautics Board implemented a policy of expanded flexibility in allowing the carriers to increase fares. . . . Delta increased its fares less than most other carriers. It is Delta's belief that the extent of these fare increases is responsible, in part, for the decline in traffic during the year. We also believe that some of the increases were implemented to support uneconomic deep discount fares, prizes, games, and giveaways initiated by some carriers in a misguided effort to achieve a competitive advantage. Delta will not allow any other carrier to maintain a pricing advantage in any market in which Delta has a meaningful

[14]*1982 Annual Report*, p. 12.
[15]*1980 Annual Report*, p. 13

amount of traffic participation. As a result, the Company was compelled to match many of these. . . fares.

In the coming fiscal year, Delta will continue to make improvements in its already highly regarded customer service in the areas of reservations, ticketing, inflight services, baggage handling, and extensive flight schedules.[16]

Anthony McKinnon discussed Delta's options in the face of competitive inroads through deep discounting: "We haven't any. If we sit idly by while competitors begin filling up their airplanes on routes shared by Delta, then we start to feel the pinch of flying with more empty seats, less revenues, and high levels of fixed expenses that erode profits. An airplane seat is a perishable commodity, so when price becomes a major factor, we have no choice but to fight to maintain our market share of available passengers.

"For example, TWA just started a three-week cut in one-way fares between New York and Dallas, down to $99 from $145, and a one-way New York-New Orleans price of $119, cut from $179. Then we have Pan Am offering a service start-up fare of $59, down from a level of $196, between New York and Atlanta. We're standing toe-to-toe with these and others, and don't intend to yield an inch."

While all this discounting was being launched, one of the casewriters wished for a Chicago-Denver-Chicago discount, but had to pay full coach fare of $470 on May 1, 1982, for a 950-mile journey, which came to about 25 cents a mile round trip. Passengers frequently are baffled by rationales underlying pricing tactics. "There is no specific, solid rationale, and fare reductions are definitely not rational," according to McKinnon, "it's simply a guess on the part of most carriers that they'll increase load factors by price cuts, with no thought as to what happens after that."

Republic Airlines, for example, continued promoting its "Nobody Serves Our Republic Like REPUBLIC Airlines" theme in early 1982 while introducing a two-for-one sale: "Now two of you can fly round-trip to any Republic city in the United States for the price of one." This offer was announced to run through June 15, 1982. Qualifications were that one ticket had to be full fare, round trip; both users had to fly on the same flight, same day, same class; and the ticket had to be purchased 24 hours in advance.

Delta decided to set the pace in one fare reduction foray early in 1982 by cutting prices as much as 51 percent on flights between points in the Northeast and Midwest and cities in Florida, in a bid to fill empty seats. As an example, one-way tickets between New York City and points in the Northeast and Midwest and cities in Florida dropped to $114, Monday through Thursday, and to $135 on Friday, Saturday, and Sunday. These fares were introduced without requirement for reservations or advance ticket purchases, and no termination date was announced immediately. There were some capacity restric-

---

[16]*1981 Annual Report*, p. 12.

tions on flights going by way of Atlanta because of frequent capacity business on such trips. While some critics of higher airline fares were saying it would be cheaper to drive, Delta came out with a study showing that a family of four could fly from Chicago to Florida, stay four days, rent a car, and save money, partly because of recently increased food prices and overnight accommodations enroute. During the promotion, no-show rates increased 15 to 20 percent, partly because some people booked tickets on two airlines, hedging to make sure they would have a seat.

While some airlines in mid-1982 began raising prices, industry experts blamed the business slump and overcapacity for keeping many fares below profitable levels. Rather than direct price cuts, either leading or meeting competitors, some carriers concentrated on providing flight credits for full-fare frequent flyers. As an example, Continental Airlines' "FlightBank" offered travel points kept in an account until the customer exchanged them for air travel. The company advertised, "There's nothing complicated about Continental's FlightBank" and touted its rate of return against points earned, calculated on the basis of earned discounts off regular fares. To encourage flyers to sign up, Continental offered a free first-class upgrade certificate "on the flight of your choice." Delta also launched its special-offer campaign targeted for heavy users of air travel.

McKinnon considered the situation in mid-1982: "Competition continues to grow. Major carrier expansion is accompanied by regionals that use the free market aspects of deregulation to extend their routes out of their traditional marketing regions into the denser long-haul markets. And they are developing hub operations of their own rather than connecting traffic at the hub cities of other carriers. Other small carriers are in the formative stage, waiting only for sufficient capital and landing slots before beginning operations.

"Many of us jumped into the fare-competition fray to fill an oversupply of seats, and some carriers capriciously cut fares in major markets, starting the much-publicized 'fare wars.' These deep discounts are uneconomic. They bear no relationship to costs or distance traveled. And they cost the industry hundreds of millions of dollars in lost revenues and increased expenses, not to mention confusion to passengers and airline personnel who try to serve flyers efficiently when making reservations and quoting fares."

THE BOEING STUDIES[17]

Characteristics of discount fares were studied between 1978 and 1980 by Boeing Commercial Airplane Company analysts, who examined three interre-

---

[17]The casewriters are indebted to Kit G. Narodick, director, analysis and support, in the Sales and Marketing Division of Boeing Commercial Airplane Company, for ideas and information in this portion of the case. The summary report, "Discount Fares and the Potential for Profit or Loss," October 1980, and additional details, if requested, were made available to Boeing's customers.

lated aspects of discount fare management:

1. **Surplus seats analysis.** Analysis of historical data to determine whether sufficient capacity is available to permit discount fares to be feasible.
2. **Market research.** Development of passenger surveys to estimate passenger behavior (diversion and stimulation rates) especially toward various discount fare plans.
3. **Profit impact program.** Evaluation of the effect on airline profitability of various discount fare plans based on the findings of surplus seats analysis and market research.

Natural variations in demand lead to vacant seats in all scheduled systems, and some vacant seats are essential to provide a buffer that allows flexibility in handling such variations, particularly those involving full-fare passengers who have made trip changes. Seats in addition to those required for the buffer are referred to as surplus seats and may be made available to discount passengers; careful analysis presumably can predict such vacancies. Seats required for full-fare traffic represent a function of the coach class capacity and the passenger spill rate (probability that a passenger cannot obtain a seat on a desired flight). The airline's tolerance for various spill rates helps to determine how many seats could be available for discount fares.

Boeing's studies in Canadian and U.S. markets found that profitability related to discount fares stayed positive and changed less under managed capacity procedures than in nonmanaged systems that were characterized by precipitous percentage drops in profits. Where demand is low, discount fares will be profitable whether or not capacity management policies are employed, since enough vacant seats exist to accommodate full-fare passengers and all passengers who fly on the discounted ticket. At higher demand levels, however, a capacity management policy limits the number of seats made available to discount flyers, avoiding the necessity to turn away full-fare flyers. The profitability of a carrier with capacity management competing with a nonmanagement carrier will improve at high demand factors because the managed airline relative profitability, but in the unrestricted case, the reverse is true. In other words, the competitor cuts losses by matching the unrestricted fare at low demand and not matching at medium and high demands.

As might be expected, very high discounts at, say, 50 percent off the regular price of a ticket, produce a substantially higher stimulation rate than a price off of, say, 20 percent. However, revenue dilution—caused by diversion from the higher discount—offsets revenue gains from those flyers responding to the promotion, resulting in lower profitability. No algorithm is available to predict it, but there clearly is price-demand elasticity, and its variations cannot be forecast accurately. It changes from market to market, and it is influenced by economic conditions and other elements involved in the packages and prices offered by competitors.

TWO QUANDARIES

Two of the quandaries confronting management in 1982 as they contemplated the desirability of ending a profit-draining fare war were recession and excess capacity. The continuing recession, which already had caused decreased demand for air travel, could create further customer resistance, not just among vacationers but among frequent flyers as well. In this price-conscious milieu, what had been a blessing to the public could turn out to be a curse to carriers, leading to curtailed boardings. The second aspect of the decision was airline overcapacity, coming to a large extent from an influx of smaller carriers. Excessive seats in virtually every part of the country contributed significantly to altering all fares on almost all routes. Getting prices up—not a simple process in any business—was thought to be especially difficult in the airline industry.

Then there was the question of protecting market share. A fare increase by one unless followed by others would likely lead to share erosion. Further, such a move, unmatched by competitors, could rigidify a two-tier price arrangement. In attempted incursions by newcomers, both Delta and United countered directly and, to a large extent, thwarted an otherwise easy entry for those who sought a piece of the larger trunk airlines' pie. But some of the old-line carriers also helped to stall attempts to raise fares toward levels existing prior to the skirmishes that led to open warfare, and some newcomers—World Airways, for example—asked for government help to prohibit what the protesters called predatory pricing by larger, entrenched rivals. Air Florida, which made its appearance on the basis of lower fares, found passenger resistance when attempting to boost its fares in early 1982, suggesting that once a low-price image has been established, if that weapon is the key element in a company's marketing mix, moving upward toward competitors' price levels is difficult.

A question posed among Delta management in 1982, was this: If some of the lower-price competitors are driven out by fare matching from the major carriers, what will this mean to the public? The answer seemed to be: higher fares near or possibly above previous levels.

MARKETING'S REORGANIZATION

A 1981 reorganization of the marketing division included absorbing the functions of the economic research department to deal with a rapidly changing airline environment. "The new marketing division organization should give Delta the flexibility and resources it needs to quickly and aggressively market its product," remarked Senior Vice President Joe Cooper. "Marketing has been so fortunate through the years to have had the benefit of the help of the economic research department; now we are delighted to have their full time efforts as we develop new marketing programs."

The work of the economic research department had become more and more marketing oriented following airline deregulation, concentrating on analyzing fares and schedules and developing new marketing ideas. Prior to regulatory changes, the group's primary work was in researching new routes and preparing for proceedings before the Civil Aeronautics Board, requesting new routes or fare changes. Frances Conner, formerly director of economic research, was named director of the marketing development department, created in the reorganization. To utilize the knowledge and talents of other economic research staff members, Delta formed a market analysis group in marketing planning to have responsibility for analyzing and evaluating fares, schedules, and other data needed by marketing planning and others in the marketing division.

The essence of Delta's organizational structure is distilled in Exhibit 13; a brief background on each key person appears in Exhibit 14.

DELTA'S ADVERTISING PHILOSOPHY AND PRACTICES

Delta Air Lines attributes part of its consistently high performance financially to the effectiveness of its advertising practices. "Several years ago," Tony McKinnon remembered, "*Advertising Age* picked Delta board chairman Tom Beebe as 'Advertising Man of the Year.' Mr. Beebe said all Delta employees made the award possible, citing the company's wise scheduling, good service, employee loyalty, and advertising. We spend about 1.5 percent of income on advertising; that puts us in the top 100 U.S. national advertisers." This is in addition to the amount spent on sales promotion items, such as posters, handout pieces, travel agency displays, direct-mail programs, and similar expenses. Distribution of Delta's advertising dollars among the media was estimated at 51 percent, newspapers; 16 percent, radio; 11 percent, television; 8 percent, magazines; 7 percent, outdoor; and 7 percent, other.

"Our heavy use of newspaper and spot radio is because of their flexibility," McKinnon continued, "and our use of what we call 'hard-sell' or 'retail' copy. Those percentages I gave you for 1981 and 1982 vary from year to year, of course."

McKinnon observed, "Delta does not allocate funds by city per se but, instead, maintains flexibility to allow us to promote any new service or meet any competitive challenge quickly. A major part of our business comes from small- and medium-sized cities, and many of those passengers, most of them actually, transfer to long-haul runs on Delta or some other carrier . So, we are geared to a reputation for frequent flights and efficient service. In Atlanta, for example [pointing to the system map,—see Exhibit 15], Delta operates more flights from a single city than any other airline anywhere in the world."

"We stick to the basics," explained L. E. Sport, system manager, advertis-

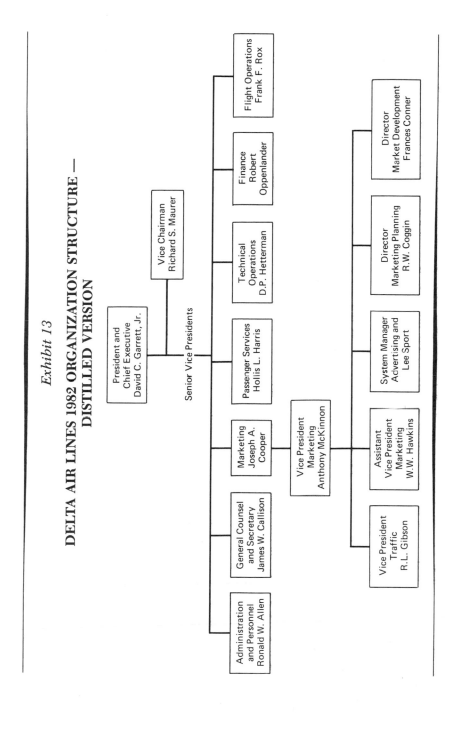

Exhibit 13

DELTA AIR LINES 1982 ORGANIZATION STRUCTURE — DISTILLED VERSION

President and Chief Executive
David C. Garrett, Jr.

Vice Chairman
Richard S. Maurer

Senior Vice Presidents

Administration and Personnel
Ronald W. Allen

General Counsel and Secretary
James W. Callison

Marketing
Joseph A. Cooper

Passenger Services
Hollis L. Harris

Technical Operations
D.P. Hetterman

Finance
Robert Oppenlander

Flight Operations
Frank F. Rox

Vice President Marketing
Anthony McKinnon

Vice President Traffic
R.L. Gibson

Assistant Vice President Marketing
W.W. Hawkins

System Manager Advertising and
Lee Sport

Director Marketing Planning
R.W. Coggin

Director Market Development
Frances Conner

Exhibit 14

BRIEF BACKGROUND ON KEY PERSONS IN ORGANIZATIONAL CHART

TOP MANAGEMENT

Garrett	Started as a Delta reservation agent in 1946
Maurer	Started as assistant to the general counsel, Chicago & Southern Air Lines, in 1943
Rox	Started as attorney with Chicago & Southern Air Lines in 1952
Oppenlander	Started as comptroller in 1958
Hettermann	Started as a mechanic in 1946
Harris	Started as transportation agent in 1954
Cooper	Started as research statistician in 1953
Callison	Started as attorney in 1957
Allen	Started as analyst in methods and training in 1963

MARKETING DIVISION

McKinnon	Started as attorney in 1972; named manager, marketing administration, in 1975 and vice president, marketing, 1980
Conner	Started in economic research department in 1951; in 1981 transferred from legal to be director, marketing development, a new department
Coggin	Started as ramp service agent in Atlanta in 1956; promoted to district marketing manager in 1964; became regional sales manager, Atlanta, in January 1979; promoted to marketing planning position in November 1979
Sport	Joined Delta in 1949 as a station agent in Knoxville; transferred to Miami in 1950, then to Delta's Atlanta office in 1956; advertising manager in 1975, until appointed to present job in December 1981
Hawkins	Started as transportation agent in Lexington in 1955; became director of advertising in 1973, general manager of passenger sales in 1975, and director of sales in 1978; promoted to his present job in 1979
Gibson	Started in 1945 as reservations agent; after serving in several cities, became director of reservations in 1968, assistant vice president, traffic administration, in 1970 and vice president, traffic, in 1975

ing. "The 'Delta is ready when you are' theme was created several years ago by the firm of Burke Dowling Adams, a subsidiary of BBDO, International, our agency since 1945."

Asked about the slogan, "Delta—the airline run by professionals," Sport called it a complementary subtheme that addressed itself to service efficiency; he then continued to interpret the role of advertising for Delta: "In the past 50 years, our airplanes have changed, but our concept of flying hasn't; the tech-

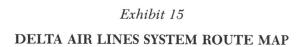

Exhibit 15

DELTA AIR LINES SYSTEM ROUTE MAP

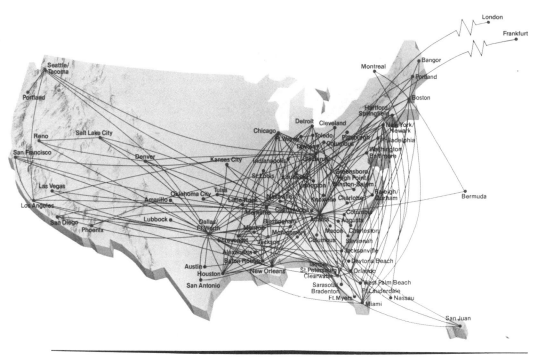

nology and administration of in-flight service has changed, but our concept of service hasn't. That 'concept' is the key to what we do. Reduced to simplest terms, we just tell the customers and prospects what the product is and how much it costs—where we are going, what time we leave, what time we get there, and the price of the ticket. It's a straightforward retail approach to selling our product."

Delta advertised in more than 300 markets, used over 350 newspapers and about 325 radio stations, a little network television, and maybe 100 TV stations on a local-buy basis. In 1981, Delta produced over 4,000 separate print ads and aired over 1,100 taped radio commercials, not to mention hundreds of live spots.

"We use only a minimum amount of national advertising where we are confined to a general approach," related Sport. "Actually, our product is different in each of the 82 domestic and 6 international cities we serve, mainly because our operating certificates vary from city to city. There's a difference between what we do in Columbus, Georgia, and in Columbus, Ohio, for example. BDA has a staff of five people who spend full time updating and monitoring our print ads alone.

"Does it work? Does advertising pay off for us? All I can say is we've shown a profit for 34 consecutive years, and you have to cast that in the framework of the last decade when airline P and L statements have had more ups and downs than a roller coaster. In that time we've consistently increased market shares and maintained position as a profit leader in the industry. A little while back, *The New York Times* rated us number one, and *Ad Age* remarked in an editorial that 'Airline marketing tactics over the past few years have been almost a textbook case of how not to do it. The airlines have been stumbling all over each other with amorphous slogans.' *Ad Age* paid Delta a compliment that pleased us so much we copied it and passed it around among our offices, 'Only Delta hammered away at one of the things passengers are really concerned about—convenient scheduling—with its Delta Is Ready When You Are campaign. And during this turbulent period for the airlines, only Delta among the big carriers was consistently profitable."

Asked why other airlines promoted general ideas instead of getting down to specifics, Mr. Sport remarked, "Some have started to emulate us; some have publicly stated they wanted to copy Delta, and believe me, they're doing it daily. Naturally, we think imitation is the sincerest form of flattery, but as you can imagine it makes our job tougher. That simply means we have to work even harder, well, smarter perhaps, to be better than those competitors."

On the P-and-L impact of advertising expenses, the advertising manager stressed consistency: "During crucial years for the industry, when so many airlines, car rental companies, and hotels were reducing promotional outlays, Delta increased its expenditures. That indicates how we feel about advertising as an important ingredient to our success, not something we can slash without feeling the impact in reduced boardings. Nobody here claims it's the sole, or even the *major,* reason for our success, but it certainly is a critical factor.

"By the way, some say we're better in print media than in others, but in the electronic media, for example, the 'Delta Is Ready When You Are' jingle was designated in 1976 one of the top 100 jingles produced in the last 50 years. We have a dozen variations of it, and we do run heavy schedules of radio spot announcements throughout the system.

"What are the central considerations in going the TV route? Well, three primary ones: (1) how to continue our retail approach; (2) how to retain the flexibility to which we are accustomed with newspaper and radio; and (3) how to produce TV spots at reasonable prices. Production costs are very high in that medium.

"Incidentally, we reject the term 'mass' media just as we reject the ideas of 'mass' transportation. Our service is personal, and we want our advertising to be personal, too. In our advertising, we want to be able to think the way our customers think and to provide information they want to help them make travel decisions. And when you handle 40,000,000 passengers a year, that is a tough goal to achieve.

"Speaking of the human side of Delta," Mr. Sport concluded, "you might be interested in knowing that we have had several task forces across the country, all volunteers—ticket agents, ramp agents, flight attendants, pilots and others—who call on travel agents and other important customers. All of this is done on their own initiative, good examples of the Delta spirit that says we are dedicated to providing superior service for our clients and we are all involved in that effort. These volunteer actions and the work of our full-time marketing people have helped make us what we are today."

SKY MAGAZINE

Sky, Delta's in-flight magazine, conveyed a strong Delta image, and advertisers in the publication supported its distribution. As on other airlines, copies of Delta's in-flight periodical were made available to passengers free of charge.

DELTA "WILL NOT BE UNDERSOLD"

When Delta's "We Will Not Be Undersold" campaign was unveiled in a special marketing division meeting, Mr. Cooper declared that the new plan is "more than just a new slogan," calling it a philosophy, the way the company "will be doing business in 1982 and beyond." The company introduced the main thrust of the plan throughout Delta's domestic U.S. and San Juan routes where the airline would "offer the best fares or would match any domestic nonstop or single-plane jet fare available from any major airline on comparable Delta flights."

> *What this means is if our existing discount fare is not already the lowest, all the customer has to do is show us any lower published jet fare on competitive service and we'll sell him a Delta seat at the same price under the same restrictions.*
>
> *At the same time, we are going to impress on the flying public that just because Delta will not be undersold does not mean that there will be any reduction in the service quality that we provide. Our reputation over the years has been that of providing outstanding service. There will be no reduction in that area.*[18]

Exhibit 16 is an ad proclaiming Delta's pricing counterattack, also mentioning the frequent flyers' promotion.

[18]*Delta Digest,* February 1982, quoting Joe Cooper, p. 6.

Exhibit 16

Delta will not be undersold!

DELTA IS UNBEATABLE

UNBEATABLE FARES!
UNBEATABLE SERVICE!

You can't beat
Delta's discount fares

We'll match the domestic* fare on nonstop or single-plane jet service of any major airline on comparable Delta flights. Just show us any published jet fare on any other major airline and we'll sell you a Delta seat at the same price under the same travel restrictions, as long as the supply of discount fare seats lasts. That means you get the lowest jet fare you can buy.

You can't match
Delta's personal service

It's the finest service in the sky, thanks to the 35,000 Delta professionals. Delta carries more passengers in the continental U.S. than any other airline. Yet we have the fewest complaints about service—by far—of any major airline, according to the latest C.A.B. records.

*Travel within domestic U.S. and to San Juan.

You can always count on
Delta's convenience

To city after city across the Delta route map you'll find we're ready when you're ready. With the nonstop or thru-jet you need. At the time that fits your personal plans.

Free flights for
frequent flyers

Enroll now in our Frequent Flyer program and start building up flights credits. They can be used for trips at big discounts or free, or for a membership in Delta's Crown Room—based on the number of credits you accumulate. Get your Frequent Flyer Membership Card application now.

Call Delta or
your Travel Agent now

Naturally with such great fares, service and convenience, Delta discount fare seats are in great demand. And the supply is limited. So get yours now—on Delta, the unbeatable airline. Check your Travel Agent or call Delta at 356-4361. ▲DELTA
The airline run by professionals

Unbeatable

DELTA IS READY WHEN YOU ARE®

Ⓗ *HAMILTON* OFFICIAL WATCH OF DELTA AIR LINES

© 1982, Delta Air Lines, Inc.

THE ROLE OF TRAVEL AGENTS

The assistant vice president for marketing, W. W. Hawkins, addressed the importance of sales contacts: "We spend a lot of time calling on the reservations, ticketing, and sales people of other airlines to keep them fully apprised of our schedules, connecting points, in-flight amenities, and the like. Inasmuch as all airlines reservations systems are automated, it is also imperative that we make sure that our flights are favorably displayed in the computers of other airlines. It is amazing how much intelligence you can pick up from airline employees who are in constant contact with the public. We keep these people adequately supplied with information on any new service features or schedules that will make their daily selling jobs easier.

"About half of Delta's total sales are made by travel agents. There are over 18,000 appointed travel agents in the United States who are authorized to sell Delta services in return for which they receive a commission. The customer does not pay a fee for this service. This is very big business to the airlines. For instance, last year travel agents sold over $1.75 billion worth of travel on Delta. Delta, in turn, paid about $150 million in agents' commissions.

"It is imperative that we stay in close touch with the needs of our agents and keep them fully aware of any changes in our service pattern. They are so important to the airline that for the last few years we have been busily engaged in placing automated reservations systems in their offices that would give them direct access from their offices into our central computer systems, just as our own reservations agents have," said Hawkins.

In 1979 Delta joined with United Air Lines as the first co-host in the APOLLO computer system; Delta marketed this automated system under the name DATAS (Delta Automated Travel Account System). Estimates in 1981 were that about half of the 10,000 travel agents in the United States with automated systems were on-line with the DATAS/APOLLO systems. This network gives travel agents instant access to over 100,000 markets with schedules reflecting all scheduled airlines. Besides airline reservations and information, the system offers hotel and car reservations. According to Joe Cooper, "The high degree of professionalism that exists in our recognition of the travel agent is especially important in the area of in-flight service and field and city ticket offices. The continued recognition of travel agents as our partners in travel will serve to keep Delta in a position of leadership in the airline industry."

Delta prepared to install a new automated reservation ticketing system in late 1982:

> Subsequent to the end of the year, the Company announced that it would offer DATAS II, an automated reservations and ticketing system, to travel agencies and large commercial customers. The fact that Delta's system displays the services of all airlines on an equal, unbiased basis is highly regarded by travel agents, as it allows them to provide their customers ef-

ficient and convenient air travel planning. Response to Delta's an-
nouncement that it will begin installing the system in the fall of 1982
has been above expectations. [19]

CUSTOMER SATISFACTION AND DISSATISFACTION

The Civil Aeronautics Board prepared a statistical report based on the number
of passenger complaints it receives. On complaints per 100,000 passenger en-
planements, Delta has consistently finished number one in fewest complaints
received. Exhibit 17 shows selected portions from a recent CAB news release.

[19] *1982 Annual Report*, p. 12.

Exhibit 17

CAB REPORT ON CONSUMER COMPLAINTS

Consumer complaints reported to the Civil Aeronautics Board in 1981
were down 42.2 percent from the 1980 level. . . . Total complaints
dropped from 22,988 in 1980 to 13,278 in 1981. The major categories . . .
remained the same, with flight problems accounting for 22.1 percent of
total; baggage, 21.8 percent; and customer service, 11.3 percent.

One reason for the complaint decline . . . may have been the increase of
new entrants in many major markets, thus challenging the performance of
the previous incumbents. Additionally, the Board has been encouraging
consumers to work directly with the airlines and state and local consumer
agencies to resolve problems before turning to the federal government for
help.

U.S. AIRLINES	COMPLAINTS PER 100,000 PASSENGERS, 1981
Delta Air Lines	0.88
Frontier	1.85
Eastern Air Lines	2.44
Continental Air Lines	2.77
American Airlines	2.91
Braniff International	4.38
People Express	10.26
Air Florida	12.85
New York Air	12.89

Source: CAB News, February 3, 1982.

A Delta ad agency spokesman said, "For the first time, we will point out in our ads that historically Delta receives the smallest number of service complaints by far of any major carrier while carrying more passengers in the continental U.S. than any other airline."

Delta's mail from customers contains occasional complaints, constructive suggestions (reflecting, according to some staffers, a personal involvement of passengers with Delta), and many letters complimenting some aspect of Delta's performance.

CROWN ROOM CLUB

Delta's Crown Room Club hospitality rooms in 19 major U.S. airports, staffed by airline personnel, provide bar service, magazines and newspapers, stationery and telephones (local calls free) away from the hustle and bustle of the terminal waiting areas and concourses. The attendant on duty in the Crown Room issues boarding passes and seat assignments (so fliers can board flights directly). The club is a source of airline schedule information and provides a personal check-cashing service. Membership also entitles new members to free luggage tags. Members of the immediate family and up to two guests may accompany a member using Crown Room facilities. In 1983 a spouse card was available for $30 in addition to the annual membership charge of $85 for the primary cardholder.

NEW SERVICES PLANNED BY DELTA

Although Eastern was historically Delta's primary competitor, some predicted that in the future American might assume that role. One feature offered by American was advance seat selection, an "extra" not currently offered nationwide by Delta but introduced by the airline in three markets in 1981. Delta planned to expand this service in 1982 and 1983.

Air-to-ground telephone linkup was scheduled for Delta in late 1982, permitting passengers to call from their seats to anywhere in the continental United States. Telephones initially were slated for the L-1011s and, when delivered, the B-767s. Then, if well received on those aircraft, DC-8-71s would also offer this convenience for Delta customers. These telephones were to be operated by inserting a major credit card into the AirFone unit, releasing a handset that the passenger then could carry to a seat to make the call. The hand-held phone contains a miniature transmitter that sends the signal to a bigger unit in the forward section of the aircraft, and from there it is beamed to one of 26 ground stations that link it to the terrestial telephone system. Call costs were estimated by Western Union, owner of 50 percent interest in the

AirFone Company, to be $7.50 for the first three minutes and $1.25 for each additional minute, a point-to-point charge regardless of distances involved.

MID-1982 INDICATORS

A spring 1982 upturn was reflected in car rental business increases and in air travel as well. Delta Air Lines happily reported over a 5 percent increase in revenue passenger miles, after a stagnant period of several months. Pointing to the projected graph, moving upward over the 1982 period, Joe Cooper, senior vice president of marketing, observed, "It's too early to say, but we have a hunch this upward turn of the revenue line signals the end of this recession; at least it indicates to us the recessionary slide could be bottoming out."

> *A better measure of the jump in business travel comes from the shuttles, which almost exclusively carry business travelers. Eastern Airlines' shuttle service to Washington and Boston had 15 percent more passengers in March than a year earlier. United, which has a Los Angeles-San Francisco shuttle, says this improved in March as well.*[20]

On April 30, for the first Friday in several months, the casewriter had difficulty booking United, TWA, and Continental flights from O'Hare westward. Agents seemed, for a change, to be both harried and happy. In May, advance airline reservations reportedly were up for summer 1982, and many hotels were experiencing surges in bookings. Part of this was no doubt attributable to vacation plans, but much of it was thought to be linked directly to increased efforts of corporations to extend their forays into the field in attempts to increase sales revenues during the continuing recession.

Delta's president and CEO speculated about the present and future:

> *Fiscal 1983 is expected to be a year of modest recovery from the slump of 1982. The economy is not expected to show any substantial improvement until early in calendar 1983. In order for Delta to show any significant improvement over fiscal 1982, we must reduce the rate of expense increases and improve productivity. The disparity between full fares and discount fares will also have to be reduced, and the impact of those fares which are not economically justified will have to be minimized. We must also work diligently to continue enhancing our competitive position in all areas of customer service.*

> *In the longer term, we have great confidence in the future of the Company. Our aircraft and ground facilities are superior. Our family of Delta*

---

[20] *Forbes,* May 10, 1982, p. 55.

Professionals is unexcelled in the industry. Our financial position is strong. We have virtually everything we need to maintain and extend our position as the leader in the airline industry.[21]

Your Task:

Advise Delta's marketing staff, particularly Vice President Anthony McKinnon.

[21] *1982 Annual Report*, p. 3.

case
33

ROUND THE CORNER
RESTAURANTS, INC.

A 1982 cartoon depicted a king instructing his nonplussed servingman to bring him, instead of his pipe, his bowl, and his fiddlers three, a burger, a shake, and a side of fries. This monarch might well have been a convert to the gastronomic delights of Round The Corner, a contender for the attention of upscale epicureans who want something more than the standard fast-food fare offered by many patty purveyors. The stature of those small, oval, flattened cakes of chopped meat was enhanced when B. Edwin (Ed) Massey and Dan W. (Bill) James II perceived a market segment of individualists with refined tastes who would appreciate that something extra to be had in charcoal-broiled beef laced with hickory sauce and other taste-tantalizing delights, served with the amenities of plates, glassware, and stainless steel utensils.

MANAGEMENT PHILOSOPHY

Ed Massey and Bill James's easygoing mannerisms and self-effacing modesty mask an intense concern for running a business that they and their associates can be proud of. What initially could be interpreted as placidity or quiet self-assurance quickly translates into enthusiastic praise of those who worked with the two partners building the enterprise known as Round The Corner (RTC), a flourishing restaurant business with stores in Arizona, California, Colorado, Georgia, and Tennessee. When they were asked to discuss RTC and the theme of success, Massey spoke of the company's camaraderie: "Being successful has more dimensions than just making money. It is very important to enjoy one's work and to feel a sense of pride in the management group that has helped the organization realize its goals. I love coming to work and so do the others; these are happy people. They're all bright. We have no jealousies and we are all motivated to perform."

Bill James commented about RTC's unique approaches: "Even though practically everything we do is public knowledge, it would not be easy to duplicate us. Our system is very difficult to master, even by someone working inside the company, let alone someone just observing it from the outside. We cook everything to order; only when your order comes in over the phone is the meat put on the grill. It is not mass produced in advance. Actually, our system is almost too complicated, so we're trying this year to streamline it to make it easier to duplicate; otherwise we can't expand rapidly enough to get the share of market we want."

RTC provides incentive programs at every level. Massey said, "People can be promoted through 11 positions at the restaurant level, and every level merits an automatic raise in pay. Management has profit-sharing pools based on five different performance categories: quality of food, ability to develop people, adherence to the fiscal plan, meeting budget, and a catchall measurement that includes their general attitude toward themselves and employees and the company. Unit managers do their own hiring. I might occasionally offer a name, maybe the daughter or son of a friend, but the unit manager makes the decision. I don't impose it. It's not fair to tell them who to hire and then expect them to make target sales and profits. This kind of freedom is why most of our key people have been with us since the inception of RTC—plenty of leeway to act, to decide. We are just 14 years old, and most of our upper-level management have been here 10 to 12 years."

The president believes in management meetings and group goal setting: "Our regional supervisors hold meetings with their people weekly and monthly. We hold upper-level management meetings quarterly and retreats and seminars annually. This year we will have a roundtable discussion with managers in a format that is under the guidance of a psychologist who'll monitor the process. This will be an idea-generating and maybe a problem-solving session for the upper-level management people. Bill James and I are always available to anyone in the organization who wants to talk to us. We encourage feedback because it gets everyone thinking. After people have been around us awhile, they feel comfortable making suggestions."

The chief executive often spoke of attempts to refine the flow of information to store managers. "I think we get overkill from our management information system. Our restaurants sometimes get too much information and can't use a lot of it. At times our managers have criticized us for this. Through continuing operations audits we are correcting this and other deficiencies. It's easy at the corporate level to forget that it is very hard work running one of the stores, day in and day out."

MANAGEMENT PROFILES AND RESPONSIBILITIES

Biographical highlights for key officers are presented in Exhibit 1. All were members of the RTC board of directors.

As an example of RTC job descriptions, responsibilities of Massey and Hawkins are summarized in Appendix A.

SELECTING LOCATIONS

Massey discussed site location: "We look for only triple-A locations, which means paying a higher price, but it costs about as much to go into a less desirable location. In choosing sites, we mainly use criteria developed and continu-

---

Exhibit 1

BIOGRAPHICAL HIGHLIGHTS OF RTC TOP MANAGEMENT, 1982

B. Edwin Massey, president, age 39. Born in Norman, Oklahoma. Managed clothing store in Norman while attending the university, majoring in business and minoring in prelaw.

Dan W. James II, secretary. Schooling in Indiana and New York before enrolling at University of Oklahoma. Co-founder and 50 percent owner of Round The Corner in 1968.

Robert D. Turrill, vice president, marketing and food service. Born in Florida, raised in Indiana, earned bachelor's degree in 1970 at University of Colorado. He bused tables and cooked at RTC's first restaurant.

Boyd E. Hoback, director of franchising. Born in New Mexico, raised in Boulder where he earned bachelor's degree in finance from the University of Colorado in 1979.

Mary Ellen Myers Ford, treasurer, age 29. Born in Hutchinson, Kansas. Graduated Beta Gamma Sigma (business equivalent of Phi Beta Kappa) at University of Colorado, major in accounting, 1975.

Greg Hawkins, vice president of operations and director of personnel, age 31. Born in Michigan. Business major at University of Colorado. Started as entry-level worker at RTC unit in 1970.

---

ously evaluated by our consultants. For example, we examine people's eating-out habits in a market, we study customer profiles of income and education, and we analyze in-and-out access of the location. Labor availability is also an important consideration."

Turning to the subject of franchisee site selection, Massey continued: "After a franchisee picks a site, we give it a second screening using our fact sheet and playing devil's advocate. Still, there's never a guarantee that any one site will prove out. As with the parent company, the primary concern is whether the intended customer is above average in income and education and is sophisticated enough to appreciate the value we offer. For that particular customer, RTC is positioned somewhere between a Houlihan's, Bennigan's, and T.G.I. Friday's and a Wendy's and McDonald's. Our average ticket runs about $5.00 a person."

MARKETING: PRODUCTS, RESEARCH, AND PROMOTION

Discussing the marketing vice president's job, Massey explained: "Bob Turrill wears two hats. He's in charge of marketing and products and must control our major costs related to these categories. But he's also responsible for getting a lot of volume, and he receives credit for that. But if he skimps on the product end, he'll lose customers and volume. It's a delicate balance. His budget consists of a combination of wholesale food costs and advertising costs, and he determines how much is to be spent for what. Wholesale food costs and advertising allowances are lumped into one budget. He controls 35 percent of our wholesale budgets and can allocate, for example, 31 percent for food costs and the other 4 percent for marketing, including market research, focus groups, and test marketing new products.

"I think this arrangement may be unique in the industry. The one who is charged with the responsibility of creating efficiencies and cost savings is the same person charged with the responsibility of bringing in and satisfying a large number of customers. In this arrangement, the traditional conflict between marketing and operations is resolved, and we get the most customer-oriented food service operations in the business."

Bill James remarked on RTC's belief in customer surveys: "We listen to our managers and to our employees, and we pay attention to what our customers say, too. The company spent $30,000 in 1980 to find out more about our customers. This survey, 'Your 2-Cents Worth' [Appendix B], was given to 11,000 customers, asking their opinions. We expected to get about half of them back, but actually got 10,000. Our customers want to tell us how we're doing, and if they didn't like us they wouldn't bother to answer. In that survey we found we didn't need to offer steak; we did need more salads, desserts, soup, and a variety of nonhamburger sandwiches. The 1982 menu [Appendix C] reflects a lot of changes made in two years' time. Of course, the major part of our menu is burgers, including what we call 'the dinner,' along with side orders, children's fare, desserts that were added based on research, and our beverages, including beer and wine."

Bob Turrill noted, "We couldn't handle preparing the specialty items [a tomato-based secret sauce, hickory sauce, baked beans, and Caesar dressing] in our company-owned central kitchen—too many manufacturing and distribution headaches—so we went to an outside firm in California, a food processor and packer that specialized in duplicating proprietary recipes for multiunit chains. This solved our quality and consistency problems. And they actually improved on our original hickory sauce and baked bean recipes. There were cost savings, too, because the packer is able to buy and produce in large quantities. As we go more into the East and South, products will be canned for us in Ohio, reducing freight costs to those areas."

Bill James returned to the subject of research data: "An example of how we use research: about three years ago the customers were telling us our decor was antiquated, that we needed something more up-to-date than the old-fashioned, gay-nineties feel of low lighting and dark paneling, something more suited to today's lifestyle. We shifted to the modern decor you see in our stores in 1982 [Appendix D] that is a lot more upbeat. This change launched us into the 1980s, and customers' enthusiasm is up, too. But doing this set us back on our timetable a couple of years because we had 10 stores that needed refurbishing. At $100,000 each, this meant spending a million dollars, which we had to borrow at 15 percent interest."

By 1982 Round The Corner was a blend of traditional and contemporary, a combination of angled ceilings, exposed beams and air conduits, earth-tone fabrics and accessories, round windows and accents of live plants, skylights, brass, copper, and arrangements of natural materials. In decor, menu, and service, Round The Corner would not be mistaken for a run-of-the-mill fast-food restaurant.

Bill James spoke of RTC's unique delivery system: "What enables us to provide fast service are the electronic phone system and an efficient kitchen staff. Diners use a telephone at the booth to call in their order. In an average time of six minutes, the phone buzzes to announce that their cooked-to-order meal is ready to pick up at the counter [Appendix D]. And the menu reminds our guests that the telephone doesn't expect a tip. During peak hours we have two order-takers working at the communication panel to minimize waiting time for customers."

Turrill explained that RTC started using TV advertising in 1978 as soon as its budget became large enough to afford the expense: "Now RTC has an 85 percent public awareness level in our major metro area; more than half of those residents have eaten at a Round The Corner store. Our ad agency helped us develop our strategy and focus; we saw a marked positive response after the ads started. Now we spend about 3.5 to 4.0 percent of our revenues for TV advertising. It's an ideal medium to reach the target markets we're after.

"Our burgers get their gourmet touch from fancy toppings, including, for example, a frozen spicy guacamole. Our suppliers tell us we sell more of this than most Mexican restaurants. With the amount we use, it would be difficult to maintain consistency from store to store, so we formulate and freeze it. In trying to boost dinner traffic, we launched the idea of the burger as part of a four-course meal and expanded our menu to achieve this. A meal for two amounts to about $10, including wine or beer. This is all part of our effort to woo the older, more affluent market."

RTC FRANCHISING

In 1978, 10 years after launching the chain with a single restaurant, the company owned 10 stores and decided to move into franchising to spread the concept and to broaden their share in this market niche. By November 1981, they added three franchised units in Atlanta, two in Memphis, three in Phoenix, one in Grand Junction on the western slope of Colorado, and a store in San Diego. The Atlanta, Memphis, and Phoenix franchisees planned to open a total of 35 stores in their regions by 1990; the goal in California was 24 stores in 10 years.

Boyd Hoback, RTC's director of franchising, responded to a question about expectations of franchisees: "We're probably more demanding than most in the industry in our requirements for financial support and business acumen. And we forbid absentee ownership." Those who aspired to a Round The Corner franchise in 1982 were required to sign the franchise fact sheet (Appendix E) and return it with their application form.

Total real estate development, equipment, and signage costs for each RTC unit ran upwards of $750,000 in mid-1982. In addition, franchise recipients were required to pay Round The Corner a $25,000 fee for developing the first restaurant and providing opening service and then to pay a monthly royalty of 3 percent on the first $500,000 gross, 4 percent on $500,000 to $1,000,000, and 5 percent on all revenues over $1,000,000. Franchisees were also expected to spend 2 percent of gross sales on local advertising.

Bill James commented on mall locations for franchisees: "Franchise owners have more difficulty than we do in getting triple-A location mall owners to believe in them—most property owners aren't very eager to give someone an entrepreneurial chance. If RTC were a public company, franchisees would be helped a great deal. Our Atlanta franchisee has four stores open. If we were a public company, he would become president of the Southern Division and make requests for capital and submit budgets just as our corporate people do now. Of course, he wouldn't have to do it alone; we would offer help from the corporate office."

Boyd Hoback reflected on other chains' franchising: "Franchising has been a vehicle to propel most of the top restaurant chains into prominent positions in the food service industry. I think we've seen a growth that can only be called impressive, in spite of interest rates and rising costs and sluggish traffic for many. McDonald's system always seems to come in with good performance, adding stores and increasing revenues and profits every year. But, on their large base, even they will see a decline in growth rate for the rest of the decade. International business is also helping them.

"Another chain that has grown rapidly by itself is Steak and Ale, but now it is throwing some stones into the franchising pond to test the waters, I believe just in the eastern states and Canada right now, but they'll expand on the basis of what they learn there. An example of the negative side is Church's Fried Chicken; they've steadily opened new units in the past two years, but a number of their licensees have closed, too, mainly because of high interest rates, increasing costs, and, in many places, local unemployment. Church's is also going into Canada and Mexico.

"McDonald's corporate takes a 50 percent interest in the international units and resident nationals have the other half. Ownership arrangements vary a lot, but equal holdings by resident nationals seem to work out well, and it's required legally in some countries. Denny's owns its Canadian restaurants—they're a moderately priced, full-service concept—but it has licensees in Mexico and Japan.

"On royalty fees, RTC is seeing a geometric progression right now. Net royalties in five years could approach $1 million a year, if we keep on the path we are committed to as of 1982."

FINANCING FOR GROWTH

Hamburger Hamlet launched a top-of-the-line burger concept in the 1960s, offering 50 different kinds of burgers in a posh setting. Its stock went from $5\frac{1}{2}$ in the spring of 1980 to $8\frac{3}{4}$ a year later. Some would say the investing public recognizes a good idea, well implemented and soundly managed, and is willing to bet on its continued success. In 1981 RTC management was considering the advantages and disadvantages of expanding beyond internally generated funds to finance anticipated growth.

Chief Financial Officer Mary Ellen Ford conjectured: "There are quite a few alternatives we could pursue in getting financing for expansion. Venture capital is out because the markup is too high at every level, including the broker's fee, which might run as high as 10 percent. Going public right around home wouldn't be the best approach because then we wouldn't be getting into the secondary markets, which would be needed if we do expand to 75 or 80 stores in the next several years."

Massey expressed a belief that the ways some operators are raising capital has become one of the more enterprising and creative aspects of the industry. "Most of the avenues open to companies searching for capital have been around for a while but have not been used in the past to any great extent; now they are becoming the rule rather than the exception," he continued. "Because of our size we cannot qualify for S.B.A. loans, but they have been a major source of capital for our franchisees. Industrial revenue bonds are always under scrutiny by the Internal Revenue Service and therefore unpredictable. Because we are established, we are unwilling to give up the percentage of equity that would be required if the capital were provided by a venture capital group, and we think that a public stock offering, merger, or acquisition would be premature right now."

Ford added that in addition to conventional bank financing, the company has turned to private placement and joint ventures. "We are offering equity in the parent company to selected individuals through common stock, subordinated convertible debentures, or subordinated convertible warrants," she said. "Each carries a different price per share, depending on the advantage to the company and the risk-reward ratio for the investor. Joint ventures will actually be structured like limited partnerships, with our company being the general partner and the investors the limited partners. The limited partner will provide all the capital required for capital improvements and the furniture, fixtures, and equipment and will receive a reasonable return on his or her investment, along with all the investment tax credit, all depreciation, and a percentage of pretax profit. RTC will provide operating expertise—selecting the location, supervising construction and opening of the restaurant, and all ongoing management. For this we will receive a management fee and a percentage of the pretax profits."

RTC'S FUTURE

Massey said, "I don't want us to become gigantic. Even 30 stores sounds big to us, and we're boggled about taking it to 75 stores in the next five years—that's our expectation—because we still want control. We want customers coming in and saying they like what we're doing. I was worried when we had 10 stores. We hit that a couple of years ago, and now, three years later, we are three times that. Maybe we will be three times that by 1990, but it may belong to somebody else by then."

Added James, "A big question is whether we can postpone opening another store until we get really good people to run it. Can we hold out for a triple-A location, meet all our budgets, and continue to grow? Can we assure that employees and investors' equity continues to grow? That growth is all the investing public cares about, and they won't criticize if we're producing an increase in equity. Ed and I don't want to be pressured to open 10 new stores when we know that 5 would make a lot more sense. Our board of directors thinks that way, and we need to educate the investors to think that way as well. As we are able to do that, we'll have more sophisticated private investors coming to us and wanting to buy stock or to become involved in joint ventures as limited partners."

On the subject of industry expansion, Massey is convinced that "the trend for people to eat out will increase. They'll do it more often as time goes by, mainly because more women are working. But our industry is maturing, so I also believe that only the well-managed companies will survive. Right now we see fewer jumping into the industry. Round The Corner has the advantage of being established, so we are able to get more of the triple-A locations needed to succeed. The mall owners are looking for the established and successful organizations, like ours; they're not willing to take chances on those who are just speculating, who are merely looking for alternative investments. The more successful the store in a shopping center, the more income for the owners of the center from percentage of sales over the base rent."

Your Task:

Advise RTC Management.

Appendix A

SPECIFIC JOB RESPONSIBILITIES
CHIEF EXECUTIVE OFFICER/PRESIDENT

Goals and Objectives. Assisting the board of directors to set goals and objectives that will maximize the company's return on the investment it has in people and physical plants.

Forecasting and Budgeting. Volume forecasting and recommending expense budgets, for approval by the board of directors.

Finance. Arranging for the capital necessary for growth and development through well-documented presentations.

Real Estate and Architecture. Finding and securing sites that meet the company's criteria and submitting plans for site and architectural review.

Law. Negotiating contracts and/or leases for the acquisition of the real property and the personal property.

Accounting. Staffing the corporate office with personnel who are trained to produce accounting information in accordance with the company's systems and standards as set forth in the accounting manual.

General Administration. Staffing the corporate office with personnel who are trained to coordinate effective communication between all entities of the company and provide timely required correspondence.

Appendix A (Cont.)

Advertising, Marketing, and Promotion. Review and coordination of the advertising materials, marketing strategies, special promotions, signage, and graphics.

VICE PRESIDENT OF OPERATIONS AND DIRECTOR OF PERSONNEL (GENERAL MANAGER)

PERSONNEL

1. The vice president/general manager must ensure that all employees meet the Round The Corner standards and must oversee that the management is doing the following properly:
   a. Recruiting
   b. Interviewing
   c. Scheduling
   d. Training
   e. Terminating
   f. Following the specific orientation program of all personnel as stated in the training program
2. The general manager and associates (regional managers and administrative assistants) personally
   a. Interview and hire all management trainees and establish training programs for the company's trainees.
   b. Maintain management records and review them on a regular basis.
   c. Monitor all labor costs and training costs throughout the year.
   d. Require personnel charts from each restaurant every year.
   e. Review personnel inspections monthly in every restaurant and are constantly aware that his or her management team and their employees are the ultimate key to the long-term success of the company (most of these tasks are delegated).

QUALITY PRODUCT

A strict adherence to product quality, as learned in the Round The Corner training program and expressed throughout the operations manual, must be maintained at all times.

CLEANLINESS AND MAINTENANCE

1. The general manager should give each restaurant a cleaning inspection every month, using the standard Round The Corner cleaning inspection form. He or she should review the scores from each inspection with the manager and develop an in-store cleaning program to cover all areas of the restaurant.

Appendix A (Cont.)

2. All equipment needs should be discussed and dates set up for necessary repairs and for preventive maintenance programs.

BUDGETS AND GOALS

1. The general manager helps each manager set monthly and yearly volume and personnel goals.
2. The general manager provides the manager with an operating budget for controllable expenses. This budget is set on an annual basis by the board of directors and adjusted when necessary.

ACCOUNTING

1. Communication with the office staff on a monthly basis to receive input on each restaurant manager's aptitude in record keeping and to relay suggestions from the restaurant managers to the office staff.
2. Periodically spot-check restaurant manager's forms (applications, daily cash reports, etc.) to make sure that they are being filled out accurately and neatly and to note any trends that could be potential problems (cash short, labor percentages).
3. Take one separate inventory "audit" each month-end that the office staff can compare to the restaurant manager's inventory.
4. Maintain a time sheet to identify for the company where supervisory time has been spent for allocation purposes.

Appendix B

RESTAURANTS

Appendix B (Cont.)

A CUSTOMER SURVEY

We know it's somewhat of an imposition to ask you to fill out our survey questionnaire. But we think you'll find it simple and painless. And we sincerely promise that your 2¢ worth will influence the way we serve you in the future.

ABOUT YOUR GROUP

1. How many people are in your group today?

One person	1	Four people	4
Two people	2	Five people	5
Three people	3	Six or more people	6

2. How many people in your group are in each of the following age categories?

Under 13	_	35-49	_
13-17	_	50-64	_
18-24	_	65 and over	_
25-34	_		

3. Which of the following relationships best describes the people you're with today?

Family members	1	By myself	4
Business associate(s)	2	Other	5
Friend(s)	3		

4. Which Round the Corner location are you eating at today?

Aurora/Buckingham Square	1
Boulder/Crossroads Shopping Center	2
Boulder/The Hill	3
Boulder/Table Mesa	4
Colorado Springs	5
Denver/Cherry Creek	6
Denver/Hampden Avenue—Adjacent to Marriott	7
Englewood/Cinderella City	8
Fort Collins/Foothills Mall	9
Fort Collins/West Elizabeth Street	10
Greeley	11

5. Day of the week:

Sunday	1	Thursday	5
Monday	2	Friday	6
Tuesday	3	Saturday	7
Wednesday	4		

6. What time did you arrive at Round the Corner today?

11:00 a.m.-1:00 p.m.	1
1:00 p.m.-4:00 p.m.	2
4:00 p.m.-7:00 p.m.	3
7:00 p.m.-11:00 p.m.	4

9. About how often do you eat at Round the Corner?

Once a week or more	1	Every 2 or 3 months	4
Several times a month	2	Twice a year	5
Once a month	3	Once a year or less	6

10. At which of the following times have you eaten at Round the Corner? (Please circle all that apply)

11:00 a.m.-1:00 p.m.	1	4:00 p.m.-7:00 p.m.	3
1:00 p.m.-4:00 p.m.	2	7:00 p.m.-11:00 p.m.	4

11. Do you think of Round the Corner more as a place to have lunch or dinner?

Lunch	1
Dinner	2
Either	3

12. Which of the Round the Corner restaurants have you eaten at previously? (please circle all that apply)

Aurora/Buckingham Square	1
Boulder/Crossroads Shopping Center	2
Boulder/The Hill	3
Boulder/Table Mesa	4
Colorado Springs	5
Denver/Cherry Creek	6
Denver/Hampden Avenue, Adjacent to Marriott	7
Englewood/Cinderella City	8
Fort Collins/Foothills Mall	9
Fort Collins/West Elizabeth Street	10
Greeley	11

13. Is the restaurant you are in now closer to your home or office?

Home 1   Office 2   About equal 3

14. About how long does it take you to get to this Round the Corner from your home and office?

	HOME	OFFICE
Less than 5 minutes	1	1
5-10 minutes	2	2
10-15 minutes	3	3
Over 15 minutes	4	4

15. Why did you choose Round the Corner today?

Appendix B (Cont.)

ABOUT YOU

7. *What do you like most about Round the Corner?*

_____

_____

8. *What is the thing you like least about Round the Corner?*

_____

_____

17. *Please indicate how important each of the following reasons are in your selection of Round the Corner, with #1 being not important and #5 being very important.*

	Not Important				Very Important
Advertising	1	2	3	4	5
Phone ordering system	1	2	3	4	5
No tipping policy	1	2	3	4	5
Quality of food	1	2	3	4	5
Price of food	1	2	3	4	5
Length of time for food to be prepared	1	2	3	4	5
Menu selections	1	2	3	4	5
Proximity of restaurant to your home or office	1	2	3	4	5
Appearance and taste of the food	1	2	3	4	5
Availability of beer and wine	1	2	3	4	5

18. *Which of the following statements best describes your feelings about the hours of operation at Round the Corner?*

The hours are fine 1
Should open earlier than 11:00 a.m. for lunch 2
Should stay open later than 11:00 p.m. 3
Other (Please specify)_____ 4

19. *Please tell us what you think about our phone ordering system.*

_____

_____

20. *Have you ever tried Round the Corner's carry-out service?*

Yes 1   No 2   Wasn't aware you had one ... 3

21. *As you know, most Round the Corner Restaurants serve beer and wine. Do you think beer and wine are adequate or would you like to also have a choice of mixed drinks?*

Beer and wine are adequate 1
Would like a choice of mixed drinks 2
Would prefer no alcoholic beverages 3

22. *How likely would you be to eat breakfast at Round the Corner if it were available?*

Very likely 1   Reasonably unlikely 3
Somewhat likely 2   Very unlikely 4

23. *What else would you like to see offered on the menu that is not presently offered?*

_____

24. *Where would you like to see Round the Corner open another restaurant?*

_____

_____

16. *What restaurants do you consider alternatives to Round the Corner?*

1. _____   5. _____
2. _____   6. _____
3. _____   7. _____
4. _____   8. _____

25. *Which of the following restaurants do you consider to be the most like Round the Corner? (If appropriate, please circle more than one)*

Arthur Treachers ...	1	Kentucky Fried		Steak & Ale	15
Azar's Big Boy	2	Chicken	8	TGI Friday's	16
Coco's	3	McDonalds	9	Ticos	17
Cork 'n Cleaver	4	Mr. Steak	10	Village Inn	18
Denny's	5	Pizza Hut	11	Wyatts Cafeteria ...	19
Ground Round	6	Red Barn	12	Other (your	
Houlihan's	7	Shakey's	13	choice)_____ ...	20
		Sizzler Steak House	14	None of the above ..	21

26. *What other restaurants have you eaten at in the last two months?*

1. _____   4. _____   7. _____
2. _____   5. _____   8. _____
3. _____   6. _____   9. _____

ABOUT YOUR FAMILY (The following questions are for statistical purpose only)

27. *How many people are in your household?*

One 1   Three 3   Five 5
Two 2   Four 4   Six or more 6

28. *What are the ages of the children under 18, if any, that live with you at home?*

Don't have any children under 18 at home 1
Have children under 6 2
Have children 6-12 3
Have children 13-18 4

29. *Please circle the number that represents your age group.*

Under 13 1   35-49 5
13-17 2   50-64 6
18-24 3   65 and over 7
25-34 4

30. *What type of work do you do?*

31. *What is the zip code where you live?* _____

32. *What is the zip code where you work?* _____

33. *Please circle the category that best represents your total annual household income.*

Under $10,000 .... 1 $25,000-$39,999 5
$10,000-$14,999 .... 2 $40,000 and over 6
$15,000-$19,999 3   Refused 7
$20,000-$24,999 4

34. *Are you:*   Male.....1   Female....2

35. *Any other comments you might have about our restaurant would be appreciated.*

_____

Please place your questionnaire at the table's edge and one of our employees will pick it up. Thank you for your assistance.

Thank you for giving us your thoughts.

Appendix C

THE SOUP AND SALAD

Monday: Split Pea Soup **Friday:** Boston Clam Chowder
Tuesday: Lumber Jack Vegetable Soup **Saturday:** Cream of Broccoli Soup
Wednesday: Cheese Soup **Sunday:** Chicken Noodle Soup
Thursday: French Onion Soup

Cup 1⁰⁰ Bowl 1⁵⁰

The Dinner Salad Tossed greens with wedges of chilled tomato. Your choice of dressings: French, Ranch, Thousand Island, Bleu Cheese or Italian. 1⁰⁰

The Chef's Salads Fresh tossed greens, tomato wedges, grated cheese and your choice of dressings.

With Sliced Ham 2⁹⁵ With Sliced Turkey 2⁹⁵ With Ham and Turkey 3⁷⁵

The Taco Salad Ensalada muy grande! A spicy concoction of beef, beans and onions on a thick bed of chilled lettuce, tomato and grated cheese. Topped with guacamole and sour cream. Taco chips and salsa on the side. 4⁵⁰

THE SANDWICH

The Chicken Sandwich Boneless breast of chicken, dipped in spicy batter and deep fried. Served with lettuce, tomato and mayonnaise on a sesame seed bun. Hickory sauce on the side. 2⁹⁵

The Chicken Cheesiano Sandwich Tender, batter-fried breast of chicken and melted Provolone cheese, smothered in our secret tomato sauce— steaming hot. 2⁹⁵

The Roast Turkey Sandwich Thinly sliced turkey (with lettuce, tomato, and your choice of cheese) heaped on a Kaiser roll spread with mayonnaise. Served hot. 2⁸⁵

The Turkey & Guacamole Sandwich The mingled flavors of white turkey meat, avocado, lettuce, tomato and mayonnaise. 2⁹⁵

The Turkey & Bacon Sandwich Turkey and cheese slices, crisp bacon strips, fresh lettuce and tomato piled high and spread with mayonnaise. 2⁹⁵

The Turkey & Ham Sandwich Layers of thinly sliced turkey and ham, with cheese, lettuce, tomato and mayonnaise. 2⁹⁵

The Hickory Cured Ham & Cheese Sandwich Thinly sliced ham, piled high and melted over with your choice of American, cheddar or Swiss cheese, garnished with lettuce, tomato and mayonnaise. 2⁸⁵

The Grilled Cheese Sandwich Thick and chewy, served on sourdough bread. Tomato and mayonnaise, add 25¢. 1⁷⁵

The Fish Filet Sandwich Deep fried, golden brown, and smothered in our own tartar sauce on a toasted sesame seed bun. 2³⁵

The R.T.C.B.L.T. Sandwich Our version of the traditional bacon, lettuce and tomato sandwich on a toasted sesame seed bun. 2⁴⁵

THE HOT DOG

The Chili Dog A ¼ pound, all beef frankfurter, smothered in steaming chili and peppered with grated cheese. 2⁷⁵

The Old-Fashioned Hot Dog Big, hot, and loaded with mustard, pickles and onions. 1⁹⁵

Appendix C (Cont.)

THE BURGER

Double. For two charbroiled beef patties instead of one, add $1.00.
Bacon. For bacon on a burger not regularly served with bacon, add 75¢.
Half Order Fries. Available with purchase of burger or sandwich. Add 75¢.

1 The Hickory Burger A savory blend of charcoal broiled beef and our rich hickory sauce. For cheese, add 35¢. **1**^{95}

2 The Old-Fashioned Burger On this menu, the closest you'll find to an ordinary hamburger. Mustard, pickles, onions. **1**^{95}

3 The Chili Burger Smothered in our famous chili, spicy hot, and topped with grated cheese. **2**^{85}

4 The Polynesian Burger An island concoction of charbroiled beef, juicy pineapple, sweet & sour sauce, and sizzling bacon. **2**^{95}

5 The Hot Radish Bacon Burger On a bed of lettuce. Topped with melted Swiss, three bacon strips and sour cream sauce with horseradish. **2**^{95}

6 The Front Range Favorite Burger With pickles, onions and our homestyle hickory sauce. For cheese, add 35¢. **2**^{45}

7 The Italian Burger Melted over with pizza cheese. Topped with secret sauce. Sprinkled with mushrooms. **2**^{85}

8 The Guacamole Bacon Burger With the mingled flavors of tomato, lettuce, avocado, spices and crisp bacon strips. **3**^{25}

9 The Thousand Island Burger Creamy Thousand Island dressing over lettuce, tomato and cheese. **2**^{85}

10 The Pizza Burger A leaning tower of pizza cheese, secret sauce and lean charbroiled beef. **2**^{45}

11 The All-American Burger The almost traditional cheeseburger, with lettuce, tomato and mayonnaise. **2**^{85}

12 The Theta Special Burger Cheeseburger graced with pickle, mayonnaise and your choice of hickory or secret sauce. **2**^{85}

13 The Mushroom Burger Smothered all in mushroom sauce and sprinkled with grated cheese. **2**^{85}

14 The Burger Stroganoff With melted Swiss cheese, mushrooms in sauce, and a generous dollop of sour cream. **2**^{85}

15 The Bleu Bacon Burger Chunky Bleu Cheese dressing ladled over crisp bacon, melted Swiss and lettuce. **2**^{95}

16 The Bacon Burger Your choice of cheddar, American, or Swiss cheese (please specify) topped with bacon, and garnished with lettuce, tomato and mayonnaise. **2**^{95}

17 The Border Burger The fiery flavor of whole green chilies, melted cheddar, sour cream, and a dash of green chili with pork. **2**^{85}

18 The Genuine Ham Burger A charbroiled cheeseburger, with hickory sauce and grilled ham, on a bed of lettuce and tomato. **2**^{95}

19 The Burger Especial Spicy guacamole and sour cream with lettuce and grated cheese, smothered in zesty pork green chili. **3**^{25}

20 The Hickory Bacon Burger Grated cheese, hot bacon strips and savory hickory sauce on a big charbroiled burger. **2**^{95}

THE DINNER

Our popular Hickory Burger with a whopping order of fries or baked beans, plus the soup of the day or a tossed green salad (with French, Ranch, Thousand Island, Italian or Bleu Cheese dressing). All for one low price. **3**^{50}

You may substitute the burger of your choice
and we'll adjust the price accordingly.

Appendix C (Cont.)

THE SIDE ORDER

The French Fried Potato Crisp, tender, long, slender, hot, golden brown, delicious, and rather massive in portion. **1**²⁵

The French Fried Onion Rings A large order, crisp on the outside, hot and oniony on the inside. **1**⁹⁵

The "Half Rings" A small order, crisp on the inside, hot and oniony on the inside. **1**¹⁰

The Baked Beans Simmered for days with bacon, onion and seasonings **85**

The Chili Some chili! With cheese and onions, add 35¢.   Cup **1**²⁵   Bowl **1**⁷⁵

THE CHILDREN'S FARE

For people with tiny little tummies, usually 10 years of age or under, we offer the following junior entres. Each comes with a proportionate order of fries and pickles.

The Jr. Burger • The Jr. Cheeseburger • The Jr. Hot Dog **1**⁶⁵

THE DESSERT

The Good News Sundae It comes in Chocolate, Strawberry or just Plain Ol' Vanilla. **1**⁰⁰

The Baby Cakes Special Fluffy pound cake heaped with creamy ice cream and hot fudge (or strawberries) and whipped cream. Great for sharing. **1**⁵⁰

The Carrot Cake Tender and moist, full of good things. If you want it à la mode, add 25¢. **1**³⁵

THE SOFT DRINK

Coca Cola, Dr. Pepper, Sprite or Tab

60 oz. Pitcher (best value)	1.75
Large	.65
Regular	.55

Coffee	.55	Milk	.55
Hot Tea	.55	Hot Chocolate	.55
Iced Tea	.55	Lemonade	.55

Shakes	Chocolate Strawberry Mocha Vanilla	.95

THE BEER & WINE

Coors and Miller Lite

12 oz. Mug	1.00
60 oz. Pitcher	3.50

Michelob

12 oz. Mug	1.25
60 oz. Pitcher	4.50

Inglenook Chablis, Rosé or Burgundy

By the Glass	1.25
By the ½ Liter	2.25
By the Liter	3.95

In the name of quality and good taste, Round the Corner proudly includes foods and beverages from these famous-brand makers.

Appendix D

Appendix E

ROUND THE CORNER RESTAURANTS, INC., FRANCHISE FACT SHEET (SELECTED PASSAGES FOR ILLUSTRATION PURPOSES)

The Round The Corner concept of franchising is based upon a strong personal relationship between the applicant(s) and RTC management. We do not believe in absentee ownership of our franchised restaurants.

1. A franchise applicant must have and present a satisfactory financial statement
2. A franchise applicant must be in good health. The operation of a Round The Corner Restaurant makes substantial physical demands.
3. The franchise applicant(s) must be prepared to devote his or her full time and best effort toward the success of the restaurant.

The applicant must come to the company's corporate headquarters at his or her own expense for extensive interviewing. The company reserves the right to reject any application without giving the applicant any reason therefor.

Upon acceptance, the franchisee will be required to undertake and satisfactorily complete a company-conducted course of training of approximately 20 weeks' duration. This training will be scheduled for the time the restaurant is under construction. Personal expenses for travel, food, lodging, and so on, during training are the responsibility of the franchisee.

The applicant must realize that Round The Corner Restaurants, Inc., does not guarantee the success of the restaurant or the security of the franchisee's investment. The success of the venture is dependent largely on the business abilities of the franchisee.

The applicant's capability or experience in site selection, lease negotiation, and capital acquisition will be a factor in determining the size of the "franchised area" to be granted. As soon as an applicant has been accepted, the company will advise the franchisee of the number of restaurants and performance (time) schedule that will (ultimately) be required in his or her area. The number will be tied to an in-depth demographic study of the area and a reasonable timetable.

In the absence of agreements to the contrary, the franchise agreement will have a term of 20 years.

The current total of the franchise and assistance fee for developing an initial restaurant and providing opening services is $25,000. In most "franchised areas," the franchisee is required to guarantee the company a franchise and assistance fee for a minimum of two or three restaurants.

Appendix E (Cont.)

Franchisee shall pay a monthly royalty of 3 percent on the first $500,000 of franchisee's annual gross sales, 4 percent on the franchisee's gross sales from $500,000 to $1,000,000, and 5 percent on annual gross sales in excess of $1,000,000. The franchisee is required regularly to submit financial data on sales and to give the company the right to examine its accounts.

Franchisee will be required to spend 2 percent of annual gross sales for local media advertising until such time as a national advertising program is available. All advertising materials will be available from the company's advertising agency at 50 percent of original production cost plus the cost of adaptation to the franchise market.

Total real estate development costs currently range between $500,000 and $750,000 with the major variables being land costs, required site work, and new construction utility fees. A build-to-suit and leaseback at a lease rental of approximately 15 percent of the total real estate development costs or 6 percent of gross sales per annum, whichever is higher, is generally the most desirable arrangement.

Restaurant equipment must meet the specifications of the company. The current restaurant equipment cost is approximately $150,000.

The sign package must meet the specifications of the company. A standard package currently costs $10,000.

Arrangements for the purchase or lease of the real estate, equipment, phones, signs, registers, and so on, will be direct between the franchisee and the owner, supplier, or manufacturer.

To assist in the development and operation of the restaurants, Round The Corner Restaurants, Inc., at its expense, will make available to the franchisee the following:

1. Site location review by full-time company real estate personnel
2. Standard plans and specifications for the building, equipment, furnishings, decor, layout, and signs identified with Round The Corner Restaurants, together with advice and consultation concerning them
3. Review of real estate leases and equipment and furnishings purchase agreements (bids)
4. Advice on purveyor selection, including but not limited to food items, paper products, and cleaning supplies
5. Information concerning volume purchasing advantages that may exist through Round The Corner Restaurants, Inc., and/or assistance in setting up approved sources of supply if the franchisee elects to purchase elsewhere
6. A preopening training program conducted at a Round The Corner Restaurant
7. Assistance in setting up the accounting system specified and used by Round The Corner and all franchisees

Appendix E (Cont.)

8. Preopening and opening assistance and supervision, including assistance in hiring and training of store staff and the presence of one or more company supervisors in the restaurant for at least two weeks following the opening date

9. The company's confidential standard **Business Policies and Operations Manual**

10. Advice on merchandising, marketing, and advertising or other data as may from time to time be deemed by Round The Corner Restaurants, Inc., to be helpful in the promotion of the restaurants

case
34

PENROSE HOSPITALS

"The future strength of health care is moving more and more toward out-patient services," remarked Sister Myra James, president of Penrose Hospitals. "We will certainly be delivering a different health care product during the rest of this decade than we have in the past 10 years," she conjectured, as she and other staff reviewed the fiscal year just ended and contemplated how the hospitals' long-range plan might address the myriad conflicting issues and increasing competition that confronted health care institutions both in their market area and nationwide. External factors included technology, rising costs of health services, people's awareness of and interest in their own health, and changing demography as reflected in the 1980 Census.

BACKGROUND

For 80 years doctors, nurses and other professionals have applied their skills and knowledge at the main Penrose facility, and for some 75 of those years the hospital has been owned and operated by the Sisters of Charity of Cincinnati, a Catholic religious order renowned for its expertise in health care. Sisters of Charity Health Care Systems, Inc., operates seven major institutions in four states, making their organization in 1981 the seventh largest not-for-profit chain in the United States.

Penrose Hospital originated as the Glockner Tuberculosis Sanitarium in 1889 when Mrs. Albert Glockner funded the embryonic organization to fulfill the request of her husband who had died of tuberculosis in 1888. Taking personal charge of operations, Mrs. Glockner headed the sanitarium, furnishing board, room, and nursing care to patients for $7.00 a week. It is not surprising that revenues failed to cover operating costs, so the founder made up the deficit for several years out of personal funds. At her request, the Sisters of Charity assumed responsibility for the fledgling venture in 1892. But for the protests of the bishop and residents of the region the nuns would have sold the institution in 1900 because of financial difficulties. With the aid of many supporters, outstanding debts were paid, heralding solvency that has been sustained since. The first major shift into another treatment area occurred some four decades after that shaky start.

Penrose Cancer Hospital, originally established as Penrose Tumor Institute in 1939, became one of the first facilities for cancer treatment and research in the country. In 1932, when Spencer Penrose was informed he had carcinoma of the larynx, he consulted with Dr. Henri Coutard, a pioneer in radiation therapy, using small doses of radiation, or "fractionation." Mr. Penrose became Dr. Coutard's patient at the Curie Institute, University of Paris. Results were favorable, and several years later, when the patient developed carcinoma of the esophagus, he purchased a radiation treatment machine, installed it in the ballroom of his home, and later persuaded Dr. Coutard to implement the idea of a tumor institute. The machine used at home by Mr. Penrose was given after his death in 1939, along with a $300,000 contribution from Mrs. Penrose, to the Sisters of Charity at Glockner Hospital to become part of Penrose Tumor Institute's original equipment. The educational program developed at today's Penrose Cancer Clinic is responsible for training about one-third of the radiation therapists in the United States. Radiotherapy and surgery, which treat localized areas, and medical oncology, which uses a systemic (drug therapy) approach, are the principal treatment methods used. Cobalt-60 and linear accelerator machines provide external radiation sources, and Iridium 192 implants is a new technique employed in treating breast cancer.

It became evident as the years passed that the original physical plant of Glockner/Penrose Hospital would not long be adequate. Hence, a campaign was launched to raise funds for a modern building. Dedicated in 1955, and at the suggestion of Mrs. Glockner, the new 12-story facility was named Penrose Hospital. "Historically," said Sister Myra James, "as an institution Penrose has never stood still; we have never been content to follow but preferred instead to accept the challenges and responsibilities of maintaining a strong leadership role in providing health care for this area." Penrose Cancer Hospital was expanded to a regional center for the southwestern United States, and a large intensive care and critical care units were constructed in the early 1960s, adjoining the 12-story bed tower.

COMMUNITY HOSPITAL ACQUISITION

In 1978 Penrose Hospital purchased Community Hospital, owned at that time by an insurance company. An 88-bed, family-oriented facility that provides primary and secondary health care services, as well as a wide variety of community education and outreach programs, Community shares with Penrose Hospital data processing, business functions, laundry, and purchasing. Ownership expenses diminished for Penrose Community Hospital under the two-hospital operation, aiding cost containment. Comparing similar time periods of 1977, 1978, and 1980, costs per patient day actually decreased. Noted Doug Farnham, administrator, Penrose Community Hospital, "This was one of the goals identified in the Certificate of Need when Penrose proposed to acquire Community and we are pleased to have realized that goal." Building plans for Community included a 20,000-square-foot medical office facility to be constructed on hospital property. "Discussions are being held about the feasibility of moving Penrose's Obstetric Department from the main facility to Community," added Mr. Farnham, "and we have already expanded the Radiology and Nuclear Medicine departments. We are constantly reviewing to see if needs of the area are being met."

In the belief that separating patients from their families can be unsettling, Community practices the philosophy of family-centered care. The hospital provides overnight accommodations for a patient's relative when conditions warrant such an arrangement. For example, the nursing mother who is hospitalized can bring her baby with her. Rooms are made available in the pediatric young adult area, and, although the infant is primarily the mother's responsibility, pediatric nurses oversee the care of both mother and child. Mother and father can be with young patients 24 hours a day if they wish. Preoperative tours for young patients and their families—even peers who are not family members—are common occurrences. A preoperative videotape is used for both young and adult surgical patients. Director of Nursing Sharon Lee observed, "Patients are invited to visit the hospital prior to admission as they are much more receptive to information given them at that time than during the stressful period when they first arrive for surgery. For the patients and their families, it gives knowledge and understanding, which will ease their fears and concerns, and this positive attitude rubs off on the patient."

A unique feature of Penrose Community is the treatment program for alcoholics, started in the spring 1979. Its mission is to provide a comprehensive facility within the hospital environment to address the total needs of alcoholics. Medical Director Larry Shoemaker, M.D., and administrator Jerry Varrone directed these activities. The philosophy is to treat alcoholism as a family disease since, in the words of Dr. Shoemaker, "The family is most closely affected by the illness; their behavior is most likely to effect change in the alcoholic. Those individuals who know and love the patient are the persons whom the staff define as family. This approach is based on the treatment model implemented at the Johnson Institute in Minneapolis—one of the most successful alcoholic treatment programs in the United States."

Mr. Varrone explains, "There are two stages of family participation in the treatment program. The first and most critical stage is called 'intervention,' a concept developed at Johnson Institute, which helps the family develop a plan to confront the alcoholic with his or her problem and to encourage the person to seek help. It's a loving and supportive approach, easy for the alcoholic to accept. Then, once admitted for treatment, the alcoholic's family participates in the second stage, starting with a week-long program of an educational film and lecture series, counseling, and group therapy. Rebonding is a major focus so the entire family can reestablish trust and mutual respect lost during the destructive period of drinking prior to starting treatment."

SUPPORT SPACE PROBLEMS

A number of support departments of the hospital such as materials management, accounting, and the business office were taking up valuable space that could be potentially used for clinical services. The question of what to do about these increasingly important but overcrowded management support areas had grown to crisis proportions.

May 15, 1981 was groundbreaking day for an administrative support center of approximately 51,000 square feet of area, 1.5 miles north of the main hospital, to contain warehouse space for storage of the hospital's materials and supplies as well as office space for the departments of materials management, print shop, data processing, medical records, accounting, and insurance services. Sister Myra James recounted the three-fold advantages of this planned facility:

1. It will enable us to alleviate overcrowded conditions presently faced by patients and staff alike on the basement level of the hospital.
2. It will enable us to provide support services more efficiently, effectively, and safely.
3. It will enable us to renovate and expand direct patient care areas within the hospital to better meet the health needs of the community.

Prior to groundbreaking and following presentation of a plan to the Council, the city approved a request for additional parking facilities at the main hospital, and the Sisters of Charity Health Care Systems Board approved a $6 million bond issue to fund the administrative support center, CAT scanner updating, laboratory computer installation, and several miscellaneous items.

MISSION STATEMENT, 1980

The mission statement of Penrose Hospitals is presented in Exhibit 1.

Exhibit 1

MISSION STATEMENT OF PENROSE HOSPITALS, 1980s

The mission of Penrose Hospitals is to provide, through the healing ministry of Christ, optimal health care, services, and programs that contribute to the physical, psychological, sociological, and spiritual well-being of people in our city and surrounding communities.

The hospitals believe that all persons are created in the image and likeness of God and that each individual has the God-given right to life, the right to health, the right to care when ill, and the right to die in dignity and peace. Sponsored by the Sisters of Charity of Cincinnati, Ohio, the hospitals' activities are based upon a philosophy of the Catholic health care apostolate and standards of medical ethics and are effected in a spirit of ecumenism. The desire to serve those in need is embodied in the motto of the Sisters of Charity, "The Charity of Christ Urges Us." Hospital administration reflects this commitment through its efforts to promote the mission of healing, of building Christian community, and of service through its governance and management process.

The hospitals are principally acute care health insitutions, but seek to develop a full continuum of preventive, diagnostic, treatment, and rehabilitative health services in collaboration with the civic and health community. The institutions will strive to provide primary and secondary health care services in the region, as well as tertiary service to the immediate community and region.

Medical, medical-moral, and health education for physicians, employees, patients, and the general public will be a continual process directed toward the improvement of patient care with opportunities provided for personal growth and professional growth. Support will be given to facilitate appropriate medical research within the resources of the hospitals.

The institutions will strive on a continuing basis to deliver their chosen range of services to the public at the lowest reasonable cost consistent with the principles of prudent financial management.

ROLE OF SISTERS OF CHARITY
HEALTH CARE SYSTEM

Relationships between local hospitals and the Sisters of Charity Health Care System have affected marketing planning and financial projections, from development of mission statements for the institutions to estimating revenues for the budget year. Exhibit 2 summarizes the director of medical affairs' conclusions about these relationships following a 1981 conference.

Exhibit 2

THE SISTERS OF CHARITY HEALTH CARE SYSTEMS

Doctors Gene Moore, O'Rourke, Wetzig, and myself were the physician participants in the recent Sisters of Charity Health Care System, Inc., Annual Trustees Meeting in San Antonio, Texas.

As part of that meeting, discussions about the relationships between the local hospitals and the Sisters of Charity Health Care System raised questions concerning how much the Medical Staff at home knows about the Health Care System of which we are a part. This article is an attempt to explain briefly some of those questions about our relationship.

As a Medical Staff, we should understand our relationship to this overall Health Care System, since it is beginning to affect us in our planning and financial projections. The Sisters of Charity Health Care System, Inc. (hereafter SCHCS), has not been in existence very long. Until about two years ago, the seven hospitals in the Sisters of Charity of Cincinnati system reported directly to the Congregational Board of the Sisters of Charity. Because of some difficulties with the arrangement, particularly differences of opinion between the educators and the health care professionals on the Congregational Board, a subsystem entirely devoted to health care was established.

The SCHCS is made up of the seven health care hospitals and representatives from the Congregational Board. The Board of Trustees of this System is made up of the Chief Executive Officer and one other representative from each of the seven hospitals, as well as representatives from the Congregation.

The System has set certain goals for itself which affect the local hospitals. These goals are broad and general. They emphasize the Christian

Exhibit 2 (Cont.)

health care mission of the Sisters of Charity and indicate that the System is a service vehicle for the local hospitals. The System also exercises responsibility on behalf of the Congregation by carefully reviewing the long-range plans for each hospital and the annual and long-range budgets. Through this mechanism they exert some control, including the power to delay, veto, or question plans which may seem important at the local level, but are not at the level of the System. Thus far, the Administration of the Penrose Hospitals has been persuasive with the Board, obtaining their approval for our long-range plan and budget projections in almost every situation of importance.

However, at the annual meetings this year (directed and devoted to the planning process) several of us were concerned about the potential for misunderstanding and differences of opinion within this System. It is important for us to let our colleague physicians know that (a) the SCHCS is beginning to play a more important role in reviewing our thinking and planning for the future, (b) they do so in an effort to assist us in making the best possible allocation of our resources and directing our efforts toward the most urgent needs in our communities, and (c) they will not understand our local situation sufficiently well without extra effort on **our** part.

It is important the Medical Staff know about this issue. We should be available, if necessary, to help participate in the planning process with the SCHCS representatives. Further, it's important for all of us to understand that we have a **System** not just a collection of hospitals, moving to share services and to address similar problems in a concerted fashion. We have continuing authority and responsibility for the direction of our local enterprise, but this authority is shared with the System. We are accountable to them for the wisdom and effectiveness of our choices.

The meeting in San Antonio underscored for all of us that the hospitals face many similar problems as the health care field is changing. Sharing with each other how these problems are being addressed was a useful experience, one that can be of help to us back home. It was important for us to recognize that the Medical Staff must become more knowledgeable about the SCHCS in the future. I hope this has been a beginning.

> Michael B. Guthrie, M.D.
> Director of Medical Affairs

Source: Internally circulated report, Penrose Hospitals.

DIRECTOR OF MEDICAL AFFAIRS

The position of Director of Medical Affairs, created in 1979, was filled by Michael B. Guthrie, M.D., a psychiatrist; the nature of his tasks evolved following Dr. Guthrie's appointment. In mid-1981 Chief of Staff Gene Moore, M.D., published in the Penrose Hospitals *Staff Bulletin* the statement in Exhibit 3.

Exhibit 3

THE ROLE OF THE DIRECTOR OF MEDICAL AFFAIRS

As a consequence of some of the discussions about the role of the Director of Medical Education, certain questions have been raised about the position of the Director of Medical Affairs. What follows is provided in an effort to clarify his responsibilities.

The Director of Medical Affairs must be a physician on consulting status who is appointed to the Medical Staff and is a member of the Administrative Council for the hospitals. His responsibilities are as follows:

1. Provide medico-administrative support to the Chief of the Medical Staff, Department Chairmen, Committee Chairmen, and the Medical Staff in general.
2. Verify and maintain custody of the credentials files of the Medical Staff.
3. Inform the Medical Staff, Board of Trustees, and Administration of the requirements for maintenance of accreditation, licensure, and educational accreditation for the hospitals.
4. Ensure that medical care review and quality assurance activities are conducted by the Medical Staff to meet the requirements of external agencies, as well as to meet the desire expressed by the Medical Staff to render medical care of the highest quality.
5. Report to the CEO and the Board of Trustees of the hospitals regarding the quality of medical care provided.
6. Provide for continuing medical education by supervising, on behalf of the Executive Committee of the Medical Staff, the Director of Medical Education and the Medical Education Department.
7. Serve as a member of the Medical Staff committees to provide liaison with the Executive Committee of the Medical Staff and Administration.
8. Perform such duties as are delegated by the Chief of Staff to support functions of the Medical Staff. Similarly, perform duties assigned by the President to support the hospitals' function as a whole.
9. Inform the Medical Staff and Board of Trustees of current issues concerning professional liability and risk exposure.

Thus, the Director of Medical Affairs essentially (1) works for the Executive Committee, the Chief of Staff and, more generally, the Medical

Exhibit 3 (Cont.)

Staff organization as a physician executive; and (2) provides on their behalf full-time liaison and communication between the Medical Staff and
Administration. He wears two hats, being both a physician and a participant, on behalf of the medical staff, within the administration.

The Director of Medical Affairs is paid by the hospital. He is evaluated on an annual basis by a committee made up of the Chief of Staff, a
member of the Board of Trustees (frequently another physician), and the
Chief Executive Officer of the hospital.

Gene Moore, M. D.
Chief of Staff

Source: Penrose Hospitals, *Staff Bulletin,* Vol. IV, no. 6, (June 1981).

CURRENT SITUATION

In 1981, Penrose Hospitals provided medical and surgical services, cancer
care, burn care, obstetrics, gynecology, intensive care, critical care, pediatrics,
psychiatric services, and an impressive array of ancillary services including diagnostic and therapeutic radiology, laboratory and pathology, inpatient and
outpatient surgery, emergency room, pulmonary diagnosis, rehabilitation
medicine, physical therapy, nuclear medicine, and ultrasound. When asked, local physicians consistently rated Penrose Hospital as the most advanced in the
availability of diagnostic tests and procedures, which was a Penrose strong
point for many years.

Exhibit 4 reflects the attitudes of 129 physicians admitted to practice at
Penrose Hospitals regarding hospitals of choice, and Exhibit 5 presents a summary of the medical staff affiliation of all physicians surveyed; both studies
were conducted by an outside consultant, so the findings were considered to
be valid. The county medical society had a membership of some 410 medical
doctors, and the Yellow Pages listed approximately 440 physicians, so it was
estimated that perhaps 30 medical practitioners in the county were not members.

The hospitals employed approximately 1,800 people and extended privileges to some 400 medical staff members, fewer than half of whom were active. As the number of inpatient days continued growing, Penrose in 1981 had
a share of market estimated at 52 percent and accounted for 50 percent of hos-

Exhibit 4

PHYSICIANS' HOSPITAL OF CHOICE
(number of cases = 129)

HOSPITAL OF CHOICE	PERCENTAGE
Penrose	51.2%
St. Francis	19.4
Memorial	14.0
Penrose Community	5.4
Eisenhower	5.4
Emory	2.3
No Preference	2.3
	100.0%

Source: I.E.C. study, 1980.

Exhibit 5

MEDICAL STAFF AFFILIATION OF ALL RESPONDENTS

Type of Affiliation	Number of Responses	PERCENTAGE AFFILIATED WITH EACH INSTITUTION					
		Eisenhower	Emory	Memorial	Penrose	Penrose Community	St. Francis
Active	150	5.3%	2.7%	19.3%	35.3%	20.7%	16.7%
Associate	35	—	—	22.9	40.0	31.4	5.7
Courtesy	121	—	5.0	28.1	33.1	20.7	13.2
Consulting	38	15.8	15.8	50.0	5.3	5.3	7.9
Total	344						

Source: I.E.C. study, 1980.

pital beds in the city. Financially, the organization was strong—combined net income for both hospital facilities was $4.6 million in fiscal 1982, on operating revenues of $59.5 million (Exhibit 6).

The total number of beds available at both facilities was 460—372 at the principal site and 88 in the recently acquired facility located in a rapidly growing section of the city. Exhibit 7 provides an overview of patient care services usage and bed capacity by service. Occupancy rose 6 percentage points in one

Exhibit 6

PENROSE HOSPITAL FINANCIAL SUMMARY, JUNE 30, 1979–1982

	1979	1980	1981	1982
Operating revenue from service to patients	$37,689,785	$44,410,784	$59,264,772	$68,547,725
Deduction from revenue				
Charity	231,872	248,252	Not reported	
Contractual allowances	3,659,338	3,848,786	separately	
Doubtful accounts	1,003,163	1,116,896		
	4,894,373	5,213,934	8,312,644	10,251,719
Net operating revenue	$32,795,412	$39,196,850	$50,952,128	$59,548,436
Operating expenses				
Salaries, wages, and fees	$17,270,097	$21,441,116	$26,827,613	$32,515,350
Employee benefits	1,876,432	2,321,418	4,235,736	4,433,728
Supplies, repairs, utilities	7,241,799	8,293,848	10,645,157	11,440,810
Interest expense	683,079	660,181	660,743	1,037,967
Other: Depreciation, insurance, Equipment rental, postage, minor equipment, etc.	3,766,295	4,432,989	5,312,218	6,699,799
Total operating expenses	$30,837,702	$37,149,552	$47,681,468	$56,127,654
Gain from operations	$1,957,710	$2,047,298	$4,306,075	$3,420,782
Nonoperating revenue	182,109	258,799	774,214	1,179,983
Net income	$2,139,819	$2,306,097	$5,080,289	$4,600,765
Net income applied to				
New facilities and equipment	$1,515,431	$1,321,054	$4,440,465	$3,430,557
Payment on principal on long-term debt	624,388	985,043	639,824	1,170,208
	$2,139,819	$2,306,097	$5,080,289	$4,600,765

Source: Penrose Hospitals annual reports.

year, 1980, up again in 1981, declining in 1982, indicating that capacity limitations, if demand trends continued, urgently needed evaluation.

Administrators developed a bed availability plan for occasions when there were more than 370 patients at the main hospital, when the number of patients reached overflow status, between 370 and 390 (yellow alert), and when the situation reached emergency status (red alert), that is, a census of over 390 patients. For the yellow-alert condition, physician members of the Utilization Review Committee were to review the circumstances, on a floor-by-floor basis, in collaboration with the head nurses. This review activity was to take place between 8:00 A.M. and 11:00 A.M. until the census decreased to

Exhibit 7

PENROSE SERVICE AND CAPACITY STATISTICS, JUNE 30, 1979–1982

	1979	1980	1981	1982
Patient care services				
Patients admitted	17,806	18,830	19,254	17,969
Patient days	122,703	132,669	140,611	130,110
Avg. length of stay (days)	6.9	7.1	7.3	7.2
Percent of occupancy	73.1	79.0	83.7	77.4
Emergency department visits	34,747	35,815	35,348	35,992
Physical medicine treatment	67,030	62,281	65,024	69,460
Nuclear medicine procedures	7,780	9,938	11,559	11,680
Surgical operations	10,300	10,663	11,107	10,188
Open-heart operations	258	308	350*	375*
Kidney dialysis treatments	6,378	3,413	NA	NA
Meals served	609,830	703,719	690,545	658,072
Full-time employees	1,269	1,347	1,323	1,297
Part-time employees	359	386	302	222
Bed capacity				
Medical and surgical	321	No change from 1979		
Gynecology and obstetrics	39			
Pediatrics	36			
ICU/CCU and sub ICU	38			
Psychiatry	12			
Alcohol recovery program	14			
	460			

*Estimated.
NA – Not available.

Source: Penrose Hospitals annual reports.

350. Further, preadmission testing and early discharge were to be encouraged and the short-stay unit was to be expanded to accommodate more inpatients. For the red-alert condition, aggressive utilization review activities were to be intensified, while limiting admissions to emergencies to be authorized only by members of the active medical staff. Penrose hoped that these steps would help to reduce strains on overcrowded facilities and provide better quality care for patients.

With increasing demands on capacity, the admitting office supervisor appealed for assistance from those involved in patient management:[1]

[1] Penrose Hospitals, *Staff Bulletin,* Vol. 4, no. 7 (July 1981).

An increasing number of discharges are being made after 1 P.M. This inter-feres with the availability of beds for your new patients arriving during peak admission times around noon. It also throws a burden on House-keeping and the Laboratory to prepare patient rooms and to provide for stat laboratory testing.

Please make every effort to discharge your patients as early as possible in the morning. Routine discharge time is 11 A.M., and discharge prior to that hour will allow ample time for room turnover for new admissions.

Your cooperation will be most appreciated by all concerned.

Ruth Heine
Supervisor, Admitting Office

COST CONTAINMENT
AND MEDICAL CARE OUTLAYS

In 1950, 4.5 percent of the nation's total output of goods and services was in health care; in 1966 this figure had risen to 5.9 percent; in 1977 it was at 8.6 percent; and by 1980 it was estimated at 9.0 percent. The public in general and many legislators in particular expressed alarm over the trend.

A shift in attention from the supply side to the demand side of the health services equation became evident in 1980 under the new administration in Washington. It was thought likely by many in the industry that consumer choice, free market competition, and changes in federal funding would at least partially replace federal regulation as cost-containment emphases. Hospitals were concerned with the impact of budget cuts on such programs as Medicare and Medicaid; many felt reductions were imminent and that eligibility re-quirements were likely to be changed. The federal emphasis was directed to-ward creating more cost-conscious consumers and to the application of free market penalties to poorly managed and undercapitalized hospitals. Reagan administration health policies echoed this by creating financial incentives for doctors, hospitals, consumers, employers, and governments to be more cost conscious in using the system.

In the market served by Penrose, there was an upward trend between 1980 and 1982 in both the average hospital bill and the hospitals' cost per pa-tient. Factors contributing to those trends were growth in salaries and benefits of personnel, growth in other operating costs, increased utilization by elderly patients, and inflation generally. It appeared that hospitals experienced their greatest impact from inflation some 12 to 18 months after that of the larger economy. The state had experienced high inflation in 1979; Penrose began to experience the impact in 1981.

As for the future, assuming that labor expenses, which account for 50 percent of the average hospital bill, would continue to increase throughout the state and region more rapidly than food, utilities, and medical supplies, it was expected that Penrose could not hold the line on patient charges. The gap between hospital costs and hospital charges at Penrose and throughout the health services industry widened during 1980 and 1981, reflecting an increase in bad debts, charity care, and Medicare-Medicaid underpayments, and, locally, development of financial reserves for growth and development. Few doubted that only the strongest, economically sound health institutions would survive in the competitive 1980s. A note of optimism: the average hospital bill in the state in 1980 and 1981 ran from 10 to 15 percent below the average of all hospitals across the country.

The problem of making up patient revenue shortfalls would likely continue to persist. Fund-raising campaigns would be a factor, but such community and philanthropic support was generally uncertain and irregular and usually allocated to capital expenditures. To meet operating expenses, some hospitals resorted to borrowing working capital, a practice that became less viable as 1981–1982 interest rates rose to 15 to 20 percent. To meet health care responsibilities to its community and to avoid unnecessary borrowing, it seemed inevitable that Penrose must build into its patient charges an appropriate percentage to cover current needs and to plan long-range improvements in physical plant, technology, and services.

The state legislature created a hospital commission in 1977 to help improve hospital cost containment but discontinued the body in 1980. Most hospitals and a number of related organizations in the state believed that the commission had not been effective in accomplishing its stated purpose. After the commission's demise, hospitals no longer were required to submit budgets and charge structures for state approval. Most institutions asserted that cost containment is more effective on a voluntary basis and that the commission, while intending to do good, provided yet another layer of bureaucracy imposed upon hospital management. Related paperwork tasks, said the hospitals, added significantly to the responsibilities of already overburdened planning and accounting staffs.

MARKET CHARACTERISTICS, TRENDS, AND COMPETITION

A relatively young population and a sizable number of retired military and active-duty personnel in the surrounding region importantly influenced medical care in the city. Two key military installations had inpatient treatment facilities and served large outpatient clinic populations. There was some spillover into the civilian health care system of patients from these facilities, but figures on this phenomenon were inconsistent and unpredictable.

The 1980 Census disclosed that the area had grown from its early origins as a resort community to an active metropolis of over 300,000 people, much of the growth attributed to the active solicitation by the Chamber of Commerce of industries in the electronics field, such as Hewlett-Packard, Digital, and TRW. In addition, the military population had grown substantially. Prediction called for continued annual growth at a 2.3 percent rate (Exhibit 8). Most of the population influx was in the areas of the city with open space, primarily to the north and east of Penrose Community Hospital.

Because of the climate and proximity to recreation and resort activities, attracting quality physicians was not difficult. The community of physicians represented the best of all the medical specialties, including a high portion of specialists and an acceptable balance of family and general practitioners as well as general internists. In 1981, approximately 88 percent of physicians were either board-eligible or board-certified. Thus, expectations of young physicians for a high-quality medical environment could be met. Physicians were actively involved in continuing medical education and were interested in establishing graduate residency programs in either internal medicine or surgery. A physician demographic profile is presented in Exhibit 9.

The city was remarkable for its large percentage of solo and independent physicians as contrasted to group practices (Exhibit 10). However, one substantial group practice did exist, an organization recently established as a health maintenance organization, which by early 1981 had begun to make small in-

---

Exhibit 8

CITY AND COUNTY STATISTICAL OVERVIEW

POPULATION	CITY	CITY/COUNTY COMBINED	RACIAL/ETHNIC PERCENTAGES OF CITY/COUNTY POPULATION IN 1980
1950	45,472	74,542	White, 85.2%
1960	70,194	143,742	Black, 5.2%
1970	135,060	235,972	Mexican American, 8.5%
1979	227,320	307,250	Other, 1.3%
1980	214,820	309,424	
1981	222,300	319,150	
1985P	276,000	371,000	
2000P	427,800	543,500	

P – Projected.

Source: Pike's Peak Area Council of Governments, El Paso County, Colorado, 1981.

Exhibit 9

PHYSICIAN DEMOGRAPHIC PROFILE BY AGE*
(number of cases = 127)

AGE (years)	% OF TOTAL
Under 35	15.0%
35–40	28.3
41–45	13.4
46–50	11.0
51–55	7.1
56–60	13.4
61–65	3.9
Over 65	7.9
Total	100.0%

*Of the physicians participating in the survey, 98.4 percent were male and 1.6 percent were female.

Source: I.E.C. Study, June, 1980.

Exhibit 10

MEDICAL PRACTICE PROFILE: DISTRIBUTION OF RESPONDENTS BY TYPE OF PRACTICE
(number of cases = 126)

TYPE OF MEDICAL PRACTICE	% OF TOTAL
Solo practice	43.7%
Single specialty group	35.7
Private medical group (general)	2.4
Multispecialty group	7.9
Staff	4.0
Government agency	2.4
Corporate	.8
Resident	.8
Retired	2.4
Total	100.0%

Source: I.E.C. Study, June 1980.

Exhibit 11

SELECTED ANNUAL STATISTICS, FISCAL YEARS ENDING JUNE 30, 1973–1980

PENROSE HOSPITALS	1973	1974	1975	1976	1977	1978*	1979	1980
Number of licensed beds	372	372	372	372	372	372 + 88	460	460
Admissions (exclude newborn)	16,886	17,403	17,871	16,256	15,005	15,832	17,806	18,830
Inpatient days (exclude newborn)	117,047	117,887	124,321	116,156	107,778	110,861	122,703	132,669
Total outpatient visits (E.R. plus other)	86,263	80,295	84,680	91,603	98,172	112,229	137,462	147,084
Inpatient revenue	$12,315,205	$13,566,841	$16,720,217	$18,819,583	$20,531,673	$25,570,193	$31,714,188	$37,083,004
Outpatient revenue	$ 1,240,238	$ 1,283,606	$ 1,863,127	$ 2,368,156	$ 3,044,468	$ 3,720,539	$ 5,165,105	$ 6,118,696
Total operating expenses	$11,640,454	$13,037,470	$16,112,855	$18,435,903	$20,321,897	$24,692,632	$30,837,702	$37,149,552

*Reflects acquisition of Penrose Community Hospital, February 23, 1978.

Source: Penrose Hospitals internal records.

Exhibit 12

CHANGES IN DEMAND FOR REPRESENTATIVE
SERVICES, 1980 VERSUS 1976

SERVICE	1980	1976	% INCREASE
Nuclear medicine procedures	7,830	4,066	93%
Ultrasound diagnostic technology	1,988	601	231
Blood bank unit demand	6,000	2,000	200
Respiratory therapy procedures	94,187	49,072	92

Source: Penrose Hospitals, Planning Department, 1981.

roads into the total patient population. Local industries expressed considerable interest in this approach to controlling health care cost increases

Changes in selected statistics for Penrose from 1973 to 1980 are given in Exhibit 11, including the impact of adding Community Hospital for approximately 10 months of 1978. Changes in demand for representative services are presented in Exhibit 12.

Penrose Hospitals' principal competitor traditionally had been St. Francis Hospital, a 179-bed general medical-surgical institution that actively pursued orthopedic surgery and general medical care. Its leaders were active in the community and aggressively promoted the hospital's services both to physicians and to the general population. Impressive gains had been made in popularity and in market recognition.

City-owned Memorial Hospital, with approximately 220 beds, had just completed construction of a new facility at a substantial cost to taxpayers. Memorial was surrounded by constant controversy. Many medical staff members avoided participating in the institution's affairs; consequently, its occupancy rate was lowest in the city in 1980. In 1980 and 1981, however, Memorial announced aggressive plans to expand cardiology and obstetrics; theirs was the only neonatal intensive care unit in the city. Memorial's deliveries were running at a level about twice that of Penrose.

The osteopathic hospital, with 123 beds, Eisenhower Hospital offered little direct competition to Penrose. Most of Penrose's medical staff did not participate in activities at Eisenhower; only recently had osteopathic physicians even been given opportunity to apply for privileges at Penrose.

Finally, a 100-bed psychiatric facility, E. J. Brady Hospital, which was purchased by a small group of private investors in 1980, was essentially separated from the mainstream of the city's medical care but was considered to be an important provider of psychiatric service for the city and region.

Exhibit 13 provides an overview of clinical services offered in the city's

Exhibit 13

CLINICAL SERVICES OFFERED AT THE FIVE LOCAL HOSPITALS

HOSPITAL SERVICES OFFERED	PENROSE HOSPITALS	EISENHOWER OSTEOPATHIC HOSPITAL	EMORY JOHN BRADY HOSPITAL	MEMORIAL HOSPITAL	ST. FRANCIS HOSPITAL
1. Alcoholism treatment (inpatient and outpatient)	Yes	No	No	No	No
2. Burn unit	Yes	No	No	No	No
3. Cardiac diagnostics	Yes	No	No	Yes	Yes
4. Chronic renal dialysis	Yes	No	No	No	No
5. Diagnostic radiology	Yes	Yes	No	Yes	Yes
6. Emergency medicine	Yes	No	No	Yes	Yes
7. Heart surgery	Yes	No	No	No	No
8. Medical education	Yes	No	No	Yes	Yes
9. Neonatal intensive care	No	No	No	Yes	No
10. Nuclear medicine	Yes	No	No	No	No
11. Obstetrics and gynecology	Yes	Yes*	No	Yes	Yes
12. Ophthalmology	Yes	No	No	Yes	Yes
13. Oral surgery	Yes	No	No	Yes	Yes
14. Orthopedic service	Yes	Yes	No	Yes	Yes
15. Otorhinolaryngology	Yes	Yes	No	Yes	Yes
16. Outpatient services	Yes	No	No	No	No
17. Pediatrics	Yes	Yes	No	Yes	Yes
18. Physical medicine and rehabilitation	Yes†	Yes‡	Yes§	Yes‡	Yes‡
19. Psychiatric services	Yes	No	Yes	No	Yes
20. Pulmonary diagnostics	Yes	No	No	No	Yes
21. Radiation therapy	Yes	No	No	Yes	Yes
22. Respiratory care	Yes	Yes	No	Yes	Yes
23. Diagnostic audiology	Yes	No	No	No	Yes

†Physical therapy, occupational therapy, rehabilitation—outpatient.
‡Physical therapy only.
§Occupational therapy only.
*Obstetrics only.

Sources: American Hospital Association, *Guide to the Health Care Field*, Chicago, Ill.: 1980 ed.; Department of Health, *Health Facilities Statistical Report*, Washington, D.C.: 1978; and other sources.

Exhibit 14

CITY HOSPITALIZATION TRENDS FOR CALENDAR YEARS 1978–1981

Hospital (beds)	1978			1979			1980			1981		
	Total* Patient Days	% Occupancy	% of Market	Total Patient Days	% Occupancy	% of Market	Total Patient Days	% Occupancy	% of Market	Total Patient Days	% Occupancy	% of Market
Penrose (372)	104,972	77.3%	45.9%	109,699	80.8%	45.4%	116,711	86.0%	45.3%	113,816	83.8%	43.5%
Penrose Community (88)	14,180†	44.1	6.2	19,553	60.9	8.1	21,233	66.1	8.2	22,560	70.2	8.6
Total Penrose Hospitals (460)	119,152	71.0	52.1%	129,252	77.0	53.5%	137,944	82.2	53.5%	136,376	81.2	52.1%
Memorial (220)	42,307	52.7	18.5	40,792	50.8	16.9	45,492	56.7	17.7	48,605	60.5	18.6
St. Francis (179)	40,934	62.7	17.9	45,160†	69.1	18.7	45,751	70.0	17.8	47,854	73.2	18.3
Eisenhower (122)	26,410	59.3	11.5	26,214	58.9	10.9	28,467	63.9	11.0	28,946	65.0	11.1
Total community hospitals (981)	228,263	63.8	100.0%	241,418	67.4	100.0%	257,654	72.0	100.0%	261,781	73.1	100.0%
	Total‡		% Change	Total		% Change	Total		% Change	Total		% Change
County population	302,740		3.1%	307,250		1.5%	309,424		0.7%	319,150		3.1%
Hospitalization days/ 1,000 population	.75 patient days per 1,000 population			.786 patient days per 1,000 population			.833 patient days per 1,000 population			.82 patient days per 1,000 population		

*Patient days as reported by Region II Health Services Agency in monthly statistical reports.
†Indicates that totals were derived from estimates made with incomplete data.
‡Population totals supplied by Area Council of Governments.

Source: Region II Health Services Agency and Pike's Peak Area Council of Governments. State of Colorado, El Paso County, Colorado Springs, Colorado, 1982.

five hospitals. Trends comparing Penrose, Memorial, St. Francis, and Eisenhower hospitals from 1978 to 1981 are presented in Exhibit 14.

QUALITY ASSURANCE COMMITTEE

The Quality Assurance Committee (QAC), organized at Penrose Hospital in the late 1970s, operated under the mission statement presented in Exhibit 15. Members of this group were also assigned to represent QAC on other hospital committees, such as the Pharmacy Committee and Therapeutics Committee. In a typical meeting, QAC members, meeting with other hospital staff and employees, might discuss arrival and assignments of newly hired anesthesiologists, problems of enforcing tubercular testing on employees and implementation of rubella innoculations, working relationships between nurses and physicians, patients' complaints about various aspects of care and communication, performance of physicians, management of patients, and problems associated with timeliness of doctors' treatment reports. This committee includes a total of 12 medical staff and lay people.

Exhibit 15

MISSION STATEMENT, QUALITY ASSURANCE COMMITTEE

To assure that patients treated at the Penrose Hospitals are afforded every opportunity to obtain maximum achievable quality of patient care from all of the clinical and professional services including physicians, nurses, technical personnel, as well as support services and administration.

To create a comprehensive, hospitalwide, and integrated approach to problem identification and problem solving that focuses not upon the rituals of record keeping but rather on identifying real and practical problems in delivering patient care and sets about to solve problems.

To create a visible program through which individuals and groups are held directly accountable for their contributions to this overall program and are held responsible for implementing actions that improve the quality of patient care.

To design insofar as possible, a program that integrates existing and successful current activities into this comprehensive program.

To assure that the board of trustees, the medical staff, and the administration of the hospital receive in a timely and useful fashion information that assures them that patient care is attended to earnestly and problems identified are resolved.

Commenting on its role, Sister Myra James observed: "The Quality Assurance Committee is appointed by the Board of Trustees of Penrose to carry out a deceptively simple function—to ensure that the quality assurance and control procedures devised by medical staff and other personnel are operating effectively. Penrose Hospital is an extremely complex organism, and although every unit here performs its own internal quality control and review, we need an organ or unit that synthesizes the information from all these groups and says publicly, 'Things are proceeding as they should throughout the entire body.' Of course, this is a difficult, perhaps impossible, task to fulfill perfectly. But the more conscientiously it is done, the more confident everyone involved in the hospital can feel about our comprehensive performance.

"Further, many institutions, hospitals included, that serve the public are increasingly considered to be accountable to those publics. For us, this accountability is being expressed in several ways: through accrediting agencies such as the Joint Commission for the Accreditation of Hospitals, through the increasing pressures of litigation, and through various legislatively appointed committees and agencies empowered to approve or disapprove modifications in the institution's operation and resources. And in official reviews of performance as well as in courts of law, trustees are expected to answer for the quality with which the hospital delivers its services.

"QAC members don't presume to institute or to perform functions that control quality—only our health care professionals do this. Rather, its members attempt to see that our procedures are in place and working suitably. This protects both the public and the hospital itself."

STAFF, EMPLOYEE, AND PATIENT EDUCATION AND MEETINGS

Special community services offered by Penrose Hospitals include, by way of example, a family-centered maternity program. Other typical programs for employees and medical staff offered weight control, aerobic dance, slimnastics, self-defense, yoga, fencing, couples communication, time management, and a golf tournament. A medical education calendar in one recent month listed the subjects of cardiovascular, chest, tumors, renal electrolytes, clinic cardiology, endocrine metabolism, clinical pathology, orthopedic, rheumatology, immunology, cancer, otolaryngology, and hematology conducted by Penrose medical staff. A special course on the health effects of low-level radiation was conducted by a professor of radiology from the state university. Penrose offered education for patients on closed-circuit channels in the hospital.

A search committee composed of the director of medical affairs and other doctors began in latter 1981 to seek an individual for the newly created post of director of medical education, someone who would devote full time to this important function.

FACING THE MAJOR ISSUES

As Sister Myra James worked together with her administrative staff and supervisors to review their current status, several major issues emerged. They felt a need for some sort of analysis to reveal where Penrose stood in terms of the overall community. Although for years the hospital had relied on the belief that it was the most respected hospital in town and provided the best care, Penrose wanted to assess what consumers in the community demanded from health care.

Several services, such as obstetrics, were losing ground to the competition. Questions arose about whether or not to continue that service, engendering a great deal of controversy among the medical staff. In general, the Sisters of Charity favored continuing the service because of their interest in maternal and child care. As the figures emerged, however, the hospital was losing approximately $300.00 per delivery and the number of deliveries had dropped by more than 40 percent for the last three years. The issue had been complicated by the suggestion that it might possibly be closed down or moved to Penrose Community Hospital with a smaller number of beds, concentrating obstetrical care in the area where most of the younger population lived. Opposition was vociferous to such a transfer from established practitioners in obstetrics and gynecology who resisted the idea of disrupting their practice patterns.

The open-heart surgery program was booming, running at about 300 operations per year in 1981. However, Memorial Hospital was actively courting the same cardiovascular surgeons and planned to open a competing heart service, if the Health Systems Agency and State Facilities Review Council would grant permission. Whether or not there was sufficient cardiovascular disease in the community to warrant opening another such unit and developing a second large-scale cardiology service remained to be seen.

Nursing care in the various hospitals was a subject of hot debate. Continuing to maintain a reputation for excellence in this area was a major item of concern, given that nurses were increasingly concerned about pay and staffing issues.

As a regional referral center for cancer patients, the hospital had begun to consider promoting itself as a regional resource for other hospital services as well, particularly cardiology and specialty surgery. Competition in this regard came not only from within the local metropolitan area, but also from several large hospitals in the state's largest city, 75 miles distant, including the major state university, and one big state hospital 45 miles to the south. The regional hospital services concept sought to improve the referral base for patients and hospital inpatient services in part by promoting continuing medical education and management service consultations to smaller rural hospitals in outlying communities.

The Cancer Hospital enjoyed a good reputation but nevertheless was losing money because of the increasing number of Medicare patients admitted to the hospital. Medicare overall had risen to 40 percent of the total number of patient days. This imposed a significant financial cost to other patients, to make up for losses from deficiencies in Medicare reimbursement by the federal government.

As was true in every community, Medicare paid only on the basis of "cost," that cost recognized as justifiable by Medicare and not the total cost of services rendered. Thus the per diem reimbursement program under Medicare rarely paid for all services, particularly where there was a high intensity of utilization such as in the treatment of cancer, cardiovascular disease, or kidney disease. As these patients became an increasing percentage of the total number of patients, they created a substantial drain on revenue, part of which was made up by increased charges to self-pay patients. But there was a limit to the acceptable amount of cross-subsidization. The Cancer Hospital particularly loomed as an increasing financial problem, and expansion plans for the cancer program were subject to careful scrutiny.

Physicians grew increasingly uncomfortable with the possibility that the hospital itself would become a competitor to their private practices, particularly in the areas of outpatient services where physicians had some vested financial interest in maintaining the community as it was. With the hospital having a limited role in providing direct patient care services to ambulatory patients, physicians provided most such care in their offices and benefited from providing their own lab and X-ray procedures. Where the delivery systems might be changed, such as emergency care or convenience clinics, medical staff in primary care specialties, such as family practice and internal medicine, began to balk, objecting to the competition posed to their livelihoods.

Further, certain promotions and advertising techniques, which the hospital had recently tried, violated the traditionalist view of many physicians. An experiment with 20 billboards, advertising the availability of quality care at Penrose Hospitals, had irritated several of the medical staff. How far to pursue such advertising methods was a question before Sister Myra James.

MARKETING ADJUSTMENT AND ADAPTATION

Exhibit 16 reflects a growing interest in health care marketing at Penrose in the early 1980s and indicates some of the Director of Medical Affairs' thoughts on the subject.

PLANNING FOR CHANGE

Given the many issues confronting Penrose Hospitals, administrators and trustees reviewed the current situation in a 1980 internal study. Penrose physicians were asked, as one part of the survey, to evaluate factors bearing upon their decisions to admit patients to one hospital rather than another. Results are summarized in Exhibit 17.

Exhibit 16

MARKETING: ADJUSTMENT AND ADAPTATION

This article is an attempt to make clear some of the basic principles that apply to marketing as a function of modern hospital administration. I am aware from discussions with various physicians that this is of interest currently. I hope that the information will be helpful.

"In industry, marketing is the matching of a company's capabilities and resources with consumers' needs and wants." Marketing is a function, like finance or production, of any business operation. It is certainly a hot topic in the hospital and health care industry today.

At its best, marketing represents a diagnostic approach to looking at the surroundings in which a business operates, a "diagnosis of the environment." As hospitals have increasingly found themselves facing inflation and financial cutbacks on payments from Medicare and Medicaid, they need to find alternative sources of revenue to improve their financial stability and support inpatient care. Hospitals have begun to use marketing tools to look for those areas in which they can improve their financial standing.

Marketing is an approach to strategic long-range planning that fits together three classes of variables: first, the potential needs or wants in the marketplace; second, the environmental opportunities and constraints; and third, the organization's intrinsic skills and available resources.

Marketing is an approach to the diagnosis of the hospital's strengths and weaknesses, as well as the needs that are unmet or underserved in the community. A marketing approach tries to match the hospital's capabilities with the community's needs.

Marketing is more than simple advertising or promotion. It is an approach to asking questions, to obtaining quantitative data on which to make decisions, to soliciting opinions from selected consumers of the service to be provided, and to future planning based on quantitative information about current trends and needs.

There are two approaches to marketing in any given environment: first, an "outside-in" approach and, second, an "inside-out" approach. The outside-in avenue is a strategy by which a business looks into the environment for a latent demand that people are waiting to express for a not-yet-invented product or service. The company can then develop such a product and market it effectively. In this fashion any hospital strategy will have been shaped by the outside environment. In many cases the demand is apparent, but the product or service is not. Sometimes, however, the demand is more latent and people have not really thought about what new service they might want. In this instance, management's central strategy becomes to create a customer.

Exhibit 16 (Cont.)

With the inside-out approach, the organization begins by asking itself what the organization's particular skills and strengths are. What does the hospital offer? What is unique about the services offered? Having identified these strengths and capabilities, we expand them to meet new applications or generalize them to serve new populations. In short, the organization has decided what it has that others could use.

What are some of the implications for Penrose Hospitals' beginning to emphasize a marketing approach? Penrose has for many years taken a marketing approach to many services, making the knowledge of our strengths and assets available to the community and publicizing the availability of modern equipment and the latest in health care capacity through the news media and word of mouth among physicians. However, Penrose has recently undertaken to formalize this approach. This has consequences for all of us.

The first consequence is the need for more opinions from our employees, our physicians, and our patients on the strengths and weaknesses of our hospitals.

Second, we will all be asked to work together to broaden our approach to the provision of health care services in the community. This will change the scope of our organization, probably moving us in the direction of becoming a "health care facility," not just a hospital where we take care of sick people.

And, finally, our formal approach to marketing will improve our strategic planning and sharpen our focus on certain new areas such as regional hospital services and relationships with various business organizations in the community.

All of this will require internal adjustment and adaptation to the changing wishes and needs of the consumers of health care services in our area.

For further information about marketing as it applies to health care, you might be interested in perusing the articles listed below. If you're interested in reprints of these articles, I have a few available in my office. Please stop by and ask for one.

1. "Marketing," by William Flexnor, Dr. PH, from **The Physician in Management,** Edited by Roger Schenki, MBA; AAMD Publications 1981.
2. "Planning and Controlling," Chapter 7, from **Management: Basic Elements of Managing Organizations,** Ross A. Webber, Irwin Publishing, Inc., 1979.

Michael B. Guthrie, M.D.
Director of Medical Affairs

Source: Penrose Hospitals, *Staff Bulletin,* Vol. 4, no. 5 (May 1981).

Exhibit 17

ATTRIBUTES AFFECTING PHYSICIANS' ADMISSION DECISIONS
(rank ordered by importance score)

ATTRIBUTE	RANK ORDER	IMPORTANCE SCORE	
Nursing services	1	96.6	
Quality/type of equipment	2	89.6	
Availability of physicians for consulting	3	88.0	
Response time for hospital services	4	86.5	
Friendliness of nursing staff toward physicians	5	81.2	
Hospital reputation with my patients	6	79.4	
The hospital management	7	76.5	
Availability of beds	8	75.6	
Surgical facilities	9	72.4	
Radiology services	10	71.2	
Hospital administration that works closely with physicians	11	70.8	
Emergency medical services	12	69.0	
Pathology services	13	68.1	
Intensive care services	14	67.6	
Geographical proximity of hospital to my office	15	53.8	
Hospital reputation with public	16	48.3	
Hospital admitting procedures	17	47.0	
Respiratory care services	18	41.9	
Hospital reputation among my colleagues	19	41.7	
Hospital reputation among area physicians	20	41.6	
Patients' hospital preference	21	41.4	
Anesthesiology	22	39.8	
Pharmacy services	23	37.4	
Costs of hospital services	24	28.8	
Outpatient services	25	23.1	
Availability of operating room time	26	17.6	
Physician parking	27	3.5	
Conference space	28	−2.6	figures
Rehabilitation services	29	−28.1	based on
Geographical proximity of hospital to patient's home	30	−28.6	scores of
Psychiatric services	31	−51.8	"not important
Religious affiliation of hospital	32	−76.0	at all"

Source: Penrose Hospitals internal document, 1980 internal study.

The 1980 study resulted in data that led to the planning assumptions listed in Exhibit 18. Although not everyone accepted these assumptions, most agreed that they provided a suitable foundation for developing a list of questions to explore in the process of preparation for long-range planning meetings to be scheduled over the coming months and years.

As part of this preparation for the anticipated series of planning conferences, a survey of physicians, nurses, administrative personnel, and members of the Planning Committee yielded a list of topics considered highly desirable for inclusion on the long-range planning agenda. Some of these items considered by the Penrose Hospital Planning Committee are presented in Exhibit 19.

Meanwhile, as both facilities' medical and administrative staffs developed a constellation of notions for brainstorming and perhaps solution at the planning retreats, Penrose Community Hospital's medical staff held two meetings, facilitated by Doctors Michael Guthrie and George Mauer, designed to consid-

---

Exhibit 18

PLANNING ASSUMPTIONS FOR PENROSE HOSPITAL

1. Health services competition in the area will continue to increase.
2. The HMO concept will grow, especially in the business sector.
3. Area population growth will continue.
4. The elderly population will be a larger portion of the population.
5. Demand for outpatient service will increase.
6. Competition among physicians will increase.
7. Closer/more interdependent relationships between physicians and hospitals will develop.
8. Roles for paraprofessionals will increase.
9. Continued increase in health care consumerism is expected.
10. Acute inpatient utilization will decline.
11. Hospitals will continue to diversify services.
12. Reimbursement and cost containment will be a major emphasis until 1985.
13. Success will lie in expanding services to targeted population groups (markets).
14. Key competitive threats to "outreach" and regional services are the Metro hospitals.
15. Consumers will be more informed and more independent regarding medical and health decisions.
16. By 1990, over 60 percent of all wives will work.
17. The mid-1940s "baby boom" will produce a "baby boomlet" through the 1980s decade.
18. Forty-nine percent of the city's population is 18 to 34 years old.
19. Intense public interest in science, including medical science, exists.

er their particular unit's strengths and weaknesses. Out of those sessions came several suggestions for consideration: (1) move the alcoholic treatment center outside the hospital; (2) add hospital beds to bring the total to between 200 and 250; (3) move obstetrics, pediatrics, and nursery services from the main unit to Penrose Community; (4) make a decision about the physicians' office building; (5) increase emergency room space; and (6) modify the Catholic code to permit tubal ligations. These six had highest priorities, among others, and are ranked in descending order of importance as listed.

Participants also submitted a list of three benefits and three liabilities of association between Penrose Community Hospital and Penrose. Most-mentioned benefits were efficiencies of scale, which foster cost containment, especially sharing of equipment, supplies, and staff; access to a large and diverse medical community pool, including specialist coverage; access to ancillary support; and planning, financial, and administrative support. Negatives received far fewer mentions than benefits: the "stepchild" syndrome experienced by community; Catholic code, as it related to tubal ligations; Penrose Community Hospital's lack of control of its own plans and activities; and poor communications between hospitals.

Exhibit 19

IDEAS AND TOPICS OF POTENTIAL INTEREST FOR PLANNING SESSIONS

Sharing services in multi-institutional arrangements.

Evaluating Penrose Hospitals' image in the city.

Increasing public's knowledge of health care in the market.

Expanding doctors' participation in hospital, including operating responsibilities.

Emphasizing "wellness" instead of just treatment of illness.

Attempting to develop measures for quality of care.

Emphasizing ambulatory (as opposed to inpatient) care.

Increasing physicians' representation on Board of Trustees.

Ensuring an adequate supply of health care professionals.

Increasing Penrose Hospital participation in national, state, and local health policy planning.

Ensuring a continued high level of capital acquisition

Becoming a referral service (tertiary) care center for high-technology services in HSA Region II.

Developing an automated information processing system for management purposes, both medical and other.

Enhancing cooperative relationship (and minimizing adversarial) between medical staff and other hospital entities.

Source: Internal planning memorandum.

ROLE OF EXTERNAL AGENCIES IN PLANNING

Penrose Hospitals are accredited by the Joint Commission on Accreditation of Hospitals, the American College of Physicians, the American College of Surgeons, the American Hospital Association, and the American Medical Association; are licensed by the State Department of Health, and as a research facility, by the U.S. Department of Agriculture; and are members of American Hospital Association, Catholic Hospital Association, American Association of Blood Banks, College of American Pathologists, Internal Association of Hospital Security, Council of Community Hospitals, Sisters of Charity Health Care Corporation, and several state health care organizations.

Agencies that could, and sometimes do, become involved in Penrose Hospitals' planning processes include the State Board of Health; State Health Facilities Review Council; Statewide Health Coordinating Council; various HSA boards and project review committees; State Department of Social Services; the State Hospital Commission (before it was disbanded by the legislature); Area Councils of Government; Department of Health, Education, and Welfare (federal); and numerous local special-interest groups.

The 22-county Region II Health Systems Agency, federally designated, is composed of volunteer members and paid staff responsible for health planning and development in the geographic area served by Penrose Hospitals, the largest institution in the region's principal city, and other health care institutions. This agency is mandated by law to gather and analyze data, establish plans and objectives, coordinate with other planning and regulatory agencies, review certificate of need applications (approval needed for all projects with capital expenditures of $150,000 or more), and make various recommendations to the state concerning health care planning, regulation, and development. The governing board of the agency must have a membership predominantly from the consumer sector. Its stated goals are "to increase the accessibility, acceptability, continuity, and quality of health services in the area; to restrain increases in the costs of providing health services; and to prevent unnecessary duplication of health resources."

Region II Health Systems Agency articulated its own set of concerns, adapted somewhat from national guidelines, related to delivery of health services. Since these affect both short-range and long-term planning for Penrose and other institutions in Region II, they are listed in Appendix A.

To illustrate how general goals were translated into specific ones, Appendix B lists selected goals of the 1980s for Region II HSA.

Your Task:

As Penrose Hospitals' administrators and medical staff start their full-scale review of the institution's current position and establish its planning process, advise them on the marketing of health care services.

Appendix A

REGION II HSA CONCERNS RELATED TO DELIVERY OF HEALTH CARE

PROMOTION/PROTECTION

1. Health promotion and protection services for the total population, actively supported by insurance carriers, members of the medical profession, health care agencies, and schools.
2. Health promotion through attention to environmental quality, to occupational safety and health, to food protection, to radiation safety, to personal wellness and third-party reimbursement mechanisms that support personal wellness, and to adequate social services.

PRIMARY SERVICES

1. Ambulatory health service availability without duplication of excess capacity, and with incentives for providers to utilize non-inpatient facilities for service and treatment.
2. Cooperative educational and health programs involving health agencies, local governments, and schools.
3. Appropriate dental care, especially for the elderly and indigent.
4. Effective prevention and detection services.

SECONDARY/INTERMEDIATE SERVICES

1. Cooperative planning between hospitals, especially rural and urban hospitals, to ensure adequate inpatient services in sufficient, but not excessive, quantities.
2. Greater use of physician extenders.
3. Improved data base.
4. Development of sufficient, but not excessive, long-term care services in conjunction with related community health and social services for the elderly, the mentally retarded, developmentally disabled, and others in need of long-term care.
5. Increased emphasis on home health care.

REGIONAL/SPECIAL SERVICES

1. Regionalized system of care for high-risk mothers and newborns, with the most efficient usage of hospital obstetrical services.
2. Moratorium on the development of new open-heart surgery service and catheterization/angiographic laboratory services until studies are conducted that demonstrate a need for more services.

Appendix A (Cont.)

3. Development of burn care services, in the most cost-effective manner possible.
4. Radiation therapy and CAT scanning equipment contained within the existing providing facilities until needs for increased services are demonstrated and plans developed accordingly.
5. Adequate services for end-stage renal disease patients, without excess service capacity or cost.
6. Communications network for poison control.

HEALTH SERVICE PROGRAMS AND SPECIAL CONSIDERATIONS

1. Coordination, nonduplication, and evaluation of health and health-related programs.
2. HMO evaluation.
3. Development of funding mechanisms to provide care to the medically indigent.
4. Training programs for minority and low-income people in health and health professions education.
5. Alcohol and drug abuse treatment and prevention programs; programs aimed at reducing child abuse, spouse abuse, and rape.

Source: Document circulated by the Health Systems Agency for the 22-county area in which Penrose Hospitals are located.

Appendix B

SELECTED SPECIFIC GOALS FOR THE 1980s, REGION II HSA

Reduce number of high-risk (teenagers and women over 35) pregnancies by 10 percent.

Reduce neonatal death rate in HSA II by 20 percent.

Reduce rate of motor vehicle fatalities in the population aged 15 to 24 by at least 17 percent, from 46.4 per 100,000 to 38.5 per 100,000.

To decrease pediatric acute inpatient beds to no more than two 20-bed units in the principal city with an overall 65 percent occupancy and to no more than two 20-bed units in the second largest city with a 65 percent occupancy.

To reduce the number of nonfederal short-stay hospital beds per 1,000 population in HSA II from the 1978 level of 4.68 to 3.56, and to increase the HSA's overall hospital occupancy rate from 65.5 percent in 1978 and 1979 to 77 percent.

Appendix B (Cont.)

To ensure the availability of primary care in every county of the HSA.

To reduce the death rate per 100,000 for heart disease in Region II by at least 5 percent, from 255.24 in 1978 to 242.48.

To increase the availability and accessibility of more highly specialized emergency services—advanced life support capability—in Region II.

To promote the effective utilization of CAT scanners so that a minimum of 2,500 medically necessary procedures per year is attained by each scanner currently in operation, prior to addition of any new scanners in HSA II.

To increase utilization of existing diagnostic nuclear medicine services to a minimum utilzation level of 12 imaging procedures per bed per year in urban areas, prior to the establishment of additional nuclear medicine services or the expansion of existing services.

To approve no new open-heart surgery units in Region II HSA unless the Penrose Hospital unit is operating, and expected to continue to operate, at a minimum of 350 adult cases.

To develop increased numbers of alternative care settings for those who are elderly, chronically, or terminally ill, or disabled.

Source: HSA II Newsletter, January–February, 1980.

case

35

U.S. GOVERNMENT AND THE AUTO INDUSTRY: DOT FACES THE ISSUES

BACKGROUND[1]

When Drew Lewis accepted his cabinet appointment as secretary of Transportation in the Reagan administration, he knew that some tough and controversial strategic decisions lay ahead. President Reagan's platform of encouraging domestic competition seemed to imply some commitment to free international trade as well.

The domestic auto industry had not anticipated the suddenness or extent of the shift of a car-buying public's preference from large, luxurious "gas-guzzlers" to smaller, more fuel-efficient models. In 1979, the industry began to suffer steep sales declines and financial losses, which continued into 1981 with no end in sight. Extraordinarily expensive efforts to adapt to new market conditions were hampered by the drying up of internally generated cash flow. As domestic automakers struggled to deal with the most wrenching structural crisis of their proud history, automotive imports—principally from Japan—made spectacular gains.

A doctrinaire hands-off policy by the federal government under such cir-

---

[1]A fictionalized scenario, based upon factual data and real circumstances.

cumstances could conceivably harm the national welfare and damage America's economic and strategic standing within the community of nations. The Republican Party had always held that the national welfare was inextricably tied to the welfare of the business community, so if the domestic auto industry did suffer permanent harm, neither Republican beliefs nor their electoral prospects would be furthered.

THE SECRETARY'S ASSIGNMENT

The president has asked Secretary Lewis to serve on a cabinet-level task force, mandated to analyze the nature and extent of auto industry problems and to make recommendations on what, if anything, the federal government should do to assist in the industry's recovery. Other members of the task force include Bill Brock, special U.S. trade representative; Murray Weidenbaum, chairman of the Council of Economic Advisers; Donald Regan, Treasury secretary; Raymond Donovan, Labor secretary; and Malcolm Baldridge, Commerce secretary. Mr. Lewis has already announced that he considers the question of trade restrictions on Japanese auto imports to be the showdown issue.

To help him evaluate whether trade restrictions should be a part of the Reagan administration's auto industrial policy, Secretary Lewis has asked his staff to prepare notes for a briefing paper, to be based primarily upon recent government studies and hearings. The notes follow:

I. Note on the Strategy and Structure of the Domestic Auto Industry to 1978

A. Value of the Industry to the Nation

1. The auto industry accounts for $8\frac{1}{2}$ percent of the GNP in the United States, for 25 percent of retail sales, and 12 percent of personal consumption expenditure every year. The U.S. auto market is easily the largest national market in the world. On average, one-third of the 30 million cars produced in the world every year are sold in the United States. According to one auto expert, "No other market in the world approaches [the U.S. car and truck market] for volume of sales, homogeneity, ease of entry, and attractiveness to competition. . . . On the average, U.S. consumers buy a combined total of more than 1,000 new passenger cars and trucks every hour of the day and night, seven days a week, all year long—even in an off year like 1980. This sales pace has held since 1963."[2]

2. Auto manufacturing consumes 21 percent of the nation's steel production, 30 percent of its ferrous castings, 60 percent of its synthetic rubber,

---

[2]Statement by David E. Cole, director, Office of the Study of Automotive Transportation, University of Michigan, at Joint Hearing before the Subcommittee on International Finance and the Subcommittee on Economic Stabilization of the Committee on Banking, Housing and Urban Affairs, U.S. Senate, 2nd sess., June 18, 1980.

29 percent of its flat glass, 11 percent of its aluminum, and 20 percent of its machine tools.

3. At its peak in the 1978–79 model year, the North American auto industry had about 300 manufacturing facilities with a capacity to produce 14.7 million vehicles. Nearly 1 million workers were employed in 1978 in auto assembly operations. Another 1.4 million were employed in component supply industries. This direct manufacturing and employment segment is concentrated in the North Central states. More than 2.3 million were employed in 1978 in the distribution, sales, and repair of motor vehicles. Thus nearly 4.7 million people owed their employment either directly or in an immediate secondary fashion to the auto industry. This amounts to nearly 25 percent of total employment in manufacturing. If motor-vehicle-related occupations such as road construction, trucking, petroleum refining and distribution, and passenger transportation are included, the auto industry contributed toward the creation of another 14.5 million jobs. Thus the auto industry can be said to be related in one way or another to approximately 20 million jobs—or 20 percent of total employment in the United States. (See Exhibits 1 and 2 for a more detailed breakdown of these employment figures. This information was drawn from *The U.S. Automobile Industry, 1980,* report to the president from the secretary of Transportation, January 1981, prepared under the direction of Neil Goldschmidt, Drew Lewis's Democratic predecessor.)

To sum up in the words of one auto expert, "Motor vehicles have . . . become a fundamental factor in the American economy. Industries that manufacture, sell, maintain, and depend on them account for a large share of the

---

Exhibit 1

NUMBER OF EMPLOYEES IN U.S. AUTO
AND RELATED INDUSTRIES

Direct	
Motor vehicle and parts	950,000
Suppliers	1,400,000
Total	2,350,000
Secondary (dealers, local purchasers, etc.)	2,310,000
Total	4,660,000
U.S. manufacturing employment	21,000,000
U.S. total employment	98,280,000

Source: Report to the President from the Secretary of Transportation, *The U.S. Automobile Industry, 1980* (Washington, D.C.: Government Printing Office, January 1981), p. 84.

Exhibit 2

EMPLOYMENT IN MOTOR VEHICLE AND RELATED INDUSTRIES BY STATE, 1977

| State | MOTOR-VEHICLE RELATED INDUSTRIES EMPLOYMENT | | | | | | TOTAL MOTOR-VEHICLE-RELATED INDUSTRIES | |
	Motor Vehicle and Parts Manufacturers	Automotive Sales and Servicing	Board Construction and Maintenance	Trucks Drivers and Other Employees	Petroleum Refining and Wholesaling	Passenger Transportation	Employment	Percentage of State Employment
Alabama	5,691	42,225	18,873	163,600	3,591	1,631	235,611	24.7%
Alaska	†	4,225	4,416	15,200	806	1,166	25,810	24.3
Arizona	852	32,234	6,314	116,000	1,265	3,014	159,684	26.3
Arkansas	4,110	24,636	8,996	135,400	2,229	912	176,283	33.5
California	46,672	290,077	44,684	1,197,900	10,861	21,208	1,611,402	24.1
Colorado	1,661	39,459	10,115	146,900	2,996	1,632	202,763	25.2
Connecticut	3,528	36,676	8,892	127,700	2,885	6,687	186,128	17.1
Delaware	‡	7,104	2,193	29,900	421	1,139	40,757	21.1
Florida	2,726	116,572	31,102	283,900	6,039	6,772	447,111	19.1
Georgia	‡	67,789	22,154	217,200	4,381	2,241	313,765	21.2
Hawaii	‡	12,566	3,002	21,200	215	3,408	40,391	15.3
Idaho	355	11,835	4,004	49,700	1,340	659	67,943	31.0
Illinois	26,403	139,633	20,780	341,600	13,915	15,585	557,916	14.3
Indiana	66,537	73,820	11,685	321,700	7,895	3,101	484,738	28.7
Iowa	7,995	40,550	10,865	165,600	3,918	1,797	230,725	28.1
Kansas	‡	32,071	12,673	149,500	2,517	2,365	199,126	30.3
Kentucky	12,012	39,972	10,173	154,500	3,083	2,033	221,773	25.8
Louisiana	989	45,168	20,635	168,100	13,186	3,237	251,315	24.1
Maine	84	13,608	4,707	55,700	1,747	1,050	76,896	27.3
Maryland	‡	53,771	9,739	123,400	2,822	‡	189,732	17.0
Massachusetts	5,841	62,607	14,771	168,000	3,956	19,647	274,822	14.1
Michigan	306,438	113,671	19,938	318,300	7,223	4,737	770,307	28.5
Minnesota	4,549	51,902	12,291	192,100	5,459	7,987	274,288	22.2

State							
Mississippi	4,529	25,400	8,953	106,700	2,701	959	149,242	26.9
Missouri	36,642	65,445	16,027	241,800	4,525	5,960	372,399	25.0
Montana	107	11,641	4,512	51,100	1,303	884	69,247	39.4
Nebraska	2,792	23,330	7,008	92,300	1,996	1,019	128,445	29.2
Nevada	90	10,719	2,882	42,700	356	2,805	59,552	25.2
New Hampshire	‡	11,530	4,174	28,700	882	1,179	46,465	18.1
New Jersey	15,140	80,803	21,850	212,500	9,496	15,329	355,118	15.7
New Mexico	546	17,110	4,107	57,100	1,895	2,061	82,819	30.1
New York	34,515	150,642	51,428	408,500	10,753	‡	656,358	11.9
North Carolina	8,186	66,841	22,942	314,300	7,027	2,959	422,255	24.5
North Dakota	‡	10,307	3,059	37,600	1,606	52	52,674	36.4
Ohio	121,909	142,575	24,080	334,900	7,869	6,507	637,840	18.5
Oklahoma	4,431	34,648	8,439	168,400	3,304	1,186	220,408	29.6
Oregon	3,723	36,087	9,082	121,000	2,325	2,739	174,956	25.2
Pennsylvania	21,685	137,236	37,241	453,200	17,442	‡	666,804	17.9
Rhode Island	‡	9,510	1,921	35,900	936	1,979	50,246	16.2
South Carolina	2,714	31,715	11,078	145,600	3,043	‡	194,150	23.1
South Dakota	435	8,927	3,542	38,400	1,549	65	52,918	35.7
Tennessee	15,113	57,466	18,048	143,700	3,525	2,914	240,766	18.8
Texas	13,480	180,869	30,198	685,000	‡	10,462	920,005	23.1
Utah	1,024	18,253	4,141	60,400	1,012	569	85,599	24.1
Vermont	82	6,015	2,174	18,800	435	598	28,309	20.7
Virginia	7,250	65,915	22,715	182,000	4,941	5,309	288,170	21.1
Washington	2,439	48,185	14,618	195,500	4,072	3,078	267,887	26.4
West Virginia	747	21,141	9,445	88,400	1,458	1,363	123,116	27.4
Wisconsin	31,111	54,809	13,898	157,400	5,033	9,247	271,748	19.0
Wyoming	†	7,319	2,350	25,600	1,761	383	37,435	33.8
District of Columbia	†	7,045	1,028	10,900	268	2,007	21,268	7.1
Total	871,368	2,691,731	730,200	9,121,500	279,433	260,277	13,956,504	21.5

*Includes some local rail and subway employees.

†Unknown or not available.

‡Withheld to avoid disclosure.

Note: Individual states may not add to totals due to rounding.

Source: Subcommittee on Trade of the Committee on Ways and Means, U.S. House of Representatives, *Auto Situation: 1980* (Washington D.C.: Government Printing Office, 1980), pp. 6–7.

U.S. gross national product. If . . . Americans stopped buying U.S.-made automobiles, the national economic structure would collapse."[3]

B. Strategy and Structure of the Domestic Auto Industry to 1973   The North American auto industry took its mature form within a generally benign environment of low energy costs, minimal government regulation, low motor vehicle and road use taxes, and the most extensive highway system in the world. The domestically produced automobile both symbolized and made possible the American people's penchant for personal mobility. Americans travel by car more than twice as many miles every year as do the inhabitants of any other nation save Canada.

While the United States accounts for only 5.3 percent of the total world population, it accounts for almost 40 percent of all the automobiles registered in the world. In 1982 there was more than one car for every two Americans. Exhibit 3 shows the growth in U.S. car ownership since 1900.

The structure of the domestic auto industry has shown a pronounced long-term tendency toward concentration and dominance by a few large producers. In 1983 four domestic firms remained: General Motors, Ford, Chrysler, and American Motors. This trend toward concentration suggests that the industry is characterized by substantial economies of scale in production and marketing. Auto experts in 1983 considered that the minimum investment needed to set up an efficient new assembly plant in the United States was $1 billion. A plant must produce at least 20,000 units per month or 240,000 units per year to break even.[4]

In general, the longer the production run and the higher the sales volume for a given model, the lower the unit cost. High production volume lowers unit costs in two ways: (1) the burden of the initial high fixed investment can be spread over more units, and (2) variable costs can be lowered through the learning curve effect. If a firm manufactures a standard product in high volume over a long period, management and labor learn how to improve internal efficiency. Thus more output can be achieved from a given level and cost of inputs.[5] Economies of scale in marketing are generated by the fact that a company with a higher sales volume can afford to spend more on advertising and other promotional activities because it can spread the cost over more units sold.

The traditional strategy of product differentiation was initiated in the 1920s by General Motors under Alfred P. Sloan's leadership. GM successfully challenged Henry Ford's pronouncement that customers could have any color Model T they wanted "as long as it is black." Product planners and marketing

---

[3]Ibid., p. 18.

[4]*Business Week*, September 26, 1980, p. 6; *The Wall Street Journal*, October 6, 1980, p. 1.

[5]Frank J. Andress, "The Learning Curve as a Production Tool," *Harvard Business Review*, January–February 1954, pp. 87–97, and W. B. Hirschmann, "Profit from the Curve," *Harvard Business Review*, January–February 1964, pp. 125–139.

Exhibit 3

U.S. AUTOMOBILE REGISTRATIONS SINCE 1900

YEAR	NUMBER OF PRIVATELY OWNED VEHICLES
1979E	120,000,000
1978	116,395,000
1977	112,968,806
1976	109,513,168
1975	106,077,384
1974	104,228,855
1973	101,412,229
1972	96,553,073
1971	92,221,291
1970	88,775,294
1969	86,414,179
1968	83,189,008
1967	79,998,511
1966	77,752,487
1965	74,909,365
1964	71,675,906
1963	68,748,863
1960	61,419,948
1955	51,960,532
1950	40,190,632
1945	25,694,926
1940	27,372,397
1935	22,494,884
1930	22,972,745
1925	17,439,701
1920	8,131,522
1915	2,832,426
1910	458,377
1905	77,400
1900	8,000

E – Estimate

Source: Motor Vehicle Facts and Figures. Detroit: Motor Vehicles Manufacturers Association of the United States, 1981, p. 16.

experts at GM discovered that consumers were willing to pay a premium for real and perceived differences in the quality of cars produced. GM set the pattern of differentiating, along two dimensions: (1) from small to large in wheelbase, frame dimension, and engine displacement and (2) from "downscale" to "upscale" in terms of the level of luxurious appointments and convenience and performance options. The marketing magic in this formula stemmed from the fact that larger, upscale models did not cost much more to manufacture than did smaller, downscale models. Variable labor costs do not differ significantly between different model production runs.

Auto companies have consistently refused to disclose their manufacturing costs by product line. However, John Z. DeLorean was quoted as stating in *On a Clear Day You Can See General Motors* that from 1950 to 1975 the manufacturing cost of a Cadillac rarely exceeded the manufacturing cost of a Chevrolet by $300 but sold at a premium of $3,000 to $4,000 over Chevrolets.[6] According to the Goldschmidt Report, the variable margin on a full-sized car before the 1979 crisis ranged between $2,000 and $2,500 in 1979 dollars. The variable margin on a subcompact ranged from $700 to $1,000. (The variable margin may be defined as factory revenue generated by each vehicle less variable costs such as direct labor and materials.) Although fixed costs would have to be allocated to give profit figures, fixed costs for large and small cars would not differ significantly. If larger cars were produced in greater volume than smaller cars, fixed costs could be allocated over more units, thus enhancing profit margins for the bigger cars.[7]

The financial logic of product differentiation dictated that domestic automakers concentrate on increasing vehicle size because profit margins were greater at that end of the market spectrum. This strategy was reinforced by minor annual cosmetic style changes and major style changes of model lines every three years. Economies of scale and gains in the learning curve were maintained since the drivetrain, suspension, and braking systems (the "go" rather than the "show" components) were not significantly modified. Technological innovation tended to focus on cost savings in the production process rather than on new product development.

The narrow profit margins at the downscale, small-car end of the market meant that domestic producers generally were prepared to concede that segment to foreign cars as long as the import market share was 10 percent or less. When the market share of imports approached 10 percent in the late 1950s, the Big Three introduced their first compacts: Ford's Falcon, GM's Corvair, and Chrysler's Valiant/Dart. Although the market shares of imports and AMC declined in the early 1960s, the import share began to recover when domestic compacts succumbed to the "bigger is better" philosophy. By the end of the 1960s many of these compacts were loaded with "luxury/sport" trim and option packages as well as V-8 engines.

C. *Response of the Industry to Environmental Turbulence in the 1970s*   The typology suggested by organizational theorists Emery and Trist can be applied

---

[6]Quoted in William Tucker, "The Wreck of the Auto Industry," *Harpers Magazine*, November 1980, p. 48.

[7]Report to the President from the Secretary of Transportation, *The U.S. Automobile Industry, 1980* (Washington, D.C. Government Printing Office, January 1981), p. 69. Also called the Goldschmidt Report.

to the volatile environment faced by domestic automakers in the 1970s.[8] They argue that the "causal texture" of business environments differs with respect to the degree of uncertainty and interdependence encountered by firms in an industry. In their mature phase prior to 1970, domestic automakers operated within a "disturbed-reactive" environment. In this stage environmental uncertainty was generated by an inability to predict how other firms in the industry would react when one firm tried to gain a competitive advantage. This reaction could leave the innovating firm no better off and could leave the industry as a whole worse off. Environmental stability was secured through a recognition by all firms that their corporate strategies to some extent should be based on a sense of interdependence, or the environment of oligopoly or imperfect competition, characterized by price leadership, relatively stable market shares, and comfortable and fairly predictable returns on sales. Competitive claims are phrased in terms of "quality" rather than price differences.

In the 1970s domestic automakers entered into a more complex and uncertain environmental stage characterized by Emery and Trist as a "turbulent field." Within this environment firms may be affected not only by interaction with other firms but also by dynamic forces arising out of the field itself. These dynamic forces were generated in part by the exogenous petroleum supply shocks of 1973-1974 and 1978-1979, forcing the industry to cope not only with these shocks but also with the federal government's policy reaction to them. There has been a strong correlation between the rising price of gasoline and increasing consumer preferences for small automobile models. Between 1960 and 1972 the price of gasoline in the United States relative to the Consumer Price Index market basket fell by 20 percent but increased dramatically during the Arab oil embargo of late 1973 to early 1974. It then declined relative to the price of other goods between 1974 and 1978. Although the nominal price of a gallon of gasoline doubled from 31.8 cents to 65.5 cents between 1960 and 1978, the real price held stable at around 44 cents a gallon (see Exhibit 4).

Government price controls caused the growing divergence in the 1970s between the domestic and world price for crude petroleum products. A democratically controlled Congress contended that permitting the price of domestically produced oil to rise to OPEC levels would be unfair to consumers—especially those on fixed incomes. Congress, sensitive to the widely held belief that the oil shortage during the 1973–74 crisis had been a ruse engineered by the oil companies to capture "monopoly profits," opted for control of prices at the pump.

The Energy Policy and Conservation Act of 1975 extended price controls over domestically produced petroleum. It also mandated that domestic automakers should improve their corporate average fuel economy (CAFE) ratings by 2 percent per model year. CAFE targets were set at 20 m.p.g. in 1980 and 27.5 m.p.g. by 1985.

---

[8]F. E. Emery and E. L. Trist, "The Causal Texture of Organizational Environments," *Human Relations,* Vol. 18 (1965), pp. 21–31.

Exhibit 4

AVERAGE GASOLINE PRICES
(in cents)

YEAR	CURRENT DOLLARS	CONSTANT (1972) DOLLARS
1960	31.3¢	44.4¢
1965	33.0	42.8
1970	37.3	40.3
1971	37.5	38.8
1972	37.8	37.8
1973	41.1	38.9
1974	54.3	46.5
1975	57.8	45.7
1976	59.8	45.8
1977	62.9	44.8
1978	65.5	43.7
1979 (all)	88.3	54.8
1979 (December)	105.2	61.7

Source: U.S. Department of Commerce, Bureau of Economic Affairs.

Corporate strategists found themselves on the horns of a dilemma. If they assumed that controls would allow only a gradual increase in gasoline prices, they might consider it justifiable to tilt their product mix toward continuing strong demand for gas-guzzlers. However, such a response could trigger fines if CAFE targets were not met. If the industry made a heavy financial commitment to a new model line of fuel-efficient cars, consumer demand (in the absence of significant price increases) could be so soft that the new models would clear the market only with reduced margins or perhaps at a loss.

The initial strategic reaction of the Big Three to the first oil supply shock was to announce, in the summer of 1974, ambitious plans to increase the proportion of compact and subcompact cars in their model lines, but these stated intentions were disrupted by rapid buildup of unsold domestic subcompact inventory in the fall. The U.S. leaders resorted to rebates to sell the smaller cars. Exhibit 5 indicates that if the big-car market is disaggregated into full-sized and intermediate models, a long-term decline in the market share of full-sized cars points to the advisability of downsizing.

Henry Ford II, chairman of the board at Ford Motor Company, reacted to the relatively sluggish sales of smaller cars after 1974 by overruling President Lee Iacocca's recommendation that a front-wheel-drive subcompact should be developed. Ford opted instead to downsize its model line gradually

Exhibit 5

TRENDS IN SALES AND MARKET SHARES BY SIZE CLASSES,
1968–1979
(includes vans)

| | SALES (000) | | | | MARKET SHARES (%) | | | |
| | Domestic | | | Import | Domestic | | | Import |
	Small	Mid	Full		Small	Mid	Full	
1968	1,500	2,451	4,661	1,030	15.6%	25.4%	48.3%	10.7%
1969	1,645	2.165	4,624	1,117	17.2	22.7	48.4	11.7
1970	1,896	1,862	3,360	1,283	22.6	22.2	40.0	15.3
1971	2,411	2,027	4,218	1,566	23.6	19.8	41.3	15.3
1972	2,616	2,390	4,341	1,621	24.0	21.7	39.5	14.7
1973	3,126	2,575	3,972	1,762	27.3	22.5	34.7	15.4
1974	2,887	2,174	2,382	1,412	32.6	24.6	26.9	15.9
1975	3,026	2,038	1,994	1,587	35.0	23.6	23.1	18.4
1976	3,065	2,716	2,532	1,498	33.3	26.9	25.0	14.8
1977	3,222	3,096	2,793	2,075	28.8	27.7	25.0	18.5
1978	3,476	3,162	2,674	2,000	30.7	28.0	23.6	17.7
1979–								
9 mos	2,898	1,910	1,638	1,814	35.1	23.1	19.8	22.0
12 mos*	3,864	2,547	2,184	2,419				

*Assumes constant growth through 1979.

Source: Data provided by Bureau of Economic Analysis, U.S. Department of Commerce. Size classification may not match that used by the industry. Treasury staff analysis of economic impact of a shutdown of the Chrysler Corporation in *Hearings Before U.S. Senate Committee on Banking, Housing and Urban Affairs*, November 14–15,1979, Part I, p. 208.

from the top end, hoping to preserve its market share in the higher-margin segment where demand seemed strongest.

Chrysler adopted a similar strategy, but it commenced developing the front-wheel-drive Omni-Horizon subcompact. However, expansion of this successful model was constrained by the fact that its engine and drivetrain were supplied by Volkswagen, which would provide only 300,000 of the units a year. Chrysler's main attention between 1974 and 1978 remained focused on improving sales of big cars.

American Motors concentrated on the lucrative off-road vehicle market. Prior to 1979, only General Motors embarked upon an ambitious and extremely expensive course of downsizing its entire model line.

The strategic predicament faced by domestic automakers on the eve of the second oil supply shock of late 1978 is summed up in the following characterization: "It is an environment in which the accelerating rate and complexity of interactive effects exceeds the organization's capacity for prediction and hence control of the compounding consequences of its actions."[9] Automakers must predict not only the direction and rate of change of world oil prices but also the U.S. government's regulatory reaction to those trends, a reaction that generated mixed signals. While it held fuel prices down, it threatened automakers with stiff fines for failure to improve fuel efficiency. Environmental signals were further confused by conflicting standards. Despite strong pressure to meet CAFE requirements, exhaust emissions restrictions set by the Environmental Protection Agency (EPA) and collision protection standards set by the National Highway Traffic Safety Administration (NHTSA) could be met only by a trade-off in lowered fuel economy and product reliability.

Corporate strategists had to deal not only with added regulatory costs but also with apparent regulatory risk—the risk of loss associated with changes in regulatory standards after productive resources were committed to meet an initial standard. The typical corporate response to increases in regulatory costs and risks was to conform to conflicting standards while lobbying or pursuing legal action to gain regulatory delay, a response that tended to intensify adversarial relationships between industry and government. Rather than accept government standards as a given, corporate strategists tried to reduce regulatory costs and risks by fighting a rearguard action, putting off major strategic decisions for as long as possible.

Theorists have suggested that the corporate strategy best fitted for survival in a turbulent field is organizational flexibility.[10] The short-term temporizing and regulatory satisfying behavior of domestic automakers in the 1970s suggests not so much flexibility as indecisiveness in the face of conflicting environmental signals. One explanation for this indecisiveness highlights the problem of structural rigidity inherent in the auto industry's mature production strategy. This strategy focused attention on potential productivity gains from the learning curve effect, to be derived from long-term mass production and assembly of relatively standardized components.

Abernathy and Wayne have drawn attention to the limits of the learning curve and to the productivity dilemma inherent in mass production technology.[11] Gains from the learning curve impose a cost in increased structural rigidity. In turn, structural rigidity limits strategic flexibility. Efforts to shift corporate strategies to meet new environmental conditions can be hampered by the enormous costs involved in developing new product and process technology. One cost is the sudden obsolescence of existing mass production technology. Another cost is the sales revenue forgone as the industry develops the new

[9]T. J. Zenisek, "Corporate Social Responsibility: A Conceptualization Based on Organizational Literature," *Academy of Management Review*, Vol. 4, no. 3 (July 1979), p. 363.

[10]Shirley Terreberry, "The Evolution of Organizational Environments," *Administrative Science Quarterly*, Vol. 12, no. 4 (March 1968), pp,. 590–613.

[11]William J. Abernathy and Kenneth Wayne, "Limits of the Learning Curve," *Harvard Business Review*, September–October 1974, pp. 109–119.

technology. These costs can be huge since producing a new car model line from design stage to sale can take three or more years.

The lead time stretches out even more if the new and old technology are significantly different. The final cost is associated with the actual development of the new product and process technology.

After 1978 the challenge of simultaneously downsizing their model lines and switching to front-wheel drive for improved interior space utilization while continuing to meet progressively more stringent fuel economy, emissions, and safety standards stretched domestic automakers up to and perhaps beyond their limits. The structural crisis triggered by the second oil supply shock in 1979 forced the U.S. auto industry to seek out new strategies and to develop at enormous cost new organizational and technological structures to meet the challenge of the 1980s and beyond.

II. Note on the Course of the Structural Crisis and Structural Change Since 1978

A. Environmental Developments that Contributed to the Structural Crisis

1. The second oil supply shock in 1979 associated with the political crisis in Iran appears to have precipitated a permanent shift in U.S. consumer preference toward more fuel-efficient cars. This was triggered by fears about fuel availability, not only sharply higher fuel prices but also the prospect of progressively higher prices over time. The market share of small cars sold in the United States increased from 49 percent in 1978 to over 63 percent in 1980. During the same period the market share of large cars fell from over 50 percent to 36 percent. Exhibit 6 shows the Congressional Budget Office projection of market shares for small, medium, and large cars on a scale of progressively higher fuel prices. If fuel prices continue to rise the market share of small cars should continue to grow. Since the product and process technology of domestic automakers was skewed toward the larger cars, the new demand trend could not be satisfied in the short run entirely from domestic supply.

2. In response to this shift in demand, the market share of imports rose from 15.2 percent in the fourth quarter of 1978 to over 28 percent in the third quarter of 1980.

3. Most of these new imports were manufactured in Japan, whose share of import sales increased from 68 percent in 1978 to 80 percent in 1980. Japan captured nearly 22 percent of the total U.S. car market in 1980.

4. The sudden surge in Japanese auto imports accentuated an already marked trade imbalance. In 1979 the value of Japanese automotive products shipped to the United States was $9.3 billion. U.S. exports of cars and auto parts to Japan were valued at $.2 billion. This gave Japan a surplus of $9.1 billion in that category. This trade imbalance contributed to U.S. balance-of-

Exhibit 6

FORECASTS OF MARKET SHARES*

Gasoline Price (in December 1979 dollars)	MARKET SHARE BY SIZE CLASS (%)		
	Small	Medium	Large
1.00	58.0	23.0	19.0
1.50	66.4	19.1	14.5
2.00	71.4	16.6	12.0
2.50	73.4	15.6	11.0
3.00	74.9	14.8	10.3
4.00	77.0	13.7	9.3
5.00	78.4	13.0	8.6

*Congressional Budget Office, March 17, 1980.

Source: Report of Subcommittee on Trade of the Committee on Ways and Means, U.S. House of Representatives, *Auto Situation: 1980.* June 6, 1980, p. 16.

payments problems and suggested that U.S. automakers were being denied access to the Japanese market.

5. A decision by the Federal Reserve Board to tighten the money supply so as to dampen inflationary pressure helped to trigger a recession in the U.S. economy. The auto industry was a principal casualty of this economic downturn that began late in 1979. Exhibit 7 shows that historically auto sales have been closely correlated with cyclical movements in the U.S. economy as a whole. However, swings in auto sales volume have been more extreme, both on the upside and the downside. When faced by the high cost (up to 20 percent) or unavailability of credit and uncertain economic conditions, prospective buyers tend to postpone the purchase of consumer durables such as cars and houses. Exhibit 8 shows the recent increase in the average age of cars in the United States as new car sales declined.

B. Consequences of These Developments for the Industry

1. *Sales and Profit Performance.* The United States produced and sold approximately 8 million vehicles in 1980. This is a 30 percent decline from the 1979 level and the lowest level of output since 1961. In contrast, Japan manufactured 11 million vehicles in 1980 to become the world's leading automotive producer.[12] The Big Four reported losses of over $4 billion in 1980, after losing $1.1 billion in 1979. Ford lost almost $2 million in 1980 in its North American

[12]*Business Week*, February 23, 1981, p. 22.

Exhibit 7

GNP AND DOMESTIC AUTO INDUSTRY'S NET SALES
HISTORICAL PERSPECTIVE, 1967–1977

YEAR	GNP (in billions of 1972 dollars)	% CHANGE IN GNP	DOMESTIC AUTO INDUSTRY NET SALES (billions of 1972 dollars)*	% CHANGE NET SALES
1967	1,007.7	—	42.9	—
1968	1,051.8	4	49.6	16
1969	1,078.8	3	50.3	1
1970	1,075.3	−1	43.8	−13
1971	1,107.5	3	54.8	25
1972	1,171.1	6	61.7	13
1973	1,235.0	5	70.4	14
1974	1,217.8	−1	62.8	−11
1975	1,202.1	−1	62.4	−1
1976	1,274.7	6	74.5	19
1977	1,337.3	5	81.3	9

*Durable goods price deflator for GNP.

Source: NHTSA study in Senate Hearings on Chrysler Loan Guarantee, November 14–15, 1979, p. 382.

operations. Profits from its European subsidiaries reduced this consolidated loss to $1.5 billion. GM reported losses of $762.5 million for 1980, the first time it had been in the red since 1921. American Motors lost nearly $140 million in 1980.[13]

2. *Unemployment.* The Big Four laid off over 300,000 auto workers in 1980. Layoffs (temporary and indefinite) peaked in July 1980 at 313,500, 25.9 percent of the industry labor force. Indefinite layoffs reached 250,000. Additionally, 350,000 to 600,000 workers in auto-related industries lost their jobs.

3. *Bankruptcies.* Over 1,000 (out of 28,000) auto dealers went out of business in 1980. High interest charges not only reduced sales volume but also increased the financial burden imposed by unsold inventory. Both Chrysler and American Motors would almost certainly have gone bankrupt in the absence of two unusual developments: (a) Renault, the state-owned French auto company, eased American Motors' desperate cash flow problems and helped to restructure its debt. In return it won an agreement that will give Renault a

[13]Report of Subcommittee on Trade of the Committee on Ways and Means, U.S. House of Representatives, *Auto Situation: 1980* (Washington, D.C., June 6, 1980), pp. 17–18; *Business Week,* November 17, 1980, January 12, 1981, March 9, 1981; and *The Wall Street Journal* (March 3 and 4, 1981).

Exhibit 8

AVERAGE AGE OF PASSENGER CARS IN USE IN UNITED STATES, 1941–1979*

YEAR	YEARS OLD	YEAR	YEARS OLD	YEAR	YEARS OLD	YEAR	YEARS OLD
1979	6.4	1971	5.7	1963	6.0	1955	5.9
1978	6.3	1970	5.5	1962	6.0	1954	6.2
1977	6.2	1969	5.5	1961	6.0	1953	6.5
1976	6.2	1968	5.6	1960	5.9	1952	6.8
1975	6.0	1967	5.6	1959	5.8	1950	7.8
1974	5.7	1966	5.7	1958	5.6	1946	9.0
1973	5.7	1965	5.9	1957	5.5	1941	5.5
1972	5.7	1964	6.0	1956	5.6		

*Estimated by the Motor Vehicle Manufacturers Association.

Source: Report of Subcommittee on Trade of the Committee on Ways and Means, U.S. House of Representatives, *Auto Situation: 1980.* June 6, 1980, p. 16.

controlling equity interest in what industry wags have called "Franco-American Motors"; and (b) Congress bailed out Chrysler.

Ford's North American operations, with losses of over $3 billion in two years, would have experienced far greater difficulty surviving if it had been unable to turn to its European subsidiaries for aid. As Ford President Donald E. Peterson reviewed prospects for 1981, he warned that the industry could last another year, but not the whole industry.[14]

C. The Debate over Trade Restrictions

The close correlation between the surge in Japanese imports and the waning of U.S. auto fortunes inspired some to suggest a causal connection.

1. *The Trade Union Reaction.* In February 1980, Douglas Fraser, president of the United Auto Workers Union, met with government officials and auto industry leaders in Japan and called for voluntary export restraint and commitment to invest in auto parts and assembly plants in the United States. (Honda announced in the fall 1982 that its Marysville, Ohio plant was open.) This would reduce the trade imbalance and increase the employment of U.S. auto workers. He delivered an ultimatum: if Japan failed to act in a responsible manner, its auto importers would soon face trade restrictions.

Disappointed with the reluctance of the Japanese to exercise voluntary restraint, on June 12, 1980, Fraser petitioned the International Trade Commission (ITC) for relief against auto imports under Section 201 of the Trade Act of 1974. ITC is a quasi-judicial body composed of five commissioners and a staff

---

[14]*Business Week,* January 12, 1981, p. 52.

of over 400 economists, lawyers, and trade experts that investigates claims by domestic interests that they have suffered "serious injury" from imports. ITC Chairman William Alberger explained that the study had to determine the extent to which imports had been a "substantial cause" of injury to the domestic auto industry. The Trade Act of 1974 stipulates that ITC will submit a report of its findings to the President of the U.S. within six months of the injury claim. If substantial injury is found, the President has 60 days to accept, reject, or modify the recommendations. If he decides to do so, the President can impose tariffs or import quotas or negotiate an orderly marketing agreement (OMA) with the offending trading nation.

The UAW proposed that tariffs on auto imports be increased from 2.9 percent to 20 percent and advocated maintenance of the 25 percent duty on light trucks, recently raised from 4 percent. The union also called for a quota limiting imports to 1975–1976 levels to be applied to imports that didn't have at least 50 percent "North American content" in parts and labor in 1981, 60 percent in 1982, and 75 percent in 1983. More, the UAW sought relief for five years with a phaseout of restrictions to begin in three years.

Fraser contended that "Basically and philosophically, we have been free traders over the years; but we cannot afford to have depression-level unemployment for three or four years while the domestic industry adjusts."[15]

2. *Auto Industry Reaction to the UAW Initiative.* Ford, even more vulnerable than other domestic producers to losing market share to imports, because it had put off developing a front-wheel-drive subcompact in 1974 when sales for small cars were sluggish, joined the union in its complaint. When the sudden shift of consumer preference toward small cars occurred in 1979, the front-wheel-drive Escort model was two years away from production. Further, the subcompact Pinto was suffering adverse publicity for its alleged safety shortcomings. In 1980 when its market share dropped from 21 percent to 17 percent as imports gained ground, Ford called upon the ITC to restrict auto imports to 2 million units in 1981–1983 and to allow 5 percent increases in 1984 and 1985, which would have the effect of rolling back the gains made by imports, primarily Japanese, since 1975 and 1976.

General Motors opposed formal trade restrictions. Chairman Thomas A. Murphy asserted that trade restrictions would be counterproductive and harmful to the long-term best interests of the country, the consumer, and the automobile industry. GM had begun downsizing its entire model line in 1976 and was better prepared than any other domestic automaker for the sudden shift toward small cars after 1978. The surge in imports barely affected GM's 46 percent share of the domestic market. It was constrained only by the time necessary to expand production of its Chevette and popular new front-wheel-drive X-body series. GM could even look forward to expanding its market share when it introduced its new J-body series in May 1981. Since its new mod-

[15]*The New York Times*, May 9, 1980, p. D-1. © 1980 by The New York Times Company. Reprinted by permission.

el lines also appeared to be compatible with market demand outside the United States, GM looked toward the possibility of producing and selling its "world cars" internationally and, therefore, was sensitive to actions that might invite retaliation by foreign governments. GM spokespersons encouraged a spirit of voluntary export restraint from Japan until the domestic auto industry could adjust to changing market conditions.

Chrysler, the U.S. distributor of Mitsubishi's popular subcompact car and light truck lines, also opposed formal trade restrictions. It was dependent on Mitsubishi as well as Volkswagen and Peugeot as suppliers of four-cylinder engines for its new front-wheel-drive models. Trade restrictions might reduce the flow or increase the price of the "captive" Japanese imports. They might even impose component supply constraints on the expansion of its locally assembled model lines. Chrysler, actively promoting joint venture investments by its foreign suppliers in the United States, needed not only new financial capital but also new process and product technology already developed abroad. While trade restrictions might encourage "import-substitution" investment in the United States by foreign producers over the long run, such restrictions could unravel Chrysler's delicately stitched international linkages over the short run.

American Motors also opposed formal trade restrictions against auto imports. Its developing association with Renault was predicated upon its role as a distributor of French-built cars and as an assembler of French-designed cars with a substantial proportion of French-made components. American Motors had prospered for a time in its niche as a producer of off-road Jeep vehicles. However, the energy crunch and Japan's introduction of more fuel-efficient four-wheel-drive light trucks left the firm with few options other than to go under or to accept the French embrace. Since American Motors lacked the capital needed to develop a competitive subcompact, trade restrictions that came between it and its French connection could well force it out of business. In general, American Motors would find tariffs against all auto imports more objectionable than import quotas because tariffs would increase the price of all imports across the board. Quotas based on import volume in 1975 and 1976 would affect European producers far less seriously than the Japanese. Of course, American Motors would not object to Japanese manufacturers exercising voluntary restraint.

D. Reaction of Imported Auto Dealers to Proposed Trade Restrictions

Speaking before the Subcommittee on Trade of the House Ways and Means Committee in March, 1980, Robert M. McElwaine, president of the American Imported Automobile Dealers Association, argued that the interests of the 4,500 imported vehicle dealers be represented and their 140,000 workers, as well. Other firms engaged in international business also needed to be considered in contemplating any trade restrictions.[16] He rejected the notion that un-

[16]Hearings Before the Subcommittee on Trade of the Committee on Ways and Means, House of Representatives, 96th Cong., 2nd sess., March 7, 1980, pp. 109–111.

employment in the domestic auto industry could be attributed to the increase of imports: "They are out of work because of the failure of the domestic industry to anticipate the market, a reluctance to make the necessary capital investments in new products and more modern plants, and a general reluctance to give up what was a very profitable type of motor vehicle long after its popularity with the American buying public had ceased to exist." According to him the market was divided between small and large cars rather than between imported and domestic cars, the root of the problem being domestic producers with their excess productive capacity and large unsold inventories of big gas-guzzlers. "The domestic manufacturers are not having difficulty selling their small cars," argued McElwaine. "Detroit's problem is simply an insufficient supply of small, fuel-efficient, modern cars. Restricting imports is not going to help that situation. Rather it is going to make the shortage of small cars even more acute than it is today. It will certainly not help Detroit sell any more of its large obsolete product."

If trade restrictions would not sufficiently reduce unemployment or stimulate demand for gas-guzzlers, McElwaine went on to speculate about the three reasons domestic auto producers were calling for mandatory or voluntary import constraints: (1) If import dealers had fewer units available to satisfy the demand for small cars, they would "virtually be able to name their own price. . . ." This would be highly inflationary. (2) Trade restrictions would reduce competitive pressure on domestic producers. They would be able to charge higher prices and so "make the same kind of profit on their new small cars as they have been able to realize on their older, larger cars. . . ." (3) Trade restrictions would limit the market penetration of imports. Consequently, when domestic manufacturers developed sufficient capacity to produce their new small cars, they would have to make fewer "conquest sales." If consumers had familiarized themselves with and perhaps had developed brand loyalty to imported models, such conquest sales necessary to recover market share could be both difficult and expensive. Domestic producers would have to make major commitments in terms of higher product quality, increased advertising expenses, price discounts, extended warranties, and other measures to win back disenchanted former customers.

McElwaine viewed these as perfectly acceptable commercial considerations. However, he did not feel that they should be "the concern of the U.S. Congress or the basis of government actions that would violate our previous trade agreements and treaties."

E. Reaction of the Carter Administration to the UAW/Ford Campaign for Trade Restrictions

The Carter administration never articulated a unified response to the call for trade restrictions, and the cabinet was divided over the trade question. Reuben Askew, the U.S. trade representative; Charles L. Schultze, chairman of the Council of Economic Advisors; and Alfred E. Kahn, Carter's anti-inflation advisor, urged continued support of a policy of trade liberalization. They argued that trade restrictions would permit domestic automakers to scale back their costly campaign to retool for the 1980s and tempt them to raise prices. A restrictive package for the auto sector might encourage other "distressed" industries such as steel or textiles to lobby for more protection from import pressure as well. Such protection would slow the process of "structural change" (rationalization to reduce capacity) in these industries while increasing prices. It might also trigger retaliation in foreign markets against U.S. exports.

This "freer trade" group in the Carter cabinet based their stand on the neoclassical trade theory of comparative advantage. This theory holds that all nations benefit if each specializes in producing those goods and services in which it enjoys a comparative advantage. All will reap gains from trade by specializing and engaging in international trade to sell their excess production and buy those goods and services in which other nations have a comparative advantage. While special interests might benefit from protection, the new result of trade restrictions would be an overall reduction in international trade and a decline in world economic welfare. Many believe it was this sort of "beggar thy neighbor" mentality that had deepened and prolonged the world depression of the 1930s. Since 1945 the United States had been the leader of a campaign for trade liberalization under the auspices of the General Agreement on Tariffs and Trade (GATT).

Neil Goldschmidt, the secretary of Transportation, headed the group in the Carter administration that favored import restraint, arguing that the problem of making the structural transition to meet radical shifts in demand outweighed the theoretical advantages of free trade. A task force headed by Goldschmidt concluded that if Japanese auto imports were rolled back to their year-earlier 1979 level of 1.6 million units (a 25 percent reduction) up to 100,000 U.S. auto workers could be reemployed. On the other hand, it conceded that trade restrictions would cost consumers an additional $1 billion in higher prices for Japanese and domestic cars (an increase of approximately $650 per car).

One of the reasons the Carter administration did not take a stronger line urging "voluntary" import restraint upon the Japanese was that the president lacked specific authority in international or domestic law for negotiating informal trade restraint agreements. Such action could invite litigation under the U.S. antitrust laws. The Justice Department warned government officials on several occasions of their potential legal liability if they engaged in informal trade talks with the Japanese. The American Imported Automobile Dealers Association threatened to initiate such legal action if given cause.[17]

The Carter administration could not legally enter into trade negotiations with the Japanese until after the ITC had issued its report or until it had been

[17]See statement by trade expert, Harold Malmgren, in "Problems of the Automobile Industry and Its Current and Future Role in the Domestic and World Economy," Joint Congressional Hearing, June 18, 1980, pp. 57–74.

requested to do so by a joint declaration of both Houses of Congress. The ITC was required to make its injury determination by November 10 and to issue its report on the UAW complaint by December 12, which tied the hands of the Carter administration until after the November elections.

Early in July, President Carter and a bipartisan group of 51 senators asked the ITC to expedite its inquiry so that the administration could act before the election. Bill Alberger, ITC chairman, and Charles W. Ervini, ITC's staff director, recommended in favor of this move; however, the five commissioners voted 3 to 2 to reject this request for a speed-up. This show of independence may have been an effort to erase the impression—in the words of a congressional aide—that the ITC bowed too readily to political pressure.

F. The International Trade Commission's Findings

Shortly after the November election, the Commission voted 3 to 2 against the UAW/Ford complaint. A majority of the commission failed to find that imports had been a substantial cause of injury. Commissioner Paula Stern spoke for the majority when she held that economic conditions—recession, the credit crunch, rising costs of car ownership—and a major, unprecedented shift in demand from large to small cars brought the domestic industry to its weakened state.

Ms. Stern argued that import restrictions would not save many jobs, asserting that productivity improvements would keep future employment lower than its 1978 high even after the domestic industry recovered. She also commented that industry spokesmen failed to give a persuasive answer when asked whether protection would help U.S. manufacturers convert to production of smaller cars.

G. Reaction to the ITC Finding

UAW spokespersons reacted with bitter disappointment, stating that the decision both ignored obvious evidence of injury and relieved pressure on the Japanese to exercise voluntary export restraint and to invest in the United States. Ford authorities expressed similar views, but reactions of other domestic automakers were more muted. The Japanese reaction to the ITC ruling was predictably enthusiastic, though hedged about by caution. The lame-duck Carter administration appeared to embrace the ITC ruling. Treasury Secretary G. William Miller told an import dealers association meeting that the only way to help the domestic industry was to speed up its transition toward producing fuel-efficient cars.

H. Concluding Note to Part II

The Reagan administration's Task Force on the Auto Industry still must decide what the government can and should do to assist producers in making the difficult structural transition to the new market conditions of the 1980s. In particular it must decide whether trade restrictions are part of that recovery program.

III. Policy Review of the Extent to Which a Broader Recovery Strategy for the Auto Industry May Depend upon Trade Restrictions

The critical question facing the domestic auto industry is: Can it generate sufficient cash flow over the next several years to enable it to continue financing an extraordinarily expensive program for restructuring product and process technology? The cost of this structural transformation has been estimated at over $70 billion (in constant 1980 dollars) between 1979 and 1985. The industry has been forced to embark upon a crash program of capital investment two to three times higher in real terms than historical trends, while suffering record financial losses, and to turn to external financial markets during a period of exceptionally high interest rates. General Motors earned a modest profit in the first quarter of 1981; Ford and Chrysler suffered losses. The national economy remains soft and interest rates high.

The Department of Transportation report concludes that the ability of the industry to generate positive cash flows sufficient to sustain its investment program depends upon

1. Increasing the volume of sales to capture economies of scale
2. Maintaining or increasing profit margins on new model lines
3. Reducing production costs to compete with the Japanese
4. Reducing regulatory risks and costs[18]

The DOT study demonstrates that unit costs are from $1,000 to $1,500 lower for Japanese cars than for U.S.-built cars, a cost differential attributed to lower Japanese labor costs, and greater productivity per worker in Japanese auto plants.[19]

U.S. automakers are aggressively pursuing long-term cost-reduction measures: reductions in administrative overhead, increased automation, improved worker training, renegotiated labor contracts, and improved production scheduling and materials management to reduce bottlenecks and inventory costs. Nonetheless, in the absence of some form of trade restriction or voluntary export restraint, domestic automakers will have difficulty in the immediate future significantly increasing their unit sales and profit margins. A production cost advantage has given the Japanese wider profit margins, so they have considerable latitude in offering price discounts to hold or expand market share. Further, they continue to expand productive capacity; by 1983 they will be able to produce 1.9 million units above their 1980 level, and by 1985 will have an export capacity of 9.5 million units.

Domestic automakers will have to earn every sale in a highly competitive market, and many sales of new domestic models may cannibalize from older,

[18]Report to the President from the Secretary of Transportation, *The U.S. Automobile Industry, 1980* (Washington, D.C.: Government Printing Office, January, 1981), pp. 80–89.
[19]Ibid., pp. 90–94.

less fuel-efficient models rather than add to sales volume. This competition will be waged in terms of price and quality. Domestic automakers apparently have a way to go before they can match German and Japanese imports in terms of perceived quality. In recent years, American perceptions of automotive quality have apparently come to be defined in terms of fit and finish, overall reliability, and operating characteristics. The traditional linkage of quality in size and luxury appointments seems to have been broken.

Although U.S. manufacturers, in order to survive and prosper, must adjust to the challenging new competitive conditions of the 1980s, government also must assume responsibility for maintaining an environment within which business can survive and prosper.

WHAT TO RECOMMEND?

Drew Lewis laid aside his staff's review of the auto industry situation, still puzzled as to what policy he should recommend to President Reagan's Task Force on the Auto Industry. He realized that there was no patently obvious "right" recommendation to be made. Any policy option—even doing nothing—carried with it a complex and, to some extent, unpredictable or unmeasurable set of positive and negative impacts on those affected. His task as a strategist would be to sort out the potential costs and benefits of policy options. Whatever path he chose would necessitate balancing the trade-offs. He hoped the decision ultimately made would inflict an acceptable level of harm in the aggregate and create a satisfactory net benefit to all concerned.

The secretary remained convinced that, at least in the short run, the trade restriction question was the showdown issue. Should restrictions be recommended in any form? If so, in what form would they induce the least harm and generate the greatest benefit? Should they be arbitrarily imposed, negotiated, or left to Japanese goodwill and initiative? If some form of trade restriction were recommended, how would it fit into the overall Reagan strategy for rehabilitating the auto industry and the economy generally? What would be best for all the American public?

The life of the strategic planner, the secretary mused, whether in a public or private setting, is not an easy one. Policies must be formulated within a maze of conflicting demands, expectations, and potential outcomes. One must negotiate the labyrinth without being able entirely to predict results at the other end. He sighed and began reviewing the notes once again.

Your Task:

As an industry adviser to Secretary Lewis, offer him your counsel on the issues outlined above.